Introduction to Psychology

L. Dodge Fernald
Harvard University
School of Public Health

Peter S. Fernald
University of New Hampshire

Introduction to Psychology
Fourth Edition

Houghton Mifflin Company   **Boston**
Dallas   Geneva, Illinois
Hopewell, New Jersey
Palo Alto   London

To G.N.F.

Cover: ''Return of the Hunters'' Pieter Bruegel,
Kunsthistorisches Museum, Vienna

Chapter opening illustrations by Norma Shaw.
Text illustrations by Eric Hieber.

Printed in the U.S.A.

Library of Congress Catalog Card Number: 77–078911

ISBN: 0–395–25815–4

Contents

PART THREE   Processes in Perceiving

PART FOUR   Learning and Symbolic Activity

Motivation and Emotional Behavior

PART FIVE

The Individual in Society   PART EIGHT

Preface

An old aphorism reflects the qualities of this fourth edition of *Introduction to Psychology*. To lead the good life, one needs: ''Something old, something new; something borrowed, something blue.''

The something old is to be found in the aim of this edition, which is similar to that of previous editions. Again, we have tried to present to the beginning student a comprehensive statement of modern psychology, emphasizing its scientific basis. Again, too, research findings and methods of all types have received careful attention, and the results have been presented in a manner which we feel reflects their interrelationships. Also, we have indicated the important research questions to which scientific psychology, just a century old, has yet to reveal answers.

The something new is called a chapter organizer, which is a brief story, anecdote, piece of research, theory, or some other theme that appears intermittently throughout a given chapter. The specific purpose is to help the student learn and remember the diverse contents of that chapter. It serves as a sort of mnemonic device, presenting the chapter contents through some idea or event which the student should find especially meaningful. This approach is based upon a widely accepted finding in modern studies in cognitive psychology: Verbal material is most readily remembered when some organizing scheme is available for learning it in the first place.

For example, one chapter begins with an anecdote about a frog in a pot of water in which the temperature is slowly but steadily increasing. Sensory psychology is the topic of this chapter, and thus the frog's plight serves as a springboard for a discussion of thresholds and the different sensory systems. This anecdote becomes the idea to which, as William James said, the ''facts will soon cluster and cling . . . like grapes to their stem.''

In another instance, a punished monk trains some unruly monastery cats to his advantage, and this story serves as the organizer in a chapter on learning. Similarly, a young man's solo voyage around the world provides the student's framework for a chapter on motivation. For purposes of variety, more subtle, abstract concepts also serve as chapter organizers. Research on dreams, the heredity-environment issue, a historical theme, and an investigation on memory, for example, are used in this way. As each idea is considered and reconsidered at relevant points, we hope that the student will recognize it as the stem mentioned by James, to which the chapter contents cluster.

So much for the old and the new. The something borrowed is from our former students; this textbook includes some of their writings. These are called response papers because in each instance the class assignment was to read a portion of the text and then to respond to a particular psychological concept by describing how it had been borne out or illustrated in personal experience. These writings appear in the margin of the text pages, and they have been keyed to this fourth edition by a small colored square (■ or □). Because of the personal content in some cases and extraneous material in others, certain data have been deleted, but the result in each instance is a clear illustration of some psychological principle, enabling the reader to learn from his or her peers, as well as from the text itself.

Finally, the something blue. That was contributed by the several reviewers of earlier versions of our manuscript. Their blue-penciling and other editorial comments were the basis for many improvements in the final product, and we gratefully acknowledge this contribution to our own efforts.

In summary, it is our belief that this fourth edition will provide an accurate and lively statement of the methods and findings in contemporary introductory psychology. We hope that, through this work, the reader will discover that psychology is an intriguing enterprise, concerned with finding answers to important questions of our times.

L.D.F.
P.S.F.

Acknowledgments

We wish to thank the many academic reviewers who contributed to this edition by reading part or all of the manuscript in its several drafts. Among these are Charles L. Brewer, Furman University; Barbara Burke, Harvard University; Russell Clark, Florida State University; Blythe Clinchy, Wellesley College; Randolph Easton, Boston College; Marjorie Fernald, Massachusetts Bay Community College; George Gourevitch, Hunter College; David Hebert, University of New Hampshire; Elissa Koff, Wellesley College; Alan Lind, Federal Justicial Center, Washington, D.C.; Roslyn Mass, Middlesex Community College, Edison, New Jersey; Joyce Clark, University of New Hampshire; Bert Moore, Stanford University; Steve Riederer, Wellesley College; Thomas Rywick, State University College, Fredonia, New York; Marty J. Schmidt, University of New Hampshire; Angelyn Spignesi, California State College, Sonoma; Robert Stutz, University of Cincinnati; Melvin B. Swartz, Pace University; Edward Wike, University of Kansas; and William Woodward, University of New Hampshire. We are also grateful to the Literary Executor of the late Ronald A. Fisher, F.R.S., and to Dr. Frank Yates, F.R.S., and to Longman Group Ltd., London, for permission to reprint a portion of a table of random numbers from their book *Statistical Tables for Biological, Agricultural and Medical Research* (6th edition, 1974).

Introduction to Psychology

PART ONE

Background and Methods

Chapter 1

Historical Perspective

Some years ago a young man was having trouble deciding what to do with his life. Bright, personable, and witty, he had received the best education available in the United States and Europe, but he still could not make up his mind.

His father warned him against an early vocational choice and even discouraged him from choosing a career in literature or science, which would limit the fullness of life. So William decided to become a painter. He enjoyed sketching and had some ability. For more than a year he worked with an accomplished artist but then abandoned the idea, although he sketched sporadically for the rest of his life.

When he was 19 years old, William entered college, planning to major in chemistry, but afterwards he changed to medicine and soon after that he was invited on a long biological expedition to the Amazon in search of new kinds of fish. The trip went well, although William caught little more than smallpox and the idea that he was destined for a less active, more speculative life.

Home again, he turned once more to his studies, but the practice of medicine now seemed a drudgery. The problem of making still another decision was delayed, however, when he became quite ill, both physically and emotionally. He suffered from stomach disorders, insomnia, and severe bouts of depression, and some of these symptoms probably were related to his problem of "finding himself."

Within just a few years, this young man, struggling with his identity crisis, was to play an important role in a whole new discipline struggling with its own identity. In an *identity crisis*, an individual searches for self-understanding and attempts to decide what sort of person he or she is and wants to become in the future. The outcome is usually regarded as most influential in the course of later events.

Emergence of a New Discipline

The new discipline also came from a broad background, but its origins occurred a bit earlier, in Europe. So before continuing with William, we turn to look at these developments in Europe and to study the role they played in establishing this new discipline. Just as young people look to more mature persons while growing up, the new field was taking some of its identity from already established fields.

Empiricism in Philosophy

One established field during the nineteenth century was philosophy, from which the concept of empiricism had emerged. The term *empiricism* comes from the Greek word for experience. It stresses that our ideas are not innate but rather acquired during our lifetime. We learn from experience.

Actually, this viewpoint could be traced back to Aristotle, who had said that all the knowledge possessed by any individual is obtained only through the senses. What one knows depends solely upon one's prior experience. In taking this position, Aristotle was speaking out against his teacher, Plato, who said that certain ideas are common to all people and therefore must be innate.

For almost two thousand years, the Aristotelian idea was virtually ignored. It was revived in the seventeenth century by an important British philosopher, John Locke, who described the human mind as a *tabula rasa*, meaning a blank sheet. One's mind is a clean slate at birth; thoughts and ideas arise during one's lifetime. While this view is certainly not new today, it was considered radical at that time.

One implication of this doctrine is that almost anyone can be made reasonably intelligent by presenting his or her senses with appropriate experiences in sufficient number. Empiricism, therefore, was regarded with much favor by educators, who stressed the importance of experience both inside and outside of school. More important in the present context is its implication for science. The way to knowledge must be through the senses—observe the environment and let the senses tell the story.

This concept of empiricism is of central importance in the *scientific method*, which begins with observation. Actually, *the* scientific method cannot be specified because there are many different approaches in science, as we shall see later, and because one of science's most enduring tasks is the development of improved methods of inquiry. Nevertheless, the basic stages in scientific studies are generally considered to be making observations, forming hypotheses, testing hypotheses and verifying the result. Thus, science begins with observation, and observations are involved in later stages as well, in the testing and verification of ideas.

The Darwinian Influence

One person who made careful observations at this time was Charles Darwin. In the mid-nineteenth century he completed a voyage around the world in a small ship and then wrote a book about what he had observed, calling it *The Origin of the Species* (1859). This book had an almost unprecedented influence on scientific and lay thought.

Theory of evolution. Specifically, Darwin had noted the wide variations in structure and behavior among various species, and he had observed the struggle for existence among all living organisms. He decided that the organisms that survive are those with variations that enable them to adapt most adequately to their environment. The poorly adapted perish and produce no offspring. This process, referred to as the *survival of the fittest*, continued over

Figure 1-1 Voyage on the Beagle. *"When on board H.M.S. Beagle, as naturalist, I was much struck with certain facts in the distribution of the organic beings inhabiting South America, and in the geological relations of the present to the past inhabitants of that continent"* (Darwin, 1859). *(The Bettmann Archive)*

millions of years and led to the appearance of distinctly different organisms (Figure 1-1).

Thus, the earliest unicellular organisms, after billions of years of life in the water, developed a capacity for existence on land. After millions of years had passed, distinctive patterns eventually emerged. Some forms of life became motionless plants, and others developed muscles and sense organs to meet different feeding requirements, and, thus, became animals. As this slow process of evolution continued over the ages, separate species evolved within the animal kingdom. Certain aquatic animals, for example, became amphibious, capable of living in water and on land, and some of these beings, through the selection process, evolved to become land-living reptiles. Other animal forms became mammalian, capable of reproducing the young within the mother's body. This specialization eventually led to the evolvement of the distinctly different organisms that we know today, such as fish, birds, cats, monkeys, and human beings.

Darwin's ideas are referred to as the *theory of evolution,* which states that any given plant or animal species has developed through modifications of pre-existing species, all of which have undergone the process of natural selection through survival of the fittest. This theory was highly controversial for a time, since it was fundamentally opposed to many religious beliefs.

The theory's implications. The theory of evolution had a tremendous effect on persons who were interested in the growing study of human behavior and experience. It suggested that if human beings are descended from animals, there may have been a continuity from the animal mind to the human mind (Darwin, 1859, 1873). Furthermore, the idea of animal instincts, which was well accepted, led to the possibility of human instincts and to the study of human motivation. In other words, if animals are our ancestors and they have instincts, perhaps we have instincts. If human beings, who we know have minds, evolved from animals, do animals have minds? By pointing out that our psychological as well as structural characteristics evolved from those of prehuman organisms, Darwin stimulated enormous interest in the study of behavior and the development of animals and human beings.

Actually, the theory of evolution, although popularly attributed to Darwin, did not originate exclusively with him. The idea that human beings are ultimately descended from animals is ancient; it even appeared in early Greek philosophy. Darwin's major contribution was to gather facts, organize them, and show their relationship to one another. The result was a more empirical basis for the concept of evolution and further interest in understanding the human mind.

Experiments in Physics and Physiology

Just one year after *The Origin of the Species* was published, Gustav T. Fechner, a physicist and physiologist, published a book from an entirely different perspective. The basic idea of his book had occurred to Fechner one October morning while he was lying in bed, apparently thinking about how he could measure mental reactions empirically. Perhaps this trait ran in the family, for Fechner's father, the village pastor, was also an empiricist. Years earlier, he had shocked his parishioners by placing a lightning rod on the church steeple, which in those days showed too much faith in his own observations and experience and too little in God (Boring, 1950).

Procedures from physics. Fechner discovered a method for measuring aspects of sensory experience. He would present some physical event in a carefully measured amount, such as a tone of specific intensity, and then note the listener's experience. Could the tone be perceived? Was it perceived on each occasion? Then the procedure would be repeated with another tone. Could the new tone be perceived? Was it different from the preceding one? With a procedure of this sort, which is adapted from physics, Fechner could study the relations between physical stimuli and sensory experience.

Fechner elaborated on the method, tested it, and published his findings under the title *Elements of Psychophysics* (1860). The significance of this work lay in its exact procedures for studying human experience. It showed that mental phenomena could be quantified by using methods from physics. Today this concept is referred to as *psychophysics*, which is the study of relationships between sensory experiences and the physical characteristics of the stimuli that produce them, as in the relationship between experiencing a certain tone and exposure to sounds of a certain wavelength.

This work provided an important contrast to that of Charles Darwin. In Darwin's approach, which is based on investigations in the world-at-large, scientists describe only what they see. This process of simply making careful observations is called the *descriptive* or *naturalistic method*. In Fechner's approach, scientists manipulate the environment while they are observing it. They place their subjects in situations in which they can control certain events and cause others to happen; then they measure the results. This procedure of controlling certain events while observing is called the *experimental method*.

Both methods are essential to scientific inquiry. Both have assets and limitations, and both have contributed significantly to a better understanding of mental life and behavior.

Studies in physiology. The experimental method also proved to be of value in physiology, in which several important feats were accomplished—including the apparently impossible. Previously, a physiologist had written: "We shall probably never attain the power of measuring the velocity of nervous action . . ." (Boring, 1950). However, empiricism had advanced to the point of determining the speed of nerve transmission in the frog. It was neither impossible to measure nor faster than the speeds of sound and light, as many had supposed. Instead, it was about 90 feet per second.

The importance of this discovery was that it showed a certain regularity in behavior. A response could follow stimulation only after a certain fixed interval, and this process could be studied experimentally. There were clear benefits to be gained from the laboratory approach, and studies continued on the brain, sense organs, and structure of the nervous system.

The Beginnings of Psychology

The following three events were fundamentally involved in the origin of psychology as a new discipline: empiricism in philosophy, evolutionary theory in biology, and experimental methods in physics and physiology. Of course, there

**Figure 1-2 Origins of
Psychology.** *These developments
were among the most important, but
practical concerns in psychiatry and
education also contributed to the
founding of psychology.*

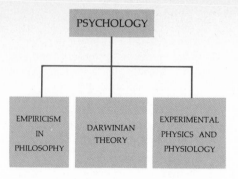

PSYCHOLOGY

EMPIRICISM
IN
PHILOSOPHY

DARWINIAN
THEORY

EXPERIMENTAL
PHYSICS AND
PHYSIOLOGY

were other factors, such as the practical concerns of psychiatry and the emergence of interest in individual differences in various body measurements and, more or less incidentally, in sensitivity and imagery (Figure 1-2).

Wundt and Structuralism

The incident usually considered, perhaps arbitrarily, to have marked the inauguration of psychology as an experimental science occurred at the University of Leipzig in Germany in 1879. A laboratory for research in psychology had been established there by Wilhelm Wundt, and in 1879 the first independent study by a doctoral candidate was completed, although laboratory work had begun several years earlier (Boring, 1965). On the basis of developing a research laboratory, Wundt is generally regarded as the father of scientific psychology (Figure 1-3).

Wundt's method. As a philosopher and physiologist, Wundt had seen the fruitfulness of the experimental method in other fields, especially physiology. His first research was an examination of the salt content of his own urine; the second was a paper on vivisection of the vagus nerve, submitted in Latin (Bringmann et al., 1975). Later, he too became impressed with the idea of determining explicitly the relations between stimulation and a person's sensory experience. It seemed that conscious experience could indeed be measured. Investigators

in his laboratory studied all kinds of mental conditions, including reaction time, sensation, and attention, and various feelings, such as dizziness and fatigue (Figure 1-4).

The distinctive feature of Wundt's approach, however, was its use of *experimental introspection.* Introspection itself was not new; anyone who examines or reflects upon his or her experiences is introspecting. But the people who made observations in Wundt's laboratory were especially trained in introspecting, which means contemplating and reporting on one's own experiences. First, they were carefully instructed in how to make their reports, and then they were exposed to some specific stimulation, such as a whirl of color, and asked to describe the basic elements of their experience. The instructions and the presentation of the stimulation were both carefully controlled; the whole research program was designed to facilitate these descriptions of personal experience.

**Figure 1-3 Wilhelm Wundt
(1832–1920).** *Many early experimental
psychologists were trained in Wundt's
laboratory. Here, in the middle of the second
row, he is shown celebrating his eightieth
birthday with other psychologists. (Keystone)*

This approach was the only acceptable method for Wundt and his followers. As one of his students wrote:

Only by looking inward can we gain a knowledge of mental processes; only by looking inward under standard conditions can we make our knowledge scientific. . . . We must always fall back upon experimental introspection. For our own mind is our only means of interpreting the mind of another organism; we cannot imagine processes in another mind that we do not find in our own. (Titchener, 1898)

Structuralism. For Wundt and his followers, psychology was the study of immediate experience. Their aim was to analyze human experience much as the chemist analyzes matter into its elements. Through proper study, the simplest units or elements of mental life could be discovered; in fact, the structure of mental life would be disclosed. This psychology is referred to as *structuralism* or structural psychology.

For example, Wundt decided that all human feelings could be described on three scales: pleasant–unpleasant, excited–depressed, and tense–relaxed. More recent research of greater complexity has given some support to this idea (Osgood et al., 1957).

Because of this preoccupation with sensations and feelings, psychology at this time was defined as "the science of conscious experience," and anything that did not lend itself to investigation through experimental introspection was thought to be outside its sphere of interest. There was narrowness in Wundt's work, but since no comparable opportunity existed for research in psychology, it attracted students from all over Europe and America.

James and Functionalism

One early visitor to the scene of Wundt's activities, who did not stay long, was William James, the young man mentioned at the beginning of this chapter. In coping with his identity crisis, he had

Figure 1-4 Early Reaction-Time Apparatus. *The weight hanging in the center was pulled to its highest point and then, at a signal, was released. As it fell, it moved gears and the pointers shown on the dials. The subject's reaction time was the interval that elapsed before he pulled on two bulbs, not shown in the photograph, which stopped the fall of the center weight. (Sheila A. Farr photo)*

Figure 1-5 William James (1842–1910). *Before he began teaching psychology, James wrote that he had four interests: "Natural history, medicine, printing, and beggary." As it turned out, he became a scientist and wrote like a novelist, while his brother Henry, the novelist, wrote like a scientist. (Courtesy of Alexander R. James)*

made still another trip to Europe, thinking a period in Germany might satisfy his scientific interests; however, he caught only a glimpse of Wundt before returning home.

Back in the United States, James finished his studies, spurned a career in medicine, and at age 30 accepted a modest teaching position in physiology at Harvard. When he began, he was unknown by the public except by the fame of his older brother, Henry, who had already achieved a substantial reputation as one of America's foremost novelists (Figure 1-5).

William James began his new role by teaching a course on physiological psychology—a natural bridge from medicine to his new interests. In 1875, four years before the date associated with Wundt's laboratory, James developed a laboratory of psychology, but it was used only for demonstrations with students, rather than for research.

James's approach. James was not particularly inclined toward laboratory work, partly because he had poor eyesight and a weak back and partly because he preferred to move ahead more rapidly in different aspects of the new field, rather than work diligently on an isolated topic, which laboratory research requires. Nevertheless, he did some studies on memory, thinking, and vision. He also performed a few practical experiments, such as whirling people around and thereby developing some ideas on the prevention of seasickness (Perry, 1920).

More important to psychology were James's accomplishments as a writer and teacher. When his two-volume textbook, *Principles of Psychology,* appeared in 1890, it was immediately successful in the United States and abroad. It earned him an international reputation, not only for its scientific basis but also for its literary style, and it did a great deal to stimulate interest in psychology. Afterwards, he wrote the "Jimmy," a shorter version of the enormously popular original text. Largely because of these books, William James is recognized as the founder of American psychology.

Functionalism. As far as Wundt's work was concerned, James could not see much value in structural psychology. In America, he advocated a much broader approach called *functionalism,* or functional psychology, which emphasized the functions rather than the contents of mental life. Wundt and other structuralists tried to describe or measure conscious experience exclusively at the human level because they could not work with children or animals. The functionalists, however, thought that consciousness should be studied from the standpoint of how its processes are related to the *adaptation* of *any* organism. Thus, Wundt asked "What is mind?", and James asked "What is mind for?"

Influenced by Darwinian thinking, the functionalists argued that when consciousness evolved, the new processes played an important part in survival. In other words, as we learn a skill, we are at first clearly conscious of our activities. Then, as the habit approaches perfection, consciousness recedes. Eventually, the act can be performed without any conscious attention to it. Consciousness is important in the origin of the habit but much less so in its maintenance.

Functionalists were more interested in what mental life does than what it is. This view was natural for the practical-minded Americans, for whom adaptation to the new environment was a key to survival. The functionalists' appeal also lay in their flexibility with respect to methods. Their approach was to use whatever method was helpful or necessary, rather than restricting themselves to a given procedure. Functionalism was, in every sense, a psychology of adjustment and clearly American in origin (Raphelson, 1973).

James once punned to a friend and former student, Mary Wilton Calkins, that structural psychology was, "structurally" considered, a will-of-the-wisp and added that its "function" was to keep professors and laboratories in employment (Perry, 1935). Calkins, as a woman, was given special permission to study under James and then went on to an illustrious career in psychology. She founded her own laboratory in 1891, published a text called *An Introduction to Psychology* in 1901, and was elected president of the American Psychological Association in 1905. In her presidential address she attempted a reconciliation between functional and structural psychology, but she attempted no reconciliation with Harvard. That institution refused to grant her a graduate degree because of her sex, even though she had completed all the university's requirements (Furumoto, 1974).

James's influence. In the context of structuralism, James wrote on such diverse topics as habit, reasoning, instinct, emotion, and even hypnotism. Gradually, mostly because of his influence, the whole area of scientific psychology broadened in scope. James's ideas on emotion, for example, are still of interest today, and his early support of the mental hygiene movement was most important in its development in this country.

Regarding James's textbook, one noted historian said:

Great books are either reservoirs or watersheds. They sum up and transmit the antecedent past, or they initiate the flow of the future. Sixty years after its publication, *Principles* appears to be one of the major watersheds of twentieth-century thought. Directly, or indirectly, its influence had penetrated politics, jurisprudence, sociology, education and the arts. In the domain of psychology, it had foreshadowed nearly all subsequent developments of primary importance. (Morris, 1950)

After 35 years at the university, James retired. He died three years later, in 1910, having clearly established an identity by his work in psychology. In turn, psychology gained much of its initial identity through James's early work. Looking back, James once noted wryly that the first lecture he ever heard on psychology was the one he gave himself (Perry, 1935).

Systems of Psychology

William James and Wilhelm Wundt are two of the great figures in the founding of modern psychology. But there are others, too. The aim of this first chapter is to present a historical introduction to contemporary psychology in the context of the lives and ideas of a few highly significant individuals. This "great person" approach should provide a scheme for organizing and remembering the various theories and details relevant to the evolution of modern psychology.

Thanks in no small way to James's efforts, present-day psychology is broadly functional. It includes all aspects of mental life and is concerned with the organism's adjustment to its environment. Today, however, this trend is so broad that it can hardly be called a distinct system. It is reflected in most psychology.

Wundt's structuralism also has disappeared, although the study of consciousness is still a subject in psychology. During the early part of this century, Wundt's approach was severely criticized, for both its subjectivity and its narrowness. *All* of Wundt's data were subjective, evident only to the experiencing individual, and thus there was great difficulty in establishing verifiable, repeatable observations. Wundt's approach was considered narrow because it showed no interest in children or animals, who Wundt believed could not give accurate reports of their experiences. Furthermore, individual differences, behavioral manifestations of inner experience, and even learning were ignored. In fact, Wundt found it necessary to train his subjects to overcome the problem of individual differences. Under all these objections, structuralism disappeared from psychology rather suddenly in America. Its demise in Europe, where the tradition was stronger, began earlier but was more gradual.

After these changes, psychology's leadership was taken up by several other people. In the early decades of the twentieth century, psychology was developing rapidly in breadth and spirit, and soon several distinctly different systems arose. Just as there are different systems or approaches in politics, economics, and religion, there have been various approaches in psychology. One of these, behaviorism, arose primarily as a protest against the overemphasis on the study of consciousness, as developed by Wundt.

Rise of Behaviorism

In simplest terms, the main point of *behaviorism* is that the only suitable topic for study in psychology is overt behavior. The study of consciousness is totally inadequate because of its subjectivity. The early behaviorists claimed that if psychology were to be a science, it must concern itself exclusively with objectively observable phenomena, which can only be overt behavior and certain physiological processes.

Early behaviorism. As the leader of a protest movement in the first decades of this century, John B. Watson was ideal in several respects. He was a colorful, active personality and was able to promulgate the new outlook in diverse ways—through research, in a textbook, and on the lecture platform.

In the course of his investigations, Watson became enamored with his research associate, Rosalie Rayner, and became front-page news in Baltimore when he obtained a divorce in order to marry her. Upon doing so, he was asked to resign his professorship, and then he abruptly left the whole educational scene, joining instead a large business enterprise in New York City. These were the times and the character of John B. Watson (Figure 1-6).

Watson argued for greater objectivity in psychology. He contended that psychology should abandon the study of conscious experience, both its structure *and* its functions. Physicists studied phenomena that any trained physicist could observe, not just privately, but in common with others of this training. Biologists studied organisms by observing what other biologists also could observe. On the other hand, psychologists had been attempting to obtain scientific data by looking ''inside their skulls.'' Watson wanted them to look outward, like natural scientists, and study human beings as any other object in nature.

Thus, a psychologist would be restricted to observing a *stimulus,* which is any factor that arouses behavior, and the *response*, which is the organism's reaction to the stimulus. Included in the reaction are the physiological mechanisms involved, such as nerves, glands, and muscles. This psychology is referred to as *stimulus-response psychology,* also called S-R psychology.

Of course, Watson's views were influenced by other developments. Memory, child development, and learning processes had recently been investigated without introspection or reference to how the individuals felt. In the case of animals, moreover, one could have a science of behavior, although there is no way of obtaining reports from the organisms. In 1913, Watson published a highly influential paper entitled "Psychology as a Behaviorist Views It." It marked the beginning of the behavioristic movement, clearly bringing into question the whole European-bred Wundtian psychology, which was concerned with introspecting on feelings and experience. For those persons following Watson, psychology was *his* psychology.

Watson's academic career was comparatively brief, and later on the job in New York City he remarked to a friend how surprising it all was to him. The earlier excitement he had found in watching the increased learning of a rat was now found in the increased profits curve of his new company. He wrote for weekly magazines and then published a popular book entitled *Psychological Care of Infant and Child.* The book was highly specific about the proper approach to childrearing, and it emphasized rather rigid feeding and bedtime schedules, which Watson felt should not be altered because the child cries. The parents of many of today's college students were probably raised on these principles.

Modern behaviorism. After Watson and others, behaviorism acquired another controversial spokesman, B. F. Skinner, who is perhaps the best known and most misunderstood of contemporary psychologists. He is known for re-

Figure 1-6　John B. Watson (1878–1958). *Watson once made the ultrabehavioristic statement: "Give me a dozen healthy infants, well formed, and my own special world to bring them up in, and I'll guarantee to take any one at random and train him to become any type of specialist I might select—doctor, lawyer, artist, merchant-chief and, yes, even beggarman and thief, regardless of his talents, penchants, tendencies, abilities, vocation, and race of his ancestry" (1925). (Historical Pictures Service, Inc., Chicago)*

search on rats and pigeons and his behavioristic novel describing a modern utopia, *Walden Two.* But there have been misunderstanding and controversy about his ideas on the control of human behavior.

In mid-career, Skinner became second-page news because of his method of childrearing. As an infant, one of his daughters was placed in a special box, which was really an elaborate crib with controls for temperature, sound, light, cleanliness, and humidity, which simply made childrearing easier. Some of the mass media suggested that she was kept there almost exclusively for two years and eventually became maladjusted. Actually, the baby was in and out of the box just as any other child is intermittently removed from the crib, and her development apparently has been quite favorable. But the "baby in a box" episode illustrates a basic premise in Skinner's approach: human behavior can be best managed by appropriate manipulation of the environment.

In this case, the crib was simply improved. It better served the child's needs, which meant that life was less difficult for both the baby and the parents (Figure 1-7).

Figure 1-7   B. F. Skinner.
Skinner's approach to psychology has resulted in many practical applications, especially in education, childrearing, and therapy. (The New York Times)

In the study of psychological questions, Skinner has continued the behavioristic tradition of emphasis upon objectivity. Thoughts and feelings are of little interest, except insofar as they are expressed in overt behavior. Instead, Skinner has studied the ways in which behavior is developed and sustained by events in the environment that reduce or satisfy the organism's needs, such as a smile, promotion, money, food, freedom, and other rewards. These events are called *reinforcement* because they reinforce or support the behaviors that precede them. That is, they increase the likelihood of that behavior's recurrence. According to Skinner, to understand any given individual's responses, one must study the reinforcements that support them in that individual's environment.

The details of Skinner's work and the behavioristic outlook in general are considered throughout this book, especially in connection with an aspect of learning called conditioning. For now it is sufficient to note that today there are many behavioristic psychologists and many opponents of this view, both within and outside the field. Behaviorism is one of the most important systematic developments in modern psychology, and applications are found in virtually all of the social sciences.

The Gestalt Protest

But behaviorism was not alone in its resistance to structuralism. Gestalt psychology arose in the same manner, except that the gestaltists' protest did not concern the study of consciousness per se. Rather, they resisted the effort to analyze consciousness into separate elements or parts. Gestalt theorists contended that the observer should assume an "everyday" attitude in his or her introspection, rather than a special analytical attitude, as in the trained introspection of structural research.

Emphasis upon wholes. The German word *Gestalt* refers to ''form'' or configuration, and so those who followed the new gestalt principles were also referred to as *configurationists*. They emphasized the *whole* configuration, of consciousness or whatever, rather than separate parts. They argued that the analytic procedures of the structuralists were artificial and that what they revealed did not represent the full or true nature of conscious experience. The whole person, whole situation, or whole of consciousness is distinctly more than the sum of its parts. Thus, the structuralists' emphasis on elements of experience was challenged.

When you look out the window, what do you see? Brightness, contours, and hues? Not according to the gestaltists. You see a whole scene of brick buildings, leafy trees, clouded sky, and so forth, rather than a series of separate sensory elements.

The roots of this view seem to go back to the turn of this century, allegedly to a moment when Max Wertheimer, a German psychologist, was riding on a train on vacation. Apparently he was still thinking about his work, for suddenly an idea came to him for an experiment that would demonstrate to the world the new gestalt psychology. A man of action, Wertheimer dropped his vacation plans, got off the train at the next stop, and went to a store to purchase equipment for the crucial test (Newman, 1944; Figure 1-8).

He bought a toy stroboscope, which creates the illusion of movement in a series of still pictures. When the pictures are shown in rapid succession, motion is perceived. Today, this phenomenon is illustrated in movies, in which the film consists of a sequence of still photographs shown rapidly, one after another, on the screen. The perceived motion demonstrates rather dramatically that the whole experience can be something more than the sum of its separate parts.

On much this same basis, gestalt psychology was also a protest against behaviorism. Certain behaviorists had

Figure 1-8 Max Wertheimer (1880–1943). *Wertheimer, a leader of gestalt psychology, disparagingly referred to Wundt's approach as ''brick-and-mortar'' psychology, meaning that in structuralism, sensory experiences were regarded as little more than a collection of bricks held together by the mortar of our associations to them. Gestalt psychologists wanted to demonstrate that this approach ignored the meaningfulness of human experience and the interrelationships among our experiences. (United Press International)*

argued that human learning is simply a chain of small habits, each one serving as a stimulus to set off the next one. But to gestaltists, learning was more than a bundle of habits. Sometimes learning appeared all at once, in the form of insight, rather than being built up gradually, piece by piece, over a long period of time, as shown in experiments with animals and human beings. For example, chimpanzees seemed to solve relatively complex problems involving sticks, boxes, and other equipment with considerable swiftness, using the apparatus as a crude tool to obtain otherwise inaccessible food. An important consequence of this research was its influence in demonstrating that learning need not be studied in isolated parts; greater understanding might be gained by examining the act as a whole.

Humanistic psychology. Even in its birthplace in Germany, gestalt psychology was a vital force for only a short time, due partly to Hitler's rise and the consequent departure of its initial leaders to the United States and Spain. Today, gestalt psychology is reflected indirectly in a movement called *humanistic psychology*, which emphasizes the complexity and uniqueness of human beings. In contrast to behaviorism, it stresses the differences between human beings and lower animals; the former comprise a unique species, with capacities and awareness not found in animals (Buhler, 1971). It also stresses that, at the human level particularly, the whole is greater than the sum of its parts.

The humanists state that modern psychology has been ignoring the subjective side of human life. We study rituals of living, work habits, patterns of friendships, and childrearing practices, but we overlook what the individual is thinking and feeling. According to humanists, this aspect of our condition has been much neglected since the criticisms brought against Wundt's work, and they argue that the most important issues facing humanity can be studied only when the researcher accepts some degree of imprecision in his or her work.

The resistance of other psychologists to the humanistic movement concerns its methods, not its goals, which most people accept in one form or another. Both behaviorism and psychoanalysis brought distinctly new procedures to the study of psychology, the former by adapting laboratory methods of natural sciences and the latter through clinical procedures for studying individuals. Humanistic psychology, by contrast, has few special methods; it developed in resistance to current practices, but has not yet formulated practices of its own. Even within the movement, it has been noted that "humanistic psychology is as much distinguished by what it is not or by what it opposes as by what it affirms" (Bugental, 1967).

Thus, the current humanistic trend has been called *third-force psychology,* meaning that it represents the most significant dimension after behaviorism and psychoanalysis (Maslow, 1962). This description may or may not be fitting; only history can verify a designation of this type in psychology or any other field. Study of the most significant advancements in the social sciences from 1900 to 1965 has indicated that there was an interval of approximately 15 years between the inception of behaviorism and its first major impact on other fields of scientific activity and society at large. Similarly, the delay of the impact of psychoanalysis was estimated to be about 30 years (Deutsch et al., 1971). Despite the accelerated nature of modern life, it is too early to know the impact of this contemporary movement. All we can say for the present is that the basic gestalt—humanistic ideas have not been as fully incorporated into the mainstream of psychological thought as have those of behaviorism and psychoanalysis, to which we now turn.

Origins of Psychoanalysis

Unlike the approaches discussed previously, psychoanalysis was not a protest against another system, unless we say that Sigmund Freud's theories were a grand intellectual protest against the rigid social code of his day and society. In any case, Freud's parents followed the traditional roles of the times. Although Freud was a precocious child, his father tolerated no suggestion of disrespect. Once he said to a friend, "My Sigmund's little toe is cleverer than my head, but he would never dare to contradict me!" (Wittels, in Jones, 1953).

Early influences. Freud graduated from medical school with no fondness for a physician's work. A man of diverse interests, he studied the anesthetizing properties of cocaine and the sexual organs of the eel and eventually, for want of income, entered clinical practice. Soon he began using hypnosis for treating patients with neurotic disorders. In *neurosis,* a person usually experiences anxiety, sometimes accompanied by symptoms such as difficulty in interpersonal relationships, strange fears, the repetition of apparently useless acts, or inexplicable paralyses or loss of feeling in parts of the body.

Freud had acquired his interest in hypnosis after spending some months in France, where he came under the influ-

Figure 1-9 **Figure 1-9 Charcot and Freud.** *The observers of Charcot's demonstration of hypnosis are physicians and medical students. The bearded figure in the apron in the front row is presumed to be Sigmund Freud. The portrait shows Freud at a later age. (The Bettmann Archive)*

ence of a widely respected French neurologist, Jean Martin Charcot. It was Charcot's belief that persons with certain neurotic disorders were particularly susceptible to hypnosis. Further, Charcot believed that persons whose paralyses and anesthesias were not affected by physiological causes—because the disorders did not conform to the patterns of neural pathways—were nevertheless somehow ill. This view was a most important contribution to clinical work (Figure 1-9).

On the basis of his experiences in Charcot's classes, and his own observations, Freud began to use hypnosis with neurotic patients, although this work made him highly unpopular with his colleagues. At the time, hypnosis as a medical treatment was regarded with considerable skepticism. Instead, baths, massages, and medicines were commonly employed. But Freud had observed that hypnotized persons behaved in strange ways and recalled desires and fears that went unrecognized when they were awake. Thus, he decided that similar unconscious residues might account for neurotic behavior and commenced with his unorthodox methods.

A self-analysis. Like his patients, Freud also began experiencing difficulties in personal adjustments during these years. He encountered financial problems, doubted his ability, was rejected by his colleagues, and was becoming bored with clinical work. Further, he feared certain types of travel and experienced strange physical ailments from time to time. During this period his father died, an event that, combined with all the others, prompted him to undergo an intense and unremitting self-analysis (Jones, 1953).

In the course of these analyses, especially dream interpretation, Freud came to a difficult conclusion. Beneath his conscious thoughts were feelings and ideas concerning his father of which he had been unaware. In short, as an unknown accompaniment of the obvious love and affection that he felt towards his father, there were also hatred and jealousy, and these feelings had prompted him to behave in previously inexplicable ways. For example, Freud finally decided that his unexpected hostility towards a long-time friend, Wilhelm Fliess, was connected to an unconscious identification of this man with his father (Jones, 1953).

In therapy sessions with patients, Freud made similar discoveries about them. When they talked openly, they also encountered previously unknown aspects of their mental makeups, and these hidden attitudes seemed to have significant consequences for their behavior. Such findings convinced Freud that unconscious impulses play an important role in human behavior.

Concept of the unconscious. The idea that behavior can be influenced by unconscious events was revolutionary to many people. Wundt had claimed that psychology was the science of conscious experience, but now Freud was writing about an unconscious realm. It could not be understood through experimental introspection, but it could be reached by a careful examination of childhood experiences and the interpretation of dreams. Freud stressed that the individual's unconscious begins in childhood, and he introduced a new method for investigating it, known as the practice of psychoanalysis. Today the term *psychoanalysis* refers both to this method of therapy, as practiced by Freud, and to his theory of personality.

This revolutionary doctrine soon developed into a whole system of psychological thought and now includes many distinct psychological concepts. Among these, the most fundamental principle is *unconscious motivation*, which states that the behavior of any individual is significantly influenced by past events of which he or she is no longer aware. This dramatic, broad approach attracted many disciples.

But there were many doubters as well. Some psychologists who opposed psychoanalysis felt there was simply not enough empirical evidence for the existence of the unconscious. Others argued that unconscious impulses do not inevitably involve sexual and aggressive urges, as Freud seemed to suggest. Still others stated that the whole influence of culture is much ignored in this system. Such resistance continues today (Jurjevich, 1974).

Nevertheless, today it is not too bold to say that anyone who is interested in the ideas that make our modern world distinct from earlier ages must give full consideration to the influence of Freudian psychoanalysis, not only in psychology and psychiatry but also in all the social sciences, art, and literature. We shall refer to Freud's system of psychoanalysis frequently throughout this book.

Contemporary Psychology

The concern with systems of psychology as such is less prominent today than it was fifty years ago. These systems still exist, but detailed comparisons are largely of theoretical interest (Fuchs & Kawash, 1974). A contemporary psychologist may regard behaviorism as the best system for him or her but not necessarily as the only road to truth. Most individuals studying psychological processes identify themselves simply as psychologists, rather than as behaviorists or psychoanalysts, and usually they pursue a rather narrow specialty within this broad field.

The demise of intense rivalries among the systems was ensured by World War II, if indeed it had not occurred already. The war increased the prestige of the growing discipline and gave psychologists an overriding goal. Suddenly they were called upon to select the best people for certain jobs, to train them for these tasks, to develop methods for raising morale and motivation and, when the war was over, to deal with the very difficult psychological problems it had engendered. Thus, specialties in psychology came into being.

Diversity of Interest
After World War II, psychology expanded enormously in many directions. Now psychology is combined with almost every field of study. For example, there is mathematical psychology, psycholinguistics, psychopharmacology, psychology and religion, and the psychology of aesthetics, just to name a few of the specialties. The different

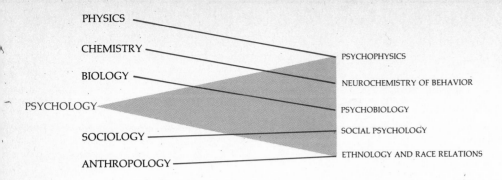

Figure 1-10 Psychology's Position among the Sciences. *Psychology lies between the biological and social sciences but has relations with virtually all scientific fields.*

areas of special interest in psychology will become readily apparent throughout the remainder of this book and they can be surveyed merely by inspecting the table of contents.

A definition. As a reflection of psychology's current diversity, contemporary psychology is often called a *biosocial science,* as it stands between biology and the social sciences. The interdependence of physical structure, mental life, and behavior is accepted by most psychologists, although the details remain unknown. In this sense, psychology is a biological science. Similarly, the influence of one's outer environment on behavior is widely accepted, and the social dimension is the most obvious aspect of this environment. People respond to other people. In this sense, psychology is also a social science. The appropriateness of this designation as a biosocial science becomes increasingly apparent as psychologists penetrate the intricacies of the human condition (Figure 1-10).

Today, *psychology* is defined as the scientific study of the behavior and experience of organisms. This definition includes animals as well as human beings.

Research and applied psychology. Psychologists who perform scientific studies for the purpose of acquiring further knowledge are called *research psychologists.* They perform the type of investigations that have resulted in the body of knowledge now called psychology. They often work in university research laboratories and also in investigation centers found in hospitals, business and governmental agencies.

The work of psychology includes more than research, however. Other psychologists are less concerned with developing additional knowledge than with solving current, practical problems. They are called *applied psychologists* because they apply, rather than discover, psychological principles. Thus Freud, although he began with a practical problem, was not an applied psychologist. He was more interested in the discovery process than in treating people, and actually he dealt with relatively few patients during his career.

Applied psychologists perform psychological services such as administering mental tests, designing equipment, assisting with childrearing, engaging in various therapies, and consulting in a variety of fields ranging from business to education. But the reader should not conclude that psychologists either do research or simply apply the results. Many psychologists do both. In fact, those who work in academic institutions, sometimes called *academic psychologists,* commonly engage in research and some other activity, such as teaching, counseling, consulting, or doing administrative work.

Areas of applied psychology. Although it directly concerns the public,

Figure 1-11   Clinical Psychology. *Like psychiatrists, clinical psychologists diagnose and treat psychological disturbances, but their work is less medically oriented. They often use psychological tests in their diagnoses, and many are affiliated with hospitals or universities. Clinical psychologists also engage in research related to psychological disorders, using the various methods available to psychology, including observation of subjects through a one-way window. (Forsyth from Monkmeyer)*

the work of applied psychology is sometimes misunderstood. There is also some confusion between related fields, such as psychology and psychiatry, but our previous definition of psychology should begin to clarify the difference. Psychiatrists generally are not interested in allegedly normal people or in the study of animals. As a specialty in medicine, psychiatry is primarily concerned with the diagnosis and treatment of mental illness and mental defect. Psychology is much broader because it is concerned with normal and abnormal behavior and experience, in any context and in any species.

Within psychology, there is a specialty called *clinical psychology,* in which the interest, as in psychiatry, is in mental illness and its treatment. Thus, the clinical psychologist engages in diagnosis and therapy of mental disorders. The psychiatrist, with a medical background, is more likely to prescribe drugs and assume responsibility for the patient's overall health. The psychologist, with greater background in testing, is more likely to become involved in diagnosis,

therapy, and perhaps basic research on these issues (Figure 1-11).

Another occupation with which modern psychology is sometimes confused is school guidance, which is a specialty within education. The guidance counselor may engage in certain activities similar to a psychologist's, but generally the counselor's concern is limited to school-related issues. Counselors advise students concerning curriculum planning, course requirements, and special education programs. The specialist in *counseling psychology,* on the other hand, is concerned not only with the school adjustment but also with vocational problems, marriage adjustment, adjustment to retirement, and related personal issues. In contrast to the clinical psychologist, counseling psychologists work within the normal range of adjustment problems of any type, and they engage in diagnostic testing, counseling, and therapy. *Educational psychology* has a broader scope, being concerned with all aspects of learning and teaching, particularly in the school environment.

The psychologist also may be found elsewhere in the community, such as in an industrial or business setting, in which he or she is concerned with training employees, selecting personnel, analyzing jobs, and developing techniques for improving work efficiency. One aspect of early *industrial psychology* was *time and motion study,* a procedure developed by an industrial engineer named Frank B. Gilbreth and his wife, Lillian, who was also an engineer as well as a psychologist. This study concerns finding the most efficient methods of accomplishing tasks. In one of their original studies, the Gilbreths analyzed bricklaying procedures and reduced the number of required movements by two-thirds. In other words, a worker following the new method could lay three times as many bricks as could one following the older system. Today, industrial psychologists use films, lectures, and various techniques to train and improve the efficiency of workers on the job. They also utilize case studies and therapeutic methods to improve management–labor relations (Figure 1-12).

The development of another field, *human factors psychology,* was given a strong impetus by the requirement of World War II for improved operation of a wide variety of machines. It has grown rapidly in recent years, as reflected in the wide variety of titles by which it has been known; these include engineering psychology, human engineering, man–machine research, and equipment design. During the war, the primary concern was with the design of equipment best suited for human use. By studying the visual, auditory, and other capacities of the human being, psychologists played an important role in the development of efficient radar, sonar, and other tracking gear. In peacetime, through the study of color blindness, night vision, and depth perception, for example, psychologists have collaborated in the construction of highway signs, traffic signals, and other safety

Figure 1-12 Industrial Psychology.
Psychologists are not restricted to the clinic or laboratory, but are also active in the world of work and business. The process of bricklaying interested the Gilbreths, the authors of a classic time and motion study, just as it evidently interests the bystanders in the photograph above. Some companies have staff psychologists or consultants who assist in the development of training and career development programs. (Upper photo by Hurst from Stock, Boston; lower photo by Herwig from Stock, Boston)

Sitting in a room full of adults, the conversation was spinning about me. I was quite detached until a familiar topic arose—Uncle Charlie, my favorite uncle. Everyone seemed to agree with Uncle Tom when he said Charlie was very dishonest. When I inquired why he thought this was true about Uncle Charlie, he groaned as if explaining to an eight-year-old were a great difficulty. He finally said, "Well, Charlie never looks anyone straight in the eye, so there can't be much honesty in him."

After this important information was given to me, I set out to see just who was honest and who wasn't. My older brother was definitely looking in my eyes while he talked, but when I turned my back he cheated at cards. My grandmother hardly ever looked at my eyes unless she was sitting, perhaps because her back hurt to bend over. I concluded that most of my friends at school were dishonest, even my teacher. The most hurting thing was to discover that Tiny, my dog, was dishonest. I explained this misfortune to my mother and she set me straight. . . .

apparatus. Today, there is also considerable interest in the design of organizations and administrative systems that are most appropriate for human functioning. Hence, the title *human factors psychology* is most commonly used.

Among the first developments in *consumer psychology* were research methods concerning advertisements. In one instance, some years ago, the manufacturers of a certain instant coffee consulted with consumer psychologists in an effort to increase sales. The psychologists constructed two identical shopping lists of several items each, except that one list simply contained the entry "coffee" while the other specified the brand name of the instant coffee. Each of hundreds of persons in grocery stores was shown one of the lists and then was asked to characterize the person who might buy that list of items. It was discovered that the person who would buy instant coffee was more likely to be perceived as being lazy, taking shortcuts in preparing meals, and thus caring less about his or her family. On this basis, an advertising campaign was developed that emphasized that the minutes saved using instant coffee would allow one to spend extra time with family members. In effect, those who served instant coffee cared more, not less, about their families. Sales were reported to have increased significantly with this campaign (Haire, 1950).

It should be noted, however, that consumer psychology applies to more than business and buying. Recently, it has been employed for noncommercial purposes, such as in promoting safety programs, emphasizing the school dropout problem, campaigning against litterbugs, encouraging environmental conservation, and attempting to achieve international understanding.

Persons in *legal psychology* are often called upon to provide expert testimony through psychological tests and research methods, as in the assessment of a defendant's intellectual and personal–social functioning. In addition, these psychologists study the reliability of testimony. They may consider the ways in which various psychological processes, such as perception, emotion, and motivation, may affect recall and thereby influence outcomes. The processes of selecting a jury and jury deliberations are also of considerable interest, as is the very difficult issue of legal responsibility and the plea of insanity.

The Problem of Deception

Confusion about psychologists' activities sometimes arises because persons whose work seems to be related to psychology may make a living from a gullible public by intentionally creating a false impression. It is one matter to have a misunderstanding of established facts. ■ It is another for individuals to establish themselves as experts, without the appropriate training, and to offer guaranteed results in dealing with complex personal problems, as has often happened.

Sometimes promoting themselves as psychologists, such persons may study a man's head, his facial characteristics, his birthdate, or all of these, and then attempt to tell him what his capacities are, what sort of person he should marry, or how he should plan for his future. Sometimes these people are referred to as *psychoquacks*, and surveys have suggested that they are considerably more common than one might expect (Figure 1-13).

A graduate student in psychology, under the guidance of a professor of clinical psychology at Columbia University, visited 14 persons in New York City who had listed themselves in the telephone directory as qualified to render psychological services. The student posed a series of realistic symptoms and

Figure 1-13   The Business of Advising Others.   *Some people, calling themselves spiritualists or advisors, make rather grandiose claims. (Hamilton from Stock, Boston)*

had a total of 23 consultations with the 14 alleged psychologists. It was discovered that more than half of the "psychologists" were quacks and that 6 had good intentions but were unqualified. Only 1 of the random sample of 14 appeared fully qualified to give psychological treatment, and he was the only one who did not guarantee a quick cure (Kursh, 1964).

These people confuse the public about the nature of psychology, and therefore in most states clinical and counseling psychologists must be certified or licensed by law. Persons who misrepresent themselves run the risk of legal penalties, but often they circumvent this legality by adopting some other professional title, which adds to the confusion. At present, extensive public education seems to be the most promising solution to this problem, which is one of our aims in writing this book.

Summary

Emergence of a New Discipline

1. The problems of psychology have interested scholars since antiquity, but psychology emerged as a clearly formulated science just a century ago, partly through a rising interest in empiricism in philosophy, which states that ideas are not innate but are acquired through experience. The emphasis is on direct observation.

2. Darwin's theory of evolution also was important in the founding of psychology, as it demonstrated the value of naturalistic, or descriptive, research and at the same time stimulated considerable interest in human and animal behavior and the possibility of human instincts.

3. A different research spirit was contributed by Fechner, in his application of

methods in physics to problems in psychology. He showed that the relations between stimuli and responses could be discovered through experimental procedures. At the same time, productive research was occurring in experimental physiology.

The Beginnings of Psychology

4. The founding of modern psychology is credited to Wilhelm Wundt, who established the first research laboratory in 1879. The chief method in Wundt's laboratory was experimental introspection by trained observers. By this procedure he hoped to analyze the structure of consciousness; therefore, his psychology was called structuralism.

5. William James, the founder of American psychology, stimulated the new movement more by creative writing and teaching than by research. He inspired a broad development of psychology and emphasized the functions rather than the structure of mental life. His system of psychology was called functionalism.

Systems of Psychology

6. Eventually it became clear that a study of behavior per se avoided many of the age-old problems of psychological inquiry, especially those encountered in structuralism. Thus, behaviorism arose in America; it emphasized the objective rather than subjective approach and focused on overt responses and their reinforcement. It was led by Watson and later by Skinner.

7. Gestalt psychology developed under Wertheimer as a protest against the analysis of conscious experience into separate elements, as advocated by structuralists, and the omission of conscious experience from psychological inquiry, as advocated by behaviorists. It stressed the study of the whole individual. As a system of thought, it has not been fully incorporated into the mainstream of contemporary psychology, but a contemporary reflection, called humanistic psychology, has prompted considerable interest. It emphasizes the uniqueness and complexity of human beings, the subjective side of human life, and the study of the whole person.

8. In contrast to the conscious experience of structuralism, the system of psychoanalysis, under Freud's leadership, focused on the unconscious processes and maladjustment. The basic concept is unconscious motivation, which states that human behavior is influenced by past events in a person's life of which he or she is no longer aware. Psychoanalysis also brought attention to the value of clinical work and procedures for the treatment of emotional problems.

Contemporary Psychology

9. Some of these systems, especially behaviorism and psychoanalysis, have changed psychology a great deal with respect to its scope, methods, and theoretical orientations. Others, after guiding research for a time, passed out of favor. Today, the research interest continues, and in addition there are numerous applied specialties, such as clinical, counseling, industrial, engineering, consumer, and legal psychology. Psychology is the scientific study of the behavior and experience of organisms.

10. Unfortunately, confusion about the nature of psychology is constantly created by persons who erroneously present themselves as experts in the study of behavior. Public education seems to be the most promising solution to this problem.

Suggested Readings

Boring, E. G. *A history of experimental psychology* (2nd ed.). New York: Appleton-Century-Crofts, 1950. A scholarly and popular description of the early history of experimental psychology.

Kasschau, R. A., Johnson, M. M., & Russo, N. F. *Careers in psychology.* Washington, D. C.: American Psychological Association, 1975. A pamphlet that describes psychologists' activities and requirements for becoming a psychologist.

Klein, D. B. *A history of scientific psychology: Its origins and philosophical backgrounds.* New York: Basic Books, 1970. A lengthy, well-illustrated volume with philosophical emphasis.

Schultz, D. *A history of modern psychology* (2nd ed.). New York: Academic Press, 1975. Concentrates on the development, influence, and decline of various systematic positions in psychology.

Watson, R. I. *The great psychologists: From Aristotle to Freud* (3rd ed.). Philadelphia: Lippincott, 1971. A comprehensive paperback that describes the development of psychology as a science.

Chapter 2

Methods of Research

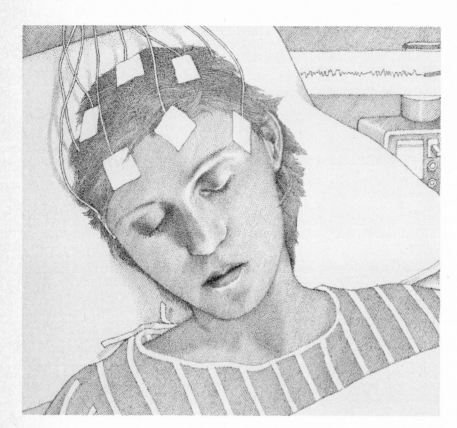

A college student wrote: "I dreamed that my father died and turned into a skeleton and made me play chess with him under the Christmas tree." This student had an interest in dreams and wanted to find out how to study them. In this chapter, we examine the ways in which psychologists study the various topics of psychology, including dreams.

Our concern is with methods of research, but the study of dreams is a useful illustration because it allows us to examine and compare each of the various approaches. Today, we can specify at least four general research methods, which fall on a continuum of control.

That is, they differ in the extent to which the investigator has control over the events being studied.

At one end, in *naturalistic observation,* subjects are studied in their own environments, unaffected by the investigator as far as is possible. In the *survey method* we intrude upon this privacy to the point of asking the subject questions by mail, telephone, or personal interview. In the *clinical method,* the investigator exerts still more control, by asking the subject to come to a clinic, private office, or other institution, where

Background and Methods

series of tests and treatments are administered. Finally, in the *experimental method* there is the fullest possible control. The subject enters a laboratory or comparable setting where the investigator manipulates the environment to a very large extent.

Naturalistic Observation

The aim of *naturalistic observation,* the most basic of the general research methods, is to study behavior in its natural setting, without asking any questions or administering tests in a clinic or laboratory. The investigator does nothing more than observe and record what is happening. For this reason, naturalistic observation is often the first step in a research program.

Precision and Inference

But before proceeding with any research, the topic of study must be identified precisely. Consider the question: What happens when we dream? This question may seem appropriate to the student taking an introductory psychology course, but the advanced researcher recognizes immediately that it is too broad. There are too many possibilities for study. There are physiological aspects, behavioral dimensions, dream contents, individual differences, and probable age differences, since infants and young children sleep a great deal more than do adults. Hence, the research question must be restricted.

To be more specific, the question might be limited as follows: What happens physiologically when we dream? Even more specific is: What changes, if any, take place in the patterns of breathing, pulse rate, and electrical brain activity when we dream? This question, assuming that we possess appropriate methods of measurement, is more answerable than the other two. As answers to such specific questions are obtained, piece by piece, they collectively constitute an answer to the broader questions.

Variables. The breathing pattern, blood pressure, and brain activity during dreams are variables that we wish to study. A *variable* is any changeable element or event that can be manipulated or studied in research. It is some aspect of the research situation that the investigator wishes to consider. Other variables might be the sleeper's mumblings, the amount of light in the room, and the type of food the person consumed before going to sleep. Commonly, such factors are studied in relation to one another.

But how do we study them? What is a change in breathing pattern? How do we know when one has occurred? How do we decide about blood pressure? We now need a system for observing and recording these variables.

Operational definitions. To deal with this problem, scientists generally use *operational definitions,* in which some specific procedure or set of operations is established for measuring a given variable, such as breathing pattern. That is, breathing pattern is identified in terms of readily observable, objective, repeatable conditions.

In earlier days, distance was determined by placing one's feet alternately in front of each other and counting the steps, a convenient procedure and certainly much better than indiscriminate guesses, since most adults' feet are nearly the same size as those of other adults. Of course, there were differences. Thus, the question arose: By whose feet was a foot to be measured? To improve the procedure, a standard, a readily observable foot of 12 inches, was selected. Today, distance is accurately measured by this standard procedure, using an operational definition of feet, yards, meters, or some other unit.

Similarly, how do we establish an operational definition of hunger in a lower animal? We cannot ask the animal how it feels, and in observing the animal we do not know whether a high degree of activity reflects a need for exercise, sexual arousal, exploratory behavior, or a state of hunger. Therefore, in many studies hunger is operationally defined in terms of the number of hours since the most recent feeding. The hunger in one rat is defined as 24 hours of food deprivation and in another, 36 hours. This definition is stated in objectively measurable units that can be understood and repeated by others, rather than in vague terms understood only by the investigator.

In studying dreams, we can define the pattern of breathing in terms of changes in the record from the *pneumograph,* an instrument that registers the movements of respiration in liters per second. Blood pressure can be defined in terms of millimeters of mercury, as recorded on a *sphygmomanometer,* and the *electroencephalograph* is used to record brain activity, measured as the number of waves per second.

Inference. Even with such apparatus to measure variables, which is helpful but not indispensable in science, another problem remains. Dreaming occurs inside the individual; it is not a directly observable event.

The college student who reported the dream at the beginning of this chapter is observed while she is in bed. She might be sleeping, resting, unconscious, dreaming, feigning sleep, or even dead. The only evidence immediately available is that she is in bed, and on this basis alone we cannot be sure of her condition or what she is doing. As we approach, we note that her chest is rising and falling. These events are not consistent with the inference that she is dead. An *inference* is a guess, hypothesis, or judgment drawn from some observable events. It concerns something not directly evident but based on available data. Accordingly, the inference that the woman is dead is no longer tenable.

Upon closer observation, we see that her breathing is deep, not shallow, so we infer that she is not unconscious.

Further, her eyes are closed and occasionally she mumbles or seems to be talking to someone who is not in the room. Hence, we tentatively discard the inference that she is resting. Instead, our observations lead to the inference that she is sleeping and perhaps dreaming.

In science it is often necessary to make inferences about conditions that cannot be observed directly. In physics, the structure of the nucleus is inferred from collision experiments; in chemistry, inferences concerning reactivity are essential. In medicine, the virus allegedly responsible for the common cold has not yet been identified, but it is presumed to exist. Medical scientists have adopted an ''as-if'' attitude; they investigate the cold symptoms as if they were caused by a virus. The use of inference has limitations because the investigator has ventured beyond the observed facts, but without this procedure some major questions about humanity would be entirely out of the realm of research.

No one has observed another person's dream, but dreams are not excluded from psychological research. Instead, researchers depend heavily, although not exclusively, on persons' reports of dreams. As we shall see, there are many other aspects of the dreaming state besides a sequence of visual scenes (Figure 2-1).

Overt and Covert Observation

With this background in scientific thinking, which applies to all methods of research, we return to naturalistic observation. Here, the basic technique is simply to be a careful observer. Equipped with recording devices, the investigator sometimes observes even his or her own behavior.

In 1892, when the study of dreams was just beginning, an American psychologist made some very careful observations about himself. He examined his own visual experiences at the moment of going to sleep, at the moment of awakening, and, insofar as possible, at the moment of dreaming. Then he wrote:

Background and Methods

technique eliciting language patterns & personality information, dream analysis, case report, 51:7839
technique for maintenance of longitudinal dream record, 52:5766
theoretical aspects of dream interpretation in terms of Freud's & Jung's & E. Erickson's & O. Rank's systems, 52:7681
therapeutic agreement technique using dreams, analytic process, personality disorder patients, 50:9386
unifying theory of dreams & nightmares, psychopathology & collective social panic behavior, 50:1235
water, dream symbolism, 50:284
written word as means to understanding & as distancing obscuring device, application to Freud's description of his dream about Irma, 52:2950

Dream Content
adaptively regressive models of experiencing, primary process expression in dreams, college women, 49:854
associations to key words from dream symbols, visual & graphic displays of language patterns & psychodynamic associations, oral-dependent 40 yr. old hospitalized male, 51:7681
birth order, dream recall & affiliative imagery in dreams, college students, 51:2545
cultural & sex differences, affiliation & achievement drives expressed in reported dream content & projective technique, unmarried college students, New York City vs. Lima, Peru, 49:2305
cultural differences, dream content, 16-18 yr. old Arabs & Israeli Jews, 50:8695
daydreaming styles, nocturnal dreaming, college students, 52:6856
dream content in laboratory dream reports, schizophrenic vs depressed patients, 52:1133
dream power, elucidation of central conflicts in psychotherapy, 52:8180
dreams about drinking, prognosis, alcoholics, 51:7356
dreams, content & relation to sleep disorders & diagnostic usage, children, 50:4604
dreams preceding hypomania, case reports, 51:11291
dreams, psychoanalytic treatment, schizophrenics, 51:7741
early memories & current daytime thoughts & current dreams about fathers, male college students, 52:7364
early primal scene observations, splitting self-representation in dreams & symptoms, case report, 51:7758
ego & present group situations & primary childhood group, dreams & dream structure, 51:9085
experiencing of dream, transference during analysis, young female borderline schizophrenic, 52:3800
extrasensory or paranormal information transfer, dreams, 52:4258
high vs. low imagery & distortion rates in dreams, hypnotic susceptibility, college students, 50:11364
hypnotic induction & suggestion, nocturnal dreaming & thinking, 51:8538
insight into symbolism of dreams, language of dream interpretation, book, 50:4901
K-complex as an indicator of phasic activation in NREM sleep associated with NREM mentation variations, 50:8360
low vs. medium vs. high levels of hypnotic susceptibility & personality characteristics, manifest dream content, female college students, 49:855
manifest dream content during pregnancy, childbirth duration, 50:1380
mental content & recall of Stage 4 night terrors, 26-52 yr olds suffering from nightmares, 52:7937
nocturnal sleep duration, aggressive & other dream content & dream recall frequency, female undergraduates, 49:3751
observations from psychoanalysis, mental life, genius & talented men, 49:7462
perimetazine vs mepromazine & ego function, dream content, neurotic vs psychotic mental patients vs normal Ss, 52:1477
personal meaning & social element in dream analysis, patient & therapist, 51:7764
precognitive dream analysis, 52:90
precognitive dreams, case report, 49:8175
presleep suggestions, nocturnal dream content solicited upon awakening from REM vs NREM sleep, 52:9141
reinforced subliminal vs. liminal vs. supraliminal visual stimuli, dream content, 49:3573
reserpine therapy, dream reports, chronic lobotomized schizophrenic patients, 52:3659
sex role orientation, dream recall & content, college students, 51:7132
sociological perspective from view of academic performance & social mobility & cultural salience, examination dreams, Hausa & Ibo & Yoruba students, Nigeria, 51:6928
success-failure decathexis, dream incorporation, male undergraduates, 49:7009
technique for maintenance of longitudinal dream record, 52:5766
telepathic influence with sensory bombardment, dream content & recall, college students, replication of S. Krippner's findings, 49:10311
troubles of conscience & roles in psychopathology, dream content & psychiatry, 51:11238
unconscious sense of time & psychosomatic significance, 25-yr-old male with bleeding ulcer in analysis, 51:9784
unifying theory of dreams & nightmares, psychopathology & collective social panic behavior, 50:1235
water, dream symbolism, 50:284

Dream Interpretation [SEE Dream Analysis]

Dream Recall
adaptively regressive models of experiencing, primary process expression in dreams, college women, 49:854
autokinetic perception, inner experience measure & daydreaming & dream recall & cognitive style, male college students, 51:3216
birth order, dream recall & affiliative imagery in dreams, college students, 51:2545
dream recall frequency & precognition & ESP attitudes, adults, 49:1599

psychoanalytic discussion, relationship between dreamer while dreaming & remembering dreams after awakening, 52:3791
psychotherapeutic use & method for self-analysis, dream interpretation, book, 50:5323
reported sleep-talking frequency, dream recall, 49:3714
repression vs interference of normal behavior, forgetting dreams, 52:10152
rigidity, dream recall, male vs. female college students, 49:2443
sex role orientation, dream recall & content, college students, 51:7132
technique for maintenance of longitudinal dream record, 52:5766
telepathic influence with sensory bombardment, dream content & recall, college students, replication of S. Krippner's findings, 49:10311

Dreaming [SEE ALSO Nightmares, REM Dreams]
actualization of dream-space, acting-out of experiences, 23-yr-old female in analysis, 51:9776
adaptive function of REM sleep, war neuroses, Vietnam war veterans, implications for psychoanalytic theories of dreaming, 49:11615
age differences & variability in individual sleep requirements, sleep disorders & insomnia & sleepwalking & enuresis & nightmares, 43:11037
alcohol, dreams & hallucinations, alcohol addicts, 51:7421
alcohol vs. caffeine, REM sleep & EEG, 47:407
alpha rhythm states, personality & self-restitution, relaxed wakefulness & dream & hallucinosis & twilight state & psychosis, 44:2518
anxiety intensity, definition & evaluation, symptom formation & amelioration & dream patterns & clinical examples, 44:2426
anxiety reduction & personality reintegration, symbol confrontation in directed daydream, case reports, 44:3760
archetypal content in remembered dreams, statistical investigation, 47:2039
attitudes toward death, dreams & "out-of-the-body" experiences, 44:4317
auditory average evoked response variability, sleep & dreaming, children & adults, 44:1911
autofellation, oral-genital auto-erotic manifestation of acts & fantasies & dreams & instinctive drive, 2 case reports, 48:7407
autokinesis as inner experience measure & daydreams & recall & content of night dreams & cognitive styles, 48:2088
awakeness & sleeping & dreaming, 51:10552
awakening during different sleep stages & phases & cycles, subjective judgments of preceding night sleep duration periods, 49:492
behavioral theory of images, 51:6168
belief in prophetic dreams, psychological mechanisms, 48:145
body image scores & varieties of consciousness, 47:4815
child analysis, dreams & autobiographical data, V. Tausk, 48:7332
clinical & experimental observations of sleep & dreaming & memory psychology, evolutionary brain formations, 52:288
communicative use of manifest dream content during analysis, 47:4941
conformational changes of body-tissue proteins, wakefulness & sleep & dreams & aging, 52:11614
conscious ordering vs. liberated visualization of unconscious, dreamwork, J. Hawkes' "The Lime Twig" & "Second Skin", 48:9364
contemporary & psychoanalytic theories of dream function, 50:11335
contentless vs. dreamless recall reports, menstrual cycle & time of report & total sleep time, 48:10247
cotherapist system in group psychotherapy, dream manifestation of latent problems of therapist, 4 dream descriptions, Japan, 44:5248
covert oral behavior during REM vs. NREM periods, conversational & visual dreams, 48:6206
creativity & imagery & dreams, review of L. Kubie, 44:5162
culturally patterned dreams & altered states of consciousness, 50:11073
culture shock, repression of symbolic links to American culture & affective imagery displaced by cultural identification & adaption, dream & memory of summer work in India, American scholars, 47:10695
day residues & recall residues & dreams, theoretical & clinical implications, 48:1188
daydreaming styles, nocturnal dreaming, college students, 52:6856
Descartes, psychological background, philosopher & scientist, dream, 44:1485
desensitization, dream changes, 47:9055
diagnostic judgment of manifest dream content, therapist vs. hospital professional vs. nonprofessional experience, hospitalized schizophrenics & nonschizophrenics, 47:9345
Dickens/C., analysis of dream representing loss of idealized object, 47:1147
dream & folktale as expression of waking thought, cognitive analysis, 44:2232
dream analysis & interpretation, personal understanding & guidance, case reports, 44:2430
dream analysis of traumatic neuroses, persons surviving dangerous experiences, 48:1187
dream as communication, symbolic expression composed in latent content of structural opposites, 48:7344
dream concept development & faulty reality testing, behavior disordered & borderline & psychotic 9-11 yr. olds, 50:5044
dream content during hypnotic dreaming, pursuit-like eye movements, 47:125
dream content, age differences, grade & junior high school students, 47:650
dream content, differential assimilation into waking consciousness & anxiety associated content, 47:10131
dream function, laboratory research vs. theories of S. Freud & C. Jung & A. Adler, 48:6203
dream groups & dynamics, use in classroom & therapeutic groups & understanding waking life, Senoi people of Malay Peninsula, 52:5996
dream hallucinations, genesis & primary contents, 47:4904
dream processing, differentiation & expansion of psychoanalytic theory & dream contents & transfer & defense & application in therapeutic methods & neuropsychological research, 47:11114
dream recall & auditory awakening thresholds in NREM sleep,

I am inclined to think that on closing the eyes for sleep the eyeballs are, as has been customarily supposed, turned upward and inward. This position is probably most favorable for the disappearance from consciousness of all visual images. . . . But I am inclined also to believe that, in somewhat vivid visual dreams, the eyeballs move gently in their sockets. (Ladd, 1892)

This observation was published inconspicuously in the back of a professional journal under a section called ''Notes.'' No one paid it much attention, perhaps because it is so difficult to make accurate observations on oneself, especially while falling asleep.

Overt observation. More commonly, observations are made of other organisms, human or animal, and in the procedure called obtrusive or *overt observation,* the investigator makes no effort to hide his or her intentions. The subject is aware of the observer, who often uses checklists, rating scales, and other instruments for keeping systematic records (Figure 2-2).

In the early 1950s an investigator in Chicago, Eugene Aserinsky, was collecting basic facts about sleeping infants. One of the chief variables in which he was interested was body movements prior to and during sleep. His operational definition of large movements was based on recordings obtained by a sensitive spring-type instrument attached to the crib. The smaller movements were observed directly and entered in a notebook. He noted the twitches of the arms and legs and movements in the face as the child went to sleep. He also noted the slow, rolling movements of the sleeper's eyes under the lids, which he had seen many times and knew to be prominent just prior to sleep. Apparently these movements were the eyeballs turning ''gently in their sockets,'' as observed more than fifty years earlier.

During one cribside visit, his attention suddenly was caught by something new. After the slow, uncoordinated, drifting eye movements, there appeared large, rapid movements, coordinated in both eyes, similar to those of someone watching a spirited game of Ping Pong in waking life. The investigator's first reaction was one of disbelief and surprise that no one had reported these rapid eye movements previously. They could be seen very clearly beneath the closed lid. Undoubtedly they had been noted, but apparently no one had seriously considered their possible scientific significance.

Immediately, Aserinsky went to his laboratory for further studies, but that is another part of our research story, which we will discuss later. As happened in this case, naturalistic observation is often the first step in scientific research. Here the investigator gathers ideas and makes hypotheses for later testing.

Afterwards, another method may be more useful. In nature, the great number of factors that influence any given event are so intermixed that cause-and-effect interpretations are commonly impossible on the basis of observation alone. As one investigator says: ''I find that during the long hours of observation in the field, I not only learn about behavior patterns, but I get ideas, 'hunches,' for theories, which I later test by experiments whenever possible'' (Tinbergen, 1965).

Figure 2-2 Classifying and Scoring Dreams. *In modern analyses, dreams are studied according to several categories, including setting, characters, aggressive elements, and emotion. A system for scoring the dream setting is illustrated here and shows in this dream that the contents concern indoor and familiar settings. (Adapted from Hall & Van de Castle, 1966)*

Portion of the Dream	Scoring
I was in MY ROOM getting dressed.	IF
We were in what seemed to be A CELLAR.	IU
I was IN A STORE buying a pair of shoes.	IQ
I was yelling from OUR NEIGHBOR'S DRIVEWAY.	OF

I: Indoors	U: unfamiliar
O: outdoors	Q: questionable
F: familiar	(familiar/unfamiliar)

Covert observation. While Aserinsky was collecting facts about sleeping babies he could readily be observed by the baby, but his presence probably had little influence on the drowsy infant's behavior. In other cases, the subject might alter his or her responses in order to please or impress the investigator, who therefore tries various methods to reduce this influence. The investigator might spend considerable time with the subjects before the study begins, so that they become accustomed to his or her presence. Automatic recording devices might be employed; while the subject is aware of them, they are less threatening than the actual presence of the investigator (Long, 1974). In unobtrusive or *covert observation*, the investigator's purpose is concealed, so that the subjects do not know they are being studied.

In investigations of animals, binoculars and high-powered cameras are common equipment, with which innumerable species have been studied covertly (Figure 2-3). A man researching the digger wasp describes his preparations for such a session:

Settling down to work, I started spending the wasps' working days (which lasted from about 8 A.M. to 6 P.M.) on the "philanthus plains," as we called this part of the sands. . . . An old chair, field glasses, notebooks, and food and water for the day were my equipment. (Tinbergen, 1958)

Problems in Observation

One problem in naturalistic observation concerns the focus of the observer's attention. As the novice investigator quickly discovers, everything cannot be noted and recorded; there is simply too much to be observed. Therefore, sometimes no special categories are used at the outset of a research program. The observer simply records as much as possible and notes those events that seem most significant, regardless of whether they are expected or unexpected. Later, as the research goals become clearer, certain variables come into focus and operational definitions are more firmly established. Then, observation becomes more selective, and specific systems are employed for noting the presence, absence, and intensity of specific behaviors. Special situations may even be

Figure 2-3 Naturalistic Observation of Animals. *Rings with numbers are placed on the flippers of birds to be studied in detail, and they can be read even at a great distance by the use of binoculars. The bird in the right foreground is No. 16. (Sladen, 1957; photo from Her Majesty's Stationery Office)*

■ *One spring day on the campus of our university, a friend and I performed a small experiment of our own design. We were interested in testing the reactions of people (relatively intelligent) to an obstacle placed in their path. We placed a string at mid-calf height across one of the most frequented paths in the quadrangle. We then sat inconspicuously on a step nearby to observe. The first guy to come along walked up to the string, stopped and then stepped over it and walked on without looking back. We were amazed when other groups came along and did precisely the same thing. About forty people had passed and not one had questioned the presence of the string or attempted to remove it. We watched a little longer and more students did exactly what the first ones had done, and later two professors stepped over the string. My friend and I came to the conclusion that the human being was an uninquisitive animal who would rather confront an obstacle than question its presence. As we were getting up to walk away disgustedly, we saw a little boy about 8 years old come up to the string and examine it closely; then he examined the trees to which the string was attached. He then proceeded to untie one end of it and stood back to examine the effect that it had. Seeing that it had none, he untied the other end, rolled the string up carefully and stuffed it in his pocket. My friend and I watched our hypothesis on human nature go down the drain.*

devised for testing hypotheses in a natural setting. ■ In short, there seems to be an advantage in a broad beginning with increased precision and focus as the work progresses.

Another difficult aspect of naturalistic observation concerns the degree to which inferences about motives and feelings should be included in the record, since they cannot be observed directly. Many investigators feel that only observable behavior should be noted, and with this procedure high agreement among observers is usually achieved. Other investigators feel that observation without some interpretation is essentially meaningless, and therefore they include some inference in the record, usually designated in a special manner (Figure 2-4)

William James recognized these problems and stated that no rules could be established in advance for naturalistic observation. He merely advised the would-be researcher to ''use as much sagacity as you possess.'' He also warned of the ''great sources of error'' in this method, which are the intrusions of the observer's personal biases. For the most part, therefore, the investigator's task is simply to observe and record. Inference and interpretation are left for another day, after the basic facts have been collected.

The Survey Method

In the survey method, the subject is not merely observed. Rather, this person is asked many questions by mail, telephone, or interview. A *survey* is an investigation of the attitudes, traits, or behaviors of a large group of people, usually accomplished by presenting them with various series of questions.

This method was first used by two cousins, Charles Darwin and Sir Francis Galton, the latter being well known for his discoveries in anthropology, sensory psychology, and statistics. About the future of their work, William James warned: ''Messrs. Darwin and Galton

Figure 2-4 Naturalistic Observation of Human Beings. *In one study, eight different observers took turns recording the behavior of a seven-year-old boy, Raymond Birch, from the moment of his waking at 7:00 A.M. until he went to bed at 8:32 P.M. This excerpt concerning his behavior at school shows that the observer occasionally made special comments or inferences about the boy's attitudes and feelings, as indicated by the italics. (One Boy's Day by R. G. Barker and H. F. Wright. New York: Harper & Row, 1951.)*

11:13 Raymond turned back to his paper and worked at it briefly.

Then he got up from his seat and walked quickly to the teacher's desk.

He stood quietly and patiently at the teacher's desk waiting for her to finish with four other children at her desk so that she might check his work.

11:14 The teacher turned to Raymond, took his paper and looked it over.

There was a brief, businesslike exchange between the teacher and Raymond about the paper.

They were too far away for me to hear what was said.

Mrs. Logan raised some question, however, about a part of the work.

Raymond tried to defend what he had on the paper.

Then, grinning broadly, he took the paper and started walking slowly back to his seat.

The grin may have been to cover up embarrassment or disappointment at his performance.

As he walked back to his seat, he carefully folded the paper. Then it disappeared. I could not see what Raymond did with it.

---

have set the example of circulars of questions sent out by the hundreds to those supposed able to reply. The custom has spread, and it will be well for us in the next generation if such circulars be not ranked among the common pests of life'' (1890).

Surveys are now too common for some people. For others, they make an important contribution to understanding humanity. In any case, they are probably the best known of the major methods of psychological research. Extensive use of this method today is due partly to the availability of high-speed computers for analyzing the data from large samples of subjects.

Sampling Procedures

Years ago, on March 1, 1932, sometime between 8 P.M. and 10 P.M., a ladder was placed against the side of a house in Hopewell, New Jersey. Someone ascended the ladder to the second floor, left a ransom note, and fled into the night with the 20-month-old son of Charles and Anne Morrow Lindbergh. This kidnapping was a national crisis and "clues" arrived from all over the country: a bottle cap was found, allegedly belonging to the baby; "Red" Johnson, the boyfriend of the baby's nurse, had the infant at sea; the baby would be dropped at home by parachute.

Incidental sample.   Amid the concern of the Lindbergh kidnapping case, two psychologists indirectly entered the case. They published in a Boston newspaper an advertisement for clairvoyant dreams about what had happened. *Clairvoyance* is the capacity to know about events without using the known sensory capacities. It is an alleged aspect of extrasensory perception (ESP). There were no restrictions on who could participate; each person sending a dream to them at Harvard University was to indicate only his or her sex, age, marital status, number of children, and the contents of the dream. This notice was picked up by other newspapers in North America, and altogether the psychologists received more than 1,300 accounts of dreams.

This procedure for soliciting information is called an *incidental sample* because anyone who happens to respond is included. There is no effort to question

people of certain ages, both sexes, and various occupational and ethnic groups. Such samples are common in survey research because they are easy to obtain.

When the dead baby's body was discovered and its condition reported to the nation, all the dreams were carefully examined for accuracy of information. To make these studies as objective as possible, the psychologists focused on only three incontestable facts—the baby was found dead, it was in a shallow grave, and it was near woods. These data were later accepted as evidence in the trial of Bruno Hauptmann, who was convicted of the kidnapping and murder.

Analyses showed that four dreams, which is less than 1 percent, reported these items correctly. According to the investigators, this figure is extremely low because the baby would have to be (a) dead or alive; (b) above ground, in the ground, or in the water; and, if in the ground, (c) in the cellar of a building, in an open area, or in the woods. Many more than four correct dreams would be expected just on the basis of chance (Murray & Wheeler, 1937). Altogether, there was no convincing evidence for clairvoyant dreams in this case.

Today, many people report dreams that seem to be clairvoyant, but successful research on this topic is difficult to achieve. The findings are mixed and the controversy continues, with evidence on both sides (Krippner & Ullman, 1970; Belvedere & Foulkes, 1971).

A representative sample.   The problem in the Lindbergh survey is that not everyone in the population had an equal chance to participate, since the advertisement was carried only in large-city newspapers. Many people in small towns might have had clairvoyant dreams, but they were not included in the incidental sample.

In most modern surveys, a concerted effort is made to obtain a small group of subjects, called a *sample*, that depicts what is true of a specified larger group, called the *population*. The population includes all people, objects, or events of a

■ *I was on the staff of the school paper and proposed that we run a survey on the popularity of the three school presidential candidates. RM, a junior, was chosen to ask 200 out of the 1400 students attending WHS which candidate they preferred, and results predicted an overwhelming victory for Louie, with Sam placing a distant second, and Melissa an almost nonexistent third. We published the survey the day before the voting began.*

Two days later our staff was rather surprised! Sam, "the surfer," won, Melissa, "the hood," placed a close second, and Louie, "the intellectual," was a close third. We asked RM how he could have gotten such incorrect results by running around school asking anyone he saw how he or she planned to vote. He said that he felt too sick the day of the survey to wander all over school, so he just asked the people in each of his seven classes.

RM's classes consisted of honors history, honors English, advanced algebra, advanced biology, chemistry, fourth-year German, and physical education. No wonder his sample predicted a huge victory for "the intellectual." . . .

particular class. It might be the general population of the United States, as defined by the census, or all the schoolchildren in New Jersey, as defined by the state board of education, or all red marbles in a certain toy store, as defined by an inventory. When any sample reflects the characteristics of a certain population, it is called a *representative sample*. It accurately represents the larger group; it is not biased by including, for example, only the tallest people, too many senior citizens, or too few females in comparison with the population.

To achieve a sample that is representative of a certain population, a *quota sample* can be used, which includes people from each subgroup in the same proportions as they appear in the larger population. A quota sample in the United States would include so many Oriental-Americans, so many Afro-Americans, so many Spanish-Americans, and so forth, depending on their numbers in the general population. The people from these designated subgroups would be selected on a random basis.

In an *area sample*, certain geographic areas are identified, such as New England, the Middle Atlantic States, the North Central Region, and the West Coast. Then, a certain proportion of subjects is chosen from each area, depending on its population relative to the whole country. Again, random procedures are used for selecting the subjects from these areas.

The random sample. From these descriptions, it should be clear that random sampling is basic to obtaining a representative group, even when subgroups have been identified. In fact, randomization is *the* fundamental principle in any research, from naturalistic observation to the experimental methods. Furthermore, as any random sample is increased in size, the influence of chance factors generally becomes less. Thus, a large random sample is more likely to be representative of the population than is a smaller one.

To obtain a *simple random sample*, each individual in the target population is designated by a different number. Then, some numbers are selected on the basis of chance, by using a table of random numbers or by placing each number on a card and shuffling the cards thoroughly. An important principle in random sampling is that each subject has the same chance of being included. Another is that each selection is independent; that is, the inclusion of any particular element or person in the study has no influence on the inclusion of any other person. To obtain a random sample of ten subjects, for example, ten numbers are selected in this way (Figure 2-5).

Interpreting the Results
Violation of these sampling principles can severely limit the value of any study. With a nonrandom sample, the investigator cannot confidently draw conclusions about a larger population. ■

Limits in generalizing. An anthropologist studied the dream content of people living in Tzintzuntzan, a small Mexican village. His sample included 42 citizens of the town, 16 men and 26 women, aged 16 to 75 years. It can be seen immediately that this distribution of 38 percent male and 62 percent female does not approximate the 50:50 ratio found in such communities. It appears that each person in the village did not have an equal chance of being chosen. In fact, the investigator states that he essentially studied his friends (Foster, 1973). Therefore, the sample was biased, not random.

Of the 334 dreams collected, 37 percent of the males' dreams were contributed by only 2 men, and 36 percent of the females' dreams were reported by just 3 women—a mother and her two daughters. Altogether, 6 persons contributed very heavily to this study, and

Figure 2-5   Sampling with Random Numbers.   *To select a random sample of 20 percent from a population of 100 subjects, all subjects are numbered and then 20 numbers are drawn according to a table of random numbers. There are various procedures for selecting a starting point in the table and determining in which direction the table is to be read. A sample could be drawn more easily by using 20 persons in one location, but such a sample might be biased rather than random. (Excerpt of table from Fisher & Yates,* Statistical Tables for Biological, Agricultural and Medical Research, *published by Longman Group Ltd., London (previously published by Oliver and Boyd, Edinburgh), and by permission of the author and publishers. Photo by Vivienne della Grotta.)*

RANDOM SAMPLE

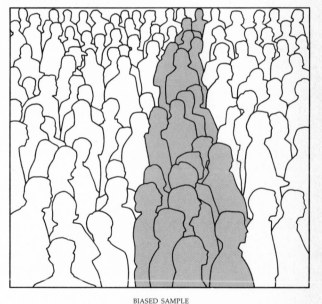

BIASED SAMPLE

TABLE OF RANDOM NUMBERS

	1	2	3	4	5	6	7	8	9	10	11	12	13	14	15	16	17	18	19	20
1	03	47	43	73	86	36	96	47	36	61	46	98	63	71	62	33	26	16	80	45
2	97	74	24	67	62	42	81	14	57	00	42	53	32	37	32	27	07	36	07	51
3	16	76	62	27	66	56	50	26	71	07	32	90	79	78	53	13	55	38	58	59
4	12	56	85	99	26	96	96	68	27	31	05	03	72	93	15	57	12	10	14	21
5	55	59	56	35	64	38	54	82	46	21	31	62	43	90	90	06	18	44	32	53

they were not selected on a quota basis, area basis, or through simple random sampling. The researcher concluded that the dreams reflected the basic character and cultural outlook of the village. More properly, it should have been concluded that the dreams perhaps reflected the outlook of an incidental sample, the researcher's friends in the village of Tzintzuntzan.

Limits of verbal reports. A further limitation in most survey research is that the investigator observes only the products of his or her subjects' behavior, such as written answers or marks on a questionnaire, rather than the behavior itself. Thus, many survey data indicate what certain people *say* about their dreams, favorite cereal, voting preferences, sexual habits, or whatever. Whether these statements actually reflect behavior is difficult to ascertain. Studies of this issue have been both encouraging and discouraging, depending partly on the survey topic (Pernanen, 1974).

Some people who respond to questionnaires answer too hastily, giving incorrect information; others intentionally falsify information; and some do not respond at all, leaving the investigator to decide whether the results merely represent characteristics of people who answer questionnaires. Various statistical adjustments for such nonresponses in survey data have been widely discussed, but no fully satisfactory solution has been achieved (Fuller, 1974; Mandell, 1974).

Despite these limitations, the survey method is widely used. The obvious reason, in contrast to naturalistic observation, is the enormous efficiency with which voluminous data can be obtained from many subjects.

The Clinical Approach

The study of dreams also has been pursued by the *clinical approach*, which means that psychological activities are carried out in a clinic or hospital, usually for the purpose of dealing with an individual's personal problems. This work involves diagnosis and treatment of various psychological functions and processes, including learning, intelligence, emotional reactions, motivation, and others. One additional benefit of such efforts is that they contribute to our general understanding of human beings, as well.

Idiographic Analysis

The other methods of research under consideration are concerned chiefly with formulating universal statements about people. Their aim is to establish principles that apply to the general population, insofar as possible. Thus, these studies are called *nomothetic*, from the Greek root *nomo*, meaning "law." The purpose of nomothetic research is to discover general laws.

Clinical and counseling psychologists, on the other hand, are usually more interested in understanding a given individual than in drawing broader generalizations. Many of them engage in *idiographic* research, which means that the behavior of any individual is best described in terms of his or her own special lawfulness. Uniqueness is emphasized in idiographic investigations; uniformities among individuals are of lesser concern.

In clinical work, the psychologist assembles all kinds of information that may be helpful in understanding the individual. Psychological, medical, vocational, and educational information is prepared in a case study or *case history*. It forms the basis of diagnosis and treatment, and hence, its preparation requires the work of well-trained persons (Schwartz, 1974).

Case of Dora. The most famous clinical investigator of dreams was Sigmund Freud, and one of his best-known cases involved a woman named Dora, who came to see him after a suicide letter written by her was discovered by her parents. At the time, she was 18 years old and lived with her parents and a 20-

year-old brother. Her father was a highly active, talented man in his late forties, whose interests for the most part were outside the family, especially in his love affair with the wife of one of his best friends. Dora's mother had less education and devoted herself almost exclusively to housekeeping chores.

At the age of 8, Dora began to show signs of maladjustment, chiefly in the form of puzzling physical illnesses. The most pronounced symptom was sudden attacks of laborious breathing, for which there was no apparent explanation. The family physician diagnosed the disorder as a nervous condition and prescribed rest, but the problem continued intermittently. At about age 12, Dora began to experience severe migraine headaches, coupled with attacks of nervous coughing, and these too persisted irregularly. Each episode lasted from three to five weeks, although one continued for several months.

Another troublesome symptom accompanied the early stages of each attack—complete loss of voice. Several different therapies had been tried and had failed, and then Dora developed a strong resistance to medical advice. It was only at her father's insistence that she consulted Freud, at which point she was suffering from a cough and hoarseness (Freud, 1905).

Freud's approach. Two of Dora's dreams served as the departure point for several clinical sessions. One was lengthy, and concerned her misadventures in a strange town; the other was recurrent, which, therefore, interested Freud considerably:

A house was on fire. My father was standing beside my bed and woke me up. I dressed quickly. Mother wanted to stop and save her jewel-case; but Father said: "I refuse to let myself and my two children be burnt for the sake of your jewel-case." We hurried downstairs, and as soon as I was outside I woke up. (1905)

Freud listened carefully and pursued the significance of each detail in a complex analysis which suggested a sexual basis of her problems. Dora recalled that Mr. K. had recently given her a jewel case, which perhaps explained the appearance of this object in her dream. But as Freud pointed out, "jewel case" is also a favorite expression for the female genitals. Perhaps it was her own "jewel case" that Dora feared was in danger, since she was in love with Mr. K.

Freud arrived at such hypotheses through a detailed study of many aspects of the case, including an analysis of Dora's dreams and her behaviors while awake, as she described them in psychoanalytic sessions. According to Freud's theory, dreams and certain waking behaviors are symbolic expressions of our unconscious thoughts. As we saw earlier, they are regarded as representing conflicts, impulses, and wishes of which we are unaware, often dating back to early childhood. ■ Freud knew that this new viewpoint would meet with resistance from his colleagues. In fact, he waited four years to publish Dora's case, which attributed forbidden sexual impulses to a young girl.

Today, not everyone agrees with Freud's conclusions; in fact, some people harshly object to them (Jurjevich, 1974). His theory of dreams has received considerable criticism, but it is widely agreed that Freud was significantly responsible for focusing attention on the importance of childhood experiences in the adult personality and for developing the clinical approach to investigations in psychology.

Interviews and Tests

Besides the case history, another feature of the clinical method is the interview. The clinical *interview* is a conversation between the therapist and another person, sometimes called the patient, that is aimed at diagnosis or treatment. The way in which the dialogue proceeds and the extent and nature of each person's role can vary

■ *A dream I particularly remember was when I was twelve years old. At the time my parents had just been divorced and my mother, younger brother, and I were fleeing the tensions of the time by moving to Florida. It was a very insecure time for me, having to leave a home I had always known and going far away where I would know only two other people. . . . I dreamt that I was walking along a beach after a vicious storm had passed. I was looking for my mother and brother for I had last seen them there. Soon I got very tired and stopped by an overturned boat lying amid the seaweed. When I stopped to turn it over, I found my family lying beneath, dead from drowning. It was a terrifying dream and was one of the few that have ever awakened me.*

Figure 2-6 Interview with a Child. *When interviewing children, communication is often facilitated by permitting the child to play with toys or to make drawings. In this instance, a five-year-old child drew a picture of her dream and then described it. The question marks indicate points at which she was queried by the psychologist: "Santa Claus is going water skiing but a monster might eat him up. The boat is going to the North Pole. . . . That's a mommy fish and the babies and they're going to the North Pole. (?) They're happy. (?) Because they're with the mommy. . . ."*

widely. Sometimes the patient is asked many questions (Figure 2-6). In other instances he or she is allowed to behave more spontaneously, raising and discussing issues as they occur, which was Freud's approach.

Types of interviews. In the traditional *psychoanalytic interview* the person lies on a couch and speaks as freely as possible about whatever comes to mind. The basic idea here is that a person is more likely to be relaxed when lying down, and therefore the interview can proceed on the basis of the subject's deeper thoughts and feelings, rather than on topics of daily conversation or the therapist's ideas. As a general rule in clinical interviews today, however, the client sits in a chair and the therapist is more active. Depending upon his or her orientation, the therapist may ask many questions, give answers, and even give advice.

An unusual example of the interview, used for selection and not therapy, is the *stress interview*, in which a tense, high-pressure atmosphere is intentionally created to evaluate the interviewee's capacity for managing himself or herself in stressful situations. Some questions are asked in a conciliatory manner, using the soft sell approach. Others are asked in a loud voice, sometimes with simultaneous cross-questioning by several people. During this process, the interviewee is studied carefully for signs of emotionality, such as sweating, flushing, and stuttering under these stressful conditions. Some people have exploded with anger, others have wept, and still others protest. Overall, the intent is to gain insight into the individual through wide variations in the interview technique.

Psychological tests. Perhaps the best-known aspect of clinical work is the use of psychological tests. They vary widely in scope and structure, and since the basic ingredient is always a set of questions, they are commonly regarded as an extension of the interview. They are used, however, in many contexts outside the interview situation.

Test questions may be highly specific, as in educational testing, or open-ended, as sometimes occurs in personality testing. Criteria may be available for judging the answers, or the answers may be rated in a more subjective manner. Tests are constantly being constructed for diverse purposes, including the measurement of dream contents (Figure 2-7).

Incidentally, Freud was not inclined to use psychological tests. He relied essentially on the interview for collecting data on human behavior, and thus one criticism of his work is that it lacks precision. His definitions were sometimes more literary than operational, and he made extensive use of inference. His procedure sometimes departed from the basic scientific principles discussed earlier, but it enabled him to consider a wide range of behavior and eventually to establish his renowned psychoanalytic theory.

Figure 2-7 A Procedure for Rating Dream Reports. *Upon awakening a sleeping subject, the investigator can ask questions such as these. Methods are available for scaling the answers and assigning numerical values. ("Dimensions of dreaming: a factored scale for rating dream reports" by P. Hauri, J. Sawyer, and A. Rechtschaffen.* Journal of Abnormal Psychology, *1967, 72, 16–22. Copyright 1967 by the American Psychological Association. Reprinted by permission.)*

1. How unreal was the dream?

2. To what extent did you, the dreamer, participate actively in the dream and attempt to influence its outcome?

3. How pleasant was the dream?

4. To what extent did you, the dreamer, engage in physical aggression in the dream?

5. How much activity was there with the opposite sex?

6. With what time in your life was the dream associated?

Experimental Methods

Through clinical studies, Freud decided that dreams are partly influenced by events that occur while we are sleeping. In fact, he said that a minor function of dreams is to preserve sleep, in the sense of incorporating loud or sudden stimuli into the sleeper's mental life and thus preventing him or her from awakening.

How could this idea be tested? In naturalistic observation, the investigator simply observes what happens and how often it happens, but it cannot be stated with any confidence that A causes B, that is, that a banging shutter prompts a dream about fireworks. Similarly, the answer cannot be found in the survey approach, and in clinical work the only manipulations that are usually permissible are those deemed beneficial for the subject, since the purpose is to provide some sort of therapy.

The most promising answer to such questions comes from experimental methods, where the essential purpose is to discover what leads to what. In the *experimental method,* the research variables are controlled in one way or another, thereby permitting the study of cause-and-effect relationships. For this reason, experimental research is often considered to stand foremost among the various methods in psychology.

The first recorded experimental studies of this "outside stimulation" theory of dreams occurred in 1861, when a Frenchman named Alfred Maury had simple experiments performed on himself, perhaps because no one else was quite so willing to be pinched, tickled, and otherwise tormented while asleep. When the sleeping Maury was pinched, he reported the next morning that he dreamed about being given medical treatment. When exposed to a heated iron, he dreamed about people with their feet on hot coals. When he was tickled on the face, he dreamed that a mask was being pulled off, peeling his skin at the same time. When metal was struck, Maury dreamed about bells sounding a French revolution (Maury, 1861).

Maury's work prompted a cause-and-effect conclusion: dream contents are caused by external factors. If the bedstead falls across one's neck, as happened to Maury, one dreams about being guillotined. When one throws off the bedclothes, one dreams about being naked. However, this view has not been fully confirmed by more recent experiments. Modern studies with better controls have shown that external factors are not of primary significance in determining dream content. When a sleeper is sprayed with water, that person may or may not dream about being wet, and furthermore, that person's dream includes a wide variety of contents not evident in the external stimulation. In the long run, the acceptability of scientific information depends not on one experiment but on the production of the same results in repeated research.

Research Variables

In a psychological experiment, the investigator purposely manipulates some variables or factors in order to observe the consequence. These variables can be any aspect of the research situation, as illustrated in Maury's work.

Types of variables. A variable that initiates some activity is known as a *stimulus,* the Latin word for "spur". The resulting activity or consequent event, if it involves action by any organism, is called a *response.* In research, stimuli are also known as S-variables and responses as R-variables. The stimulus of shaking the sleeping Maury probably would awaken him, which is a response.

Aspects of the *organism,* or subject, are known as O-variables. If Maury were sick or drugged, these conditions would influence his response to the stimulus of shaking him. A person's age, weight, sex, educational level, and personality traits also are organismic variables. Some of these factors are difficult to define, but since they are separate from the external stimuli, and influence the individual's response, they are of considerable interest to many experimental psychologists.

S-O-R and S-R approaches. For some people, the basic formula for psychological research is: $R = f (S,O)$. This expression indicates that any particular response is a joint function of the stimulation and the conditions of the organism. The research problem is to discover which stimuli and which organism conditions lead to which response(s).

The ways in which S–O–R variables act, react, and influence one another may be complex indeed, but in our simple example of awakening Maury, the important S-variables include how hard we shake him, how long, the noise level in the room, and so forth. Significant O-variables are the sleeper's degree of fatigue, length of sleep, and general state of health; R-variables include mumbling, twitching, talking, sitting up, and even getting out of bed. These three categories of variables are specified in much but not all research.

Other psychologists prefer to minimize the importance of the individual or-

ganism. They are not as interested in differences among individuals as in the characteristics of a species. They think primarily in terms of S- and R-variables, and are referred to as S-R psychologists. Another reason for the S-R approach is that certain O-variables are difficult to specify. Some that are relatively stable, such as attitudes and intelligence, can be considered as responses, while those that are less enduring, such as fatigue and hunger, can be considered as stimuli.

The Classical Experiment

Regardless of one's orientation, the experimenter must decide which stimulus or organism variables to study in relation to which response variables. That is, in the classical experimental method all significant aspects of the environment and characteristics of the organism must be controlled or held constant *except one,* which is purposely manipulated. If an effect is observed, that is, if a change is observed in some other variable, then it is assumed to be the result of the manipulated factor, especially if the control procedures are well established (Figure 2-8).

Independent variables. Since the experimenter determines which variable or variables are to be manipulated, they are referred to as *antecedent variables* or *independent variables.* Changes in these factors are not dependent on any other aspect of the experiment, except the investigator's decisions. The independent variable is the S- or O-factor that the experimenter manipulates in accordance with the basic question in the study. If the investigator wants to know the influence of loud noises on sleeping, he or she makes a loud noise, which is then the independent variable.

The reason for traditionally limiting experimental observations to a single independent variable can be readily illustrated. Suppose that a loud noise occurred at the same time that Maury was jostled. If he awoke, it would be difficult to decide whether the noise, the jostling, or both brought about this response.

Dependent variables. In addition to introducing some independent variable, the experimenter observes and measures the subject's responses. These are called *consequent variables* or *dependent variables* because their presence, absence, or degree of intensity seems to depend on the independent variable. In the case of the sleeping Maury, a loud noise or bright light might be the independent variable, and mumbling, talking, or other R-variables, separately or collectively, could be the dependent variables. The choices of variables are decisions of the experimenter (Figure 2-9).

In Maury's experiments, being pinched was the stimulus chosen for study in the first experiment and therefore it is the independent variable. The dependent variable was his report of his dream about receiving medical treatment. In the next instance, exposure to

Figure 2-8 A Controlled Environment. *In the anechoic chamber, reflected sounds are negligible and, thus, hearing can be studied without interference from echoes. (NASA)*

STIMULUS VARIABLES	ORGANISM VARIABLES	RESPONSE VARIABLES

STIMULUS VARIABLES	ORGANISM VARIABLES	RESPONSE VARIABLES
C ANCILLARY TEXT MATERIALS (NONE)	C AGE (30 TO 49)	EXTRACURRICULAR ACTIVITIES
C FACULTY SUPPORT (NONE)	C HEALTH (GOOD)	DV ACADEMIC SUCCESS
IV COMPUTER-ASSISTED INSTRUCTION	C SEX (MALE)	INTEREST IN ELECTRONICS
C TYPE OF CURRICULUM (ENGINEERING)	C PRIOR EXPERIENCE WITH CAI (NONE)	AND OTHERS
C AND OTHERS	C AND OTHERS	

Figure 2-9 Independent and Dependent Variables. *Here the experimenter has selected computer-assisted instruction (CAI) as the independent variable and is studying its influence on academic success, which is the dependent variable. (Sheila A. Farr photo)*

Methods of Research

heat was the independent variable and the description of the dream of hot coals was the dependent variable. The reader should be cautioned, however. In many psychological experiments the independent and dependent variables are more complex and cannot be identified so readily in terms of stimuli and responses, respectively.

Multifactor Studies

The reader also should be cautioned about the fallacy of the single cause, as suggested in aphorisms such as: "Spare the rod and spoil the child." One is just as likely to hear the opposite view: "You catch more flies with sugar than with vinegar." Such statements are occasionally true and thus perhaps are remembered, but invariably they are oversimplified. In human behavior, few one-to-one relationships are observed; more often several factors are involved.

Multiple basis of behavior. One condition, such as sparing the rod, is unlikely to bring about one predictable outcome, a spoiled child, because children, parents, rewards and punishments, and environments all differ. Hence, outcomes also differ. Even if a child is "spoiled," there are undoubtedly other reasons besides whether or not the rod was used. Thus, we speak of the *fallacy of the single cause.*

A central theme of this book, in fact, is the *multiple basis of behavior.* Behavior is influenced by many factors; scientific investigations are concerned with identifying these factors and determining their interdependence.

Additive and interactive effects. Because behavior is influenced by many factors, modern psychologists often study the influence of two or more independent variables simultaneously, a procedure that is possible with the use of refined statistical methods. These investigations, known as *multifactor studies,* are preferred by many contemporary in-

vestigators because of their efficiency, although the basic procedure is similar to that of the single-factor model.

The interest in multifactor studies lies not only in efficiency but also in what happens when two or more factors are combined. Sometimes the result is an *additive effect,* meaning that the total influence of all the factors is the sum of their separate influences. In other words, no independent variable influences the effect of any other independent variable; the final result is simply their cumulative sum. For example, a sleeper may awaken slightly to a loud noise and slightly to a tap on the shoulder, and in the additive effect both factors combined are sufficient to arouse the sleeper almost completely.

In other instances, the result is an *interactive effect,* meaning that the effect of a given independent variable depends on the presence or level of one or more other independent variables. Or the effect of one independent variable changes with changes in some other variable. Thus, moderate consumption of alcoholic beverages before going to sleep has no significant effect on a sleeper's health. Similarly, ingestion of a moderate dose of phenobarbital should have no significant effect. But when taken together, even in normal amounts, these two factors can have an extremely powerful and adverse effect on one's physical condition, sometimes even resulting in death. The effect of the alcohol is markedly altered by the phenobarbital, and vice versa. In brief, interaction effects are present whenever the influence of any given factor varies with the presence or level of other factors.

Design of Experiments

Maury's work was a beginning in the experimental study of dreams, but it suffered from serious defects. How could anyone be reasonably certain that the heated iron, for example, caused the dream about hot coals? Other factors, apart from the independent variable, were not well controlled.

Almost a century later, when Eugene Aserinsky made his discovery of rapid eye movements in sleeping infants, experimental techniques had advanced considerably, and improved controls were possible. Thus, in the laboratory Aserinsky and a colleague checked to confirm the regularity of these movements, painting sleepers' eyelids black and using a flashlight to observe more carefully. Later, they took motion pictures and then performed a controlled experiment on these movements.

The hypothesis in this research was that the extremely *rapid eye movements* (REMs) that occurred during sleep had some relationship to dreaming. The plan was to use ten subjects who would be awakened sometimes during REM periods and sometimes when there were no rapid eye movements. In all cases, the subject would be asked whether he or she had just been dreaming.

When the subjects were awakened under these conditions, almost 80 percent of the REM cases reported dreams, compared to only 20 percent of the non-REM cases (Aserinsky & Kleitman, 1953, 1955). With this finding, a whole new realm of research was opened—the experimental study of dreaming. It was the most notable advance in the study of dreams since the work of Sigmund Freud (Figure 2-10).

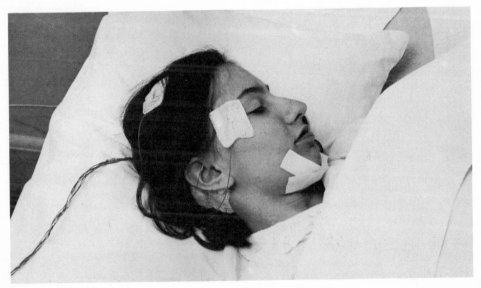

Figure 2-10 Laboratory Studies. *The subject is prepared by attaching electrodes beside the eyes to record REMs, to the scalp to record brain waves (EEGs), and under the chin to record muscle tonus. In most laboratories, the subject is alone in one room with a light and tape recorder while an experimenter monitors electronic recording equipment in another room. (From* The Biology of Dreaming *by Ernest Hartmann, M.D., published by Charles C. Thomas, Springfield, Ill., 1967.)*

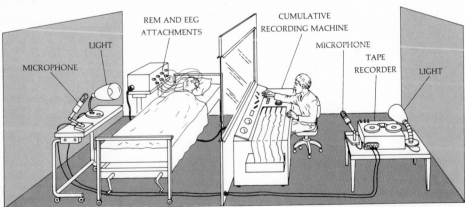

MICROPHONE   LIGHT   REM AND EEG ATTACHMENTS   CUMULATIVE RECORDING MACHINE   MICROPHONE   TAPE RECORDER   LIGHT

SLEEP ROOM   OBSERVATION ROOM

■ Can dogs construct recognizable images from a television screen? Experimental group: Place some dogs that have not eaten for eight hours in front of a TV that is broadcasting an ad showing various types of dog food. Control group: Place dogs of the same age and breed that have just eaten in front of the same TV . . .

□ Is it true that blondes have more fun? This is a question that has puzzled me for some time for, unlike certain advertisers who feel confident that they know the answer, I wonder. Before one even begins to construct an experiment by which to investigate this question, a major problem concerns what is meant by "fun" and even "blonde". . . . Then we have to select an arbitrary age range—16 to 30 may be useful . . . . Then approximately half of the nonblondes would be required to dye their hair blonde, and half of the blondes would have to dye their hair dark. About six months later we'd have to change the whole thing around, having the dyed blondes do their hair dark and . . . .

Use of Control Conditions

The two different circumstances under which the subjects were awakened are referred to as the *experimental condition,* in which the independent variable is present, and the *control condition,* in which it is absent. In a traditional experiment, the investigator assesses the influence of the independent variable by comparing the results under these two conditions, which are alike in all important respects except for the presence of this variable. Since unwanted influences, if any, should occur equally in both conditions, any difference in the subjects' behavior must be due to the influence of the experimental or independent variable. ■

Perhaps Maury had been sitting by a warm stove much of the day, which caused him to choose the heated iron as a stimulus that night and also to dream about hot coals. Similarly, he may have been thinking about a French revolution during a particular day, which prompted him to have the iron struck and to dream about bells. In the overall plan of his work, called the *design of the experiment,* Maury ignored certain aspects of control.

There are many subtleties in experimental design, including the choice of variables, subjects, and apparatus, but no issue is more important than control. The reason is that extraneous variables, such as what Maury did during the day, may influence the independent or dependent variables of the experiment. Such extraneous variables are called *confounding variables* because they give an uninterpretable result to the experiment. The purpose of controls is to eliminate these influences, in order to provide a clearer indication of the effect of the specific variables that are selected for study.

Using one set of subjects. In the REM study, the method is called *own controls* or *within-subject controls* because the same subjects are used in both conditions—experimental and control. The advantage is that each subject is compared with himself or herself; except for the independent variable, differences in favor of the experimental or control condition are minimized because each subject serves under both conditions (Greenwald, 1976). The REM study also illustrates the importance of obtaining numerous measurements in most experiments. Each subject was observed on several occasions, which gives greater reliability to the result.

A special procedure is necessary in this method, however. The subject must be assigned to the two different conditions according to a *random schedule* of trials. If all the experimental trials are accomplished first, the subject may become steadily more fatigued and perform more poorly in the control condition. Or the subject may gradually improve, learning how to better recall dreams, and thus give a superior performance in the control condition. These progressive changes, in either direction, must be spread evenly throughout both conditions, and for this purpose a random sequence of experimental and control trials is often employed.

If it is impossible to randomize the trials, they are presented in a *counterbalanced order,* whereby half the REM trials are made, followed by all the non-REM trials, and finally the remainder of the REM trials. For example, a subject might be given 25 REM trials, 50 non-REM trials, and then 25 more REM trials. This procedure, sometimes referred to as the ABBA sequence, distributes the effects of certain progressive changes, such as practice and fatigue, equally on the two conditions, providing these changes occur at a uniform rate.

In another procedure, the two conditions are presented in the opposite order to half the subjects. Half of the group receives an A-B sequence and the other half a B-A sequence. The experimenter then compares the results of the two equal groups to determine whether the sequence is an important factor. □

Using two sets of subjects. In many experiments the same subjects cannot be used in both conditions, and therefore two similar groups are employed. For example, when control of inherited factors is desired in studying human beings, identical twins are used; one twin is placed in the experimental group and the other in the control group. This method of *co-twin control* is effective because identical twins have the same heredity and also because maturation is largely influenced by hereditary factors (Figure 2-11). A similar procedure occurs with animals in the *split-litter technique,* in which a rat's litter of six pups is divided, three in the experimental group and three in the control group. Again, these assignments are randomly determined.

In other experiments, the investigator is interested in the control of acquired characteristics, such as level of education, occupation, marital status, and so forth. Thus, it is customary to form two groups from pairs of subjects who have been matched in these respects; these groups are called *matched groups.* In research on dreaming in schizophrenia, for example, a male patient of a certain age, occupation, educational level, and psychotic condition is paired with another male who has these same characteristics, except for the psychosis. The first man is assigned to the experimental group and the other to the control group. In such studies, it has been found that the amount of dreaming in schizophrenic persons is much less predictable than in psychiatrically normal people (Hartmann, 1967).

When matching procedures cannot be used or are inappropriate, *random groups* may be used. Here large groups are formed entirely on a random basis, without evaluating the subjects and then matching them in pairs. It is assumed

Figure 2-11   Twins as Identical. *Identical twins are the product of a single fertilized egg that splits soon after fertilization, but at birth it is often difficult to determine whether the two people are physically identical. When necessary, studies are made of their blood types, the mother's placenta, skin grafts, and even certain behavior characteristics, such as handedness. (Harbutt from Magnum)*

that the extraneous or potentially confounding factors are controlled or evenly distributed by this procedure. With true randomization, the average age, intelligence, and educational level, for example, should be approximately the same in each group. This method is less exact than matching, but it is particularly useful when hundreds of subjects are involved.

Control of Set

When we say that perhaps Maury dreamed about hot coals or ringing bells because of the influence of earlier activities, we are speaking of set. *Set* is a readiness to respond in a specific manner based on prior experience, and the control of set is most important in psychological experiments.

Subject's set. Recently, psychologists wanted to investigate influences on dream content. Before going to sleep, some people were exposed to a hypnotic procedure and others were not; similarly, some received certain suggestions on what to dream about, while others were not told anything in particular.

These psychologists were investigating set; this factor was the independent variable.

With control subjects, the investigators avoided the influence of set, giving these subjects no expectation one way or the other. The results of the experiment showed that hypnotic induction and suggestions prior to sleep can have various influences on dream content (Barber et al., 1973).

Controlling set is especially important in pharmacological investigations, in which it is necessary to test the physiological effects of a certain drug, such as a pill for airsickness, apart from whatever psychological benefit may be derived from the knowledge that one has received medication. In many such investigations, the experimental group receives the actual drug while the control group receives a sugar pill, identical in appearance, with no medicinal properties. This pill is called a *placebo* which, freely translated, means "I shall please." It suggests to the control subjects that they have received the drug; it gives them the same set or expectation as those in the experimental group. ■

Experimenter effects. Similarly, the experimenter's set can be a concern in research. Numerous studies have indicated that the experimenter's expectancies and personal characteristics can influence the results of the investigation, without his or her knowledge. Collectively, these potential influences are referred to as experimental bias or *experimenter effects* (Rosenthal, 1966). Ivan Pavlov, whose work is considered in detail in later chapters, was aware of this problem. He suggested that the results of one series of investigations, which showed improved learning ability in successive generations of mice, probably were attributable to increased teaching efficiency on the part of the experimenter (Gruenberg, 1929). More recently, it has been suggested that several investigators participate in various ways in the same experiment in order to

randomize the experimenter effect. But this procedure has not yet been followed sufficiently (Silverman, 1974).

In REM research, one experimenter should awaken the subject and another investigator, without knowing the condition under which the subject has been awakened, should record the dream. In this way, the potential experimenter bias—to obtain much dream information with REMs and little in their absence—is eliminated. Another method is to use a mechanical device for recording the dream report and then have the report evaluated by someone who knows nothing of the experimental hypothesis or of the different treatments of the various subjects. Thus, in many experiments today, the "dream detector" awakens the sleeper automatically at moments of REMs, recording the subject's dreams in the experimenter's absence (Okuma et al., 1970).

When the subject's set is controlled by preventing that person from knowing which treatment he or she has received, the procedure is called a *single blind*. It is illustrated in the use of the placebo. But when even the experimenter, at any given moment, does not know the subject's condition, this procedure is called a *double blind*. Neither the investigator nor the subject knows to which group the subject belongs. Decisions regarding which subjects receive what treatment are made by a third party and coded so that the evaluation of each subject's responses can be made without knowledge of the treatment received. Under these conditions the experimenter's set or expectancy cannot influence the outcomes of the investigation.

Animal Research

Sometimes people wonder why some psychologists spend so much time studying animals. In fact, one occasionally hears a particular psychologist referred to as a "rat man" or "monkey

■ *I have had occasion to see "psychology in action" several times as a sort of therapy or trick in the pharmacy where I worked. I remember one case in which a doctor ordered capsules with a harmless, virtually useless, glucose mixture inside. Although the capsules performed no medical function, they did much to appease his very "neurotic" patient; indeed he* thought *he felt much better!*

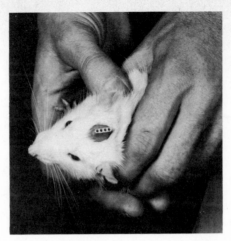
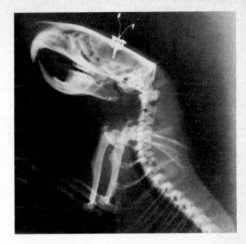

man'' in recognition of such interests. There are several reasons for animal research, including an interest in understanding the lower species per se. Another reason is that knowledge of lower animals may aid us in understanding human beings. Research accomplished on this basis, called *comparative psychology,* involves the study of lower organisms in relation to one another and especially in comparison with human beings.

Through animal research, psychologists have discovered that pigeons dream, sea turtles do not, and elephants stand up to sleep but lie down to dream (Hartmann et al., 1967). More specifically, we should say that pigeons show the REM state, sea turtles do not, and it is evident in elephants when they lie down, since dreams and REMs are not perfectly correlated. Dreams also occur outside the REM state.

Another important reason for animal experiments involves the increased control that is possible. Genetic factors can be manipulated and controlled through selective breeding. Surgical operations that would not be permitted with human beings can be performed (Figure 2-12). Environmental conditions can be controlled in ways that would not be possible at the human level, especially when lengthy time periods and new materials,

such as drugs, are necessary to complete the experiment (Schuster & Johansen, 1974).

In one instance, investigators wished to discover the importance of REM sleep for the individual's health. It is a known fact that prolonged loss of sleep is detrimental to health, but is loss of dreaming also important to us physiologically?

The experimenters began with volunteer human subjects. For five nights some of them were awakened every time they began to show the REM state. During this same period, control subjects were aroused for comparable intervals of non-REM sleep. Results of the study showed that REM loss, compared to simple sleep loss, makes one even more tense, anxious, irritable, and forgetful. After this study was finished, the experimental subjects compensated for this loss, dreaming at more than double their usual rate (Dement, 1960).

Questions regarding the reliability of these findings have been raised by subsequent research, but our concern here is with methods, not results. After the testing, the original investigators decided that the experiment should be repeated, this time lasting for two or three months, but obtaining subjects for such a lengthy study would be difficult or impossible. Consequently, the additional research was accomplished using lower animals. Cats were kept on a treadmill where they could catch quick naps but could not enter deep sleep, in which dreaming occurs. After ten weeks in this condition, the animals became hyperactive, gulped their food, mounted members of their own sex, and fought much of the time. It seemed that the REM loss resulted in an increase in several physiological drives (Dement et al., 1967). This energizing effect of REM deprivation also has been shown in later investigations (Giora, 1971).

Still another advantage of animal research is the faster maturation rate; the lower species are more convenient in studies of growth and development. An investigator can obtain results of developmental animal research within a year or two, but with human beings the psychologist might have to wait two decades before a comparable level of maturity is reached.

With all these advantages, one important limitation must be kept in mind. It is difficult to know the extent to which research findings with animals can be applied to human beings. The generalization is especially risky when the species is quite different from human beings in physical structure and natural environment.

The Research Continuum

With the discovery of REMs as signs of dreaming, research programs sprang up throughout the country and around the world. Dreaming could be studied in an objective fashion, and soon many physiological accompaniments to dreaming were identified (Snyder, 1971). Most important was the disclosure that certain types of brain waves, those of low voltage and high frequency, also characterize dreaming. These waves are more like those of a person who is awake rather than asleep, but it is difficult to awaken a sleeper who is showing such a brainwave pattern. Thus the REM or dream state is also known as *paradoxical sleep*.

Using such physiological measures, and waking people at specified moments, we now know that nearly everyone dreams, that dreams also occur during non-REM sleep, and that on the average we have several dreams per night. But how much one dreams also depends on one's age. Adults spend one-twelfth of their lives dreaming, but babies spend much more time in REM sleep, although they also spend more time sleeping (Figure 2-13).

Figure 2-13 Age and Dreaming. *As people grow older, not only do they spend less time dreaming, but also a decreasing proportion of their nightly sleep is devoted to dreams. (After Hartmann, 1967)*

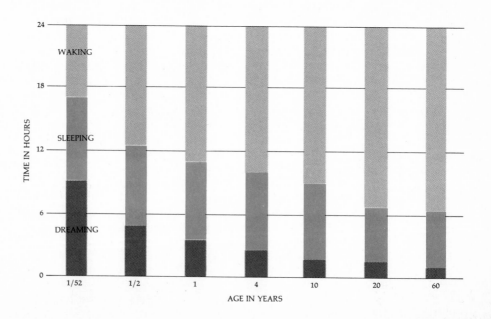

Today, the prevailing but tentative view is that dreaming is not primarily a response to external stimuli that occur during sleep. Rather, it is a nightly process whereby we review and sort out the day's activities and ideas. By this procedure we discharge accumulated tensions and, thus, awaken refreshed mentally as well as physically. In this way, dreaming acts as a sort of safety valve (Hall, 1966; Dallett, 1973).

However, credit for this progress in understanding dreams does not belong exclusively to one research method. The first external signs of dreaming were discovered through naturalistic observation. Further data on dream content have been accumulated by means of the survey method. In clinical work, Freud perhaps overemphasized the importance of childhood experiences and symbolic meanings in dreams, but he successfully focused on the potential value of dream interpretation and rightfully emphasized the role of psychological factors, including events in the individual's recent past (Langs, 1971; Foulkes & Vogel, 1974). Finally, through various experimental methods we have begun to understand the numerous physiological characteristics of the dreaming state.

Each method has its assets and limitations and each has made its special contribution to our understanding of human functioning. Since these methods also differ in the degree of control and artificiality in the research situation, they are often used in various combinations in modern research.

Summary

Naturalistic Observation

1. To increase precision in research, investigators use operational definitions, whereby a given variable is identified in terms of certain measurable events. Many important behavioral events, such as dreaming and memory, cannot be observed directly, and therefore the scientist has the choice of ignoring them or making inferences, dealing with them in an ''as if'' manner. Inferences are made on the basis of related events that can be observed, and they make possible a broader research perspective.

2. In naturalistic observation, behavior is observed in its usual setting, using note taking, movies, and tape recordings for collecting data. In overt observation, the researcher's presence is known to the subjects; in covert observation, the research purpose is concealed.

3. Naturalistic observation does not appear to be a complex procedure, but the observer needs considerable training. One often begins by being unselective and then gradually gains increased precision, identifying specific behaviors to be observed. In addition, the observer must know how to make and indicate inferences and minimize personal bias.

The Survey Method

4. To obtain information from a large number of subjects, a survey can be used, in which many people are asked a series of questions by mail, telephone, or interview. Commonly, an incidental sample of subjects is obtained, but a representative sample is preferable. It can be identified by using a quota sample, area sample, or simple random sample.

5. Unless the investigator has obtained a representative sample, no generalizations can be made concerning a larger population. Another limitation of the survey is that the behavior in question is rarely observed; the investigator usually examines what the subjects say about their behavior.

The Clinical Approach

6. The purpose of the clinical method is to assist disturbed individuals in achieving a more satisfactory adjustment. Because it focuses on a given individual, it

involves idiographic analysis, which asserts that the behavior of any individual is best described in terms of that person's own special lawfulness. Such studies also have contributed to our general understanding of human beings.

7. Besides the case history, extensive information on the maladjusted person is gained through a series of interviews, which can differ widely in method. Psychological tests also have proven useful in this regard.

Experimental Methods

8. The experimental method involves controlling or manipulating variables. The concern is with the ways in which various stimulus (S) and organism (O) conditions result in various responses (R).

9. In the classical experiment, the investigator isolates the influence of one variable while keeping the others constant. This independent variable, usually a stimulus or condition of the organism, is studied for its influence on a dependent variable.

10. Because of the multiple basis of behavior, modern psychologists often study the influence of several independent variables simultaneously. These multifactor studies can reveal additive effects, where the influences are simply cumulative, and interactive effects, where the influences are interdependent.

Design of Experiments

11. In planning an experiment—experimental design—a most important consideration is the methods of control used to eliminate confounding variables. Commonly, the subjects are studied under two equal conditions, experimental and control, except that the independent variable is absent in the control condition. Thus, comparisons of the two groups show the influence of this factor. In one method of establishing these conditions, called own-controls, the same subjects are used for the experimental and control conditions. In other methods, two sets of subjects are used, placed in comparable groups by matching pairs or by procedures for randomization.

12. Single blind procedures can be used for control of the subject's set. The subject does not know what treatment he or she is receiving. Double blind methods can be used for the control of experimenter effects, as well. Here neither the investigator nor the subject knows what treatment the subject is receiving.

13. The advantages of animal research usually concern the increased control that is possible. Selective breeding, surgical operations, and environmental restrictions are more readily permitted, and the length of time necessary for developmental studies is relatively short in comparison with studies of human beings. However, one must be cautious about the generalization of results to include human beings.

The Research Continuum

14. Research methods differ in degree of control and, therefore, in artificiality. Each of the various methods has its advantages and disadvantages and makes its own contribution to our understanding of human and animal behavior and experience.

Suggested Readings

Christensen, L. *Experimental methodology.* Boston: Allyn & Bacon, 1977. An undergraduate text that aims to convey the process of experimental research in step-by-step fashion.

Deese, J. *Psychology as a science and art.* New York: Harcourt, Brace, Jovanovich, 1972. A challenging paperback that describes limitations and failures in scientific psychology.

Doherty, M. E., & Shemberg, K. M. *Asking questions about behavior: An introduction to what psychologists do.* Glenview, Ill.: Scott, Foresman, 1970. This paperback attempts to approach psychological research with questions of particular interest to students. In the process of trying to answer such questions, the student is introduced to the requirements of scientific research.

Kerling, F. N. *Foundations of behavior research* (2nd ed.). New York: Holt, 1973. This comprehensive volume, sophisticated in parts, describes research methods and statistical techniques and measurement that are considered later in the present text.

Siegel, M. H., & Zeigler, H. P. (Eds.) *Psychological research: The inside story.* New York: Harper & Row, 1976. A collection of reports by 24 psychologists describing the details of their research projects.

Chapter 3

Statistical Methods

Typing involves work, but it is obviously faster and more efficient than writing by hand. In fact, not long after Christopher Sholes developed the first successful typewriter in 1873, there was considerable interest in finding out just how much energy its use required and what changes might be made to improve its design.

To determine the amount of energy involved, scientists studied changes in metabolism. They determined the increase in calories required for typing as opposed to merely resting. Thus, energy expenditure was quantified; it was defined in terms of calories per hour.

This idea of quantification is fundamental in science. Statistical methods, whether or not they are mentioned explicitly, are involved in almost all scientific research, from naturalistic observation to experimentation.

In a study of 100 typists, the following calories-per-hour scores were obtained:

```
27 24 21 30 25 26 24 23 26 28
25 26 25 28 24 25 23 28 27 28
28 29 26 25 25 27 26 25 27 23
25 26 25 23 24 25 24 27 25 26
26 27 24 23 26 28 23 26 26 29
19 30 26 25 27 24 25 23 27 26
29 27 27 25 24 23 25 22 23 27
26 26 28 29 27 24 26 25 23 24
24 27 26 31 25 23 25 24 22 25
27 28 25 23 24 26 28 27 25 21
```

What can be said about these scores? What is the additional caloric output required in typing?

Descriptive Statistics

When there are so many *raw scores* or *raw data,* as the original scores are called, sometimes the major characteristics of the group cannot be perceived readily. There are too many scores to be understood all at once, and so there is a need for some general method for describing them. One such procedure is the *frequency distribution,* which indicates the number of times that each score occurred in the group. More succinctly, it shows the frequency of the different scores in the distribution. From this simple tabulation, the observer can tell at a glance which are the most common scores, the least common scores, and those of intermittent frequency (Figure 3-1).

The frequency distribution sometimes is used as an end in itself, and sometimes it is considered as a step in constructing a graph. A *graph* is a visual display of the same data, showing the group trend by lines of a certain length or form. The graph is used because it is more pictorial than a frequency distribution. In the *histogram* or *bar graph,* for example, the lengths of the columns indicate the frequencies of the different scores. In the *frequency polygon,* the heights of the figure above the baseline indicate the frequencies (Figure 3-2).

Insofar as a picture is worth a thousand words, graphs are a useful device. Provided they are constructed correctly, they can be informative and persuasive. But there is another way to present group data that is more efficient in terms of space and more useful for those familiar with basic statistical methods.

All the energy scores can be presented by *descriptive statistics,* in which just a few numerical values summarize the performance of the group as a whole. Generally, there are two basic types of descriptive statistics: some values indicate the typical scores and others show the extent to which all the scores differ from those typical values. The very important advantage in these descriptive statistics over the graphic display is that they then can be used in additional, more complex analyses of the same raw scores.

Measures of Central Tendency

A typical score is some *measure of central tendency,* so-called because it indicates the performance of subjects near

Score	Tallies	Frequency
31	I	1
30	II	2
29	IIII	4
28	HHT IIII	9
27	HHT HHT HHT	15
26	HHT HHT HHT III	18
25	HHT HHT HHT HHT I	21
24	HHT HHT III	13
23	HHT HHT II	12
22	II	2
21	II	2
20		0
19	I	1
		N = 100

Figure 3-1 **The Frequency Distribution.** *This figure is constructed by listing all possible scores, as shown at the left, and then indicating the number of times each score occurred in the group.*

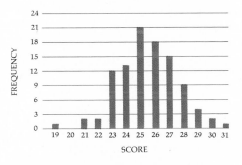

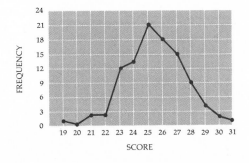

Figure 3-2 **Histogram and Frequency Polygon.** *The histogram is made by constructing columns that are proportionate to the number of tallies for each score in the frequency distribution. It is the frequency distribution simply turned on its side. The frequency polygon is constructed by again indicating the possible scores on the horizontal axis, or* abscissa, *and then plotting the frequency of each score against the vertical axis, or* ordinate. *This polygon shows the same data as the histogram; the plotted points represent the midpoints of the tops of the columns in the histogram.*

the center of the distribution. Casual inspection of the 100 energy output scores shows that the central tendency is approximately 25 calories per hour. This figure is close to that obtained in early laboratory studies (Carpenter & Benedict, 1909).

Mode, median, mean. There are several types of typical scores, one of which is called the *mode* because it occurs most frequently. This name can be remembered by thinking of pie à la mode, which literally means "pie according to the fashion." The score that is most in fashion, or the most frequent, is the mode. Among the 100 energy scores, 25 is the mode. It occurs more times than any other score in the distribution and, therefore, also represents the highest point on a graph of these scores.

Another measure of central tendency is the *median,* which is the middle point in a distribution when all the scores have been ranked according to size. It has half the scores above it and half below it, dividing the group into sections of 50 percent each. The meaning of this term can be remembered by thinking of an expressway or turnpike where the sign says: "Keep off the median strip." The median divides the highway in half, just as it divides the ranked scores in half. When there is an odd number of cases, the median is the middle score; with even-numbered groups, it is that point equidistant from the two middle scores. In the group of 100 energy-expenditure scores, the median is 25.

Generally, the most useful measure of central tendency is the *mean,* which should be remembered as simply the arithmetic average. It is obtained by adding all the scores and dividing this sum by the number of scores. For the 100 calories-per-hour scores, the sum is 2550 and the mean is 25.5.

The normal curve. When the scores in the graph accumulate near the center and decline symmetrically on both sides at a given rate, the distribution is called a *normal probability curve* or *normal curve.* Experience has shown that this curve occurs whenever many random factors act in a complex, often unknown way, to determine a single event. In all normal curves, also called *bell-shaped curves,* all three measures of central

tendency have approximately the same value (Figure 3-3).

All normal curves are bell-shaped, but all bell-shaped curves do not necessarily constitute a normal distribution. Sometimes the curve looks generally like a bell and is symmetrical, but the scores are too spread out or too close together to represent the normal curve (Figure 3-4).

Skewed curves. At times, the scores pile up at one end or the other, and the distribution is clearly nonnormal. In this instance, called a *skewed distribution,* the three measures of central tendency provide different indications of the typical score. Here one must be careful in selecting any measure of central tendency as representative of the entire distribution (Figure 3-5). ■

Consider another example. Energy expenditure may be of chief interest to the typist, but work output undoubtedly is of most interest to the boss. Hence, the operator's proficiency generally is indicated by the number of words typed per minute. For the following typing-speed scores, what are the mode, median, and mean?

54 61 47 56 43 50 61 52 44 55

The most frequent score, or most in fashion, is the mode, which is 61. The median, falling in the middle of the ranked scores, is 53. The mean, which is the arithmetic average, is 52.3.

Interpretation. As a rule, the mode is the least dependable measure of central tendency, particularly when the number of scores is small. It may change markedly when just one score is changed or added to the sample because it represents only the most frequent score. If one of the typists who achieved 61 words per minute had felt ill on the day of the test and scored 44, the mode for the whole group would have decreased by 17.

The median is more stable, particularly when extreme scores are involved, because all the scores in the group are

■ *A skewed distribution occurs in the arrival of students at a cafeteria. Most people get there just a few minutes before the cafeteria opens, and then a few continue to drift in during most of the rest of the dinner hour.*

considered. Thus, the change from 61 to 44 in the case of one typist would alter the median by only 2 points, making it 51 instead of 53. The median is a good measure of central tendency for skewed distributions because the ranks of the scores are involved.

The mean, based on the values of all the scores and not just the ranks, is generally the most widely used measure of central tendency because it is the most stable value. In the change just mentioned, the mean would be altered by less than 2 points, from 52.3 to 50.6. The mean includes the most information about the performance of each subject or item in the group, and thus it is a basic point of departure for many statistical methods.

Measures of Variability

In addition to mean speed, however, we also want to know something about the typist's consistency. Suppose an employer has two beginning typists as candidates for a job. Both type at an average rate of 50 words per minute, as shown by their scores on 10 different days:

X: 51 48 45 49 53 52 50 47 49 56
Y: 58 42 52 40 59 46 54 50 41 58

Which one should be selected? They have the same average scores, but closer examination shows that they are not equally consistent. Typist Y is much more variable. On any given day Y's speed might be fairly high or just barely acceptable. X's scores are more consistent. Hence, it is useful to know not only the typist's typical score but also the extent to which he or she varies from this typical score. *Measures of variability* indicate the degree to which the scores differ from some typical score.

MODE = 25   BECAUSE IT OCCURS 21 TIMES, MORE OFTEN THAN ANY OTHER SCORE

MEDIAN = 25   BECAUSE THERE ARE 50 SCORES LESS THAN OR EQUAL TO 25 AND THERE ARE 50 SCORES GREATER THAN OR EQUAL TO 25

MEAN = 25.5   BECAUSE THE SUM OF ALL SCORES, 2550, DIVIDED BY THE NUMBER OF SCORES, 100, GIVES 25.5

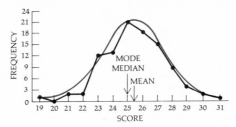

Range and standard deviation. The simplest indicator of variability is the *range,* which is the difference between the lowest and highest scores. Thus, the range for typist X is 11, and for Y it is 19. Like the mode, however, the range is an unstable measure. It takes into account only two scores in the whole group.

Compared to the range, the *standard deviation* (SD) is less well known and more complex, but it is greatly preferred in statistical work because, like the mean, it is based on every value in the

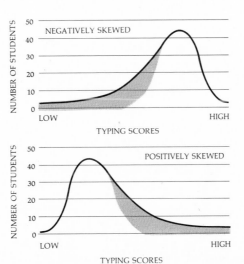

Figure 3-3   A Normal Curve. *This figure, presenting the same information as the histogram and polygon, is an approximately normal distribution. Hence, the mean, median, and mode are nearly the same. This figure also illustrates a third type of graph, called the frequency curve. It is made by plotting the necessary points, as in the other graphs, and then connecting them by the best-fitting continuous line, which is necessarily curved. If more energy scores were obtained, the other graphs presumably would approach the shape of this smooth curve.*

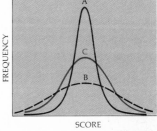

Figure 3-4   Nonnormal Distributions. *Curve A is too tall and narrow and curve B is too low and wide to be a normal distribution, although both curves are symmetrical and approximately bell-shaped. Curve C represents a normal distribution.*

Figure 3-5   Skewed Distributions. *The curves shown here, representing hypothetical data, illustrate skewed distributions. When there is a spread of several low scores away from the mean, as in the shaded area, the curve is said to be negatively skewed. The other curve, with a spread of additional high scores, is positively skewed. In these cases, the measures of central tendency differ from one another.*

Figure 3-6   Computation of Standard Deviation

	Typist X				Typist Y		
1 *Trial*	*2* *Score* (X)	*3* *Deviation* (d=X−M)	*4* *Deviation* *Squared* (d²)	*1* *Trial*	*2* *Score* (X)	*3* *Deviation* (d=X−M)	*4* *Deviation* *Squared* (d²)
1	51	+1	1	1	58	+8	64
2	48	−2	4	2	42	−8	64
3	45	−5	25	3	52	+2	4
4	49	−1	1	4	40	−10	100
5	53	+3	9	5	59	+9	81
6	52	+2	4	6	46	−4	16
7	50	0	0	7	54	+4	16
8	47	−3	9	8	50	0	0
9	49	−1	1	9	41	−9	81
10	56	+6	36	10	58	+8	64
Sums	500	0	90	Sums	500	0	490

Mean (M) = 50

Computation:

$$SD = \sqrt{\frac{sum\ d^2}{N}} = \sqrt{\frac{90}{10}} = \sqrt{9} = 3$$

Mean (M) = 50

Computation:

$$SD = \sqrt{\frac{sum\ d^2}{N}} = \sqrt{\frac{490}{10}} = \sqrt{49} = 7$$

Figure 3-7   Approximately Normal Distributions.   *These data were obtained from 100 college students. In the second graph, each student, tested individually, was instructed to indicate when 30 seconds had elapsed after the instructor said "Begin." Try it.*

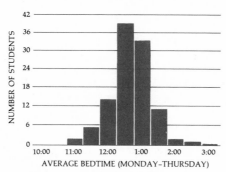

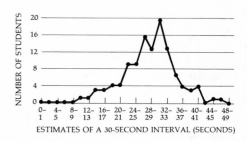

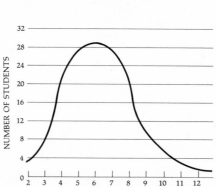

group and is, therefore, more dependable. It indicates the degree of dispersion or variability from the mean among all the scores in the distribution.

Computation of the standard deviation. More specifically, the formula for calculating SD involves the number of scores *(N)* and the deviation of the scores from the mean *(d)*. In operational terms, SD is approximately the average deviation of the scores from the mean, except that squaring and a square root are involved to make the final value more sensitive to extreme scores. Squaring a high score greatly increases its importance in the distribution. Thus, the formula is:

$$SD = \sqrt{\frac{\text{sum } d^2}{N}}$$

For typist X, the number of scores is 10 and the sum of the squared deviations from the mean is 90. Hence, SD becomes $\sqrt{9}$, or 3. For typist Y, the number of scores is again 10 but the sum of the squared deviation equals 490. Thus, SD equals 7 (Figure 3-6).

Interpretation of SD. The value of determining SD is evident when the performances of the two typists are compared. The range suggests that typist Y is more variable from day to day, and SD, determined from all the scores, confirms this conclusion. In this case, as in all others, we can say that the larger the SD, the greater the variability or dispersion of the scores from the mean.

Differences in variability are of interest to laypersons as well as statisticians. For example, there is greater variability in dress on the street than at a wedding. There is less variability in typing speed among students in a typing class than in the general population, which includes experts and complete beginners. Statistically, these differences are most accurately and most usefully reflected in calculation of the SD.

The SD is also useful in another respect. With large samples of subjects, the scores for most human characteristics distribute themselves approximately according to the normal curve. Height, weight, intelligence, and typing speed show this distribution. In the United States, where there are people of diverse ethnic backgrounds, even the number of letters in surnames shows this trend (Figure 3-7). When the SD is calculated in such instances, it identifies a certain segment of the population.

For any normal distribution, the distance between one SD below the mean and one SD above the mean always includes 68 percent of all the scores in the group. Similarly, approximately 95 percent of all the scores are included between 2 SDs below the mean and 2 SDs above the mean. Finally, the distance between −3 SD and +3 SD includes approximately 99 percent of all the scores (Figure 3-8). This relationship between SD units and percent of the cases under the normal curve is basic to inferential statistics, which we shall consider later.

Use of Statistics

When Christopher Sholes assembled his first typewriter, the idea was simply to make a contraption that would work, without the keys striking or colliding with

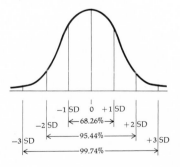

Figure 3-8   Areas of the Normal Curve. *This figure shows the percent of cases between various SD units in the normal curve.*

Figure 3-9 Early Type-writer. *This machine, developed a few years after Sholes's first successful typewriter, included a shift-key, which was much more suited to the touch method of typing. Thus, only half the number of keys were required on the keyboard for making capital and lower case letters. (Smithsonian Institution)*

one another. He planned the typewriter for use by only a few fingers (Figure 3-9).

At the turn of the century, the modern approach, now called touch typing, was on the scene. It has proven to be of tremendous significance, particularly when special training methods are used. Today, average speeds of at least 40 to 50 words per minute are required for most typing jobs (Bureau of Labor Statistics, 1974).

With this background in statistical methods, how can we solve a psychological problem, such as improving the design of a typewriter? Designing instruments that are best suited for human use is an area of psychology known as *human factors* research or *engineering psychology*. The latter dates back to an era when this field was generally limited to improving machine design. Today it includes the improvement of all kinds of systems in which human beings are involved—environmental, social, and governmental, as well as industrial (Alluisi & Morgan, 1976).

Confronted with this task, a human factors psychologist would consider two

sets of variables—the work to be performed and the worker's capabilities. The work is essentially a transcription skill. The typist must be able to translate written or auditory symbols, which serve as input, into a prescribed sequence of letters, which is the output (Shaffer & Hardwick, 1970). The worker's capabilities concern chiefly finger and hand dexterity, in addition to adequate vision. To obtain accurate information in both respects, statistical methods are essential.

Graphic data. Years ago, when the typewriter was still relatively new, some psychologists began studies to improve the standard typewriter keyboard. The first step was a detailed study of the letter frequencies and spelling patterns of the English language, which represented the work to be performed. Letter counts were made in four samples of text—a common spelling list, the gospel according to St. Mark, some business correspondence, and a newspaper editorial. Then, the average frequency for each letter of the alphabet and for each punctuation mark was found for all samples (Figure 3-10).

These data are impressive. For every one thousand times the letter *E* is used, the letters *K, J, X, Q,* and *Z* appear little more than one hundred times altogether. In fact, *E* is used more often than twelve other letters of the alphabet combined.

The most common letters are *E, T, A, O, S,* and *I*. These 6 letters constitute more than 50 percent of the letter usage in common English. When the data for all 26 letters are presented in the form of a graph, the differences in frequency of letter usage are readily apparent (Figure 3-11).

Central tendency and variability. After determining the letter frequencies as a measure of work output, the next step was to determine the average worker's capabilities as measured by the differences in ability between the hands and among the fingers. Males and females, all young adults, were tested by having them tap in various ways on the typewriter and on a table top, with the wrist held stationary. Then, the average rate of tapping was calculated separately for each finger, excluding the thumb, and separately for each hand.

When the group means for 54 female college students and teachers were obtained in this manner, the right index finger proved most capable, followed by the left index finger. Next were the middle fingers, then the little fingers and finally the ring fingers (Hoke, 1922).

Then came the question of variability. How consistent are the different fingers? Does the index finger, for example, vary more from one person to another than does the ring finger, which is the least capable? These data could be influential in designing a new keyboard. The SDs showed no such variations, however; finger consistency was not an issue (Figure 3-12).

In describing a set of data, generally the mean and SD are reported together, conveying information about central tendency and variability. In the case of finger dexterity, we can conclude that while the fingers differ in mean rate of tapping, they are similar in variability. No one of them is significantly less predictable than the others.

	Spelling List	Bible	Business Letters	Newspapers	Average
E	1,000	1,000	1,000	1,000	1,000
T	609	605	686	841	685
A	571	572	720	876	684
O	524	325	711	685	561
S	420	340	463	723	486
I	498	321	446	673	484
N	508	391	557	420	469
R	591	247	386	468	423
H	232	565	411	409	402
L	350	232	420	396	349
D	263	340	274	169	261
C	298	85	265	276	231
U	233	137	260	263	223
M	210	151	214	216	198
Y	146	192	205	157	175
B	132	74	146	289	160
P	219	92	94	228	158
W	123	137	137	132	132
F	154	85	51	120	102
G	153	48	86	109	99
V	82	44	69	71	66
K	49	22	34	60	41
J	19	7	17	49	23
X	18	0	25	37	20
Q	4	4	8	24	10
Z	7	11	8	11	9
.		70	124	64	86
,		125	140	81	115
:		22	12	0	11
;		41	0	7	16

Figure 3-10 Scores for Letters and Punctuation Marks. *To make comparisons easier, all totals were proportionately raised to the base of one thousand for E, the most common letter. (From "The Improvement of Speed and Accuracy in Typewriting" by Roy Edward Hoke. The Johns Hopkins University Studies in Education, No. 1, 1922.)*

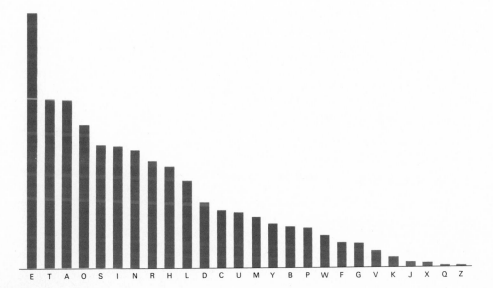

Figure 3-11 Frequency of Letter Usage. *This bar graph represents the average scores from the four samples in the survey (Hoke, 1922).*

E T A O S I N R H L D C U M Y B P W F G V K J X Q Z

Figure 3-12   Finger Dexterity.
The mean and standard deviation for rate of tapping are shown for all fingers except the thumbs (Hoke, 1922).

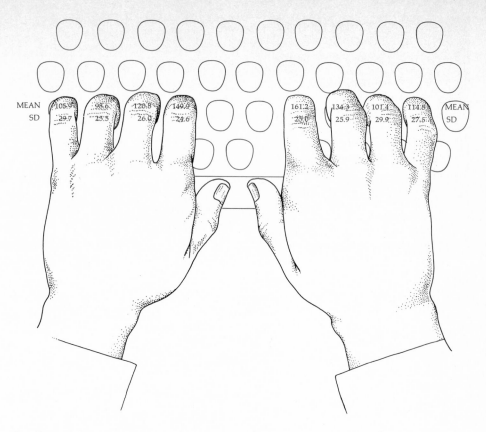

MEAN 105.8 98.6 120.8 149.9 161.2 134.3 101.4 114.8 MEAN
SD 29.7 25.5 26.0 24.6 25.0 25.9 29.9 27.5 SD

Studies of Correlation

We now know something of the work to be performed, defined as letter frequencies, and something about the worker's capability, defined as finger dexterity. The next step in this human factors problem is simply to discover whether the most work is assigned to the most capable fingers. If so, the keyboard is well designed for human use.

In science, however, one always searches for verification of results. Are we confident that our samples of letter frequencies represent letter usage in the language as a whole? Fortunately, there is a convenient method for checking these data. We can compare them with the printer's font, a large box-like affair for holding the metal molds of all the letters and punctuation marks used in typesetting. The font includes a separate bin for each letter and each punctuation mark, and these bins vary considerably

in size, depending on how often the letter or mark is used. On the basis of our letter-count data, we would guess that the bin for *E* is the largest, containing the most molds, and that the bin for *Z* contains the fewest (Figure 3-13).

Types of Correlation

In discovering whether our letter frequencies agree with those in the printer's font, we are interested in *correlation*, meaning the extent to which two sets of scores are related. Age and illness are highly correlated; the older a person, the more likely he or she is to have an illness. Similarly, height and weight are highly correlated; tall people tend to weigh more than people of lesser height. In correlation, however, there are two aspects—direction and magnitude.

Background and Methods

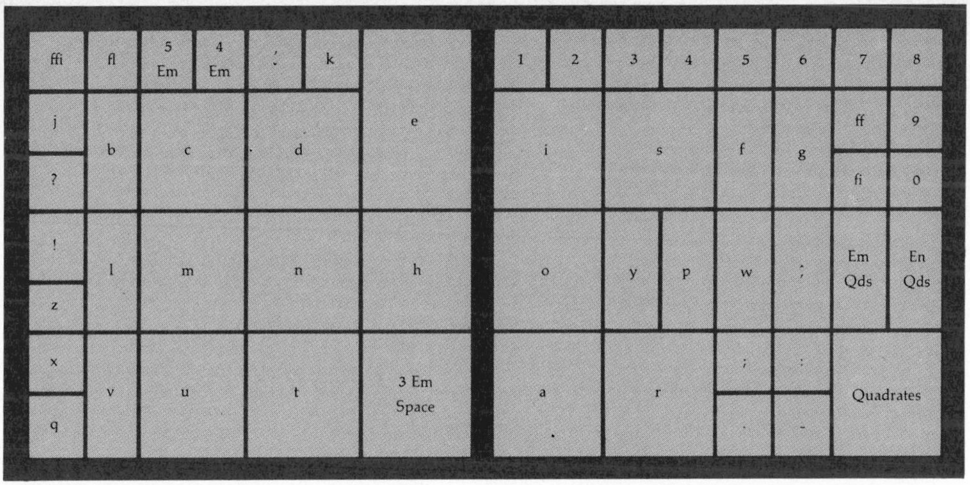

Figure 3-13 Printer's Font.
Note the different sizes of the bins, depending on the letter involved.

Direction of correlation. In the preceding examples, the relationships are positive, meaning that both scores go in the same direction. When age is high, the probability of illness is high, and when age is low, the probability of illness is low. The two sets of scores increase and decrease together in *positive correlation.* For a given individual, both scores tend to be low, moderate, or high. Expressed differently, we say there is a *direct relationship* between the variables.

When we examine the printer's font, we find that the most common letter is *E,* which is also the most common letter in our survey. The next-most-common letter in the font is *T,* which is second in our survey, and so forth down through *Z,* which is least common in both sets of data. This comparison suggests a high positive relationship. That is, although there are a few exceptions, the most common letters in the bins are the most common in our survey, and the least frequent in the bins are the least frequent in the survey (Figure 3-14).

In other sets of data, there may be a *negative correlation,* meaning that a high score on one variable is associated with a low score on the other. In other words, the two sets of scores go in opposite directions. For example, amount of cigar smoking and health of the lungs are

negatively correlated. The more an individual smokes, the less likely he or she is to have healthy lungs. Prejudice and tolerance for ambiguity also are negatively correlated. Persons who are highly prejudiced generally have a low tolerance

Figure 3-14 Survey and Font Frequencies. *This table shows the letters in the printer's font compared with the averages from the survey. (From "The Improvement of Speed and Accuracy in Typewriting" by Roy Edward Hoke. The Johns Hopkins University Studies in Education, No. 1, 1922.)*

	Printer's Font	Survey Average
E	12,000	1,000
T	9,000	685
A	8,500	684
O	8,000	561
S	8,000	486
I	8,000	484
N	8,000	469
R	6,200	423
H	6,400	402
L	4,000	349
D	4,400	261
C	3,000	231
U	3,400	223
M	3,000	198
Y	2,000	175
B	1,600	160
P	1,700	158
W	2,000	132
F	2,500	102
G	1,700	99
V	1,200	66
K	800	41
J	400	23
X	400	20
Q	500	10
Z	200	9

for unstructured situations. In other words, there is an *inverse* or *indirect* relationship between these two variables.

No particular merit is attached to a positive as opposed to a negative correlation. Both indicate a relationship, but then we are confronted with the second aspect of this relationship—How strong is it? What is the magnitude of the correlation?

Magnitude of correlation. The numerical value of any correlation can range from 0 to +1.00 for positive correlations and from 0 to −1.00 for negative correlations. No correlation can exceed 1.00, which indicates a perfect relationship, something rarely found in psychological studies. Thus, a statistical computation that yields a result larger than ±1.00 must be in error.

Correlations close to ±1.00 are regarded as high; those that approach 0 are described as low. Between these extremes there are mild and moderate correlations. For example, the relationship between our letter frequencies and those in the printer's font seems to be high and positive. Now we turn to methods for determining this magnitude.

Determining the Relationship

Earlier, we saw that a large group of scores could be presented graphically, as a histogram or frequency distribution, or numerically, by indicating the mean and SD. With two sets of scores, the same two methods are available.

Scattergrams. In the graphic display, each subject or item has two scores. In this case, each letter has two scores; one score is plotted against the horizontal axis and the other against the vertical axis. Then, the point of intersection of the two axes is marked, and this procedure is repeated for every entry. The result, called a *scattergram,* is a visual display of the degree of relationship between the two sets of scores.

The purpose of a scattergram is to show how widely scattered are the plot-

ted points. The less the scatter, the stronger is the relationship. In fact, if the relationship is perfect, the points will fall in a straight line. Thus, such a correlation is also called a straight-line or *linear* relationship. When the plotted points are widely scattered, forming no particular pattern, the relationship is close to zero. And when they show a cigar-shaped pattern, they indicate a correlation of intermediate numerical value (Figure 3-15).

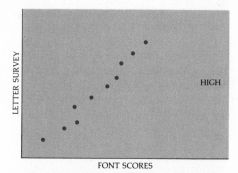

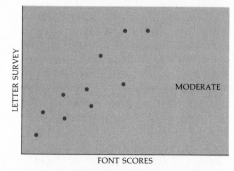

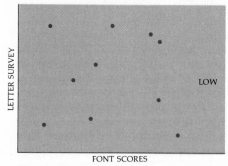

Figure 3-15 Scattergram Patterns. *The more widely dispersed the plotted points, the lower is the relationship between the two sets of scores.*

Background and Methods

When the survey and printer's font data are plotted in this way, the points take a definite shape. They fall generally in a straight line, indicating an unusually high relationship (Figure 3-16).

Numerical computation. The scattergram gives a visual representation of the relationship but not an exact numerical value. Again, the numerical value is more useful, so we determine the *coefficient of correlation*. There are several methods of calculating this coefficient, one of which is the Spearman *rank-order* method, based on the ranks of the scores, not the scores themselves. It produces a coefficient called *rho*.

The first step in calculating rho is to convert all scores to ranks for both the survey and printer's font data (Figure 3-17). Next, the difference *(D)* is determined between the two ranks for each item, or letter. If these differences are small, the letters were ranked in the same way in both instances, and the correlation is high. Since we are interested in some expression of the average of these differences, the sum of the differences is divided by an expression of *N*, representing the number of pairs of scores involved. Again, squaring is used for weighting purposes, and this time a constant, 6, is included. The result is then subtracted from 1, so the formula becomes:

$$rho = 1 - \frac{6 \ (sum \ D^2)}{N(N^2 - 1)}$$

As can be seen by inspection of the formula, when the differences *(D)* are 0, the numerator becomes 0 and therefore so does the whole fraction, leaving nothing except +1.00, a perfect correlation. As the differences increase, the correlation decreases. In the pairs of scores for the survey and printer's font, there are only a few slight differences and rho = .98, which is an extremely high correlation.

Figure 3-16 **A Scattergram.** *When the scores from the survey and the printer's font are plotted, the result indicates a high relationship.*

	Scores		Ranks	
Letters	Survey	Font	Survey	Font
E	1,000	12,000	1	1
T	685	9,000	2	2
A	684	8,500	3	3
O	561	8,000	4	5.5
S	486	8,000	5	5.5
I	484	8,000	6	5.5
N	469	8,000	7	5.5
R	423	6,200	8	9
H	402	6,400	9	8
L	349	4,000	10	11
D	261	4,400	11	10
C	231	3,000	12	13.5
U	223	3,400	13	12
M	198	3,000	14	13.5
Y	175	2,000	15	16.5
B	160	1,600	16	20
P	158	1,700	17	18.5
W	132	2,000	18	16.5
F	102	2,500	19	15
G	99	1,700	20	18.5
V	66	1,200	21	21
K	41	800	22	22
J	23	400	23	24.5
X	20	400	24	24.5
Q	10	500	25	23
Z	9	200	26	26

Figure 3-17 **Ranking the Scores.** *In the survey, E received a score of 1,000 and, therefore, it is ranked 1. T, with 685, is ranked 2, and so forth down through Z, which has the lowest score and is therefore ranked 26. For the printer's font, E again has the highest score, T again is 2, A is 3, and so forth. In the case of ties, each letter receives the average of the ranks involved. (From "The Improvement of Speed and Accuracy in Typewriting" by Roy Edward Hoke. The Johns Hopkins University Studies in Education, No. 1, 1922.)*

Another method for determining correlation, called the Pearson *product-moment method,* is also used frequently, and it produces similar results. This finding, symbolized as *r,* is sometimes more precise than *rho* because the values of the scores are used, not just the ranks. The calculations, based on the concept of standard deviation, are more laborious, however.

Interpretation of Correlation

Our findings on the frequencies of letter usage in the English language are therefore verified by the contents of the printer's font. There is high agreement. We are confident that *E* is the most common letter, *T* is next, and so forth. We now need verification of our findings on finger dexterity, and fortunately, although we do not have numerical data, our results are supported by reports of experienced musicians. Skilled pianists and others indicate that the right hand is usually more capable than the left and that the strength and agility of the fingers occurs in this order: index, middle, little, and ring finger, respectively. If, for expediency, we accept this evidence, both sets of data are verified and we can proceed to the crucial question.

To what extent are the most frequent letters typed by the most capable fingers? In other words, what is the relationship between finger workload and finger capability?

Calculation. Again, the first step is to determine the ranks for the two sets of scores. For finger capability, the right index finger is ranked first, the left index finger second, and so forth down to the left ring finger, which is last. The full sequence for finger ability is: 1R, 1L, 2R, 2L, 4R, 4L, 3R, and 3L.

Next the fingers are ranked according to workload. This ranking is accomplished by noting the letters for which each finger is responsible and the frequency with which each of these letters is typed. The left index finger, for example, types 6 letters, thus having a total frequency score of 1,535, which places it first in workload. The right little finger ranks eighth; it types only the letter *P* plus 3 punctuation marks and the shift key, for a total score of 296, the lowest in the group. The other fingers rank in intermediate positions and the full sequence is: 1L, 2L, 1R, 3R, 4L, 3L, 2R, and 4R. This ranking is somewhat different from that for finger ability (Hoke, 1922; Figure 3-18).

Right Hand					
Fingers	1	2	3	4	Total
	y 175	i 484	o 561	p 158	
	h 402	k 41	l 349	; 16	
	n 469	, 115	. 86	: 11	
	u 223			? 11	
	j 23			Shift 100	
	m 198				
	1,490	640	996	296	3,422

Left Hand					
Fingers	1	2	3	4	Total
	r 423	e 1,000	w 152	q 10	
	f 102	d 261	s 486	a 684	
	v 66	c 231	x 20	z 9	
	t 685			Shift 100	
	g 99				
	b 160				
	1,535	1,492	658	803	4,488

Figure 3-18 Finger Workload. *This shows the work of the different fingers on the conventional keyboard, with the total strikes of the shift key equally divided between the right and left fourth fingers. Note also the much greater overall workload of the left hand. (From "The Improvement of Speed and Accuracy in Typewriting" by Roy Edward Hoke. The Johns Hopkins University Studies in Education, No. 1, 1922.)*

The difference in ranks for each finger is squared, which when summed and entered into the formula, indicates that rho is + .43 (Figure 3-19).

Interpretation. In interpreting this value of +.43, we note first that the correlation is positive, meaning that high scores on one variable are associated with high scores on the other, and low scores on one variable generally are associated with low scores on the other. But we also note that the numerical value of the coefficient, .43, is only intermediate. Considering the extremely wide usage of the standard keyboard in today's world, this relationship is not as

	Scores		Ranks			
Fingers	Ability	Workload	Ability	Workload	D	D²
1R	161	1,490	1	3	2	4
1L	143	1,535	2	1	1	1
2R	134	640	3	7	4	16
2L	121	1,492	4	2	2	4
3R	101	996	7	4	3	9
3L	99	658	8	6	2	4
4R	115	296	5	8	3	9
4L	106	803	6	5	1	1
						48

Figure 3-19   Computation of a Rank-Order Correlation

Sum $D^2 = 48$

$$rho = 1.00 - \frac{6(Sum\ D^2)}{N(N^2-1)}$$

$$rho = 1.00 - \frac{6(48)}{8(63)}$$

$$rho = 1.00 - .57$$

$$rho = .43$$

strong as one might expect. There are certain instances in which less capable fingers are doing more work than more capable ones.

It should be noted here that this correlation, or any other, does not necessarily mean that one variable causes the other. In other words, this moderate correlation between the two variables does not mean that finger dexterity causes workload, or vice versa. Sometimes a third factor is involved, such as Sholes's preference for printing when he assembled the keyboard. For instance, among children weight and memory are positively correlated, but one would not conclude that gaining weight improves a child's memory. This correlation occurs because both conditions increase with a third variable, age. The influence of age becomes evident when we correlate weight and memory scores in children of the same age, for then the relationship is negligible.

Furthermore, correlation does not indicate percentage. A coefficient of +.43 indicates considerably less than 43 percent interdependence between the two variables. For example, a correlation of .50 indicates only 25 percent interdependence, which can be roughly calculated by squaring the coefficient (.50 × .50 = .25). The correlation merely indicates the degree to which two variables are in agreement, increasing and decreasing together in magnitude.

Finally, it should be noted that this discussion has been limited to linear or straight-line relationships. Another type of relationship, nonlinear, also can occur in two sets of scores. The values on one trait might go up and then down as the values on the other trait steadily increase. There is a predictable relationship here, but it is not in a straight line. For example, as anxiety increases steadily, performance on a given task is likely to improve up to a point, but when the subject becomes highly distraught, performance is likely to become steadily

Figure 3-20 Nonlinear Relationship. *Clearly, in this hypothetical example concerning running speed and age, the data are not linear, but there is a predictable pattern.*

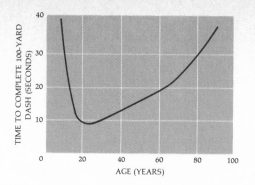

poorer (Figure 3-20). To determine nonlinear coefficients, other statistical techniques are necessary, but they are not of concern in this context.

Additional data. This information on the relationship between finger capability and workload makes it clear that the keys on the standard typewriter could be arranged more efficiently, but there is

other evidence as well. For instance, ask any one of today's million typists to type the word "million" using the touch system. Determine what happens yourself by referring to the standard keyboard (Figure 3-21).

You will find that this word is typed entirely with the right hand; the left hand is completely idle. Such a discovery is disappointing, but imagine typing *Afterwards we were sadder.* Again, refer to the standard keyboard (Figure 3-21).

There are thousands of such words that are typed entirely with the left hand, which in the course of normal typing does more work than the right hand. The standard keyboard is not the *greatest;* efficiency is sometimes at a *minimum.* The keyboard for the French language has been found similarly inefficient, with the left hand carrying two to three times the workload of the right hand (Navarre, 1947). Sometimes you can detect this inefficiency simply by listening to a fast

Figure 3-21 Standard Keyboard. *The arrangement of the letters and position of the hands are shown for the standard keyboard.*

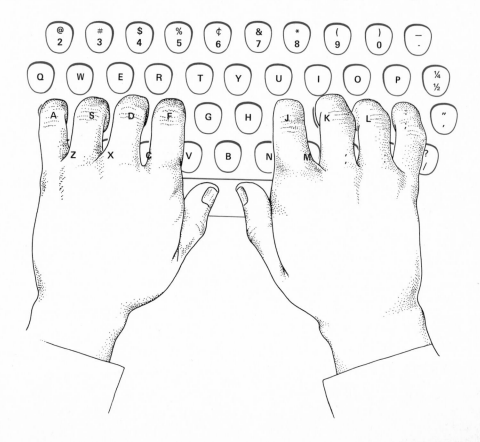

Background and Methods

typist striking a one-handed sequence. The rhythm is disrupted and the tempo is forced to half its speed, like temporary slow motion.

Obviously, both hands should be used simultaneously, if possible. While one hand is moving downward to strike a letter, the other should be moving upward into position to strike the next letter. To achieve this condition, the letters must be assigned so that they are struck alternately by each hand, the time of the down stroke for one hand being used for the up stroke for the other. In English words, consonants often follow vowels, and vice versa, so some alternation is possible. In short, the letters should be assigned to the hands in accordance with the consonant–vowel alternation principle, and the letters should be assigned to fingers in accordance with ability. Using statistical methods, we can make these assignments.

Furthermore, the typewriter keyboard has three rows of letters, and it is easiest to type on the home row, where the fingers are stationed initially. Since it is easier to stretch a finger to the row above the home row, than to reach below it, the next-most-frequent letters should be in the upper row. Again, using simple descriptive statistics, we find that this arrangement does not occur on the standard keyboard. Approximately 20 percent more typing is done in the upper row than in the home row. Ironically, in a mostly right-handed world we have a

Row	Total Strokes (percent)
Upper	52
Home	32
Lower	16

mostly left-handed typewriter, and the fingers are stationed in a position where they do less than one-third of the work (Figure 3-22).

Inferential Statistics

Taking all these factors into account forty years ago, Augustine Dvorak, a psychologist, redesigned the standard typewriter keyboard. It became known as the Dvorak (Dvôrźhäk) or modified keyboard. The five vowels appeared in the home row of the left hand and the five common consonants in the home row of the right hand. The least-used letters were placed in the bottom row and the intermediate letters in the top row. Then a number of tests were made to discover the efficiency of this new keyboard (Dvorak et al., 1936; Figure 3-23).

Row	Total Strokes (percent)
Upper	22
Home	70
Lower	8

Figure 3-22 Row Workload on the Standard Keyboard. *More typing is done in the upper row than in the other two combined (Dvorak et al., 1936).*

Figure 3-23 Dvorak Keyboard. *The strongest fingers do most of the work and, with the placement of vowels and consonants, the hands typically are used alternately. The typing is also largely in the home row (Dvorak et al., 1936).*

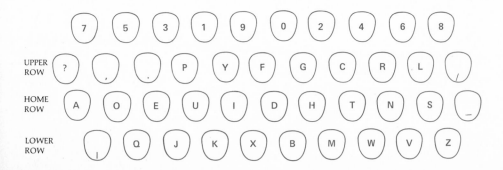

Sampling and Estimation

In any research, it is usually impossible to test all the subjects who might be of interest to the investigator. With regard to speed of learning to type on the new keyboard, for example, there are thousands of beginner typists in schools in the United States, but all these people cannot be included in a single experiment. Thus, the investigator selects a *sample,* which constitutes only a portion of the total cases in which he or she is interested. All possible cases, such as the two hundred thousand beginner typists, are referred to as the *population.* The investigator makes estimates about the corresponding characteristics of the population from the information obtained by studying the sample. In short, the investigator decides whether the findings obtained with the sample are likely to recur regularly if the experiment were repeated several times with the same subjects or even with other subjects from the population.

Point estimation. In the typewriter problem, we select a representative sample of beginner typists, test them on the Dvorak keyboard, and then infer how the whole population would perform with the same keyboard. This procedure is sometimes called *point estimation,* as the investigator estimates a point or value, in this case the population mean, on the basis of a sample. If the average score for the sample of beginning students on the Dvorak keyboard is 41.7 words per minute after 45 hours of instruction, we might infer that the whole population would learn at this same speed.

Using a sample to make an inference about a population is called *inferential statistics,* which include point estimation and studies of differences, as we shall see later. They enable the investigator to decide to what extent his or her findings can be generalized to subjects not included in the sample. On the other hand, descriptive statistics are used simply to describe the group from which the scores were obtained, without inferences regarding a larger population.

The most widely recognized use of inferential statistics occurs in political polls, where not every voter is asked how he or she plans to vote. Yet, the winner can be predicted successfully. In all such cases, the accuracy of the estimate depends on the nature of the sample. If it is representative of the larger population, the prediction should be fairly accurate. Various methods of random sampling are used to ensure a representative sample.

Sampling error. We wonder about our sample of Dvorak typists: Is their mean speed of learning to type representative of the whole population? The only way to answer this for certain would be to test all typists, but since that is impossible, we accept some uncertainty as inevitable and take steps to deal with it. In short, we make use of a procedure for estimating the probable sampling error, which is possible because chance errors in sampling, in the long run, tend to be distributed according to the normal curve.

Our sample mean was 41.7, but for other samples the means might have been 41.3, 40.5, 42.9, and so forth. If we continued taking successive random samples from the total population and continued finding their means, eventually we would discover that this distribution of sample means is very nearly a normal distribution. Furthermore, the mean of this group of means would be close to the population mean—that is, close to the true mean of the population of two hundred thousand beginner typists.

The problem, however, is that we simply cannot take endless samples. We have only one, but by employing the laws of chance, statisticians have developed a method for determining how much our one sample mean is likely to be in error. This statistic is called the

Background and Methods

standard error of the mean. It is calculated from the number of scores in the sample and their standard deviation, which shows how closely the scores cluster around their mean. When there are many scores and their deviations from the mean are small, the sample mean is most likely to reflect the population mean.

Using this method for estimating the standard error of the mean in the Dvorak sample, we find, for example, that the chances are 95 out of 100 that the true mean for the population lies somewhere in the interval from 40.42 to 42.98 words per minute. This statement of probability is our best estimate of the performance of the whole population of Dvorak typists had it been possible to assess everyone using this method. If we wished a still higher degree of confidence in our estimate, then we would obtain a wider interval, but the details of these calculations are not of interest here. Instead, we can summarize by saying that it appears extremely likely that the population mean is some value close to 41 words per minute.

Studies of Differences

In statistical inference, we sometimes are interested in knowing the probability that the sample mean represents the population mean. Finding this probability is called *point estimation,* as just described. At other times we want to know the probability that a difference between two or more sample means represents a true difference between the population means. This issue is called *hypothesis testing* or *studies of differences,* to which we now turn. The essential feature of much psychological research is a comparison between two or more groups, representing experimental and control observations. In the case of the Dvorak keyboard, the obvious procedure is to test equivalent groups of subjects on the two keyboards, one standard and one Dvorak, and then to examine any difference in performance.

Determining the difference. First we find the difference between the two sample means. In several tests of hundreds of high school beginner typists using a standard keyboard in the 1930s, the mean score was 25.0 words per minute after 90 hours of instruction. For 21 high school beginner typists learning on the Dvorak keyboard for less than half of the 90-hour period, the average performance was 41.7 words per minute—a difference of 16.7 words per minute in favor of the Dvorak keyboard.

This difference seems to be large, but would it appear in subsequent samples? In short, what are the chances that a similar or larger difference would be found in the total population?

The statistic of interest in this instance is called the *standard error of the difference.* In brief terms, it is the difference between two sample means divided by the probable sampling error in determining that difference; the procedure in many respects simply goes one step beyond the calculation of the standard error for a single mean. Again, however, we consider only the general method and then turn to a more important point, the interpretation of this statistic.

Here the investigator again makes use of the normal curve. The probability is determined in this manner because the distribution of differences between the means that would be found in many repetitions of this experiment—that is, in repeated samplings—also takes this shape. The procedure is similar to that used in point estimation, except that now we are concerned with the difference between two points.

Since we are testing the difference between two means, we consider the means and the dispersion of the scores around the means, which involves the standard deviations of both sample distributions. The smaller this dispersion, the more likely it is that a difference between the sample means is significant. In other words, when the scores within each group are close to one another but

Figure 3-24 Differences between Means. *The difference between the means in case x is smaller than that for y, but it is more reliable because there is less overlapping of the scores in the two samples. With further samples from the same populations, the y difference is less likely to reappear.*

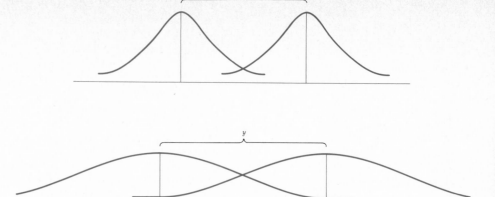

there is a substantial difference between the group means, this difference is likely to be reliable (Figure 3-24).

Drawing conclusions. If no difference is found between the two sample means, it is inferred that there is no difference between the population means. The independent variable had no significant effect. If a difference is found, then, taking dispersion into account, a probability statement is made regarding the likelihood that such a difference, or an even larger one, also would be found in the populations. This probability is expressed in terms of chances out of one hundred.

Usually, a difference between the means is regarded as statistically significant if the probability is 95 or more out of 100 that an equal or larger difference would be found between the populations. *Statistically significant* means that the finding probably is not due to chance. The obtained difference still could have occurred through some chance factors, but the investigator is confident, at least at the 95 percent level, that it was due instead to the influence of the independent variable.

In other words, if the experiment is repeated 100 times, in 95 instances we should find a difference between the means at least as large as the one obtained in the first try. This result is described as $p < .05$, which means that

the probability of finding a smaller difference on the next trial is less than 5 in 100.

To be even more stringent, the scientist can raise the standard to $p < .01$, meaning that the probability of finding a smaller difference in the next experiment is 1 in 100, or less. In studies of difference, just as in point estimation, we cannot know for certain because we cannot test all members of the population, and so our conclusion remains a probability statement.

All scientific statements are probability statements; the conclusions simply indicate the likelihood that the same result will appear again in a repetition of the experiment. In the case of the modified and standard typewriters, it is very unlikely that the difference of 16.7 words per minute between the sample means occurred on a chance basis ($p < .01$). In short, we are quite confident that the rearrangement of the keyboard was responsible for the improved score.

Statistics in Psychology

The superiority of the Dvorak keyboard was shown in several other tests. In one instance, the average gain in speed was .20 words per instructional period for learners using the standard keyboard

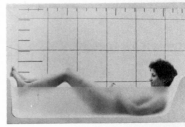
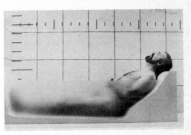
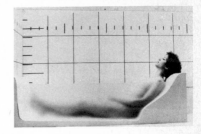

and 1.12 words for those with the Dvorak model, a difference that again does not appear due to chance ($p < .01$). Further, experienced Dvorak typists won 7 first places in the International Commercial Schools Typing Contest (Dvorak et al., 1936). In one instance, it was reported that operators using the redesigned keyboard typed at a rate of more than 100 words per minute, as compared with 50 to 65 words per minute on the traditional keyboard. With all these reports, the reader undoubtedly wonders why the Dvorak design has never been widely adopted.

There seem to be several answers, one of which is that many people do not realize the system is available. Second, with other improvements, such as electrical power, the workload of all fingers is relatively light; the keys need only be stroked, not pushed, as in Dvorak's day. Finally, and perhaps most important, manufacturers of any product commonly do not make expensive improvements if sales continue at a high level. A change today would require not only new keyboard arrangements but also massive retraining programs, probably without any significant sales increase.

Unfortunately, the typewriter is older than scientific psychology, especially the field of human factors. The ideas and techniques for studying human performance were developed mainly in the last 30 to 40 years, when the keyboard was already 60 years old, and many of the statistical procedures are of more recent origin. However, both statistics and human factors engineering have had significant impact on the design of later equipment, such as safety devices, office equipment, and household implements (Figure 3-25).

Moreover, statistics are now involved in virtually all aspects of psychology. They are obviously useful in experimental work and are indispensable in surveys, various clinical procedures, and even naturalistic observation. Today, there is almost no area of psychology that has not benefited from the use of statistical methods. Thus, our discussion is concluded with two general statements about statistics.

Figure 3-25   Advances through Human Factors Research.   *For most adults, the sink should be higher and the tub shaped differently for optimal use. One should be able to identify here the conventional sink and tub and the modifications recommended by human factors psychologists. Studies in human factors also have indicated that the toilet should be lower, for most hygienic use, and the controls for the shower should be nearer the entry. (From* The Bathroom *by A. Kira, Bantam Books, 1976.)*

First, the results of a psychological study, or of any scientific investigation, do not constitute conclusive proof of any phenomenon. They merely indicate what was found in a particular set of circumstances. Statistics are used to describe these findings in a systematic fashion and to determine the probability of obtaining the same findings in the future. All generalizations based on scientific statements are, in the last analysis, probability statements.

Second, statistical foundations and probability statements underlie most of the findings reported in this book. Although the procedures are not discussed in detail again, the studies considered later are almost invariably based on statistical analyses.

Summary

Descriptive Statistics

1. Information obtained in psychological studies is usually described and analyzed by means of statistical methods. A group of scores can be described by a graph or by certain summarizing values, indicating the typical score in the group. These summarizing values are of two types—measures of central tendency and measures of dispersion. The three most common measures of central tendency are the mode, which is the most frequent score; the median, which is the middle score in a ranked series; and the mean, which is the arithmetic average. These values are identical in a normal distribution.

2. Measures of variability are used to indicate the extent to which scores in a group differ from one another. The simplest measure is the range, which is based on only the two most extreme scores and therefore is unreliable. The standard deviation, based on the values of all the scores, is most reliable and is used in most statistical analyses. It is the square root of the average of the squared deviations from the mean.

3. Statistical methods are indispensable in modern psychological research, as illustrated in human factors psychology, which is concerned with the design of instruments best suited for human use. Here a group of scores, such as work output or operator capability, can be analyzed and summarized by descriptive statistics.

Studies of Correlation

4. Statistics can be used to study a single group of scores or the relationship between two sets of scores for the same subjects or items. In the latter case, a coefficient of correlation is computed, which can be positive, meaning that high scores on one trait are associated with high scores on the other, or negative, meaning that high scores on one trait are associated with low scores on the other. The correlation also can vary in magnitude from 0, which shows no relationship, to ± 1.00, which indicates the highest possible relationship.

5. The magnitude of this relationship can be indicated by plotting all the scores on a scattergram. When the plotted points are widely scattered, showing no particular pattern, the relationship is close to 0. When the points tend to fall in a straight line, they show a high degree of correlation. Also, the relationship can be indicated by computing a coefficient of correlation, which gives a numerical result somewhere between 0 and ± 1.00.

6. However, this coefficient is not a percent, and it does not imply causality. It merely indicates the degree to which two factors are associated, increasing and decreasing together in magnitude.

Inferential Statistics

7. For practical purposes, an investigator generally cannot study all potential subjects for a given experiment. Instead, a small representative group, a sample, is selected for study; then estimates are made of the extent to which characteristics of the larger population are reflected in this sample. This process is called inferential statistics. In point estimation, inferences are made that a sample mean, for example, reflects the population mean.

8. In another aspect of inferential statistics, called hypothesis testing or studies of differences, an inference is made about the difference between two or more population means, judging from the difference between sample means. These samples might represent experimental and control groups in a research investigation. If a difference is found, a probability statement is made regarding the likelihood that an equal or larger difference would be found in the population.

Statistics in Psychology

9. Statistical methods are used in psychology to describe research results in an efficient, systematic manner and to determine the likelihood of obtaining similar results in subsequent similar investigations. They do not constitute conclusive proof of any phenomenon, but they do enable investigators to make objective statements regarding the phenomenon under investigation.

Suggested Readings

Blommers, P. J., & Forsyth, R. A. *Elementary statistical methods* (2nd ed.). Boston: Houghton Mifflin, 1977. A basic text illustrating the use of statistical methods in research.

Huff, D. *How to lie with statistics*. New York: Norton, 1954. An amusing, illustrated little book that shows how to use statistics unfairly to your own advantage and how to be on guard when others do the same.

Linton, M., & Gallo, P. S. *The practical statistician: Simplified handbook of statistics*. Monterey, California: Brooks/Cole, 1975. This book presents statistical tests, beyond those covered in this chapter, in a step-by-step manner.

Tanur, J. M., & ASA-NCTM Joint Committee on Statistics (Eds.). *Statistics: A guide to the unknown*. San Francisco: Holden-Day, 1972. A sprightly volume illustrating applications of statistics in many fields, prepared for the novice with diverse interests.

Van Cott, H. P., & Kinkade, R. G. (Eds.). *Human engineering guide to equipment design*. Washington; D.C.: U. S. Government Printing Office, 1972. Describes principles and practices in human engineering, especially in relation to communications work and training methods.

PART TWO

The Human Organism

Chapter 4

Human Development

In the Caune Woods of Aveyron, France, in the late eighteenth century, a wild boy, completely naked, had been reported running free in the forest for some years. Toward the end of September 1799, a group of French hunters captured this "human-animal" as he was climbing a tree to evade their pursuit. Later the boy escaped, was captured again, and eventually was sent to Paris for further study.

His arrival in the capital city aroused considerable interest. People of all backgrounds came to see him, expecting to encounter the "noble savage" in all his dignity, uncontaminated with civilized ways. It was anticipated also that the "Wild Boy of Aveyron," after a few months of education, would be able to give a most interesting account of his earlier life in the woods. But instead, the spectators saw a dirty, frightened creature who crawled and trotted like a wild beast, ate even the most filthy garbage, and emitted only unintelligible grunts and shrieks. About eleven years old, he spent most of his time rocking forward and backward like an animal in the zoo. His only concerns were to eat and to sleep, and apparently to escape the attentions of sightseers (Humphrey, 1962).

The famous French physician, Philippe Pinel, renowned for developing more positive attitudes toward mental illness, was asked to examine the boy. Afterwards, he declared that the child was simply mentally retarded and perhaps had been abandoned for this reason. On the other hand, a younger physician, noted for his successes in teaching deaf mutes, attributed the boy's subnormality to his lack of experience with human beings. Hence, Jean Itard took up the case, named the boy Victor, and devised various ways of teaching him. Itard persisted in this difficult task for five years, but the boy never did learn to speak and never did rise above the severely handicapped level (Itard, 1894).

When Victor died at forty years of age, the issue was still unanswered. To what extent was his lack of human development due to a prolonged earlier life in the woods, as Itard believed? To what extent did Victor inherit a low mental potential in the first place, as was Pinel's view? This case and others like it raise the issue of the relative roles of environment and heredity in human development. Clearly, both factors are involved in all our lives, but how are they related? This problem is the central issue of this chapter, and we follow it from the earliest point in life, the moment of conception.

Role of Heredity

Each of us begins life as a single cell, smaller than the head of a pin, which results from the union of a male sperm and a female ovum. All our *heredity,* the characteristics and potentialities transmitted from the parents, is contained in this cell. During our prenatal life, this cell multiplies into many cells (Figure 4-1).

Determiners of Heredity

Within the fertilized cell there is a complex organization of chemical materials. These materials, which were first seen by scientists as colored strands in stained cells, were named *chromosomes* because the Greek roots of this word mean "colored bodies." They contain the basic determiners of our biological inheritance.

Microscopic studies have shown that there are 46 chromosomes in every human cell. In all individuals, 44 of these can be arranged on the basis of size and form into 22 pairs. The remaining pair consists of the sex chromosomes, called X and Y, which result in the development of a male (XY) or female (XX). The male receives an X from the mother and a Y from the father, while the female receives an X from each parent. All our inherited characteristics are represented in these 46 chromosomes (Figure 4-2).

Genes. Within these structures are the more basic determiners or blueprints of heredity, called *genes,* which specifically direct the development of most of our physical characteristics and certain behavioral traits. In a series of continuing studies it has been discovered that the genes of bacteria are deoxyribonucleic acid (DNA), which is the basic genetic substance of all kinds of living

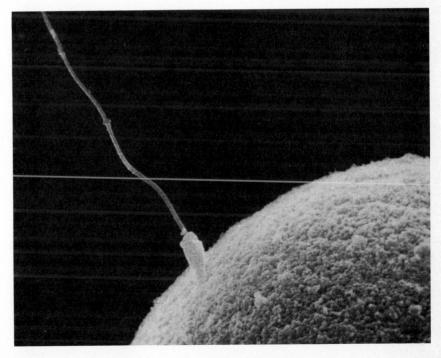

Figure 4-1 Conception. *This photograph, taken with a powerful electron microscope, shows the moment of conception, as the sperm of a sea urchin makes contact with the egg. (Courtesy of D. W. Fawcett and E. Anderson)*

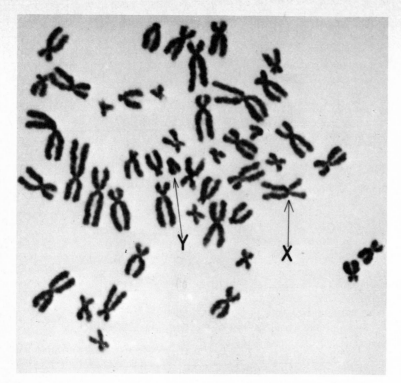

Figure 4-2 Human Chromosomes. *These chromosomes are of a human male cell, since the Y chromosome is present. (Courtesy of Dr. J. H. Tjio)*

genes received from the parents. On the other hand, his dirty, frightened appearance seemed to be the result of his life with animals.

Reproductive cells. Beginning at puberty, the reproductive cells, the *sperm* cells in the male and the *ova* or egg cells in the female, undergo a division that is different from that just described. Instead of being split and duplicated, only one member of each pair of chromosomes goes to the new cell. Ova receive half of the female's chromosomes, and sperms receive half of the male's chromosomes. Different ova produced by the same individual receive different sets of 23 chromosomes, and the same is true with sperms. Furthermore, the chromosomes are so thoroughly shuffled in this process that the probability of any two ova or any two sperms having exactly the same set is extremely small.

There are millions of possible combinations of chromosomes in the reproductive cells of any female. There are also millions of possible combinations in the male. Taken together, the potential different inheritances for any given individual, with a contribution from the male and female, rise into the billions. They become even higher when, during the cell-division process, chromosomes occasionally split apart, and a segment of one chromosome is exchanged with a segment of another split chromosome.

It is not surprising that we never meet our double. The only exception occurs in the case of *identical twins,* where the ovum divides soon after fertilization, forming two or more organisms with the same genetic makeup. In short, identical twins are alike not on the basis of two independent assortments of genes that turned out to be identical but rather by sharing the same initial assortment. *Fraternal twins* develop from separately fertilized ova, rather than from the division of one ovum. Their heredity is no more alike than that of children born to the same parents at different times.

organisms, including human beings. All genes are composed of DNA molecules. Since the structure of this molecule has now been established, genes can be studied at the molecular level. This work is greatly aided by the electron microscope, which provides a highly magnified view.

When a cell divides, its chromosomes and thousands of genes are duplicated. The complete genetic code is passed on to each of the resulting cells, giving all except the reproductive cells an identical inheritance (Figure 4-3).

Thus, genetic inheritance controls the development of our hair color, eye color, and other physical characteristics. It also makes a most important contribution to our potential physique and potential for learning, although these traits also are influenced by other factors. In the case of Victor of Aveyron, for example, his facial features were primarily determined by a particular assortment of

The Human Organism

FERTILIZATION

NUCLEI COMBINE

CHROMOSOMES
ARE FORMED

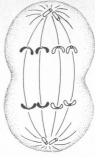
CHROMOSOMES
ARE DUPLICATED

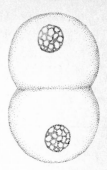
TWO-CELLED STAGE

CELL DIVIDES

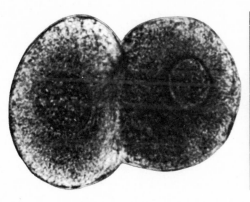

Figure 4-3 Cell Division. *After fertilization, a division process produces two cells, then four, eight, and so on, until billions have been produced. Even when full growth is attained, the process continues in many tissues, so that sloughed-off cells are replaced. The photographs, taken by a scanning electron microscope, show embryo cells in the process of division and replication. (Photos courtesy of Dr. Landrum B. Shettles)*

Genetics and Behavior

We know that Victor of Aveyron had an XY combination for the twenty-third pair of chromosomes because he was born a male, but what about the other 22 pairs? What genetic structures might they have included, and how are these genes related to physical characteristics and behavior? Many psychologists are especially interested in the relationships between genetics and behavior.

Since human subjects cannot be manipulated in selective breeding experiments for studying these questions, investigations in genetics often involve animals. Furthermore, when the researcher is interested in behavioral characteristics, the electron microscope is of little use. Instead, the investigator makes inferences about hereditary processes based on observations of the animals' responses.

Single-pair traits. Since genes come in pairs, let us refer to the genes in a mouse with normal running ability as *RR*. The capital *R* is used because the gene for running is a *dominant* gene throughout the species. Another mouse might have *Rr,* and it would also be a runner because of the dominant *R*. Still another mouse might have *rr*. The lower-case *r* denotes the gene for a defective type of locomotion known as whirling or waltzing, which is a recessive trait, determined by a *recessive* gene. A recessive gene will influence the organism's behavior or physical appearance only if it is paired with another recessive gene of the same type. Thus, a waltzer must have the *rr* combination.

If we mate an *RR* mouse with an *rr* mouse, all the offspring will be *Rr*. Each newborn receives one gene from each parent, and we would correctly predict that all of them will run normally.

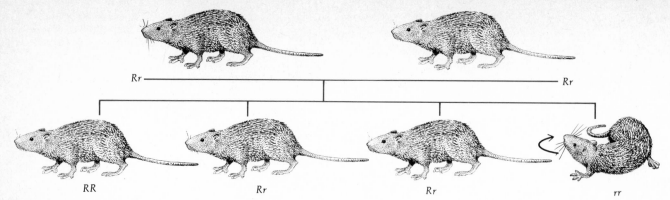

Figure 4-4   Locomotion in Mice. *The presence of the dominant gene (RR or Rr) results in normal running. Absence of the dominant gene (rr) results in a defect in locomotion, called waltzing. (Adapted from Dunn, 1932)*

Suppose we mate *Rr* and *Rr*. With a sufficiently large sample, chance distributions will result in approximately one-fourth of the offspring having an *RR* combination, receiving a capital *R* from each parent; approximately one-half will be *Rr*, receiving an *R* from either parent and an *r* from the other one; finally, one-fourth will be *rr*, inheriting an *r* from each parent. Of these, three-fourths will be runners, as *RR* or *Rr*, and only one-fourth waltzers, all *rr* (Figure 4-4).

Among human beings, the same result is found, for example, with Huntington's chorea, an inherited nervous condition in which symptoms appear about midlife. It becomes manifest in jerky movements, involuntary twitching, and convulsions, as well as mental deterioration, lasting for about 15 years. In this case, the gene for this abnormality *(H)* is dominant, and that for the normal condition *(h)* is recessive. A union of *Hh* and *Hh* will produce the same distribution as just seen in mice, but the offspring have a 75 percent chance of manifesting the disease. Fortunately, this dominant gene is rare.

Multiple-pair traits.   Not all human and animal characteristics can be explained so simply, however. Even in eye color, there are variations from the traditional blue and brown, and in traits such as intelligence and physique, the variations are innumerable. In fact, most human characteristics do not appear in one specific category. They are evident in countless variations, and thus it seems that they are influenced by *multiple pairs* of genes. Even characteristics of the lowly fruit fly seem to depend on dozens of pairs of genes.

In one extensive experiment with animals, 142 rats were tested for their capacity to learn a maze. Those making few errors were designated *bright,* and those making many errors were designated *dull.* Keeping the environment constant, the experimenter then mated the brightest rats in each generation with one another, and he also mated the dullest with one another. Initially, there was not much difference between the offspring in the two groups, suggesting that maze-learning is not controlled by a single dominant gene. If a single gene had been dominant, a more pronounced difference in intelligence would have appeared in just a few generations. It was only after seven generations that two distinct types of rats—maze-bright and maze-dull rats—were developed. Marked differences in learning ability and emotionality were produced by this selective breeding (Figure 4-5).

In such cases it is speculated that multiple pairs of genes are involved, each with two degrees of expression but with no dominance. One pair might be *A* and *a,* another *B* and *b,* still another *C* and *c,* and so on, for as many genes as are relevant. Thus, it is assumed that a rat with the *AA* combination is, in this respect, brighter than the rat with *aa,* and a rat with *Aa* falls between the two. Similarly, a rat with *BB* is, in this respect, brighter than *Bb*, which in turn is brighter than *bb*. It is also assumed that, within the species, no dominance exists in the various gene pairs that contribute to the complex trait.

If we assume that each pair of genes functions in these ways, the relevant genes possessed by the brightest possible rat would be *AABBCCDD*; the dullest rat would have the genes *aabbccdd*; and a cross between the brightest and dullest would produce many combinations. Presumably, combinations such as *AaBbCcDd* and *aABbcCDd* would occur with the highest frequency, and there would be gradations towards the extremes of the distribution.

Finally, if the inheritance of maze-learning ability is determined in this way, we would expect that crossing bright and dull rats would yield a continuous distribution rather than the separate classes, such as one obtains when single pairs of genes are involved. That is, instead of having a new generation of bright rats and dull rats, as we had runners and waltzers, we would have rats with all degrees of maze-learning ability. This result was found when bright and dull rats were mated.

Studies in behavior genetics. The whole field of research, when it focuses on the role of heredity in the organism's responses, is known as *behavior genetics*. In the past, geneticists have emphasized physical characteristics, which are easier to study than behavior, but currently there is much interest in the hereditary foundations of emotionality, aggressiveness, learning ability, and even responsiveness to others in the species. The study just cited, on maze-learning in rats, is one example.

Besides the possibilities for selective breeding, another advantage in using animals is that the laboratory surroundings can be intentionally simple and

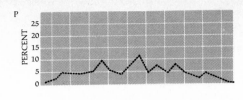
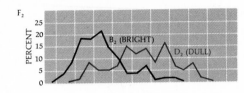
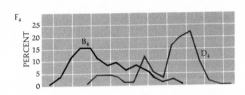
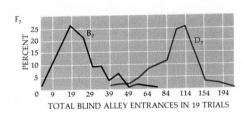

TOTAL BLIND ALLEY ENTRANCES IN 19 TRIALS

Figure 4-5 Inheritance and Maze-Learning Ability. *Successive generations of selective breeding for brightness and dullness in maze learning eventually produced two separate distributions. The parental group (P) and the second, fourth, and seventh generations are shown (Tryon, 1940).*

constant; they can exclude environmental factors that might affect certain behaviors. In these studies, it has been shown that there are genetic antecedents to right and left ''handedness'' in mice, that rats and guinea pigs have an inherited susceptibility to *audiogenic seizures,* which are convulsions induced by exposure to high-frequency sounds, and that the responsiveness to light of moths and other flying insects can be influenced by breeding procedures (Collins, 1970; Schlesinger & Griek, 1970; McClearn & DeFries, 1973).

Although human investigations cannot be controlled in this manner, there have been numerous studies of genetic determinants in schizophrenia, intelligence, and other areas of human behavior. Schizophrenia is a severe psychiatric disorder usually involving irrational thinking and emotional upset, commonly requiring hospitalization or out-patient medication. If there is a significant hereditary factor in this condition, one would expect that children of schizophrenic parents would tend to manifest this disorder, just as they inherit certain of the parents' physical traits. Thus, when a group of foster children was studied in this respect, it was found that this disorder occurred more commonly among those who had a biological parent considered to be schizophrenic than it did among those with parents considered to be normal (Wender, 1969). On the basis of many such studies, there is considerable evidence for some hereditary component in schizophrenia.

The contribution of heredity in intelligence also has been studied widely, especially by using sets of identical twins. We will turn to this evidence later in this chapter and elsewhere in this book. Estimates of the hereditary component range up to 70 percent and higher, although the figures and the whole issue have been widely debated (Herrnstein, 1973; Kamin, 1974). On the other hand, in certain forms of mental retardation the behavioral limitations due to inherited factors are readily apparent.

As a result of advances in genetics and behavioral studies, an interdisciplinary specialty called *genetic counseling* has been developed. Here prospective parents, especially those with a family background of some abnormality, can consult with experts in genetics about the probability of transmitting these characteristics to their offspring. In addition, they can be informed about treatments for certain inherited disorders.

Role of Environment

The environment, of course, is also of importance in human development. No organism grows in a vacuum; there is always some context in which heredity unfolds, and it can have a vital influence on the growing individual.

Figure 4-6 Prenatal Environment. *The growing organism is surrounded by amniotic fluid and attached to the mother by its umbilical cord, through which nourishment is obtained and waste products are excreted. This environment is extremely important, for normal development can proceed only if the liquid that surrounds the organism has the proper thermal and chemical properties. (United Press International)*

Prenatal Influences

The first environment for any organism is inside the mother. Before birth, the human fetus exists within the amniotic sac, which is simple and constant compared to the world outside (Figure 4-6). On this point, George Bernard Shaw quipped: "We are never quite so well able to manage our affairs as during the first nine months of life."

Sometimes even this environment can be difficult; we know that a variety of maternal conditions can disrupt normal development of the fetus. These include nutritional deficiencies, infections, exposure to radiation, and chemical changes in the blood, many of which can pass the placental barrier and enter the fetal environment, thus influencing the unborn. It is also known, for example, that certain viruses can produce neurological damage and mental deficiency in the fetus.

At one time the placenta was considered a barrier to the transfer of drugs, but today it appears that almost all drugs ingested by the mother are transferred to the fetus. In fact, the placenta may even concentrate some toxic substances. Thus, some drugs can cause severe physical malformation in fetal life; others are recognized as contributing factors in lack of responsiveness in the newborn offspring (Hill, 1974).

The influence of the prenatal condition also is evident in the case of twins. The average IQ of identical and fraternal twins is about four to seven points below that of people who do not have a twin. Apparently, this result is due to the fact that twins share the intrauterine space and nutrition (Jensen, 1969; Zajonc & Markus, 1975). However, twins share the mother, father, and others in the postnatal environment, which also influences intellectual development.

Further, smoking by the expectant mother is related to the size of the newborn. The more the mother smokes, the less the newborn is likely to weigh, but no causal relationship is necessarily indicated (MacMahon et al., 1966). Emotional factors, for example, may prompt both outcomes. Maternal smoking is also related to premature birth, although, again, it does not necessarily cause premature birth (Figure 4-7). Researchers are just now beginning to identify the ways in which diverse maternal conditions can influence prenatal development.

Postnatal Influences

At birth, the infant is suddenly exposed to a radically different environment composed of a wide variety of physical and chemical energies, as well as social forces that arise from contacts with

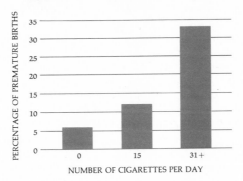

Figure 4-7 Maternal Smoking and Pregnancy. *Premature births occur at the rate of about 6 percent among nonsmoking mothers, 12 percent among mothers who smoke 15 cigarettes a day, and 33 percent among mothers who smoke 31 or more cigarettes a day. (Adapted from Simpson, 1957; photo © Paul Kellogg)*

other human beings. This complex environment lasts the rest of the individual's life, and for the growing child the problem is to find or create an environment best suited for his or her favorable development.

The Skeels-Skodak children. There are countless illustrations of the influence of environment on human development, but here we have chosen to consider one in detail. Later, it will be followed by various types of experimental evidence.

In an Iowa orphanage in the 1930s, a change of environment seemed appropriate for two young girls who seemed to have received an unfavorable assortment of genes. In fact, these infants, 13 and 16 months old, were noticed by psychologists because they were so undersized and unresponsive. With tearful eyes, stringy hair, and runny noses, they spent most of their time rocking, rolling, and crying in their cribs.

Nobody was much surprised at that time. The mothers of these children were both known to be retarded and, while there was no information on the fathers, they too were presumed to have poor genetic endowments.

The hospital administration agreed with the two examining psychologists, Harold Skeels and Marie Skodak. The girls were hopelessly retarded, the orphanage was overcrowded, and a transfer could be arranged. Within two months, the girls were placed in a state institution for the mentally retarded.

Follow-up studies. About six months later, Skeels visited the state institution again. In his ward rounds, he noticed two smiling, playful children running around like most others of their age. They were hardly recognizable as the two "hopelessly retarded" children of a half year earlier. In disbelief, he tested them again, and the results were remarkable.

The girls' intelligence quotients had more than doubled, approaching the normal range. The change in physical development was obvious, and the girls seemed happier and more stable emotionally. The difference was so dramatic that Skeels and Skodak believed it was perhaps only temporary and made no change in the children's lives. They made plans, however, to test them again later.

Once more, a year later, unmistakable signs of favorable development were found. One child showed a fully normal

intelligence and the other had progressed to a borderline level. What had happened?

The institution for retarded women, as it turned out, was a favorable environment for the improved development of the two children. Each had been placed in a ward with older girls and women, who were from age 18 to 50, and had been "adopted" by one of them. The other patients became adoring "aunts," while the hospital attendants and nurses also played with the children and gave them affection. Both girls had received much adult attention, they enjoyed many toys and picture books, and they were often taken on shopping trips and other excursions. The setting, in short, was abundant in affection and interesting stimulation for the preschool child, despite the fact that most of the women had no more mental ability than a nine-year-old child.

By contrast, the orphanage was a bleak place; earlier it had been an army barracks for troops during the Civil War. Medical and physical care was provided, but there was little interaction with adults or even with other children. There were only two nurses and one or two older girls occasionally serving as assistants. The staff was overworked, there was little time for play, and the children seldom left the nursery, except for brief walks outdoors.

An experimental program. This unexpected development in such an unlikely place so impressed Skeels and Skodak that they made another radical proposal. A whole group of hopeless orphanage cases would be sent *early* to institutions for the mentally retarded, before reaching the usual age for transfer. There were misgivings among the orphanage administrators, but it was pointed out that little could be lost. If a child did not attain normal functioning, that child would simply remain where he or she was eventually destined to be anyway. Furthermore, the children would be considered only house guests at the institu-

	Experimental Group						Control Group			
Case	IQ Before	Months of Transfer	IQ After	IQ Change	Case	IQ Before	Months at Orphanage	IQ After	IQ Change
1	89	5.7	113	+24	1	91	43.1	62	−29
2	57	23.7	77	+20	2	92	25.3	56	−36
3	85	11.9	107	+22	3	71	27.3	56	−15
4	73	8.1	100	+27	4	96	39.4	54	−42
5	46	24.8	95	+49	5	99	27.4	54	−45
6	77	14.5	100	+23	6	87	29.3	67	−20
7	65	10.4	104	+39	7	81	35.6	83	+2
8	35	24.6	93	+58	8	103	32.8	60	−43
9	61	12.3	80	+19	9	98	21.4	61	−37
10	72	22.0	79	+7	10	89	28.2	71	−18
11	75	23.6	82	+7	11	50	30.1	42	−8
12	65	12.0	82	+17	12	83	28.3	60	−23
13	36	52.1	81	+45					

Figure 4-8 IQ Changes. *The transfer and control periods are expressed in months. (After Skeels, 1973)*

tion, in order to escape the stigma of being committed as mentally retarded at an earlier age than usual. Their names would remain on the orphanage roster.

Under this plan, 11 more children were transferred, making a total of 13. Their average age was 19 months and average IQ was 64 at the time of transfer, and none possessed any known gross physical handicaps or were ineligible for placement for legal reasons. At the time of selection, it was not planned that they would become the subjects of an investigation, but in order to have some basis for later evaluation, a control group of 12 children was identified from among those who remained at the orphanage. These children were selected by using comparable age and intelligence scores and potential for placement as the chief criteria. Thus, the control subjects' average age was 17 months and average IQ was 87 at the time observations were started.

The transferred children remained in their new institutions for approximately two years, after which they were seen and retested. The basic purpose of this follow-up investigation was to study the development of all the children in their new environment, noting any changes that had occurred over the two-year period. Afterwards, the children were returned to the orphanage or transferred elsewhere, depending on the individual needs of each child. Similarly, the members of the control group were restudied and treated according to the best available plan.

When the results were analyzed, it was found that the experimental group showed an average *gain* in IQ of 28 points. Among the control group there was an average *loss* of 26 points. The chief factor accounting for this difference, according to the investigators, was the amount of stimulation and adult-child relationships for the transferred children (Figure 4-8).

Heredity and Environment

All human development is of interest to psychologists, but cases such as the Skeels–Skodak children arouse special interest about the contributions of heredity and environment in the developmental process. In what ways does each of these factors influence human growth? This question is a difficult one for which the answers are decidedly incomplete, but we can understand some of the complexities by considering other types of evidence. Hence, we begin with the issue of maturation.

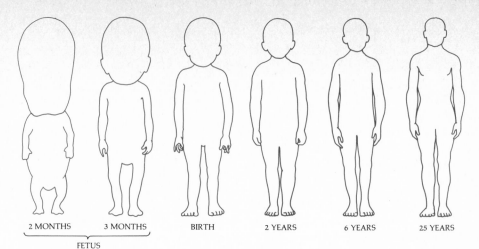

| 2 MONTHS | 3 MONTHS | BIRTH | 2 YEARS | 6 YEARS | 25 YEARS |

FETUS

Figure 4-9 Changes in Proportions. *At birth, the ratio of head length to total body length is 1:4; at maturity, it becomes 1:8. The ratio of head length to length of limbs shows a similar change (Jackson, 1923; Civa Symposium, 1943). Note the ratio of head length to arm length in the child in the photograph, and compare it with your own. (Photo by Mazzachi from Stock, Boston)*

Process of Maturation

There is a universal pattern of development among all normal members of a given species. This pattern of development, called *maturation,* depends on biological conditions and takes place almost inevitably within the species. In short, it is essentially a function of heredity and suggests a common inheritance among the group members. The changes, once they begin, are usually predictable (Figure 4-9).

Prenatal sequences. Even during the prenatal period, there is a universal tendency in vertebrates to develop faster at the head than at the tail. The head region of the six-week-old human fetus has reached a greater proportion of its ultimate size than the lower body parts. Since the head is referred to as *cephalic* and the tail as *caudal,* this development sequence is known as *cephalocaudal.*

There is also a universal tendency for structures close to the center of the body to develop faster than those at the extremes, as a comparison of the trunk region and arms and legs of the six-week-old fetus suggests. This sequence is known as *proximodistal* development, since *proximo* means "nearby" and *distal* means "away from the center."

Postnatal changes. Immediately after birth, the sensory capacities improve rapidly. Newborns cannot readily perform automatic functions such as focusing the eye lens and coordinating eye movements, but the relevant muscles and visual mechanisms develop quickly, and infants begin exploring their environment visually many weeks before they have achieved sufficient motor coordination to move themselves from place to place. In fact, infants have pattern vision just a few hours after birth.

In one series of studies, infants from age 48 hours to 6 months were tested in a special "looking chamber." This apparatus consisted of a large frame for holding visual stimuli over the infant's bed, a series of visual targets, and a peephole whereby the investigator could observe the direction and length of fixation of the infant's gaze. Each of the 43 infants was exposed to patterned stimuli and to some unpatterned but colored stimuli that were repeated up to 8 times each. The results showed considerably more visual attention to the patterned surfaces than to the plain but colored ones, and most attention to a human face, indicating that the visual world of even the very young infant is not entirely formless (Figure 4-10).

Hearing also appears quickly after birth. The newborn is responsive only to loud noises, but soon pitch, quality, and

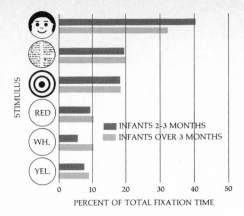

STIMULUS

INFANTS 2-3 MONTHS
INFANTS OVER 3 MONTHS

0   10   20   30   40   50
PERCENT OF TOTAL FIXATION TIME

Figure 4-10   Study of Infant Gazing.
The infants' visual interest is indicated in the fixation times. The object being fixated was determined by noting its reflection in the subjects' eye, and the length of each fixation was recorded electrically. The photograph shows the experimental setup and the drawing shows the stimulus patterns, including the red, white, and yellow circles. (From "The Origin of Form Perception" by Robert L. Fantz. Copyright © 1961 by Scientific American, Inc. All rights reserved. Photo courtesy of David Linton.)

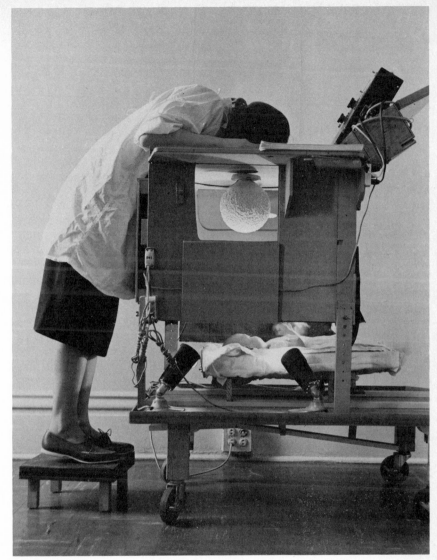

other aspects of sound are discriminated. Sensitivity to temperature and other stimuli and the capacities for taste and smell, although present in the fetus, continue to increase in the weeks following birth.

The most obvious postnatal developments are not sensory but *motor,* meaning that they pertain to the muscles and glands; these changes reflect the prenatal sequences in a minor way. The baby learns to control the head before the legs, illustrating the cephalocaudal sequence. The baby moves the arms as a whole before gaining effective control of the hands and fingers, demonstrating proximodistal development.

As the muscles grow, the normal infant also progresses to successive *developmental stages.* A developmental stage is a period in this process of change; it is a point or an interval in the sequence. In locomotion, for example, the infant progresses from lying to sitting, to standing, and finally to walking

with assistance within the first year. These four stages are predictable, and ages have been identified at which they often occur, although there are distinct variations in the rate at which children reach them.

Deviations always occur, even in the normal child, but sometimes they are so extreme that they suggest abnormal development. The two little girls at the orphanage, for example, were much behind the normal schedule. When first observed by Skeels and Skodak, they

When my sister was nine months old the doctor discovered that she had a dislocated hip and suggested surgery. After the operation, she had to be in a body cast for six months. She was unable to move her legs or body, but when the cast was finally removed and the stiffness was exercised out of her legs, she walked right away. She never even really learned to crawl.

could not even sit up in bed. With normal development, the younger one, at 13 months, would be climbing stairs, and the older girl, at 16 months, would be standing and walking alone (Figure 4-11).

In terms of finger dexterity, the older child should have been using her thumb and forefinger in opposition to one another, as in picking up beads and perhaps a piece of thread. Instead, neither girl had developed beyond the level of a normal six- or seven-month old baby.

These cases suggest the possibility of a defective inheritance, which sometimes occurs. But they also suggest that maturation, a factor of heredity, can be influenced by environmental conditions, as illustrated when the children were transferred. The extremely rapid and positive physical, mental, and emotional changes that were observed after the children were placed outside the orphanage suggest that environmental conditions can play a role in the maturation process. While based in heredity, maturation proceeds in the context of suitable environmental influences.

Maturation and environment. More precise demonstrations of this relationship are also found in animal studies, in which the environmental factor can be controlled more readily. The development of locomotive responses in lower animals has been studied in this way, as, for example, in the swimming response among salamander tadpoles.

In the very earliest stages of growth, a group of tadpoles was placed in ordinary tap water and another group was placed in water containing a mild anesthetizing solution of chloretone. The experimental tadpoles continued to grow normally, but they were rendered inactive by the anesthetizing chloretone. The control subjects, as they matured, showed the usual series of preswimming movements and eventually the normal swimming response. Then the experimental subjects were removed from the chloretone solution and placed in pure tap water. After

half an hour, the time required for the effects of the chloretone to disappear, the experimental subjects were swimming normally in the water. As a rule, an interval of several days is required between the tadpole's initial movements and the appearance of the full swimming response. Thus, the investigation demonstrated that the swimming response in these tadpoles is based on inherited changes within the organism (Carmichael, 1927). ■

However, another study presented evidence for the environmental factor. When the tadpoles were maintained in the anesthetizing solution for two weeks, which was much longer than the usual developmental stage for beginning to swim, they showed a definite loss of swimming ability (Matthews & Detwiler, 1926).

Experiments with infant monkeys also have shown the importance of early environment on maturation. In a series of extensive studies, it has been demonstrated that monkeys that do not receive the usual maternal stimulation and affection in infancy fail to develop into normal adults. Their social relationships are infrequent or ineffective and adult sexual behavior is decidedly disrupted. Furthermore, the females, if they do become mothers, show grossly inadequate maternal responses. Even adult intellectual functioning appears disturbed (Harlow & Harlow, 1962; Harlow et al., 1971). These widely cited experiments are considered in further detail later, as are other studies showing the importance of influences during the early, critical periods.

Such research demonstrates that some degree of environmental stimulation is necessary to initiate even the appearance of maturational responses, that these responses may be modified by learning, and that eventually they merge with other learned behavior. In short, under normal conditions the influences of heredity and environment proceed simultaneously.

The Human Organism

Figure 4-11 Development of Locomotion. *The numbers indicate the average approximate ages in months, but completely normal children reach these stages at widely different ages. (After M. M. Shirley,* The First Two Years. *Child Welfare Monograph No. 7, University of Minnesota Press, Minneapolis. Copyright © 1933 by the University of Minnesota.)*

Limitations of feral cases. At the human level, apart from such rare investigations as that of Skeels and Skodak, the evidence is more anecdotal. For example, it is said that more than half a century ago a group of Europeans and Asians gathered in a remote area of Bengal, India, to observe with field-glasses what might emerge from an animal den approximately two hundred yards away. Eventually, three wolves ventured from a tunnel-like passage, followed by two cubs, and later a human head covered with bushy hair. It gazed

Human Development

Figure 4-12 Wild Boy of Aveyron. *The story of Victor has inspired poems, plays, a movie, and even music—the "Wild Child." The bust shows his likeness in 1800 after he was captured. (From* The Wild Boy of Aveyron *by H. Lane, Harvard University Press, 1975.)*

from side to side for a time, and then a whole human form appeared, with another close at its heels.

Excavation of the den took place a week later, and it revealed two female wolf-children, about six and eight years old, respectively. They were later named Amala and Kamala. They were entirely naked, crawled on all fours, uttered no sounds, and ate raw meat readily. It was soon discovered that they tore clothes off themselves, howled in a peculiar voice that was neither human nor animal, and apparently saw better at night than during the day (Squires, 1927). When they were made to stand, their toes remained perpendicular to the ground, due to their extensive crawling, and there were hard callouses on their knees (Zingg, 1940).

Although these details of the girls' capture are controversial, their existence is well substantiated. Amala died shortly after she was taken to live with a human family, but Kamala spent nine years in a human environment. During this period she acquired only a few human habits and mastered only about

fifty words, which she used in rudimentary fashion. Amala was a feral child, like the "Wild Boy of Aveyron" mentioned at the beginning of this chapter (Figure 4-12). The term *feral child* refers to a young person who lacks a human personality as a result of being reared apart from human contacts.

There have been reports of similar cases. Years earlier, Wild Peter was found wandering about the German countryside, reputedly the perfect specimen of man in nature, but later it was discovered that he had the mark of a tan on his legs, suggesting the presence of breeches earlier, and even the fragment of a shirt hanging around his neck (Tylor, 1863). Similarly, the Swine-girl of Salzburg, the Lithuanian Bear-boy, and others are of questionable reliability (Zingg, 1940). Such accounts were especially common after the Napoleonic wars, which left many children without parents or friends, uncared for in the wilds.

Even less substantiated is the historical report of Kaspar Hauser. Not long after birth, he allegedly was prevented from gaining his rightful throne to a small German kingdom by being shut alone in a dungeon with only two hobby horses and feedings of bread and water. According to the reports, when released from his tiny dark cell at age 17, he was almost totally unable to walk, talk, or eat anything but his usual fare. He was barely able to lift a hobby horse across the threshold.

In five years of training after his release, he apparently developed much greater human capacities than did Victor. One possible advantage was that Kaspar had no animal behavior to unlearn, and perhaps he had significantly greater mental potential in the first place. He never learned to walk or run well, but he reportedly developed into a capable horseman, partly because his legs were well adapted to riding. Gradually, his language ability developed and he began writing his life story. Unfortunately, he was then assassinated, apparently by those who had isolated him soon after birth (Zingg, 1940).

The Human Organism

Type of twins	Height	Characteristic intelligence	Personality
Identical	.93	.88	.46
Fraternal	.64	.63	.27

Although dramatic, these examples of feral children are not sufficiently systematic or well documented to constitute substantial findings. They are suggestive of the importance of environmental conditions in the unfolding of inherited potential, but they do not have a rigorous approach to the data. As such, they are inadequate means by which to understand the complexities of the issue, and better methods have been sought.

Heredity-Environment Relations

The most convincing procedure for studying the influences of heredity and environment on personality, intelligence, physique, and other characteristics would be to hold either heredity or environment constant while varying the other, but again the possibilities of carrying out such experiments with human beings are limited. We cannot mate persons of known heredity to control the inheritance of their offspring as we can with mice and rats, and we cannot confine a human being to a constant environment.

By producing twins, nature has provided us with some help in this regard. In fraternal twins, as noted already, heredity is no more similar than between any other pair of siblings, but with identical twins, heredity is exactly the same. Normally, however, identical twins are reared in close proximity, and the influence of subtle differences in environment cannot be readily assessed. Hence, there is considerable interest in those instances where identical twins are adopted into different localities.

Comparisons of twins. Information about identical twins being reared in separate environments has come from extensive searches in Europe and America, and in some instances the results have been analyzed collectively. When the twins were brought together again and tested, data on special traits became available, such as physical characteristics and appearance, in which the identical twins were found to be very much alike (Erlenmeyer-Kimling & Jarvik, 1963). In height, for example, there was a close resemblance. On the other hand, there was an average difference in IQ of about eight points, but an important factor here is whether the twins had received comparable schooling. Differences in educational opportunity can produce significant differences in intelligence (Anastasi, 1958). Finally, in personality traits the separately reared twins were sometimes similar and sometimes very different. By and large, however, there were larger differences in personality than intelligence (Newman et al., 1937; Gottesman, 1963). ∎

These findings permit some generalizations about the relative influence of heredity and environment, providing we ignore extreme circumstances. Environmental factors influence physical appearance, but generally they are more influential with respect to intelligence and are especially influential in development of personality, where one's parents, friends, and cultural milieu play decisive roles. The opposite statement also might be made. Under normal conditions, heredity is highly influential with regard to height, influential with regard to intelligence, and least influential—but certainly not without importance—in the development of personality (Figure 4–13).

∎ *My twin and I have been brought up in a similar environment, obviously not identical, but very similar. Being identical twins we have the same genes, so our heredity is much more similar than is our environment. I am 5′ 3½″ tall. K, my twin, is 5′ 3¼″ tall. In school we have performed equally, although I scored consistently higher on the SATs and Achievement Exams. We have been told that our IQs are separated by only two points. But the slight differences in our environments definitely have affected our personalities. I am more trusting and naive than K, and my conscience, at times annoyingly so, seems to speak to me more often than does K's. I am the domineering twin, although K is far from being shy and retiring. These few examples are evidence of the subtle and not so subtle differences in our personalities brought about not by our identical genes, but by our similar, slightly different environments.*

■ *I was very young when the first of many attempts was made to teach me to tie my shoelaces; but I did not learn. A few years later, with no further experience, in one quick lesson I tied my shoelaces easily. Sometime between these two attempts, I must have reached a readiness for that task.*

The qualification concerning normal circumstances should be emphasized, however. In extreme cases, when heredity is at such a low level that the individual does not have the capacity to understand language or to move in a coordinated manner, environment will have little influence on the development of intelligence and personality. Similarly, if the early environment is extremely adverse, as when an individual receives grossly inadequate nutrition, sunlight, exercise, fresh air, and other conditions necessary to health, the hereditary potential will have little chance to unfold.

A more important conclusion, however, concerns the *relationships* between heredity and environment—an interplay of forces that can be extremely complex. In fact, the influences of heredity and environment are so intermixed that it is almost impossible to determine on which basis any given trait or behavioral change occurred. Through studies of identical twins and laboratory investigations of animals, it is now apparent that the heredity-environment question, also called the *nature–nurture issue,* is not an either/or issue. The contributions of both factors are widely acknowledged, and the main focus of contemporary research is on discovering the ways in which nature and nurture *combine* to bring about a given characteristic.

The interaction principle. An example of this interaction is found in studies of *readiness,* which is the time at which an organism is first physiologically capable of responding correctly in a given situation. In an early study of 141 schoolchildren, it was discovered that a large proportion of them began to read when they reached the mental age of six to six and one-half years. The children first were able to profit from reading instruction at this stage, and for most of them there was little value in advancing or postponing it (Morphett & Washburne, 1931). But today we know that age six and one-half is not the "magic age" at which to learn reading because readiness also depends on environmental factors, such as the size of the typeface and prior exposure to letters and word elements. The most precise conclusion that can be drawn from the earlier study is that six and one-half years was the average mental age of readiness for reading as it was then taught in the schools. With different instructional facilities, children learn two and three years earlier and, of course, later. ■

A word about the "November boy" might be added in this context. Boys develop more slowly than do girls in the early years, and in many school districts in the United States, November is the birthday month of the youngest children in any particular grade. Children with a December or January birthday begin school a year later. Hence, the boys born in November are often the least mature and most lacking in readiness compared to their classmates. In one classroom, all eight children experiencing school difficulties were boys born in November or December (Ames, 1967). These children's lower level of maturation, as significantly influenced by heredity, generally requires a far less advanced scholastic environment in order for them to meet with success.

We cannot engage in controlled studies of the interaction concept with human beings, but we have done so with animals. In one instance, rats were selectively bred for either brightness or dullness and then, after weaning, their offspring were maintained for 40 days in one of three environments—restricted, neutral, or enriched. Later, when the offspring were tested for learning ability, it was found that heredity made little difference for those animals brought up in the extreme environments. The average scores for the bright groups differed by fewer than 9 points in both instances, but there was a difference of 47 points between the bright and dull groups in the neutral environment. In short, heredity had a marked influence in one environment but not in the others (Cooper & Zubek, 1958; Figure 4-14).

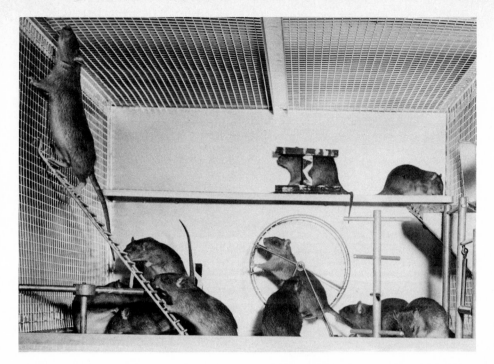

This principle is also well known among cattlemen. With regard to the production of beef, for example, Galloway cattle fare better than Aberdeen Angus in poor grazing areas, while the Angus thrive better and produce more beef in the good grazing areas (Haldane, 1946). Whether the Galloway or Aberdeen Angus have the more favorable heredity for beef production depends on the area in which they are grazing—that is, on the environment. Conversely, whether the environment, sparse or lush, is particularly favorable or unfavorable depends on which strain of cattle is involved.

At the human level, an individual does not inherit a specific behavioral trait but rather a tendency or predisposition that becomes manifest in one way in one situation, differently in another, and perhaps remains latent in a third. The result of any given inherited potential inevitably depends on the environment with which it interacts. ■ This condition is known as the *interaction principle*. Ultimately, the

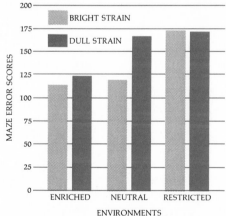

Figure 4-14 Interaction Effect. *Maze learning by bright and dull rats showed the effects of heredity only in the neutral setting; they were obscured by environmental influences in the extreme conditions. The photo shows an enriched rat environment. (Graph after* A Profile of the American Negro, *T. F. Pettigrew. Copyright 1964 by D. Van Nostrand Company. Reprinted by permission. Photo by Bennett and Rosenzweig, University of California, Berkeley.)*

■ *When we lived in our other house on the other side of town we always grew day lilies in the front of the house and marigolds in the back. We took great pride in the flowers and every year the neighbors would remark at how beautiful they were. Five years ago when we moved into our present house, by habit we planted the same flowers in the same places—day lilies out front and marigolds in the back.*

Well, we didn't get any remarks from the neighbors that year—they were nice enough not to tell us how miserable the flowers were! Hoping that it was only some fluke of nature, we planted the flowers in the same places the next year with the same results—horrible!

Then we found out what was wrong, through the help of a 90-year-old neighbor. He said that it didn't much matter how well we kept the flowers watered, fertilized, and bug-sprayed if we didn't take into consideration the amount of sun the flowers got. Our old house was shady in the front (O.K. for day lilies) and sunny in the back (advantageous for marigolds), whereas our new house was just the opposite. This is what caused the plants to do so well at our old house and poorly at our new one.

In other words, marigolds didn't inherit the specific characteristics of being large and bushy, but rather a predisposition that manifests itself in sunny situations and less so in shady ones. However, day lilies can do O.K. in shade.

Figure 4-15 Prenatal Brain Growth. *The brains, shown in actual sizes, indicate the growth of the fetal brain and its increasing complexity. (Division of Medical Sciences, National Museum of History and Technology, Smithsonian Institution)*

6 MONTHS

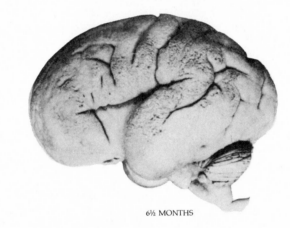

6½ MONTHS

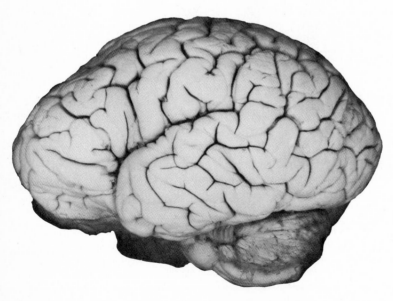

9 MONTHS

influences of heredity and environment depend on one another. Both factors are *always* present for everyone; they combine in various ways to bring about a given trait, and it is this complex interaction that must be better understood.

Study of Human Development

Studying these interactions and understanding the bases of individual variations are difficult tasks. They require a number of research methods, some of which have been considered already. To illustrate the basic procedures further and to indicate some of the difficulties, we now turn to consider human mental development. Human development proceeds in many areas—perception, thinking, motivation, emotion, personality, language, and so forth—but these topics are considered later, under their respective titles. The study of mental development not only is of special evolutionary significance, but it also was the major factor under investigation in the Skeels-Skodak research.

Early Mental Growth

The brain, primary organ of human intelligence, develops remarkably during the fetal period. From the third month to birth, it increases in weight by about 90 times. The front portions of the brain, especially in comparison with those of lower animals, show a pronounced development; the hemispheres become larger; and the convolutions or folds, which allow for a greater brain surface, become deeper and more numerous. At birth, the normal human being has a brain with considerably greater potential than that of any other species (Figure 4-15).

New brain cells apparently are added even in the first year after birth, but afterwards the growth is confined to cells already present and to the interconnections among those cells, which become increasingly complex. In the first postnatal year, the brain mass increases from about 25 percent to 60 percent of

The Human Organism

its normal adult mass, and over 90 percent is achieved by the end of the fifth year. The postnatal growth of intelligence is doubtless related to these changes.

Despite this knowledge of the brain's physical growth, success in measuring the infant's mental capacity has been slight. Ideally, we would like to find some measure that would have predictive value for later life, but researchers have not been successful. After several decades of research in which the same individuals have been tested again and again as they grow older, the conclusion forced on most investigators is that test scores from the first one or two years of postnatal life show little relation to those of later childhood and adulthood. Perhaps the scores somehow represent the infant's current mental development, but they do not successfully predict that individual's IQ in later years (Bayley, 1970; Rutter, 1970; Eichorn, 1973).

It is on this basis that the Skeels-Skodak investigation has been criticized. The intelligence scores of all the children in both groups were obtained at around age 18 months, an age at which the data are still unreliable. Hence, we do not know to what extent the differences reported in later years are due to mental growth, inaccurate measurements in the earlier years, or both. Was the capacity much higher but incorrectly measured at the earlier age? We cannot know the answer to this question, although Skeels and Skodak used some of the best testing instruments available at the time.

Generally, an extremely low score on infant tests has greater predictive significance than an average or high score. A severely retarded person is unlikely to overcome this handicap, whether it is primarily environmental or hereditary, while a person of higher intelligence, for various reasons, may encounter later deficits. The Skeels–Skodak cases are interesting in this respect.

One reason for this general lack of predictability in infancy is that the intelligence tests for this age are necessarily limited largely to sensory and motor responses, such as noticing where an object has been hidden or manipulating blocks according to a model. For the first 18 months of postnatal life these activities are the only discernible responses. Behavior typically called intelligent during this period is certainly of this nature. Even in language development, the sensory-motor aspect appears. In cooing and babbling, infants provide themselves with auditory stimulation, as well as the opportunity for motor behavior.

Another explanation for the low predictability in infancy is that the major aspects of the infant's mental life are constantly changing. Especially during infancy, it may be unwise to assume that intelligence is a constant, singular trait. The marked qualitative shifts in behavior and skills from one age to another suggest a more complex basis of intelligence. It has even been suggested that the term *mental* is inappropriate in describing the infant's test performance and behavior.

From still another viewpoint, that which we call "mental" in the early years may be more a factor of personality. The infant with an extroverted personality style, according to current mental tests, appears brighter than a more socially inhibited peer (McCall et al., 1972).

Identifying Developmental Patterns

At six to nine years of age, the IQ finally begins to have predictive value for adult intelligence (Eichorn, 1973). Above age seven but below old age, the correlation at different times in the life span is rather high; out of a possible perfect correlation of 1.00, it is approximately .80 (Herrnstein, 1973).

At this age in childhood, we can say that intelligence reflects verbal comprehension, general information, memory, and a few other characteristics, insofar as intelligence is operationally defined by the tests with which it is measured.

At all ages, *intelligence* is more generally defined as the capacity to learn from experience and adapt to new situations, but this definition does not indicate the different facets of this complex concept.

Longitudinal studies. In studying intelligence or any other aspect of human development, persons are sometimes tested and retested several times during their lives. These investigations are called *longitudinal studies;* the same individuals are followed during childhood and sometimes into adulthood. Such studies, illustrated in the Skeels–Skodak research, indicate changes occurring during the life span. They are relatively rare because several years must pass before any effects can be observed, and in the interim many subjects are lost from the sample.

One major longitudinal investigation, the *Berkeley Growth Study,* has followed individuals from birth to adulthood. Beginning in 1928, monthly observations were made of 61 infants from the first through the fifteenth month of life. Then more children were added to the study and observations were made of all subjects every three months until three years of age, annually until age seven, and semiannually from pre- to post-adolescence. At this point, with the rate of change much slower, observations occurred at ages 21, 26, and 36 years, and they are continuing today.

In this study, mental tests of all sorts have been used; routine medical examinations have been made; periodic behavior ratings have been obtained from parents, teachers, and psychologists; personality tests have been included irregularly since the age of eight years; and intensive interviews with the subjects have been conducted and analyzed by persons with no knowledge of the sample group (Eichorn, 1973). Lately, subjects from the *Oakland Growth Study* have been merged with the Berkeley subjects in an intergenerational study, which includes children, grandchildren, and spouses of the original subjects. Because successive generations are so much larger and more widely scattered around the world, the data-collection schedule now has become more limited (Eichorn, 1973; Haan & Day, 1974).

The group trend. The pattern of mental growth that has emerged from these studies is fairly constant between the third year and the early teens. On the average, mental growth increased steadily with chronological age. In the late teens, the average yearly increments became progressively smaller until age 20, when a plateau *began* to appear (Figure 4-16).

This pattern is representative of mental development for persons of average or above-average intelligence, assuming some constancy in environmental influences. It is a group trend only, with many individual variations, as we shall see shortly. For persons of below-average intelligence, the trend occurs but the leveling off appears earlier. In general, the higher the intelligence, the later the age at which peak growth is attained.

Individual fluctuations. For the individual, on the other hand, there are considerable fluctuations within the general pattern. These irregularities do not seem attributable to deficiencies in testing methods but rather to true variations in the intellectual capacities and styles of growing children. In one study, more than half the cases showed a change in IQ of 15 points or more over a 12-year period (Honzik et al., 1948). Among the Berkeley cases, the average change between ages 6 and 9 years was 12 IQ points (Bayley, 1940).

All possible patterns have been observed—abrupt increases and abrupt decreases, steady changes, uneven changes, and essentially stable conditions (Eichorn, 1973). There is an overall smooth group trend, but this pattern is not necessarily shown by any individual. It is the product of many individuals who may show very different and uneven developmental rates (Figure 4-17).

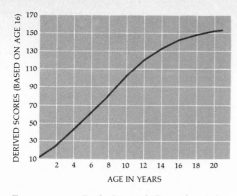

Figure 4-16   Early Mental Growth. *The scores are composite scores derived from several tests administered to the same subjects at different ages (Bayley, 1970).*

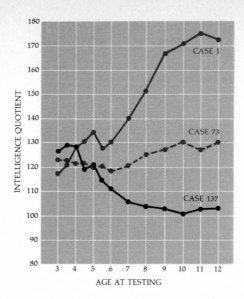

Figure 4-17   Differences in Mental Growth. *These 3 cases were selected from 140 in the longitudinal research. (After Sontag et al., 1958)*

Control of Cultural Factors

The chief problem in longitudinal research is that one must wait 5, 20, 40, or more years, or even a lifetime, for the results. A quicker method would be useful, especially one in which the data could be collected all at once.

Cross-sectional studies. A method has been employed in which different subjects at different age levels are studied at the same time. Subjects in the total sample include infants, older children, adolescents, and adults. A cross-section of the population is represented at each age level in which the investigator is interested; hence, the term *cross-sectional study* is used.

In one early cross-sectional investigation of 50 years in the life span, 500 subjects, male and female, from diverse occupations were carefully selected from among thousands of possibilities. The age range was from 20 to 70 years and intellectual performance was determined for several intervals. In all instances the findings showed peak performance by the early 30s. These findings were not surprising and, in fact, essentially verified several earlier studies (Schaie, 1958; Figure 4-18).

However, there are also limitations in this research. First, there is a loss of less-healthy subjects at the older age levels. Second, due to steady cultural improvements, younger subjects have received a better education than older ones. The difference in performance may not be due to a leveling off or decline in the older person but rather to improvements in the performance of younger ones. Even in the longitudinal study, cultural change is a factor, although there it operates in the other direction. Ideally, the only difference between a subject at a young age and the same person at an older age is that he or she has grown older, but in our rapidly changing society, this same individual at an older age generally is benefiting from a much greater availability of knowledge and vastly improved means of disseminating it. In other words, cultures grow older just as people do, and generally there is improvement with age.

The adult pattern. Improved studies using chiefly the longitudinal method, but including procedures to establish controls for cultural influence, now show that there can be continued mental

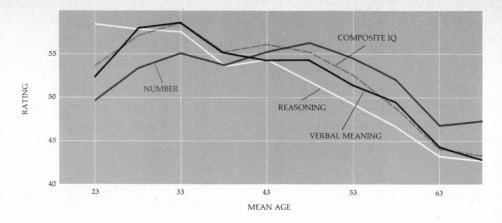

Figure 4-18   Age and Mental Ability: Cross-sectional Results. *According to these data, which were obtained from different individuals of different ages studied at the same time, mental abilities begin to decline early in the third decade of life. (After Schaie & Strother, 1968. Copyright 1968 by the American Psychological Association. Reprinted by permission.)*

growth in the adult years. Overall, there is a gradual gain in total ability, at least among college-educated subjects (Figure 4-19). The idea of an inevitable intellectual decline beginning in early adulthood is a myth (Schaie, 1974).

Reasoning seems to improve and verbal ability increases markedly, apparently remaining high at least through age 50. One investigator suggests that general intelligence does not reach its highest point until about 60 years (Maxwell, 1961). But gains do not occur in all categories. Numerical ability shows a gradual decline, and tests emphasizing speed show the most rapid decrement (Birren, 1973). In any case, the overall peak performance certainly does not occur anywhere near adolescence or young adulthood; growth apparently continues at least until the forties and probably later (Honzik & MacFarlane, 1973).

Role of experience. One point needs to be emphasized—gradual gain is not inevitable. It is related to social and economic success, independence, and physical vigor. Most vital is one's occupation and the type of mental activity it demands (Owens, 1966). College graduates have served as subjects in the most fully controlled studies, where increments appear in later life, and they are more generally employed in positions that demand a high level of mental

activity (Figure 4-20). The aged are not a homogeneous group, any more than any other age level, and the mental gain in later life seems significantly related to exposure to the advantageous circumstances already mentioned (Schaie, 1974).

In summary, intellectually active people should show a slight but steady gain in mental growth from 20 years of age upwards, continuing for two or more decades. Again, as in all areas of human development, the environment is of great importance. Those who are not intellectually active will experience an earlier point of peak ability, perhaps in the early twenties, and a slow but steady decline thereafter.

Development in the Life Span

With an understanding of human development and research methods, we close with a broader perspective, approaching the full life cycle in terms of a theory. A *theory* is a set of principles with some explanatory value, but it is based on inferences, some of which have little empirical support. Thus, this viewpoint is not only more general but also more speculative than the research perspective considered in the preceding sections.

The Human Organism

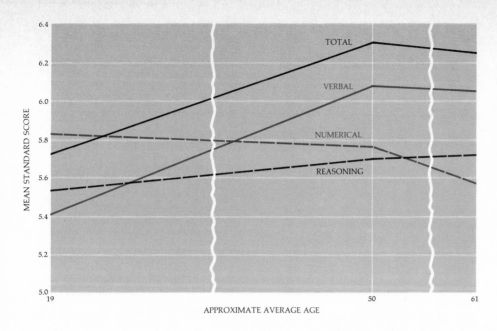

Figure 4-19 Age and Mental Ability: Longitudinal Results. *This figure, in which adjustments have been made for changes in environmental influences, shows gains in mental ability at least through age 50. Straight lines have been used to connect the scores, but we do not know the exact pattern of this trend. (Adapted from Owens, 1966. Copyright 1966 by the American Psychological Association. Reprinted by permission.)*

Psychologists differ with regard to the value of such an approach. Some contend that theory plays an indispensable role in integrating previous research. It is a method for explaining diverse data and a means by which research findings can be related to one another. In addition, it stimulates further research.

Opponents argue that theory may impede advancement—it may prompt biases among investigators, encourage nonproductive research, or define problems that cannot be approached experimentally (Brogden, 1951). It also may fail to consider existing evidence.

These opposing viewpoints are illustrated in the work of two prominent figures in modern psychology. Sigmund Freud's important contributions are widely recognized as theoretical in nature. His hypotheses were presented with relatively little systematic evidence. B. F. Skinner, on the other hand, feels that psychology should begin with research. In his view, theory is unscientific, or at least inappropriate, at this stage of our knowledge of human behavior (Skinner, 1950).

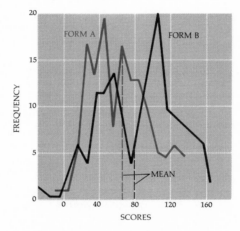

Figure 4-20 Gains in Middle Adulthood. *The subjects are husbands of gifted women. Form A of the intelligence test was administered during the second or third decade of life, and Form B was administered 12 years later. (After Bayley & Ogden, 1955)*

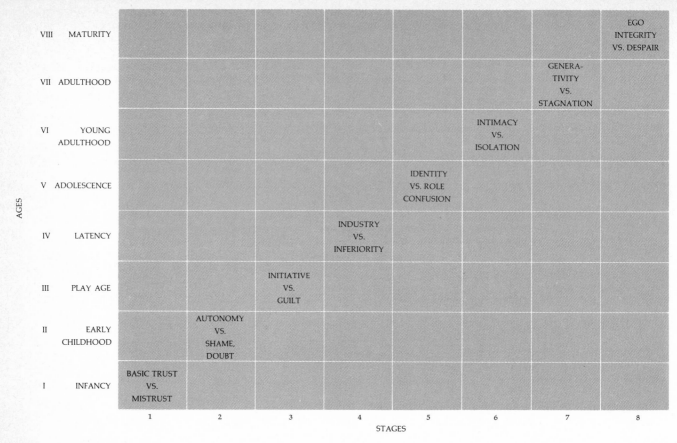

AGES		1	2	3	4	5	6	7	8
VIII	MATURITY								EGO INTEGRITY VS. DESPAIR
VII	ADULTHOOD							GENERA- TIVITY VS. STAGNATION	
VI	YOUNG ADULTHOOD						INTIMACY VS. ISOLATION		
V	ADOLESCENCE					IDENTITY VS. ROLE CONFUSION			
IV	LATENCY				INDUSTRY VS. INFERIORITY				
III	PLAY AGE			INITIATIVE VS. GUILT					
II	EARLY CHILDHOOD		AUTONOMY VS. SHAME, DOUBT						
I	INFANCY	BASIC TRUST VS. MISTRUST							

STAGES

Figure 4-21 Developmental Stages. *The diagonal indicates the progression to be followed as the individual attempts to achieve a favorable outcome in each crisis. The blank spaces adjacent to each crisis indicate that there is room for individual variation in tempo and intensity. (Reprinted from* Childhood and Society, *Second Edition, Revised, by Erik H. Erikson. By permission of W. W. Norton & Company, Inc. Copyright © 1950, 1963 by W. W. Norton & Company, Inc.)*

To illustrate the life cycle and the use of theory in developmental psychology, we consider now the work of Erik Erikson, a psychoanalyst who acknowledges a debt to Freud. Erikson's work is not the only development theory, and in later chapters we consider others. Nor has his theory been spared criticism. But it has stimulated much interest in developmental psychology and, unlike many other theories, it considers the whole life span (Erikson, 1963; Figure 4-21).

Childhood Changes

According to Erikson, human development occurs in eight stages, which are called *psychosocial stages* because they emphasize interpersonal behavior at various points in the life cycle. In each instance the focus is on our relationships with other people.

Trust. The newborn's first awareness, in Erikson's view, is of physical needs, most obviously the need for nourishment. According to his theory, if the child's caretaker anticipates and fulfills these needs consistently, especially during the first year, the infant will learn to trust others. As the caretaker supplies nourishment and the child responds with smiles and sounds, gradually a mutuality occurs and confidence develops in the child. Thus, basic trust is established, although not permanently, during the first year.

Inevitably, the child will experience moments of anxiety and rejection, but if trust is established early, it can be re-established more easily later. According to Erikson, early deprivation of physical and psychological needs, as in feral children, is devastating to the emerging

The Human Organism

personality. All infants express their basic needs, and the degree to which the caretaker is sensitive to these signals is most important for future personality development.

Autonomy. By the time a child begins the second year of life, the muscular and nervous systems have developed rapidly. Eager to acquire new skills, the child is no longer content to sit and watch but wants to move around and explore. However, the child's capacity for judgment has developed more slowly. What the child wants is not necessarily wanted by adults, who are concerned about health, safety, and the rights of others.

The child has the muscle control that allows walking and talking, but enormous physical and mental limitations prevent the child from gaining independence. The child needs guidance, and the caretaker's decision about how much freedom to allow is very important. In an extremely permissive environment, the child encounters difficulties that he or she cannot yet handle and can easily become overwhelmed and lose a developing sense of independence. Similarly, if the control is too severe, the child begins to doubt himself or herself, feeling worthless or shameful of being capable of so little.

Initiative. Once a sense of independence has been developed, the child wants to explore his or her capabilities in order to try various possibilities. Through fantasy, the child can become a hunter, a hairdresser, an airplane pilot, or any other character who captures the imagination. Vigorous play at this stage, in the fourth and fifth years, often involves "getting into things," such as shaving with a razor or weeding the garden and pulling up flowers or vegetables by mistake. There is no other time in life when the child is more ready to try new things.

The environment, however, greatly influences the child's initiative in this regard. If the caretaker recognizes the child's creative effort in attempting to

paint the house, rather than the resulting mess, freedom of expression is enhanced, and it should influence initiative in future years. The child should be stimulated towards self-expression and finding solutions to life's problems at a later age. It was partly during this period, as well as the preceding one, that the Skeels–Skodak orphans were in the supportive environment of "mothers and adoring aunts."

Industry. During the ages 6 to 12 years, the child has a greater attention span, needs less sleep, and is gaining rapidly in strength; therefore, he or she can expend much more effort in acquiring skills (Figure 4-22). The child is eager to learn real skills, rather than pretend to have them. Particularly in this stage, the child needs a feeling of accomplishment, regardless of his or her level of ability.

The key concept here, which was considered earlier, is readiness. Is the child ready to perform the tasks to which he or she is exposed? The fortunate child is guided to tasks that are appropriate to his or her capabilities at the given moment, as shaped by the interplay of inherited and environmental factors.

Figure 4-22 Learning New Behaviors. *Between the ages of approximately 6 and 12 years, most children are interested in learning how to do things they have not done before. In this way they master new skills and attitudes, some of which will be important in their later lives. (Franken from Stock, Boston)*

The Adolescent Crisis

When the child reaches the teens, or sometimes earlier, the focus of his or her environment shifts from parents to peers. This change is brought about by rapid physiological developments, matched in swiftness only in the first years of life. The term *adolescence* means "growing up," and it refers to the transition from youth to adulthood.

The chief changes associated with adolescence are stimulated by secretions in the body, called *hormones,* that occur for the first time or in much greater amounts than previously. They act on various body parts but especially the sex organs, the muscles and body hair in males, and the mammary glands, hips, and body hair in females. On the average, they appear about two years earlier in females than in males. There are, however, very broad differences within both sexes. These changes are complete in some individuals before they commence in others of the same sex, and there is wide variation in the time at which puberty is reached. *Puberty* is defined as the onset of menstruation in females, at about age 13, and the presence of sperm cells in males, at about age 15 (Figure 4-23).

The identity crisis. One problem for the adolescent is that these changes propel the individual from childhood to adulthood at an alarming rate. Or the opposite problem occurs; in contrast to peers, the changes take place much later or more slowly. Once present, they have enormous implications for the individual's sexual, social, emotional, and vocational life. The new crisis, amid this "storm of puberty," is finding an *identity,* which means developing an understanding of oneself, deciding who one is and the goals one wishes to achieve in life.

In developed countries of the twentieth century, where sons and daughters commonly do not follow in parents' footsteps, this identity crisis can be especially difficult. Temporary support during this period of confusion or indecision is sometimes found in exclusive groups and cliques, or in intolerance of those with different values, such as older people. Allegiance to a cause also provides some sort of self-definition. It satisfies the need for someone or something to believe in, which is present at all mature stages but most prominent in adolescence.

Puberty and the interaction concept. Two generations ago, the average British girl reached puberty at 15, but now it occurs just before age 13. This change is found throughout western Europe, in the United States, and in other developed parts of the world. One wonders what has brought about this change, since the onset of puberty seems to be biologically determined.

A general warming of the earth from the mid-nineteenth to mid-twentieth century has been cited as a possible factor, but there is little substantial evidence as yet. Another contributing factor may be increased psychosexual stimulation; the shift from the nuclear family to close relationships with members of the opposite sex has been greatly facilitated by the automobiles, telephones, and television of modern life. The most likely contributor, however, is improved nutrition, beginning with conception and continuing throughout the

Figure 4-23 Differences in Adolescent Development. *The graph illustrates the wide variations in height spurt for each sex. (Adapted from W. A. Marshall and J. M. Tanner,* Archives of Diseases of Childhood, 45, *1970, 13.)*

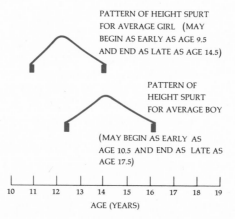

PATTERN OF HEIGHT SPURT FOR AVERAGE GIRL (MAY BEGIN AS EARLY AS AGE 9.5 AND END AS LATE AS AGE 14.5)

PATTERN OF HEIGHT SPURT FOR AVERAGE BOY

(MAY BEGIN AS EARLY AS AGE 10.5 AND END AS LATE AS AGE 17.5)

10 11 12 13 14 15 16 17 18 19

AGE (YEARS)

growth period. Comparisons of well-nourished and poorly nourished populations clearly support this idea, showing a sharp difference in the median age of the beginning of menstruation (Tanner, 1971).

Recently, the trend towards earlier onset of menstruation seems to be lessening, but this change nevertheless demonstrates a long-term interaction effect. The "adolescent spurt" is a universal inheritance, but the time of its occurrence depends partly on the interplay of environmental factors.

Patterns in Adulthood

As an adult, the individual takes a firmer place in society. Usually, he or she has a job, contributes to his or her community, and maintains a family. Erikson, influenced by Freud, often cited the latter's brief definition of a healthy adulthood—*lieben und arbeiten*, which means "to love and to work." In Erikson's stages, the young adult, having struggled with his or her own identity, is now ready to share it with others, especially through love and work.

Intimacy and generativity. The new responsibilities of adulthood can create tension and frustrations, and in the young adult they can be relieved by *intimacy*. An intimate relationship with someone else, physical or psychological, provides relief from the strain of work. But a commitment to someone else also requires abandoning one's own goals to a degree, something that is not easy to do.

In middle or later adulthood, there is an ever-broadening concern, called *generativity*. This stage involves expanding one's interests to include the next generation, but the issue is not just breeding and bearing children, for the biological parent is not necessarily interested in future generations. The success of the whole of humanity is at stake. Therefore, this stage is manifest in teaching and caring for the young, in the products and ideas of the culture, and in a more general "belief in the species."

Perhaps the reader has noted a change in the terms used to describe these stages of adulthood, in comparison with those of childhood and adolescence. There is a reason. Compared to the earlier stages, the adult stages in Erikson's theory are not nearly so closely tied to physiological conditions within the organism. The perspective at this point becomes more philosophical and perhaps ethical than biological, and the theory has been criticized for this reason. Skeptics ask: What are the operational definitions for these concepts? What is the evidence? Others also maintain that the stage of intimacy should appear before identity, on the grounds that many people achieve self-understanding only after intimacy with another individual. But in spite of these criticisms, especially of the adult stages, Erikson's conception gives more attention to the later years than most other developmental theories.

The Skeels-Skodak children as adults. Emphasis on the full life span is regarded with increasing interest in modern developmental psychology and, therefore, more than 25 years after his earlier work, Harold Skeels decided to do further longitudinal studies of the orphanage children. He tried to find all 25 original children, from the transferred and control groups, who were now adults about 30 years old. Some lived not far from the orphanage site, but others had to be traced across the country to Florida and California. Once located, each person was interviewed, along with the adoptive parents, if possible.

The results were dramatic. None of the people in the experimental group, transferred to live with the "mothers and adoring aunts," were wards of any state institution. They were essentially self-supporting. Among the control group, which had remained at the orphanage, 4 were still institutionalized and another had died in an institution. Altogether,

Experimental Group			Control Group		
Level of Education	Subject's Occupation	Spouse's Occupation	Level of Education	Subject's Occupation	Spouse's Occupation
11	Staff sergeant	Dental technician	2	Institutional inmate	Unmarried
5	Housewife	Laborer	2	Dishwasher	Unmarried
15	Housewife	Mechanic	4	Deceased	—
15	Nursing instructor	Unemployed	3	Dishwasher	Unmarried
10	Housewife	Semiskilled laborer	0	Institutional inmate	Unmarried
12	Waitress	Mechanic, semiskilled	13	Compositor/typesetter	Housewife
12	Housewife	Flight engineer	8	Institutional inmate	Unmarried
12	Housewife	Foreman, construction	2	Dishwasher	Unmarried
6	Domestic service	Unmarried	3	Floater	Divorced
14	Real estate sales	Housewife	6	Cafeteria worker	Unmarried
16	Vocational counselor	Advertising copywriter	2	Gardener's assistant	Unmarried
12	Gift shop sales	Unmarried	3	Institutional inmate	Unmarried
13	Housewife	Pressman-printer			

Figure 4-24 Adult Characteristics of the Skeels-Skodak Subjects. *For the state of Iowa, the maintenance costs were five times greater for the control group than for the experimental group (Skeels, 1966). (Skeels, H. M., "Adult status of children with contrasting early life experiences," in Monographs of the Society for Research in Child Development, 1966, 31, serial no. 105. Copyright © 1966 by the University of Chicago Press.)*

the 13 members of the transfer group had spent a total of 72 years in institutional residence, while the 12 people in the control group had been in these circumstances for a combined total of 273 years.

Regarding Freud's statement that a healthy adulthood is shown in love and work, 85 percent of the experimental group was married, compared to only 9 percent of the control group. It should be stressed that love certainly is not a requisite for matrimony, and love certainly is not absent among unmarried persons, but the very large difference here suggests an overall *group* difference in interpersonal relations. As for work, all of the transferred persons were housewives or employed outside the home. Among the control group, only half were employed, sometimes intermittently. No intelligence tests were applied, out of concern for the individuals' privacy, but on the basis of what we know about the influence of occupation on adult mental growth, one would certainly expect the transferred subjects to show more continued growth, or at least less decline, than the control group (Figure 4-24).

The average salary was almost five times greater in the experimental group, although one member of the control group deserves special mention. He was higher in educational level than most members of the other group, and his income was more than all the other incomes in his group combined. Whatever his inherited potential, somehow it apparently interacted favorably with his early circumstances. Because of a moderate hearing loss, he eventually attended a school for the deaf, where he received individual attention, which perhaps was a significant factor in his development.

The case of this person emphasizes that the interaction of heredity and environment is difficult to predict. It also reminds us again that early measures of intelligence, as in this study, are not highly reliable. This individual's capacity, and indeed that of all the children in these relatively small samples, might have been quite different from that indicated at the early age. Another limitation in this research is that the rate of adoption for the experimental children was higher than for the controls, and this circumstance could have influenced adult status considerably. The study is impressive, but its limitations must be kept in mind.

The Human Organism

The Period of Old Age

As people reach the last decades of a long life, their horizons and abilities become more limited. If the criterion for entering old age is the generally accepted retirement age of 65, then every day about four thousand people enter this life stage in the United States, and the quality and style of life for the aged become of increasing concern (Poorkaj, 1972).

According to Erikson, if an old person can find meaning in memories, then integrity is possible. *Integrity* implies emotional integration. It is accepting one's life as one's own responsibility. It is based not so much on what has happened as on how one feels about it. If a person has found meaning in certain goals, or even in suffering, then integrity has been achieved.

Whether or not one accepts Erikson's view, involuntary separation from most of society is a fact of old age. Some say that it is a more difficult problem for the elderly than facing death (Kinsey et al., 1972; Schaie & Gribben, 1975).

We observe the completion of the life cycle in the physiological changes of this stage. The infirmities of the elderly remind us of the inabilities of the young, prompting the phrase ''second childhood.'' In walking, talking, and making sense, in strength and the need for rest, in susceptibility to disease and injury, the elderly become more and more limited, and the earlier issues—industry, initiative, autonomy, and even trust—arise again. In autonomy, for example, the individual's problem is finding an environment where he or she can develop and maintain a sense of independence, without getting into difficulties or danger (Figure 4-25).

In fact, according to Erikson, all the issues in all these stages of human development arise time and time again throughout life. As pointed out earlier, autonomy is not permanently established in the second and third years, but it is easier to re-establish if a promising

Figure 4-25   Activity in Old Age. *The embroidery of aged women in southeastern Siberia ranks among the finest examples of handicraft in the Soviet Union. With such skills, elderly persons often can cope successfully with the problems of initiative and autonomy in later life. (Sovfoto)*

basis has been laid earlier. The same is true for identity. In the view of many writers, especially in these times of rapid environmental changes, maintaining a sense of identity is a recurrent issue throughout the life span.

Whether or not one accepts this particular theory of lifelong development, as postulated by Erikson, there is no doubt that the human organism is always in the process of developing. Physical and psychological changes occur continuously throughout life, and we are faced with different tasks at different stages of the life span. In one way or another, the life of every human being is being shaped and reshaped every day.

Summary

Role of Heredity

1. At conception, the human organism begins a life-long process of development based on two ever-present influences—heredity and environment. Our biological inheritance is determined by the chromosomes or, more specifically, by the genes within the chromosomes. Except in the case of identical twins, genes differ from one person to another, and this variation is the hereditary basis of individual differences.

2. Certain traits, such as eye color in human beings and type of locomotion in mice, apparently are determined by single pairs of genes. Others, including most human traits, seem to depend on the interaction of multiple pairs of genes. In behavior genetics, scientists are concerned with the relationship between inheritance and behavior.

Role of Environment

3. No organism develops in a vacuum; therefore, environment is also important. In human beings, the relatively simple prenatal environment can be influenced by several factors, including nutrition, infection, exposure to radiation, and even the mother's emotional states. These circumstances can disrupt the normal development of the fetus.

4. This situation changes at birth, when the organism begins an exposure to a highly complicated social environment. Stimulation early in postnatal life appears to have extremely important consequences for the infant's ultimate development. Intelligence, for example, apparently depends not only on our inborn potential but also on the ways in which this potential is modified in the course of experience. Similarly, social development and personality can be profoundly influenced in the early years.

Heredity and Environment

5. When developmental responses appear in a given sequence at about the same age in all members of a species, they are said to be due to maturation. Most human beings progress from lying to sitting to standing and then to walking on this basis, but environmental deficits, if sufficiently prolonged, can severely retard this development.

6. It is difficult to specify the precise developmental influences of heredity and environment, particularly at the human level. For years, scientists attempted to discover which factor was most important to human development, but today it is recognized that both are always present and always in interaction with each other, producing a wide range of individual differences among people. The ultimate influences of heredity and environment depend partly on each other.

Study of Human Development

7. In infancy, intelligence is extremely difficult to measure; behavior labeled intelligent is essentially sensory-motor in nature. Measurements of intelligence do not successfully predict the IQ in later years until a child is from six to nine years old.

8. The pattern of early mental growth has been discovered through longitudinal studies, where the same children are tested and retested as they grow older. In the group trend, there is a constant, rather sharp increase from the third year to the early teens, after which the increments become smaller; at about age 20 leveling off begins to appear. For any given individual, there may be considerable fluctuation within this general pattern.

9. In cross-sectional investigations, different subjects are studied at different age levels. The defect in this approach, as well as in the longitudinal method, is that cultural change can produce a biased result. When control procedures

are used in such studies, it is found that mental growth sometimes continues into the fifth decade of life and later, providing the individual is engaged in stimulating mental activities. The highest levels of performance for the different abilities, such as reasoning, verbal skills, and numerical ability, are reached at different ages.

Development in the Life Span

10. The most rapid developmental changes in the life span take place in childhood. According to one theory, the significant issues during this period concern the development of trust, autonomy, initiative, and industry. If these characteristics are not established in the early years, they are difficult to establish later.

11. A second period of rapid development occurs during adolescence, when hormonal secretions produce physiological changes having repercussions for social, emotional, and sexual life, as well as personality. The most significant psychosocial issue at this stage is that of establishing a personal identity.

12. Healthy adults, according to this viewpoint, express themselves through love and work. The psychosocial issues related to this stage are intimacy and generativity, which concerns future generations.

13. The rapid increase in the number of older persons in modern society has prompted concern about an appropriate environment for this segment of the population. Such persons are confronted with the psychosocial issue of achieving integrity, a problem brought about largely by increasing physical limitations.

Suggested Readings

Cox, R. D. *Youth to maturity.* New York: Mental Health Materials Center, 1970. A long-term study of 63 college graduates in the first ten years after college, based on six tasks—further education, work, marriage, parenthood, relations with one's own parents, and management of money.

Lane, H. *The Wild Boy of Aveyron.* Cambridge, Mass.: Harvard University Press, 1975. The story of Victor in readable style, with emphasis also on the philosophical and scientific questions it raised.

Newman, B. M. & Newman, P. R. (Eds.) *Development through life: A case study approach.* Homewood, Ill. Dorsey Press, 1976. These cases illustrate the chief psychological issues at different life stages.

Stone, L. J. & Church, J. *Childhood and adolescence* (3rd ed.). New York: Random House, 1975. A traditional, well-respected text on virtually all aspects of early development.

Whitehurst, G. J. & Vasta, R. *Child behavior.* Boston: Houghton Mifflin, 1977. A text with a behavioral orientation for the first undergraduate course in child development.

Chapter 5

Physiological Bases
of Behavior

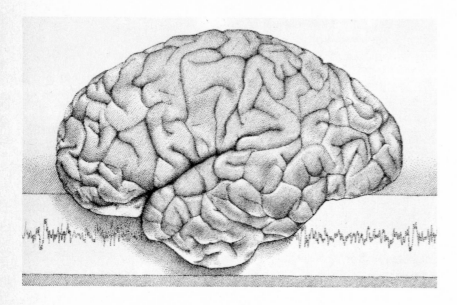

At the beginning of the nineteenth century, the brain was recognized as the organ of thought, which is what the Greeks had decided centuries earlier. But little more was known. One popular conception held that devils were influential in its operation.

The major nerves had been identified at this time, but it was thought that they were all the same type. Any given nerve could be responsible for both our sensations and our movements. In some unknown fashion involving the brain, it could bring about a feeling of warmth under the collar and at the same time a movement of the neck. How was it possible? How could the nerves transmit both reactions simultaneously?

Pathways in the Body

A Scottish physiologist, Sir Charles Bell, eventually attempted to answer this question. He doubted that any nerve could transmit both types of impulses, and he had observed in dissection studies that nerves extend down the spinal cord in the front *and* the back. Possibly, different functions were involved.

Peripheral Nervous System

In one series of experiments with animals, Bell stimulated the nerve going up the back, and there was no reaction. He observed no change in the animal's behavior. In other experiments, he touched a nerve extending up the front, and immediately the animal showed a muscular contraction. Impressed with this result, Bell made a series of tests and concluded that there are *two* basic types of spinal nerves and that each serves a different function in its connection with the brain (Bell, 1811).

Not wanting to be too bold, Bell wrote a book on these findings just for the benefit of friends, but it aroused enormous interest among scientists. He gave it the title *An Idea of A New Anatomy of the Brain.*

Sensory and motor nerves. Bell had identified a motor nerve, which transmits impulses to the muscles. Almost immediately, other investigators identified sensory nerves. Today, these two types of nerves are the basic components of the *peripheral nervous system.* Peripheral means ''outlying,'' and this system includes essentially all the nerves lying outside the brain and spinal cord. The peripheral nervous system is not a coordinating system; it serves primarily to conduct impulses to and from the central concentration of nerve tissue in the brain and spinal cord (Figure 5-1).

The *sensory* nerves transmit impulses from the sense organs, such as the eyes, ears, and skin. When such an impulse reaches the brain, we see, hear, smell, or have some other sensory experience. These nerves are also known by the term *afferent,* which means ''carrying towards'' or ''input.'' The afferent nerves make an input into the brain.

The *motor* nerves enable us to make movements; they transmit impulses to the *effectors,* which are the muscles and glands of the body. These organs carry out actions and create ''effects,'' as when one turns one's head or moves one's limbs. Hence, the motor nerves are called *efferent,* which means ''carrying away'' or ''output.''

Nerve tissues typically appear in bundles, like wire cables, and the term *nerve* specifically refers to such a bundle, although it is loosely used in other ways too. A *neuron,* on the other hand, is a single nerve cell; it is the fundamental structure of all nerve tissue. It is composed of a *cell body* and two types of fibers—axons and dendrites. The *axon,*

often a very long fiber, characteristically carries impulses away from the cell body towards other neurons. The *dendrite,* which is shorter, receives impulses and carries them towards its own cell body. Thus, dendrites of either type of nerve, sensory or motor, carry impulses towards cell bodies, and axons carry them away (Figure 5-2).

Spinal and cranial nerves. On the basis of location, nerves of the peripheral nervous system have been identified as spinal or cranial; 35 pairs of *spinal nerves,* sensory and motor, extend outward from the spinal column. We speak of pairs because the human organism is bilateral, meaning two-sided, and each

Figure 5-1 Peripheral Nervous System. *The peripheral nervous system, shown in color, extends to and from the body's extremities. This system has been suggested but not fully represented here.*

Figure 5-2 Structure of Neurons. *A sensory neuron and a motor neuron are shown. Nerve impulses cross from the axon of an afferent neuron to the dendrites of an efferent neuron, but other neurons may be involved also. The myelin sheath is a white fatty substance that covers the fibers of some nerve cells.*

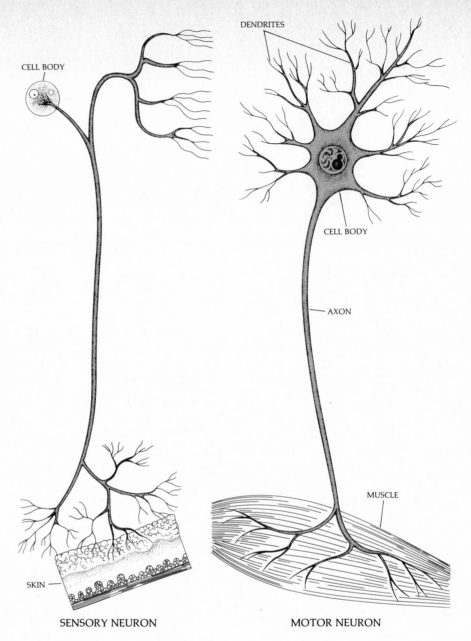

CELL BODY

DENDRITES

CELL BODY

AXON

MUSCLE

SKIN

SENSORY NEURON

MOTOR NEURON

side of the body has one member of each pair. The spinal nerves serve the chest, trunk, and extremities. Impulses traveling across the afferent spinal nerves give rise to sensations of the skin, muscles, and glands in these regions, while impulses traveling over the efferent spinal nerves are involved in moving these body parts, as Bell noted, and in stimulating the glands.

Twelve pairs of peripheral nerves connect directly with the brain and are known as *cranial nerves,* since that portion of the skull containing the brain is the cranium. These nerves extend from the head, neck, and certain body parts directly into the cranial cavity. The sensory nerves transmit visual, auditory, and other impulses to the brain, while the motor nerves enable us to move our eyes, tongue, jaw, and other parts of the head and face. ∎

Ten years after his first studies, Bell examined some cranial motor nerves in detail by means of experimental studies of the donkey and medical treatments of human beings. He noted the influence of such nerves in using the jaw, wrinkling the forehead, and opening and closing the eyes (Bell, 1821). The condition of facial paralysis, where such actions are impossible as a result of some injury to the cranial motor nerves, is now called Bell's palsy.

The overall function of the peripheral nervous system is the transmission of nerve impulses throughout the body and, therefore, some of these fibers are quite long. One spinal nerve extending to the toe can be 4 feet in length.

The nerve impulse. The transmission of nerve impulses is accomplished by electrochemical activity. Basically, the nerve impulse consists of an exchange of electrical charges outside and inside the nerve fiber. Each fiber, according to the generally accepted evidence, has a semipermeable membrane with more positive than negative electrical charges outside; inside, the negative charges are more numerous. In this resting state, the fiber is said to be *polarized*—it has opposite poles or charges on either side of the membrane. Each segment of the nerve fiber is, in effect, a tiny battery with positive and negative poles, but the poles in this case are the fiber's inner and outer surfaces.

When the fiber is stimulated, either by receptor activity or by adjacent fibers, the membrane becomes more permeable or porous in that region. In simplified terms, the positively charged particles on the outside of the membrane move to the inside for an instant. Thus, the nerve segment in this part of the fiber is *depolarized*. The resultant

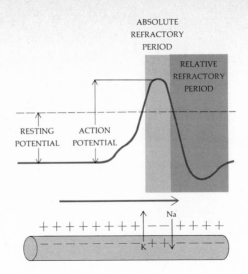

ABSOLUTE REFRACTORY PERIOD

RELATIVE REFRACTORY PERIOD

RESTING POTENTIAL   ACTION POTENTIAL

+ + + + + + + + — — + + + +
Na
K + +
— — — —

Figure 5-3   The Nerve Impulse. *The upper figure depicts the electrical impulse as it is experienced at a single point on the nerve fiber. The dashed axis represents the passage of time from left to right.*

The lower figure shows what happens as the action potential moves along the fiber from left to right. Sodium (Na) ions enter the fiber, making it positive, whereas in the normal resting state potassium (K) ions keep it negative. Thereby a successive release of energy travels along the fiber. (Adapted from "The Nerve Impulse" by Bernhard Katz. Copyright © 1952 by Scientific American, Inc. All rights reserved.)

action potential, which is what we refer to when we speak of the nerve impulse, then produces a similar increase in permeability, or depolarization, in the immediately adjacent part of the fiber, causing an influx in the next part of the fiber, and so on, until the electrical/chemical disturbance has traveled the length of the fiber. The impulse is self-propagating. Its maximum speed in human nervous tissue is about 4 miles per minute, and it is fastest in the relatively thick fibers (Figure 5-3).

All impulses traveling along a particular nerve fiber have the same potential, regardless of the nature or intensity of the activating stimulus. This is because a stimulus does no more than release energy already in the fiber; it does not contribute energy. This property of the nerve fiber, responding at full speed and full strength or not at all, is known as the *all-or-none law*, which is illustrated whenever a doorbell is pressed. If you press hard enough, the bell sounds; if you press harder, it does not sound any louder.

The nerve fiber is like a doorbell in another sense—the bell cannot be reused until the button pops out again, and a waiting or restoration period, known as

∎ *Having had an older sister struggling with anatomy in medical school, I couldn't help learning some of her "curriculum" myself: "On old Olympus' treeless tops, A Finn and German viewed aging hops."*

The first letters of the words in this poem help you to remember the twelve cranial nerves: Olfactory, optic, oculomotor, trochlear . . . and so forth.

the *refractory period,* also is necessary with the nerve fiber. This refractory period has two phases. Immediately after activation, no stimulation of any strength will start a nerve impulse. This *absolute refractory phase* differs from fiber to fiber, but it is very brief, usually only about one-thousandth of a second.

After this phase, there is a progressive increase in excitability so that stronger than normal stimulation may produce another response. This interval between the absolute refractory phase and restoration of the normal resting state is known as the *relative refractory phase,* and it lasts only a few thousandths of a second. During this phase, the nerve responds only with intense stimulation.

It should be remembered that nerve fibers typically appear in bundles and, thus, thousands of fibers can be activated simultaneously. The optic nerve, for example, has an estimated 400,000 fibers. When a stimulus excites some of these fibers, an increase in intensity can activate still more fibers. Hence, increasing the stimulus intensity can have two effects: it can increase the frequency of discharge in each responding fiber during the relative refractory phase and it can activate more fibers.

Central Nervous System

In animals with a backbone, called vertebrates, there is a thick, rope-like structure of nerve fibers running up the spine, called the *spinal cord.* This structure and the brain, which has an even greater concentration of nerve cells, comprise the central nervous system. The *central nervous system* is an extensive organization of nerve cells that serves primarily as a coordinating system, receiving impulses from the peripheral nervous system and from its own subdivisions. It is the supreme example of a neural integrating and control center, and it gives vertebrates far greater versatility in behavior than is found in animals not possessing such a central concentration of cells (Figure 5-4).

Figure 5-4   Central Nervous System.   *The human being, with a central nervous system (shown in color) and innumerable peripheral connections (shown in black), can perform an endless variety of behavior patterns.*

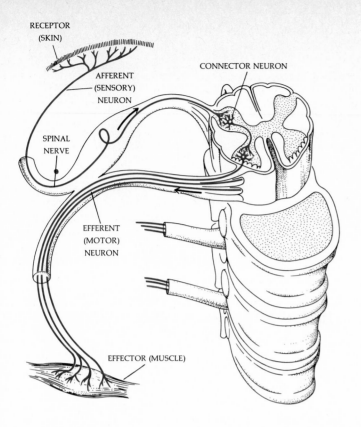

RECEPTOR
(SKIN)

AFFERENT
(SENSORY)
NEURON

CONNECTOR NEURON

SPINAL
NERVE

EFFERENT
(MOTOR)
NEURON

EFFECTOR (MUSCLE)

Figure 5-5 Reflex Arc. *The pathway shown schematically here is simplified. Actually, there are many incoming, connector, and outgoing fibers, as well as connections with ascending and descending paths in the spinal cord. This reflex has three types of neurons.*

Spinal cord. The most complex neural integration occurs in the brain, while less complicated operations occur within the spinal cord. A *reflex,* for example, is a relatively simple, inborn, automatic response integrated completely within the spinal cord. When a tendon in the knee is struck in a typical physical examination, the foot kicks forward automatically because of the activation of sensory and motor nerves in the spinal cord. Hence, we speak of spinal reflexes, and the simple neural circuit is known as a *reflex arc.*

In much human behavior the response is more complex, and a connection is necessary between the sensory and motor nerves. Hence, a third type of neuron is involved, called a *connector* or *association neuron,* which serves to carry the message to other parts of the central nervous system, thus completing a more complex reflex arc or involving other nerve mechanisms in a highly intricate circuit between incoming and outgoing messages. When you smell a pie and walk into the kitchen, sensory neurons carry the incoming message, motor neurons carry the outgoing message, and connector neurons provide various complex interconnections within the nervous system that are required in this behavior (Figure 5-5).

Synapses. The flexibility of mammalian behavior is due not just to connector neurons in the spinal cord and brain, however. It also results because, instead of being welded together in a fixed network, the ends of nerve fibers actually do not touch one another. They terminate

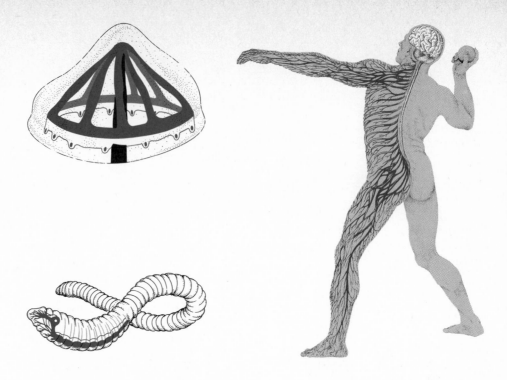

Figure 5-6 Neural Organization. *The neural mechanisms of the jellyfish take the form of a fixed nerve ring. The worm's nervous system is segmented and bilateral, much like a ladder in appearance. In the human being there are countless synapses and a central organization.*

only in very close proximity, and this region is called a *synapse* or *synaptic cleft*. The synapse, a microscopic distance, is the location at which the nerve impulse travels from one neuron to another, passing from the axon of the first to the dendrite, or directly to the cell body, of the second. At some synapses, the nerve impulse is slowed and goes no further. At others, it activates a few connecting fibers. In other instances, the impulse entering the synaptic junction activates one hundred or more fibers, which is often what happens in the spinal cord and brain.

In the jellyfish there is only one basic possibility for response because all the fibers are joined. With no synapses, any impulse potentially can influence the entire system. The jellyfish responds diffusely or hardly at all. Behavior in organisms with this type of nerve network is typically slow, repetitive, and without significant variation. The nervous system of the worm, on the other hand, is segmented, thus permitting greater complexity in behavior than in the jellyfish.

Sections of the worm can move separately, enabling it to crawl or inch along, extending one segment, then the next. In the human being, our literally countless synaptic connections permit the movement of many or few body parts. This versatility in response is the essential advantage of the synaptic nervous system over more primitive systems (Figure 5-6).

But how does the nerve impulse cross the synaptic cleft? It does not jump the space like a spark, as was believed earlier. Use of the electron microscope and improved methods of research in chemistry have indicated that a chemical *transmitter substance* is involved in synaptic connections. At the ends of all presynaptic neurons are small vesicles containing a substance that is discharged into the synaptic space, where it immediately acts on the membrane of the adjacent fiber. Activation of the adjacent neuron is presumed to be caused by a chemical that depolarizes the receiving membrane, thereby increasing the volatility of discharge in that fiber. Inhibition is presumed to be caused by a different chemical substance, which makes the dendrite, a receiving membrane, more polarized and thus more resistant to firing. Thus, the nerve fibers carrying messages that lead to activation or inhibition apparently do not differ in the type of electrical impulses involved (Eccles, 1965; Figure 5-7).

Because synapses serve as relay stations and filtering systems, most of them are found in the spinal cord and brain. Furthermore, the presence of these and connector neurons means that most nerve impulses entering the spinal cord do not remain confined to that particular region, as in the reflex. Rather, they ascend the cord, transmitting impulses in innumerable circuits to and within the brain. These activities give rise to other impulses that descend the spinal cord to connect with efferent neurons.

It should be noted that the ascending and descending paths form definite spinal tracts, most of which cross to the opposite side of the organism. Thus, impulses descending from the brain's motor control regions eventually reach effectors on the other side of the body, just as ascending sensory impulses cross over to reach the opposite side of the brain. Within the spinal cord, these tracts appear white because the fibers are covered by the white, fatty myelin sheath. They are readily distinguished from connector neurons and other cells, which form a butterfly-shaped mass of gray matter at the center of the spinal cord (refer to Figure 5-5).

Human brain. In the brain, the ascending impulses activate the so-called higher mental processes, sometimes referred to as our second level of integration. These processes include reasoning, remembering, and other forms of thinking, rather than mere reflexes.

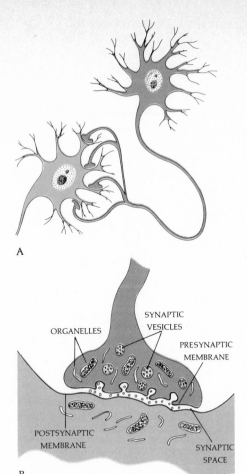

A

B

ORGANELLES

SYNAPTIC VESICLES

PRESYNAPTIC MEMBRANE

POSTSYNAPTIC MEMBRANE

SYNAPTIC SPACE

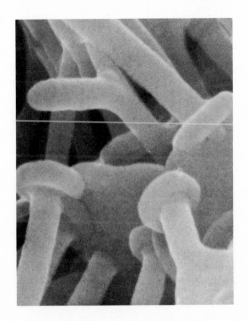

Figure 5-7 The Synapse.
Drawing A shows how the nerve fibers terminate in close proximity, called a synapse. Note that the end of the axon, known as a synaptic knob, converges on a dendrite or cell body. Drawing B shows that synaptic vesicles, which contain the transmitter substance, are found only in the membranes of the presynaptic neuron. When released into the synaptic space, they travel across the cleft in a few microseconds and act upon the adjacent nerve cell membrane, called the postsynaptic membrane. The organelles are important in the development of cells.

The photo, taken with the electron microscope, shows the trumpet-shaped synaptic knobs magnified to a great degree. (E. R. Lewis, Y. Y. Zeevi, and T. E. Everhart)

The activities confined to the spinal cord, which is lower and simpler, are known as first-level integration.

Casual observation suggests that it is the brain's size and weight that makes human beings so much more capable in diverse environments than other creatures. Bird and fish brains weigh only a few ounces, and the average gorilla brain is less than a pound, while the human brain weighs approximately 3 pounds. However, elephant brains and whale brains are even larger, recorded up to 10 and 14 pounds, respectively, and these creatures are much less intelligent than human beings.

The size of these bigger brains might be explained by the much larger bodies to which they must be responsive. Perhaps the important factor in intelligence is brain size relative to body size. In whales, this ratio is 1:10,000. Thus, there is 1 pound of brain tissue for every 10,000 pounds of whale flesh. Elephants appear more intelligent, having a ratio of 1:500. Human beings have a ratio of 1:50. The problem is that some monkeys have this same ratio, and certainly they are less intelligent than people (Wheeler, 1940; Blinkov & Glezer, 1968).

Another explanation might be the weight of the brain in proportion to the weight of the spinal cord. If the weight of the brain is about equal to that of the spinal cord, the brain presumably can do little more than serve the elementary requirements of the cord, relaying impulses and coordinating automatic movements. The frog, not noted for intelligence, has a brain that is actually lighter than its spinal cord. As the weight of the brain increases in proportion to the weight of the spinal cord, more intelligent behavior is found. The brain weight of the gorilla is 15 times that of the spinal cord, and the average human brain weighs more than 50 times the spinal cord, far in advance of all other species (Carlson & Johnson, 1948;

Blinkov & Glezer, 1968). In the context of other nervous systems, the human brain is truly "the great unraveled knot" in the study of behavior.

Outer Structures of the Brain

For more than half a century after the discovery of sensory and motor nerves, little was known about the brain. It was believed that direct stimulation by touching the surface of the brain had no effect. Mechanical and chemical stimuli had been tried with animals with no significant result, and the brains of fully conscious human beings had been operated on without producing sensory or other phenomena. Scientists were completely puzzled about the way in which the motor and sensory impulses were integrated in the brain, believing that the brain functioned only as a whole—as an excitable mass.

In the 1860s, two young German physiology professors, Gustav Fritsch and Eduard Hitzig, found fault with the view that the brain functioned only as a whole, and with the previous experiments on animals. They pointed out that the surface of the brain had not been explored in a systematic manner and, therefore, if regions for sensory and motor responses did exist, the chances were slight that they could be identified.

Furthermore, Hitzig had noticed that a weak electrical current applied to an area of the head of a human patient produced eye movements. These movements could only be attributed to the direct stimulation of the brain. Hence, the two men did a preliminary study using a rabbit, and when this method yielded positive results, they decided to use it in a study of the dog's brain. Operating on a dog, they applied the electric current directly to the outer surface of the brain, as others had done earlier, but in a more organized approach (Fritsch & Hitzig, 1870).

In most tests, the current they used was so weak that it just barely evoked a

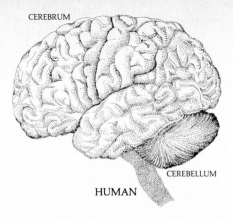

HUMAN

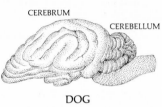

DOG

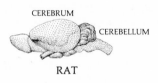

RAT

Figure 5-8 Species Differences. *Note how the cerebrum (Cb) becomes proportionately larger than the cerebellum (C) as one ascends the evolutionary scale. Note also that the brains from animals high on the phylogenetic scale are more convoluted than those of lower animals. These convolutions are important because they provide a large effective surface for our billions of brain cells; without them it would take a brain of enormous size to provide the same capacity.*

sensation on the human tongue, but it worked well on the surface of the dog's brain. They found that application at one point aroused movement of the dog's neck; in another region, leg movement was induced; at still another point, facial movements were the result. Contractions in the back, stomach, and tail muscles were brought on by stimulation of other areas.

Motor and Sensory Functions

Fritsch and Hitzig had shown that the human brain was not just an excitable mass. Certain parts were specifically related to certain body movements, as shown by direct stimulation. Other workers immediately sought to further this advance in knowledge, and within a few years most of the surface areas of the brain had been identified with respect to motor or muscular control. Study of sensory areas followed, and this procedure was called *brain localization,* or mapping the areas of brain function.

Hemispheres and lobes. The outer covering of the brain is known as the *cerebral cortex,* which comes from the Latin words *cortex,* meaning "bark," and *cerebrum,* which is the uppermost and largest part of the human brain. This structure becomes larger and more elaborate as we ascend the evolutionary scale, and its surface, which is smooth in lower animals, shows many more *convolutions,* or folds, in higher animals. From the side it looks almost like a gray, wrinkled boxing glove. The brain is divided in half, with a "glove" on each side; these halves are called the *cerebral hemispheres* (Figure 5-8).

The two hemispheres are separated by the longitudinal fissure, a large crevice that runs from front to rear. In addition, each hemisphere is divided into four sections or lobes. The *frontal* lobes are over the eyes, the *temporal* lobes are behind the ears, and the *occipital* lobes are at the extreme back of the head. The

Figure 5-9   Areas in the Cerebral Hemisphere. *The chief lobes and fissures are labeled in black. The specialized motor and sensory areas, as described in the text, are labeled in color.*

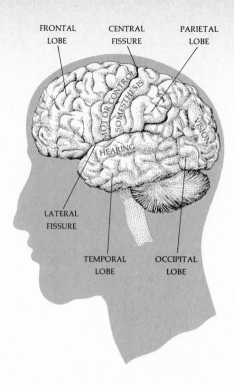

FRONTAL LOBE

CENTRAL FISSURE

PARIETAL LOBE

MOTOR CONTROL

SOMESTHESIS

VISION

HEARING

LATERAL FISSURE

TEMPORAL LOBE

OCCIPITAL LOBE

parietal lobes are separated from the frontal lobes by another crevice, the central fissure (Figure 5-9).

Area for motor control.   We now know that the primary area for controlling body movements is a narrow strip of tissue at the rear of the frontal lobe directly in front of the central fissure. The body parts are represented in this strip by an inverted sequence with reference to an upright human being. Control of the toes, feet, and legs appears near the top; the trunk is toward the middle; and the arms, hands, neck, and head are near the bottom of the hemisphere. When you begin to walk, impulses occur at the top of the cerebral cortex. When you are speaking, impulses occur much lower down the side. In both cases, the locations are just forward of the central fissure (Figure 5-10).

Research on the sensory areas proceeded more slowly because sensations are not readily observed. The experimenter can watch for movements, but he or she must infer sensations in animals or find a human subject who will

talk about them in an experiment. By such procedures, vision and hearing eventually were localized in the cerebral cortex.

Areas for vision and hearing.   The primary visual areas are in the occipital lobes. Visual experience depends on the dispersion of impulses in this region. Surgeons have noted that direct electrical stimulation of the occipital cortex leads to experiences such as flashing lights and whirling colors. After a blow to the back of the head, you may "see stars," even with your eyes closed.

Advances in research have enabled recent investigators to study highly specific portions of the visual cortex, even to the point of examining the response of a single nerve cell to a given visual stimulus. These studies are called *visual coding* because they are concerned with the way in which visual symbols are translated or coded in the brain. They have shown that the single cell is not generally responsive to any visual stimulus but rather uniquely responsive to certain visual features. One nerve cell, for example, is activated by a straight line in a vertical position but not by a straight line in another position. Another cell responds to a different visual feature, such as a straight line in a nonvertical position (Hubel & Wiesel, 1962). Activities in billions of such cells prompt responses that, when they are integrated with one another *and* with responses from other brain areas, ultimately result in visual perceptions.

Impulses for auditory experiences are received chiefly in the temporal lobes. Direct stimulation of these areas produces humming, buzzing, and similar experiences, but the experience of hearing is also dependent on the integration of activities in other brain areas. In *auditory coding*, microelectrodes are used to record electrical responses from single nerve cells in the temporal region. An experimental subject is exposed to a certain type of auditory stimulation and then the researcher attempts to "follow" the information transmission from

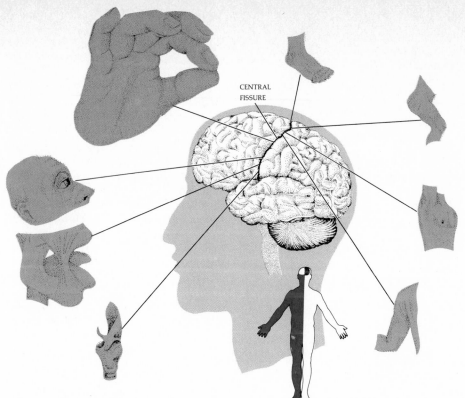

CENTRAL
FISSURE

Figure 5-10 Motor Control Areas. *Motor control areas appear just forward of the central fissure. The relative sizes of the body parts reflect the relative amounts of neural tissue devoted to motor control in that area. Note that large amounts of tissue serve the hands, face, and speech organs. The drawing shows only one side of this system; there is a counterpart on the other side of the brain, serving motor functions on the opposite side of the body.*

one neural site to another by observing the associated brain activity. In this manner, electrophysiologists are discovering which cortical cells in various brain regions are responsive to which aspects of auditory, visual, and other forms of stimulation.

Other senses. The primary area for body feeling, called *somesthesis,* is the front part of the parietal lobes, immediately adjacent to the central fissure. Actually, somesthesis has two divisions, *cutaneous,* which is sensitivity of the skin, and *kinesthetic,* which involves feelings in the muscles, tendons, and joints. Thus, this brain area receives impulses from receptors throughout the body. In a patient whose cortex has been exposed prior to brain surgery, electrical stimulation of this area is often followed by statements such as ''My hand feels warm,'' ''I have electrical feelings in my leg,'' or ''I can feel my leg

moving,'' even though these limbs have not been stimulated (Penfield, 1958).

Again, the body is represented in an inverted sequence. The lower part of the body is represented near the top of the brain, the trunk in the middle, and the upper body towards the bottom of the cortex.

Our other senses apparently do not have such clearly represented locations. Even pain, one of the somesthetic senses, is not well localized. While operating, surgeons have cut into every part of the cerebral cortex without reports of pain, except the pain produced while the covering tissues are being penetrated prior to the actual operation, which can be prevented by a local anesthetic. Possibly, pain is mediated at subcortical levels of the brain.

Association Functions

As emphasized already, none of the motor and sensory areas is the exclusive seat of any function. Rather, they are centers of neural activity when that function is taking place. No complex function is completely controlled by any one area of the cerebral cortex or nervous system; inevitably, that control is at least influenced or shared by other structures in other areas (Vander et al., 1975).

Location of association areas. Adjacent to the sensory areas are sensory association areas, which integrate sensory information. Rather than receiving information directly from the sense organs, these areas receive information from other parts of the brain. They process stored information and the relationships between stored information and present stimulation; thus, reactions in the association areas are significantly influenced by prior learning.

The experience of the color red is initiated by impulses that reach the visual area of the occipital cortex, but this color can produce reactions such as "danger" or "stop." The reason is that the visual association area has been aroused, awakening memories of former experiences with red. Thus, meaning is added to the primary stimulation. In this way, other sensory experiences are given meaning in accordance with stored information.

Significance of association areas. The significance of the association area for touch can be illustrated by reference to a disease known as *astereognosis,* literally meaning "without tactual knowledge of space." If you were blindfolded and asked to handle a small cube, ball, or pyramid, you would have no difficulty identifying these objects, but if you subsequently suffered a serious impairment of the association areas for touch, you would be unable to recognize them by touch alone. Loss of the association tissue causes impressions of touch to lose the meaning they once had for you. Differences in sharpness and roundness could be experienced, assuming the sensory areas remained intact, but they could not be identified.

When such disorders involve language functions, we speak of *aphasia,* meaning "without language." The visual impressions reaching your eyes from this printed page have meaning for you only because the relevant association areas retain what you have learned previously about the significance of these characters. When the visual association area is seriously disturbed, the corresponding functions are impaired. The disturbance may be so serious that although a formerly literate individual sees written words and can even trace them, he or she does not understand what they mean.

In closing, it should be indicated that apparently there are some exceptions to this three-way division of the cortex. Nonsensory functions have been observed in sensory areas, nonmotor functions in motor areas, and nonassociative functions in the association areas. The distinction is useful, but it is not complete (Masterton & Berkley, 1974). Undoubtedly, references to sensory and motor cortex will continue, and these areas do have distinctive features, but one region is not exclusively sensory and the other is not exclusively motor.

Deeper Structures of the Brain

In the years following Fritsch and Hitzig's work, the deeper areas of the brain remained inaccessible to investigation. A method of stimulating them without destroying any significant brain tissue was needed. At the same time, to study the behavioral effects, the subject would have to be in a normal condition, moving freely in the environment, rather than lying inert on an operating table with a head wound. In the 1920s, a Swiss physiologist, Walter Rudolf Hess, devised such a method.

Hess commenced his studies on the cat because it has a brain fundamentally the same as that of a human being, but it is not extremely complicated. The cat also has well-developed sense organs, and it often sits quietly for long periods, in which it can be readily observed by the experimenter.

To achieve access to the hidden brain regions, Hess used a needle electrode so fine that it could be implanted anywhere without major damage to the brain tissues. To keep this electrode in place, it was planted in a socket permanently fixed to the animal's skull. Whenever stimulation was to be delivered, the needle was connected to a weak electric current by means of a flexible steel spring with long lead wires. Even under experimental conditions, the cat could move around the room with little or no resistance. If some strain was placed on the wires, the connection was immediately broken, and when the testing session was finished, the wires were disconnected (Hess, 1957).

Emotional Arousal

Using the needle electrode, Hess stimulated a group of nerve centers situated beneath the cerebral cortex in a fully functioning cat, which immediately became aroused. It pulled back its ears, lashed its tail, crouched, snarled, and showed other signs of rage. The animal was ready to fight (Hess, 1954; Figure 5-11).

The same result was obtained in later tests, although one investigator labeled it "sham rage" because the response seemed so stereotyped. This difference is not important to the present discussion, however. What is significant is the fact that Hess had opened up a new mode of brain research and had demonstrated experimentally the role of the hypothalamus in emotional arousal.

Hypothalamus. On the basis of many related investigations, the *hypothalamus,* lying below the cerebral cortex near the bottom of the brain, is now

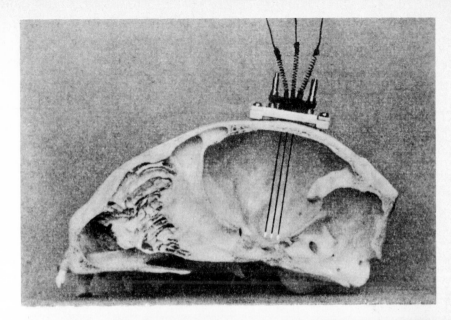

Figure 5-11   Brain Stimulation and Arousal. *The upper photo shows the mount and long electrode needles in place in a halved skull. The lower photo shows that when the electrodes were activated in a live cat, the animal attacked readily. Note the lead wires at the top of the head. (From* The Functional Organization of the Diencephalon *by W. R. Hess, published by Grune and Stratton, 1957. By permission of Grune and Stratton, Inc.)*

Figure 5-12   Brain Stimulation and Decreased Responsiveness.
Spanish bulls used in bullfights are especially bred for aggressiveness. Here, the charge of one such animal is stopped by stimulating the bull's brain with a transistorized device and an implanted electrode. Electrical stimulation of the brain can result in inhibitory as well as excitatory processes. (Courtesy of José M. R. Delgado)

considered a coordinating center for emotional expression. Earlier, it had come into prominence through clinical observations. Neurologists had noted that injuries in hypothalamic regions produced apathy in human beings, and destruction of this area in animals brought about a similar condition.

This concentration of neural mechanisms is considered a coordinating center in emotion because sensory impulses pass through it on the way up to the cortex and motor impulses pass through it coming down from the cortex. It prompts muscular activities associated with emotion and it activates several visceral organs, as when it stimulates the adrenal gland to secrete adrenalin. In addition to these arousal activities, the hypothalamus plays an important role in inducing sleep.

No one has shown that the hypothalamus is responsible for full emotional experience, but an intact hypothalamus is clearly a necessity for emotional arousal. When the cerebral cortex is removed from the cat, an integrated emotional reaction still occurs, but it is absent when the hypothalamus is removed.

Septal area.   An adjacent brain region, lying just forward of the hypothalamus, is called the *septal area*. Literally, *septum* means "wall" or "partition," but this group of nuclei has an important connection with the hypothalamus and serves many of the same functions. It plays a role in the strength of emotional reaction by sending impulses to the hypothalamus. Using an electrode implanted in this area, a Spanish scientist was able to control the charge of a wild bull. A transistorized transmitter was used to send an electrical impulse, and the bull stopped in its tracks (Figure 5-12).

Similarly, the aggressive behavior of a leader of a monkey colony changed when this region was stimulated by an electrode implant. His dominance decreased, and other monkeys on the fringes of the play area became more assertive. They went on the swings, played with other apparatus, and generally were more possessive of the territory. When the electrical stimulation ceased, the docile former leader became his old self again, once more dominating the group (Delgado, 1971).

Pleasure centers. In the mid-1950s, James Olds, another psychologist, used Hess's technique in a different context and discovered still another dimension of the brain. He placed a rat with an implanted electrode in a Skinner box, which has a bar that delivers food or some other reward when it is pressed. In this case, a press of the bar activated a weak electrical current, transmitted via the electrode to the animal's brain. Thus, the animal was capable of shocking itself and, to the investigator's surprise, it did so at the rate of five hundred to five thousand times per hour. Some animals engaged in this apparently pleasurable stimulation two thousand times per hour for a full day. So the researcher dubbed this particular brain region, discovered partly by accident, the *pleasure center* (Olds, 1956).

Following this lead, other rats were put on a food-deprivation schedule on which they lost more than one-fourth of their original weight. Yet, when offered a choice of food or electrical stimulation in a maze, they chose this electrical stimulation rather than food. Control rats with electrodes implanted in other brain regions preferred the food reward (Figure 5-13).

Eventually, this technique was used with persons who were chronically depressed or suffering from a terminal illness. Stimulation of the septal region in some cases produced ''a glowing feeling'' and other positive sensations; further stimulation was sought, just as with the animals (Monroe et al., 1954; Sem-Jacobsen & Torklidsen, 1960).

But the nature of these pleasure centers is still largely unknown. They are especially puzzling because sometimes they do not seem to have a temporary satiation point, at which the organism no longer seeks such stimulation. Satiation occurs in eating, sexual activity, and so forth. In fact, the motivating effects of this stimulation may be more readily interpreted as some sort of addiction (Gallistel, 1966).

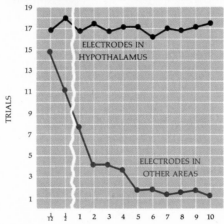

DAYS OF FOOD DEPRIVATION

Figure 5-13 Electrical Self-stimulation in Animals. *Subjects receiving electrical stimulation of the brain in the hypothalamic region showed no sign of preferring the food reward, even as the number of days of food deprivation increased. (After Spies, 1965. Copyright 1965 by the American Psychological Association. Reprinted by permission. Photo courtesy of Professor Elliot S. Valenstein, University of Michigan.)*

Furthermore, a very small difference in placement, such as $\frac{1}{500}$ of an inch, can make a very large difference in reaction, and in some cases with animals, sites initially appearing as pleasure centers have become aversive later. The animal abruptly terminates this type of stimulation for long periods. Depressive reactions have been observed in some psychiatric patients. Such experiments provide rather clear evidence that these brain areas are involved in emotional states, but their specific operation is still unclear.

Organization of the Brain

Through such studies, psychologists' attention has been drawn from the obvious characteristics of the cerebral cortex to more careful scrutiny of other structures. From an evolutionary viewpoint, the cerebral cortex is a late development, and therefore is part of the *forebrain*, which is the most recent of the three brain divisions. The forebrain also contains other important structures, such as the *thalamus*, which serves as a switchboard for relaying sensory impulses. Located just below the thalamus is the *hypothalamus*, which influences emotional behavior and other motivational systems, as we have seen. These are referred to as *subcortical structures* because they lie beneath the cortex (Figure 5-14).

The *midbrain*, so-called because of its location, is also subcortical. It is at the end of the brainstem, near the center of the brain, and forms a connection between the more recently developed forebrain and the long-recognized hindbrain. Portions of the midbrain, particularly the *tectum*, meaning "roof," have a special role in processing nerve impulses involving visual and auditory information.

The oldest division of the human brain is the *hindbrain*, located in the lower rear portion of the brain, where we would find the boxer's wrist, in the boxing glove analogy. Its most prominent structure, the *cerebellum* or "little brain," is a major mechanism for coordinating body movements and maintaining posture.

All these structures and many others are important in most brain activities. In localizing any function, it must be remembered that certain areas are the most essential neural links, but by themselves they are not sufficient to produce the responses involved.

The Brain and Consciousness

One area of the brain that for years did not appear essential to any neural activity is the *corpus callosum*. This structure is the chief connecting link between the two hemispheres, and its role seemed so insignificant that it prompted irreverent comments. Its function was said to be only structural, to prevent the hemispheres from sagging, or perverse, transmitting epileptic seizures to the other side of the brain. Curiously, the brain semed to carry on undisturbed even when its largest central-fiber system, the corpus callosum, had been destroyed (Sperry, 1964).

Clinical studies of human beings in whom this structure had been surgically cut because of disease or accidentally damaged showed that the damage had no noticeable influence on behavior. In animal research, investigators destroyed this mass of brain tissue and found only a small loss of vision. The influx of sensory information, outflow of motor impulses, and integration with the many lower-brain centers remained intact.

The first major breakthrough came in the late 1950s when Ronald Myers performed split-brain surgery on cats. In the *split-brain technique* the corpus callosum is completely cut, as are the optic chiasma and another structure, leaving the two hemispheres joined only at subcortical centers. Cutting the *optic chiasma*, which transmits visual information to both hemispheres, means that information presented to one eye travels directly only to one hemisphere. Visually, the two hemispheres are separated (Figure 5-15).

The Human Organism

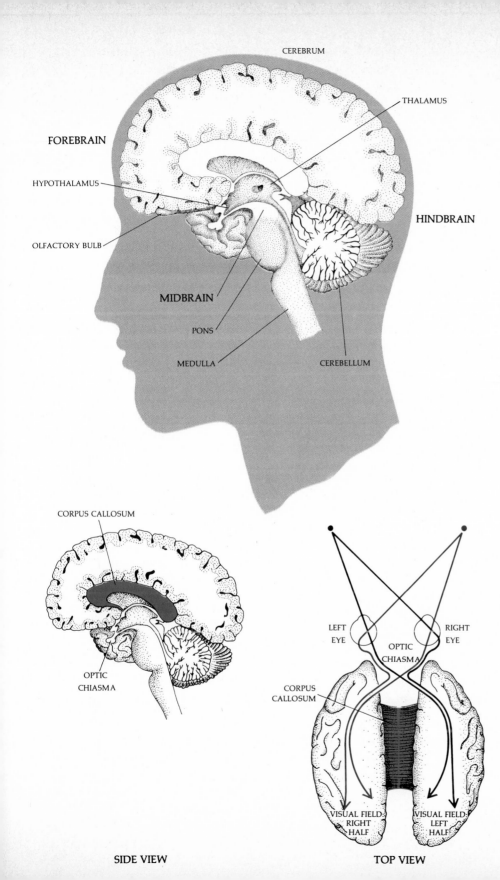

CEREBRUM

THALAMUS

FOREBRAIN

HINDBRAIN

HYPOTHALAMUS

OLFACTORY BULB

MIDBRAIN

PONS

MEDULLA

CEREBELLUM

Figure 5-14 Division of the Brain. *Here the "thumb" is removed from the boxing glove, showing a cross-section of the brain from the left and the basic structures in each of the major brain divisions.*

CORPUS CALLOSUM

OPTIC CHIASMA

Figure 5-15 Location of the Corpus Callosum. *The first drawing shows the right half of the human brain, seen from the midline, with the corpus callosum indicated in color. The second drawing is a simplified view of the brain from the top. When the optic chiasma is cut, each eye provides information only to the brain hemisphere on its own side.*

LEFT EYE

RIGHT EYE

OPTIC CHIASMA

CORPUS CALLOSUM

VISUAL FIELD: RIGHT HALF

VISUAL FIELD: LEFT HALF

SIDE VIEW

TOP VIEW

Functions of the Hemispheres

Next Myers trained the cats to solve problems in visual discrimination that could be observed with only one eye. They learned normally under this condition, and after a consistently high level of performance was achieved, then the animal was required to perform with the untrained eye. The animal behaved normally except that success on the discrimination task immediately dropped to a chance level. One hemisphere had mastered the task, but the other had not done so (Myers, 1956).

Two consciousnesses. Later, several detailed follow-up experiments demonstrated convincingly that the memories stored in one hemisphere were not available to the other. With the midconnections destroyed, each brain functions adequately alone, and a strong case is made for two consciousnesses or two minds housed in the same skull (Sperry, 1961).

Moreover, when the animal learns opposite or conflicting responses in the two hemispheres there seems to be no interference. Through the left eye it can learn that a square is the correct choice, and through the right it can learn to choose a circle. Furthermore, it shows no signs of indecision when the circle is presented to the right eye, as does an animal with an intact brain that has already learned to choose the square. This discovery, that a split-brain monkey sometimes can deal with twice as much information as a normal one, has prompted speculation whether human beings could learn twice as much with their "two minds" separated (Sperry, 1964).

The split-brain technique already has been used with human beings in cases of persistent, generalized epilepsy, and it has been remarkably successful, as judged by two criteria. First, the epileptic brain activity does not spread to the other hemisphere; and second, for some unknown reason there is a decreased frequency of attack in the initiating hemisphere. After split-brain surgery, previously hopeless cases have gone years without a seizure (Gazzaniga et al., 1965; Sperry, 1968). Otherwise, individuals who have had such an operation are completely normal, and an untrained observer would not even know that brain surgery had been performed (Gazzaniga, 1972).

A chief function of the corpus callosum, it seems, is to mediate the development of duplicate memories in the two hemispheres. When learning is deliberately restricted to one hemisphere, the intact corpus callosum is utilized by the untrained hemisphere to gain information from the trained one. It thereby tends to make the two hemispheres equal in terms of new learning. In addition, it integrates certain sensory-motor reactions across both sides of the body.

Different consciousnesses. What is the purpose of the two hemispheres? Apparently they serve different functions, as illustrated when split-brain people are studied carefully. If the right hemisphere knows the answer in a simple square-versus-circle test, the individual cannot *say* the correct answer. The person will reply that he or she does not know or did not see the test objects. The reason, apparently, is that in most persons the left hemisphere is dominant in language, especially spoken language. If you ask the person to grasp the correct object or point to the correct word instead, the person can do so.

The right hemisphere, although generally subordinate, also has special capabilities. It can manage only rather simple numerical problems, for example, but it exceeds the left hemisphere in assembling objects, such as blocks and puzzles. Split-brain persons using the right hemisphere and therefore their left hand perform better than when they use the left hemisphere and right hand, even when they are naturally right-handed. In short, the right hemisphere appears to be the locus of control for analyzing and utilizing spatial information (Gazzaniga, 1972; Webster, 1972).

Further evidence is obtained by measuring the brain activities in different hemispheres of split-brain persons. Impulses in the left hemisphere increase during language problems and those in the right hemisphere increase in spatial relations problems. Clinical studies of injured children suggest that the overall dominance of the left hemisphere can be reversed early in life, but a change in dominance in adulthood is unlikely. In summary, it is now hypothesized that the left brain is more dominant in traditional academic tasks such as using words, analyzing, and reasoning, while the right side is more involved in spatial relations and synthesizing and, thus, is perhaps more holistic in function (Phillips, 1976).

Measuring Brain and Body States

To measure electrical activity in the split or intact brain, investigators commonly obtain a record called the *electroencephalogram* (EEG). This term indicates that the measurements are taken directly from the brain, also known as the *encephalon,* and that they involve electronic recordings.

EEG method. In the EEG procedure, no surgery is involved, and the subject can be prepared in a few minutes. Pad electrodes simply are placed on the skull, and as the brain waves are emitted and amplified, the patterns are recorded by a writing stylus on a moving tape.

When the individual is resting, a regular EEG rhythm, called an *alpha wave,* may appear. This wave occurs at a rate of about 10 cycles per second. Sometimes an irregular rhythm occurs, indicating some type of brain disorder.

Some of these disorders are temporary, as among people who have changed time zones rapidly in transcontinental flights and among those who have been deprived of sleep. After an appropriate wake–sleep schedule, the deviant pattern disappears. Other irregular rhythms are permanent, as in some psychoses and certain forms of brain damage, such as epilepsy. In the split-brain condition, there is an irregular pattern from one hemisphere, if it involves brain injury, but a normal pattern may be transmitted from the other side.

Other patterns are associated with different states of consciousness, such as the various stages of sleep. Of particular interest in sleep is the stage in which dreaming occurs, but all the sleep stages reappear predictably every one and one-half to two hours (Figure 5-16).

The absence of recordable brain waves is known as a *flat EEG,* indicating no measurable brain activity. It occurs in death and also in traumatic injuries, and this finding has led to a controversial issue.

Figure 5-16   EEG Stages.   *The alpha waves occur when a person is relaxed. As shown by the one-second indicator, they are much less frequent than those in excitation. (Brain waves from Penfield and Erikson,* Epilepsy and Cerebral Localization, *1941. Courtesy of Charles C. Thomas, Publisher, Springfield, Illinois. Photo by Percy W. Brooks.)*

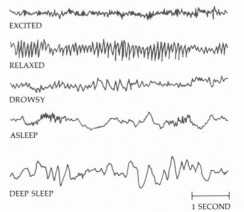

EXCITED

RELAXED

DROWSY

ASLEEP

DEEP SLEEP

1 SECOND

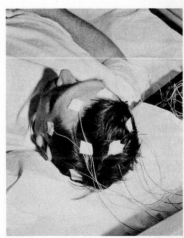

It is possible for a person's brain to be permanently injured, as shown by the total absence of recordable waves for several minutes, yet, due to the action of subcortical centers, there can be faint heartbeats. In all medical history, no one has recovered consciousness from this condition, but death has been interpreted as the cessation of heartbeat. With modern life-support apparatus the heart can continue to function in spite of irreversible brain damage such that the person can never regain consciousness. Thus, the question of life and death now involves the quality of life and the degree of consciousness, and it has ethical, legal, physiological, and psychological dimensions.

Measuring body states. For measuring changes in the rate and rhythm of the heartbeat, the electrocardiograph is used, and the record obtained from this instrument is known as an *electrocardiogram* (EKG). In this procedure, an electrode is attached to each arm and each leg and another is placed at various positions on the chest. With additional apparatus, tracings are made by a stylus on a moving sheet of paper. The examiner looks for various patterns in this record, of which about a dozen have been established, indicating different aspects of heart activity.

Another body response that has been of particular interest to psychologists is the activation of the sweat glands during emotional arousal. The resulting perspiration, especially in the palms of the hands, causes a lowering of the electrical resistance of the skin, called the *galvanic skin response* (GSR). The skin becomes wet and thus a better conductor of electricity. To measure this change, two electrodes from a galvanometer, which records electrical potential, are connected to the palm of the hand. The lowered resistance, or GSR, is registered by a swing of the needle of the galvanometer.

Finally, changes in muscle tension, breathing rate, and blood pressure also can be measured by appropriate instruments. One device that includes most of these measures and receives frequent attention in the public press is the so-called lie detector or *polygraph*. The latter name indicates that a number of physiological records are made simultaneously.

When the polygraph is used in a lie detector test, sound recordings are made as the subject answers questions, some relevant and some irrelevant to the act that he or she is suspected of committing. It is assumed that the subject who committed the crime or has knowledge of it will be more aroused by the relevant than the irrelevant questions. For several reasons the lie detector is not foolproof, however, and its results are not readily admitted as legal evidence. It has sometimes been useful in narrowing the field of suspects and in influencing alleged offenders to confess (Reid & Inbau, 1964).

Maintenance Systems

There are many other systems within the human body besides the central and peripheral nervous systems. Most of them are maintenance systems, devoted to sustaining respiration, circulation, the use of food, and other conditions within the body. They provide an appropriate internal environment for the central and peripheral nervous systems to cope with the external environment, but they too can influence behavior.

Hormonal Influences on Behavior

The second great communications network, after the nervous system, is the *endocrine system,* which is composed of a series of interlocking glands that secrete fluids directly into the bloodstream. These secretions then are carried to all parts of the body and have a broad influence. In contrast, the *exocrine glands* secrete through ducts, as in salivation and perspiration, and therefore they influence only specific parts of the body.

The Human Organism

The endocrine secretions, called *hormones,* ensure certain chemical activities within the whole organism. They control bodily growth, provide appropriate utilization of food, help conserve energy, stimulate reproductive reactions, and play an important role in emergency situations. Directly or indirectly, they are involved in almost every aspect of bodily functioning.

Endocrines and the nervous system. The endocrine glands are small, each usually weighing less than an ounce. Eight are well known, including the placenta, which appears only in the pregnant female, but four of them have special significance for physiological psychology: the pituitary, thyroid, adrenals, and gonads. These tiny glands secrete incredibly small amounts of hormones, yet they form an interlocking system to the extent that disturbance in any one of them may lead to malfunctioning of the others (Figure 5-17).

Furthermore, it has become evident that there is an interaction between the endocrine and nervous systems. The central nervous system, especially the hypothalamus, serves a crucial role in regulating hormone secretions. In return, these secretions markedly alter neural functions and, of course, influence behavior. The significant extent to which these two systems operate as a single interrelated system has given rise to the specialty known as *neuroendocrinology* (Vander et al., 1975).

The endocrine glands. The most important gland, in the sense of influencing others, is the *pituitary,* a small structure located near the brainstem. Often called the ''master gland,'' the anterior portion of this gland secretes several hormones, including growth hormones that have much to do with the determination of physique. The dwarf may have an underactive anterior pituitary and the giant an overactive one. Through their effect on the gonads, these hormones also influence sexual behavior. The posterior

pituitary is closely associated with the central nervous system through hormones from the hypothalamus, and its action is more complicated than can be described here.

Another hormone from the pituitary gland, the adrenocorticotrophic hormone, or ACTH, stimulates the *adrenal* gland, which has two basic parts. The adrenal medulla secretes adrenalin, a substance that serves to increase our energy in emergencies, as we shall see in a moment.

The adrenal cortex secretes several substances necessary for general maintenance. When there is inadequate secretion here, called *hypofunction,* the individual becomes weak and lethargic, loses his or her appetite for food and sexual activity, and suffers a widespread breakdown of physiological functions. With medical treatment to make up the deficiency, general vigor and other functions are restored. On the other hand, *hyperfunction,* or overactivity, in this part of the adrenal gland may produce sexual maturity at an unusually early age.

General bodily vigor is affected by the pituitary, the adrenal cortex, and the *thyroid* gland. Early undersecretion of thyroxin, the thyroid hormone, results in cretinism, a condition of various bodily defects and low intelligence. Undersecretion at later ages often produces lethargy. Both of these conditions can be corrected by the injection of thyroxin (Kashgarian & Burrow, 1974). Overactivity seems to result in tension, which can be diminished through surgery or radium treatment. ■

The testes in men and ovaries in women, collectively known as the *gonads,* are key factors in sexual behavior. They produce hormones responsible for the major physiological changes that occur at puberty, and they contribute significantly to the accompanying psychological developments.

■ *While I was working permanent shift as a nurse in an intensive care unit, I was followed on nights by Miss P. I knew her to be a likeable and pleasant person. Her only quirk was her extreme flightiness, but after a few months in the unit, she became quarrelsome and demanding. People spoke to her of this change, which she realized was taking place, but she felt that she couldn't do anything about it. In time she decided the tensions of the unit were causing her trouble and she decided to leave. After a while, a hyperthyroid condition was found by her physician and she underwent a thyroidectomy. Now her friends tell me she is a much calmer person, having the responsibility of a large ward in another hospital, and continuing to be a pleasure to be with. The tense atmosphere of the hospital unit can contribute to changes such as she experienced, but I think Miss P's physiology was important also.*

**Figure 5-17   The Major
Endocrine Glands.**   *Malfunctioning
of the endocrine system may exert a
powerful influence on one's personality,
but one must not conclude that every
lethargic person has an underactive
thyroid, that every tense individual
has an overactive thyroid, or that the
most sexually frigid or driven persons
have abnormal gonads. Similar changes
are produced by other physical
conditions and psychological factors.*

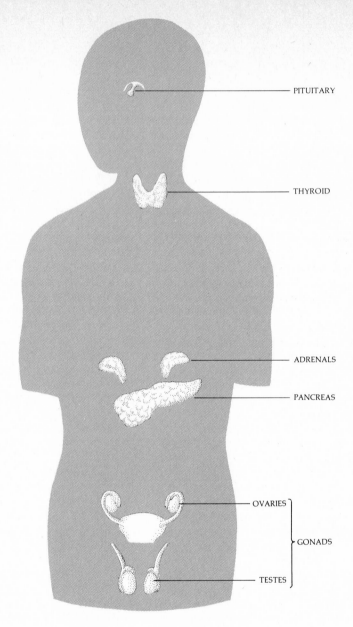

PITUITARY

THYROID

ADRENALS

PANCREAS

OVARIES ⎫
        ⎬ GONADS
TESTES ⎭

Endocrine research.   Some other endocrine glands have been tentatively
identified but are only vaguely understood. There are also bodily processes
that today seem related to endocrine
functions, yet they cannot be connected
to any of these specific glands. There
must be still other secreting organs
(Vander et al., 1975). At this time even
the total number of endocrine glands
seems uncertain.

Research in this area has been advanced by new techniques for detecting
increasingly minute amounts of hormones. For example, a generation ago
the *basal metabolic rate,* concerned with
the building up and breaking down of
living cells, was the most common test
of thyroid function. But the results were
often inaccurate. They were distorted by

The Human Organism

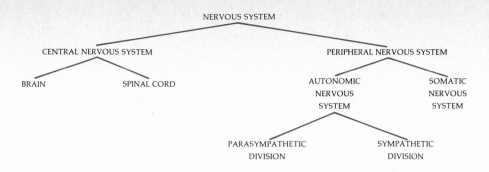

Figure 5-18 Overview of the Human Nervous System. *The diagram, which depicts the separate systems, does not indicate their interlocking nature. All of them have reciprocal influences. The somatic system, not discussed in this text, has nerve fibers going to the skeletal muscles and therefore is primarily concerned with voluntary actions in the outer environment, such as running and writing.*

a variety of nonthyroid conditions, including leukemia, starvation, congestive heart failure, Addison's disease, certain psychiatric states, and even perforated eardrums.

Today, a more direct measure of thyroid condition focuses on the iodine bound to protein. In the normal state this iodine is virtually all thyroxin iodine, and therefore provides a measure of thyroid function. This method also has limitations, as when the gland function is normal but thyroxin levels are elevated through oral contraceptive therapy. Nevertheless, the protein-bound iodine test is much superior to the older method and currently the most common single measure of thyroid operation (Ezrin et al., 1973).

Autonomic Functions

The extent to which human physiology is a series of interlocking systems is illustrated by the adrenal gland, which responds in emergencies. This gland is part of the endocrine system and also part of another maintenance system known as the autonomic nervous system. The *autonomic nervous system* is so named because it was once thought to be automatic, self-regulating, and not susceptible to voluntary control. As the name also suggests, it is part of the human nervous network (Figure 5-18).

Two divisions. The autonomic nervous system controls much of the internal environment through its two major divisions—the sympathetic and parasympathetic—which operate essentially but not completely in opposition to one another. If one division activates or accelerates an organ, the other usually checks it. The sympathetic connection with the heart, for example, increases its activity while the parasympathetic connection decreases it. Stomach activities are reduced by the sympathetic system and activated by the parasympathetic.

The *sympathetic* division plays a dominant role in emotion. The heart pounds, gastric secretions are checked, and secretion of adrenalin is accelerated, all in an integrated fashion because the sympathetic system has assumed control. This division also causes blood vessels of the intestine and stomach to constrict, permitting more blood to flow to the arms and legs in anticipation of "fight or flight." Altogether, it acts as an *emergency* system, providing for an immediate expenditure of energy, especially through the flow of adrenalin, and generally it is controlled by the hypothalamus. If portions of the hypothalamus are damaged, as we saw earlier, the individual acts in a stuporous fashion, unprepared for emergency activity.

When the crisis subsides, the *parasympathetic* division resumes control and the activity of the related organs returns to its usual level. The heartbeat becomes more normal, saliva returns to the mouth, and blood flows more readily in the stomach. This division serves as a *routine* system, providing for normal body functioning and conservation of energy (Figure 5-19).

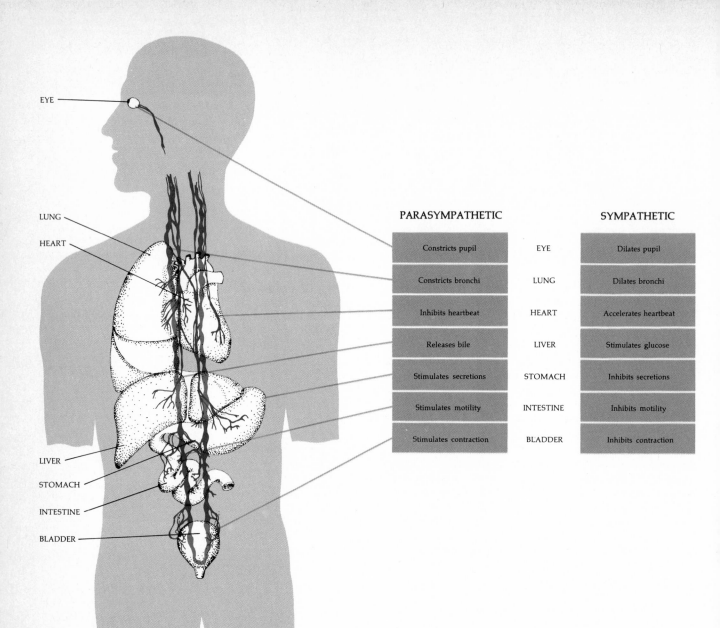

| | EYE | | | LUNG | | | HEART | | | LIVER | | | STOMACH | | | INTESTINE | | | BLADDER | |

PARASYMPATHETIC   **SYMPATHETIC**

PARASYMPATHETIC		SYMPATHETIC
Constricts pupil	EYE	Dilates pupil
Constricts bronchi	LUNG	Dilates bronchi
Inhibits heartbeat	HEART	Accelerates heartbeat
Releases bile	LIVER	Stimulates glucose
Stimulates secretions	STOMACH	Inhibits secretions
Stimulates motility	INTESTINE	Inhibits motility
Stimulates contraction	BLADDER	Inhibits contraction

Figure 5-19 Autonomic Nervous System and Related Activities.
The functions of organs such as the heart, lungs, stomach, bladder, intestines, and the pupil and lens of the eye are controlled by the autonomic nervous system. This system is made up of bundles of nerve fibers, shown in color, along each side of the spinal column. The loose interconnections with the central nervous system are highly complex.

The Human Organism

Biofeedback studies. The traditional conception of the autonomic nervous system as completely involuntary has been brought into question on two bases. First, there are numerous reports of voluntary control of the circulatory and respiration systems among Eastern peoples. These outcomes, brought about through forms of meditation long ignored in our own culture, have been at least partially verified. Second, similar changes apparently have been achieved by subjects in Western experiments on biofeedback (Wallace & Bensen, 1972).

The *biofeedback* procedure is not a system whereby some chemical or electrical impulse is delivered to the body. It is simply a condition wherein a device monitors the activities of bodily organs and then makes this information available to the individual. With this information, the individual sometimes can achieve more control over the organs in question.

This research was inaugurated partly by Joe Kamiya, a psychologist who was studying sleep in the early 1960s. In the midst of his investigations, he decided to find out whether his subjects could become better aware of the relaxed alpha state if they observed their own alpha brain waves as they occurred. To his surprise, they not only became more aware of the state but eventually learned to enter and sustain it at will. Later, he improved the technique by including a tone whenever alpha waves were being generated. With this additional information, the subjects learned to control these waves even more readily (Kamiya, 1968, 1969).

Alpha waves are not part of the autonomic nervous system and are not directly controlled by any peripheral organ, as far as we know, but at almost the same time the influence of biofeedback procedures on the autonomic nervous system was demonstrated with animals. A curare derivative was administered to a group of rats, thus suppressing all voluntary muscular responses.

However, some rats learned to control their heart rate and others learned to control their intestinal activity when they were rewarded by electrical stimulation to a pleasure center of the brain. The usual forms of reward, such as a food pellet, could not be used because the animals were paralyzed, but the electrical brain stimulation served well. The animals' autonomic activities increased, decreased, or remained unchanged, depending on how this reward was used (Miller & Banuazizi, 1968).

The nature of science. Biofeedback appears to be a promising enterprise. In future years, persons with heart problems, headaches, ulcers, tired muscles, and various aspects of hypertension might use it as part of a prescribed treatment for malfunctioning organs (DiCara, 1970). Already it has been advocated for promoting self-regulation in counseling and for facilitating classroom learning. But on the practical side, application with human beings is an imposing task. Their daily environment is infinitely more varied than that of rats in a laboratory and even of patients in a medical setting. Biofeedback learning may not prove to be enduring weeks, months, or years later in a person's normal life (Shapiro & Schwartz, 1972). So far, there is little long-term evidence, and even in short-term studies many patients cannot maintain control in their home environment (Engel, 1972).

Moreover, some doubts have been raised about the reliability of biofeedback experiments, including the repeatability of studies with animals (Jonas, 1972; Miller & Dworkin, 1973). And there is the question of whether the induced physiological changes are the same as those occurring on a more natural basis. Altogether, before biofeedback becomes a well-established research area, and certainly before it moves from research to widespread applications, the magnitude of the effect, its duration, and its transferability to human contexts must be better demonstrated (Blanchard & Young, 1973; Melzack, 1975).

This condition illustrates the nature of science in all fields, including the study of the human body. For thousands of years investigators have struggled to understand the mysteries about physical structures and functions, especially in relation to behavior. Each success, from Sir Charles Bell to all the others, has brought some satisfaction but has also posed further questions. Whenever one question is answered, new ones immediately arise in its place. The business of science in any field is never finished; almost always, it grows increasingly more complicated.

Summary

Pathways in the Body

1. The chief integrating system of the body is the nervous system. The peripheral nervous system, composed of spinal and cranial nerves, is essentially a transmitting system; it sends impulses to and from the central nervous system. Some of these nerves are sensory, which enable us to become aware of our environment; others are motor, which enable us to respond.

2. The central nervous system is composed of the spinal cord and brain. The spinal cord contains connector neurons, whereby it can convey impulses from sensory neurons directly to motor neurons in the form of a reflex arc, and to other regions of the central nervous system, where more complex behavior is involved. The synapses, which are the junctions between neurons, also play a most important role in the flexibility of human behavior. They can inhibit nerve impulses, activate a few nerve fibers, or activate many adjacent fibers, thus influencing the distribution of nerve impulses over all parts of the body.

Outer Structures of the Brain

3. The most highly developed part of the human brain is the cerebral cortex, which has four lobes. Visual areas are located in the occipital lobes, auditory areas are in the temporal lobes, and somesthetic areas are in the forward part of the parietal lobes. Voluntary motor activities are mediated in the back part of the frontal lobes.

4. These lobes also have associative functions, relating especially to the respective sensory and motor activities represented by them. They are significantly involved in making associations between current stimulation and prior stimulation, stored as memory. In all these areas, however, some other functions have been found. These distinctions should be regarded as general, rather than absolute.

Deeper Structures of the Brain

5. Substantial portions of the brain are subcortical structures, lying beneath the cortex, and several of them, including the hypothalamus and septal area, play an important role in emotional reactions and arousal. Through electrical stimulation studies, it appears that there is also some form of pleasure center in these regions.

6. From an evolutionary standpoint, the brain can be considered in three parts: the most recent division, the forebrain, includes the cerebral cortex and hypothalamus; the smaller midbrain connects the forebrain and hindbrain; and the oldest division, the hindbrain, contains the cerebellum, which is concerned with coordinating body movements and posture.

The Brain and Consciousness

7. A relatively new approach to brain studies involves split-brain research, where the cerebral hemispheres are essentially separated by cutting the corpus callosum. The results show two consciousnesses, one in each brain half, and tentatively suggest some important differences between these consciousnesses.

8. An indispensable record in studying consciousness is the electroencephalogram (EEG). It shows the patterns of brain waves in various stages and types of consciousness. For investigating changes in the rate and rhythm of the heart, the usual record is the electrocardiogram (EKG). For detecting emotional arousal, investigators often examine the electrical conductivity of the skin, observing a reaction called the galvanic skin response (GSR).

Maintenance Systems

9. Other body systems are primarily concerned with internal functioning. The system of endocrine glands regulates growth, helps conserve the body's energy, and plays an important integrative function. Disturbance in the functioning of any one of these glands may lead to a malfunctioning of the others and have wide repercussions in the individual's physical structure and behavior.

10. The interlocking nature of the systems in human physiology is also illustrated in the autonomic nervous system, which has connections with the endocrine system, the central nervous system, and the peripheral nervous system. It has two divisions: the sympathetic operates in emergencies and the parasympathetic is dominant in routine functioning. Recent research involving biofeedback has offered evidence that this system is not completely involuntary or automatic.

Suggested Readings

Gardner, E. *Fundamentals of neurology: A psychophysiological approach* (6th ed.). Philadelphia: Saunders, 1975. A basic text in this area for over 30 years.

Jaynes, J. *The origin of consciousness in the breakdown of the bicameral mind.* Boston: Houghton Mifflin, 1977. A highly speculative, novel theory of the origin of human consciousness, with reference to modern brain research.

Luria, A. R. *The working brain: An introduction to neuropsychology.* New York: Basic Books, 1973. A leader in brain research presents neurological and behavioral sciences for a broad readership.

Munn, N. L. *The evolution of the human mind.* Boston: Houghton Mifflin, 1971. Traces the concept of the mind from our animal ancestry to its contemporary evolution.

Thompson, R. F. *Introduction to physiological psychology.* New York: Harper & Row, 1975. Intended for the first course in physiological psychology, this version of a more advanced text is still comprehensive.

PART THREE

Processes in Perceiving

Chapter 6

Sensory Processes

A story, probably legendary, is told about a frog placed in a pot of water. Beneath the pot a low fire was lit, and the amphibian continued to sit there, half in and half out of the water, apparently undisturbed.

Later, the heat was increased by a very slight amount, and the frog remained where it was, blinking and staring impassively, as usual. Still later, the temperature was raised again by the slightest amount, and again the change did not seem to bother the frog.

In similar fashion, the temperature was raised again and again, each time without any reaction on the part of the frog. Eventually, the water reached the boiling point and the animal still failed to move. It is said that the poor creature was boiled alive without making any effort to escape.

If the event was ever attempted, would the frog have come to such an untimely end? This question concerns several aspects of sensation, which is the topic of this chapter.

Awareness of Stimulation

Sensation and perception are at the beginning of any behavioral sequence. The organism usually responds to some information received via the *sense organs*, such as the eyes, ears, and skin. These organs enable us to detect energy in the environment, known as *stimulation*. In the case of the frog, the heat of the water is one form of stimulation, and the noise of the bubbles is another.

Inside the sense organs are tiny but very important receiving mechanisms called *receptors;* ultimately, it is these specialized nerves, also known as end organs, that are responsible for our sensitivity to different types of stimulation. The ear contains receptors for sound waves; the eye contains receptors for light waves; and the skin contains receptors that are responsive to pressure and stimulation by heat. It is these mechanisms in the frog that allegedly were insensitive to the small changes in stimulation.

The Detection Question

The fact that the frog did not respond to increasing temperatures also might be explained in another way. At some point perhaps the animal detected that the water was hot, but its muscular abilities had been rendered ineffective by the extremely high temperature. This outcome is not likely, as we shall see, and so the following discussion focuses on the issue of sensitivity. The first question is detection: When is a stimulus likely to be detected or noticed?

Absolute threshold. The frog in the pot of water is like a person in a quiet room. If we present a sound of gradually increasing intensity, when will it be heard? The point at which it is first observed, as determined by series of tests, is known as the *absolute threshold,* which is that level of intensity at which a stimulus can just be detected by a given individual. All organisms experience stimuli only when they are at or above the absolute threshold.

The absolute threshold varies among different people and also within the same individual from time to time, depending on fluctuations in mood and physiological condition. Hence, it is defined as that level of stimulus intensity that can be detected in one-half of many trials. By studying a large number of people, investigators offset individual variations and obtain information on absolute thresholds in general.

Stimulus	Threshold
Light	A candle seen at 30 miles on a dark, clear night.
Sound	The tick of a watch under quiet conditions at 20 feet.
Taste	One teaspoon of sugar in 2 gallons of water.
Smell	One drop of perfume diffused into a 3-room apartment.
Touch	The wing of a bee falling on your cheek from a distance of 1 cm.

Suppose that a man has crept into a dark, quiet room. Will his presence be noticed just by the ticking of his watch? If one drop of perfume has been spilled in a three-room apartment, will it be noticed? Such questions have been answered by research on thresholds, which has been extremely useful in the construction of radar, sonar, and x-ray apparatus, and also for such household purposes as quiet telephones and artificially scented foods (Figure 6-1).

Another word for threshold is *limen.* Accordingly, stimulation below the absolute threshold is occasionally referred to as *subliminal,* and in past years some advertisers have attempted to use subliminal stimulation to influence potential buyers. In a movie theater, for example, advertisements for certain foods and drinks were flashed on the screen so rapidly that the audience presumably was unaware of their presence, and it was reported that the purchase of these articles increased. Much public concern arose over *subliminal advertising,* as the procedure was called, but its effectiveness has not been demonstrated (McConnell et al., 1958). One problem is that the audience is composed of many different individuals and, thus, the advertiser cannot be certain that the message is above, below, or just at the absolute threshold for each person concerned.

Figure 6-1 Approximate Absolute Thresholds. *(From* New Directions in Psychology, *Vol. 1, edited by Roger Brown, Eugene Galanter, Eckhard H. Hess, and George Mandler. Copyright © 1962 by Holt, Rinehart and Winston. Reprinted by permission of Holt, Rinehart and Winston.)*

In the case of the frog in the pot of water, the heat undoubtedly was not subliminal. At some point it must have passed the absolute threshold, and the animal then would have detected the warmth of the water.

Terminal threshold. Perhaps the frog stayed in the water until the heat reached the terminal threshold, when it became painful. Then it certainly would have jumped out of the pot. The *terminal threshold* is that point at which a stimulus of increasing intensity first produces pain; that is, the normal sensory response changes to pain, as in the case of strong light, loud sound, or intense heat.

Besides the terminal threshold, we observe another phenomenon in seeing and hearing. The human eye does not respond to wavelengths greater than 700 nanometers, which means 700 billionths of a meter. The human ear does not respond to frequencies greater than 20,000 hertz, formerly called cycles per second. In these instances, there is no sensitivity at all. These points are not terminal thresholds because there is a change in the nature, not intensity, of the stimulus, and it causes the absence of sensitivity, not pain.

The Discrimination Question

The frog's plight seems sad partly because of the way the story is told. It seems that the creature had no cause to escape, and here we encounter the discrimination question: When is a change in stimulation likely to be noticed?

Detection involves awareness of a stimulus; discrimination involves awareness of the difference between two or more stimuli. At each increase in heat, the frog apparently could not tell the difference between the preceding and successive intensity.

Difference threshold. The smallest perceptible difference between two stimuli of the same type is known as the *difference threshold.* Very small differences may pass unnoticed; in the frog experiment, each change was below the animal's difference threshold, and so it produced no reaction. The size of the difference threshold varies with different organisms, and it depends on which sense organs are stimulated, such as the eyes, ears, or skin. ■

If three candles are burning in a room and you add one more, there will be a noticeable increase in illumination. The change will be far above the difference threshold. If one hundred candles are burning and you add one, there may be a perceptible or *just noticeable difference* (j.n.d.), which represents the difference threshold. Now suppose that two hundred candles are burning and we add another. No matter how much you are prepared to perceive the difference, you cannot do so. The change in illumination is not a j.n.d.; it has not reached the difference threshold.

Weber's law. This simple example illustrates that the size of the difference threshold, or j.n.d., depends on overall stimulus intensity. In other words, with a slight stimulus, a mild change is noticeable; with a strong stimulus, a change of much greater magnitude is necessary before it will be noticed. This finding is known as *Weber's law,* named for E. H. Weber, a German physiologist who investigated this principle.

In studies of Weber's law, one stimulus is held constant and referred to as the standard intensity. Then we determine what other stimulus can just be discriminated from it. If the standard or original intensity, S, is 100, and the change, ΔS, is 1, then the ratio is $\frac{1}{100}$ or .01. Therefore, to produce a j.n.d. in brightness with five hundred candles, we must add one for every 100, or five. The increase or decrease must be a constant fraction of the standard intensity.

The Weber fraction depends on the kind of stimulation being measured, such as weight, illumination, odor, and so forth. In typical psychophysical experiments, it is larger for visual brightness than for auditory pitch. It also differs with the intensities involved, being constant only within the normal or intermediate range (Figure 6-2).

Perhaps the frog failed the discrimination problem. Whatever the Weber ratio might have been, maybe the frog could never tell the difference between one heat level and the next, but certainly it would have passed the detection problem. Somewhere between the absolute and terminal thresholds, the frog must have perceived that the overall temperature was too warm for comfort and leaped for safety.

The Traditional Senses

If the hypothetical frog did leap for safety, where it would land is another matter. On land, frogs do not see well at a distance, and in the water, vision is limited even for close objects. Frogs and similar creatures often stay partly submerged, on the lookout for nearby insects and predators.

Visual Experience

Light, the stimulus for visual experience, is considered to be waves of radiant energy emanating from a source. These waves occur in sequence, but the human eye is attuned only to a narrow range of light wavelengths, from approximately 400 to 700 nanometers. Within this range, the shorter wavelengths are perceived as violet, the intermediate ones as blue, green, and yellow, and the longer ones as red. White light is a mixture of all wavelengths. The experience of *hue,* which refers to what we commonly call color, is largely a function of wavelength (Plate 1).

Stimulus	Ratio
Pitch, at 2,000 cycles/second	.003
Brightness, at 1,000 photons	.016
Heaviness, at 300 grams	.019
Smell of rubber, at 200 olfacties	.104
Taste of saline, at 3 moles/liter	.200

Figure 6-2 Difference Thresholds. *These are also known as Weber ratios. (From* Foundations of Psychology *by E. G. Boring, H. S. Langfeld, and H. P. Weld. New York: Wiley, 1948. Reprinted by permission of Mrs. Lucy D. Boring.)*

Visual phenomena also can be described in terms of intensity or *brightness,* which means that the experience may vary from dark to bright. Even a yellowish hue may be dark or light. This experience is correlated chiefly with wave amplitude, which is the size of the wave (Figure 6-3).

Finally, colors vary in richness or *saturation.* Highly saturated colors are the reddest reds and the yellowest yellows, as determined by several physical properties of light, including the mixture of different wavelengths. When we speak of saturation, we are referring to differences in purity among hues of the same level of intensity. In other words, we are referring to the degree to which any given hue differs from gray of the same brightness (Plate 2).

Although we do not have names for all the hues, a human being with normal color vision can identify more than one hundred different hues. When the brightness and saturation dimensions are included, it is not surprising to find that we have the capacity for several thousand different color experiences.

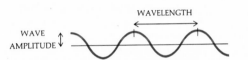

Figure 6-3 Wave Characteristics and Sensations. *Wavelength is the distance between consecutive waves; amplitude is the maximum displacement of a wave.*

Figure 6-4 Eye Structures. *Light rays pass through the cornea, which is a transparent outer covering; the aqueous and later the vitreous humor, which are transparent jelly-like substances that help maintain the shape of the eye; and the lens, which focuses the light when its curvature is changed by actions of the ciliary muscle. Another adjustment is made by the iris, which determines the amount of light entering through the pupillary opening. The choroid coat blocks all other light from entering the eye, and the sclerotic coat protects the mechanisms from injury.*

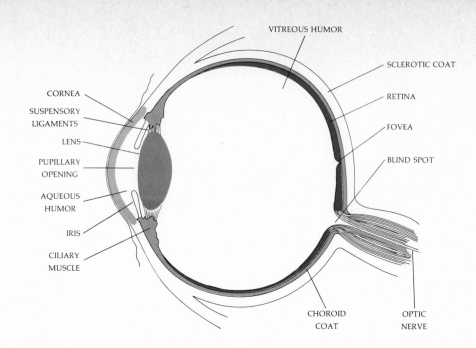

The retina. After these light waves pass through various receiving mechanisms of the eye, they strike the photosensitive surface known as the *retina,* which contains the receptors necessary for vision. When these receptors are stimulated, impulses are carried to the brain via the optic nerve and arouse visual experiences (Figure 6-4).

The human retina, which in limited ways is analogous to the film in a camera, actually contains two types of receptors. When the *rods* are stimulated, patterns of black, gray, and white are experienced, while the *cones* are responsible for color vision. The *fovea* of the human eye, near the center of the retina, is thickly packed with cones but is without rods. Here color vision is best and images are the clearest. Outside the fovea there are both cones and rods, but the cones become less dense towards the periphery and therefore there is less color vision in these regions.

Another special area of the retina is the *blind spot,* where vision is absent. There can be no receptors here because it is the point at which the optic nerve leaves the eye (Figure 6-5). It does not constitute an important visual defect, however, because there are two eyes and the blind spot for each eye involves a different part of the visual field. Furthermore, the head and eyes are constantly in motion, permitting a visual image to change its location on the retina. If our eyes were not moving constantly, our capacity to see would soon fade and then disappear.

Sensation and stimulus change. A series of ingenious experiments illustrates the significance of the eyes' continuous movements. Since it is virtually impossible to stop them, as they occur at a rate of up to one hundred per second, a device was developed in which the visual field moved with the eye. A small projector was mounted on a contact lens placed over the subject's cornea. Eye movements caused the lens and projector to move and, thus, the projected image always matched the

Processes in Perceiving

Figure 6-5 The Blind Spot.
Close your left eye and look at the small cross on the kicker with your right eye. Then, beginning at about 15 inches, move your head slowly towards or away from the book until the soccer ball disappears. With your head in this position, the image of the ball is falling on that point in the retina where the optic nerve leaves the eye.

eye movements. The retinal image could not change, despite eye movements. Under these conditions, the unchanging retinal image disappeared within a minute and did not reappear until there was some change in stimulation (Riggs et al., 1953).

It is well known that the frog eats only small, moving objects, ignoring dead flies right in front of it because it cannot see them (Manturana et al., 1960). The frog's visual system is nonfunctional in this case, just as the human system becomes nonfunctional when the images are artificially immobilized on the retina. This common outcome points to an important property of many sensory systems: they operate primarily in response to changes in the environment. We are generally more responsive to changing than to unchanging stimulation.

Adaptation. All sensory capacities gradually change under certain environmental conditions, a process known as *adaptation.* Two illustrations in the visual realm are dark and light adaptation. A gradual increase in visual sensitivity under conditions of low illumination is known as *dark adaptation.* This improvement is due partly to pupillary dilation but chiefly to changes in the retina, especially the production of a substance in the rods called *visual purple,* which improves our responsiveness to weak visual stimuli. After remaining in a dimly lit theater for a few minutes, one sees

more clearly, even though the illumination has not changed. In low illumination, vision involves only the rods and there is virtually no color vision.

An interesting aspect of vision in partial darkness results from the cones' showing different sensitivity under different degrees of illumination. In ordinary light the cones are most sensitive to yellow–green hues, but in dim light the maximum sensitivity shifts down the spectrum to green. Hence, when illumination changes, the comparative brightness of certain hues also changes. For example, if you are viewing red and green flowers of equal brightness as twilight approaches, at a certain time the red hue seems to lose brightness while the green and blue–green seem to retain their brightness. This change in relative brightness with decreasing illumination is called the *Purkinje shift.* As illumination decreases further, all hues lose their brightness and eventually appear gray and then black.

A gradual decrease in sensitivity in bright illumination, on the other hand, is referred to as *light adaptation.* Again, the eye adjusts to the prevailing light intensity partly as the result of pupillary constriction but largely because of photochemical changes in the retina. For example, a skier emerging into the intense glare of sunlight on icy snow gradually becomes accustomed to this condition and sees better after a time.

An unusual form of light adaptation, known as the *Ganzfeld effect,* has been demonstrated in laboratory experiments involving a completely uniform color field. *Ganzfeld* means "entire field." When one is exposed steadily to a completely red field, uninterrupted by figures or other colors, the red gradually ceases to be seen. It fades and then disappears. This effect may be obtained by placing well-fitted halves of pingpong balls over the subject's eyes and illuminating them by a slide projector equipped with a colored filter. One of the authors was exposed in this way to a homogeneous field of red, and the red faded to a neutral gray after several minutes.

Color vision.   While it is clearly established that cones mediate color vision, investigators know very little about how this result is accomplished. One theory, called the *Young-Helmholtz* theory in honor of two of its earliest proponents, assumes that there are three types of cones especially responsive to the long (red), intermediate (green), and short (blue) wavelengths. Studies of vertebrates' retinas have supported this view, indicating that color is discriminated by three pigments that are segregated in each of three types of cone receptors. These pigments appear to correspond approximately to the red, green, and blue wavelengths (MacNichol, 1964). Supporters of this theory believe that the experience of yellow depends on the simultaneous stimulation of red and green cones, and it is indeed possible to obtain yellow by overlapping red and green patches of light. Yellow also is obtained when one eye is stimulated with red and the other with green by using a special stereoscopic device (Hecht, 1928).

The *Hering theory* also postulates three types of receptor mechanisms in the retina, but proponents of this theory assume that these receptors respond to red–green, yellow–blue, and black–white stimulation, each functioning in reciprocal fashion. When the yellow–blue structure is stimulated by yellow, it

supposedly develops increasing sensitivity to blue and decreasing sensitivity to yellow. The Hering theory remains relevant despite discovery of the three different types of cones proposed by the Young-Helmholtz theory. It was revitalized by evidence indicating that there is such pairing of colors as blue–yellow and red–green, although this pairing does not necessarily occur at the receptors. One type of nerve cell, for example, is stimulated by red and inhibited by green (Wagner et al., 1960). Thus, evidence seems to favor a combination, supporting the Young-Helmholtz theory at the receptor level and the Hering theory at a level closer to the brain (Hurvich & Jameson, 1957).

The phenomenon of *visual afterimages* also is pertinent to color theory. When you look at a bright green light, for example, the experienced greenness may remain for a moment after you cease looking at the light. This outcome is a *positive afterimage.* This carry-over of the stimulus color is soon replaced, however, by an image of the complementary color, known as the *negative afterimage,* which in this case will have a reddish hue. In the red–green, yellow–blue, and black–white pairings of positive and negative after-images, we have the basic elements of the Hering theory (Plate 3).

Further information on color vision has been provided by studies of *color blindness,* particularly in those rare instances where an individual is color blind in one eye but has normal vision in the other. The most common form of color deficiency is red–green blindness. To be adequate, a theory of color vision must explain why the periphery of the human retina is not as sensitive to red and green as to blue and yellow and why so many people have a deficiency in red–green vision (Plates 4, 5). ■

I knew a guy who was color blind and didn't even know it until he took a test for the army. He passed the rest of the test easily and had 20/20 vision, but they made some kind of restriction on what he could do as a GI because sometimes he couldn't tell red and green apart very well.

Hearing Ability

Sound waves, the physical stimuli for hearing, are set up by vibrating bodies in our environment and transmitted through the air to our eardrums. In the ear, they arouse mechanical activities that stimulate nerve fibers. When these impulses reach the brain, auditory experiences occur.

The *pitch* of a sound is determined primarily by the frequency of vibrations per second, which is a function of wavelength. The note middle *C,* for example, depends on vibrations at a frequency of 256 hertz. Lower frequencies produce tones of lower pitch; higher frequencies produce tones of higher pitch. Although frequencies to which the human ear is attuned range from approximately 20 to 20,000 hertz, it is most sensitive between 2000 and 5000 hertz.

The *loudness* of a sound is primarily a function of the sound pressure that activates the eardrum. It is related to amplitude of the sound wave—that is, to the degree of displacement of the vibrating body from the resting position. As an example of this displacement, consider the vibrations of a tuning fork or harp string.

Vibrating bodies usually vibrate complexly. The harp vibrates as a whole, in thirds, in fourths, and so on, all at the same time. This complexity of mixture determines the *timbre* or quality of a sound. A harp and a horn playing the same tones sound different because of the different periodic vibrations. Aperiodic vibrations give rise to noise rather than tone.

In a sense, when we consider the chief properties of sound and light, timbre corresponds to saturation because both are types of mixtures. Loudness and brightness are both aspects of wave amplitude, and pitch and hue are related to wavelength. Hence, there is some parallelism in these two realms of sensory experience.

The cochlea. When we hear, sound waves actually stimulate three divisions of the ear. They set up vibrations of the eardrum in the *outer ear,* which is a collecting system. These vibrations are transformed into tiny bone movements in the *middle ear,* which is a transmitting system. Finally, in the *inner ear,* which is a converting system, they become liquid pressures, sending impulses to the brain via the auditory nerve (Figure 6-6).

In the inner ear, the *cochlea* serves a function somewhat similar to that of the retina in the eye; it contains the receptors, which in this case are *tiny hair cells* on the *organ of Corti.* This organ is located in the cochlear canal, which is filled with liquid. Whenever the liquid moves in response to movements originated by the eardrum and transmitted through the middle ear, the hair cells are induced to bend and, therefore, to send impulses to the brain, which produces hearing (Figure 6-7).

The frog's ear operates in much the same way, but its structure is simpler. It has three divisions, but in the middle ear there are just two connecting bones instead of three. In the outer ear, there are no skin folds to collect the sound waves and no auditory canal to carry them to the eardrum. There is nothing except the eardrum itself, which appears merely as a large, disc-shaped region of skin on each side of the animal's head.

Theories of hearing. In hearing, just as in color vision, there are two major theories. According to *place theory,* different regions of the hair cells are especially attuned to different vibration frequencies. Although these structures do not vibrate in the manner of wires in a piano, as suggested by Helmholtz, who originated the place theory, they do respond differently to different frequencies (von Békésy, 1960).

In this theory it is also assumed that impulses aroused in different hair cells go to somewhat different regions of the

Figure 6-6 Ear Structures. *The outer ear includes the auditory canal, down which the air waves travel, and the eardrum, which then vibrates. The middle ear changes these vibrations into tiny movements of the oval window by movements of the hammer, anvil, and stirrup on this window. In the inner ear, the oval window exerts pressure on the liquid in the cochlear canal, which activates the auditory receptors. Thus, the mechanical motions become electrochemical signals.*

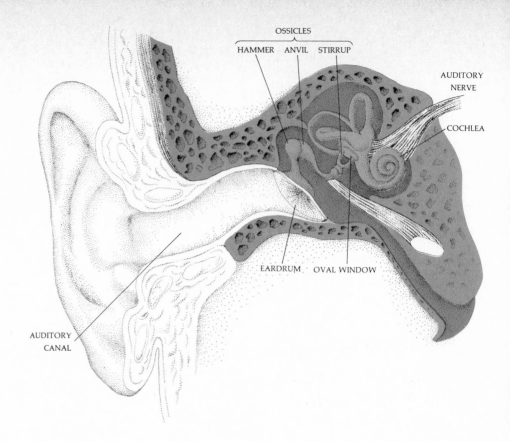

OSSICLES
HAMMER   ANVIL   STIRRUP

AUDITORY NERVE

COCHLEA

EARDRUM   OVAL WINDOW

AUDITORY CANAL

Figure 6-7 The Cochlea. *Part A shows the cochlea coiled as it is in position in the inner ear. The cochlea is partly extended and sectioned in part B, indicating the cochlear canal. Part C is a cross-sectional view showing the organ of Corti, containing the hair cells that stimulate hearing. The round window serves as a safety device, absorbing excessive pressure in the canal.*

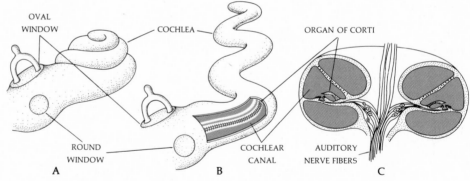

OVAL WINDOW

COCHLEA

ORGAN OF CORTI

ROUND WINDOW

COCHLEAR CANAL

AUDITORY NERVE FIBERS

A   B   C

auditory cortex and that pitch thus depends on both the place in the cochlea that is most activated and the place in the auditory cortex that receives the resulting nerve impulses. The assumption that there are precise cortical localizations for high-pitched and low-pitched sounds has yet to be verified, however.

According to this theory, loudness depends on the spread of disturbance in either direction from the place in the cochlea most involved. Two tones of the same frequency and intensity would activate the same range of fibers, but if the two tones differed in intensity, the range of activated fibers would be greater in the case of the greater intensity.

The *volley theory* is an extension of an earlier viewpoint known as the frequency theory, which was the most logical theory to account for our capacity to hear sounds below 1000 hertz. A limitation in the frequency approach, however, is that frequencies up to about 4000 hertz are somehow transmitted by the auditory nerve, even though no single fiber responds more frequently than 1000 times per second. This finding suggests that perhaps nerve fibers work in groups, and that some fibers in the group, because of their greater excitability, discharge more often than others (Wever, 1949). This concept of group activity is central to the volley theory.

On this basis, for a tone of 3000 hertz, a spurt of neural activity called a *volley* would occur in the auditory nerve every .003 second, with different groups of fibers responding each time. Some fibers, because of their greater excitability, would contribute to more of the spurts than others. According to this theory, pitch depends on the frequency of volleys rather than the frequency carried by the individual fibers.

Loudness is thought to increase as more impulses occur in each volley. We have already seen that an increase in the intensity of stimulation causes more fibers to respond. Thus, a sound wave of increased amplitude might activate one hundred instead of fifty fibers, and the effect would be to produce more impulses per volley without changing the frequency of the separate volleys.

As in the case of vision, the two theories are not necessarily competing. The volley factor may play a major role in mediating the lower frequencies, up to around 4000 hertz, and the place factor may play a more significant role in the higher frequencies. Recent research suggests that both aspects are involved in the neural basis of human hearing, and higher-level processing in the brain is currently being stressed.

Sensitivity in Smell

In human beings, the sense of smell is less important than in other species. It does not alert us to predators, as it does in animals, although it puts us on guard when certain foods are unfit to eat and warns of other dangers, such as fire or gasoline. Smell, also called *olfactory sensitivity*, might be of greater significance in human life except that we move about in an upright position, with our nose away from many odors, and our visual and auditory senses usually serve us quite well.

An interesting characteristic of human smell, as opposed to vision and hearing, is that it detects only the strongest stimulus present. Weaker odors are readily masked by stronger ones, a principle that is operative in the use of perfumes, heavily scented disinfectants, and breath mints. Furthermore, olfactory adaptation is very rapid; to detect an odor in a room, one may have to leave for a while and then re-enter.

The olfactory epithelium. Smell occurs in response to gaseous chemicals, and the receptors in human beings are long *thread-like structures* extending from the olfactory bulbs down into the nasal cavities. They lie in the *olfactory epithelium,* a thin layer of tissue at the extreme top of the nasal cavity, above the main current of air moving from the nostrils to the lungs (Figure 6-8).

The frog is similarly constituted, as shown by experiments where tiny electrodes are attached to the olfactory epithelium. A brief puff of odorous air elicits an electrical response, measured by the electro-olfactogram (EOG). It is not obtained with pure air and, furthermore, the response increases as the concentration of odorous material increases (Ottoson, 1971).

Theory and application. One theory of smell, called the *sterochemical theory,* assumes that we experience an odor when gas molecules of various shapes fit into similarly shaped ''sockets'' in the

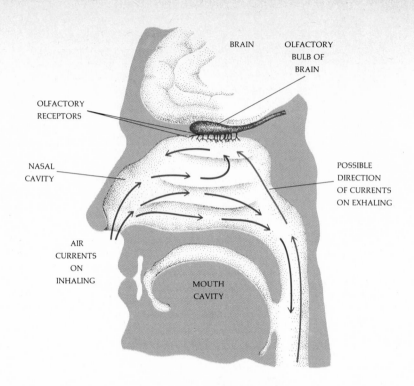

Figure 6-8 Structures of the Nose. *Sniffing is helpful in identifying an odor because then, as the arrows indicate, the air currents are more likely to reach the olfactory receptors.*

BRAIN

OLFACTORY BULB OF BRAIN

OLFACTORY RECEPTORS

NASAL CAVITY

POSSIBLE DIRECTION OF CURRENTS ON EXHALING

AIR CURRENTS ON INHALING

MOUTH CAVITY

receptors. Molecules from the odor of musk, for example, are considered to have a particular shape and therefore fit into a socket of that shape, while floral molecules, which have a different shape, fit into their own kind of socket (Amoore et al., 1964). Research has not yet provided convincing support for this view, however, and there has been little success in identifying the basic odors. One popular classification includes six odors—flowery, fruity, spicy, resinous, smoky, and putrid—but there are other classifications as well.

On the practical side, smell plays a subtle but important role in our enjoyment of our environment. Years ago, three pairs of stockings were scented with attractive odors and one pair was left unscented. Then 250 New York housewives were asked to select the pair they liked best. More than 50 percent chose a narcissus-scented pair, approximately 20 percent selected each of the other scented pairs, and only 8 percent selected the pair with the natural smell.

Furthermore, when they were asked afterwards it was evident that only 6 of the women even noticed that the stockings had been scented (Laird, 1932).

Factors in Taste

The adequate stimulus for taste, as in smell, is chemical energy, but it must be soluble in form to reach the receptors. The human tongue has many slight elevations, called *papillae*, and the *taste buds* lie in the crevices between the papillae.

Taste buds and receptors. The taste buds are flask-shaped and each one is accessible through an opening called a *pore*. Inside each bud are several *taste cells*, which are the taste receptors. On the basis of this embedded location, it is apparent why substances must be in liquid form to stimulate the receptors. They must seep into the crevices and then into the pore of a taste bud (Figure 6-9).

Processes in Perceiving

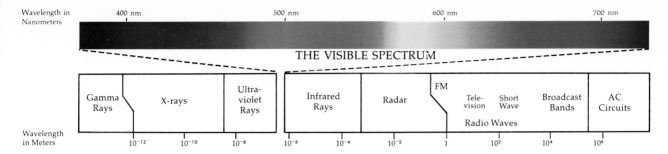

Plate 1   The Visible Spectrum
(p. 139) The visible range of wavelengths extends from approximately 400 to 700 nanometers (nm).

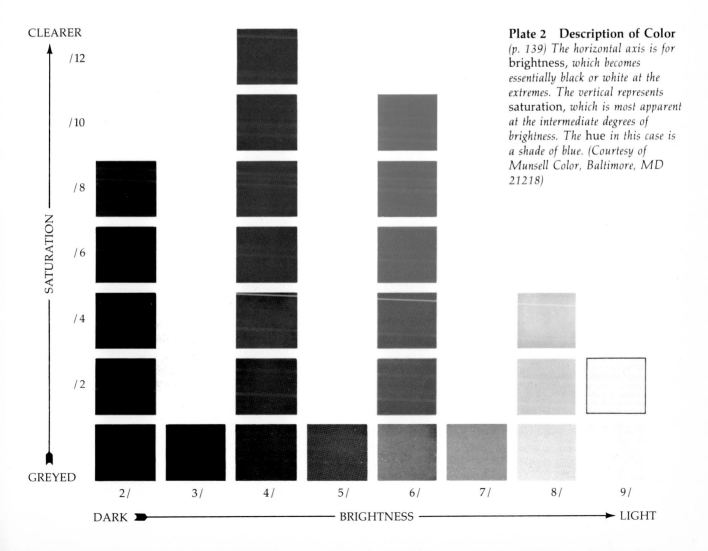

Plate 2   Description of Color
(p. 139) The horizontal axis is for brightness, *which becomes essentially black or white at the extremes. The vertical represents* saturation, *which is most apparent at the intermediate degrees of brightness. The* hue *in this case is a shade of blue. (Courtesy of Munsell Color, Baltimore, MD 21218)*

Plate 3   Negative After-image
(p. 142) After looking steadily at the center of this flag for approximately 30 seconds, look at a brightly illuminated white sheet of paper. The negative after-image which you will experience involves the complementary colors of those shown here. The phenomenon is due to receptor adaptation.

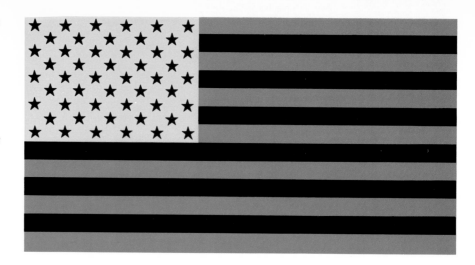

Plate 4   Detection of Color Blindness *(p. 142) This plate, from the AO Hardy-Rand-Rittler Pseudo-isochromatic Test, is used to detect specific deficiencies in color vision. A person with red-green blindness probably will not see the circle and triangle in the left-hand plate. Persons with a less common* *deficiency, blue-yellow blindness, will be unable to see the X and triangle in the right-hand plate. For testing color vision, a large number of these plates must be administered under carefully controlled conditions. (Courtesy of American Optical Corporation)*

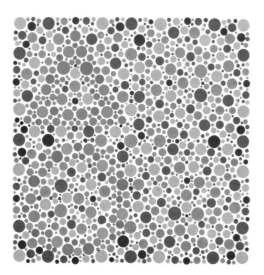 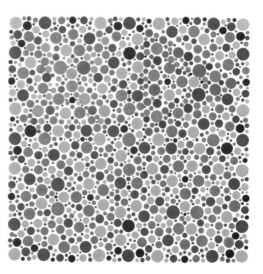

Plate 5 Forms of Color Blindness *(p. 142) A person with normal color vision colored the first parrot, and then two subjects with color blindness performed the same task. Note the difficulty with red and dark green. (After R. J. S. McDowall,* The Handbook of Physiology and Biochemistry. *London: John Murray)*

Plate 6 Study of Creative Persons
(p. 237) Persons chosen at random and persons judged as highly creative were given colored squares and asked to construct mosaics. Patterns such as that shown at the left were often constructed by randomly selected persons; the mosaic at the right is typical of the designs made by the creative persons. The creative individuals "expressed what can only be called aversion for the figures which were simple and obviously symmetrical" (Barron, 1958, p. 155). (Courtesy of Dr. Wallace B. Hall)

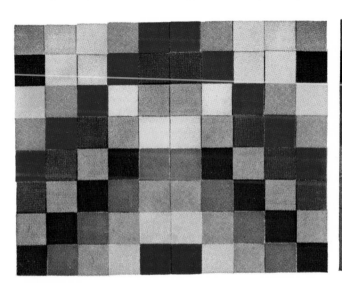

Plate 7 Psychosis: Flight from Reality (p. 441) The work of Louis Wain, known for his realistic paintings of cats, began to suggest a lack of contact with reality. Note the strange eyes and background in the first composition, done during the onset of his delusions, and the progressive distortion in the later paintings. This change in Wain's behavior, his delusions of persecution, and his incoherent speech were regarded as psychotic symptoms. Unusual paintings per se, however, are not considered evidence of psychosis. (Copyright © Guttmann Maclay Collection, Institute of Psychiatry, London)

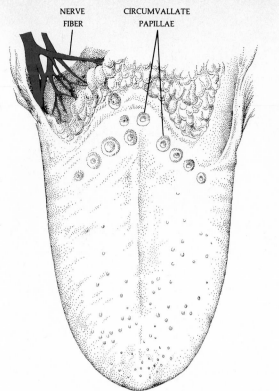

NERVE FIBER   CIRCUMVALLATE PAPILLAE

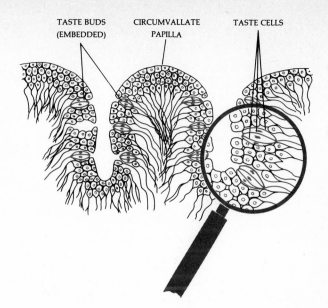

TASTE BUDS (EMBEDDED)   CIRCUMVALLATE PAPILLA   TASTE CELLS

Figure 6-9 Taste Receptors. *Each taste bud has more than the two or three cells shown in the diagram. Moreover, each of these cells has its own nerve fiber, although only one is represented.*

The cells at the back of the tongue are particularly sensitive to bitter substances, those at the sides are particularly sensitive to sour substances, and those at the tip are sensitive to sweet substances. Still others, scattered all over the tongue except at the center, are most sensitive to salty substances. The central part of the tongue towards the front does not have any *gustatory sensitivity,* as the sense of taste is called (Figure 6-10).

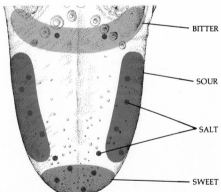

BITTER

SOUR

SALT

SWEET

Figure 6-10 Taste Areas. *The tongue is not uniformly sensitive to bitter, sour, sweet, and salt.*

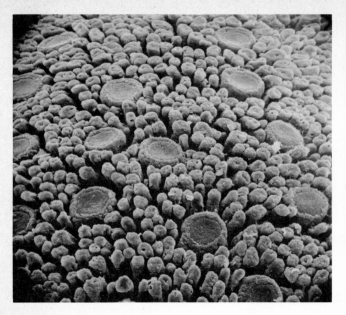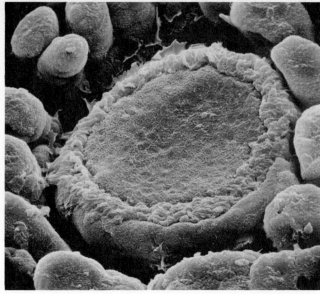

Figure 6-11 Frog Papillae. *The first photograph shows a portion of the surface of a frog's tongue magnified. In the second photograph, at greater magnification, the disc-shaped surface of the individual papilla is clearly visible. (Courtesy of P. P. C. Graziadei, M.D., Florida State University, Tallahassee, Florida)*

In certain lower animals the taste buds are not as inaccessible. Many fish have them in the skin of the body, and in the ubiquitous frog they are disc-shaped structures on the surface of the papillae. They are sensitive to salty, sour, and bitter substances, but not to sweet substances (Figure 6-11). On this basis, one investigator suggests that the sweet taste is a later evolutionary development than the others (Moncrieff, 1967).

Taste research. A persistent research question has concerned the ways in which we mediate the many tastes available to us. All of them seem to be one or a combination of four fundamental tastes—salty, sour, sweet, and bitter. Some studies indicate that the taste conveyed by any given fiber depends on the activity in other fibers. If a certain fiber is activated, the taste may be salty, but if nearby fibers are also activated, the taste may be sour. The role of the adjacent nerve tissue is emphasized in this theory, called the *pattern theory* of taste (Pfaffmann, 1964).

Taste is also influenced by other factors, such as smell. With the nostrils blocked to prevent air from reaching the olfactory receptors, a subject has little success in recognizing substances placed on the tongue. A drop of lemon juice is experienced merely as something sour, and a drop of Coca-Cola as bittersweet. Other senses are important too. Coffee and Coca-Cola taste quite different at different temperatures. Still other substances taste different depending on whether they have a smooth or rough texture, as in oysters and oyster soup, which suggests that touch is involved as well.

Pressure, Pain, and Temperature

The experience of an oyster on the tongue involves pressure, while hot coffee involves temperature and, if it is too hot, includes pain. Collectively, these experiences are known as *cutaneous sensitivity,* meaning that they arise through the skin. They constitute the last of the traditional five senses enumerated by Aristotle; he simply referred to them collectively as touch. An interesting aspect of both pressure and temperature sensitivity is the rapid adaptation. After a few minutes one usually ceases to notice the ring recently placed on a finger or the apparent chill of an air conditioner.

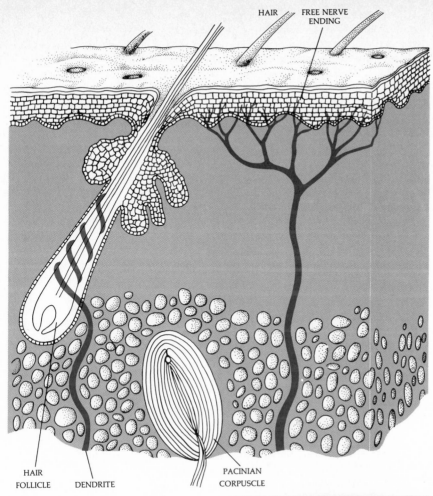

HAIR FREE NERVE
ENDING

HAIR
FOLLICLE   DENDRITE

PACINIAN
CORPUSCLE

Figure 6-12   Skin Receptors.
*Dendrites around hair follicles, and
other unknown mechanisms, mediate
light pressure. Pacinian corpuscles,
located beneath the skin's surface,
apparently are the receptors for heavy
pressure. Free nerve endings mediate
pain sensitivity. (Photo of hair follicle
from Winkelmann, 1959; photo of
Pacinian corpuscle by Dr. Malcolm R.
Miller, Department of Anatomy,
University of California, San Francisco)*

Unknown receptors. Relatively little is
known about the underlying receptors
for cutaneous sensitivity in human
beings. The experience of *light pressure*
is induced by stimulation of a hair follicle, but transitions in the life cycle of
free nerve endings also may be responsible (Altman, 1966). The experience of
heavy pressure involves tissues lying beneath the skin's surface. Since Pacinian
corpuscles are subcutaneous and relatively numerous, they are considered by
some to be receptors for heavy pressure
(Figure 6-12). Certain laboratory experiments have supported this conclusion
but considerable uncertainty remains
(Hahn, 1974).

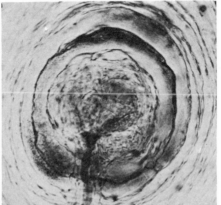

PACINIAN CORPUSCLE

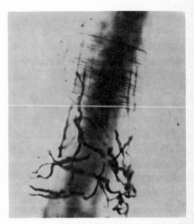

HAIR FOLLICLE

One condition for pain is sufficiently high stimulus intensity, as we saw in the terminal threshold. Another is the stimulation of free nerve endings, found just below the surface almost everywhere on the body. Some of these appear to transmit pain without being associated with any other sensitivity; hence, they are likely candidates for pain receptors. However, the experience of pain can be markedly changed by one's thoughts and by other sensory experiences, as in the use of recorded music as an anesthetic in dentistry. The apparent effectiveness of acupuncture, in which needles are inserted in various places on the human body to relieve pain, also suggests that we have much to learn about the mediation of pain. This predominantly Eastern procedure has been used as an anesthetic in surgery and also as a treatment of painful conditions, such as arthritis and headaches, but its physiological basis remains essentially unknown.

In human beings and many animals there is a sensitivity to warmth and cold just a few degrees above or below normal body temperature, but the structural mediators of *temperature* sensitivity are not known either. Free nerve endings and the microscopic blood vessels (capillaries) that run to every part of the skin are currently mentioned as possibilities, but progress in understanding temperature receptors has been slow (Hahn, 1974).

Cutaneous research. Despite the lack of success in identifying receptors for cutaneous sensitivity in human beings, research on the skin has told us a great deal about their distribution over the body. Sensitivity to light pressure is most likely on the most mobile parts. There are approximately 135 pressure-sensitive spots per square centimeter on the end of the thumb, compared to only 30 on the back of the hand (Guilford & Lovewell, 1936). The areas of greatest sensitivity are on the fingers and lips, which thereby serve us well in explorations based on touch (Figure 6-13).

Pain is experienced at many points, but not everywhere. The mucous lining of the cheek, which has no free nerve endings, the cerebral cortex, and certain visceral organs fail to yield pain.

Receptors for cold are much more numerous than those for warmth throughout most of the human body. But the cold spots themselves are not evenly distributed. There are many more per square centimeter on the tip of the nose than on the forearm (Figure 6-14).

Not long ago, there were sensational reports of people being able to "see" colors by using their fingers. When this claim was tested in the laboratory in carefully controlled conditions, it was found that the reports were much exaggerated. Some people can make such discriminations but only at a minimal level, and the capacity being used is not vision but temperature sensitivity. Certain people, some of the time, apparently can tell one colored cloth from another by small differences in reflected warmth from the different-colored surfaces (Youtz, 1965; Makous, 1966).

The Proprioceptive Senses

Just as there are receptors for stimuli coming from outside the body, there are receptors for stimuli within it. This recognition has led to the identification of several more senses since Aristotle's time. The term *proprioception* refers to these senses as a group; the root *proprio* means "belonging to the body."

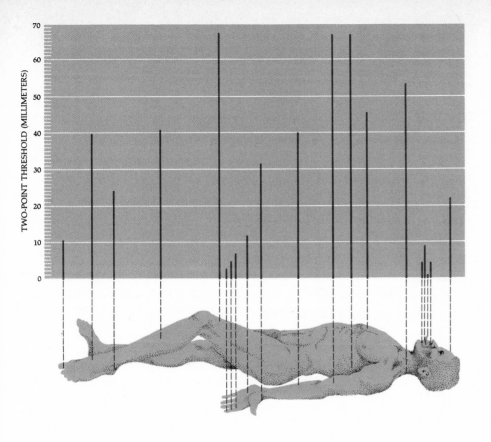

TWO-POINT THRESHOLD (MILLIMETERS)

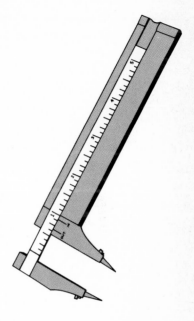

Figure 6-13 Studying Pressure Sensitivity. *Sensitivity to light pressure is investigated by using an aesthesiometer. With this adjustable instrument, two points of pressure can be applied simultaneously to nearby regions of the skin. The aim is to discover how far apart the two points must be in order to be perceived as different points. In general, it is found that the skin is most sensitive to different points of pressure on the most mobile parts of the body, such as the tongue and fingers.*

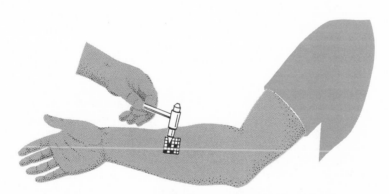

Figure 6-14 Studying Temperature Sensitivity. *In this early method of investigating sensitivity to temperature, a grid is stamped on the subject's skin and then a heated or cooled cylinder is applied at various points within this area. After each trial, the subject reports his or her experiences; it is found that sensitivity to different temperatures varies considerably at different points on the skin.*

Figure 6-15 Role of Kinesthesis.
This capacity for body control in physical activities is largely dependent on kinesthetic feedback from the muscles and tendons, informing the individual when the correct response has been made. (Herwig from Stock, Boston)

Active Movement and Body Position

The capacity for sensing the voluntary movements of our own body and the positions of its parts was first brought to scientific attention by Sir Charles Bell. In 1826, he called it the "muscle sense"; later it was known as the sixth sense, and today we call it *kinesthesis* or kinesthetic sensitivity. On this basis any normal individual can stand with his or her eyes closed without swaying, tie his or her shoe without looking, or carry on a conversation without thinking about the movements of the tongue and jaw (Figure 6-15).

Kinesthetic receptors. Information concerning voluntary movements is made possible by receptor mechanisms in the muscles, tendons, and joints. They are subject to pressure and release of pressure as parts of the body are moved or held in a firm position and the resulting nerve impulses travel to the brain. Impulses then are sent back to the muscles, tendons, and joints, stimulating further activity. Through this feedback mechanism, motor activities act as stimuli for their own re-arousal, thus proceeding more or less automatically.

Research has readily demonstrated this sensitivity in various lower animals, including the frog. This amphibian wipes its back with a front or hind leg, depending on what point has been stimulated (Corning & Labue, 1971). The animal knows which area to wipe through cutaneous sensitivity, but how does it reach the right spot? The answer lies in kinesthetic sensitivity, which guides the limb forward or backward or to one side or the other through feedback from the muscles.

A clinical example. Few people realize how much our normal behavior depends on kinesthesis unless they are afflicted by *tabes dorsalis*. This disease, sometimes caused by syphilis, follows damage to certain nerve tracts of the spinal cord. When these tracts are no longer intact, kinesthetic sensitivity below that level is destroyed. Impulses come into the spinal cord as before, but they have no pathway to the brain. The individual cannot lift his or her foot onto the curb without looking at it, walks with a peculiar (tabetic) gait, and if the destruction is high in the cord, cannot accurately touch other body parts with the eyes closed—all because he or she is receiving little or no information concerning the location and movement of the body parts.

Orientation in Space

If all the traditional senses and kinesthesis were eliminated, it would still be possible for a person to know whether he or she was literally right side up or upside down. This sensitivity is part of the *sense of balance* or *equilibrium*, made possible by a responsiveness to the pull of gravity. The mechanisms that mediate it are part of the inner ear, but they have nothing to do with hearing.

The vestibular system. In human beings, the portion of the inner ear that contains the equilibrium mechanisms is called the *nonauditory labyrinth,* meaning that it is not related to hearing (non-auditory) but is maze-like (labyrinthine) in

Processes in Perceiving

structure. It is entirely filled with a liquid known as *endolymph* and has two types of chambers, sacs and canals. At the moment we are interested only in the sac-like chambers, the *saccule* and *ventricle,* which are collectively known as the *vestibular system.* The receptors for the position of the head and body with respect to gravitational force are hair cells in this system, and they operate in almost the same way as those for audition. The hairs are weighted with calcium particles called *otoliths,* and any change in the position of the head causes them to bend in the liquid. A movement of the head is associated with a lag in adjustment of the otoliths, which bends the hairs in the opposite direction. Then the aroused nerve impulses go from the vestibule to the brain via the vestibular branch of the auditory nerve (Figure 6-16).

Even when this system is functioning properly, an individual may show poor balance. The problem in this case is usually that the auditory nerve has been damaged and, therefore, does not carry the vestibular impulse to the brain. Some people who have poor hearing also have poor balance, not because the same receptor mechanisms are involved but because the neural impulses in both cases are transmitted to the brain by the same nerve pathway.

Studies in lower animals.   In lobsters, the otoliths, or weighted particles, must be replaced periodically as the organism acquires a new shell, and the substances used for this purpose are generally stones and sand obtained from the ocean floor. In some early experiments, conditions were arranged so that no materials other than iron filings were available for replacing the sloughed-off stones, and so the animals used them. Later, when a magnet was placed above these aquatic creatures, they turned over on their backs and remained in this position (Prentiss, 1901). This action

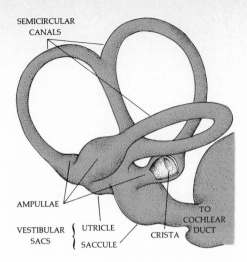

SEMICIRCULAR CANALS

AMPULLAE

VESTIBULAR SACS { UTRICLE / SACCULE

CRISTA

TO COCHLEAR DUCT

Figure 6-16   Nonauditory Labyrinth. *The vestibular sacs serve the sense of body position and rectilinear motion. The semicircular canals contain receptors for rotary motion. The entire structure basically provides a sense of balance, and its location in relation to the auditory mechanisms can be seen in Figure 6-6, just above the stirrup.*

Figure 6-17   Role of the Labyrinth. *The first drawing shows a water frog with an inoperative nonauditory labyrinth on the right side shortly after the removal operation. The second drawing shows recovery of normal functioning by means of the remaining labyrinth and other senses.*

returned the normal gravitational pull, which comes from the animal's underside rather than its back.

When one vestibular system is damaged in the frog, it immediately turns its head towards that side. After a while, this symptom disappears. Apparently the frog learns to compensate for this loss through the use of other senses, especially vision (Figure 6-17).

Changes in Passive Motion
Besides the sense of moving one's body and knowing one's position in space, there is the sense of *passive motion,* which occurs whenever one is moved about in space without any effort on one's part. As we discover from elevators and roller coasters, this sensitivity can be pronounced at times.

■ *I've often wondered if our "tastes" don't change a good deal as we grow older. I really have noticed a change in myself when it comes to a taste for dizziness. As a kid I loved to twirl around and around or roll over and over down a hill until my head was "spinning" so much I couldn't stand up. Now I have no desire at all for that kind of feeling. Is it possible that something in my ears has changed so that I am more sensitive—or less sensitive—to that kind of motion?*

Generally, two types of passive motion are specified. *Rectilinear motion* involves movement in a straight line. It is sensed whenever one's *rate* of straight-line movement is changed, as when a train slows down abruptly. *Rotary motion* involves circular movement. It occurs whenever someone is spun or twisted, as in carnival rides, and it too is experienced through a change in rate.

Rectilinear motion, as well as orientation in space, is indicated by the vestibular system. A change in movement in any straight-line direction is associated with a lag in adjustment of the otoliths of the vestibule. This adjustment bends the hairs in the opposite direction and nerve impulses are aroused.

The semicircular canals. In addition to sacs, the nonauditory labyrinth contains canal-like chambers, which are comprised of the three *semicircular canals*. They are responsible for sensitivity to rotary motion. In the human being, these three canals are positioned so that we are sensitive to all varieties of rotation. Each canal is at right angles to the others, one corresponding to each of the three planes of space. Turning the head in any direction produces movements in at least one canal.

At the base of each canal is a swelling (ampulla) into which projects a small structure containing the receptors. The *hair cells of the crista,* as this structure is called, are the receptors for rotary motion, and when they are bent by changes in motion, they send impulses to the brain via the auditory nerve.

Motion sickness and space flights. Generally, human beings are exposed only to mild rotary motion, such as when a car rounds a curve or when some brief spinning motion is required in a dance or athletics. When the movement is pronounced and sustained, motion sickness can result; this nauseous feeling is caused partly by activity in the nonauditory labyrinth. Sometimes, further experience enables the individual to become accustomed to this feeling, and adaptation can be accelerated even by simulated exposure to the situation, as in motion pictures (Parker & Howard, 1974). ■

Despite the absence of prolonged rotary and rectilinear motion in most of our lives, the possibility of life in space has prompted closer study of the nonauditory labyrinth and its related experiences. Departure from and re-entry into the earth's atmosphere involve immense changes in acceleration and deceleration, and zero gravitational pull requires definite readjustments in order to maintain positions and coordinate movements. Living comfortably in spacecrafts and rotating space platforms will require a better understanding of our sensitivity to these types of motion.

Sensation and Perception

What we know about the world is due to more than the stimulation of our various sense organs. This information is combined with that already stored in the brain, in the form of memories. In other words, we add past experience to current sensations. We make some interpretation or derive some meaning from the stimulation in a process called *perception*. We experience more than redness, warmth, and putridness; we perceive a fire engine, a fire, and burning rubbish.

Intersensory Perception

A perception is generally considered an organized, unified experience that can arise from several sensory processes. In fact, our senses usually operate in conjunction with one another and we speak of multisensory or *intersensory perception*. By this term we mean that information is obtained from two or more sensory processes simultaneously and is added to information already acquired from prior experience (Figure 6-18).

Type of Sensitivity	Physical Stimulus	Sense Organ, Receptors	Area of Cerebral Cortex	Types of Sensation
Visual	light waves	eyes: rods and cones in retina	occipital lobe	hue, brightness, saturation
Auditory	sound waves	ears: hair cells in Organ of Corti	temporal lobe	pitch, loudness, complexity
Olfactory	gaseous substance	nose: hair cells in olfactory epithelium	none: mediated in lower brain centers	——
Gustatory	soluble substance	tongue: taste cells in taste buds	parietal lobe	salty, sour, sweet, bitter
Cutaneous	mechanical or thermal stimulation	skin: free nerve endings	parietal lobe	pressure, pain, warmth, cold
Kinesthetic	change in movement and position of body parts	muscles, tendons, and joints: nerve endings	parietal lobe	movements of body parts
Equilibrium	body position	ears: vestibular system	——	upright, tilted
Passive motion	rectilinear motion	ears: vestibular system	——	acceleration, deceleration
	rotary motion	ears: semicircular canals	——	turning or spinning

Senses as interrelated. In daily life, almost all of us are regularly exposed to interrelated sensory experiences, even when simply eating a meal. What is commonly called "taste" is a composite of gustatory, olfactory, and cutaneous sensitivity. Slices of uncooked potato and apple are discriminated only when the sense of smell is added to taste. Gustatory sensitivity alone is insufficient. However, uncooked cauliflower can be identified by noting the different texture on the tongue, which is a cutaneous experience.

From the laboratory there is evidence for intersensory perception even in *touch typing,* a term that is a misnomer because the primary sensation is kinesthetic. It is often thought that the expert typist never looks at the keyboard, but research shows that typing is a kinesthetic-visual task, especially with regard to accuracy. The importance of visual cues for beginners is obvious, but even the "skillful typist is . . . not aware of the frequency with which he or she steals

Figure 6-18   Sensory Experience.
Consider how many of the senses are involved in the activity shown in this photograph. (Photo by Gscheidle from Magnum)

corner-of-the-eye glances at the keyboard and/or typescript'' (West, 1967).

Senses as active. The fact that skilled typists unconsciously steal glances at the keyboard also illustrates that the senses operate in an active and exploratory nature. They *seek* information. It has been said that the eye is like a camera, but this analogy is partly misleading. The eye is active and the camera is passive. The eye is constantly compensating for blur and refocusing on a new stimulus whenever the head comes to rest (Gibson, 1966).

We orient ourselves in space not only by receptors in our inner ears but also by those in our eyes. A person who is tipped backwards in the dentist's chair is aware of the situation through vision, as he or she seeks information, and through information from the semicircular canals and vestibule. People with defective vestibular systems maintain themselves reasonably well in an ordinary environment until they wear blindfolds; then their defect is obvious.

People with normal vestibular systems can lose their orientation in space through abnormal kinesthetic information. Citizens of Niigata, Japan who constantly occupied a building that had been tilted by an earthquake, reported that they felt upset much of the time and that the world seemed to be spinning or ''swimming about'' rather than stationary. Their symptoms were in marked contrast to other persons who lived in the same buildings but spent most of their time away from home (Kitahara & Uno, 1967). Because this condition occurred when there was no abnormal condition in the vestibule, we might say that the sense of balance should also include vision, kinesthesis, and even cutaneous sensitivity.

Extrasensory Perception

Finally, when all these various senses are unavailable, is it still possible to perceive something? Can we know about things without the use of our normally recognized sense organs? Most psychologists would answer negatively, despite many extraordinary stories suggesting the contrary.

Anecdotal reports. In one of their first meetings, Sigmund Freud and the famous Swiss psychoanalyst, Carl Gustav Jung, had an astonishing experience. They were discussing psychic phenomena when suddenly the bookcase went ''bang!'' Then, for some reason that he was never able to explain, Jung predicted that another loud noise would occur, and it did, just as he spoke. This event made a profound impression on both of them (Jung, 1963).

Freud apparently was quite shaken at the time, but later he decided that there was some obvious physical reason involving the furniture for the loud noise they heard. He never knew quite what to make of psychic experiences and vacillated on the issue most of his life. On the other hand, Jung regarded the event as another convincing demonstration of *psi,* a general term that includes ESP and most psychic phenomena. ESP, or *extrasensory perception,* is perception without any known sensory basis. It takes place, allegedly, without the use of any of the sensory processes currently identified (Figure 6-19).

Outside the field of psychology, Sinclair Lewis gave an extended account of ''mental radio,'' by which he meant mental telepathy, also called reading another person's mind. Mark Twain reported unexpected encounters with people he had not seen for a very long time, just after thinking about them. Thomas Edison's associates said he had several uncanny psychic abilities. The problem in all such instances is that we do not know the details. Perhaps, through uncontrolled circumstances, the ordinary senses were simply being used in extraordinary ways. ■□

■ *I dreamt that we were being bombed by the Germans. They were dropping bombs all around our yard, and one fell and hit the tree and it blew up and fell over. The dream scared me and I woke up. I went downstairs and told my mother the entire dream, pointing out the tree in our yard that had been bombed. It was a bright and sunny day. In less than five minutes the sky went black and there was a big electrical storm and lightning hit the tree directly behind the one I saw bombed and it fell the way I dreamt it did.*

Processes in Perceiving

Photograph taken at Clark University in Worcester, Massachusetts in 1908. Freud is at the left in the front row; Jung is at the right. (The Bettmann Archive)

□ *On two separate occasions, Peter had an experience that he attributed to ESP. Peter lived in Florida in his own apartment, and rarely went home to visit his parents, who also lived in Florida. On both occasions, he suddenly felt an urge to drop in at home. Each time, within 15 minutes of his arrival, his girl friend, Carol, called from Massachusetts. He had no outside "warning" of her call, but felt certain that she would contact him on those nights. His first assumption was that he had some form of ESP, and could tell when his girl friend would call.*

In this situation, I would tend to look for situational cues that could have aroused a suspicion or belief within Peter that Carol would call. The best source of cues would be the letters they exchanged and perhaps previous patterns of telephone communication. In examining the letters, it became apparent that one day prior to both the events, Peter had received a letter from Carol revealing some depression or general emotional upset. He perhaps perceived these cues and assumed that she would call the next day; thus he made the trip to his parents' home. In patterns of communication, it was clear that Carol generally called every four weeks and past experience showed that it was usually on a Sunday night, when Peter began to expect a call.

Need for controls.

There is a need for careful study, even in animal observations. For example, when a frog is put in a box in which there is a window, it will turn and face the light, perhaps hopping in that direction. If we cover that window and put another one in the opposite side of the box, the frog will turn in the new direction, face the light, and jump towards it. Apparently it sees the light and moves towards it.

If we block the frog's vision, it still knows the direction of the light and turns towards it. It does so even when there is a pane of glass preventing air currents from reaching the skin and arousing cutaneous sensations. At first glance the frog seems to have ESP, knowing where the light is without seeing it and without using any other senses.

Through further experiments, we discover the answer. The skin of the frog is sensitive to light (Milne & Milne, 1962). The animal can locate the light source by seeing it or by feeling it on its skin.

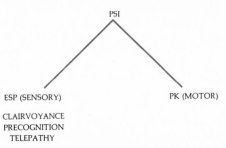

Figure 6-19   Types of Psi.   *Psychic phenomena, sometimes referred to collectively as psi, can be considered as sensory and motor. On the sensory or ESP side, there are clairvoyance, in which an event is somehow known as it occurs; precognition, in which an event is known before it occurs, as happened to Jung in the second sound from the bookcase; and telepathy, in which someone else's thoughts are known. On the motor side, called psychokinesthesis (PK), people make things happen, as would have been the case had Jung made the bookcase go "bang."*

Figure 6-20   Testing for ESP. *In some tests, cards with five different designs are used and the subject tries to guess which design is on each card in a large deck. If success is significantly greater than 20 percent, the result is presumed to be a demonstration of ESP. If the subject scores significantly lower than 20 percent, the presence of negative ESP, in which the subject unconsciously is avoiding the correct answer, is postulated.*

Earlier we noted people who could "see" colors with their skin, an ability that was discovered to be a sensitivity to thermal stimulation.

Research methods. Because of reported occurrences of ESP, its study has been brought under closer scrutiny. In controlled studies, people attempt to indicate the symbol on a hidden card, the next number in a random series, or the content of another person's dreams. Statistical methods are used for data analysis, taking chance into account. The results may suggest that something other than guessing is taking place. Thus, the ESP hypothesis is maintained (Figure 6-20).

Tests of this hypothesis take place in all forms all over the world, within and outside the laboratory. In Argentina, a man was brought to the laboratory for study after several anecdotes about his personal life led researchers to believe that he might be a high-scoring ESP subject. He was tested in 15 experimental sessions, during which he attempted to reproduce several drawings made in another room by one of the experimenters. Then four judges ranked each of these drawings for degree of similarity to the experimenter's "target" drawings, and analyses suggested a correspondence above the level of chance (Musso & Granero, 1973).

In Sweden, each student in a regular university course received a special packet of test materials for a written examination. The test questions were on the outside of the opaque envelope, which could not be opened. Inside, unknown to the students, were the answers to some of the questions. After the students completed the examination, their results were scored by independent judges. They found a better-than-chance difference in some instances in favor of the questions in which ESP might have been used unconsciously to discover the correct but hidden answer (Johnson, 1973).

Problems remain. ESP research has always been subject to criticism, partly because it is extremely difficult to apply adequate controls when the basic research variable is essentially unknown. Thus, fault has been found with the various rating procedures, such as those used in the drawing experiment, and objections have been raised that nonsignificant results are too often ignored, as perhaps occurred in the exam study.

But not long ago ESP research received a far more severe setback than criticism raised against experimental designs, which occurs in any research. It was discovered that the director of one of the leading ESP laboratories in the world was falsifying research results (Rhine, 1974a). Ironically, this announcement came less than three months after the foremost American investigator of extrasensory perception had declared that deception was no longer an issue in ESP investigations (Rhine, 1974b).

In addition, there is still another fundamental problem in ESP research, apart from the possibilities of deception. The results in support of extrasensory perception generally become weaker as the controls against normal sensory awareness are improved. This circumstance is contrary to what one finds in other psychological research. Usually the effect grows stronger when extraneous variables are eliminated.

Still another difficulty is the lack of any conceptual framework for studying psychic phenomena. Despite a century of scientific investigation, there is no useful theory, not even according to Robert Thouless, one of the leading British figures in this field (Rhine, 1970). If ESP does exist, we have no adequate approach to interpreting such events at the present time.

Current investigators commonly assume that ESP does exist, based largely on statistical probabilities, and interest has turned to discovering those variables in the situation and in the personality that relate to its occurrence. Many researchers add, furthermore, that extrasensory perception is such a delicate capacity that the laboratory is just where it will not be found.

In all likelihood, the final outcome in the ESP question will not be a single, simple conclusion. Even the answer to what makes a person feel hungry, apart from the fact that he or she needs food, is very complex, and we are still learning the many secrets of vision, an area in which the basic variables apparently have been identified for years. Every month hundreds of new studies on vision alone are published. To believe that there is a single, simple answer—*the* answer—to the numerous incidents that raise the ESP hypothesis is probably unrealistic.

Summary

Awareness of Stimulation

1. All that we know of the world and of our own bodies comes from the brain's decoding of neural messages received from the sense organs, but we do not receive all the information that is potentially available. A stimulus must be above the absolute threshold to be perceived, and it must be below the terminal threshold in order not to be painful.

2. The difference threshold concerns sensitivity to a difference between stimulus intensities. In the normal ranges of intensity, it follows Weber's law, which states: the least amount of change in a stimulus that can be noticed is a constant fraction of that stimulus. This change is called a just noticeable difference (j.n.d.).

The Traditional Senses

3. Visual experience depends on the light transmitted to the eyes, physiological reactions in the cortex, and the individual's interpretation of these reactions. The human eye focuses an image on a light-sensitive surface known as the retina, which contains rods and cones. Rods concern black and white vision, while cones initiate color vision. When these receptors are activated, nerve impulses pass along the optic nerve to the brain. The Young-Helmholtz theory of color vision postulates that there are three types of cones, which are especially responsive to red, green, and blue wavelengths, with the other hues depending on simultaneous stimulation of combinations of these receptors. The Hering theory also postulates that there are three types of receptors, but they supposedly function in reciprocal fashion for certain pairs of colors.

4. The stimuli for hearing are sound waves entering the outer ear that make the eardrum vibrate. This vibration is carried through the middle ear and into the cochlear canals of the inner ear, where a liquid is set in motion, causing the bending of small hair cells. The movement of these cells arouses nerve impulses that travel over the auditory nerve to the brain. According to the place theory of hearing, certain regions of hair cells are especially attuned to certain vibration frequencies. According to the volley theory, nerve fibers operate in groups and thus the pitch of any tone depends on the frequency of volleys rather than on the frequency of vibration within any individual fiber.

5. Smell plays a subtle role in everyday life, especially in its contribution to what is usually considered to be taste. The olfactory receptors are located high in the nostrils and are stimulated only by substances in eddying gases.

6. Gustatory sensitivity consists of four primary qualities—salty, sour, sweet, and bitter. The receptors are small cells located in buds within the walls of the papillae of the tongue and, therefore, substances must be soluble to stimulate them. Olfactory and cutaneous cues are also important in taste.

7. The primary skin senses, once referred to as the sense of touch, are pressure, pain, and temperature. Cutaneous sensitivity to light pressure is mediated by hair follicles and unknown mechanisms, heavy pressure is probably mediated by the Pacinian corpuscles, and pain sensitivity is mediated by free nerve endings. No specialized receptors have been identified for warmth or cold.

The Proprioceptive Senses

8. Kinesthetic sensitivity results from activation of receptors in the muscles, tendons, and joints. Muscular activities and posture provide their own feedback, which underlies the automaticity of well-established motor responses.

9. Awareness of body position in space, such as being right side up or upside down, is based on activities in the nonauditory labyrinth of the inner ear. Hair cells in two small sacs, collectively known as the vestibular system, provide this information.

10. Awareness of rectilinear motion, which is passive movement in a straight line, also arises through events in the vestibular system, and the only adequate stimulus is a change in rate of movement. Sensitivity to rotary motion comes from another part of the nonauditory labyrinth. Hair cells in the semicircular canals are stimulated to bend one way or the other, and then they transmit impulses to the brain. Again, change in motion is the adequate stimulus. Vision, kinesthesis, and other sensory systems also contribute to our sense of body position, motion, and balance.

Sensation and Perception

11. Awareness usually involves intersensory or multisensory perception, which is information based on several sense organs and data previously stored in the brain. The various sensory systems operate in an interrelated and active manner.

12. Extrasensory perception implies perception without the involvement of any currently known sense organs. Most psychologists currently regard the evidence as not yet convincing; further research is necessary.

Suggested Readings

Carlson, N. *Physiology of behavior*. Boston: Allyn & Bacon, 1977. Prepared as an introduction to physiological psychology, this text contains chapters on receptor organs and sensory coding.

Gregory, R. L. *Eye and brain*. New York: World University Library, McGraw Hill, 1966. An abundantly illustrated, readable account of the psychology of seeing.

Gulick, W. L. *Hearing: Physiology and psychophysics*. New York: Oxford University Press, 1971. A brief illustrated text on methods and findings.

Schiffman, H. R. *Sensation and perception*. New York: Wiley, 1976. A basic text describing topics discussed in this and the next chapter.

Somjen, G. *Sensory coding in the mammalian nervous system*. New York: Plenum Press, 1975. Deals with the representation of sensory information at the receptor level, in the various modalities, and with the handling of such information in the central nervous system.

Chapter 7

Perception

In our daily lives we are literally bombarded with potential stimuli. Even as we sit in front of the television, it is impossible to respond to all the sights, sounds, and smells available to us, as well as to the subtle changes in temperature and pressure that impinge on our sense organs. Hence, we respond selectively to the environment.

What we see, hear, smell, taste, and otherwise experience, furthermore, is influenced by our past experience and present psychological state. Our perceptions are a function of stimulating circumstances both outside and inside the organism. In this chapter we are concerned with the ways in which human beings perceive their environment and find stability in such a potentially confusing world.

The Problem of Attending

For the most part, we perceive only those aspects of the environment to which we attend. *Attending* is a readiness to perceive; it is an expectancy based on our interests and motivations, as well as the nature of the stimuli to which we are exposed.

Aspects of the Stimulus

Advertisers are usually interested in catching our attention and thus much research has been devoted to the attention-getting value of various stimuli, as the reader well knows. For example, turn on a TV set, leave the volume constant, and observe the change in loudness when the commercials appear. The programs' sponsors want you to notice what they are selling, so they increase the intensity of the stimulating conditions. By *intensity*, we mean the strength of the stimulus, such as the brightness of a particular color or the loudness of a sound.

The *size* of the stimulus is related to intensity. In most of the words printed here, the letters are approximately the same size. Hence, a word printed in CAPITALS has greater attention-getting value than lower-cased words.

Another important determiner of attention is the *location* of the stimulus. The best position for a visual stimulus is directly in front of the eyes, but when this position is not possible on a magazine page or on the television screen, an advertisement placed in the upper portion of the page or screen is more likely to receive attention than one in the lower portion. A left-hand page receives more attention than a right-hand page, especially in the Western world, where people read from left to right and top to bottom.

We also know that certain *colors* are more attention-getting than others. Red and orange are high in attention value, but contrast is also important. If all the words here were in the same reddish color, a single word printed in black would stand out the most.

Also, *movement* or apparent movement is more likely to attract attention than a stationary stimulus. The neon signs of Broadway and the use of animated letters on the TV program "Sesame Street" illustrate this principle. A most important reason for the interest in television, as opposed to a newspaper or picture magazine, is the movement involved.

Finally, when other factors are approximately equal, the *novelty* of a stimulus is obviously important. A familiar item in unexpected surroundings or an unfamiliar item in common surroundings usually catches attention. A stimulus becomes novel in contrast to what is customary or expected. As we have seen, senses are designed primarily to be responsive to changes in the environment rather than to unchanging stimulation.

State of the Perceiver

All these factors are important, however, only to the degree that they arouse or pertain to an individual's interests, attitudes, and values. What an individual perceives is determined not only by the type of stimulation involved but also by the state of the perceiver (Figure 7-1).

Adjustments of the organism. Observe a person watching television or, better yet, ask someone to examine something he or she has never seen previously. Note the person's eye movements as he or she scans the screen or the object, the posture changes as he or she observes it from various angles, and how the facial muscles are drawn tighter as he or she tries to interpret the stimulation. These reactions are some of the bodily adjustments required in attending.

An example of the increased muscle tension in attending was shown in an experiment where subjects listened for a barely audible click and one known to be obviously audible. In both instances recordings were made of the electrical activity in four different muscle groups of the body, and as soon as the sound was heard the subject was required to press a key. Analysis of the results showed a general thickening of the muscles when the subjects were attending to both types of sounds, but the response was greater when the subject was expecting the weaker sound (Freeman, 1931).

When a dog "pricks up" its ears, we see another adjustment. Some animals not only point their ears but also turn them to permit better reception of sound waves. Most of us cannot move our ears, but sometimes we move our heads to facilitate auditory reception, an adjustment that is especially evident in a person who has hearing in only one ear.

These adjustments in attending are collectively known as the *orienting response*, that is, an organism's initial constellation of reactions to any given stimulation. As illustrated, many aspects are not observable without special apparatus. These include dilation of the blood vessels, changes in the skin's electrical activity, altered heartbeat rate and greater rapidity of brain waves. Russian psychologists, in particular, are interested in this series of reactions, having demonstrated, for example, several influences on the skin's electrical activity. It increases with the novelty of the stimulus, with motivating instructions, and even when the stimuli are simply incongruous with one another (Berlyne et al., 1963).

Processes in attending. Unfortunately, the stimulus characteristics in attending and even the organism's adjustment reactions have been far easier to identify and describe than the attentive processes within the individual. The state *seems* simple—the organism is simply ready to perceive. But in what way is it ready and how is the selection process accomplished?

For example, does the selection of stimuli in attending take place at the receptors in terms of what information enters the organism? Or does it occur later, in the central nervous system? These questions have been studied for decades, often with conflicting results, but improvements in methods have led to recent advancements. First, human attention to an acoustic signal now can be measured by the electrical activity evoked in the cerebral cortex and, second, the response of the auditory nerve

can be recorded from the auditory canal by use of a needle electrode. The latter procedure can cause some discomfort, however, and so in one study, four experimenters served as their own subjects. Sometimes they listened for faint clicks presented through earphones and at other times they read a book, ignoring the clicks. The findings showed an increase in evoked potential from the scalp when the subjects were attending to the clicks rather than reading, but there was no effective change from one condition to the other in the auditory nerve. The recorded action potential of the nerve remained essentially stable under the varying conditions of attention (Picton et al., 1971). In short, there was no evidence that the basic selection process occurs through some sifting or percolating system at the receptor level.

But evidence for where stimulus selection occurs does not tell us how it takes place. What happens in the central nervous system? This question is extremely difficult to answer, but recent experiments suggest that two kinds of conscious selection processes may be involved, as illustrated in the following study. A series of 12 unrelated words was projected onto the same place on a screen in front of the human subject. The total elapsed time for the entire series was less than 1 second, which means that each item appeared instantaneously. In observing this sequence, the subject was asked to identify a certain word, such as the word in capital

Figure 7-2 Influence of Set.
What do you see, a letter or a number? Persons who have just seen D, P, and E tend to see B, but those previously exposed to 38, 52, and 74 see 13.

■ *A few weeks ago, a group of relatives and friends were watching home movies of my brother's wedding. . . . Having been an usher, I was mostly concerned with how many times I appeared, and how I looked. While thinking that I had really looked pretty good, a "friend" perceived that I looked 15 pounds overweight, my mother distinctly noticed that I appeared with a cocktail at least 5 times, and my fiancée thought I looked a bit smug while dancing with a bridesmaid.*

letters when all others appeared in lower case, or the name of an animal when the other words all referred to something else. It was found, as the reader may suspect, that the first task was far easier than the second, apparently because so little information is required concerning the irrelevant stimuli. Deciding that the words do not appear in capital letters demands the gathering of less information than deciding in each instance that they do not concern animals (Lawrence, 1971).

The two types of attentive processes illustrated in this experiment have been called filtering and pigeonholing. In *filtering,* a stimulus is selected because it possesses some specific sensory feature not found in other events. In *pigeonholing,* however, the stimuli in question do not necessarily differ by just a single, readily discernible feature. They must be distinguished by various combinations of features and thus this kind of attending requires far more processing of information than is the case in filtering (Broadbent, 1977).

Focusing on the more complex operation, investigators have tried to understand how we make the decisions involved in pigeonholing. They have asked: Is pigeonholing an active process, in which the perceiver seeks information relevant to the percept in question, or is it a more passive process, in which the data initially are admitted unselectively? While it is still early, recent experiments seem to suggest a two-stage process. In the first stage, the incoming information is handled in a global, more passive manner, being processed only into different segments or groups of data. Then there appears to be a later, more active stage in which further inquiry is made into the details in the original segments. This viewpoint is still highly speculative, but the data upon which it is based represent a significant advance in our understanding of the attending processes in recent years (Broadbent, 1977).

Attending and set. Attending is a readiness to perceive; it involves an expectancy. But as some of the previous experiments suggest, a person can attend with a *specific* expectancy or frame of reference in mind. Thus, there is a condition known as *set,* also called *perceptual set,* which is more than attending; it is attending or a readiness to perceive *in a certain manner* (Figure 7-2). ■

This expectancy is based on past experience and personal characteristics, temporary or relatively enduring. Thus, a psychiatrist says: "Think of your mother. If you and I see her at the same time, we certainly see very different persons. I, of course, do not know what you see; but I may see an attractive mature woman . . . or a fat, frowsy, old bore, or an interesting example of some obscure skin disease" (Preston, 1940). Here, rather pompously, the psychiatrist is indicating that his personal interests influence what he sees. Hopefully, he would be more interested in the skin disease in the clinic and in the mature woman as at a party.

Set is enormously influential in perception, so much so that people sometimes seem to have lied about what they have perceived. Witnesses and even experts in court often differ dramatically, not necessarily because they wish to deceive but because of perceptual distortions imposed on them by their hopes, fears, and expectations.

There is no doubt that people find in their environments the things they are looking for, the sorts of things that they are motivated to see in the first place. As Shakespeare said:

Or in the night, imagining some fear.
How easy is a bush supposed a bear!
  (Midsummer Night's Dream)

The Perception of Objects

Set is always a factor in any perceptual experience. It determines, in part, what we see, but it does not explain how we see. After attending, we are still left with the famous question posed by Kurt Koffka: "Why do things look the way they do?" Koffka was one of the founders of the field of gestalt psychology, in which there was much interest in the problem of perception, as we shall see. The gestalt psychologists began, as we do here, by trying to understand the ways in which individuals organize stimuli into basic patterns.

Organizing the Perceptual Field

In our simplest perceptions a *figure* or pattern is perceived as having a certain shape or contour, and it stands out against a *background* or ground. There is a certain theme and surroundings, which comprise the *figure-ground relationship*. Thus, a television set is perceived in a room or a figure is seen on the television screen. This perception is so basic that it is usually considered the starting point in organized perceptual experience (Haber & Hershenson, 1973).

Figure-ground relationships. As a rule, the figure and background are relatively unchanging, prompting stability in the perceived environment. As you read this page, you do not reverse the figure and ground. You do not focus on the background, which is the white paper, rather than the black print. Usually, the separation of figure from ground is accomplished rather easily.

It would be difficult to prove that these perceptual tendencies are inborn, although animals, children, and diverse groups of adults behave as if the stimulating properties were the same for them as for us. The discrimination of figure from ground is certainly present early in life, but investigations suggest that it is not automatically achieved by observing a stimulus pattern (Haber & Hershenson, 1973). In fact, clever artists' drawings indicate that we can sometimes be misled (Figure 7-3).

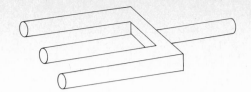

More important for understanding perceptual processes, however, are those occasional instances in which we unintentionally reverse figure-ground relationships. After a few moments' observation, the figure in some stimulus patterns becomes the background, and the ground becomes the figure (Figure 7-4). The viewer can create these shifts intentionally, but they increase automatically as the viewing time is lengthened, which suggests a process of

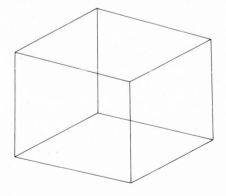

Figure 7-3   Impossible Figure-Ground. *The tines of the fork sometimes seem to be the figure, sometimes the ground.*

Figure 7-4   Reversible Configurations. *The figure and ground alternate. Sometimes you see a white vase against a dark background; other times you see two dark faces against a white background. When reversals occur with the cube, the cube sometimes seems to be above the viewer, and at other times it seems to be lower than the viewer.*

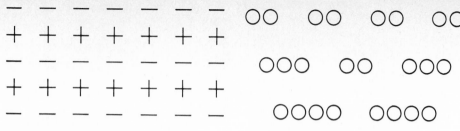

Figure 7-5 Principles of Grouping: Similarity. *The signs are viewed as five rows rather than seven columns, even though the distances between the rows and columns are approximately equal.*

Figure 7-6 Principles of Grouping: Proximity. *The rows of eight circles are seen as forming groups of two, three, or four, depending on their nearness to one another.*

■ *This past summer I worked in the same supermarket that I did last year and it didn't take me long to get used to the prices again. All of the items are supposed to be properly marked, but often the figures are smudged or one of the digits is unclear. If the item is a common one, however, and the price is not entirely clear, I can usually check the item right through, ringing up the proper amount, without even realizing that one of the digits is missing. Although incomplete, I recognize the total price by the digits that are present.*

stimulus satiation in the central nervous system. With prolonged observation, the neural mechanisms become fatigued, and the figure begins to fade; eventually, it is replaced by the ground, which becomes the figure for a time, until the nervous system is again satiated, and another reversal occurs. As each point of fatigue is reached more quickly, the shifts take place more frequently. Earlier, we noted that the sensory system of the human organism is responsive chiefly to changes in stimulation, and in studies of motivation it has been demonstrated that human beings confined to an unchanging environment actively seek sensory variation.

Perceptual grouping. Since a pattern usually has several parts, the next problem concerns how the parts of the figure are organized. Again, the earliest gestalt psychologists described certain principles of organization. As we mentioned earlier in the book, *gestalt* means "form" or "configuration," and the different stimulus elements were said to be grouped on the basis of certain configurational principles.

According to the *principle of similarity,* stimuli of similar shape, size, or color tend to be grouped together. With neither figure on the television screen, for example, you could still identify the words spoken by a husband and wife by the similarity of the tones in each person's speech. You know the players on

one basketball team from those on another by the color of the uniforms (Figure 7-5).

The *principle of proximity* refers to the tendency to perceive stimuli near one another as belonging together. Grouped one way, these letters read: MAC HIN ERY. Grouped differently, they indicate MACHINERY. This principle also applies in the auditory realm. Ask a friend to listen while you tap twice in rapid succession, wait an interval, and tap twice again. When asked how many taps he or she has heard, your listener probably will report two pairs of taps, rather than four altogether (Figure 7-6).

Sometimes the viewer cannot see the whole figure, as when a person is partly hidden by someone else or partly excluded from the television image, but we ignore the absence of the unseen parts. In the *principle of closure,* one would still perceive this person, providing enough of the body is visible. When a band strikes up in the distance, the music is heard only intermittently or may be obscured by traffic noises, but the song is often recognized (Figure 7-7). ■

In the *principle of continuity,* any line or movement tends to be perceived as continuing in the direction already established. Stimuli that form a continuous pattern are perceived as a whole; they make an obvious or "good" pattern. If a hat and walking stick are lying together, we would decide which lines belong to the hat and which to the stick on the basis of the natural continuity, although

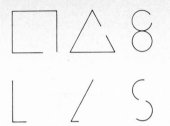

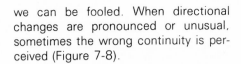

Figure 7-7   Principles of Grouping: Closure. *The top figures are recognized as a square, triangle, and number. The bottom figures are too incomplete to be recognized as such symbols.*

Figure 7-8   Principles of Grouping: Continuity. *The upper figure is more likely to be perceived as a hat and a cross than as four segments, because we perceive patterns on the basis of continuous forms to which we are accustomed.*

we can be fooled. When directional changes are pronounced or unusual, sometimes the wrong continuity is perceived (Figure 7-8).

Problems in grouping. Stimulus conditions, necessarily described sequentially here, usually appear simultaneously in a stimulus pattern. Furthermore, they usually support one another, making a readily discernible figure-ground pattern, as when green wine bottles are together at one end of the table and brown ones are at the other end. Both similarity and proximity prompt the observer to perceive two groups of bottles, or two figures, against a single background. But what happens when the green ones form a semicircle on one half of the table that connects with an identical semicircle formed by the brown ones on the other half? Most likely, through the principle of closure, the observer will perceive one full circle of bottles. This illustration is not to say that closure is ascendant over the others but rather that each principle usually occurs in the context of the others, and it is their interaction that influences perception.

At other times, these principles are used intentionally to render objects less visible, and the result is called *camouflage.* All the principles of grouping can

serve this purpose, but certainly the most important is color, which is an aspect of similarity.

Perception as information processing. The gestalt approach generally emphasizes apparently inborn ways of perceiving the world, as illustrated in the figure-ground relationship and the principles of grouping. Since these perceptual tendencies appear in diverse human cultures, it has been assumed that they are imposed on us by the nature of the stimulus and the ways in which our sensory and neural structures are organized. These principles are not the subject of much current research, however, because they cannot be readily studied in the laboratory. They are essentially descriptions of the perceptual outcome rather than statements of the underlying processes.

More recently, studies of perception have emphasized the perceiver's role in interpreting the stimuli to which he or she is exposed. That is, the perception of any stimulus is influenced by the way the perceiver processes the information, even in figure-ground relationships. In this more recent approach, called *information processing,* it is assumed that the incoming messages are selected, analyzed, and then organized, as necessary, according to the individual's best interpretation of the data. In trying to

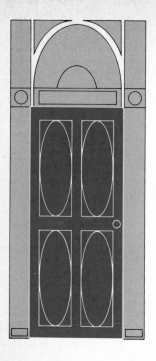 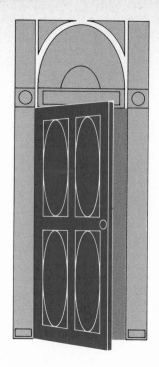 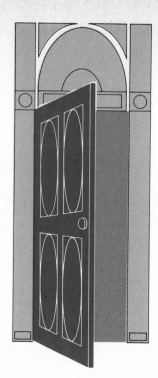 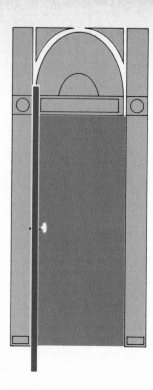

Figure 7-9 Shape Constancy.
The retinal image is trapezoidal in the second and third instances, yet the door is perceived as rectangular. (After J. J. Gibson, The Perception of the Visual World, p. 170. Copyright 1950 by Houghton Mifflin Company.)

understand the stimuli to which he or she is exposed, the perceiver does so actively, not automatically; he or she is selective in the message that is being considered and is constantly forming interpretations. This approach was illustrated in our earlier discussion of attending, especially in the concepts of filtering and pigeonholing.

Perceptual Constancy

If you were typical of millions of television viewers in the 1970s, you might have turned to "All in the Family" and said that Archie Bunker was on TV because an image of that well-known bigot appeared on the screen. But as you looked at Archie, his image actually changed a great deal from moment to moment. When he walked across the stage, the image on your retina via the TV screen was different at different moments, depending on his location and body positions and the locations of the cameras. When he was far away, the image was small and it may have been green because of the stage lighting. Yet

you did not perceive him as distorted in shape, six inches tall, or greenish in complexion. This tendency for objects to look essentially the same under different viewing conditions is known as *perceptual constancy*.

Types of perceptual constancy. The door in the Bunkers' hallway appeared rectangular regardless of the position from which it was viewed. Here we have an example of *shape constancy*, which occurs whenever an object appears to maintain its form or shape despite marked changes in the retinal image (Figure 7-9).

Look at some small familiar object, holding it close to your eyes and then gradually moving it away. The probability is high that its perceived size does not change a great deal, although the retinal image has become smaller. This demonstration illustrates *size constancy*. Similarly, actors on the opposite side of the stage have a smaller image than those closer to you, but they all look about the same size.

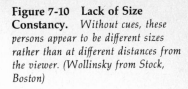

A white rabbit in the setting sun is reflecting orange rays, but it is not seen as orange. It is perceived as white, and *color constancy* has occurred. Actually, the rabbit appears a little less white than usual because some compromise occurs in all constancies. The actors on the other side of the stage, especially if they are unfamiliar, look a bit smaller than their actual stature, and Archie Bunker, in the green lighting, looks a bit greener than usual.

Three terms are often usefully employed in discussions of constancy and other perceptual phenomena. The term *distal stimulus* refers to the stimulus "out there" in the world. It is physical energy at its source, such as the light waves emanating from the figure of Archie Bunker. The term *proximal stimulus* refers to the physical energy at the receptor; it consists of the light waves impinging on the observer's retina. The difference between these stimuli is created not only by molecules of the air, as the light waves are scattered, but also

by the lens of the viewer's eyes, which refocuses the light again, and the humors and other eye mechanisms as the light passes to the retina. The paradox and also the blessing of the constancy phenomena is that the *perceived stimulus,* which is the viewer's experience as he or she looks at the world, corresponds not so much to the proximal stimulus, on which it is based, as to the distal stimulus (Weintraub & Walker, 1969).

Importance of context. All the constancies depend partly on environmental cues and they tend to disappear when the cues are removed. When the props are taken away and we have no other cues to distance, actors on the other side of the stage, because they are not seen as more distant, appear to be much smaller in size than those nearby (Figure 7-10). The rabbit, if we do not know it is in the setting sun, appears to have some color mutation. In the maintenance of constancies, knowledge of the context and prior experience with the viewed object are most important (Wohlwill, 1960).

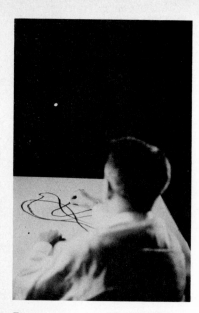

Figure 7-11 Autokinetic Effect.
Sometimes the person draws on paper the movements he or she perceives in the stationary point of light. Special arrangements were made for this photograph; the illusion occurs only in a fully darkened room. (Fritz Goro, Life Magazine, © Time, Inc.)

A correct interpretation of the proximal stimulus is also readily achieved because there is so much redundant information in the environment. Archie Bunker is always with the same people and often wearing the same clothes. Except with reversible figures and other demonstrations, which must be carefully prepared, there is usually more information than necessary for interpreting the stimulus. Even with intentionally ambiguous figures, such as the Rorschach inkblots, we are generally not confused. We simply decide what the blots *seem* to look like, knowing that the stimulus pattern is imperfect.

The relative constancy of perceived objects is obviously essential. Think of the confusion that would exist if we responded to every aspect of our world in terms of retinal images alone. Objects would seem to be constantly shrinking or enlarging or changing their shape or color as corresponding changes occurred in the retinal image. Even the simplest routines in daily life would be almost impossible to accomplish.

Movement, Space, and Illusions

Sometimes our perceptions do involve changing retinal images, and then we may see movement. But the perceptual phenomena of movement are not that simple, and we have a great deal more to learn. Even when there is no change in the distal stimulus, the perceived object is sometimes reported to be moving, as we shall see in the autokinetic effect.

Awareness of Movement

The basic condition for the visual experience of movement is successive stimulation of different rods and cones. As a distal stimulus moves within our visual field, the proximal stimulus activates different receptors. A man is sitting in a chair and a woman is walking towards him. His image is stationary while her image stimulates one and then the other side of the retina.

Real and induced motion. The visual experience of movement becomes more complex when you are sitting on a train in the station, looking out the window. You can see only the train on the next track, and suddenly your train seems to be moving, although you have experienced no jolt at the start. The images on your retina are successively stimulating different receptors but, without further information, a misperception has occurred. When you look out the window again and do not experience successive images with respect to a telephone pole, you know it is the other train that is moving.

To perceive *real movement,* you need a reference point. When you have none, the movement is sometimes attributed to the wrong stimulus; then it is called *induced movement.* Movement is perceived in a stationary stimulus because another stimulus is moving. In looking at the sky on a moonlit but cloudy night, you sometimes experience induced movement. The moon seems to dart behind the clouds, but when there are treetops in your visual field, the clouds show the movement.

Autokinetic effect. Perceived movement also can occur when both the distal stimulus and the viewer are stationary. You can observe this result yourself by covering the front end of a flashlight with black paper, making a pinhole for the light to shine through, and then placing the lighted flashlight on a table 10 to 20 feet away in a *completely* dark room. For almost every observer, this small, fixed spot of light seems to move around in different directions, as though transported by a silent machine (Figure 7-11).

This phenomenon is called the *autokinetic effect* because the light seems to move by itself. Its bases are essentially unknown, but two comments are relevant. First, the apparent motion immediately ceases when another light is displayed or when the illumination is increased. Thus, the absence of a reference point is essential. Second, this

Figure 7-12 Eye Fixations. *An eye-movement camera was used to photograph the subject's gaze as he or she looked at the picture. The numbers show the sequence of fixations. Unshaded circles indicate constriction of the pupils, light circles indicate normal pupillary openings, and dark circles indicate dilation of the pupils, suggesting special interest in what is being perceived. The woman and man apparently were interested in different aspects of the picture. (After Hess, 1965)*

Museum of Art, Carnegie Institute, Pittsburgh

WOMAN'S FIXATIONS

MAN'S FIXATIONS

illusion may be related to our continuous eye movements, which occur as we seek visual information in the world around us. In fact, one would expect the world to be a constant blur before our eyes because they are moving constantly. Some of these movements are evident when someone is scanning a line of print or watching a ball go back and forth at a tennis match.

These voluntary and involuntary movements are known as *saccadic movements,* during which we are temporarily blind. They occur whenever we change our point of fixation (Figure 7-12). The human eye is in almost constant motion, yet the world appears stable because we actually see only during the fixations.

Cues in Space Perception

The human eye has an extremely thin retina, less than one-half a millimeter in thickness. It has no significant depth, and the proximal stimulus has no significant depth, even when it contains the images of two objects at different distances from the eyes. How then do we see in three dimensions?

The answer, at least in terms of *what* stimuli we use, is fairly clear. Psychologists have uncovered a number of *monocular* cues, available to just one eye, and *binocular* cues, requiring both eyes. Most monocular cues are also called *psychological,* meaning that they depend on characteristics of the visual image, rather than on the structure of the retina.

Monocular cues. One obvious distance cue is *interposition,* which occurs whenever one image on the retina partially obscures another. The obscured object loses its contour and therefore is judged as more distant. Another cue comes from *shadows,* as when the sunlight falls from certain angles.

As objects become distant, they decrease in size and seem closer together. This condition is known as *linear perspective.* Trees, telephone poles, and other objects seem to grow smaller and railroad tracks seem to converge as they recede into the distance. *Aerial perspective* is quite different, referring to the increasing haziness of distant details due to atmospheric conditions, as when a nearby mountain is seen in greater detail than a more distant one.

Another cue to distance is the *relative speed and direction of movement* of viewed objects. When an object moves by rapidly, it is perceived as close at hand, partly because it obscures more objects than when it is moving at a distance. When the viewer is moving, or simply moves his or her head, nearby objects seem to move past in the opposite direction and those at a distance seem to move in the same direction as the viewer's movement. However, both sets of objects cannot appear to move at the same time. When the point of fixation is a nearer object, the distant ones seem to move, and vice versa.

Finally, a most important monocular cue is the *size of the retinal image,* which is normally larger for nearby objects than for distant ones. ■ But one must be acquainted with the actual size of the object to make this distinction. Clouds might be of almost any size; hence, it is difficult to know whether we are seeing a large cloud far away or a small cloud nearby.

Usually, these cues are available at the same time, although occasionally there may be some conflict. Perhaps a tree partly obscures a building, yet it is hazier, due to unusual atmospheric conditions. Then the overall evidence is evaluated; as in this case, interposition is usually considered the stronger cue. More often, the cues support one another and depth perception is readily achieved.

All these monocular cues are called psychological because they depend on characteristics of the visual image, but another monocular cue is considered *physiological* because it arises from the structure and movement of the eyes. In *accommodation,* the curvature of the lens changes, or accommodates, as the perceiver focuses on objects at different distances. It increases for objects close at hand and decreases when more distant objects are brought into focus. This adjustment, made by muscles attached to the eye mechanisms, evokes nerve impulses that apparently provide the brain with information about the relative distance of the perceived objects (Figure 7-13).

Binocular cues. There are two generally recognized binocular cues, both of which are physiological. In *convergence,* the eyes turn inward as we look at objects, and they do so more for nearby

■ *As a child, while I was supposed to be napping, I used to hold my thumb in front on my face and line it up with a door across the room. I was fascinated by the effect because my thumb appeared to be the same size as the door. I knew it wasn't, but because it was close to my face, the image was large.*

Figure 7-13 Monocular Depth Cues. *All the monocular cues to depth perception except movement occur in this Paris street scene. (Photo by Henri Cartier-Bresson, © Magnum Photos Inc.)*

SIZE OF RETINAL IMAGE

INTERPOSITION

LINEAR PERSPECTIVE

SHADOWS

AERIAL PERSPECTIVE

ACCOMMODATION

Figure 7-14   Principle of the Stereoscope.   *The left-hand and right-hand pictures are directly in front of the left and right eyes. However, as the two images pass through the prisms, they are thrown toward the outer parts of the retinas, where they would be if only one object was being viewed, with depth, straight ahead. As a result, the two images are perceived as one, at a point midway between the two pictures, where the dashed lines meet. (Sheila A. Farr photo)*

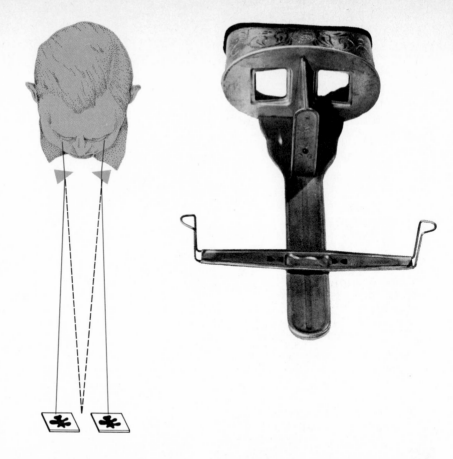

Figure 7-15   Stereoscopic Effects.   *Notice that the two images were photographed from slightly different viewpoints. Place a piece of thin cardboard twelve inches in length vertically between the two images and place your nose at the edge of the cardboard, so that each eye is exposed to only one image. Looking straight down at the pictures, if you can fuse the two images together, you will experience a single photograph in three dimensions.*

objects than distant ones. The aroused nerve impulses travel to the brain, serving as cues to distance. For distant objects, however, the movements are so small that they are of doubtful value. The purpose of these movements is to prevent blurred vision by placing the image closest to the fovea, where vision is clearest.

Since the eyes have different locations in the head, each obtains a somewhat different picture of the same situation, as can be experienced by holding a small object near your face and alternately closing one eye and then the other. The right eye sees more of one side while the left eye sees more of the other. This difference is referred to as *retinal disparity,* and the closer the object is to the viewer, the greater the disparity, which is therefore another distance cue. ■

The principle of *stereoscopic vision* is based on retinal disparity. When a stereoscope is used, the right eye sees only the picture taken by a camera on the right, and the left eye sees only the one taken by a camera on the left. The function of the prisms is to throw the disparate images on the same regions of the retina that would be stimulated if the original scene were viewed by the two eyes under normal circumstances (Figure 7-14). Stereoscopic effects also can be obtained without prisms, but here the observer must fuse the two images himself (Figure 7-15).

Development of space perception. The existence of these spatial cues in animals and young children has prompted observers to wonder whether they are inherited and therefore fully present at birth. For example, animals that are born with their eyes open and able to move around soon after birth avoid a cliff without learning. Such findings suggest innate depth perception. Human beings cannot be tested until they are able to crawl, at the age of six months or more. They avoid a cliff at this time, but considerable learning already has occurred (Figure 7-16).

Figure 7-16   Testing Early Space Perception. *This apparatus is called a "visual cliff" because it only presents the appearance of a cliff. Its purpose is to test depth perception in infants without exposing them to any danger. On one side of the board in the center the patterned squares are directly under the glass, and on the other side they are on the floor. When human infants are induced to leave the firm middle board, almost all of them crawl onto the "shallow" cliff. Such experiments in various species suggest that depth perception is often present soon after birth (Gibson & Walk, 1960). (William Vandivert photo)*

■ *When I was younger I would stare for hours at distant things, pointing my finger directly at things with both eyes open, and then close first one eye, then the other. The object I focused on seemed to move its position, and I used to think that there was something wrong with my eyes.*

It is possible that moving about in the environment aids in the development of depth perception, and this hypothesis was tested with kittens. All the animals were reared in darkness, and some were given a ride every day in a small carousel, from which they could see their environment but could not move around in it actively. Others were given the same visual experience, but it was achieved by walking around instead. How would the two groups perform when presented with some problem in depth perception, such as a cliff?

The results were quite clear. Depth perception did not develop adequately in the passive kittens. Those that rode in the carousel showed no awareness of the precipice. On the other hand, none of the walkers went over the cliff. For them, apparently the visual cues came to have meaning through association with muscular and tactual experiences (Held & Hein, 1963; Hein et al., 1970).

In another experiment, human beings were tested at ages 6 to 20 days with an object moving towards them, of which they showed an awareness. The head moved backwards, the eyes opened wide, and the hands sometimes were raised in front of the face (Bower et al., 1970). Confirming results were found in other experiments (Ball & Trodnick, 1971). Apparently some space cues are available to human beings very soon after birth, but undoubtedly further experience helps us develop and refine the use of these cues, especially those for longer distances.

Investigations of blind people further underscore the potential contribution of learning. In one instance, investigators studied more than 60 people, all of whom were congenitally blind but later had vision restored through cataract removal. After the operation they had no significant problems dealing with colors and certain figure-ground relationships, but they were quite confused about distance and other aspects of their new visual world. They were even unable to identify familiar objects through vision.

After being allowed to touch and trace them, sometimes practicing for weeks, they gained more normal use of visual cues (Senden, 1932).

Auditory and other cues. Another reason we perceive in three dimensions with a two-dimensional retina lies in the nonvisual cues we use, as illustrated by blind persons. Some decades ago, an extensive series of investigations by psychologists showed that, apart from touch, blind people rely most heavily on auditory cues in detecting unseen objects. The helpful sounds come not only from the objects themselves, as in the motor of an engine, but also from reflected sound waves, such as the individual's footsteps echoing from a wall, building, or other obstacle (Supa et al., 1944).

In general, increasing *loudness* is associated with decreasing distance; when a sound grows louder, we know that the object is approaching. Increasing *complexity* is also associated with decreasing distance. Only a low hum is audible when an airplane is far away, but when it is close we hear a great variety of sounds. Furthermore, the perceived *spatial volume* is also a cue. Nearby sounds seem to fill more space than distant ones. The roar of a jet taking off nearby seems to be everywhere, but at a distance it appears to take up relatively little space.

In perceiving the distance and *direction* of sounds, we are often aided by previously acquired knowledge. We know that the aircraft is overhead and, therefore, we look in that direction. We know that the traffic sounds come from the road and look over there to find them.

Without vision and knowledge of the situation, we need the use of two ears in order to locate the direction of a sound, which must stimulate each ear differently. There can be a *time difference*, which occurs when the sound reaches one ear before the other. There can be an *intensity difference,* when the sound stimulates the closer ear more strongly. Finally, there can be a *phase difference,* which occurs when a sound reaches the two ears at different points in its cycle, striking the nearer ear at one stage in its cycle, such as the crest of a wave, and the farther ear at another, such as the trough. When none of these differences occurs, as when the sound is equidistant from the two ears, it cannot be located by auditory cues alone.

Having an ear on each side of the head is not like having a spare part, as in the case of kidneys. Both ears are essential to locating sound only by hearing, called *auditory localization,* just as having two eyes in different positions provides the spatial cue of retinal disparity.

In addition, our space perceptions come from olfactory, cutaneous, and kinesthetic cues. The sense of smell, although not highly developed in human beings, makes it possible to determine the direction and distance of some odor-giving objects and organisms. Temperature sensitivity aids us in the detection of a draft or a warm gust of air, and the skin tells us about the sizes and shapes of objects that we handle without looking at them. Muscle movement also plays an obvious role in the perception of nearby space.

The Problem of Illusions

Sometimes, even with practice and continued exposure, we still perceive a given stimulus incorrectly. In this case, the stimulus pattern probably constitutes an *illusion,* which is a common but erroneous way of perceiving the world; it does not correspond to the objective situation as determined by physical measurement. This term is perhaps an unfortunate one, however, suggesting the idea of magic or deception, which is not involved (Figure 7-17).

Shape: *The right-hand circle is the same shape as the one on the left.*

Direction: *The diagonal lines are parallel.*

Size: *The three cylinders are the same size.*

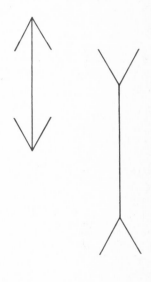

Length: *The vertical lines are the same length.*

Figure 7-17   Illusions.

Movement: phi phenomenon. We all experience the illusion of movement whenever we see a motion picture or a movie on TV. A succession of still images, each appearing in a slightly different position, one after the other at a suitable rate, gives this illusion. We observe the same result in electrical advertising signs when the figure that appears to move from one position to another is actually two figures in different locations, flashed alternately.

If the interval between flashes is too long, one light is seen to go on, then the other, and there is no apparent movement. If the interval is too short, two lights are seen flashing at approximately the same time. If one flash follows the other at an appropriate interval, which depends on the space between the lights, their size, and their brightness, a light is seen moving from one position to the other. When this illusion was first demonstrated experimentally around 1912, the experience was considered so basic yet so impossible to analyze in terms of its components, that it was simply described in terms of a Greek letter—the *phi phenomenon*.

Immediately, a counter-argument was offered: the illusory movement was due to kinesthetic sensations in the eyes. In looking from one figure to the other, the eyes were in motion. These muscle movements produced the phi phenomenon.

Thus, the phi phenomenon was studied in such a way that eye movements could not be responsible for the outcome. Two pairs of figures were used, one above the other, and the intervals between exposures were set so that the perceived movement would be left to right in one instance and right to left in the other. In this arrangement, the movement was perceived to occur in two opposite directions at the same time, which would be impossible if the illusion was based on eye movements from one position to the other.

The phi phenomenon apparently is dependent on some fixed reaction of the visual system to these particular stimulus relationships. It is speculated that this reaction perhaps ensures that we perceive very fast-moving objects as moving (Rock, 1975).

Shape: Sander's parallelogram. Illusions involving distance and shape are even more common than illusions involving movement. Adults, children, and animals respond to many configurations in a manner that suggests that they experience an illusion. One wonders, therefore, whether learning plays a role in these instances.

To study this issue, a group of investigators formulated the "carpentered-world" hypothesis: people constantly exposed to carpentered objects, such as doors, tables, walls, platforms, benches, and other rectangular objects, should respond differently to illusions involving these patterns than should people who are less familiar with rectangular forms. If learning is important, the Zulus, for example, should be less susceptible to a parallelogram illusion than residents of a carpentered world. The Zulus spend much time outside, recognize the circle as the dominant pattern, and have little experience with rectangles. When they were tested and the results were compared with those from residents of Illinois, group differences were found. The carpentered-world hypothesis was supported, and the role of learning was suggested (Herskovits et al., 1969; Figure 7-18).

Since susceptibility to illusions was found in all the 15 cultures tested, biological factors are clearly involved to some degree. However, the large group differences indicate that experience is an important augmenting factor. In fact, the chief thrust of this chapter so far is that human perception, while dependent on inherited sense organs and neural structures, is something more than a simple reception of information "out there" in the world around us. To this stimulation we inevitably add the influence of earlier learning.

In short, perception involves a synthesizing or creative process. We try to make something meaningful out of the information coming from the environment and previous experience. To some degree, we create our own perceptions. This circumstance has prompted the following remark: "Our perceptions come from us, not from our surroundings. The perceiver decides what an object is. . . . He makes it what he chooses to make it, and can make it, in the light of his unique experience and purpose'' (Kelley, 1955).

The Perception of People

Perhaps the most obvious instance in which people ''add to'' the stimulation in the environment is the perception of other people. Human beings are endlessly trying to make accurate judgments about other human beings, but often they meet with little success. What factors make person perception so much more difficult than object perception?

Obstacles in Person Perception

First, when people perceive one another they usually try to go beyond physical characteristics. They try to understand the other individual from a psychological standpoint as well.

Archie Bunker has a large forehead, is rather fat, and wears nondescript clothes, but these characteristics are not as important to the viewer as his feelings, attitudes, and personality traits. The viewer usually is looking for internal and abstract qualities, although his or her information is limited to physical and behavioral characteristics. Thus, the viewer makes an inference about the inner qualities. The stimulation received from the environment is combined with previously established ideas, now stored in the brain, in forming an impression of Mr. Bunker. The perceiver is being creative in his or her perceptions, but also may be making an error.

In passing, we should note that the relationships between physical characteristics and personality have been studied extensively, and the findings have not been impressive. If Mr. Bunker has a large forehead, we cannot say very much about what that means in terms of personality characteristics. There is no significant relationship between the size of one's forehead and his or her intelligence, and the relationship between

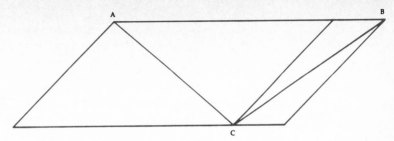

Figure 7-18   Sander's Parallelogram Illusion. *The AC diagonal appears about the same length as BC, but it is 16 percent shorter. If the parallelogram actually were a table top seen from one side and slightly above, the left-hand diagonal would represent a greater distance across the surface than the right-hand diagonal. Hence, it is judged longer. Note the circular huts, the circular cattle pen, and the circular kraal used by the Zulu of South Africa, who are not as susceptible to this illusion as are people from more ''carpentered'' cultures. (Photo by James W. Fernandez, Princeton University)*

body type and personality is doubtful. Even in the few instances where correlations have been found, they pertain to groups of people rather than to individuals (Rees, 1961; Walker, 1962). Archie may have been rather fat, but he was not necessarily good-natured, as a common stereotype suggests.

A second problem is that the qualities being perceived are changing. In object perception, the size, shape, and color of a stationary object can change, in terms of the retinal image, as the perceiver moves about in space. To achieve object constancy, the observer must make generalizations based on different perceptual experiences. In person perception this problem is considerably increased because the perceived individual also moves about, grows older, becomes emotional, changes physically, and acquires new ideas and interests. By contrast, a table is far less changeable.

Finally, person perception can be a two-way process. When a man looks at a table, the table does not look back, but when you meet Archie Bunker in real life, as the actor Carroll O'Connor, you perceive him and he perceives you. This condition might prompt you to become angry, flustered, or excited, depending partly on your impression of O'Connor's reaction, and thereby further perceptual distortions may occur. Your ideas about how you are perceived are likely to influence your perception of the other individual.

Altogether, more inferences are made in person perception than in object perception. The perceiver makes inferences about psychological traits and internal states, about changing qualities, and often about how *he* or *she* is perceived. This process, dealing as it does with aspects of emotion, motivation, learning, and personality, is indeed complex.

Forming Impressions of People

In recent years psychologists have expended considerable effort trying to understand how people arrive at the ideas they each have about one another. This area of psychology is called *attribution theory* because it concerns the process by which people attribute characteristics to others. Its purpose is to identify the procedures or implicit "rules" that people use in making inferences about other people's behavior and personality (Jones et al., 1972).

Perhaps the most important finding in attribution theory thus far concerns the relatively little weight we tend to give to the circumstances in making judgments about another individual. Commonly, the influence of the context is ignored.

In forming an opinion, we tend to perceive the other person's behavior as more the result of enduring personality dispositions than due to the situation in which that person is involved (Mischel, 1971). As a rule, the customer who makes a sharp retort to the cashier while waiting in line is more likely to be regarded as having a nasty disposition than as being in a hurry.

It has also been found that our descriptions of others reflect our own personality to a surprising degree. Mr. A's perception of Mr. B can tell us a great deal about Mr. A, especially when he is relatively unfamiliar with Mr. B (Dornbusch et al., 1965). A viewer's description of Archie Bunker presumably could reveal aspects of that person's personality.

Central traits. People normally dislike ambiguity in dealing with others. They want to form a definite impression, especially when dealing with stangers. Thus, they are apt to jump to a conclusion based on relatively little information.

One idea people immediately want to form about another person is his or her degree of social warmth. How accepting is this person of others? This characteristic, the warm-cold dimension, is influential in our estimates of many other personal traits and, thus, is called a *central trait*. A person described as intelligent, skillful, industrious, cold, determined, practical, and cautious is considered to be significantly different from one described in exactly the same way, except with the substitution of *warm* for *cold*. Other traits have not shown this effect. The substitution of *polite* for *blunt,* for example, does not change the overall ratings significantly. Warmth and coldness are central traits; politeness and bluntness, by contrast, are peripheral traits and much less important (Asch, 1946).

In one study, a person was introduced to different groups of people by brief biographical notes that described him as "very warm" or "rather cold." After a 20-minute discussion with his observers, he left the room and was rated on several characteristics. Again, the suggestion of warmth or coldness produced a widespread effect in the overall ratings, and it had additional consequences for the perceivers' subsequent degree of interaction with this person (Kelley, 1950). ■ At present, no other central traits of this magnitude have been identified, but the degree to which any trait is central or peripheral clearly depends on the context.

Out-of-role behavior. Despite the findings in attribution theory, context can play a role in our judgments of others, and in out-of-role behavior it can serve to strengthen our convictions considerably. This behavior is illustrated at a polite dinner party at which someone uses loud, abusive language. It is called *out-of-role behavior* because it is not typical of people in this circumstance, but it may or may not be typical of the person involved.

In one experiment involving inappropriate role behavior, the subjects listened to a tape on which people sometimes showed the behavior expected of a job applicant and on other occasions acted contrary to expectations, making irrelevant comments and asking inappropriate questions. The result was that persons acting contrary to the expected role were perceived as "showing their true colors" more than those acting in accordance with expectations. Furthermore, the subjects placed much greater confidence in the personality estimates obtained from out-of-role behavior (Jones et al., 1961).

Since it is not called forth by any obvious aspect of the external situation, and in fact is contrary to social custom, out-of-role behavior is most commonly assumed to be a function of underlying personal characteristics. Hence, it is given considerable weight in forming impressions of people.

Prejudice as a Set

Central traits and out-of-role behavior are aspects of the stimulus "out there," outside the perceiver, but in judging someone else, the state of the perceiver is also critical. Earlier we referred to *set*, or perceptual set, as a readiness to perceive in a certain way. □ It is well illustrated in connection with Archie Bunker and others in "All in the Family."

This TV show broke with tradition in the early 1970s by focusing on rather than avoiding racial and ethnic issues. It also broke records for popularity. What were the reasons? The successful direction, script, and acting were obviously important, but there must have been other factors as well.

Ethnocentrism. Archie Bunker, the acknowledged star of this program, was a slightly paunchy, outspoken, white, working-class American, prone to derisive comments about those not of his ethnic background. Much of the program's intended humor was derived from his bigotry. Edith, his wife, was presented as lovable, sometimes flighty and simple-minded, but never sharply critical of her hard-working, patriotic husband. That role was left for the daughter and son-in-law, Gloria and Mike, who lived with the Bunkers while the unemployed young man finished college. Besides being jobless, Mike was extremely liberal, had long hair, and was of Polish ancestry, all of which were offensive to Archie. One basic theme of the program was the endless conflict between Archie and Mike (Figure 7-19).

■ *Before I met Bill I was told that he was very intelligent and scientific, and preferred to work math problems in his spare time. From this description, I immediately categorized him as "cold," and I had no desire to talk with him or even to meet him. Later, when I first saw him, my negative impression of him was intensified—he was quite ugly. . . . I judged him as dull and uninteresting, and excluded him from any parties I had, though I invited our mutual friends.*

A year later, I had finally grown up enough to accept him as a person, and I discovered him to be friendly and easygoing, with many talents. The next year we became very good friends, and now I consider him my best friend. . . . I no longer consider him a "cold" person due to his scientific interests, and now other factors about him far outweigh his physical appearance.

□ *In a junior high school initiation trial called a blind-walk, we were blind-folded and led by older girls through a maze that had a series of objects in it. We were told what each object was and had to examine it without the use of sight. Two objects, in particular, affected me in such a manner as to bring on feelings of nausea and intense fear. I was told to thrust my hand into a can and to allow the contents to slither around it. Worms! Thousands of slimy worms. I became ill! I could just see them crawling all over my body. Next, I had to feel the contents of a can of fish eyes. Sure enough, there they were! Hundreds of gooey eyes, looking at and touching my skin. Later, I learned that the first can contained spaghetti and that the second can contained wet blueberries. . . .*

Figure 7-19 "All in the Family." *The four major characters in this popular television series are shown. (United Press International)*

The program was organized around Archie's *ethnocentrism,* which is the belief that other cultures are necessarily inferior to one's own. Although we may completely disapprove of ethnocentrism, there were widely different views in the national press concerning the reason for the show's popularity. It was pointed out by some that the humor brought prejudice into the open and thereby decreased racial tension. Others argued that the program helped diminish prejudice by giving people insights into their feelings and biases. People who were against the show argued that it taught prejudice, especially to children who did not understand its satirical intent.

Influence of set. When social scientists studied the influential factors, two groups of people were used, 237 high school students in the United States and 168 adults in Canada. All subjects were white and both groups were rated on degree of prejudice or ethnocentrism. In

the U.S. sample, measurements were made regarding American Indians, Afro-Americans, and Spanish Americans. In Canada, the subjects' attitudes were measured towards Canadian Indians and French Canadians. In this way, the subjects were measured as being high or low on prejudice. *Prejudice* is defined as a tendency to prejudge someone or something, positively or negatively, ignoring the evidence. It is a form of set, a readiness to respond in a certain way.

Afterwards, all the subjects were asked about "All in the Family." Almost all of them had viewed the program and found it humorous, but sharp differences occurred when they were asked which character they admired most, which one made better sense, and which one seemed to be most successful at the end of each program.

The highly prejudiced people from both countries admired Archie, and they perceived Archie as triumphant in the interpersonal rivalries. Even the highly prejudiced adolescent Americans, closer to Mike's age, saw Archie as making better sense. On the other side, persons who were extremely low on prejudice were more evenly divided, more perceiving Mike as admirable and fewer regarding Archie in this manner. The two groups of people, viewing the same persons under the same circumstances, perceived them very differently, according to their own set or prejudice (Figure 7-20).

This selective perception, brought about by the viewers' set, also served to maintain their existing attitudes, and perhaps the program was popular for this reason. Persons constantly strive to find confirmation of their views in the environment, and they try to avoid ambiguity and disconfirmation. Many prejudiced viewers, for example, were not even aware that the program was intended as a satire on bigotry (Vidmar & Rokeach, 1974).

Processes in Perceiving

	U.S. Adolescents		Canadian Adults	
Character	High Prejudice	Low Prejudice	High Prejudice	Low Prejudice
Archie	38%	24%	40%	26%
Mike	18	20	13	21

Figure 7-20 Most Admirable Character in "All in the Family" According to High-Prejudice and Low-Prejudice Viewers. *(Vidmar & Rokeach, 1974)*

Altered States of Perceiving

Observations of philosophers also indicate that set is important in perception, even in altered states of perceiving, such as drug-induced states and hypnosis. As early as 2737 B.C., the Chinese emperor Shen Hung described the use of marijuana in this manner. One reason for the widely differing reports of drug-induced states is that the results are so dependent on the expectations or set with which the drug is used.

Drug-Induced States

Another reason for the widely differing reports is that drugs are sometimes used for very different purposes, therapeutic or experiential. In therapy, they are prescribed to alleviate anxiety, depression, and other conditions associated with mental disorder. Our purpose here, however, is to outline the experiential use and the factors influencing these outcomes.

Usage and terms.   Not long ago, LSD was referred to as a *psychotomimetic* drug, meaning that it produced psychotic-like symptoms, among which are hearing unspoken voices and seeing strange images, such as those occurring in schizophrenia. This idea came from the use of LSD in clinical work, for controlling severely depressed and hyperactive patients. Later, when LSD was used in experiential settings, it was referred to as *hallucinogenic,* but this term is not accurate either because the visual reactions are not necessarily hallucinations. They are not solely subjective; often, they have a substantial basis in reality.

Eventually, the term *psychedelic* was promoted as a neutral word; it refers to many different states of consciousness and simply means "mind-manifesting." In short, the "normal" or usual effects of psychedelic drugs are not known with any certainty. Results vary markedly according to the psychological pressures to which the consumer is exposed (Tart, 1969).

Usage and outcomes.   Users of marijuana, for example, commonly report that they must learn new ways of perceiving under the influence of this drug. The change is not automatic, as emphasized by the first-time users who say they experienced nothing different. With practice and a drug of certain potency, which unfortunately is very difficult to assess, a person under the influence of marijuana might experience *time expansion,* by which a momentary scene seems quite prolonged, and *sensory intensification,* by which colors seem more saturated, shapes more distinct, and variations more noticeable. When these two features are combined, one can understand why a person in a drug-induced state may find a fascination that lasts for hours in some color or in the face of a clock. ■

The diverse unpleasant experiences involved in drug-induced states are known as "bad trips," which are difficult to predict. There are also "flashbacks," in which severely disturbing false perceptions reappear several days, weeks, or even months after using LSD (Horowitz, 1969). This result is related to the biochemical characteristics of the individual and the ingested drug, rather

■ *This past Saturday I was under the influence of an hallucinogenic drug. . . . I remember looking at a single leaf; it was in no way unusual in shape or color and it was lying with hundreds of other leaves that looked just like it. Yet, it attracted and held my attention for a long time and I was able to perceive unforgettable, fine details. . . .*

Walking next to a wall that had been built to the contour of a hill, I became very upset. . . . I could not understand how the wall was changing size, why I could sit on it at one point and not at another. I attempted to express to a friend how frightening and yet fantastic it was to have the world so drastically altered. . . .

Figure 7-21 Painting Under the Influence of Drugs. *The painting on the left was done in normal consciousness and the one on the right while under the influence of psilocybin. (Courtesy of Dr. H. Leuner)*

■ *I was sitting in Southdale Hall last night watching the movie and I guess there were only 20 minutes left until the end. All of a sudden I started having a recurrence of an acid trip. (I haven't done any hard drugs since last March and I have never worried about having a flashback. So I didn't bring it on through worry.) I tried to talk myself down and concentrate on the movie but it just wasn't working. I felt as though I couldn't breathe—the air was there but it wasn't doing me any good and I could see it. I couldn't understand what "space" was. I can't explain the rest of it but I left the movie and sat outside on the stairs. I felt better for a minute and then it started happening again. There was a breeze but I couldn't feel it. I ran back to my dorm, cried a little, and I guess you could say I flipped out . . .*

Now I'm not sure it was the acid trip hitting me again, but it's the only way I can explain what I suddenly felt. . . .

than to any particular set. ■ Psychological damage from drug abuse, incidentally, seems to be associated with the stability of the personality; the less stable the individual, the greater is the likelihood of a long-term disturbance (McWilliams & Tuttle, 1973).

One reliably reported result of LSD ingestion is that shape and size constancy are disrupted. Under LSD influence, a hand held close to the face is perceived as being larger than normal rather than closer than normal. Such perceptual changes have obvious repercussions for the individual's functioning (Figure 7-21).

Until recently, there was little concern and less research on altered states of awareness in the Western world, despite one early effort with marijuana by an American experimental psychologist before the turn of the century (Delabarre, 1899). In contrast, the varied states of consciousness are of much interest to certain African tribes and Eastern civilizations (Figure 7-22).

The Hypnotic State

Set is also influential in hypnosis. There are many reports that the behavior of a hypnotized subject is influenced by what he or she thinks the hypnotist hopes to achieve. According to one viewpoint, set is the most significant factor in the so-called hypnotic condition (Barber, 1969; Spanos & Barber, 1972).

Set as the most significant factor. To create the hypnotic state, a person is usually asked to relax and then concentrate on something in a methodical way—an object, a thought, or someone else's words. As the person relaxes, he yields control of himself and enters a trance-like state. Under this condition, certain reactions occur that are said to be characteristic of the hypnotic state. These include *analgesia,* which is insensitivity to painful stimuli, *amnesia,* which is loss of memory, and *age regression,* where the subject behaves as he did at an earlier stage in life.

Among those who stress the importance of set, however, the idea of a special hypnotic state involves circular reasoning. A person is said to be under hypnosis when he or she is insensitive to pain and acts as he or she did in childhood, yet when these acts are explained, invariably they are attributed to the hypnotic trance. According to this view, these behaviors can be best explained on the basis of suggestion and the subject's motivation, without reference to an unusual state of consciousness (Barber, 1969).

In one instance, university students were hypnotized and made to regress to the day of their sixth birthday, but biographical information and analyses of their behavior under hypnosis showed marked inconsistencies. One subject

Processes in Perceiving

asked the time and looked at his wrist-watch, although he had not worn one at age six. Another subject spoke English, although German was his only language until adolescence. Apparently, they were not behaving as they did at age six but rather trying to simulate this condition (Orne, 1951).

Recent experiments on analgesia, muscular rigidity, and forgetting have demonstrated similar results. When subjects' hands were immersed in ice water or a heavy weight was attached to the finger, they were told to consider their hand as numb or to think of something very pleasant. Under these instructions they reported little or no pain and exhibited none of the accompanying physiological changes (Barber, 1969). The implication is that suggestion and motivation, collectively referred to as set, can produce much of the behavior attributed to the hypnotic "trance" state. But the evidence is not complete (Hilgard, 1972).

Neodissociation view. A very different approach to the study of hypnosis shows some relationship to split-brain research, in which it has been found that the right and left hemispheres of the brain apparently process different kinds of information in different ways. Each brain hemisphere is dominant in only part of our overall mental functioning. Similarly, in the *neodissociation view* of hypnosis it is postulated that there is a shift in the locus of brain control under hypnosis. The lower brain centers apparently become influential in what is experienced or not experienced, remembered or forgotten, reported or not reported. Certain typically voluntary activities become involuntary as the dominance of the normal brain controls is reduced. There is, in effect, a dissociation or split in the hypnotized person's overt and covert responsiveness.

For example, a hypnotized woman places one hand in a pail of cold water and experiences no significant pain. However, the physiological measures of heartbeat and blood pressure show little

Figure 7-22   Drugs and Religious Ritual. *In this ceremony, celebrated by the Fang of Africa, a certain drug traditionally was used to depress the appetite and enable men to make endurance marches over a wide territory for many days. Here this same drug is used to induce visual experience. The chalk on the participants' faces is symbolic of the bones of their ancestors. (Photo by James W. Fernandez, Princeton University)*

difference from the nonhypnotic state, in which the pain is fully experienced. At some level the subject is responsive to the cold. Furthermore, when the subject is capable of automatic writing under hypnosis and is asked to write with the other hand about her experience, she indicates that she is aware of the pain. She writes or presses response keys in an enclosed box, where she cannot see what she is communicating, and then she describes the experience as painful, though in conversation with the experimenter she reports no conscious pain (Hilgard, 1973).

Other demonstrations have been accomplished with automatic talking, in which subjects also report pain. Again, the hypnotized individual seems to be in contact with a part of his or her consciousness that has been dissociated from normal awareness. This consciousness is aware of information that is otherwise unavailable and thus is referred to as the "hidden observer," meaning that it is a dissociated consciousness. This "hidden observer," however, is highly rational, as opposed to the very different irrational unconscious postulated in psychoanalytic theory.

Perspective. The idea of multiple layers of consciousness is not new. William

James did some experiments of this nature, and the concept antedates the founding of psychology. But the neodissociation theory, coupled with our modern knowledge of sensory experience, may bring us a step closer to understanding human mental life. The fact that, as yet, we have so little comprehension of centuries-old hypnotic phenomena suggests that we still have a long way to go in attempting to identify the functions of the human brain.

Eventually, it may be discovered that hypnosis, like sleep, is not a single, unitary state, since several dimensions have been described. These include the subject's efforts to behave as a hypnotized person, his or her degree of awareness of the immediate environment, and the extent to which deep-seated aspects of his or her personality enter into the hypnotic condition (Shor, 1962). Further understanding of these factors may clarify the issue, but today for *some* people, hypnotism, more than showing the remarkable powers of the hypnotist, demonstrates the remarkable capacities of a motivated, suggestible, normal human being.

Summary

The Problem of Attending

1. What we perceive is partly a function of the nature of the stimulus. Aspects of the stimulus that are important in catching attention include intensity, location, movement, and color. When all these factors are approximately equal, novelty becomes most important.

2. What we perceive is also a function of the organism. An organism attends to certain stimuli and not to others. Attending is a readiness to perceive, based on the organism's internal state. This selection of stimuli apparently takes place in the central nervous system, rather than at the receptor level, and may be a two-stage process. Set is more than attending; it is a readiness to perceive in a certain way. It arises from the perceiver's personal traits, interests, and motivations, and it can be highly influential in perception.

The Perception of Objects

3. Discrimination of figure-ground relationships seems to be the starting point in organized perceptual experience. According to gestalt psychologists, the parts of a figure, or several figures, are grouped on the basis of similarity, proximity, closure, and continuity.

4. A stable perception of the world is also based on object constancy, which is the tendency to perceive any given object as the same, even though it stimulates us in a variety of ways. Important aspects of object constancy are shape, size, and color.

Movement, Space, and Illusions

5. Movement is perceived whenever successive areas of the retina are differentially stimulated. Without a frame of reference, however, induced motion, rather than real visual movement, is likely to be experienced.

6. Space perception arises from the integration of diverse cues from several senses. The monocular cues include interposition, shadows, linear perspective, aerial perspective, relative movement, size of the retinal image, and accommodation of the lens. Among the binocular cues are convergence, which is of doubtful value except at close distances, and retinal disparity, which occurs because the different locations of the eyes give rise to different retinal images.

7. An illusion is a perception that does not correspond to the external situation as indicated by physical measurement. Extensive cross-cultural studies have shown that learning contributes significantly to the illusory experience; thus, perception is partly a creative process.

The Perception of People

8. Person perception is more complex than object perception for several reasons. The perceiver tries to determine

psychological as well as physical characteristics; the perceived person moves about in space and changes as he or she grows older; and if both perceivers know that they are being perceived, their perceptions may be influenced still further.

9. Attribution theory is concerned with the processes by which people describe the behavior of others. It appears that, in making these judgments, they generally place less emphasis on the stimulus situation and more emphasis on the concept of enduring personality traits. In forming impressions of people, the warm—cold dimension is often important, even outweighing other traits, but out-of-role behavior is also considered significant.

10. Probably the most crucial determinant in person perception, or any perception, is the observer's set or expectancy regarding the other individual. People with different sets are very likely to perceive the same individual quite differently, especially when the set is strong, as in much prejudice.

Altered States of Perceiving

11. In drug usage, dosage and potency are important in the obtained reaction, but the response is also influenced by the subject's set, including the context of the usage and the person's prior experience with drugs. The major psychedelic drugs, such as LSD, may create severe, undesirable effects.

12. According to a new view of hypnosis, the essential feature is the subject's motivation and suggestibility, rather than the special trance created by the hypnotist. From another viewpoint, the most important feature in hypnosis is a shift in the locus of brain control, from the higher to lower brain centers. Regardless of what views eventually prove to be correct, it is clear that set and learning are important in almost any altered state of perceiving.

Suggested Readings

Cohen, J. *Secondary motivation: I. Personal motives.* Skokie, Ill.: Rand McNally, 1970. A book in a paperback series discussing drug usage and hypnotic motivation; it has numerous historical references.

Cole, M., & Scribner, S. *Culture and thought.* New York: Wiley, 1974. Goes beyond the topics of this chapter into such related issues as learning and memory.

Epstein, W. (Ed.). *Stability and constancy in visual perception: Mechanisms and processes.* New York: Wiley, 1977. Presents the views of 15 contributors on the development and breakdown of constancy.

Gibson, E. J. *Principles of perceptual learning and development.* New York: Appleton-Century-Crofts, 1969. Emphasizes theories and the experimental approach to perceptual learning.

Haber, R. N., & Hershenson, M. *The psychology of visual perception.* New York: Holt, Rinehart & Winston, 1973. A thorough textbook for the advanced student.

PART FOUR

Learning and Symbolic Activity

Chapter 8

Conditioning and Learning

Consider what would happen if everything you have learned somehow were removed. You would be like a helpless infant, perhaps aware of your needs but unable to do much about them. Cats could steal your food, as they do in a story concerning a Spanish monk, to be told shortly, and you would be unable to deal with the problem. Your whole environment would be strange, and you would perish without the assistance of others. On the other hand, you would not be anxious about college grades or concerned about rejection by others. For better and for worse, human beings are creatures of learning.

Learning is any relatively permanent change in behavior that results from experience. Exceptions to this rule include those changes due to injury or physiological adjustments, such as adaptation and fatigue, and those due to maturation, as when a person's voice changes in pitch during adolescence.

Classical Conditioning

At the turn of this century our understanding of certain aspects of the learning process was advanced by Ivan Pavlov, a Russian physiologist who was interested in various gastric secretions. In fact, Pavlov received the Nobel prize for his research on digestion.

Figure 8-1 Ivan Pavlov. *Before his appointment at the Russian Academy of Sciences, Pavlov (third from the left) was Professor of Physiology at the Military Medical Academy in Petrograd. (The Bettmann Archive)*

Background of the Method

To study salivation in a live dog, Pavlov and his assistants made an incision in the dog's cheek and inserted rubber tubing, through which the saliva passed into a glass container. Here it could be measured in a precise, objective manner. When meat was presented, the dog naturally salivated, and then studies were made of this process (Figure 8-1).

Eventually something happened that caused Pavlov's interests to be redirected. As the experiments progressed it was noted that the sight of the bowl, the sight of the experimenter, and eventually even the sound of the experimenter's footsteps produced salivation. Pavlov called these reactions *psychic reflexes* in order to distinguish them from the physiological ones elicited by the food itself. Since they were interfering with his purpose, he felt he should either eliminate them or study them directly. Grasping the possible significance of these events, Pavlov changed the focus of his research from physiological to psychological processes, and a special laboratory was built for this purpose.

For a long time it had been known that one's mouth waters at the sound of a dinner bell or some other indication that food is nearby, but Pavlov saw in this circumstance a controlled method for investigating mental phenomena and studying brain physiology in animals and perhaps in human beings. The term *classical* means "in the established manner," and the term *conditioning* refers to learning. Hence, *classical conditioning* means the study of learning in the manner established by Ivan Pavlov.

The conditioning procedure. Although pervasive, classical conditioning is a simple form of learning; it usually involves a relatively simple modification of behavior. In fact, classical conditioning has been described as merely *stimulus substitution*. A previously neutral stimulus is substituted for a stimulus that originally elicited the response. The sound of the experimenter's footsteps in Pavlov's experiments became a substitute for food; it too evoked the salivary response. The idea of stimulus substitution is somewhat oversimplified, however, because the response to the new stimulus is not identical to the response

Figure 8-2 Diagram of Classical Conditioning. *Figure A shows the situation before conditioning, where the neutral stimulus may elicit arousal reactions but salivation does not occur. Figure B shows the conditioning process.*

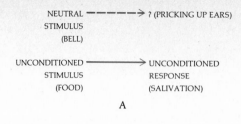

A

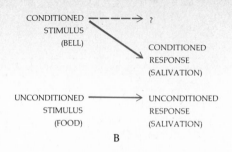

B

to the original one. It may be more abbreviated, of lesser intensity, or slightly different in other ways.

The first step in the Pavlovian method is to ensure that the new stimulus is neutral. It should not elicit the response in question, which in this case is salivation. If the sound of a bell does not elicit salivation, it is a neutral stimulus for this response and thus it can become conditioned.

Conditioning takes place when the bell is sounded, each time followed by food, which evokes the inborn, automatic salivary response. As this pairing is repeated, eventually the sound itself elicits salivation. ■ Conditioning has occurred when the bell alone, a previously neutral stimulus for salivation, elicits the salivary response (Figure 8-2).

Basic terms. Food automatically elicits salivation, and therefore Pavlov called this stimulus the *unconditional stimulus*. It led naturally to the salivary response, which he called the *unconditional reflex*. But when the sound of the bell led the dog to salivate, Pavlov designated this response a *conditional reflex,* which emphasized that it depended upon some stimulus other than the natural one—the *conditional stimulus*.

In translation, the Russian word *ouslovny* became "condition*ed*" rather than "condition*al*"; hence, the widespread adoption of the adjective *conditioned*. In later research it became apparent that many conditioned reactions, strictly speaking, are not reflexes. For these reasons, the following terms have come into general usage today: the *unconditioned stimulus* (US) leads to the

unconditioned response (UR); similarly, the *conditioned stimulus* (CS) leads to the *conditioned response* (CR). The essential feature of the classical conditioning process is that a previously neutral stimulus acquires the capacity to elicit a certain response (Figure 8-3).

Conditioning Principles
The early findings from Pavlov's laboratory have been amplified by modern research that focuses on how this form of learning originates, how it is modified, and how it disappears. In all this research, the primary concern is with the learning process, not with salivation or some other response used for studying it.

Acquisition. The acquisition of a conditioned response is still understood much as Pavlov reported it. In fact, the basic process was depicted years earlier by the Spanish dramatist Lope de Vega in a story of a punished monk. This man was made to sit on the floor all day and eat his meals with the monastery cats. They stole his food, but he was constantly watched and not permitted to drive them away. The monk describes how he eventually retrained the cats:

I put them all in a sack, and on a pitch black night took them out under an arch. First I would cough, and then immediately whale the daylights out of the cats. They whined and shrieked like an infernal pipe organ. I would pause for awhile and repeat the

■ *Two years ago I worked in a factory located alongside a railroad track. Each morning at approximately 10:30 A.M. a freight train would go by. This was also the time assigned as the beginning of my coffee break. After working there two months I took a better job in a factory located around 50 miles north of my original place of work. This factory was situated alongside the same railroad track. The same freight passed each day, but it went by this factory almost an hour earlier. For the first two weeks I felt the desire for a cup of coffee whenever I heard the train go by, whereas when I began my first job I never even considered drinking coffee at that hour of the morning.*

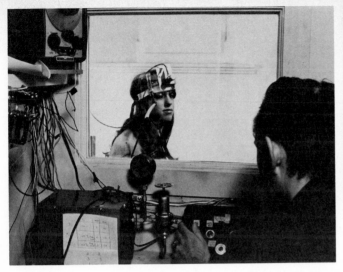

Figure 8-3 Study of Classical Conditioning. *Note the similarities between this modern laboratory and the early Pavlovian laboratory. In both instances, there are separate rooms for the subject and the experimenter, and the apparatus enables the experimenter to make controlled presentations of stimuli. The modern laboratory, designed for study of the human eyeblink response, includes a one-way vision window. In the Pavlovian laboratory, the saliva passed through an opening in the dog's jaw, while the harness held the dog in position. Each drop of saliva, upon entering the calibrated test tube, activated a lever and stylus, which recorded the secretion on a revolving drum.*

operation—first a cough, and then a thrashing. I finally noticed that even without beating them, the beasts moaned and yelped like the very devil whenever I coughed. I then let them loose. Thereafter, whenever I had to eat off the floor, I would cast a look around. If an animal approached my food, all I had to do was cough, and how that cat did scat! (Bousefield, 1955)

In modern terminology, this example illustrates response acquisition through trace conditioning. In *trace conditioning* the conditioned stimulus is removed before the unconditioned stimulus appears. The coughing is terminated before the beating begins. Only a neural or memory trace remains when the unconditioned stimulus is presented, and learning depends on this trace.

There are two other variations by which a classically conditioned response can be acquired. In *delayed conditioning* the conditioned stimulus also appears first, but it continues to be present until the appearance of the unconditioned stimulus. The monk starts coughing and before he finishes, he hits the cats with the stick. In *simultaneous conditioning,* both stimuli, the coughing and the beating, are present only at the same time.

Considerable laboratory research has shown that the conditioning process is most effective when there is some interval between the CS and US. Thus, the trace and delayed procedures result in faster and stronger learning, but especially when the interstimulus interval is short. The most effective CS-US interval has been said to be approximately one-half second, although it varies considerably with different responses and different species. The least effective of all stimulus arrangements is *backward conditioning,* where the US appears first. Generally, a dog will not learn to salivate to a bell, for example, if the sound appears after the meat (Tarpy, 1975).

Among human beings the timing of the CS and US may not be quite as important as among lower animals. The reason is that human beings have greater ability to make mental connections among temporally distant stimuli.

Stimulus generalization. Often the conditioned response occurs not only to the conditioned stimulus but also to similar stimuli not directly conditioned. This phenomenon is called *stimulus generalization,* and here the magnitude

■ *My sister had a bladder ailment when she was a little girl and, as a result, had to visit the doctors in Boston every three weeks and go through a lot of discomfort in the treatments. She developed a fear of the doctors who wore white coats because she associated their presence with the discomfort of treatments and examinations. One day, my family decided to eat at a restaurant that happened to have bus boys who wore white jackets. My sister got scared the minute she saw them.*

Figure 8-4   Differential Conditioning.   *One dog in Pavlov's laboratory learned to discriminate between the narrow black T and each of the other figures. (From Conditional Reflexes by I. P. Pavlov, translated by G. V. Anrep, published by Oxford University Press.)*

T

of the response depends on the characteristics of the new stimulus. The greater the similarity of the new stimulus and the conditioned stimulus, the larger will be the response. ■

Pavlov attributed stimulus generalization to the spread of effects from one region of the brain to other parts not previously excited. In his experiments, a buzzer produced the same reaction as the sound of the bell. In the case of the monastery cats, if the monk were unable to cough, he might snort through his nose, inducing the same conditioned fear reaction in the cats.

Differential conditioning.   To prevent stimulus generalization, which could occur in many instances, Pavlov taught his laboratory animals to make a discrimination between the two stimuli, using the process of *differential conditioning.* When a bell is sounded on several occasions and food consistently follows, the bell sound becomes a CS. When a horn is sounded, the dog may salivate at first, but if this sound reappears time and again without being followed by food, salivation in response to this stimulus will soon disappear. Discrimination has then occurred; the bell sound has been followed by the reinforcement of food, while there has been no reinforcement for the horn (Figure 8-4). In classical conditioning, the term *reinforcement* means that the conditioned stimulus is followed by the unconditioned stimulus and the conditioned response is thereby strengthened.

Suppose that the monk gives a whistle instead of a cough and the cats do not respond. They have made a discrimination between the two stimuli. In this case differential conditioning is unnecessary.

Trials	Latency in seconds	Drops of Saliva
1	3	10
2	7	7
3	5	8
4	4	5
5	5	7
6	9	4
7	13	3

Figure 8-5   Extinction.   *As extinction trials were continued in Pavlov's laboratory, the saliva drops were slower to appear and fewer in number. (From Conditional Reflexes by I. P. Pavlov, translated by G. V. Anrep, published by Oxford University Press, 1927.)*

Extinction.   Once a conditioned response has been formed, how can it be eliminated? The obvious method is to present the CS continually without the US, as just illustrated in the case of the horn. When this procedure, called *extinction,* was used in Pavlov's experiments, the conditioned salivation response gradually disappeared (Figure 8-5). If the monk coughs many times at the cats without providing reinforcement for this stimulus by striking them, eventually they no longer will be frightened by the cough.

Spontaneous recovery.   Much research has shown that extinction is not necessarily permanent. After an interval of time, the conditioned response to the CS reappears, even when there has been no intervening reinforcement. This outcome is known as *spontaneous recovery.* But the recovered response grows weaker each time the conditioned stimulus is presented. Without further reinforcement, there is less and less spontaneous recovery, until eventually the conditioned response fails to appear (Figure 8-6).

Learning and Symbolic Activity

This phenomenon also is illustrated with the monk. Caught and punished again a week after his release, the monk frightens the cats with his cough on the first few trials, even though extinction had occurred earlier and there had been no new beating in the bag. But unless the cough is reinforced, the cats, again, will be afraid no longer.

Higher-order conditioning. Finally, it has also been found that a well-established conditioned stimulus can be used as an "unconditioned" stimulus. For example, if an animal has been conditioned to salivate in response to a bell, the bell then can be used to obtain conditioning to some other stimulus. This process is known as *higher-order conditioning*, and the first new level is called second-order conditioning (Figure 8-7).

Pavlov failed to obtain more than second-order conditioning in dogs because the conditioned stimulus became extinguished after being used many times without the US, and this process would not be particularly useful with other lower animals. But Pavlov believed that third-order, fourth-order, and higher levels of conditioning are possible with human beings. In fact, he believed that there is no discoverable limit to the orders of conditioned responses that human beings acquire in everyday life.

Higher-order conditioning also illustrates that a given stimulus cannot be identified as an unconditioned stimulus or a conditioned stimulus without reference to the way in which it is used. A loud bell can serve as a neutral stimulus in salivary conditioning, and later it can become a CS for this response. But the bell also can serve as a US for awakening someone, if it automatically elicits that response.

Influence of Classical Conditioning

As a consequence of these studies, Pavlov stated that "different kinds of habits based on training, education and discipline . . . are nothing but a long chain of conditioned reflexes" (1927). Today

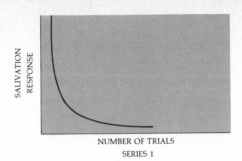

SERIES 1

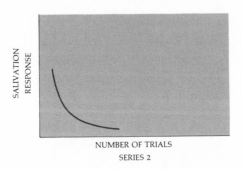

SERIES 2

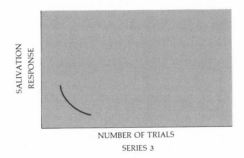

SERIES 3

Figure 8-6 Spontaneous Recovery. *In several series of tests for spontaneous recovery, the response reappears at a much lower strength each time and disappears after fewer trials. Eventually, it will not appear at all.*

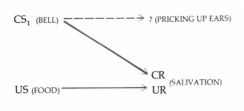

ORIGINAL CONDITIONING

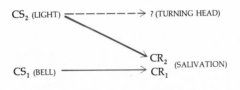

SECOND-ORDER CONDITIONING

Figure 8-7 Higher-Order Conditioning. *First the subject is conditioned to salivate to CS_1, the bell. Then the sound of the bell is used as an "unconditioned stimulus" in developing a conditioned response to CS_2, the light.*

this generalization seems too broad, but most psychologists believe that the principles of classical conditioning are applicable in a wide variety of learning situations.

Treatment of a behavior problem. Classical conditioning is used in the treatment of certain behavior problems, such as the child who wets the bed while asleep. The purpose here is to make the child more responsive to bladder tension, which is a neutral stimulus for awakening since it fails to wake the child. The sound of a bell is an unconditioned stimulus in this context, since it always wakes the child. Hence, the bell is wired to a special bed pad that makes a complete circuit when it is wet by urine, setting off the alarm. In the early stages of conditioning, the bladder tension does not wake the child; instead the child urinates and is awakened by the bell. But as it is continually followed by the bell, the bladder tension eventually becomes a conditioned stimulus, waking the child before the bell sounds, and waking up is a conditioned response to this tension.

This procedure is useful with children who are not sufficiently sensitive to nocturnal bladder tension to be awakened by it. It can lead to undesirable outcomes if used with a child who lacks bladder control for some emotional or physiological reason, especially since increased anxiety, which may result, leads to decreased bladder control. Many other therapeutic uses of classical conditioning are available, however, as discussed later.

Study of sensory capacities. Classical conditioning procedures are also used to assess the sensory abilities of infants, handicapped persons, and even animals. In a clinic for hearing and speech disorders, for example, there is an infant who does not respond to sounds of any kind, but when the foot is pricked, the leg is withdrawn. If a bell is sounded in advance of the pinprick on several occasions, eventually the baby withdraws the foot at the sound of the bell alone. In this case, we know that the infant's auditory mechanisms are functioning satisfactorily and that some other factors must be causing the lack of response to sounds.

Development of emotional reactions. Probably the most important role of classical conditioning lies in the development of attitudes and feelings. In fact, there is reason to think that all classical conditioning involves some emotional reaction. The CR seems to include not only a physiological response, such as salivation, goose pimples, or a change in heart rate, but also a diffuse emotional reaction on a pleasure-pain continuum (Tarpy, 1975).

Three centuries ago this outcome was described by the brilliant English philosopher, John Locke. In reading the following passage, remember that the schoolchildren of his day were corrected for mistakes by a spanking or beating, which is an unconditioned stimulus for pain and discomfort. The conditioned stimuli were textbooks and other materials, which immediately preceded the beating:

Many children imputing the pain they endured at school to their books they were corrected for, so join those ideas together, that a book becomes their aversion, and they are never reconciled to the study and use of them all their lives after; and thus reading becomes a torment to them, which otherwise possibly they might have made the great pleasure of their lives. There are rooms convenient enough, that some men cannot study in, and fashions of vessels, which, though ever so clean and commodious, they cannot drink out of, and that by reason of some . . . ideas which are annexed to them, and make them offensive. (Locke, 1690)

In most cases, the conditioned emotional reaction is built up through a series of such pairings. However, a conditioned response also can occur after just a single trial, providing the unconditioned stimulus is of sufficient intensity. This outcome is called *one-trial conditioning*. After a car accident, for example, an individual might readily fear roadways, signs, a certain color, or any other stimulus associated with the incident. ■ In the acquisition process, several previously neutral stimuli can become conditioned at the same time, but the strongest CS is the one most closely associated with the US.

Positive feelings also can be learned in this way. Not long ago, one of the authors entered an animal psychology laboratory and encountered what he considered to be the usual foul odor. His daughter exclaimed, "Oh, I love that smell." Then she added, "It reminds me of Snoopy." Snoopy was a pet white rat that provided her with warmth and cuddliness in her younger days. Odors commonly become such conditioned stimuli. □

Responses and Reinforcement

Despite Pavlov's optimism, his discoveries do not appear adequate to explain all learning or even the whole situation with regard to the hungry cats and the monk. Our discussion thus far has been limited to physiological reactions, such as salivation and pupillary constriction, and to emotional responses. At the monk's cough, the cats became fearful and showed certain visceral changes, such as the secretion of adrenalin.

Types of Responses

These physiological and emotional acts apparently arose through classical conditioning, but nothing yet has been said about the important response of running away. It appears to be brought about by another process, called operant conditioning. This distinction in types of responses, although not without limitations, is important in understanding the two types of conditioning, and it must be made before we explore further the concept of operant conditioning.

Respondent and operant behavior. Reactions such as fear and trembling upon being struck with a stick are often called *respondent behavior* because they occur in response to a specific, identifiable stimulus. Tropisms and reflexes are excellent examples of respondent behavior. A *tropism* is a forced movement on the part of a plant or lower animal. Some plants inevitably turn toward a source of light. A cockroach runs from it, and a moth is attracted to it. The response is automatic and puppet-like, the direct result of the stimulus involved.

In other organisms, including human beings, we see responses that are equally puppet-like, called reflexes. A depressor is applied to the back of the tongue and the person immediately chokes, demonstrating the gagging reflex. Exposed to cold air, a person shows the pilomotor reflex, called goose-bumps. These inborn behaviors also occur in response to a specific stimulus.

Still other respondent behaviors are acquired during the lifetime of the organism, through the process of classical conditioning. Unusual fear reactions, such as that displayed by the cats in reaction to the monk's cough, are among the many examples of respondent behavior. They are directly triggered by some specific stimulus, such as a cough, the smell of yellow jasmine, or the sight of a punitive schoolmaster.

The act of running away, on the other hand, is described as *operant behavior* because the organism operates on its environment in some fashion. A child throws pebbles into a pond; an adolescent fixes old automobiles; an adult balances the family budget. All these behaviors have an effect on the external situation, but they are not *controlled* by some explicit stimulus, as far as we know. We are not sure why someone throws pebbles in the pond, fixes autos, and so forth. Sometimes these actions are called *instrumental* behavior, signifying that they are instrumental in achieving some result.

■ In late May of my junior year in high school, just after my last semester exam, I went for a drive in the country to celebrate the beginning of summer. While enjoying the fresh air and heavy fragrance of yellow jasmine, one of the spring flowers blooming at the time, an oncoming car careened from its side of the highway directly into my lane. There was no head-on collision, but the impact sent my car to the right into a field of yellow jasmine; the other car, whose driver had fallen asleep, also ended up in the field. No one was seriously hurt, except the cars, but now, whenever I smell yellow jasmine, my stomach tightens up as it does when something frightens me, and I have chills.

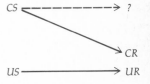

CS: Smell of yellow jasmine
US: Auto crash
CR ⎫
   ⎬ Anxiety
UR ⎭

□ In childhood, when my mother went for long rides in the car, she often became nauseous and experienced what is called motion sickness. Her mother always handed her a perfumed handkerchief in the hopes that it might distract her from her sickness or help her in case of an accident. To this day, the smell of perfume has a nauseating effect on her.

A continuum. The difference between operant and respondent behavior is most accurately expressed when the word "identified" is used. Respondent behavior is identified by its stimulus, although directly or indirectly it has some effect on the environment. Operant behavior is identified by its effect in the environment, although it is always influenced in some unknown way by various stimuli (English & English, 1958).

In other words, we can say that the two types of behaviors differ in the *degree* to which they are under external control; both exist on a reflexive-nonreflexive continuum. Any respondent behavior, near the reflexive end, varies in the strength, immediacy, and facility with which it can be elicited by a given stimulus (Turner & Solomon, 1962). Similarly, any operant response towards the nonreflexive end takes place in the context of diverse stimuli, some of which, although not readily identifiable, may have a significant influence in arousing it. The respondent-operant distinction indicates that responses differ in the degree to which they are stimulus-bound, and therefore it is useful in understanding the difference between classical and operant conditioning.

The Reinforcement Principle

In learning, we are interested in the appearance of a response, and therefore we encounter the concept of *reinforcement,* which is any event that increases the probability of a given response. This definition has the advantage of applying to both classical and operant conditioning, although the event is different in each case.

We have already encountered this concept in classical conditioning. Reinforcement occurs whenever the conditioned stimulus is increased in strength by being paired with the unconditioned stimulus. The likelihood that the CS by itself will be capable of eliciting the conditioned response is thereby increased. The response, of course, is essentially respondent.

In operant conditioning, the term *reinforcement* means that some event follows the response rather than a given stimulus. This event is something that can satisfy a basic drive, such as hunger and thirst, or some acquired drive, as we shall see later. The organism operates on its environment in some way and thereby receives a "reward," which increases the probability that it will operate on its environment in this same way in the future. The response is sometimes called a "free operant" to emphasize that the organism can choose to emit or not to emit the behavior in question.

Recently, there has been research showing some exceptions to this rule. Elements of operant-type reinforcement, for example, have been found with respondent behavior, as in biofeedback procedures. These investigations have theoretical significance, and they have led to reconsideration of the basic distinction between the two procedures, but at this time the conventional rule is still a good one. There are two kinds of conditioning procedures and two kinds of responses (Bolles, 1975). The classical procedures are particularly effective with respondent behavior, as just described, and the operant procedures are particularly effective with operant behavior, to which we now turn.

Operant Conditioning

Near the beginning of this century, while Pavlov was studying Russian dogs in harness, an American psychologist, E. L. Thorndike, had been investigating cats roaming freely in a specially constructed box, called a "puzzle box." The cat's problem was to find out how to escape. The food-deprived animal walked around, scratched, bit, pawed, and so forth, and eventually it pushed a latch in the proper manner. Then, the door opened and the cat was released to receive food. In subsequent trials it pushed the latch earlier and earlier. Finally, as soon as it was placed in the box, the cat operated the latch and escaped (Figure 8-8).

The same result occurred when the cat was required to pull a loop, scratch its ear, bump a pole, or produce some other response to gain its release. The animal tended to repeat the action that immediately preceded its escape. This outcome reminds us of the monastery cats; they repeatedly ran away, thereby escaping a fearful situation. Thorndike called this result the *law of effect:* an organism tends to repeat those behaviors that bring about satisfaction, and it tends to discard those that bring about discomfort.

A man of many interests, Thorndike later developed intelligence tests for human beings, word lists for spelling and vocabulary, scales for judging handwriting, methods of teaching specific subjects, and procedures of educational and vocational guidance. In effect, he began educational psychology in the United States.

Background and Principles

In the 1930s, another psychologist began to study the same phenomena that Thorndike had observed with the cats, but he started with a simpler setting, measured the response more precisely, made the delivery of reinforcement more controlled, and, as his concepts developed, applied the principles in the analysis of more complex learning. Today, B. F. Skinner's work in operant conditioning, which states basically that responses are modified through reinforcement, is widely recognized.

The conditioning procedure. In this conditioning procedure, an experimental animal is placed in a small box called a *Skinner box,* or, more technically, an operant chamber, which contains a lever for the animal to manipulate and a device for dispensing food or water.

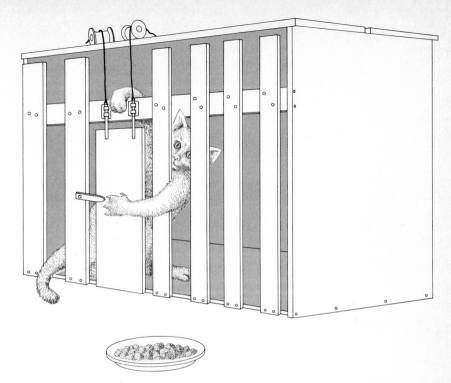

Figure 8-8 Study of Animal Problem Solving. *To obtain the food, the cat must remove the obstructions that lock the door of the box. The cat tries many kinds of responses before opening the box the first time. After a few trials, the cat learns to escape more readily. (After Thorndike, 1898)*

Skinner and his followers are *not* interested in lever-pressing per se, but, as in Pavlov's work with salivation, this behavior is convenient for studying the learning process.

A food-deprived rat is placed in the box and is free to move within the confined area. Usually it explores, and eventually it presses the lever which triggers the food-delivery mechanism, producing a food pellet. After gaining this reinforcement, the subject continues its apparently random activity—sniffing, stretching, and cleaning itself—but sooner or later it presses the lever again. This bar-press produces another pellet and, as time passes, the bar is pressed more frequently. Finally, a point is reached at which the rat is consistently pressing the bar and receiving food (Figure 8-9).

Figure 8-9 Operant Conditioning.
When the lever is pressed, a pellet of food or drop of water appears. The graph shows that no lever-pressing response occurred for the first few minutes, after which the responses increased gradually, and after two hours rose sharply. (Sheila A. Farr photo)

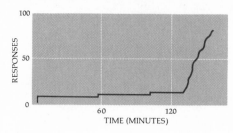

When a rat has acquired this response, usually it begins pressing the bar immediately after being placed in a Skinner box, and it continues to do so many times, providing that it continues to receive food pellets. When the bar-pressing response finally becomes infrequent or does not appear at all, it is presumably because the subject no longer is motivated to receive food (Skinner, 1953).

Basic terms. The concept of reinforcement in operant conditioning has been explained already, and the reader probably has noted its similarity to the law of effect. It indicates that the learning of a given response depends upon its consequences. Sometimes the consequence is the appearance of food or water, which is called a *positive reinforcer* because its *appearance* increases the probability of the response being repeated on another occasion. Other times the consequence involves the disappearance of a loud noise or extreme heat, called a *negative reinforcer* because its *removal* increases the probability of that response being repeated. Occasionally, people use the terms *reward* and *punishment* in these ways, but these terms also have popular meaning and therefore are less precise in this context. The term *punishment,* for example, might refer to the appearance of a beating or to the removal of one's allowance.

Other elements in operant conditioning are less specific than those for classical conditioning, primarily because it is so difficult to identify the original stimulus, which first evoked the response, as in bar-pressing. It may have been the sight of the bar, smells associated with the box, stimuli within the rat or some combination of these factors. Nevertheless, the rat did press the bar, and this *operant response* (R_O) operated on the environment to produce a positive reinforcer or *reinforcing stimulus* (S_R). The situation is represented as $R_O \rightarrow S_R$

Gradually, the organism in this circumstance begins to recognize a certain stimulus as indicating that reinforcement is available if the proper response is made. This stimulus might be the originally initiating but unknown stimulus, such as the sight of the lever, or it might be something else. In any case, it is called a *discriminative stimulus* (S_D) because it signals the availability of reinforcement. It does not elicit the response, as in classical conditioning, but it becomes the occasion on which that response is emitted. Thus, the sequence eventually becomes $S_D \rightarrow R_O \rightarrow S_R$, and it tends to be repeated until the stimulus conditions change or until the organism is no longer motivated to seek the reinforcer (Figure 8-10).

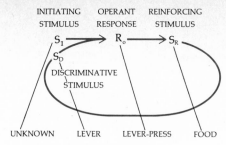

INITIATING   OPERANT   REINFORCING
STIMULUS   RESPONSE   STIMULUS

$S_1 \longrightarrow R_o \longrightarrow S_R$

S_D

DISCRIMINATIVE
STIMULUS

UNKNOWN   LEVER   LEVER-PRESS   FOOD

Figure 8-10 Diagram of Operant Conditioning. *S_1 is the unknown stimulus that first prompts the rat to press the lever. The rat's operant response (R_O) results in the availability of food, which is a reinforcing stimulus (S_R). This reward may prompt a behavior cycle, provided the organism can discriminate the stimulus (S_D) that indicates its availability.*

In this sequence we have an interpretation for the operant behavior of the monastery cats. The discriminative stimulus was the monk's cough, the response was to run away, and the reinforcement was escape from or avoidance of aversive stimulation.

Conditioning principles. With the cats, the monk's cough was a conditioned stimulus in the classical context and a discriminative stimulus in the operant model, which may not be the case in all instances. The two conditioning procedures are different, as far as we know, although they share some of the same principles.

In operant conditioning, for example, the *acquisition* of the response is measured as the rate of responding, not the amount of the response, as in classical conditioning. The reason lies in the fact that operant behavior, not elicited by any recognized stimuli, therefore cannot be measured as a function of the stimulation (Hilgard & Bower, 1975). Thus, operant conditioning is measured as the rate at which a given response occurs.

To demonstrate acquisition, a base rate must be established first, by placing the organism in an operant chamber with a lever and food dispenser but no food. The animal's base rate is the amount of bar-pressing that occurs

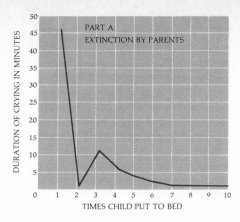

PART A:
EXTINCTION BY PARENTS

DURATION OF CRYING IN MINUTES

TIMES CHILD PUT TO BED

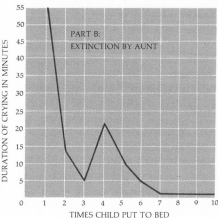

PART B:
EXTINCTION BY AUNT

DURATION OF CRYING IN MINUTES

TIMES CHILD PUT TO BED

within a given time interval without reinforcement. Later, when the food pellets are made available for correct responses, the rate of acquisition is determined by a comparison of the number of responses under the two conditions.

Other principles discussed in classical conditioning also appear in some form in operant conditioning. Insofar as a discriminative stimulus can be identified, *stimulus generalization* and *discrimination* can be demonstrated. *Extinction*, on the other hand, occurs when reinforcement is no longer available for a response (Figure 8-11). This phenomenon can be followed by *spontaneous recovery* when the appropriate conditions are met.

Figure 8-11 Extinction. *Because he was seriously ill, an infant required considerable attention during the early months of his life. Later, when he regained his health, it was necessary for one of his parents to spend up to two hours in the child's bedroom to prevent temper tantrums at bedtime. Part A shows how extinction of crying occurred when the parents left the room immediately after he went to bed. Part B shows that it was necessary to repeat the extinction process after an aunt put the child to bed and returned to his room when he began crying. The child shown in the photograph was not the subject of this study. (Graphs adapted from Williams, 1959. Copyright 1959 by the American Psychological Association. Reprinted by permission. Photo © Paul Kellogg.)*

Finally, it must be emphasized that operant conditioning is not limited to the availability of food, water, and other reinforcers that satisfy physiological needs, called *primary reinforcement*. Some animals and most human beings will respond for long periods of time to *secondary reinforcement,* which satisfies acquired needs rather than inborn ones. Money satisfies physiological needs only indirectly, yet it is a powerful form of secondary reinforcement. The words "Well done," the mark of "A," and countless other events constitute secondary reinforcement, which is extremely potent in the control of human learning.

Secondary reinforcement acquires its reinforcing properties through association with primary reinforcement, as in the classical conditioning procedure. Suppose the rat's bar press is followed by a tone and then a food pellet. After many repetitions, the rat will continue to press the bar for long periods of time when this response is followed only by the tone. When neither food nor the tone follows the response, the animal's response is extinguished much more rapidly. Furthermore, the animal's rate of response to the tone alone is a function of the number of times the tone and food have been previously paired. Money is constantly paired with all sorts of reinforcing circumstances, which makes it powerful indeed.

Improving the Response

Whether it is primary or secondary, operant conditioning is most efficiently achieved when reinforcement immediately follows the desired response. As a rule, the smaller the interval between response and reinforcement, the faster the conditioning. Even a delay of a few seconds can retard the conditioning process.

In addition, there are two other major considerations in developing an operant response. The first concerns the efficiency with which it is established. In conditioning a rat to emit the bar-press response, for example, we could simply wait for this behavior to appear on several occasions, or we could shorten this process considerably.

Method of approximations. In the operant chamber, perhaps the rat moves from one part to another without even approaching the lever. To avoid a long wait for the animal merely to reach that vicinity, we could supply a food pellet whenever it has moved in the direction of the lever, even a short distance. We give it a few more reinforcements if it remains in the closer area, but then no further reinforcement occurs until it moves still closer to the lever. As this procedure is repeated, the animal is brought to the wall containing the lever, and then it receives no reinforcement until it touches the lever, perhaps sniffing it on the first occasion. Later, it must touch the bar with a paw before the reinforcement appears; still later, it must actually push the bar. At last, the rat's behavior is shaped so that it pushes the bar through a complete arc because only these responses are reinforced. Thereafter, bar-pressing increases in frequency as it is reinforced each time.

Utilizing this procedure, called the *method of approximations,* entertainers have taught animals to perform remarkable feats in a very short time. Many readers no doubt have seen these acts at circuses and on television. The circus pig is not really clever; the method of approximations has been cleverly used to shape its behavior. Hence, the procedure is also called *shaping* (Figure 8-12).

In human behavior, this method is widely used. In our educational systems, the tasks gradually become more difficult each month and each year. In a mental hospital, a patient who had been mute and passive for 19 years was induced to talk by this procedure. The experimenter (E) noted that the subject's (S) glance followed a package of gum when it accidentally fell on the floor, and so he used chewing gum as a positive reinforcer:

Figure 8-12 Shaping of Behavior. *This raccoon has become proficient at shooting baskets through the application of operant conditioning principles, especially the method of approximations. (Animal Behavior Enterprises, Inc.)*

Weeks 1, 2. A stick of gum was held before S's face and E waited until S's eyes moved toward it. When this response occurred, E as a consequence gave him the gum. By the end of the second week, response probability in the presence of the gum was increased to such an extent that S's eyes moved toward the gum as soon as it was held up.

Weeks 3, 4. The E now held the gum before S, waiting until he noticed movement in S's lips before giving it to him. Toward the end of the first session of the third week, a lip movement spontaneously occurred which E promptly reinforced. By the end of this week, both lip movement and eye movement occurred when the gum was held up. The E then withheld giving S the gum until S spontaneously made a vocalization, at which time E gave S the gum. By the end of this week, holding up the gum readily occasioned eye movement toward it, lip movement, and a vocalization resembling a croak.

Weeks 5, 6. The E held up the gum, and said, "Say gum, gum," repeating these words each time S vocalized. Giving S the gum was made contingent upon vocalizations increasingly approximating *gum*. At the sixth session (at the end of Week 6), when E said, "Say *gum, gum*," S suddenly said "Gum, please." This response was accompanied by . . . other responses of this class, that is, S answered questions regarding his name and age. (Isaacs et al., 1960)

Later, the patient responded to other questions. Eventually, he even made spontaneous requests, saying "ping-pong" when he wished to play a game. ■

Reinforcement schedules. Another way to improve an operant response is to increase its frequency, which is achieved by controlling the instances in which the organism receives reinforcement. During the acquisition phase, the organism is reinforced for every correct response, using a schedule called *continuous reinforcement*, or 100 percent reinforcement. Once the desired behavior is acquired, it then can be made to

■ *Both Skinner and my music teacher make use of the method of approximation. Each sets up a simple requirement and advances gradually to the final goal by immediately reinforcing all correct responses. For example, first we were told to "feel" the beat of the music, next to clap it, then to clap the accent louder, and finally to translate the music into shorthand. At first we would write only a measure at a time—later we had to do two at a time, and, today, we graduated to three at a time, and thus my inspiration for this paper.*

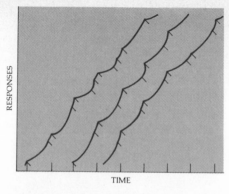

Figure 8-13 Fixed-Interval Responding: Animals. *A scalloped curve is produced, regardless of the species. Near the end of each time unit, as indicated on the horizontal axis, the response rate rises sharply. A pigeon, rat, and monkey produced these curves, but which is which? (After Skinner, 1956. Copyright 1956 by the American Psychological Association. Reprinted by permission.)*

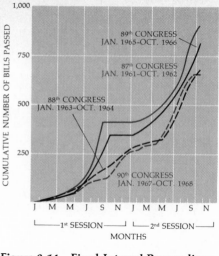

Figure 8-14 Fixed-Interval Responding: Human Beings. *The graph shows that the number of bills passed by each of four Congresses is extremely low at the beginning of each session and then rises rapidly just before adjournment (Weisberg & Waldrop, 1972).*

appear more frequently through partial or *intermittent reinforcement,* in which the response is not reinforced on every occurrence.

On a *fixed ratio* (FR) schedule, the subject is rewarded for only a proportion of the correct responses, and as this proportion increases, the organism responds at a higher rate. The subject might begin at FR2, meaning that one reinforcement is received for every two correct responses, but then the ratio changes to FR3, FR4, FR5, and slowly up to FR30, over the course of days and weeks. As the ratio increases, the subject performs more efficiently and at a higher rate. Payment for piecework in industry illustrates this schedule.

Reinforcement is available only after a certain interval of time on a *fixed interval* (FI) schedule. After another interval of the same length, reinforcement is available for the next correct response. Thus, the response rate gradually increases just before the end of each successive interval. In fact, many animals learn to discriminate the fixed interval between

reinforcements quite accurately (Figure 8-13). At the human level, a fixed-interval schedule occurs in a wide variety of contexts, from college to Congress. When an instructor administers a test every Friday, students usually study this subject at a low rate from Saturday through Wednesday, but then studying rises to a high rate on Thursday night, just before the next opportunity for reinforcement (Figure 8-14).

To maintain a consistently high rate of responding, variable schedules are used, in which the individual never knows when the next reinforcement will occur. On a *variable ratio* (VR) schedule, proportions or ratios are used, but reinforcement is provided only according to a certain average. On a VR6 schedule, the organism receives, on the average, one reinforcement for every six responses, but perhaps the individual emits eight responses and receives a reinforcement, then three responses and receives a reinforcement, and then

Learning and Symbolic Activity

Figure 8-15 Pigeon Missile Guidance. *Pigeons have been trained in the guidance of wartime missiles. Each pigeon is trained by a control signal to keep the target in the center of the viewing scope by pecking on a device that makes the necessary correction. The photo shows a pigeon being placed in a missile. For several reasons, these birds never became bombardiers. (From Skinner, 1960)*

seven responses and receives a reinforcement. The average is one reinforcement for every six responses, but the subject never knows how many responses are required for the next reinforcement, a situation similar to that in many gambling establishments where a high response rate occurs. The VR schedule can be increased gradually, leading to an extremely high rate of response.

The *variable interval* (VI) schedule also varies around some average, but here time intervals are used. On a VI8 schedule, the organism might respond 15 minutes before receiving a reinforcement, then receive a reinforcement for the first response just 1 minute later, then after 6 minutes, then 10 minutes, and so forth, averaging one reinforcement every 8 minutes. Under such conditions, pigeons have pecked for hours at the rate of 5 pecks per second; some have responded 10,000 times without any reinforcement whatsoever (Skinner, 1953). Human beings act in much the same way, although without the pigeon's incredible persistence.

By way of summarizing these various possibilities, we can say that all ratio schedules, fixed or variable, are maintained by some device or method for counting the responses. On the other hand, the various interval schedules are maintained by a timing apparatus.

Influence of Operant Conditioning

Operant conditioning procedures are pervasive, both in the training of animals and human beings (Figure 8-15). With these methods, pigeons have been trained as inspectors in a pill factory, a job for which they are well suited because of their high visual capacity. Using their beaks, they identified defective products with a 99 percent accuracy,

My ten-year-old brother was having difficulty learning some knots in order to pass a Tenderfoot test for Boy Scouts. My mother, noticing that he was having a hard time with them, tried to help him. Being the youngest, my brother enjoys attention and saw a good opportunity to keep it for a while. He became very obstinate with my mother, and played up the act of being totally frustrated with the whole procedure. She in turn had to become progressively more cajoling. Suddenly, without warning, she stood up quietly and suggested that he work on it by himself. No amount of sighing and frustrated exclamations could draw her back into her role of helper. Finally my brother settled down and began working in earnest on the knots. At this juncture, my mother returned to his side and he successfully learned the knots.

I particularly remember a camper I had last summer. Every time we would go anywhere he would always lag way behind the group and if I asked him to hurry up, he would go slower. If the group stopped to look at something, he would run ahead and tell everyone else to hurry up. His mother told me that he always did this sort of thing to get attention at home and in school. I then decided to ignore him at these times, but I did give him attention at other times when he was not aware of having an audience to perform for. Eventually he stopped always doing the opposite of what the group was doing.

selecting them as they passed by on a conveyor belt. Their performance was superior to that of the human workers in the same role, and special safeguards were set up against possible errors. Nevertheless, they were not employed, partly due to management's fear of adverse publicity (Verhave, 1966). Dogs have been trained for police work, horses for farming, monkeys for the circus, and other species for countless other tasks.

At the human level, the procedures are sufficiently widespread in childrearing, industry, education, and therapy that, in this context, we shall merely mention a few instances and indicate others appearing elsewhere in the book. ■ Earlier in this chapter we described how they were used for reinstating speech in a psychotic patient. Later, we shall discuss their use in behavior therapy (Figure 8-16). Programmed instruction is a teaching procedure based on operant conditioning principles. In short, this approach has been found useful in such diverse contexts as treating sex problems, developing antilitter behavior, and enabling a hyperactive child to sit still longer (Reckers & Lovaas, 1974; Clar et al., 1972; Twardosz & Sajwaj, 1972). □

In the novel *Walden Two*, B. F. Skinner advocates operant conditioning techniques, known as "cultural engineering," for establishing a utopian society. He has urged their use in redesigning cultures and improving human life, and communities have been created on this basis (Kinkade, 1973). Also, a great deal already has been written on training parents in operant methods (O'Dell, 1974). This issue is highly controversial, however, for it seems to call for shaping and reshaping human behavior by social scientists (Skinner, 1961b, 1974). These views have found support, however, as evidenced by the following statement:

There have been many revolutions in our time, but . . . in the long run this psychological revolution that we see beginning here in

the theory and practice of shaping behavior of the young will be the most important of all for the success and happiness of man on this planet. (Platt, 1966)

In another book, *Beyond Freedom and Dignity*, Skinner argues that redesigning a culture involves changing the environment so that different responses are selected for reinforcement. There is a selection process in any environment, which went virtually unnoticed until Darwin stated his ideas, and supporters of operant conditioning emphasize that selective reinforcement pertains to responses as well as to the structure of species. According to Skinner, the way we organize our environment determines our responses; virtually all our major problems of overpopulation, depletion of natural resources, pollution, and the possibility of nuclear war stem from our lack of environmental control over human behavior.

The difference between our present society and the one Skinner proposes is that the control would be more carefully planned, rather than springing up haphazardly from the self-interests and the political successes and failures of so many different people. The evolution of our present culture is the result of a massive but prescientific effort at controlling ourselves. As Skinner has said, we see what humanity under these circumstances has made of itself, but we have not discovered what scientific human beings, using a behavior technology, can make of themselves (Skinner, 1971).

Many people who disagree consider the causes of behavior as residing primarily within the organism, rather than in the environment. A person who works tenaciously at a task without success has will power, rather than a history of intermittent reinforcement. It is said that the use of conditioning procedures divests the individual of his or her dignity and represents an extreme encroachment on the individual's freedom. Skinner recognizes these concerns, as reflected in the title of his book.

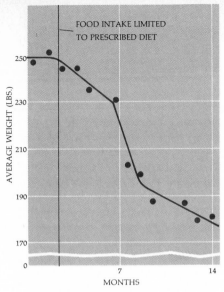

Eating Problem
Whenever the patient stole food, she was removed from the dining area. The graph shows her weight loss with this procedure.

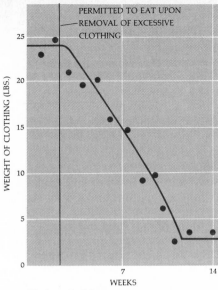

Clothing Problem
If the patient's clothing weighed more than a specified amount when she entered the dining room, she was not allowed to have her meal. The graph shows the amount of clothing worn by the patient.

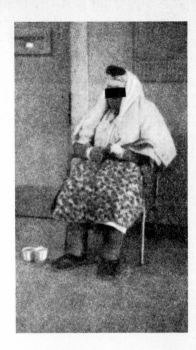

Figure 8-16 Operant Conditioning in Therapy. *The use of operant conditioning techniques in therapy is illustrated in the case of a 47-year-old woman hospitalized as schizophrenic. This woman, weighing more than 250 pounds, overate and stole food from others in the dining hall. As shown in the upper photo, she wore several dresses, stockings, and sweaters at the same time and carried cups and saucers from the dining hall wherever she went. She also wore several of the hospital towels on her head like a turban. In an effort to change these behaviors, her meals were made available only upon the appearance or disappearance of certain responses. The lower photo shows the patient after treatment. (After Ayllon, 1963)*

Conditioning and Complex Behavior

Skinner's viewpoint on operant conditioning is not so much threatening or dangerous as it is impractical, in the view of those who disagree. These people charge that it does not apply to complex human behavior. Even if it is a plausible interpretation of simple habits, the ideas are insufficient to account for the broad range of human behavior (Neal, 1973; Bindra, 1974).

Developing Behavior Chains

A moment's reflection shows that human behavior usually does not occur in separate segments, as just described, but in a more or less continuous flow. A batter hits the ball, runs down the baseline, touches first base, and watches the coach for further signals, all in a rapid, integrated sequence. Up to this point we have considered incidents of learning as discrete phenomena, occurring essentially in isolation from one another.

Learning a series of related behaviors, according to Skinner, is known as *chaining,* and the result is a *behavior chain.* The driver of an automobile, for example, must emit a sequence of interconnected behaviors in order to transport himself or herself from place to place, and these acts cannot occur in a random order. In fact, except for minor variations, only one sequence will achieve the goal.

Response-produced cues and reinforcement. In a behavior chain, each response results in a set of conditions that constitutes reinforcement, usually secondary, for that response, and it also serves as a stimulus for the next response. After the driver of an automobile has reached into his or her pocket and withdrawn the keys, the condition of having the keys in hand constitutes reinforcement for the act of putting the hand into the pocket, and it also serves as a stimulus for using the key in the lock of the door. Once the key has been turned, the click of the lock, as well as the kinesthetic cues from the turning movement, indicate that the door is unlocked. Thus, the response of turning the key has been reinforced, for the door now can be opened, and it also has provided a stimulus to operate the door handle, the next important act in the chain. Similarly, the act of opening the door is reinforced because the car can be entered, and it also provides a stimulus for making the entrance. Entering the car is reinforced because the individual gains access to the ignition, and the presence of the ignition cylinder is a stimulus to insert the ignition key, and so forth.

Each successive cue in such a sequence is termed a *response-produced cue* because the stimuli that arise from each response serve as cues for the next act of the chain. Such cues are discriminative stimuli (S_D). The external cues are usually visual or auditory, while the internal cues are largely kinesthetic, which arise from turning the key in the lock, depressing the accelerator, or turning the wheel. Other senses also may be involved, such as the sense of rotary motion when the steering wheel is turned too suddenly. With training, rather complex behavior chains can be developed in lower animals (Figure 8-17).

We also form verbal chains, as evidenced in our memorization of telephone numbers, poetry, and other materials. In conversation, the chain is verbal and interpersonal. One person says "Hello," which is a stimulus for the other person to say "Hello" or "How are you?" This behavior is a stimulus for the first person to talk again. Each person's response is both reinforcing and the stimulus for a reply. If the other person's reaction is unpleasant or merely covert, it may be a stimulus to break the chain or modify it in some way.

Levels of integration. Behavior chains also can develop at successively higher levels of integration. A complex skill may be the final product of a series of smaller behavior chains synthesized earlier.

Consider the problem of learning to operate a typewriter. First one learns responses designated as *letter chains,* so that when typing the word "YES," the chaining proceeds as follows: *Y* is struck and this response is reinforced by the presence of the letter on paper, and its presence on the paper is a stimulus to strike *E,* and so forth. After the individual is fairly proficient at this level, he or she begins developing *word chains,* in which the letters for a whole word arouse a single response, instead of noticeably separate responses. The letter responses seem to take care of themselves. Eventually, *phrase chains* appear, in which whole series of words are typed without much attention to the separate letters or the separate words (Figure 8-18).

A child may bake a cake in a most laborious fashion, performing each step as a major task in itself. The completion of any one act is not a sufficient stimulus to begin the next one, and the child must try to remember what to do next. Gradually, the separate acts are chained in longer sequences, with fewer mistakes. Eventually, the child may not refer to the cookbook or even pause to think what to do next; the entire sequence is performed almost as a single response, which then serves as the signal for the next response, preparing to serve the cake. In such instances, the separate chains are linked together at higher and higher levels of complexity; complicated skills, after they have been practiced a long time, tend to proceed automatically. ■

■ *Because of the cost of skeet shooting, I reload my shells, using a handloading press. In operating the press, the empty shell case is resized, primed, filled with powder, wadded, then filled with shot, and finally crimped and placed in a box. When repeating this procedure over and over, my mind wanders off the task sometimes. Suddenly I remember what I am doing, and I cannot recall completing the last couple of shells. The shells seem to turn out perfectly, however, even better than if I were conscious of doing them.*

Learning and Symbolic Activity

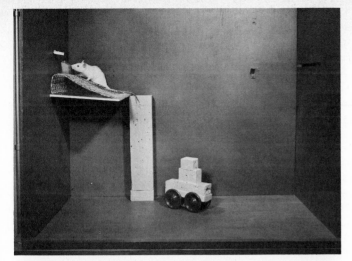

Figure 8-17 A Behavior Chain. *The rat has learned to push the car to reach the stand to jump on the ramp to climb to the food. But this chain is learned backwards. The rat first learned to climb the ramp leading to the food dispenser. Next, it learned to jump to the stand, thus reaching the ramp. Later, it learned to climb on the car so it could get to the stand. Finally, it learned to push the car into position, from where it could make the jump. (R. W. Kelley, Life Magazine, © Time Inc.)*

Type of Chain	Response
Letter	Y E S S I R , T H A T ' S M Y B A B Y !
Word	YES SIR, THAT'S MY BABY!
Phrase	YES SIR, THAT'S MY BABY!

Figure 8-18 Chaining in Typing. *According to the chaining viewpoint, the separate responses are developed into larger and larger units.*

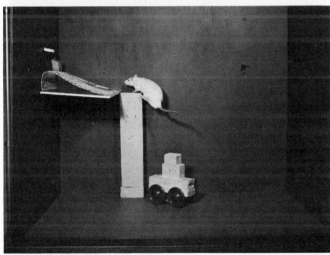

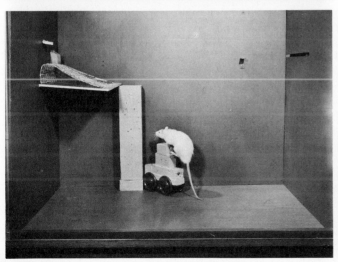

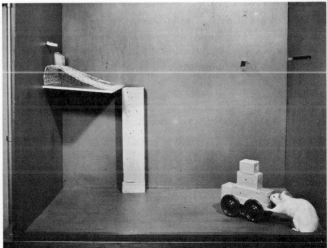

Response Hierarchies

In most learning situations an individual acquires more than one potential response that may initiate a behavior chain. Furthermore, these initial responses generally are established in some order of probability of occurrence, in an arrangement called a *response hierarchy*. In understanding complex behavior, we must consider not only the relationships among responses chained at the same level but also the relationships among hierarchically ordered responses that initiate these chains.

A young man failing a college course might emit any one of several responses. He might go to see the dean first, in hopes of being allowed to drop the course; next, he might consult with the professor in an attempt to obtain extra help; then, he might try to rationalize the whole affair, stating that he didn't care what grade he received in the course; and finally, he might decide to leave school for a semester. The most dominant or potent response in this hierarchy is consulting the dean, presumably because it has been reinforced most on previous occasions. The next-strongest response is dealing directly with the professor, which has been found somewhat less helpful in the past, and so forth, through the entire response hierarchy for this particular situation.

Thus, the student goes to see the dean, and if he or she is receptive, a behavior chain has commenced in which the student follows procedures for dropping a course and perhaps adding another one. If the dean is not receptive, the student consults with his professor and thus begins a different chain. Whether or not any particular chain is enacted depends on the position of its initial response in the hierarchy and whether or not the more potent initial responses in that hierarchy have been successful. Another student who is failing a course goes to visit the professor immediately, probably because he or she has found that response most reinforced on previous occasions.

The behavior of the monk, in the example cited earlier, can be interpreted on these bases. The most potent response in his hierarchy undoubtedly was to strike the cats immediately, but he was prevented from doing so. Perhaps the next most potent response was to ask to eat his meal elsewhere, but the rules of the punishment did not permit this. Somewhere lower in his hierarchy was the complex response of secretly going out at night to punish the cats.

We can also imagine the behavior chain in this reaction. The response of looking in the storage house was reinforced by finding the bag, which was then the cue to go look for the cats. Finding the cats served as reinforcement for the monk's search and also as the signal to put them in the sack. The response of putting them there was reinforced because then they could not escape, and it was also the signal to creep out under the arch in search of a big stick.

Two-Factor Theory

But the cats' behavior, once they were released in the kitchen, requires further scrutiny. Part of their reaction, the fear response, was induced by classical conditioning, and the other aspect, running away, was based on operant conditioning. How do these two types of conditioning interact, if at all?

A possible answer involves the two-factor theory of conditioning, illustrated in laboratory experiments on avoidance conditioning. In *avoidance conditioning* the organism's response prevents the occurrence of some negative reinforcer, such as confinement or a shock.

Avoidance conditioning. In one early laboratory experiment, guinea pigs were placed individually in a revolving drum that turned whenever they ran, and initially they all received an electric shock on several occasions shortly after a buzzer was sounded. Through classical conditioning the buzzer became a conditioned stimulus, and all the animals acquired a conditioned emotional reaction to this signal. They showed trembling and rigid posture whenever the buzzer (CS) sounded. However, each animal in one group could avoid the shock by running at the onset of the signal, while those in the other group always received a shock, regardless of their behavior. Those that could avoid the shock soon began to run at the sound of the buzzer, and this operant response was reinforced, resulting in the termination or prevention of the shock. For these subjects, both classical and operant conditioning had occurred (Brogden et al., 1938; Figure 8-19).

The fear reactions in both groups constituted the first factor in the two-factor theory. In addition, one group learned the operant running response, and this behavior can be identified as the second factor. Both groups acquired the fear, but only the avoidance group learned, in addition, a way of coping with it. More recent experiments have shown similar findings (Kamin, 1956; Singh et al., 1971). ■

On such bases, some psychologists claim that emotions are learned following the laws of classical conditioning and that the responses for coping with emotions are acquired through operant conditioning. Complex behavior is thus viewed as a combination of classical and operant conditioning, wherein each contributes a different aspect to the total learning situation.

The situation with the cats can be interpreted on this basis. Their original training, in the sack, was in a classical framework; their behavior there in no way influenced their receiving a beating. Coughing, which was associated with the beatings, eventually became the signal for this painful treatment, and it elicited a conditioned fear response. Later, when the animals were placed in an open situation, they ran away whenever the monk coughed. This behavior did influence the situation; it provided a solution to the problem. The reinforcement for this operant response was the reduction of fear.

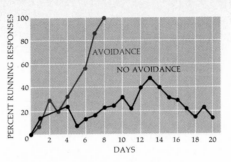

Figure 8-19 Two-Factor View. *Both groups learned to fear the sound of the buzzer through classical conditioning. The group that could avoid the ensuing shock (color line) did so by running, which was learned through operant conditioning. (After Brogden et al., 1938. Copyright 1938 by the American Psychological Association. Reprinted by permission.)*

The concept of tension reduction as reinforcing has been applied to all sorts of aversive situations, including *escape conditioning,* which is similar to avoidance conditioning except that the organism cannot completely avoid the noxious stimulus. Instead, it can perform an appropriate response to remove it once it has commenced.□ Incidentally, the difficulty in removing an irrational fear of a harmless object, as in a phobia, also involves tension reduction. In order to avoid the tension, the organism never approaches the feared object. Thus, in this avoidance behavior it cannot discover that the object in question is essentially harmless.

A two-factor interpretation also can be made for approach behavior. A person begins to like a certain perfume or incense through its association with a newly found loved one; then, he or she purchases some in order to ensure the presence of this odor. Again, classical conditioning is considered a basis for learning attitudes and emotional responses, and operant conditioning is considered to be the basis for learning what to do about them.

■ *When I was a young child and I did something wrong my father would approach me with a strap, which didn't bother me until he hit me with it. It wasn't long before I started running when I saw my father with the strap.*

□ *Tensions were running high among the members of our family last spring. We were about to move from New Hampshire to New York. One day my mother lost her temper at my brother for some reason or other and out of habit I made a move towards the dishwasher. Suddenly I realized that this was a move of habit and that Mom was not mad at me nor did her anger have anything to do with the dishes not being done! Now I realize that Mom had unknowingly conditioned me to do the dishes every time she became really angry.*

The conditioning started when Mom was trying to train the three girls in our family to do their share of the dishes. Quite often she would get mad because one child had been left by the others to do the dishes alone. She would praise the child who had stayed to do her share of the job and "tongue-lash" the others for running off. I soon learned the value of doing dishes voluntarily whenever she was angry. I would escape her rage and would be praised at the same time. I also had the pleasure of seeing my siblings suffer.

Research challenges. One purpose of theory is to provide an interpretation of research findings, and in this respect the two-factor theory has proven useful. Results from a single experiment can be viewed from both the classical and operant framework, and the viewpoint has been advanced that both types of conditioning take place in every experiment (Tarpy, 1975). Another purpose of theory is to stimulate further research on the issue, and here the two-factor theory also has been of value. Especially in recent years, some investigations have challenged the two-factor theory.

The question has been raised as to whether one or two different processes are ultimately involved (Terrace, 1973). Biofeedback-type experiments have served to stimulate this interest, and other studies have shown that experimental animals sometimes shape their own behavior, without the method of approximations. In this case, called *autoshaping,* there is some evidence that operant responses follow the laws of classical conditioning, rather than the usual operant model (Braun & Jenkins, 1968; Gamzu & Williams, 1973). Further, studies in avoidance learning suggest that innate behavior patterns in certain lower animals may restrict the application of the two-factor theory (Bolles, 1970).

On the other hand, the two-factor theory has maintained a prominent position in learning theory for more than 25 years. For any theory to be useful, research must continue, some of which undoubtedly will raise further issues. At this point, some modification may be in order, but some version of this theory still appears warranted.

In any scientific field, challenges are continually raised, as illustrated even with regard to the basic components of conditioning. When three different neutral stimuli—sugar water, lights, and noise—were paired with the same unconditioned poisonous stimulus for a group of rats, only the sugar water became a conditioned stimulus. Apparently, this stimulus was associated most easily with the unconditioned response, which was severe nausea. However, the other two stimuli, when paired with electric shock, readily became conditioned (Garcia & Koelling, 1966). These findings suggest that conditioning is not equally applicable to all types of stimuli and responses. Organisms are neurologically prepared to acquire certain associations more readily than others (Seligman, 1970). Research with infants has shown several applications of the principles of conditioning but also some exceptions to the findings obtained with adults and animals (Fitzgerald & Brockbill, 1976).

Extension of Conditioning Principles

In closing we should make a final observation concerning the monk and the monastery cats. The monk exerted an influence over the cats, but advocates of operant conditioning also emphasize that the cats influenced the monk.

Operant conditioning as reciprocal. In operant conditioning, each participant reinforces the other; the relationship is reciprocal. For the monk, then, the discriminative stimulus was the approach of the cats, his response was to cough, and his reinforcement was the cats' running away, leaving him to consume his meal in peace. He had them conditioned but they, in return, had him conditioned. They kept him coughing, while he kept them running.

Operant conditioning occurs in this way in any sustained relationship. The individual operates on his or her environment, and the environment, which includes the living organisms in it, operates on the individual, as well. ■The parent controls the child, but the child, as any parent knows, also controls the parent. A government creates and amends laws to control the people, but it does so according to how well the people respond to them.

The monk also thought up the whole procedure of training the animals in the first place. How do we understand this behavior in terms of conditioning?

■ *Because I would do almost anything to avoid hurting my father's feelings, I taught myself at an early age to laugh, or at least smile, at his poor jokes. Each time I laughed, however, I was increasing the likelihood of his telling another joke.*

Conditioning and thinking. As a rule, psychologists interested in conditioning are not concerned with thinking as a research topic. They study overt responses, focusing, for example, on the monk's finding the sack, catching the cats, and so forth. When referring to complex behavior, the concepts of chaining and response hierarchies are emphasized.

Thinking is assumed to involve a complex interaction of these components, the result of many diverse behavior chains at all levels of complexity. Most important are the internal or mental chains, where the responses are merely thoughts, and the reinforcement is imagined as success or failure. Each thought serves as a cue for the next one. The monk produced chains and response hierarchies in symbolic fashion, until he discovered the solution; then, he put this solution into practice in an overt manner.

This viewpoint, since it describes learning as the formation of stimulus-response connections, is known as *S-R psychology*. The objection to this approach has been that the contribution of the organism (O) is ignored. For this reason, some psychologists interested in thinking change the formulation to S-O-R: stimulus, organism, and response. They try to make inferences about the organism's internal processes as well as about relationships between stimuli and responses.

In any case, the emphasis in conditioning is on S-R associations. Sometimes the association is among stimuli, as in classical conditioning; sometimes it is between a response and reinforcing stimulus, as in operant conditioning; and sometimes it is in the interaction between these circumstances. For these reasons, S-R learning or conditioning is said to be based on *associative processes*. Sometimes it is known simply as association learning.

In another approach to learning, the role of associative processes in the acquisition of simple habits is acknowledged, but these processes are not considered to be sufficient to account for higher levels of behavior. The enormous difference between human beings and other animals is emphasized, and it is pointed out that human learning, through the capacity for thinking, is the most outstanding development of psychological evolution. As we shall see in the next chapter, special higher-level processes, called cognitive processes, are said to be involved.

Summary

Classical Conditioning

1. Learning is generally defined as a change in behavior that is a result of experience, excluding changes due to maturation and physiological adjustments. Classical conditioning is a simple form of learning typically involving physiological reactions and emotional responses. It occurs whenever some previously neutral stimulus arouses such a response, as when ringing a bell can be made to produce salivation. To achieve conditioning, the neutral stimulus is regularly paired with an unconditioned stimulus, which automatically elicits salivation.

2. Some of the important principles of classical conditioning are:

   a. stimuli that resemble the conditioned stimulus also elicit the conditioned response—the principle of stimulus generalization;

   b. when two different stimuli are presented, only the one that has been followed by the unconditioned stimulus elicits a response—the principle of discrimination;

   c. repeated presentation of the conditioned stimulus without the unconditioned stimulus eventually results in the disappearance of the conditioned response—the principle of extinction;

d. after an interval, there may be a return of the previously extinguished conditioned response—the principle of spontaneous recovery;

e. a conditioned stimulus, such as a bell, can be used as an "unconditioned" stimulus to produce further conditioning—the principle of higher-order conditioning.

3. The procedures of classical conditioning are useful in treating certain behavior problems and in studying sensory capacities. Probably the most important role of classical conditioning lies in the development of diffuse emotional reactions and certain attitudes.

Responses and Reinforcement

4. Two types of responses have been identified: respondent behaviors, which occur in response to a specific, identifiable stimulus, and operant behaviors, in which the organism operates on its environment in some fashion. These behaviors exist on a continuum of reflexiveness; that is, they differ in the degree to which they are under external stimulus control.

5. Reinforcement is any event that increases the probability of a response. In classical conditioning, it occurs whenever the conditioned stimulus is paired with the unconditioned stimulus. In operant conditioning, it occurs whenever a certain event follows the response.

Operant Conditioning

6. Habits are acquired through operant conditioning, where responses are followed by reinforcing stimuli. The originally initiating stimulus for any given operant response is unknown, but gradually a discriminative stimulus develops, which signals the availability of reinforcement. Secondary reinforcement is an important aspect of operant conditioning; objects and events acquire reinforcing properties through their association with primary or physiological reinforcement.

7. In operant conditioning, the organism's response can be developed by shaping, where each closer approximation to the desired behavior is reinforced. Responses also can be reinforced regularly or intermittently and on variable or fixed schedules. The highest rate of responding and greatest resistance to extinction are achieved with variable types of intermittent reinforcement.

8. Operant conditioning procedures are used extensively with animals and also in childrearing, industry, education, and therapy among human beings. According to this view, many of our major problems stem from a lack of scientific control over human behavior, which could be achieved by a more carefully planned environment.

Conditioning and Complex Behavior

9. Complex behavior is accounted for partly by chaining, which is the process of learning a series of related responses. Each response serves as reinforcement for the previous response and also as a stimulus for the next one. The series is known as a behavior chain.

10. Complex behavior also is accounted for partly by response hierarchies, in which an individual acquires several potential responses to a given situation. These are ordered in terms of their previous reinforcement history and they appear on this basis. When a given response in the hierarchy fails to yield a certain reinforcement, the next one in the hierarchy is emitted.

11. Aspects of classical and operant conditioning are combined in the two-factor theory. According to this view, the organism learns attitudes and emotional reactions on the basis of classical conditioning; responses for coping with these feelings are learned through operant conditioning. While issues have been raised, this theory still appears warranted.

12. From the conditioning viewpoint, thinking is assumed to involve a complex interaction of S and R components, resulting in internal behavior chains at all levels of complexity. Since the emphasis in learning is always on S-R associations, the whole process is sometimes known as association learning.

Suggested Readings

Hilgard, E. R., & Bower, G. H. *Theories of learning* (4th ed.). Englewood Cliffs, N.J.: Prentice-Hall, 1975. A primary source for 30 years for students of learning theory.

Hill, W. F. *Learning: A survey of psychological interpretations* (3rd ed.). New York: Crowell, 1977. Considers a variety of viewpoints and includes a separate chapter on Skinner's approach.

Sahakian, W. S. (Ed.). *Learning: Systems, models and theories* (2nd ed.). Skokie, Ill.: Rand McNally, 1976. Provides original source materials for the various theories of learning.

Skinner, B. F. *Beyond freedom and dignity*. New York: Knopf, 1971. A controversial book which argues that a successful behavioral technology can develop only when we cease to attribute responses to an individual's inner state.

Tarpy, R. M. *Basic principles of learning*. Glenview, Ill.: Scott, Foresman, 1975. Emphasizes the recent research in animal learning, generally presented in historical perspective.

Chapter 9

Cognitive Processes

The study of the development of thinking from infancy to adulthood is one of the liveliest areas in psychology today. Much of this ferment arises from the work of one person, a Swiss psychologist named Jean Piaget.

Piaget began his studies as a biologist, publishing his first article in the *Journal of Natural History of Neuchâtel,* in which he described a rare albino sparrow. The article was well received, although Piaget was only 11 years old. Further efforts brought him the offer of a job as curator at the Museum of Natural History in Geneva, but he had to decline in order to finish high school (Ginsburg & Opper, 1969).

Upon completing graduate studies in biology, Piaget turned to a question usually considered only by philosophers: What is the nature of knowledge? This question was not novel—philosophers had been considering it for centuries—but there was novelty in Piaget's search for answers. He decided to talk with young children, who presumably have less knowledge than adults, since they are in the early stages of acquiring it.

Through these conversations, Piaget came to the view that the reasoning of normal children is *qualitatively* different from that of adults. It is not just an inferior version of adult thought. The results of this work also led him to conclude that the development of human thinking can be divided into four periods or stages, approximately according to chronological age (Figure 9-1).

Stages in Cognitive Development

Before considering Piaget's four stages of development we should point out that he has his own meanings for certain terms. He generally uses the word *learning* to refer to the acquisition of low-level activities, specific habits, and

Figure 9-1 Jean Piaget. *Piaget developed his major ideas through observation of comparatively few subjects, usually his three children and a nephew. Other psychologists have engaged in laboratory and large-scale studies to confirm his views. (de Braine from Black Star)*

other simple responses. Albany is the capital of New York, and this fact can be taught by conditioning. It is low-level learning; no reasoning is involved; and most people are not especially interested in learning the capital of New York anyway, so reinforcement is helpful.

On the other hand, *development* is considerably more complex. It involves acquiring useful ways of thinking, applicable across broad situations. It is not the acquisition of facts and habits but rather problem-solving and wisdom in the widest sense. Development is not the amount you know but rather the strategies you have for dealing with information, especially in solving problems.

It is clear from these definitions that Piaget is interested in higher-level processes, such as conceiving, recognizing, judging, interpreting, and reasoning, collectively called thinking or *cognitive processes*. The emphasis here, in contrast to associative learning, is on knowledge and understanding.

Sensory-Motor Period

From birth to approximately 18 or 24 months of age, according to Piaget, children do not think in the sense that older children do, but they have a kind of intelligence that he calls ''practical intelligence.'' It manifests itself not in thinking about things but rather in experiencing them and acting on them, and therefore this stage is called the *sensory-motor period.*

During this stage, the infant's intelligence develops rapidly in several respects, especially in forming the concept of *object permanence.* Initially, young infants cannot distinguish between themselves and other objects, and they do not conceive of objects as having any permanent, independent existence apart from their own actions. Adults know that if they put an object in a drawer it continues to exist, but babies seem to think otherwise. Piaget dangled a rattle in front of his daughter's face, and Jacqueline wriggled with delight. Then he hid it under a blanket as she watched; she instantly lost interest. Apparently, at this age an object ceases to exist when one is not looking at it, handling it, or otherwise acting upon it.

A few months later Jacqueline was observed to behave differently, as did Gérard when his ball rolled under an armchair. He retrieved it with difficulty, and then it rolled under the sofa at the other end of the room. He looked there, could not find it, crossed the room again, and explored the place under the armchair where the ball was previously (Piaget, 1954). Gérard knew that the ball continued to exist even when it was out of sight; he had acquired the concept of object permanence.

The end of the sensory-motor period is signaled by the acquisition of the concept of the object as a permanent, independent entity. This step is enormously important because now children can represent objects to themselves. They need not act on a thing in order for it to exist in their minds. They can carry things around in their heads—images of rattles, balls, and other things—which is perhaps the beginning of thinking. Children have something to think about; they can plan sets of actions.

Preoperational Thought

Gradually, children's representational abilities become more sophisticated and, most important, children learn to use language to communicate ideas to others. They become truly social beings. However, there are also serious deficiencies in thinking during this *pre-operational period*, which lasts roughly through the preschool years, from age 18 months to age 6 or 7 years.

Egocentrism. Preoperational thought is said to be extremely egocentric, but the term does not mean that children are unaware of other perspectives. Rather, *perceptual egocentrism* means that preschoolers, for example, do not realize that other people see things from a viewpoint that is different from theirs. A young boy playing hide-and-seek shuts his eyes and says to an adult: "Ha, ha! Can't see me!" ■

In one experiment, a child was seated at a table that held a model of some mountains; seated in a different location

was a doll. The child's task was to select from a series of pictures the one that represented the way the mountains looked from the doll's viewpoint. The child could walk around the table and observe the model from the doll's viewpoint but had to return to his or her own seat to select the picture. Preschoolers had little success with this task; they consistently selected the picture that matched the model seen from their own vantage point (Figure 9-2).

By school age or earlier, most children have overcome this *perceptual egocentrism*. The five-year-old who stands in front of her brother, giggling as he tries

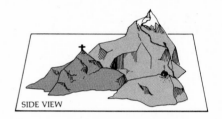

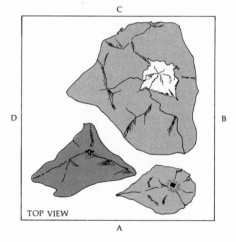

Figure 9-2 The Three Mountains Test. *The model is approximately 1 meter in length and width and varies in height from 12 to 30 centimeters. The child, first seated at position A, sees in the foreground a green mountain with a little house on top. Slightly behind and to the left is a higher, brown mountain with a red cross on its summit. The tallest mountain is in the background, colored gray, with snow on its peak. While at position A, the child is asked to indicate by various means the perspectives at positions B, C, and D. (From Piaget & Inhelder, 1967. Copyright by Humanities Press Inc. and Routledge & Kegan Paul Ltd.)*

■ *One day I was eating lunch with my sister, Emily, who was five at the time. Toward the end of the meal she apparently wanted more French fries because she shut her eyes and took one of mine. After she had swallowed it she opened her eyes again and continued the conversation as if nothing had happened.*

After a few minutes she closed her eyes again and repeated the process. I said nothing and she repeated the action three more times, each time returning to the conversation as if nothing had happened. Finally, when she opened her eyes I said "Well, Emily, that's five, you've only got three more French fries to go and I'll be cleaned out."

Of course I had meant this humourously, but Emily looked up, furious, and accusingly said, "You were peeking!"

to watch a television program, is able to take her brother's viewpoint and thus annoy him. But a kind of *cognitive egocentrism* lingers into later life. Children who can imagine how the world looks from a different perspective still find it difficult to understand that other people do not know their thoughts. Cognitive egocentrism is reflected in children's communication difficulties, in which they forget to put themselves in the role of the listener and adapt their message to that person. ▪

When children were asked to explain a new game to a blindfolded listener, one child gave the following instructions, illustrating cognitive egocentrism:

You put that thing in the cup and then you pour it out and you move your pig up and then you put it back in and then you move your pig up again. And when you put it in there sometimes you can't move it up. (Flavell et al., 1968)

Figure 9-3 Conservation Experiment.
The child under age six typically agrees that the amounts of marbles in the tall beakers are about equal. Then, after watching the contents of one jar being poured into a wider jar, he or she usually says the taller one has more marbles. (Sheila A. Farr photos)

Centration. Another characteristic of preoperational thought is that it tends to focus on a single, striking feature of an object or event, ignoring other aspects. This perceptual tendency is called *centration.* The most widely cited of Piaget's investigations, the conservation experiment, illustrates this principle. Here the idea is to discover whether a child recognizes that an amount of something is not increased or decreased when only its appearance is changed. The amount remains the same and the question is whether the child has formed this concept of *conservation.*

Two identically shaped, tall jars containing equal amounts of liquid, marbles, or some other substance are placed in front of the child, who asserts that the contents are equal. Then, as the child observes the process, the contents of one are poured into a third jar, which is low and wide. The amount of the marbles has not changed; it is conserved. But the preoperational child maintains that there are more marbles in the tall, thin beaker than in the short, fat one. His or her attention is caught by the difference in the height of the beakers of marbles (Figure 9-3).

▪ When I was growing up, we had a large ginger-colored tomcat named Precious, to which I was very attached. When I was about five, I used to pretend that I was a cat. This naturally included crawling under the sofa and perching up on the top bunk, which were Precious's favorite places, and rubbing against my mother's ankles, purring and meowing when I wanted something.

I remember the best part of this game was being under the sofa watching feet go by, or on the top bunk looking down on everything. It was fascinating to me that the cat didn't see things the way I normally did, and that I could put myself into his position. The thing that made me stop playing this game was that no matter how expressively I meowed at my mother, she wouldn't understand me. This was very confusing, and it made me sad to realize that she couldn't understand me unless I used people talk, and that poor Precious was probably continually frustrated.

The preoperational child tends to focus on states rather than on transformations, on how things appear rather than on how they were constructed. The child knows that the two quantities originally were equal and that the contents of one beaker were merely emptied into another but does not use this knowledge in making a judgment. The child thinks only of the contrast before his or her eyes between the very tall column of marbles and the short one. This type of thinking is called *preoperational* because the child cannot yet perform certain basic mental operations. The child reasons in terms of the dominant perceptual experience, not the procedures involved. ■ □

Concrete Operations

Around age six, the child begins to master the concept of conservation. Once a firm nonconserver, the child starts to waver. For example, one child and an experimenter each dropped marbles, one by one, into different beakers. The child's fell into a short, wide beaker and the experimenter's into a tall, thin one. The child, who could count to 30, counted the marbles as they dropped, and at first she maintained that she and the experimenter had the same amount. "How do you know?" she was asked. "Because I counted 'em. You've got 10 and I've got 10."

Confusion as growth. As the column of marbles mounted more impressively in the tall beaker, she began to hesitate. Even though she counted 20 in each, she finally decided that the experimenter had more. Then she became confused: "You've got more, 'cause they're spreaded out more. No, I don't know" (Clinchy, 1975).

This confusion is a sign of cognitive growth. The younger child attends to only one aspect—the height of the beakers. The older child thinks about one aspect and then another, in rapid succession, and six months later will integrate the two aspects. The child will see

that the height of the tall beaker is compensated for by the width of the shorter one. As one child later said: "They're just the same. This one's short, but it makes up for that one's being longer by being fat."

Furthermore, the child knows that appearances can be deceiving: "They look different, but they're really the same." Here the decision is based not on the final state of the two beakers but on the procedure that was performed.

Awareness of operations. During the stage of concrete operations, which lasts until age 11 or perhaps longer, the child becomes capable of reversing the transformation in his or her head. The experimenter makes two straight clay "worms" of equal length and then forms the child's into a curly worm. When asked if they are still the same length, the child says: "Acourse. If you pull my worm straight, he'll look like yours. They were both the same to start."

Similarly, the child can solve problems requiring classification, ordering, and sequencing. The child can arrange a series of sticks from tallest to shortest without making errors. Previously, he or she could not think of a given stick as both shorter than the preceding one and longer than the next one. The child could think only in terms of shorter *or* longer but now can deal with both concepts at the same time. Persons at this stage have mastered the operations required in solving such problems, providing the materials are concrete, which is why we speak of *concrete operations* (Piaget, 1950).

Suppose, however, we ask the child to find the area of a square containing a circle just touching each of its sides, the radius of which is two inches. This problem can be difficult even for college students, and the child probably will not attempt it unless he or she can see a drawing of the square, circle, and radius. Then the child will approach it on a trial-and-error basis, if at all, perhaps drawing the radius in one position and

Learning and Symbolic Activity

then the other, trying to see relationships between properties of the circle and square (Figure 9-4).

Formal Operations

To solve the circle-in-a-square problem most readily, the child needs *formal operations*, which is the capacity for reasoning apart from concrete situations. It is abstract reasoning, and usually the child age 11 or older can engage in this type of reasoning, although at a less sophisticated level than that of most adults. The child well into formal operations will approach the circle-in-a-square problem readily and, rather than drawing new radii immediately, will sit back and think, trying to generate all the possibilities for a solution.

Abstract thinking. In the previous stage of cognitive growth, the child was able to classify, enumerate, and place objects and events in time and space, but at the stage of formal operations he or she can *imagine the possibilities* inherent in a problem. The child now can deduce what should occur if a given possibility is true, perform useful experiments, and think about these conclusions in a practical way.

Probably the most important feature of formal operations is that it acknowledges various possibilities. Reality is seen as just one aspect of what might be. The adolescent can engage in this type of reasoning, generating hypothetical possibilities, and testing them to see which one seems most valid. The adolescent can leave reality altogether, reasoning entirely in terms of abstract propositions.

Implications. Extension of the capacity for formal operations means that the cognitive world of the adolescent and adult is very different from that of the child. Children live largely a here-and-now existence. Family, friends, and school are seen as relatively unchanging. Adolescents and adults live more in the future. Adolescents, in particular,

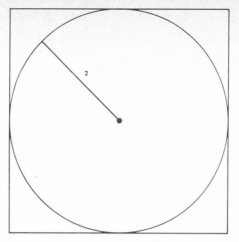

Figure 9-4   A Problem in Reasoning.   *If the radius of the circle is 2, what is the area of the square? The answer is on the next page. (After Dunker, 1945. Copyright 1945 by the American Psychological Association. Reprinted by permission.)*

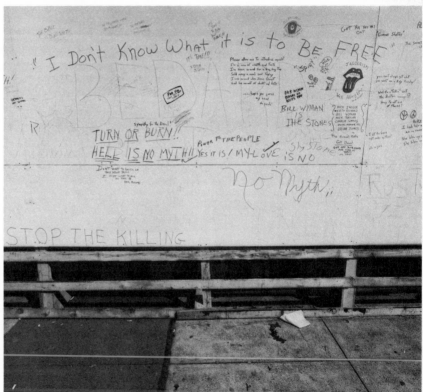

Figure 9-5   Development of Principles.   *The abstract thinking of adolescents often leaves readily visible traces in the urban environment. These graffiti suggest the development of principles of morality. (Siteman from Stock, Boston)*

imagine other worlds, especially ideal ones; they compare these imagined situations with their own and often rebel or change their life styles. As formal operations develop, the adolescent can move beyond conventional standards of morality towards the construction of his or her own moral principles (Figure 9-5).

Figure 9-6 Six Concepts. *These labels represent the concepts involved in each case, not the specific pictures. The answers for rows II and III are at the bottom of this page.*

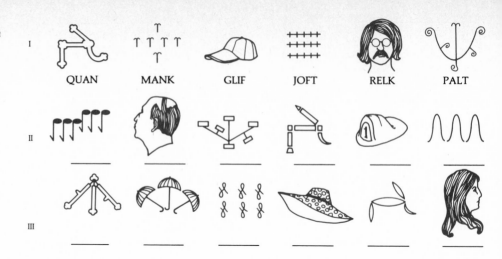

Piaget views formal operations as the last stage in the development of thinking. No further qualitative changes occur, but after adolescence, we do not all reason perfectly. The evidence suggests that all normal adults everywhere acquire concrete operations, but not everyone acquires formal operations (Bynum et al., 1972). Moreover, even those who do have this capacity commit errors in reasoning, as we shall see later.

Concepts in Thinking

A *concept* is a general idea formed from experience, usually expressed by some label. Thinking is based on concepts, as we just saw in the case of the conservation experiment, but concepts are also developed by thinking. Now, use your own capacity for acquiring concepts by solving the following problem:

There are six figures in three rows (see Figure 9-6). Examine the first figure in the second row and decide what it should be named by making comparisons with the figures in the first row. Discover the names of all the other figures on this same basis.

In this process you are developing concepts. For example, a "Mank" is a figure with six identical components.

More specifically, the term *concept* refers to a class of things that are considered equivalent. Although they are not identical, they show certain similarities. Most words in any complex language represent concepts, such as "tree," "liquid," "beauty," and "mother," each of which indicates a class of things that also can differ in some ways. The concept "mother" refers to all women who have given birth to a baby, regardless of their individual characteristics. On the other hand, "Mother," meaning your mother, refers to just one person, and therefore it is not a concept. Similarly, "Christmas" and "Japan," which refer to unique instances, are not concepts.

Without concepts we would have to treat every object as a completely separate event. Meeting a strange dog, we would have to examine it to see if it barked, had fur, ate meat, and so forth. Having the concept "dog" allows us to identify this object quickly and, as we think about it, to assume that it has the characteristics shared by other members of that class.

Answer to Figure 9-4: The area of the square is 16 units.

Answer to Figure 9-6

II MANK RELK PALT QUAN GLIF JOFT
III PALT JOFT MANK GLIF QUAN RELK

Learning and Symbolic Activity

Acquisition of Concepts

A child is helping to bury a dead dog and asks, ''When is she going to wake up?'' ''Does she like being down there?'' ''How is she going to get out?'' On this basis, you realize how limited the child's concept of ''death'' is, and perhaps you explain that animals that are dead never wake up, cannot get out by themselves, and, as far as we know, neither like nor dislike being buried. This process of observing, questioning, and receiving answers goes on for years before the child forms an adult concept of life and death.

Actually, adults are not quite sure what they mean by the concept of ''life,'' as shown in the controversies over abortion and euthanasia. Does it begin with conception or birth? Does it end with the cessation of brain waves or the cessation of heartbeat? Many of our most important concepts are the most difficult to define. Nevertheless, adults agree on the most basic features of this concept, and they are very different from those of a young child. ■

Concept formation. Children form the concept of life gradually, apparently in a regular series of steps, and under age six the major criteria seem to be usefulness, human characteristics, and movement. With regard to usefulness, for example, a child says that a watch is alive ''because it tells you what time it is, so you won't be late'' and a pencil is alive ''because you write with it.'' Concerning human characteristics, the child states that a cat is alive because it can breathe but then incorrectly adds that a watch is alive ''because it eats grease'' and a flower is not ''because it has no feet.'' Many young children think that anything that moves is alive, such as a mountain ''when it erupts'' and snow ''when it's falling.''

Around age six or seven, as they reach Piaget's stage of concrete operations, most children abandon such criteria. They insist on autonomous movement; a thing is alive only if it moves by itself.

Bicycles, pencils, and other human-made objects are not alive because people must make them go, but cats move of their own volition. Certain natural phenomena are also considered alive, however, such as fires, which ''grow by themselves and don't need help to move.'' Clouds are alive because ''they can become bigger or smaller.'' Plants may remain a puzzle. They grow, but doesn't somebody have to plant them?

The age at which a mature concept of life appears, as shown by classing all instances correctly, varies a great deal. Some children arrive at the concept at about age 6 but others not until age 14. At present, we do not know why these differences in rate occur (Piaget, 1929; Laurendreau & Pinard, 1962).

Concept attainment. The process whereby concepts evolve naturally in daily life over a period of years without much explicit teaching is called *concept formation.* It is distinct from *concept attainment,* in which concepts are acquired relatively quickly, often by some sort of training procedure in the laboratory. For reasons of efficiency and practicality, there is a great bulk of research on concept attainment, rather than the more natural process of concept formation (Neimark & Santa, 1975).

The concepts of ''Mank,'' ''Quan,'' ''Glif,'' and the others serve to illustrate some of the early laboratory tasks, and these concepts were relatively easy to attain because they are defined by just one attribute. A ''Mank'' has six items, and a ''Glif'' is something to go on the head. A complex concept has more than one attribute (Figure 9-7).

In laboratory studies, complex concepts involve several attributes, such as form, shading, number of figures, and number of borders. Furthermore, each attribute might be expressed in any of several ways. The form might be a square, circle, or cross; shading might be absent, light, or dark; there might be one, two, or three figures; and there might be one, two, or three borders.

■ *When I was a child, my older brother used to take me down to the creek to ''Elephant Rock''—the largest rock I had ever seen. Naturally I wanted to know why it was so big and Sandy, with the knowledge of a seven-year-old, explained the phenomenon to me. Rocks grow. In fact, rocks keep growing until someone walks on them. For all these years, ''Elephant Rock'' had been growing, but when Sandy and I discovered it and began to climb on it, we stopped its growth. His reasoning also took into account the gravel on our driveway. Our car had run over the gravel and our family had walked on it and it therefore had stopped growing at a much smaller size. Sandy's theory was perfectly logical. I was thrilled with my increase in knowledge, and promptly went on to explain the growth of rocks to my little sister.*

Figure 9-7 Concept Attainment. *What is a cruddledink? The answer is on page 226.*

ALL OF THESE ARE *CRUDDLEDINKS*

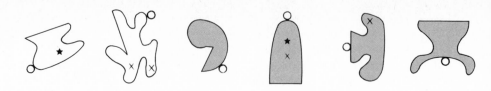

NONE OF THESE IS A *CRUDDLEDINK*

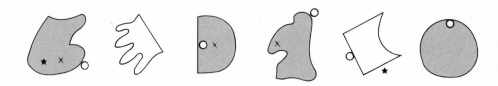

WHICH OF THESE ARE *CRUDDLEDINKS?*

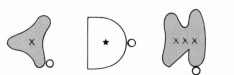

When the concept can involve any one of these three expressions for each of the four attributes, it can be very difficult to attain (Figure 9-8).

Generally the best way to attain such concepts is by using the strategy of *conservative focusing*, in which the subject focuses on only one attribute at a time, determining whether it is relevant or irrelevant, and then discards the attributes that prove to be irrelevant. Suppose, for example, that the concept is three circles in a triple border. Thus, the subject's first task might be to find out which form is relevant. Then the subject might focus on the number of figures, perhaps finding it is three, and then the type of border, eventually discovering that shading is not relevant (Bruner et al., 1956). In the course of solving such problems, systematic strategies often develop spontaneously (Millward & Spoehr, 1973).

Abstracting and generalizing. Because conditions in the laboratory are different from those in daily life, it is risky to conclude that concept attainment is the same as concept formation, but we do know that two common features of these processes are abstracting and generalizing. For example, an individual who acquires the concept "tree," in the laboratory or in daily life, must observe that all such objects, regardless of how much they differ, have some things in common, such as bark, a trunk, branches, and some type of greenery. This process of observing the essential feature(s) of an object or event is called *abstracting.*

After a series of experiences with a variety of trees, the person may see a willow for the first time. If the person designates this object as a tree, he or she must have observed something of what the willow has in common with other trees. Reaching the conclusion that this object is in the same category is *generalizing.* In the acquisition of a concept, both processes are involved, often in cyclical fashion.

Role of Language

In acquiring concepts, words are often helpful. They represent concepts, which can be extremely useful in acquiring still more concepts. Is it possible, therefore, to think without words?

Thought without language. Introspection suggests that language and thought, although related, are not identical. If they were identical, why would people have such trouble at times expressing their thoughts in words? In fact, some psychologists believe that the "inner speech" involved in thought is a stage that follows thinking. First we

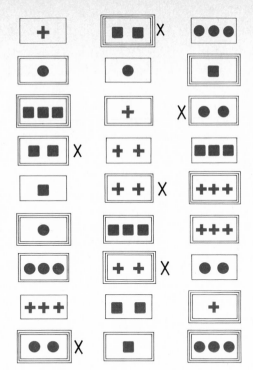

Figure 9-8   A Complex Concept. *The cards designated by the cross illustrate the concept. What is it? In these experiments, two additional sets of cards are included, one red and one green, making 81 cards altogether; thus, the attribute of color must be considered too (Bruner et al., 1956). The answer is on the next page.*

think, then we clothe our thoughts in words, and afterwards, we hear the words. The process of thinking, in this view, is unconscious; we are aware only of the products of thinking—the words in our heads (Furth, 1966).

Early laboratory experiments indicate that organisms with apparently no language can do things that seem to involve thinking, such as attaining concepts. In a typical experiment, a rat is required to discriminate between two geometric forms, such as a triangle and a circle. The experimenter reinforces the subject for responding to the triangle but not the circle, and these objects are randomly switched from side to side. After the triangle is consistently selected, a square is substituted for the circle, in order to ensure that the subject is responding positively to the triangle and not negatively to the other form. If correct performance continues, the triangle is inverted; then the accuracy of response is not much better than chance. Some animals respond as if confronted by a

Figure 9-9 Thought in Animals.
This apparatus is called a temporal maze because the correct turn, at point X, depends on what the subject has just done previously, not the place in the maze. In a double alternation problem, for example, the animal must make two series of right-hand turns, then two left-hand series, then two right-hand series again, and so forth. Triple alternation requires three consecutive turns to the right, three to the left, and so forth. The advantage of this maze to the researcher is that there are no external cues to guide the subject. Monkeys can solve many such problems, but rats and raccoons cannot. It should be noted that this problem involves an abstract rather than a concrete concept.

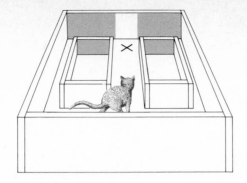

Answer to Figure 9-7: A cruddledink is any figure with at least one straight edge and only a circle on the outside. The second, third, fourth, and sixth figures in the bottom row are cruddledinks.

Answer to Figure 9-8: The concept is two objects enclosed by more than one line.

completely new problem. Apparently, certain lower animals do not form the concept of triangularity but rather a response to a particular pattern of black and white.

Monkeys, on the other hand, continue to select the inverted triangle; they react in terms of triangularity, three-sidedness, or some other abstracted property. They also respond correctly with triangles of different sizes, colors, and brightness. We can say that these animals have developed a basic geometric concept, although the few concepts that animals seem to form in a laboratory are essentially concrete (Figure 9-9).

Some clinical studies also indicate that language is not essential for thought. Most people born deaf never fully learn the language of their society, rarely progressing beyond the language competence of the average four-year-old child, yet they can think beyond this level. The cognitive deficits in the congenitally deaf seem to be caused more by deficits in experience than by the specific language disability. Deaf children, typically deprived of a wealth of information available to hearing children, might be helped through the use of ingenious teaching techniques, sign language, and other methods of supplying more diverse experiences (Furth, 1966). In short, we can conclude that in some instances there seems to be thought without language (Neimark & Santa, 1975).

Linguistic determinism. Language is useful in thought. *Thinking* is manipulating the world internally, using symbols that represent previous experience; word-symbols greatly facilitate this process.

The Eskimos have many words simply to indicate the texture and recency of snow. In the English language, we have a few such adjectives, for example, powder and granular. The Aztecs are reported to have used the same basic word for ice, cold, and snow (Whorf, 1956). Presumably, an individual whose language encompasses many such terms can think about snow in a greater variety of ways than a person who knows only a single word. This hypothesis, that language determines thought, is called *linguistic determinism.*

It seems clear that language does determine thought to some degree, but in turn, one's experiences in the culture determine one's language. Today we speak of the automobile, brain waves, and biofeedback, using words and combinations not used in earlier years. New ideas and events occur, and language is expanded to accommodate them. Furthermore, when terms are not available or the speaker is not aware of them, they are invented. The child asks for ''the drink that prickles,'' not knowing the name for ginger ale, and speaks of ''big tweezers'' rather than pliers.

The overall evidence suggests that language shapes thought in restricted ways. It apparently does not determine our overall conceptions of the nature of reality, but its influence may be powerful in those instances in which we accept approximate terms because more specific ones are not important to us or are not readily available. It seems likely, furthermore, that language becomes more important as thinking becomes more abstract. Most of the concepts formed by lower animals are concrete, but it is difficult to conceive of a monkey acquiring a concept such as ''justice.'' Words are not necessary in achieving solutions to simple, nonverbal problems, but they can be most important in solving complex ones and acquiring complex concepts.

Reasoning

Using concepts such as ''heavier'' and ''equal,'' try to solve the following problem:

Eight coins are all identical in appearance, but one of them is heavier than the others. Using a balance scale with two pans, find the odd coin by only two weighings.

This problem can be difficult, but before reading further, try to devise a method for solving it.

Arriving at the solution requires a type of thinking in which you logically manipulate concepts, called *reasoning*. Perhaps there was some trial-and-error in your work, but then reasoning showed whether you were on the right or wrong track. If you began with one or four coins in each pan on the first trial, you quickly saw that you still might not find the odd one on the second weighing. Thus, you engaged in successful reasoning, even if you did not find the answer.

To achieve the full solution, there must be three coins in each pan on the first trial. If the pans are even, then weigh the two remaining coins to find the heavier one. If the pans are uneven, weigh two of the coins from the heavier pan. An uneven balance here will show the heavier coin, but if the scale still balances, the remaining coin must be the odd one.

As demonstrated in this instance, reasoning is basically problem-solving; a conclusion is reached by making and evaluating propositions, known as *premises*. Modern investigations of this process have their roots in early gestalt psychology, in the later study of language, and most recently in computer technology. Even Sigmund Freud's concept of mental processing, while not correct in many details, has had an impact on the development of cognitive psychology.

The Gestalt Contribution

Piaget commenced his work in cognitive psychology in the 1920s, not long after the gestalt approach began to flourish in Germany. Originating as a protest against behaviorism, gestalt psychology stressed that human behavior should be studied as something more than a series of learned associations. Higher-level processes were involved.

This movement was founded by three men, led by Max Wertheimer, who eventually published an influential book called *Productive Thinking* (1945), in which he described successful problem solving. He emphasized the importance of formulating the problem correctly, restructuring the components when necessary, organizing the basic information, and then searching systematically for solutions. It was pointed out that habits and certain types of school drills, recognized as aspects of associative learning, sometimes prevented the attainment of successful solutions.

The second man, Kurt Koffka, developed a view of cognitive growth that reflects the first stages of Piaget's conception. Koffka described forms of sensory-motor development in the earliest years, followed by ideational development, in which the first use of language appears. His book, *The Growth of Mind* (1924), was a success in its time.

The transposition experiment. The youngest of the three men, Wolfgang Köhler, is best remembered, chiefly for studies of cognitive processes in lower animals. In a typical experiment aimed at this purpose, chickens were exposed to two shades of gray, light and dark. Grain or some other food was always presented with the dark stimulus. With the light gray figure there was no food, and eventually the chickens learned to respond regularly to the darker of the two stimuli. With this training established, the crucial question arose: How would the chicken respond when presented with the rewarded shade of dark gray and another shade of still darker gray? Would it continue to respond to the rewarded stimulus, or would it transpose or "cross over" to the still darker one? According to the behavioristic or S-R view, the subject has learned a specific response to a specific stimulus and therefore will choose it again. According to the gestaltists, the subject has learned a general principle of dark*er* and therefore will choose the darker gray (Figure 9-10).

Köhler discovered, as have many investigators since his day, that the subject makes its choice on the basis of a comparison between these stimuli. Whether it is a chicken, chimpanzee, rat, or human being, it will generally respond in terms of the relations between the stimuli, choosing the still darker figure in this case. This study is called a *transposition experiment* because the subject crosses over to the other stimulus; the subject seems to be following some general principle, such as darker than, smaller than, and so forth, suggesting an elementary form of reasoning.

However, the explanation of this finding has not been so simple. It was immediately pointed out that the results can be interpreted in the S-R view, on the basis of stimulus generalization and related principles, and it has been argued that all transposition phenomena are predictable from the S-R approach (Spence, 1937). More recently, after an extended series of investigations from diverse viewpoints, it appears that both explanations are oversimplified. The subject's response apparently depends on its perception of the ratio of the current stimulation to some internal standard, developed from past experience (Zeiler, 1963). In short, both the present and prior contexts are involved in complex ways. Thus, the transposition experiment has proven to be of continuing interest for psychologists concerned with discovering the ways in which cognitive processes are involved in learning.

NO FOOD   FOOD   ?

ORIGINAL TRAINING   TRANSPOSITION PROBLEM

Figure 9-10 The Transposition Question. *How will the animal respond in the new situation?*

The instrument problems. The most widely cited of Köhler's experiments were the stick or *instrument problems,* in which chimpanzees were required to use some instrument as a tool. For example, Köhler placed a banana in the ceiling of the chimpanzee's cage and a box in a distant corner, and then observed the result. Almost all of the chimpanzees repositioned the box so that it was directly under the banana. Then they obtained the food by climbing on top and jumping (Köhler, 1925).

In another instance, Köhler placed a stick in the play cage while the chimpanzees observed him, and then he took all the animals back to the living cage for the night. The next morning, shortly after being placed inside the play cage, one of the chimps obtained the stick, poked it out between the bars, and drew in some nearby bananas as a prize.

Another stick problem required that the animal join together two separate poles to rake in food that was too far away to be obtained by only one stick. A particularly bright chimpanzee named Sultan began to react to this problem in a random trial-and-error fashion, but suddenly he seemed to see the relation between the two sticks, which were lying in different parts of the cage. He collected one and then the other, immediately joined them together, and solved the problem with such apparent suddenness that Köhler called it "learning in insight" (1925).

Learning and Symbolic Activity

By *insight*, Köhler meant that the solution did not occur through a gradual building up of S-R connections but rather through a *sudden understanding of relationships* among the stimuli. Obtaining the solution is perhaps synonymous with what at the human level is known as ''seeing the point'' or the ''Aha!'' experience. The correct solution is then repeated immediately each time the same problem is presented. Once solved, the problem is no longer a problem (Figure 9-11).

Variables influencing insight. The results of these experiments also afford several interpretations. During play, chimpanzees will stack boxes and put sticks together for long periods of time, with no obvious reinforcement. Furthermore, whether or not they demonstrate ''insight'' apparently depends partly on their prior experience.

In a later experiment by another investigator, chimpanzees were presented with an extremely simple stick problem, which merely required pulling on a hoe to rake in a banana. Only two subjects, both with previous experience with sticks, solved it within the 30-minute test period. Then all the animals were returned to their home cages, where they were permitted to play with a dozen sticks, including the hoe type, for three days. When re-examined on the hoe problem later, all of them solved it within 20 seconds (Birch, 1945).

With human subjects and complex laboratory tasks, discussion after the experiments often reveals that a ''sudden'' solution appeared gradually. In describing how they solved a particular problem, the subjects describe the use of *covert trial-and-error,* by which they tried out several solutions implicitly, in their minds, before resorting to overt behavior. Rarely do we solve a complex problem without making several attempts.

Figure 9-11   Sequel to Insight Learning. *The orangutan has learned to use the stick to push the candy out of the tube, and now he does so readily on each occasion. (Yerkes Regional Primate Research Center of Emory University)*

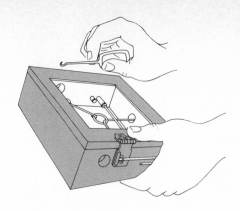

Figure 9-12 Covert Trial-and-Error. *When this complicated problem box was given to a student, she studied it for a long time and then opened it immediately, without error. To do so, the button hook must be inserted through the various holes, releasing the cords in the correct manner and sequence.*

The extent to which the solution appears suddenly depends partly on our prior experience with similar materials and partly on our use of covert trial-and-error methods (Figure 9-12).

Information Processing and Computer Models

At this point it should be emphasized that neither the associative nor the cognitive approach by itself is adequate to explain all learning. Each viewpoint makes its own contribution to our understanding of human learning and has its limitations. The two aspects apparently are combined in some way in most instances. When all possible learning tasks are considered, there is clearly a *learning continuum* from simple habit formation to complex learning with understanding (Figure 9-13).

An excellent example of this continuum lies in language learning. Here, classical and operant conditioning seem to account for our basic letter and word habits, such as associating certain words with certain objects and using these words in proper contexts. But speaking a language is far more complex than simply using single words with certain objects and events. In its fullest sense, language usage involves an enormous variety and novelty in syntax and sentence structure. In fact, many linguists feel that a thorough understanding of our language production and comprehension would provide a basic understanding of the human mind.

Concept of information processing. The proof that the child's correct grammatical constructions cannot be explained in terms of S-R principles, according to cognitive theorists, is that "speakers are clearly able to produce, and hearers to understand, utterances composed of words which were never associated with each other before" (Anisfeld, 1966). In learning a language, children learn not just a series of words but, more important, a set of rules, implicit and explicit, by which the basic materials of a language, the words and phrases, are transformed into novel sentences and understood in the same terms. This emphasis on rules and transformations in language learning is similar to Piaget's concept of conservation across transformations, as shown in the conservation experiment with children. In both cases, a set of rules is implicitly derived for combining a finite number of elements into an almost infinite number of possibilities.

Cognitive psychologists are especially interested in this enormous human capacity for information processing. Broadly defined, *information processing* is the ability to analyze and organize information from the environment in diverse, systematic ways. In language learning, for example, it includes the capacities for receiving verbal messages, sorting them out, storing them, utilizing them, and constructing rules about them. In memory, it is hypothesized that there are the following phases: selection, where an item is chosen for memory; "rewriting," where it is transformed into a suitable format; description, where its features are registered; and elaboration, where it is made more readily memorizable (Bower, 1972). The basic concern is how information is handled in the human mind.

The concept of information processing in cognitive psychology is considered relevant to perception and memory, as well as reasoning and other forms of thinking. It is clearly not as well defined as the concept of conditioning in behavioristic psychology, but it emphasizes

Learning and Symbolic Activity

| CHILD FEARS ANIMALS AFTER BEING BITTEN BY DOG | NAMING VARIOUS ANIMALS | SPELLING THE NAMES OF ANIMALS CORRECTLY | IDENTIFICATION OF DIFFERENCES IN VARIOUS ANIMAL SPECIES | SCIENTIFIC STUDY OF PHYSIOLOGICAL PROCESS IN ANIMALS |

Figure 9-13   A Hypothetical Learning Continuum.   *All five situations involve responses to animals. Dark colored areas represent conditioning and simple habit formation; light areas represent the role of thinking or understanding. The figure is hypothetical and shows only relative proportions rather than absolute amounts.*

that the symbolic processes must be further understood if we are to gain a more fundamental comprehension of complex behavior. Research on higher-level learning now regularly employs this concept rather than the less useful notion of insight.

Use of computer models.   The concept of information processing was taken over initially from observations on the distribution and use of information by computers. It came into prominence in the study of thinking in the 1950s, especially with the realization that many of the gestalt ideas were difficult to test.

Eventually, it became evident that human mental capabilities could be studied in a rigorous, systematic fashion by using the high-speed digital computer as a model. A model is generally something to be copied, but in this context it is not to be taken literally. In research, a *model* is regarded as a limited but sometimes useful method for understanding the parts of a system in relation to the whole. In this case there is no effort to represent the physiological aspects of human thought but rather the manner of processing information in the human mind. Thus, computers are used to simulate human thinking in psychology and also to study human thinking (Apter & Westby, 1973).

The LT and GPS.   A research team in industry developed the Logic Theorist (LT), a computer program that simulated human thought. This program was particularly significant because it enabled the computer to provide proofs for 73 percent of the theorems in Newton's *Principia Mathematica* without considering all the possibilities at each step. Instead, the LT used a *heuristic method,* which means that it selected the approach most likely to yield the correct solution at each step, rather than making a systematic search of all possibilities. A heuristic approach utilizes strategies to bring about discovery more readily.

The LT's heuristics offered a chance for quick success by ignoring the less likely alternatives. In this case, an exhaustive search of all the possibilities would have required hundreds of years instead of a few minutes of computer time (Newell et al., 1950). Hence, the LT works like human thought; strategies are used rather than extensive searches.

Later, by combining several computer programs, including the Logic Theorist, the General Problem Solver (GPS) was developed. The GPS idea illustrates even more precisely how machines can be programmed to use the same sort of problem-solving techniques that many

Figure 9-14 Simple Illustration of the GPS Procedure. *To understand the GPS idea in practice, consider how a computer might determine the steps needed to go from one place in the country to another. In this simple example, the place of origin corresponds to the current state, and the destination point corresponds to the goal state. For this particular problem, the distance in miles between the two points is a convenient measure of the difference between states. Once the problem is thus phrased, one can create a table relating differences to actions. (Photo on left by Falk from Monkmeyer; photo on right by Herwig from Stock, Boston)*

Suppose we are in a car in downtown San Francisco and wish to go to some historic landmark in Boston. Equipped with the GPS formalism, the following plan would evolve:

1. The initial distance between states is considerably greater than 1,000 miles. The table says to take a plane, but first we must be at the airport. Thus, going to the airport is a subproblem.

2. The distance from San Francisco to its airport makes taking a car appropriate. Since we are in the car already, we proceed and go as far as the airport parking lot.

3. We now need to arrive at the plane itself. The table suggests walking.

4. We are now prepared to carry out the action originally suggested in step 1. This action puts us at the Boston airport where similar steps will enable us to arrive at the desired location.

psychologists believe human beings use. It involves the notion that problems can be considered in terms of some problem solution or goal state *and* a current state. Problem solving then becomes an attempt to move from the current conditions to the goal state.

For this purpose, the GPS notices the difference between the current state and the desired goal state and then tries to apply an operation that is relevant to reducing that difference. Each appropriate operation causes a change in the current state, thus diminishing the difference by a small amount. The relevant operations for all possible differences are made available to the program through a table supplied by the programmer. By applying the process repeatedly, the GPS eliminates the difference between the two states, thereby solving the problem. In the case in which an operation is selected from the table but cannot be applied, a subproblem arises that consists of moving from the current state to a state in which the operation can be applied. The solution to this subproblem is attempted using the same difference-reducing technique (Figure 9-14).

Computers and people. Not all psychologists are in agreement regarding the value of computers as models for studying human thought, although there is no dispute about their value as agents in solving problems. Computer models are in an early developmental stage, and their ultimate value in our attempts to understand higher mental processes has yet to be determined.

One limitation of computers in simulating human thought is that they are too stable, too willing to work on long problems without experiencing frustration. Human beings become distracted more readily and make gross errors. They are partly emotional creatures, and recent developments have attempted to include these characteristics in computer models. Even neurotic thought has been programmed now (Apter & Westby, 1973). Whether we are studying animals or machines, however, we are still

Learning and Symbolic Activity

It is possible to force almost any problem into this GPS framework, but researchers in artificial intelligence today prefer newer schemes that permit knowledge about a problem domain to be entered more naturally than does the rigid, table-oriented GPS idea.

	Action			
Difference	Airplane	Train	Car	Walk
More than 1000 miles	X			
Less than 1000 miles but more than 500 miles		X	X	
Less than 500 miles but more than ½ mile			X	
Less than ½ mile				X

left with the difficult problem of deciding to what extent the findings can be generalized to humanity.

Inductive and Deductive Reasoning

In computer and human thinking there are two basic processes. *Inductive reasoning* is reasoning from the known to the unknown, as in discovering a new principle or premise. *Deductive reasoning* is involved in determining the logical validity of inferences drawn from premises. This sort of reasoning is used to arrive at a specific conclusion. Both types of reasoning occur in almost all phases of human thought. ∎

Inductive reasoning. A four-year-old boy has been punished several times and tries to figure out why this has happened. His mother describes the situation:

When I smack him, he'll have a good cry—''What did you smack me for?''—so I sort of tell him. So he'll sit and think and then say, ''Well, if I did so-and-so, you wouldn't smack me *then*, would you?'' Then he keeps saying, ''You know if I . . . if I spilt that tea, would you smack me then?''—''No.''—''Why?''—''Well, if you did it on purpose I might.''—Working out why, you see. (Newson & Newson, 1968)

In ''working out why,'' this child is engaged in inductive reasoning. Like a scientist, he is attempting to discover the regularities underlying the apparent flux of his mother's behavior, the principles that govern whether or not she will punish him.

Suppose your car stops unexpectedly, without apparent cause. You ask, ''Have I run out of gas?'' ''Is there something wrong with the gas line?'' ''I wonder if the carburetor is broken again.'' These possibilities constitute hypotheses, arrived at through reasoning. Reasoning from specifics—the car sputtered and stopped—to the general involves inductive reasoning (Figure 9-15).

∎ When I was young, one of my great pleasures was visiting the duck pond in the local park. I loved to watch the sassy creatures glide up to me, propelled by some invisible motor, and I always responded to their peremptory demands for food with bread crumbs or other such goodies. One aspect of the ducks' behavior bothered me, however. I couldn't understand why they kept standing on their heads. One day when my Aunt Lola was with me I asked her the reason for this strange behavior.

''Oh,'' she said, ''the sun beating down on their heads makes them hot and they cool off by putting their heads under water.''

That seemed logical, and I worried no more about it until one cloudy fall day when Mother and I went to the park together. I expected the ducks to be cold and huddled together in the middle of the lake, but they were swimming around as usual, and standing on their heads. I was confused, and asked Mother how they could possibly stand on their heads when the sun wasn't out.

''They stand on their heads to get plants and things out of the water for food,'' she said. ''It has nothing to do with the sun.''

This was my first encounter with duplicity . . . and I brooded about it for some days. Then I realized that my Aunt Lola had been brought up in the city and probably didn't know about ducks and had interpreted the facts as best she could.

Figure 9-15 Inductive Reasoning. *What words would you interpolate to complete the sequence? What is the principle involved? The answer is on page 238.*

A, By, ... Horrible

Inductive errors. Highly intelligent people commonly make errors in inductive reasoning. For example, the series of numbers 2-4-6 illustrates a certain principle governing the relation between three numbers. Try to discover the principle.

Like many people participating in such an experiment, you probably began with the hypothesis: Intervals of two between ascending numbers. How would you test it? In the experiment, you can test the hypothesis by offering examples, and you will be told whether each one is correct or incorrect. Probably you would begin with some series that conforms to the hypothesis, such as 6-8-10 and 3-5-7. After receiving a "Yes" in each case, you would announce that the principle indeed was intervals of two between ascending numbers, and you would be wrong. The correct principle is simply ascending numbers with intervals of any magnitude between them (Wason, 1960).

The best way to test the hypothesis is to include a series that does *not* conform to it, such as 2-7-10. If you repeatedly offer samples consistent with your hypothesis, you collect no new evidence, which is what most of us do in daily life. The secret is to look deliberately for negative or disconfirming evidence as well. If you hypothesize that the stopped car has run out of gas, you should still check the carburetor, which may have some fuel but be malfunctioning once more.

Deductive reasoning. Scientists trying to understand atoms, and children trying to understand mothers can never be sure that they have arrived at the correct explanation of a phenomenon. All they can do is render one explanation, arrived at through inductive reasoning, more and more probable by eliminating alternative explanations. Deductive reasoning, on the other hand, leads to conclusions that are logically necessary. It does not involve a search for other explanations or principles, but rather an effort to decide, by reasoning from the general to specifics, whether the conclusion is correct.

Thus, the boy decides through inductive reasoning that his mother punishes him when he intentionally makes more work for her. Then, through the deductive process his reasoning might be as follows:

Mum smacks me when I make work for her. Pouring tea on the tablecloth makes work for Mum. She will smack me when I do it.

Similarly, he can deduce other specifics. He will be punished when he makes his clothes dirty, does not pick up his room, or forgets to turn off the bathroom faucet, but there may be other general principles as well, such as being punished whenever he endangers himself. The conclusions from these general principles can be worked out in this same way.

Deductive errors. Mistakes in deductive reasoning are common. In fact, they occur so often that some psychologists have concluded that human beings simply do not reason logically. Others argue that the error often is not in the deductive process itself but in the way in which the task is interpreted.

In one experiment, the following problem was presented to a group of graduate students:

Mrs. Cooke had studied home economics in college. "Youth is a time of rapid growth and great demands on energy," she said. "Many youngsters don't get enough vitamins in their daily diet. And since some vitamin deficiencies are dangerous to health, it follows that the health of many of our youngsters is being endangered by inadequate diet." (Does it follow that the health of many youngsters is being endangered by inadequate diet? Give your reasoning.) (Henle, 1962)

A number of subjects accepted the conclusion. One answered: "This follows . . . youth do not get enough vitamins. Vitamins are necessary or bad health results. Therefore, youth are endangered." However, this subject has restated the premises, making "some" vitamins into "all" vitamins. She was working with a different problem, and her conclusion does not follow from the problem as originally stated. As another student indicated: "Correct if we assume that the vitamins the youngsters are lacking are those vitamins which are essential to their health." Still another pointed out that it followed only ". . . assuming that the deficient vitamins are the vital ones."

This tendency to distort or omit a premise, or include an additional one, is an important source of error in deductive reasoning. Apart from this difficulty and lack of familiarity with such problems, people generally can deduce correctly from the premises (Ceraso & Provitera, 1971; Steinberg, 1972).

Actually we go around solving *syllogisms*, as deductive problems are called, every day. These problems involve a major premise, one or more minor ones, and a conclusion. For example: "It is too far to walk to the Public Library; I must take a subway or bus. The Fifth Avenue bus passes the Public Library. I must take the Fifth Avenue bus" (Henle, 1962).

Combinations. Most problem solving in daily life involves a mixture of inductive and deductive reasoning. If the car stops suddenly, you hypothesize that you are out of gas; this is inductive reasoning. Then you use deductive reasoning to see if the principle is correct: "If I am out of gas, the gauge will indicate empty. The gas gauge does not indicate empty. Therefore, I am not out of gas." Similarly, in the coin problem mentioned earlier perhaps you used inductive reasoning to hypothesize that you should begin by weighing half the coins first, two on each scale. Then through deductive reasoning you could see that this approach was incorrect, so you developed another hypothesis.

Creative Thinking

In solving the following problem, you cannot routinely test a limited number of hypotheses, as was the case with the coin problem. There is no obvious procedure, so you must create more novel hypotheses:

Suppose that you are a physician and your patient has an inoperable stomach tumor situated at point X. A special medical instrument emits rays that, if sufficiently intense, can destroy organic tissue. How would you use it to eliminate the tumor without injuring the surrounding healthy tissues?

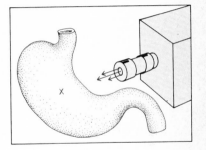

Achieving a solution to this problem requires reasoning, but it must be creative too. *Creative thinking* is problem solving that is more independent, less routine than other types of reasoning, resulting in novel and useful or aesthetic products. Hence, this type of thinking is difficult. As the physician, one way you might treat the tumor is by using rays from many different directions, all coming to a focus only at the malignant tumor site.

Creative thinking has an important basis in imagination. It is problem-oriented, but the problem is not dealt with routinely. *Autistic thinking* also has an important basis in imagination and sometimes it too is problem-oriented, but this type of thought is removed from

When I was four years old, I was at a loss to comprehend exactly why my mother was so enthralled with the idea of having another baby, and subsequently my disappointment in her obviously wrong choice of a new child over a new dog rapidly began to deteriorate into resentment. I had no qualms about becoming increasingly vocal in my requests for her to change her plans. But try as I might, I could not convince her to exchange "the baby" for my much-desired puppy. Gradually I started to tell myself that mother was merely joking; she didn't intend to have a baby after all, but rather a puppy. This notion so entranced me that I decided the world should be informed of this spectacular occurrence. Therefore, to every inquisitive person—be it stranger or relative—who asked about the baby's expected arrival date, I would excitedly remark, "Baby? She's having a dog!" Although my parents attempted strenuously and in vain to correct my illusions, I persisted in supporting my "dog theory." As the time for the "big event" approached, my excitement and anticipation skyrocketed. Mother went to the hospital, and I anxiously awaited her return, envisioning her with a furry, warm bit of fluffy puppy cradled in her arms. Appalled is almost too mild a word to describe my reaction to "Dicky"; totally disillusioned and incredulous at being the victim of such a dirty trick, I retreated to my room, refusing to marvel and gawk at that red, wrinkled object constantly being referred to as "your new baby brother." I can't recall precisely how long it took for the feelings of resentment, aversion, and disappointment to subside, but I do know that it required a lot of coaxing . . .

reality. It is wishful thinking and a form of escape from reality. Autistic thought is more characteristic of children and some disturbed persons than of the creative individual, although all of us engage in fantasy and daydreams from time to time. ■

Correlates of Creativity

Creativity, by definition, is an infrequent phenomenon, and the creative process is relatively difficult to establish in the laboratory. Therefore, we know more about the characteristics of people acknowledged to be creative than we do about the process itself.

Creativity and intelligence. Many studies have shown that creativity is associated with high intelligence, but it alone clearly does not identify creative people. In fact, correlations between intelligence and creativity for highly intelligent high school students are low to moderate, ranging from .11 to .49 (Getzels & Jackson, 1962). Above an IQ of approximately 120, intelligence appears to be a negligible factor (Barron, 1961). High intelligence is often an accompanying but certainly not the only condition for creativity; many intelligent persons certainly are not creative.

More and more, intelligence is being considered a diverse capacity, and the kind of intelligence most closely associated with creativity seems to be *divergent thinking,* which is thinking in different directions, searching for many answers, and seeking variety. The goal in this type of thinking is to create a large number of alternatives to fit a given situation, whether it is simply naming things, seeing implications, or producing solutions to problems. This type of thinking can be readily assessed in laboratory settings (Figure 9-16).

On the other hand, *convergent thinking* leads to one answer, generally recognized as the correct or best answer to a given problem. It involves solving a problem with a well-defined solution, as

Name everything you can think of that is edible and white.

DESERT, FOOD, ARMY: Write as many sentences as possible using these three words.

Suggest clever titles for the problem about the inoperable stomach tumor and special medical instrument.

 Indicate all possible occupations of persons who carry a bell or wear one on their clothing.

Figure 9-16   Measures of Divergent Thinking. *These problems illustrate standardized tests that have precise time limits in each instance. (After Guilford, 1975)*

in finding the area of a trapezoid or translating a thought from English into German. This type of thinking is more often measured on tests of intelligence and achievement. But such tests commonly do not measure divergent thinking and, therefore, they are criticized as being deficient in assessing creativity.

Independence, humor, and interest in novelty. In comparison with others, creative persons are more interested in being alone. They show a high concern for independence in thought and action. In one study, creative high school students displayed relatively little interest in "success" and traits favored by their teachers and they were not as interested in becoming "model citizens." As might be expected, they were viewed by teachers as less desirable students than members of an equally intelligent but less creative group (Getzels & Jackson, 1962).

Compared to their colleagues, creative architects see themselves as more independent and more individualistic; the less creative ones describe themselves as reliable, dependable, tolerant, and understanding (MacKinnon, 1962). In fact, it has been suggested that creativity is partly a product of loneliness and may serve to mitigate that feeling (Barron, 1975).

Among creative high school students, a high regard for a sense of humor is also apparent. When ranking a series of desirable traits, these students placed "sense of humor" second, whereas a group of students of the same intelligence but less creativity ranked it lowest among all the traits. When both groups drew pictures of various themes, over half of the creative students made drawings judged as humorous, and studies of essays showed this same difference.

Still another characteristic of creative individuals is their interest in novel or complex tasks. When given a choice, creative persons prefer more unusual and irregular drawings and paintings, and they introduce these same qualities in their own production (Plate 6). They also show less restraint in unstructured situations (Figure 9-17).

An illustration. One of the most famous descriptions of the behavior of a creative person concerns Sir Alexander Fleming's discovery of penicillin. While talking with Pryce, a colleague who had stopped by to see him, Sir Alexander began to examine some Petri dishes containing old cultures of staphylococci. As the event has been described:

Several of the cultures had been contaminated with mould—a not unusual occurrence. "As soon as you uncover a culture dish, something tiresome is sure to happen. Things fall out of the air." Suddenly he stopped talking, then, after a moment's observation, said, in his usual unconcerned tones: "That's funny. . . ." On the culture at which he was looking there was a growth of mould, as on several of the others, but on this particular one, all around the mould, the colonies of staphylococci had been dissolved and, instead of forming opaque yellow masses, looked like drops of dew.

Pryce had often seen old microbial colonies which for various reasons had dissolved. He thought that probably the mould was producing acids, which are harmful to the staphylococci—no unusual occurrence.

COMMON RESPONSES
1. SMUDGES
2. DARK CLOUDS

RESPONSES OF CREATIVE SUBJECTS
1. MAGNETIZED IRON FILINGS
2. A SMALL BOY AND HIS MOTHER HURRYING ALONG ON A DARK WINDY DAY, TRYING TO GET HOME BEFORE IT RAINS

COMMON RESPONSES
1. AN AFRICAN VOODOO DANCER
2. A CACTUS PLANT

RESPONSES OF CREATIVE SUBJECTS
1. MEXICAN IN SOMBRERO RUNNING UP A LONG HILL TO ESCAPE FROM RAIN CLOUDS
2. A WORD WRITTEN IN CHINESE

Figure 9-17 Creativity and Unstructured Stimuli. *When asked to respond to inkblots, creative subjects show greater originality and synthesizing ability than do subjects chosen at random (Barron, 1958).*

Figure 9-18 Fleming and the Mold. *Sir Alexander Fleming appears in the hospital laboratory where he made his discovery. Also shown are his notes and drawings on the occasion. (From* The Life of Sir Alexander Fleming *by A. Maurois, Jonathan Cape Ltd., 1959. Courtesy of Lady Amalia Fleming.)*

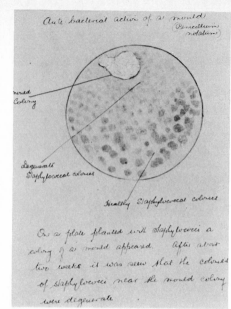

Answer to problem in Figure 9–15: Each word must begin with the next letter of the alphabet and be one letter longer than the preceding word. Thus, one correct answer would be: Can, Door, Every, Floods, Gunners.

But, noting the keen interest with which Fleming was examining the phenomenon, he said: "That's how you discovered lysozyme." Fleming made no answer. He was busy taking a little piece of the mould with his scalpel, and putting it in a tube of broth. Then he picked off a scrap measuring about one square millimetre, which floated on the surface of the broth. He obviously wanted to make quite sure that this mysterious mould would be preserved. [Figure 9-18]

"What struck me," Pryce says, "was that he didn't confine himself to observing, but took action at once. Lots of people observe a phenomenon, feeling that it may be important, but they don't get beyond being surprised—after which, they forget. That was never the case with Fleming. I remember another incident—One of my cultures had not been successful, and he told me to be sure of getting everything possible out of my mistakes. . . ."

Fleming put the Petri dish aside. . . . He showed it to one of his colleagues: "Take a look at that," he said. "It's interesting—the kind of thing I like; it may turn out to be important." The colleague in question looked at the dish, then handed it back with a polite: "Yes, very interesting." But Fleming, in no way discouraged by this manifestation of indifference, temporarily abandoned his investigation of the staphylococci, and gave himself entirely to studying the surprising mould.*

Fleming's approach to the mold shows his independence of thought—his capacity to see something significant in the apparently trivial and his quick willingness to pursue a new problem. As he was over forty on this occasion, he was a bit older than most famous persons at the time of their most significant achievements (Figure 9-19).

* From *The Life of Sir Alexander Fleming* by André Maurois, translated by Gerald Hopkins. Copyright © 1959 by Jonathan Cape Ltd. Published in the United States by E. P. Dutton, and reprinted with their permission and with the permission of Jonathan Cape Ltd. on behalf of the Executors of the André Maurois Estate and the translator.

Learning and Symbolic Activity

Type of Contribution	Percent at Each Age Interval							
	Under 20	20 to 29	30 to 39	40 to 49	50 to 59	60 to 69	70 to 79	80 to 89
Chemistry (993)	1	23	39	23	11	3		
Mathematics (938)	1	19	34	20	15	7	2	
Physics (141)		21	35	27	11	5	1	
Astronomy (83)	1	4	28	37	18	5	4	1
Practical inventions (554)	3	27	38	20	8	3	1	
Chess championships (236)		29	47	19	5			
Electrical development (170)	1	28	45	16	9	1		
Entomology (86)	1	15	32	22	16	11	2	1
Genetics (147)		18	30	26	16	9		
Psychology (65)		22	36	21	15	5	2	
Short stories (1,396)		18	37	24	13	6	2	

Figure 9-19   Age and Achievement. *In all fields except astronomy, the largest percentage of important contributions occurred when the individuals responsible were 30 to 39 years old. For example, of the 933 significant contributions to chemistry, only 1 percent occurred when the respective chemists were less than 20 years old, 23 percent when they were 20 to 29 years old, and so forth. (From* Age and Achievement, *by Harvey C. Lehman. Princeton University Press; copyright © 1953 by the American Philosophical Society. Table 1, p. 19, and Table 2, p. 20. Reprinted by permission of Princeton University Press.)*

Importance of Flexibility

Flexibility is essential in solving novel problems. The following problem is even more difficult than those discussed earlier in this chapter:

Three native women are at the fireside. One, sitting on a goatskin, has a son who weighs 120 pounds. Another, perched on a deerskin, has a son who weighs 160 pounds. The third Indian woman, sitting on a hippopotamus skin, weighs 200 pounds all by herself. What principle of mathematics can be derived from this circumstance?

If you cannot solve this problem, it may be because you are thinking of it in the same way as the others, rather than as a riddle. The answer is that this problem illustrates the Pythagorean theorem: the squaw on the hippopotamus is equal to the sons of the squaws on the other two hides! Had you approached it differently, you might have discovered this solution.

Rigidity.   In trying to solve the problem just presented, perhaps you formed one hypothesis after another concerning the numbers; perhaps you added the weights of the boys and found they were more than the weight of the woman; perhaps you noted that they were all even numbers; perhaps you made calculations on that basis, maybe even discovering the illustration of the Pythagorean theorem. In any case, if you took the problem literally, you made an improper assumption, which hindered its solution. *Rigidity* is the inability to change one's actions, attitude, or outlook.

Similar examples occur in daily life. A man in his forties begins having dizzy spells, decides that he has serious heart trouble, and consults his physician, who finds nothing wrong with his heart. Instead, the physician asks the man some questions about his eyes. The man recalls for the first time that he finds it easier to read if he holds the paper at arm's length, that he has difficulty reading small print on labels, and that his dizziness comes when he looks suddenly from a near to a more distant object. The man did not see the relationship between any of these experiences before the checkup because his thinking had been dominated by the idea that there must be something wrong with his heart.

**Figure 9-20 Nine-Dot
Problem.** *Connect these dots by
drawing four straight lines without
taking the pencil from the paper and
without retracing any lines. If you have
difficulty, notice carefully the theme of
this section. The answer appears on
page 242. Before turning to it in
despair, however, think beyond the
dots!*

■ *Once someone gave me a riddle
to solve. I had to find the solution
to the story about a man and his
son who were driving in a car and
hit a pole. The father was killed
and the son needed surgery. When
the boy reached the hospital the surgeon exclaimed, "My son!"*

*The solution to this riddle is that
the surgeon is the boy's mother. I
never thought of the surgeon as
being a woman. I couldn't solve the
problem because I had a wrong
approach.*

A checkup indicated that the man
needed bifocals, and after wearing them
his dizziness disappeared (Figure 9-
20). ■

Functional fixedness.   A special case
of rigidity in problem solving, called
functional fixedness, occurs when an
object is perceived as useful only in its
originally intended way. A pencil is regarded only as a writing instrument and
not as a doorstop, window prop, or perhaps measuring instrument, depending
on the interests of the potential user
(Figure 9-21).

In one experiment, the subject is led
into a room where two strings are hanging from the ceiling and is asked to tie
them together. The strings are long
enough to be grasped but they are too
far apart to be grasped simultaneously.
How is the problem solved? The solution
eludes some people, especially those
who have not just learned about functional fixedness (Figure 9-22).

In another instance, one group of
subjects was trained to use a switch to
complete a circuit; another group was
trained to use an electrical relay to complete the circuit; and a third group received no training at all. Then all the
subjects were given the two-string problem just described, with both the switch
and the relay lying on the table. The
question was not whether the subjects
solved the problem; to ensure that they
did, a hint was given after some time
had elapsed. Instead, the question was
how they solved it. It was found that all
the subjects trained on the relay used
the switch to make the pendulum, and
nearly all those trained with the switch
used the relay for the pendulum. In the
control group, without any training, the
results were about evenly divided. Apparently, using an object for one purpose constituted a barrier to using it for
a second, different purpose (Birch & Rabinowitz, 1951).

A school principal in New Orleans,
charged with creating an innovative
school in an old, cramped building, had
to overcome functional fixedness before
she could begin the program:

We had been trapped into looking at resources as unchangeable. Classrooms were
for learning, halls were for walking through,

**Figure 9-21 Overcoming Functional
Fixedness.**   *At county fairs, a tree makes an
excellent display-case window. The merchandise
is hoisted into the air for all to see. (Alberto
Rodríguez Rey)*

coatrooms were for coats, and basements were for assemblies. When we realized no one was going to give us any more space we began looking at what we had differently. What were its possibilities? Could children learn in hallways? Could children learn in coatrooms and basement corners? Could children even learn outdoors? Heavens! We had a lot more room for learning than we ever suspected. Now that we look upon the entire building and small yard as experiencing and learning space for *all* of us we find we've got even more than we're yet able to use. We have chickens in what was the custodian's lodge yard, a kiln and clay room in a closet, a children's lounge, game and reading area in a basement wasteland and paint and art areas in the halls. (Carmichael, 1975)

Often in everyday life we use an habitual approach to a problem when a better solution is available. One constant problem for all educators is how to help students to think in new ways.

Summary

Stages in Cognitive Development

1. According to the Piagetian view, there are four stages of cognitive development. In the sensory-motor stage, lasting for about the first 18 months, the child begins by simply acting on and experiencing his or her environment, apparently without significant thought. Gradually, the concept of object permanence is acquired.

2. In the preoperational stage, which lasts from age 18 months to age 6 or 7 years, the child slowly overcomes perceptual egocentrism, perceiving the world from others' viewpoints as well as his or her own. The child's thoughts are still primarily in terms of the dominant characteristic of objects, ignoring the procedures performed on them.

3. As concrete operations are achieved, which usually takes place before age 11 years, the child masters the procedures required in solving concrete problems. The child is capable of ordering and classifying things and understanding the concept of conservation.

4. Formal operations, which are not necessarily achieved by all adults, involve the capacity for solving abstract problems. The important aspect of this thinking is imagining the possibilities

Figure 9-22 Two-String Problem. *How can the woman manage to grasp both strings at once? The answer is on the next page.*

that are inherent in a given situation. It includes the formulation of diverse hypotheses and testing their validity.

Concepts in Thinking

5. Thinking is a symbolic process based on the use of concepts, which are properties common to a class of objects or events, derived through abstracting and generalizing. Concept formation occurs in daily life, and concept attainment is studied in the laboratory.

6. Language is not necessary for thought, but it plays a most important role in abstract thinking, in which concepts represented by word symbols are manipulated. It shapes thought to some degree but apparently does not determine one's overall conception of reality.

Reasoning

7. The gestalt contribution to the study of cognitive learning lies largely in early research on problem solving. In the transposition experiment, the subject apparently learns a general principle, rather than a specific stimulus-response association; in the instrument problem, the solution appears suddenly, seemingly based on a perception of relationships. This process is called insight in gestalt psychology.

8. The concept of information processing refers to the organism's capacity to receive, analyze, organize, use, and construct rules about information from the environment. This concept, considered useful in research on various forms of perceiving, thinking, and remembering, was adapted from studies of the processing of information by computers. It is now being used as a model in the study of human thought, including irrational thinking.

9. Both inductive reasoning, which involves discovering hypotheses or principles, and deductive reasoning, in which one decides about the logical validity of a conclusion or inference, are part of most problem solving. Errors in inductive reasoning often occur because one does not look for disconfirming evidence; errors in deductive reasoning are commonly due to distortion of the premises.

Creative Thinking

10. Creative thinking is more independent and less routine than other types of reasoning. Creative individuals have at least moderately high intelligence and are likely to be humorous and interested in novel tasks. Creativity cannot readily be brought into the laboratory, so we still know relatively little about the actual thought processes involved in it.

11. The biggest obstacle to creative problem solving is usually rigidity, which is a lack of flexibility in approach. One example is functional fixedness, in which a tool is not considered to have any function other than its originally intended use.

Suggested Readings

Anderson, B. F. *Cognitive psychology: The study of knowing, learning, and thinking.* New York: Academic Press, 1975. Basic studies in the psychology of perception, learning, and thinking.

Answer to Figure 9-20: Begin at the top left corner and follow the arrows. In attempting to solve this problem, you probably formed an improper set, one that made you keep all lines within the area bordered by the dots. The only way to solve it is to remain flexible and eventually think of the possibility that the lines may go outside this area.

Answer to Figure 9-22: Tie the pliers (lying on the table) to one of the strings. Set the string with pliers attached swinging. Grasp the other string with one hand and, when the string with pliers attached swings within range, grasp it too.

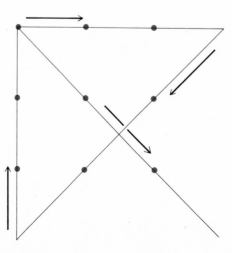

Learning and Symbolic Activity

Bourne, L. E., Ekstrand, B. R., & Dominowski, R. L. *The psychology of thinking.* Englewood Cliffs, N. J.: Prentice-Hall, 1971. A collaborative work that describes theories and research on cognitive processes.

Crovitz, H. F. *Galton's walk: Methods for the analysis of thinking, intelligence, and creativity.* New York: Harper & Row, 1970. A paperback that provides a novel approach to the study of thinking based on the work of Sir Francis Galton.

Ginsburg, H., & Opper, S. *Piaget's theory of intellectual development: An introduction.* Englewood Cliffs, N. J.: Prentice-Hall, 1971. A concise, thorough effort, and more sophisticated than the subtitle suggests.

Taylor, I. A., & Getzels, J. W. (Eds.). *Perspectives in creativity.* Chicago: Aldine, 1975. A series of diverse papers, some advanced.

Chapter 10

Remembering and Forgetting

When Benjamin Burtt was 15 months old, his father began giving him "Greek lessons." During these periods he was not permitted to have toys or other playthings and could not run around the room. Instead, this English-speaking child living in Ohio was asked to listen while Sophocles's *Oedipus Tyrannus* was read aloud in the original Greek. These sessions inevitably resulted in some restlessness on the part of the child, but every day his father read him three passages in iambic hexameter, and three months later three new passages were read. This procedure of daily readings, using three new passages every three months, was repeated again and again, until Benjamin was three years old (Figure 10-1).

Altogether, 21 passages of approximately 240 syllables each were read aloud 90 times, making a total of

Age (Months)	Passages from Sophocles
15	I, II, III
18	IV, V, VI
21	VII, VIII, IX
24	X, XI, XII
27	XIII, XIV, XV
30	XVI, XVII, XVIII
33	XIX, XX, XXI

Figure 10-1 Benjamin's Listening Schedule. *Each of the passages was approximately 20 lines in length. (From Burtt, 1937)*

453,600 syllables to which the boy listened—testimony to the father's perseverance and the youngster's patience. Then, the whole matter was dropped for more than five years.

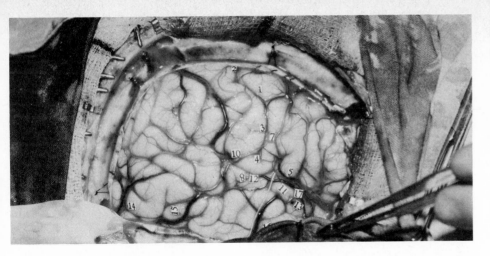

Figure 10-2 Brain Stimulation and Memory. *Weak electrical stimulation at point 13 produced memories of voices and of seeing a circus wagon. Stimulation at point 17 elicited memories of watching a play and of an office in which the subject once had worked as a stenographer. (From Penfield,* The Excitable Cortex in Conscious Man, *1958. Courtesy of Charles C. Thomas, Publisher, Springfield, Illinois.)*

Physiological Basis of Memory

The father's idea behind all this work was to find out what happens to memory with the passage of time. We all have early "memories," but these accounts might be a mixture of what we actually remember and what we have been told by others who also remember that event. Ideally, there should be some specific body of information about which a person could be tested, without contaminating influences. Since no member of Benjamin's family except his father had any knowledge of Greek, it seemed that these lessons would provide suitable material. But before looking at the outcome, we should consider what processes seem to account for memory in the first place.

Nature of the Trace

Memory of any sort must be based on some change within the individual as learning occurs. This change, sometimes called a *memory trace* or engram, presumably is somewhere in our nervous system, representing the physiological basis of memory; however, we do not understand what structures or functions are modified. Some psychologists prefer to make no assumptions and speak merely of associative strength, by which they mean the probability that a given response can be reproduced when an appropriate stimulus is present.

Reappearance hypothesis. Among those who speculate, some think that the physiological changes in memory are analogous to the electromagnetic rearrangements of particles that occur in a magnetic recording tape. In some way memory involves a similar realignment of molecules. This structural alteration, created by prior experience, is the memory trace; when it is activated, the event is remembered.

Some spectacular incidents that seem to support this view have occurred in brain surgery. During operations for epilepsy, the cerebral cortex has been stimulated with a weak electrical current, which has brought forth sensory experiences, such as seeing lights and hearing sounds. Stimulation of other areas has produced reports of other memories. As a certain point was stimulated in one patient, she reported that she heard a mother calling her boy, not in the present but years ago. She was told that the stimulation would be repeated, but it was not, and she made no report. Then the same point was stimulated again, eliciting a further report about the sound of someone's voice. Details were added, such as the observation that this scene was taking place in a lumber yard. Stimulation of still other points on the cerebral cortex produced detailed memories of other earlier experiences (Figure 10-2).

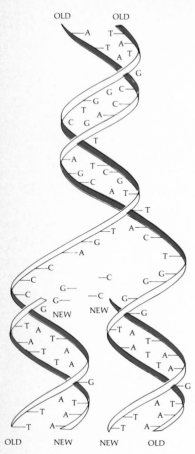

OLD   OLD

OLD   NEW   NEW   OLD

Figure 10-3   Division of DNA. *The discovery of the twisted structure of the DNA molecule is quite recent. In replicating itself, the molecule apparently untwists and unzips down the middle. Then, as shown in the drawing, each half forms a new molecule. The letters C, G, T, and A refer to the four basic units of the DNA structure.*

According to the scientists involved, these results suggest that memories are somehow stored in the brain as permanent records, to be elicited in detail by the appropriate stimulation. This view, which has been popular for centuries, is sometimes called the *reappearance hypothesis,* since it implies that a full memory will somehow appear whenever it is properly retrieved. There is no memory loss; the complete experience is retained, somehow filed away in static fashion. Forgetting is not a failure of storage but rather a failure to retrieve the existing information.

Reconstruction hypothesis.   Others consider memories not as fixed images but as reconstructions. There are memory traces, and today's experience is built on these remnants of the past, but this working residue involves chiefly prior mental acts, not fixed and filed copies of prior experience. In the utilization or *reconstruction hypothesis,* prior acts and experiences are used in assembling a memory.

A helpful analogy concerns the paleontologist, who gathers a few pieces of bone and then is able to reconstruct an entire dinosaur. The actual bone fragments are not necessarily part of the model he or she builds, but they are used in the construction process. They are merely some old parts that indicate *how* to reconstruct the object or event (Neisser, 1967).

William James was an advocate of this view, believing that a permanently existing memory image was highly unlikely. This position seems to be the more probable today, especially according to cognitive psychologists (Bransford & Franks, 1971). It is pointed out that in the reappearance experiments there is no convincing evidence that the patient's experience is a memory rather than a fantasy, that it is accurate, or that it is complete. The vivid imagery is not necessarily an accurate memory, and the feeling of familiarity, as we shall see

later, often can be misleading. Even if the patient's reports do constitute accurate memories, there is still no evidence that past events are never forgotten (Neisser, 1967).

Biochemical basis.   Whether memories exist in toto or are reconstructed, it seems that there must be some biochemical basis, as suggested in experiments with planarians, or flatworms. At the outset of one series of studies, it was demonstrated that administering an electric shock to these creatures caused a contraction of their bodies. A bright light produced no response. Then, using the process of classical conditioning, these two stimuli were paired for many trials, and afterwards the animals contracted to the light alone (Thompson & McConnell, 1955). Somehow, the animals retained this conditioning experience.

Furthermore, since these worms are cannibalistic, trained worms later were fed to untrained worms, and the latter were found to learn the original conditioning task more readily than control subjects, which devoured only untrained worms (McConnell, 1972). Such results have suggested that memory can be transferred through chemistry, but these experiments have not been verified.

Through various studies, scientists have theorized that the potential chemical basis begins with *deoxyribonucleic acid* (DNA), which is responsible for "memory" across any given generation of human beings in the sense that it is the basic substance of genes. All our innumerable inborn characteristics are retained and transmitted by these sets of tiny DNA molecules within the genes (Figure 10-3). This DNA in every living cell, in turn, manufactures a substance called *ribonucleic acid* (RNA), which apparently directs chemical activities that influence cell development, including the production of protein. DNA, which is relatively stable, carries our biological inheritance or species "memory" into every living cell, while RNA, which is less stable, may be responsible for the individual memory of every living organism. Such a viewpoint has been developed, and it has some support (Hydén, 1967).

Administration of a substance that increases the manufacture of RNA seems to result in improved memory in lower animals; use of another substance, which destroys RNA, results in poorer memory. Some of these studies have been criticized as perhaps facilitating learning in a general way rather than involving memory per se, but in certain experiments this possibility has been eliminated and the effect still occurs (Brand, 1970; Brand & Hoffman, 1973). On these bases, we can conclude that perhaps RNA molecules play a special role, serving as the ultimate repository of memory.

On the other hand, along with other parts of the nervous system, they may simply undergo alterations that reflect past experience but do not constitute the localized storage function. Quantitative changes in RNA and protein synthesis occur during learning, but as yet there is little substantial evidence that these changes are qualitatively different from those occurring in other forms of behavior (Gaito & Bonnet, 1971).

The Time Factor

Another puzzling aspect of the memory trace is its duration. How long does it last? At a party you are introduced to several people you have never met before; you smile, repeat each name, and remember it for the moment. After further conversation, you discover that you cannot remember any of these names, or very few. When you arrive home, you find that you also cannot remember most of what other people said, what they did, the clothes they wore, and the furnishings of the house. Most of the information that we take in each day is recalled only for a moment and then forgotten—perhaps to our benefit, for otherwise our minds would be quite cluttered.

Three phases. It is now postulated that three systems or phases are involved in human memory, the first of which is concerned merely with sensory input. At a party, the images of people's faces and the sounds of their voices impinge on your sense organs. The input for potential memory is large indeed, but once the stimulation ceases, these experiences are only momentary—a function of the residual stimulation in your sensory systems. This phase, therefore, is called *sensory memory.*

Sensory memory involves only information encoded at the receptors. Investigators now speak of *iconic* memory, for example, referring to visual representation, since the term *icon* means "image" or "symbol." *Echoic* refers to auditory images. In all cases, sensory memory lasts only briefly.

Information in the sensory system is then transferred to *short-term memory* (STM), which in most studies has been defined arbitrarily as any time interval considerably less than 30 seconds. During this period, the incoming information is processed in some fashion. Most of it is ignored, lost, or discarded, since STM is a limited-capacity system. Only a small portion of all the sensory input can be managed. STM apparently involves the sorting out and rehearsal of information that is to be transmitted for more permanent storage, called long-term memory. One reason for the interest in short-term memory is that material that cannot be retained for even a few seconds probably cannot be recalled a few hours or days later.

Study of short-term memory may shed light on the nature of the memory trace, since investigations have shown that people sometimes are unable to remember a three-letter nonsense syllable for even a few seconds. In one instance, the experimenter told the subject to remember a syllable and then, to prevent opportunities for rehearsing it, required the subject to count backwards by three or by four from a randomly selected three-digit number. At a later signal the subject was instructed to

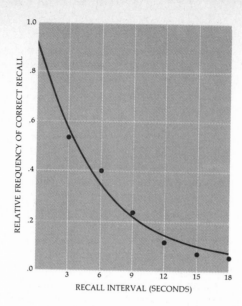

recall the syllable, but even after just three seconds, it was repeated correctly only about half the time (Figure 10-4).

Napoleon was concerned about his STM, particularly his inability to remember someone's name just after being introduced. Unlike the people in the experiment, he overcame this problem by silently rehearsing the new name several times after first hearing it.

In the third phase, *long-term memory* (LTM), information is retained for extended intervals. These intervals are defined as anything from 30 seconds to the full life of the organism, sometimes many decades. LTM has a much larger capacity than STM and it is final storage, not an interim stage. Presumably, it is an irreversible modification of the nervous system. Most of the research described in this book, and on learning elsewhere, concerns long-term memory.

Two viewpoints.   Some psychologists believe that a continuum exists between short-term and long-term memory. They regard the two processes as essentially the same, except for the time factor.

Others regard the two processes as different. Thus, short-term memory involves some type of neural activity, during which incoming information is "stored" or "dumped," depending on the organism's interests and whether or not repetitions occur. Experiences that are not coded and then transferred for permanent storage become irretrievable (Postman, 1975; Reitman, 1971). Long-term memory, however, is an irreversible neural modification, brought about by the period of consolidation, where prolonged activities produce a permanent structural change, the memory trace. The short-term component disappears rapidly, but under appropriate circumstances long-term memory is always retrievable.

Both views have support. In one study, rats were taught an avoidance response, and then different neural structures were stimulated in an effort to disrupt the ongoing neural activity. Stimulation of one brain area resulted in low retention shortly after the learning activity; in other animals, stimulation of another area produced low retention at a later retest. Thus, it appears that STM and LTM involve different parts of the brain (Kessner & Connor, 1972). At the human level, various studies on the recall of verbal materials support a distinction of this general nature (Klatzky, 1975). On the other hand, systematic reviews of all the relevant research on this topic suggest that there is not yet enough evidence to support the concept of two dynamically different memory traces; most of the data are equally consistent with the hypothesis of a single process (Wickelgren, 1973; Postman, 1975).

Measures of Memory

If we postulate two separate memory processes, we can state in the case of young Benjamin Burtt that the sound of the Greek words stimulating his auditory receptors constituted the data for sensory memory. The decay of the traces in this sensory system was extremely rapid, but some of the information was transmitted to short-term memory, where it was either discarded or rehearsed for storage. The question Benjamin's father wished to answer was: How much of this information, if any, went into permanent storage and for how long?

Although psychologists have not yet identified the physiological basis of the memory trace, they can study its existence by any one of three methods—recall, recognition, and relearning. With Benjamin Burtt, the recall method was used about five years after the passages were read to him. Unfortunately, the boy showed no memory whatsoever, which seems like an insignificant result when one considers all the effort that went into the study. Hence, let us consider in further detail this method and some of the results it yields.

Recall

During an address on the nature of evidence by Erle Stanley Gardner:

A woman burst into the room and rushed at him shouting "You got my brother hung!" She then unsuccessfully attacked him with a pointed can opener before being escorted from the room by the regular instructor . . . who had planned the stunt to dramatize the great variance of eye-witness accounts to the same event. (Houts, 1954)

After the incident, 34 students were asked to describe the woman's complexion; 3 said "dark," 2 "ruddy," 1 "medium," 5 "fair," 7 "pale," 3 "heavily powdered and made up," and 13 said they did not know. Actually, she was fair, had freckles, and wore no makeup. Accurate recall of events witnessed only once is surprisingly poor, partly because *recall* is memory that occurs without any significant prompting or cues.

Sometimes, given certain cues, a witness can recall almost an entire scene, a phenomenon referred to as *redintegration* or recall from reduced cues. The

stimuli enable him or her to reassemble or reintegrate memory traces from other aspects of this experience. This memory is not pure recall because the subject is given some of the previously learned material. In fact, it illustrates an aspect of classical conditioning. When two phenomena have occurred together, the reappearance of one of them is likely to evoke the other.

Perfect recall: eidetic imagery. Certain people, especially children, can give exceptionally accurate testimony without any prompting, as if the scene or object is still before their eyes. This recall is known as *eidetic imagery*, a term that suggests that the individual has a "memory image" as clear as a photograph or hallucination. In a common test of eidetic imagery a detailed picture is presented, then removed, and the observer is asked to describe it (Figure 10-5).

A child with eidetic imagery can observe in the mental image dozens of details that he or she has not described earlier, when looking at the real picture. Acoustical images also occur. A child with acoustical eidetic imagery can repeat long lists of digits after hearing them once. One eidetic child looked at a desk while a list of a dozen or so digits was read to him; then he "read" the list off forward and backward while still looking at the desk. The image, however, is not static, like a photograph, but dynamic and fluctuating, and it can be altered voluntarily (Gray & Gummerman, 1975).

Eidetic imagery appears in retarded as well as normal children. In fact, one study showed 26.5 percent eidetic imagery among retarded children as opposed to only 7.9 percent in normal children (Haber & Haber, 1964; Siipola & Hayden, 1965). Since most of the retarded children were brain-injured, these findings might have significance for diagnosing brain injury, but much more reliable measurement is needed.

PRACTICE TRIALS

EARLY TEST TRIALS

LATER TEST TRIALS

Figure 10-5 Studying Eidetic Imagery.
The subject is seated before an easel and asked to stare at a colored paper for several seconds, which produces a negative after-image when the paper is removed. This procedure provides the subject, especially a child, with practice and encouragement in describing something that is not really present.

After a few trials, the actual testing begins. The subject is shown a simple scene in silhouette and is instructed to move his or her eyes around, studying all parts of the picture. After several such trials, detailed scenes are studied in the same way (Gray & Gummerman, 1975).

The photograph on which the drawings are based is shown at the right. Eidetic recall of such a complex scene would be extremely difficult. (Photo by Alberto Rodríguez Rey)

Pablo Picasso, Bull, *1946. Lithograph, printed in black, 11¾" x 16⅛". Collection, The Museum of Modern Art, New York. Acquired through the Lillie P. Bliss Bequest.*

Partial recall: distortion. When memory is not perfect, certain types of errors seem to occur. In other words, our incorrect responses involve predictable changes.

These changes have been demonstrated when students try to recall a story or drawing to which they have just been exposed. If some parts of the story do not appear in the reproduction, the process of *simplification* has occurred. If other parts are overemphasized, there has been *elaboration.* If unfamiliar items are changed into more familiar form, *conventionalization* has taken place (Bartlett, 1932). All these processes often occur together (Figure 10-6).

The same changes take place as a rumor is passed around, perhaps because rumor involves "social memory." Such stories, like legends, have a basis in fact, but eventually some details are omitted, others are emphasized, and still others are incorporated as group values. Any story not so assimilated into the culture could not persist for long (Allport & Postman, 1947). These processes are obviously parallel to simplification, elaboration, and conventionalization in individual memory.

Partial recall: rate of forgetting. Most of us do not have eidetic imagery or anything like it. We forget constantly, sometimes at a seemingly very rapid rate.

Hermann Ebbinghaus, a significant figure in the early history of experimental psychology, is well remembered for his extensive studies on the rate of forgetting. He served as his own subject and memorized over two thousand nonsense syllables altogether, most of which were formed by placing a vowel between two consonants, such as YIL and MEB. He developed these syllables to provide a large quantity of unfamiliar material for memorization. Experimenters since Ebbinghaus have found that some syllables have a higher association value than others and, therefore, are easier to memorize. Nonsense syllables, at least of the type Ebbinghaus devised, are not entirely nonsense.

Ebbinghaus memorized each list until he could recite it once perfectly. Then, when he tested himself 20 minutes later, he found that about 47 percent of the material was forgotten. Forgetting

Figure 10-6 Changes in Recall. *The Picasso bull was drawn from memory by several students, after observing it for 20 seconds. Simplification and elaboration are illustrated in the top drawing: simplification in the omission of the shadow on the ground, elaboration in the shading of the rump. Simplification and something akin to conventionalization are suggested in the bottom drawing in the handling of delicate details.*

Figure 10-7 Memory Curves. *The curves illustrate that retention is the obverse of forgetting (Ebbinghaus, 1913).*

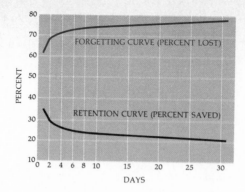

FORGETTING CURVE (PERCENT LOST)

RETENTION CURVE (PERCENT SAVED)

PERCENT

DAYS

was 62 percent after one day, 75 percent in 15 days, and 78 percent at the end of a month. Altogether, the rate was rapid at first and then slow (Ebbinghaus, 1885; Figure 10-7).

Later investigators, using many subjects and averaging the results, have verified the general shape of the curve found by Ebbinghaus, but usually they have found less overall forgetting. One possible reason is that Ebbinghaus used only himself as a subject. Memorizing all these syllables in early experiments, as we shall see, could have interfered with his memory of other syllables learned later. In all such studies, the *recall score* is generally expressed as the percent correct responses out of the total number possible.

Recognition

When a subject cannot recall any details of a preceding event, another method for measuring memory is used. More specifically, if the recall score is low, a recognition test is applied. For example, when a witness cannot recall any characteristics of a suspect, the suspect is placed in a police lineup and the witness tries to pick him or her from the group. This type of memory, by which the correct object or individual is merely identified, is called *recognition,* and it is an easier memory task than recall.

In a typical laboratory experiment, the subject chooses among words, drawings, or other items. The procedure is similar to instances in daily life in which, for example, you forget a book title and

Figure 10-8 Recognition Task. *Which photo is the one that appeared in Figure 2-9? (Sheila A. Farr photos)*

someone prompts your memory by suggesting several possibilities. If you select the correct alternative, recognition has occurred (Figure 10-8).

Tip-of-the-tongue feeling. When memories seem very strong but the words to describe them are momentarily elusive, we sometimes say that the words are on "the tip of my tongue." For example, a person warmly greets an old friend and then finds, when about to say that friend's name, that it cannot be recalled. The person says: "I know your name. I just can't say it!"

When this tip-of-the-tongue feeling is measured, by having the subject choose between correct and incorrect alternatives, it is found that persons are able to recognize characteristics of the elusive word, such as the number of syllables, the initial letter, or a sound with which it is associated (Brown & McNeill, 1966). These results indicate that our "feeling of knowing" has a good basis and that our capacity for recognizing the correct item depends on how carefully it was perceived and stored in memory in the first place (Bower & Karlin, 1974).

The déjà experience. Sometimes we find ourselves in almost the opposite situation, thinking we recognize a certain person or place even though we know that cannot be possible. This feeling is referred to as a *déjà* experience, coming from the French word meaning "already." Something in the present experience leads us to think that we have already experienced it.

In one form, called *déjà entendu,* a voice or sound appears familiar. Another, called *déjà vu,* refers to a visual experience that seems familiar. These experiences are not false recognitions because they are characterized only by a vague feeling of familiarity, apparently because some part of the new stimulus situation, something as subtle as a slight odor, texture, or rhythm, is similar to a stimulus encountered previously.

These two types of recognition experiences point to an important characteristic of human memory. Our capacity for recognizing prior stimulation is considerable, although sometimes we cannot recall specific aspects of the situation.

Recognition score. People often remark on their poor memories, but usually they are considering only recall. When the task is recognition, we quickly note our tremendous information-processing capacity. When students were required to recognize 600 randomly selected visual stimuli, the median correct recognition score was 88 percent for sentences, 90 percent for words, and 99 percent for pictures (Shepard, 1967). Another study demonstrated the human capacity for recognizing 10,000 pictures; the researcher concluded that there is no recognizable limit for this type of visual memory (Standing, 1973).

Another conclusion that can be drawn from this work is that there is no absolute standard for judging a good or poor recognition memory. Any recognition score depends heavily on the nature of the alternatives, as demonstrated in almost any multiple-choice test. The procedure in the laboratory is to mix the original stimuli with an equal number of similar new items, obtaining the *recognition score* as:

Recognition =

Correct responses − Incorrect responses
Total possible correct responses

As Benjamin Burtt showed no memory when tested by the recall method, his father then used the recognition procedure. The boy was presented with several of the original selections, which had been read to him more than five years previously, and several others written by Sophocles. Benjamin again failed, however. After inspecting them, he could not tell the old from the new. His father repeated the procedure using still other original passages, but the boy showed no recognition.

Relearning

Thus, the father tested his son's memory by the method of relearning after Benjamin had failed both recognition and recall tests. Not knowing the purpose, the eight-year-old boy learned 10 Greek passages, repeating each one aloud over and over until he could recite it perfectly without prompting. Among these passages were 7 of the original 21 selections, mixed with 3 new ones. Would Benjamin relearn the original selections more easily than the new ones?

The boy worked at this task twice a day for more than a year, after which it was found that the average number of trials for relearning the original passages was 317, compared to 435 for learning the new ones. Some memory of the earlier experience had remained for five to seven years (Figure 10-9).

These results showed some sort of memory trace, and they seem to support the reconstruction hypothesis. The complete experience apparently was not retained, but the memory was reconstructed from remnants of the past.

Type of Passage	Trials Required
Original	
1	382
2	253
3	385
4	379
5	328
6	226
7	265
Average	317
Control	
1	409
2	451
3	445
Average	435

Learning trials for control passages	435
Relearning trials for original passages	−317
Difference	118

Figure 10-9 Relearning at 8½ Years. *(From "A further study of early childhood memory" by H. E. Burtt, in* The Journal of Genetic Psychology, *1937, 50 (1), 187–192.)*

However, in tentatively rejecting the reappearance hypothesis we cannot be sure that the underlying trace, whatever its nature, was fully aroused.

Follow-up studies. In the method of *relearning,* the subject is required to relearn the original task to a specified criterion. This effort is then compared with that required to learn some control task, and Benjamin's father followed this procedure on two other occasions.

When the boy reached age 14, he memorized seven more of the original passages, together with three new ones, again without any idea of why he was doing so. After about 100 trials, he began to recite some of the selections spontaneously, when he was out walking, riding, or even swimming. His father disliked this apparently innocent pastime because it perhaps involved ''unfair'' practice of only certain passages. Nevertheless, the results were as expected. Benjamin was now a much faster learner and the memory trace was still there, but it was unquestionably weaker. The youth required 149 trials for the original selections and 162 for the new ones (Figure 10-10).

When Benjamin became 18, the relearning test was repeated for the final time, with the last 7 of the original 21 passages. This time he learned more slowly than four years earlier, perhaps because of lower motivation at this point in the experiment, but the results were· clear. The original and new passages required 189 and 191 trials, respectively, indicating no significant difference. Altogether, the effect of the earlier learning was clearly manifest at age 8½, still apparent at age 14, but no longer evident at age 18 (Figure 10-11).

Savings score. Thus, on this basis, we see the increasing inaccessibility of the memory trace with the passage of time, some further tentative evidence for the reconstruction hypothesis at age 14, and the value of the relearning method

Figure 10-10 Relearning at 14 Years. *(From ''A further study of early childhood memory'' by H. E. Burtt, in* The Journal of Genetic Psychology, *1937, 50 (1), 187–192.)*

Type of Passage	Trials Required
Original	
1	142
2	139
3	169
4	151
5	145
6	169
7	127
Average	149
Control	
1	169
2	151
3	166
Average	162

Learning trials for control passages	162
Relearning trials for original passages	− 149
Difference	13

for measuring poor retention. When the three methods are ranked in order of capacity for measuring small amounts of memory, the sequence is relearning, recognition, and recall. Technically, the method was not exactly relearning in Benjamin's case because as an infant he did not memorize the passages to a specified criterion, but the procedure shows a saving of effort, which is the essence of the method.

When the original and subsequent trials are compared to obtain a *savings score,* the procedure is:

$$\text{Savings} = \frac{\text{Original trials — Relearning trials}}{\text{Original trials}}$$

Figure 10-11 Relearning at 18 Years. *(From "A further study of early childhood memory" by H. E. Burtt, The Journal of Genetic Psychology, 1937, 50 (1), 187–192.)*

Type of Passage	Trials Required
Original	
1	202
2	190
3	181
4	220
5	160
6	175
7	193
Average	189
Control	
1	205
2	193
3	175
Average	191

Learning trials for control passages	191
Relearning trials for original passages	− 189
Difference	2

If the subject demonstrates full memory on the first practice trial, which does not count as an attempt at relearning, the savings score is 100 percent—memory is perfect. If the earlier and later trials are the same, apparently there is no memory because there has been no savings in relearning. On the three occasions with Benjamin, the savings scores were 27 percent, 8 percent, and 1 percent, respectively (Figure 10-12).

Theories of Forgetting

The inability to recall, recognize, or relearn at an improved rate is called *forgetting*. This condition can be due to a *storage failure*, in which the trace was never satisfactorily created or consolidated initially, or it can be due to a *retrieval failure*, in which the trace is intact

but an appropriate cue for evoking it is lacking. Several theories have been offered to explain how these failures occur.

The Decay Theory

According to the *decay theory*, the memory trace deteriorates unless it is used; there is a storage failure, possibly as a result of the continuous metabolic action of the cells of the nervous system. Merely the lapse of time may be responsible for forgetting. This theory has much popular appeal. When we look up a telephone number and fail to remember it moments later, it seems that the memory has just faded away (Figure 10-13).

It is extremely difficult to provide clear evidence in support of the decay theory, however. The case of Benjamin Burtt apparently gives some support, but it could be interpreted from another viewpoint also, as we shall see. Other evidence comes from a human adult who lost his sight at age two years; when he recovered his sight years later, he showed no memory of prior visual learning, behaving in the same fashion as someone who was born blind (Hebb, 1966).

Some support for the decay theory is seen in short-term memory experiments, in which much information is lost in just a few seconds. Decay theorists stress the notions that there is a limited information-processing system and that rehearsal prevents decay. They point out that a person can process only so much information during a given period of time and that rehearsal prevents the decay process, chiefly by keeping the material active in memory. When the individual stops rehearsing, decay begins, quite independently of any interference. While this theory is still unproven, it is equally difficult to demonstrate that there is no deterioration of the memory trace with time.

Figure 10-12 Savings Scores at Different Ages. *(From "A further study of early childhood memory" by H. E. Burtt, The Journal of Genetic Psychology, 1937, 50 (1), 187–192.)*

$$\frac{\text{Age } 8\frac{1}{2}}{435} = \frac{118}{435} = 27\%$$

$$\frac{\text{Age } 14}{162} = \frac{13}{162} = 8\%$$

$$\frac{\text{Age } 18}{191} = \frac{2}{191} = 1\%$$

Figure 10-13 Decay Theory. *According to this theory, the memory trace, like skywriting, gradually disappears with the passage of time. (United Press International)*

■ *Martha had planned to go to a concert in Washington, D.C. for a long time. After much persuasion, she convinced her parents to let her drive. The big day finally arrived and while she was getting ready, her parents took the car for shopping, promising to be back in a half an hour. An hour passed and Martha grew quite impatient. After an hour and a half had passed with no sign of her parents, Martha received a telephone call and a strange voice told her that her parents had had an accident and her mother had died on the way to the hospital; her father was in critical condition. She was stunned. She called me and when I arrived at her house, she was sitting in her living room with a dazed expression on her face.*

Martha was extremely upset after the accident and was sent to live with her grandparents to recover. She also began to see a psychiatrist. Apparently, this had been such a shock to Martha that she could remember none of the other events that took place that day. She could not even remember planning to go to a concert.

One month later I went to visit her and found her cleaning out her purse. She found a small piece of colored paper and looked at it with an odd expression. I realized that it was some sort of ticket, and I asked her what it was for. With a blank expression, she said that she honestly couldn't remember. She sat a while longer looking at the ticket. Finally, she burst into tears. After calming down, she explained that she suddenly realized what the ticket was for. It was for the concert that was held on the day her mother died. She was then able to remember all that had happened that day. Previously, she had been unable to recall any events of that day other than the phone call from the hospital.

Obliteration of the Trace

Another view of forgetting that postulates a storage failure focuses on sudden destruction of the new trace, rather than slow deterioration through disuse. The *obliteration theory* postulates that certain conditions occurring soon after the experience eradicate the trace before it becomes permanent.

ECS and protein synthesis. In electroconvulsive shock (ECS) treatments with psychiatric patients, a weak electric current is passed through the brain by means of electrodes placed on the skull. The patient experiences a mild convulsion followed by unconsciousness. Usually a series of treatments is given, and sometimes they are helpful in leading to recovery. However, such patients usually forget the trip to the hospital or clinic and even other events immediately preceding the treatment (White, 1956).

In the laboratory, experimental mice subjected to ECS showed lower retention than control groups that received ether or remained untreated (Herz et al., 1966). Further animal studies have shown that the time factor is important in obliteration. Electroconvulsive shock immediately after learning produces more forgetting of a given experience than the same shock administered a while after learning. In an investigation with rats, ECS was given at several different intervals following the original learning, and a test of retention 25 hours later showed that the sooner the ECS was administered, the greater was the disruption (Pinel & Cooper, 1966).

Other studies have demonstrated memory disruption by preventing protein synthesis, which we considered earlier as a possible chemical basis of memory produced by RNA. In one experiment, goldfish learned to avoid an electric shock, signaled by a light, by swimming to the darker end of the tank. Immediately after reaching the criterion for learning, some of the fish were injected with puromycin, a substance that interferes with protein synthesis. These fish seemed to forget completely what they had just learned. With other fish, the experimenter waited an hour and injected puromycin, and memory was unaffected. When the injections occurred approximately one-half hour after the training was completed, they resulted in an intermediate memory loss (Agranoff, 1967). Again, the amount of memory loss seems to be closely related to the time of the obliterating stimulus.

Emotional shock. Several decades ago, college students sat alone in a small room, learning a list of nonsense syllables, and afterwards they recalled as many as possible. On another occasion, just before the recall test, the back of the chair collapsed, scrap metal fell from the ceiling, a pistol shot rang out, and the lights went out, producing total darkness. When the commotion ceased, each subject was asked to recite all the syllables he or she could remember, and as might be expected, retention was considerably poorer than under the earlier control condition (Harden, 1930).

In daily life, persons often have amnesia for events immediately preceding emotional upset, but investigators do not know how these shocks, emotional or electrical, interfere with retention. Nor do they fully understand the way in which lack of protein synthesis disrupts memory. It seems clear, however, that the memory trace needs time to consolidate or set, and these events interfere with this process. ■

Interference Theory

Earlier, we noted that Hermann Ebbinghaus, in learning many lists of nonsense syllables, found more overall forgetting than did more recent investigators. Today, it seems that this result probably was due to an interference factor. The numerous syllables that he learned in his early work perhaps interfered with the recall of those learned later. Similarly, there was some confusion in young Benjamin's efforts to relearn the passages at age 18. Material from the trials at age 14 sometimes reappeared (Burtt, 1941). Such observations form the basis of the *interference theory* of forgetting, and it is this possibility that makes the decay theory so difficult to prove.

Proactive inhibition. When testing the interference theory in the laboratory, one group of subjects learns Task A while another rests, and then both groups learn Task B. The test of memory comes when both groups try to recall Task B. *Proactive inhibition* is found when the memory of the earlier learning interferes with recall of the material learned later (Figure 10-14).

In an impressive demonstration of proactive inhibition, a psychologist compared studies of memory by more than a dozen different investigators. The studies were selected for this analysis on the basis of several stringent criteria. Two features of each investigation were recorded—the average amount of recall of a certain list of verbal material 24 hours after the original learning and the average number of similar lists learned *before* the critical list. It was found that the accuracy of recall on the selected list was directly related to the number of lists previously learned. The more lists learned earlier, the poorer was the recall (Figure 10-15).

Group	First Learning Session	Second Learning Session	Recall
Experimental	Task A	Task B	Task B
Control	—	Task B	Task B

Figure 10-14 Proactive Inhibition. *During the first learning session, the control group rests or practices a task unrelated to Task A.*

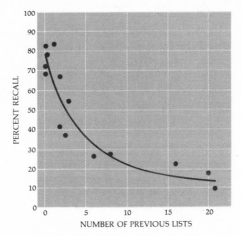

Figure 10-15 Interference of Prior Experience. *Each point represents the findings of a single study. These results show that the larger the number of previously learned lists, the lower the accuracy of recall. (After Underwood, 1957. Copyright 1957 by the American Psychological Association. Reprinted by permission.)*

Retroactive inhibition. With both Hermann Ebbinghaus and Benjamin Burtt, material memorized at an earlier age interfered with the memory of material learned later, so the result was proactive inhibition. Another type of interference follows a different paradigm. In *retroactive inhibition*, later learning interferes with the recall of earlier learning. In the laboratory, both the experimental and control groups memorize Task A; then the experimental group learns Task B while the control group performs an unrelated activity; finally, both groups try to recall Task A (Figure 10-16).

Group	First Learning Session	Second Learning Session	Recall
Experimental	Task A	Task B	Task A
Control	Task A	—	Task A

Figure 10-16 Retroactive Inhibition. *Here the control group rests or practices an unrelated task during the second learning session.*

In one instance, two college students memorized lists of nonsense syllables and then either engaged in various activities or went to sleep. Retention was tested at intervals of one, two, four, and eight hours, and it was found that retention was better after any amount of sleep than after a comparable amount of time spent in activity while awake (Figure 10-17).

The students did not go to sleep immediately, although they tried to do so; thus, it was claimed that if someone could be put to sleep right away, perfect retention might be expected. Since there is danger in inducing unconsciousness quickly in human beings, cockroaches were used, for they can be rendered inactive suddenly without the use of drugs or agents that might damage the nervous system. They were placed in a state of tonic immobility or "animal hypnosis" by inducing them to crawl between layers of tissue paper, where they remained motionless until removed and tested for retention.

At the outset of the experiment, every cockroach was trained to avoid the shaded area at the end of the training box by giving it a shock through the floor. The animal's natural response is to run toward this region, but gradually each cockroach learned to swerve around the end of a glass partition and return without entering the shaded area. Then the experimental subjects were placed in a state of tonic immobility, and control subjects were allowed to be normally active elsewhere, after which their memories were tested by the relearning method. In these tests, it was apparent that the active group required far more trials to relearn the task. This outcome suggests that something happens in the passage of time that causes forgetting, but it does not necessarily rule out the possibility of trace decay (Figure 10-18).

Research on interference theory. In proactive and retroactive inhibition, the interference might involve a storage

Figure 10-17 Activity and Recall. *The curves indicate that recall by two subjects after one, two, four, and eight hours of normal activity is consistently less than after sleeping for intervals of the same length (Jenkins & Dallenbach, 1924). Suppose the boys are given an arithmetic lesson just before their bus ride, during which they sleep. They will probably recall more of the lesson at the end of the bus ride than they would if they had played baseball or Scrabble instead. (Photo by Moon from Stock, Boston)*

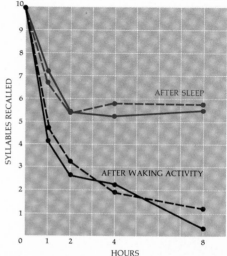

problem, due to the intervening activities, and it might be a retrieval failure, in which the wrong cues are used. Either or both circumstances could result in incorrect responses or none at all.

Since its inception in the 1930s, the interference theory has held a special attraction for experimental psychologists. Of all the theories of forgetting, it continues to be the most stimulating for research, and contemporary laboratory investigations have been highly analytic (Greeno et al., 1971). One recent shift has been towards increased interest in proactive inhibition, especially concerning the effect of long-standing language habits on the outcomes of laboratory studies requiring only the temporary learning of new materials (Hilgard & Bower, 1975). On the other hand, there have been relatively few attempts to study the concepts of interference theory in the context of business, education, and other applied areas.

Figure 10-18 Activity and Trials for Relearning. *The graph shows the savings scores for trials required to relearn the original task, which was to proceed around the barrier without entering the shaded area. Note that the inactive animals showed higher savings scores. Note also the similarity between these curves and those for active and inactive human beings. (After Minami & Dallenbach, 1946)*

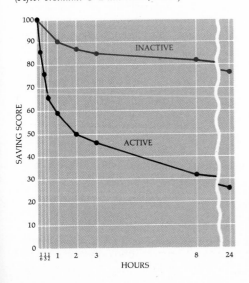

Repressive Forgetting

In the last view of forgetting to be discussed, the memory trace apparently remains intact and is not disrupted by some other trace. The full memory is potentially available and the problem is generally considered to be one of retrieval, not storage.

According to Sigmund Freud, this type of forgetting is caused by factors within the individual, such as hopes, anxieties, and frustrations that make him or her want to forget. ■ Freud called this exclusion of unwanted thoughts from awareness *repression,* and such forgetting is now referred to as motivated or *repressive forgetting.* For Freud, repression is a key factor not only in memory but in the whole personality.

No one has illustrated this concept more fully than Freud, who included examples from his own life:

In the days while I was engaged in writing these pages the following almost incredible instance of forgetting happened to me. On the first of January I was going through my medical engagement book so that I could send out my accounts.

■ *I was at a friend's house one day and decided that I would go out to the store to buy a pack of cigarettes. When I looked in my pocket to see if I could afford them, I found the exact amount of change needed to buy the cigarettes and a five dollar bill. When I was about to go out the door my friend asked me to buy him a newspaper while I was out but he did not give me any money for it. As I was leaving, my friend called out to me, "Don't forget the paper!" and I yelled back, "I won't!"*

I left the house and as I got into the car, I felt a little aggravated at the thought of having to break a five dollar bill for a newspaper. I finally got to the store and bought the cigarettes and returned to my friend's house. When he asked me for his newspaper, I realized then that I had completely forgotten to buy it. I wondered why I had forgotten even after he had warned me not to.

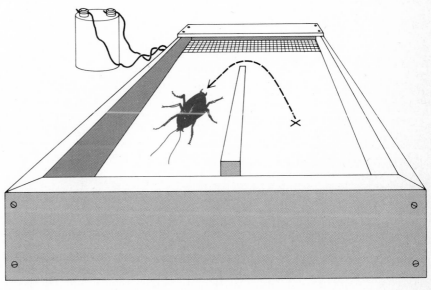

■ *I have always been able to recall events that occurred in the past. Members of my family are sometimes amazed at my total recall of incidents at the age of two or three. However, I could not for the life of me remember my great-uncle Martin.*

According to my family, Uncle Martin died when I was about eight years old. They tell me that I was Uncle Martin's favorite and he used to take me everywhere. All I could remember was attending his funeral. And even then, all I could remember was riding in a black car wearing a white lace dress. This was the only recollection I had of Uncle Martin or his funeral until I attended another funeral last summer. It was the funeral of a former schoolmate. The dead boy's mother was so overcome with grief that she pulled the corpse from its coffin and began to cry. . . . At that very moment I felt a jolt go through my whole body. I suddenly remembered myself dressed in white lace tugging at Uncle Martin's hand, begging him to leave "that old box." I could still feel that same smooth coldness of those stiff fingers and gave an involuntary shudder.

Under the month of June I came across the name ''M____l'' but could not recall who it belonged to. My bewilderment grew when I turned the pages and discovered that I treated the case in a sanatorium and made daily visits over a period of weeks. A patient treated under such conditions cannot be forgotten by a doctor after scarcely six months. Could it have been a man, I asked myself, a case of general paralysis, an uninteresting case? Finally the record of the fees I had received brought back to me all the facts that had striven to escape my memory. M____l was a fourteen-year-old girl, the most remarkable case I had had in recent years, one which taught me a lesson I am not likely to ever forget and whose outcome cost me moments of the greatest distress. The child fell ill of an unmistakable hysteria, which did in fact clear up quickly and radically under my care. After this improvement the child was taken away from me by her parents. She still complained of abdominal pains which had played the chief part in the clinical picture of her hysteria. Two months later she died of sarcoma of the abdominal glands. The hysteria, to which she was at the same time predisposed, used the tumour as a provoking cause, and I, with my attention held by the noisy but harmless manifestations of the hysteria, had perhaps overlooked the first signs of the insidious and incurable disease.*

Repressed thoughts are unconscious and generally not accessible to the individual, except through certain techniques aiding recall, such as psychoanalysis or experience in a situation that is highly similar to the original learning. ■ Suppressed thoughts, on the other hand, are accessible but intentionally kept in the background. Repression is essentially involuntary; suppression,

as we saw earlier, is voluntary. If cultural or individual restrictions are sufficiently stringent, however, suppressed thoughts eventually may become repressed.

Years ago, college students were asked to report all their experiences during a recent Christmas vacation, marking them *P* for pleasant or *U* for unpleasant. After a period of six weeks, the students again were asked to recall their experiences during the Christmas vacation. Comparison of the two sets of data showed that approximately 42 percent of the pleasant experiences had been forgotten as opposed to 60 percent of the unpleasant ones, and the large number of subjects involved makes it highly unlikely that this difference was due to chance. The investigator interpreted it as an illustration of repression (Meltzer, 1930).

Another experiment tested the concept of repression as an active process. Thus, it was hypothesized that memory for previously known verbal material, a list of 15 syllables, would be inhibited when this material became associated with failure on a motor task. Furthermore, it was hypothesized that memory for the verbal material would be restored when the ego threat—that is, failure on the related motor task—was removed by success on this same task. The subjects in the experimental group were tested under both conditions, while those in the control group learned and recalled the syllables without any related success or failure. Comparison of these results showed that failure on the associated motor task served to reduce the ability to recall the previously known verbal material and that success on the related motor task served to increase one's ability to recall the original verbal material (Zeller, 1950).

Not all psychologists are satisfied with the concept of repression, however, and one review of relevant studies has failed to provide support for it (Holmes, 1974). Some psychologists look for alternative explanations, and some point

* Reprinted from *The Psychopathology of Everyday Life* by Sigmund Freud. Translated from the German by Alan Tyson. Edited by James Strachey. By permission of W. W. Norton & Company, Inc., and Ernest Benn Limited. Translation copyright © 1960 by Alan Tyson. Editorial matter copyright © 1965, 1960 by James Strachey.

out that the forgetting of negatively toned material may occur because there is simply no effort to mark or "tag" the experience for later recall. This "forgetting," it is argued, may be due simply to the lack of relevant information that would provide cues for recalling the experience.

Principles in Memorizing

Cues for recalling an experience are essential factors in successful memory, but what are the others? Answers to this question should be of interest to any student. Can memory be improved merely by exercise, as one strengthens a muscle by exercising it? This question also should be of interest, and some years ago it was studied by William James.

He began by memorizing 158 lines from the works of Victor Hugo, applying himself to the task for 8 consecutive days. Keeping a careful record of the time, he found that he required an average of 50 seconds to memorize each line. That was the "strength of his memory" before any program of exercise.

Next, he engaged in intensive memory work for 38 days. He tried to strengthen his memory by memorizing Milton's poetry, spending 20 minutes each day in this activity. Was his memory stronger after this effort? The way to find out was to return to Victor Hugo's works and see if he could memorize new lines more easily than the earlier ones.

James employed the same procedures as before, using another 158 lines from Hugo, and this time he memorized them at the rate of 57 seconds per line, just a bit slower than previously. The slightly poorer performance, he said, was due to his becoming "perceptibly fagged" at the end of the experiment. He concluded that one's basic memory capacity—or native retentiveness, as he called it—cannot be changed by exercise alone. Later, he verified this finding by requesting friends to serve as sub-

jects in the experiment, with the same result (James, 1890).

Memory cannot be developed simply by exercise, but it can be improved by using certain memory systems and devices. Perhaps the most important factor is motivation.

Role of Motivation

What appears to be forgetting may occur because there was no impression, or only an inadequate one, initially. Frequently, we fail to remember names because we were not attentive when they were spoken. Such conditions do not constitute instances of poor memory, for nothing has been learned to be forgotten later.

Consider the thousands of stimuli around you at any given moment and how few of them you remember. You may be unable to recall even the most general features of the trees and shrubs nearby, but a botanist, because of past learning and current motivation, may recall many small details after a single visit. Lack of motivation to perceive a situation clearly can be an important factor in the inability to recall. ■

In this regard, we can raise the question of Benjamin Burtt's motivation. The passages were read to him, but it is extremely doubtful that he had the intention to learn them. If he had, undoubtedly there still would have been a gradual weakening of his memory for Sophocles's works, but it probably would have occurred at a slower rate.

Zeigarnik effect. Observations of waiters in a busy German restaurant in the 1920s supplied one psychologist with a hypothesis about the role of motivation in memory. One of Bluma Zeigarnik's professors noticed that the waiters remembered very large orders with complete accuracy until the bill was paid, and then they promptly forgot them.

Back in the laboratory, Zeigarnik gathered a number of subjects and presented them with a variety of different

■ *Since my fiancé and I became engaged four months ago, we have gotten into the habit of driving to the Golden Frog for muffins and hot chocolate three or four nights a week. I had been there so often that I could have sworn I knew the place inside and out. I described it to Steve in complete detail before we left, and then we drove over there.*

I took a good look around and received the shock of my life. The only thing I had remembered correctly was that it had four walls and wooden chairs. I didn't remember the beautiful painted murals or the bright red carpeting. The white painted ceiling I had envisioned was brown with wooden beams. The waitresses' orange and white uniforms were white shirts, red skirts, and black bow ties. What I thought were red and white checkered tablecloths turned out to be wooden tables without tablecloths. . . . I might as well have sat there every night with my eyes closed. I had no trouble describing the muffins or the hot chocolate, because these satisfy my need for food—but I hadn't remembered anything else at all.

■ *In my senior year in high school a teacher expected us to memorize several French poems. One poem especially stands out in my mind as it was the longest one (approximately 15 stanzas), and I spent the most time on it. I have forgotten the title, yet I can remember and recite the first stanza perfectly. However, my memory of what comes after this first stanza is very cloudy.*

When I set about memorizing this poem I would start from the beginning and memorize it in order by stanza. Every time I would start with the first stanza. Thus, I went over it considerably more than the middle or end stanzas. I think I overlearned the first stanza by going over it so many times. Thus, I have been "resistant to forgetting" this one for over a year and a half.

□ *I was trying to remember the starting players on the 1963 New York Yankees baseball team. At first I started to reel off the names that just came to mind: Pepitone, Mantle, Maris, Howard. But when I could not remember the rest, I went by the batting order, beginning to end, and remembered it readily. The line-up changed somewhat after Mantle got hurt, but I remembered this early one easily: Kubek, Richardson, Tresh, Mantle, Maris, Pepitone, Howard, Boyer, and usually Ford.*

tasks. Each subject worked busily, sometimes being interrupted and sometimes being allowed to finish the task, and after the entire series had been presented each person was instructed to name as many of the tasks as possible. It was found that 80 percent of the subjects remembered more of the unfinished tasks while only 12 percent remembered more of the completed tasks. The remaining 8 percent recalled the two types of tasks equally well. Further analysis showed that some individual subjects recalled up to five times as many unfinished tasks as they did completed ones (Zeigarnik, 1927).

Zeigarnik hypothesized that the waiters and laboratory subjects forgot the completed tasks because there was no further motivation to remember them. Apparently a "tension system" builds up within the individual, to be dispersed only when the task is finished. A similar tension is experienced when you enter a room and momentarily forget the reason for entering it. When the purpose is recalled and the task completed, the tension disappears.

The *Zeigarnik effect,* which is the tendency to recall more unfinished tasks than completed ones, will not appear in all circumstances, however. If the uncompleted tasks are especially threatening or much too difficult for the individual, he or she may unconsciously want to forget them (Alper, 1946; Morrow, 1938). This process, presumably of repression, further suggests the role of motivation in remembering.

Overlearning. The role of motivation is most readily evident in *overlearning,* which means learning a task beyond the point at which it has just been mastered. In overlearning, a person knows a poem or a chemical analysis "forwards and backwards." Its value is illustrated in an experiment in which adults learned lists of nouns beyond the criterion of one perfect recall. Having half again as many practice trials as required to reach the

first perfect recall was designated as 50 percent overlearning. Having twice as many was 100 percent overlearning. These two groups were compared with a third group which engaged in no overlearning, and the results showed a distinct advantage to both amounts of overlearning (Figure 10-19). ■

Actually, the term overlearning is not a particularly good one because it suggests that there has been too much practice, which is not the case. The highly motivated learner almost always passes beyond the point of initial mastery, but he or she has not learned the task too well.

The almost perfect retention of some motor skills, such as riding a bicycle, buttoning clothes, and eating with utensils, has led some to suppose that motor skills are naturally better retained than verbal skills, but this conception seems to be false. In experiments in which predominantly verbal activities and predominantly motor activities are practiced an equal number of trials, motor skills are no better remembered than verbal ones (McGeoch & Melton, 1929; Van Tilborg, 1936). A problem in most of these experiments is equating the tasks for level of difficulty. Nevertheless, it seems that the superior retention of certain motor skills, as compared with verbal skills, occurs because some of them are overlearned.

Memory Techniques

Suppose now that you must memorize something and that you are motivated to do so. You want to remember the names of all the endocrine glands or a list of important dates in history. What is the best system? Should you use *free recall,* where you simply reproduce the list in any order, or should you use *serial recall,* in which you remember the items in a particular sequence? The answer is an interesting one and illustrates a most basic principle of successful memorizing. □

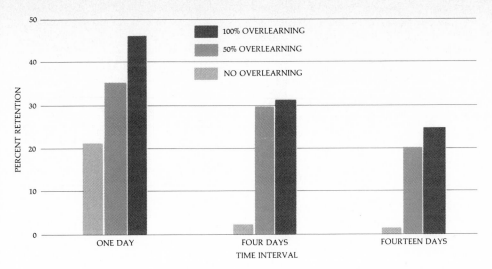

Figure 10-19 Overlearning and Recall. *In this experiment, recall was improved with overlearning. Without overlearning, it was almost negligible after four days. (After Krueger, 1929. Copyright 1929 by the American Psychological Association. Reprinted by permission.)*

Organization.   When free and serial recall are compared, using tasks too difficult for success on the first trial, it is found that on the first few trials the subject using free recall responds with the easiest words, wherever they appear in the list. Therefore, free recall is best at this point; however, in learning a complete list of several items, the subject remembers more of these items when required to do so serially (Earhard, 1967; Waugh, 1961). In studying for a history exam, use serial recall if you have a lot of dates and places to remember.

The superiority of serial recall for long lists has created a strong case for the view that successful memory is chiefly the result of an organization imposed on the material by the learner, called *subjective organization*. It is the learner's tendency to form groups among the items on the basis of his own experience. Mere repetition is ineffective unless some sort of organizational arrangement is made among the items (Mandler & Boeck, 1974; Tulving, 1966). ■

The importance of organization in recall was demonstrated when subjects sorted a pack of cards containing single words into categories. Up to approximately seven, the larger the number of categories the subject used, the better was the recall. Recall by subjects using seven categories was approximately twice as successful as that of subjects using only two (Mandler, 1967).

One investigator emphasizes organization based on ''chunks'' of material. According to this view, the average adult memory span appears fixed at approximately seven separate entries, unless the material is subjectively organized into larger chunks or categories. Then the individual is often able to recall seven such categories, each including several smaller items, prompting the expression the ''magical number seven'' (Miller, 1956). Regardless of the exact number of categories, the degree to which an individual can organize small pieces of information into larger units is a vital factor in the amount of information that he or she is able to recall (Figure 10-20). Today this organizational process in memory, called encoding, is of immense interest in research (Bower, 1972; Postman, 1975).

■ *When I was younger, I never remembered how to spell my older brother's name, but I finally did so by thinking of it as two repeating syllables enclosing a word I previously knew: ''Ge'' or ''ge.''*

Figure 10-20 Chunking the Chapter. *The information in this chapter is already organized into chunks, as indicated in the outline on the first page. To facilitate recall of each chunk, cues such as 2T, 3R, 4P, and Principles can be used.*

2T's
    TRACE
    TIME
3R's
    RECALL
    RECOGNITION
    RELEARNING
4 PUZZLES
    DECAY
    OBLITERATION
    INTERFERENCE
    REPRESSION
PRINCIPLES
    MOTIVATION
    TECHNIQUE

Building up associations among various parts of a memory task and associations between them and previously acquired learning is most important in linking the "chunks" or categories together. As William James once said:

Of two men with the same outward experiences and the same amount of mere native tenacity, the one who THINKS over his experiences most, and weaves them into systematic relations with each other, will be the one with the best memory. (1908)

Imagery. Most memory systems emphasize organization. In doing so, they also stress the importance of acquiring associations or visual images, in addition to those provided by the system itself. We remember not only in verbal terms but also in visual terms. It appears that words are most useful for encoding or storing abstract concepts—for instance, the meaning of a difficult word, such as "heuristic"—while concrete events, such as a close play at home plate, are best represented by visual imagery. The effectiveness of *visual imagery,* or mental pictures, in memory has been very well demonstrated (Paivio, 1971; Postman, 1975).

The tremendous capacity of the normal human adult for remembering visual stimuli was indicated earlier. Pictures are recognized with a very high degree of accuracy—more so than words. When subjects are presented with three types of verbal materials to be memorized—pictures, concrete nouns, and abstract nouns—the accuracy of recall appears in that order. The apparent reason is that pictures and concrete nouns can be remembered in both visual and verbal terms, while abstract nouns are generally remembered only by words (Paivio, 1971). In experiments of this nature, subjects sometimes report that they remembered the abstract words by associating them with some mental image.

Recent research suggests that imagery also is an effective means of organizing things to be remembered. Vividness is sometimes helpful, but vividness per se is not as important as one might expect (Bower, 1970). In fact, the value of extremely bizarre, weird images has been strongly questioned (Nappe & Wollen, 1973; Wollen et al., 1972).

Cues. To retrieve the associated chunks of information, with or without visual images, the individual needs cues. A *cue* is a signal for some particular action, in this case retrieval of stored information. After taking a test, for example, a student may say that he or she "knew" the material but was unable to recall it; in other words, there was storage but no retrieval. Therefore, in studying for an exam one should carefully code or "cue" the information, saying to oneself: "This information is what I would want if I were asked a question about memory, and these are the cues by which I would retrieve it." Such cues can be verbal or visual, including the image of the course outline and handwritten notes. ∎

The selection of cues is most important, for memory storage apparently is more organized than haphazard. Remember, for example, the systematic searching that occurs when a person expresses aloud his or her efforts to retrieve information "at the tip of the tongue." The person often tries to use as cues certain words associated with the forgotten event or elements of associated visual images. Some theories of memory storage have been proposed, usually suggesting a hierarchical organization (Collins & Quillian, 1972).

Method of loci. One means of establishing readily available cues is based on the *method of loci,* which is typical of most memory systems. The *loci* are "places," and many of us have familiar routes and places that we visit. A commuter returning home typically drives a car up the driveway, parks it in the garage, enters through the front door, hangs his or her coat in the closet, and then goes into the kitchen. Now suppose at some point during the day this person must remember a shopping list of hot dogs, cat food, tomatoes, bananas, and whiskey. What procedures should be used?

In the method of loci, each of these items should be associated with a specific place in this accustomed pathway, which serves as a cue for recall, and each one should be put in its place with mild imagery. Thus, the commuter perhaps thinks of large hot dogs lying in the driveway, a hungry cat having its supper in the garage, tomatoes splattered all over the front door, a bunch of bananas hanging from the hook in the coat closet, and the contents of a whiskey bottle bubbling into the kitchen sink. In order to remember these items, the individual merely proceeds mentally down the accustomed path, stopping occasionally—in the driveway, in the garage, at the door, and at other cues—to ask: "What did I put here?" (Bower, 1970; Figure 10-21).

The method of loci illustrates that success in memory comes largely from the three sources mentioned earlier. There is the organization, which in this case is the habitual route; there are the cues, which are the stopping places; and there are the visual images, which are formed on an individual basis, such as the tomatoes splattered on the door, bananas on a hook, and whiskey bubbling down the sink.

When more complex material is involved, such as the reasons for the development of the Industrial Revolution in England, efficiency in organizing masses of information into units is essential. At the first stopping point might be an entire description of the coal mining industry in England and its role in providing the energy necessary for the revolution. At the seond, there might be a comparable discussion of iron mining and its contribution to the construction of machines essential for large industrial changes. Then there might be information on England as a world power, and later the concept of the English as a

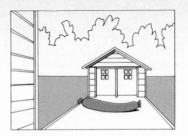

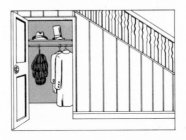

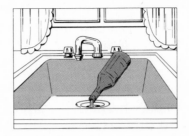

Figure 10-21   Method of Loci: A List of Items. *The individual uses the places on his habitual route as the framework for remembering a series of items.*

Figure 10-22 Method of Loci: Complex Concepts. *The method of loci is based on the principles of organization, cues, and associations. Here it is used for remembering the underlying factors in the origins of the Industrial Revolution in England.*

Organization	Cues	Images/Associations	Concepts
One's habitual route, as in traveling from home to work	Descending stairs	Entering coal mine	Role of coal as source of power
	Passing a mailbox	Constructed of iron	Use of iron in making machinery
	Climbing a hill	On top of the world	England as a leading nation
	Passing a beauty parlor	A place of business	Business-like character of the people
	Observing traffic light	Modern machinery	Importance of James Watt's steam engine

business-like people, and at another stopping place there might be the contribution of James Watt and the steam engine. Notice that these background factors are not necessarily in historical order; they simply have been placed with visual cues with which they are readily associated (Figure 10-22). Try this system sometime with your own material and habitual pathway.

Summary

Physiological Basis of Memory

1. It is hypothesized that memory is based on some change in the nervous system, called a memory trace or engram. According to the reappearance hypothesis, the memory trace remains intact in the brain and is some structural alteration. When the trace is properly aroused, the memory reappears. In the reconstruction hypothesis, memories are not fixed and filed in the brain but rather reassembled, chiefly on the basis of remnants from past experience. The biochemical nature of the memory trace is suspected to involve RNA, a substance manufactured by DNA, which influences cell development.

2. Speculation also occurs about two different memory processes, short-term and long-term memory, chiefly because it is sometimes very difficult to remember small bits of information for very short periods. Some investigators feel that short-term memory is a limited-capacity, processing system, in which incoming information is coded and rehearsed or discarded. Long-term memory is the final storage, an irreversible modification of neural structures.

Measures of Memory

3. Long-term memory can be measured by any of three methods. Recall is the most difficult memory task because related stimuli are essentially absent. Thus, systematic distortions often occur—there is loss of details in simplification; certain details are accentuated in elaboration; and changes that fit the individual's expectations and past experience occur in conventionalization. In terms of amount, the rate of forgetting is rapid at first and then relatively slow.

4. Recognition is an easier memory task than recall. An individual simply identifies the familiar and unfamiliar.

5. In a test of relearning, used to measure very small amounts of memory, the subject attempts to regain information or a skill that has been partially or completely forgotten. This procedure results in a savings score, where the time or number of trials involved in relearning is compared with those required in the original learning.

Theories of Forgetting

6. Forgetting is the inability to recall, recognize, or relearn some previously acquired information or skill at an improved rate. There may be a storage failure, in which the memory trace was never established or has disappeared, or a retrieval failure, in which an appropriate cue for evoking the memory is lacking. In the decay theory, forgetting is presumed to involve a storage failure. Through disuse and the passage of time, the trace has deteriorated.

7. Emotional and physical shock can cause forgetting, especially of recent events. According to the obliteration theory, the severe shock destroys the currently forming or newly formed trace, causing a storage failure.

8. There is also evidence that forgetting is produced by what happens in time, apart from some shock immediately after learning. Interference from the activity that preceded the learning is known as proactive inhibition. Interference from activity that followed the learning is known as retroactive inhibition. Either type of interference might create a storage or a retrieval problem.

9. Forgetting apparently can occur even when the memory trace remains. If so, there is a retrieval problem, as in repressive forgetting. It is hypothesized that through repression, unpleasant thoughts are unconsciously excluded from awareness.

Principles in Memorizing

10. A most important aspect of an effective memory is motivation; without motivation there is often no original impression. The Zeigarnik effect suggests that forgetting can be very rapid when one has no desire to remember.

11. The chief aspects of most memory systems include creating an organization in the material to be learned, building up associations or imagery for the various aspects of the task, and establishing reliable cues by which the memorized information can be retrieved. The method of loci illustrates these aspects.

Suggested Readings

Flaherty, C., Hamilton, L. W., Gardelman, R., & Spear, N. E. *Learning and memory*. Skokie, Ill.: Rand McNally, 1977. A textbook in both learning and memory with historical and contemporary perspectives.

Freud, S. *The psychopathology of everyday life*. New York: Norton, 1965. A paperback of Freud's classic work on the relation of unconscious motives to "slips of the tongue" and the forgetting of names.

Klatzky, R. L. *Human memory: Structures and processes*. San Francisco: W. H. Freeman, 1975. A readable presentation of major topics in this field.

Luria, A. R. *The mind of a mnemonist*. New York: Basic Books, 1968. The fascinating account of a man with an incredible memory, written by a noted Russian psychologist.

Norman, D. A. *Memory and attention: An introduction to human information processing*. New York: Wiley, 1976. A series of integrated papers and discussions, "designed for the sophisticated beginner."

Chapter 11

Learning and Instruction

Henry Adams once said of children: "They know enough who know how to learn." There is much to be said for this view, for complex learning does not take place automatically. Carefully planned instruction is often helpful.

In this chapter we move beyond theory and research to consider the application of learning principles in practical situations. The central question is this: Given a certain task to be learned, such as a geography unit, how does one go about planning the learning environment?

Components of Instruction

In educational psychology, three elements of the instructional process, apart from the learner, are widely recognized—the learning objective, which concerns what is to be learned; the instructional method, which involves how it is to be learned; and evaluation, by which one discovers the extent to which the objective has been attained. Each element serves a special function and complements the others (Figure 11-1).

Learning Objectives

Learning goes on constantly at school, at work, and in recreation, but much of it is incidental or unintentional. That is, a person learns something without intending to do so. Our concern here is with planned learning and, therefore, we begin with objectives.

Levels of objectives. The specific outcome that the learner hopes to achieve is called the *learning objective*. It is what the student should be able to do as a result of the learning experience. Generally, the objective is stated precisely, as in this example from a geography unit: to be able to locate on a blank map of a given region all the states and capital cities.

Learning objectives can be set at various levels of difficulty, however. The objective just stated is a *knowledge objective,* meaning that it requires only recall of specific facts. An *application objective* requires greater competence. The learner must apply certain principles of geography in a new situation, such as: to be able to indicate why certain areas have become urban and why other areas have remained rural. At a still higher level, an *evaluation objective* would require that the learner assess the development of certain urban areas and support his or her conclusions. This objective might be stated as: to be able to decide which geographic areas are most appropriate for urban development and redevelopment and which are least appropriate. Clearly, objectives can exist in a hierarchical order, from those that are relatively simple to attain to those that are more complex (Figure 11-2).

Domains of objectives. Regardless of the level, some objectives involve responses that are essentially mental, such as reciting vocabulary, forming concepts, and learning geographic features. The objectives are said to fall in the verbal or *cognitive domain.* Other objectives require responses that are predominantly muscular, as in drawing a map or

driving a car, and they are part of the psychomotor or *motor domain.* This general distinction does not mean that all objectives fall neatly into either one of these categories; more commonly, there is a mixture. Making a speech involves primarily verbal learning, but it is based on complex motor learning, as well. Locating cities on a map involves motor behavior, but is supported by cognitive learning.

There are also objectives in the *affective domain,* which concerns the learning of attitudes, feelings, and values. This learning, also called emotional learning, can be extremely important for the performance of both cognitive and psychomotor skills. A student with a negative attitude towards certain minority groups is unlikely to study their customs and folkways in social science, and even if they are learned initially, he or she probably will not remember or use the information.

Learning through Modeling

Once objectives are established, in any domain and at any level, the next concern is developing methods for achieving them. Today, printed materials, films, sound tapes, computer programs, laboratory equipment, self-instructional materials, closed circuit television, and innumerable other methods are available. Many of them are relatively new and represent outgrowths of interdisciplinary work in psychology, education, and electronics. Students can learn effectively from all of these instructional activities, but thus far the new technology has served primarily an enrichment function, rather than replacing teachers (Jamison et al., 1974).

Our discussion of instructional activities, therefore, focuses on the teacher. In addition to the concepts of conditioning and cognitive processes, there is another approach to learning that is especially relevant to the teacher's role. It is called *social learning theory* because it stresses that much learning occurs through social activity, by observing and

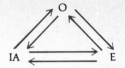

Figure 11-1 Interrelations between Objectives, Instructional Activities, and Evaluation. *The loss of any of the three vertices in the triangle makes education inefficient or unsuccessful. Without objectives, there is no goal; without instructional activities, there is no way of achieving goals; and without evaluation, there is no way of knowing whether or not the objectives have been achieved.*

Figure 11-2 Levels of Educational Objectives. *In one hierarchical classification, six levels are specified. The descriptions below are illustrative but not all-inclusive. (After Bloom, 1956)*

Evaluation:	Judgments are made on the basis of specified criteria.
Synthesis:	Ideas are rearranged or combined into a new form.
Analysis:	Interrelationships are identified and inconsistencies detected.
Application:	Principles are applied in new situations.
Comprehension:	Facts and principles are restated or interpreted in another form.
Knowledge:	Facts and principles are recognized and recalled.

interacting with others. It applies broadly to *any* learning situation in which other people are observed, not just to the classroom.

The concept of modeling. According to this concept, human learning develops partly through direct experience. The individual acquires new behavior on the basis of continuous, direct interaction with the environment; responses that produce desirable effects are retained, and those that produce undesirable effects are discarded. This rudimentary form of learning follows the laws of conditioning, but if human learning occurred only in this way it would be extremely laborious.

Think how much time and effort would be required for a child to learn to tie a shoe if he or she could never copy someone else. It would also be hazardous if we had to learn everything by direct experience, rather than having someone else demonstrate the correct behavior. According to social learning theorists, most human responses are acquired by following an example, or model, either deliberately or inadvertently. Thus, the concept of *modeling* is central to social learning theory (Bandura, 1973).

Consider how often children adopt the habits of their parents and also other models to whom they are regularly exposed, such as teachers and coaches (Figure 11-3). In research, it has been shown that young children of aggressive mothers are more likely than others to be aggressive in school (Sears et al., 1957). Ironically, when an adult punishes aggressive behavior in the child, he or she is demonstrating the very behavior that the child, at some later time when away from the influence of the punitive model, probably will imitate.

Models also can induce desirable behavior. In another experiment, some withdrawn children observed a schizophrenic child who eventually joined other children playing together and interacted with them in a satisfying manner. After this incident, the children who were observers showed a much greater increase in social interaction than did a comparable group of children not exposed to a favorable model (Bandura, 1969).

In these and other instances, behaviors are adopted and abandoned even when no reinforcement is involved. The observer's behavior seems to change simply on the basis of what happens to the model—that is, on the basis of vicarious reinforcement. Children watching aggressive adults who eventually received rewards were more likely to be aggressive. When the aggressive model was punished, the children displayed fewer aggressive acts (Bandura, 1965).

A distinction between learning and performance is necessary in this context, however. *Learning* can occur through modeling when the only reinforcement is vicarious, but the *performance* of any learned act, aggressive or otherwise, is also influenced by the availability of rewards and punishment for the learner (Bandura, 1965). Without reinforcement, the learned act is unlikely to be emitted often.

Processes in modeling. Research such as that discussed in the preceding section illustrates that several processes are involved in modeling—the need for attending to the model, the mental representation or memory, the reproduction of the motor behavior, and the need for reinforcement (Bandura, 1971). Attending and memory are cognitive processes, and sometimes there is mental practice of motor behavior. Therefore, social learning theory has a cognitive orientation. But reinforcement has a role, since the appearance of a learned response can be affected by reward and punishment. Modeling, in this respect, involves conditioning too.

Virtually everything that human beings learn through direct experience also can be learned vicariously, by observing other people and noting the consequences of their behavior. This learning is sometimes very rapid, and for this reason modeling has been used in diverse learning situations, including therapy. Its special value in therapy is that many different behaviors can be approached from a single framework, especially when symbolic modeling is involved. In symbolic modeling, the model is not actually present but is imagined or viewed in pictures by the patient. In this way the patient can participate vicariously in a variety of learning situations, involving such responses as social relations, emotional reactions, and complex motor skills. Modeling is considered an important link between various types of therapy and daily life (Krasner, 1971).

In the classroom, the teacher's behavior can be highly influential in the learning outcomes of the students. The student who observes his or her professor working enthusiastically in preventive medicine is more likely to consider this field for a career than is one whose instructor is interested only in areas of curative medicine. As a role model, the teacher can be particularly effective in teaching attitudes as well as psychomotor skills (Segall et al., 1975). Much teaching in the later years of professional schools, such as schools of medicine and dentistry, is accomplished on this basis.

Evaluation of Learning

Evaluation should indicate the extent to which the student has achieved the learning objectives. But no one has observed learning directly. It occurs somewhere inside the organism, in the form of neural or other physiological changes, the nature of which has not been established. Learning is thus a construct. A *construct* cannot be observed directly but is inferred from the observed data and provides a way of thinking about them. Thus, learning is evaluated by studying overt performance.

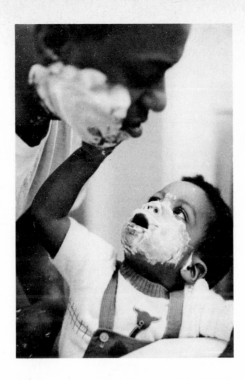

Figure 11-3 Modeling. *Deliberately or inadvertently, we learn partly by observing influential others. (Uzzle from Magnum)*

Measures of performance. The sailor who ties a complex knot quickly and the basketball player who is successful in nine out of ten free throws are credited with learning. In these instances, learning is defined in terms of the speed of response and number of correct responses, respectively. Such measures are common criteria for evaluating learning.

A novice basketball player, nevertheless, may be acquiring greater proficiency even though missing on every trial. A child may be learning to use language even without saying a word. In short, the learner may be making improvements that are not evident in performance. On the other hand, the learner may show a worsening of performance because of other factors, such as fatigue, anxiety, and misunderstanding of instructions. For a variety of reasons, learning may seem to appear or disappear from one moment to another. Any measure of performance must be interpreted with caution when used as evidence of learning.

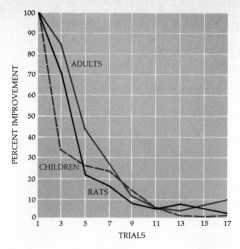

Figure 11-4   Performance Curves for Maze Learning. *Rats, children, and adult human subjects served in this experiment. The human maze was large enough to walk through; rats learned a comparable scaled-down maze. Improvement is shown as a percentage of the score obtained on the first trial. (After Hicks & Carr)*

Learning curves. Using some measure of performance, the acquisition of most behavior can be represented graphically by a curve, which shows the general trend of the responses. This curve is known as a learning curve, even though it is technically a *performance curve.* It is plotted by representing some measure of time or trials on the horizontal axis and the subject's behavior on the vertical axis. When the measure of learning on the vertical axis is the number of correct responses, a rising curve results; if errors are plotted, a falling curve is expected (Figure 11-4).

Performance curves for individual subjects may differ widely. One subject might progress for a trial or two, regress for a period, and then show further improvement. Another subject might do poorly for several trials and then improve quickly. For purposes of establishing trends, individual data are usually combined and averaged to produce a group curve, but the reader should not make the assumption that the average of the group performance is representative of a typical individual in the group. Sometimes the group curve is not similar to the performance of any given individual.

Often, after improvement has occurred, an individual curve will show no further progress for several trials, and the flat region in the curve is referred to as a plateau. An *intermediate plateau* can occur while the subject is perfecting certain aspects of the performance, after which additional improvement takes place. A *terminal plateau* is set by the problem itself or by the subject's capacity. In an arithmetic problem, the subject cannot improve a score of no errors. In track and field events, lung capacity and leg length are among the factors that impose a physiological limit, but it is never fully known when such a limit has been reached. For decades the four-minute mile was believed to be physically impossible, but after Roger Bannister ran it in less than four minutes in the early 1950s, a number of other runners have done so too.

Applications of Learning Principles

Given a learning objective, a wide array of possible instructional activities, and the potential for evaluation, how does one structure the learning environment? What theory of learning or principles of learning should be followed?

The problem of moving from basic to applied science can be a difficult step due to significant differences between the laboratory and classroom. The conditions of the laboratory are more readily controlled than those in the classroom, and the subjects are more carefully selected. The experimenter generally deals with each person individually while the teacher often has a large group. In the laboratory there is less interest in the outcomes for the learner and more interest in discovering which factors influenced the learning (Bugelski, 1964). Nevertheless, basic research does suggest some prescriptions for planning learning at school, on the job, or elsewhere.

Learning and Symbolic Activity

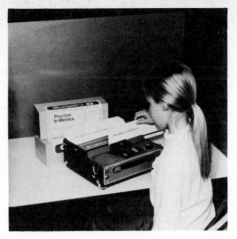

Figure 11-5 Teaching Machine.
This machine is designed to aid in teaching reading. The student reads the problem, records his or her answer, and then can listen to the correct answer on a recording. (Califone International Inc.)

The Programmed Approach

From the conditioning viewpoint comes the idea of a *programmed approach,* which indicates that complex patterns of behavior can be developed through careful elaboration of simpler responses, provided the learning environment is properly structured. Terminal and intermediate objectives are specified for each learning unit, and the material to be mastered is presented to the learner with careful instructions. In short, the learner is guided step-by-step towards well-established goals. The leader in this approach is B. F. Skinner, who has contributed not only basic research but also some practical applications.

S-R principles. Within the stimulus-response framework, the most relevant principles are the method of approximations and the use of certain schedules of reinforcement. In the former, a gradual series of steps is used, and each step is slightly more complex than the one preceding it. During the acquisition phase, the learner receives reinforcement for every success, but as refinements in learning occur, intermittent reinforcement is more often employed.

One technique that illustrates these procedures is *programmed instruction.* It consists of a set of step-by-step materials—verbal, graphic, or both—called a program and sometimes a device for presenting this material, popularly known as a *teaching machine.* The latter term is a misnomer because the machine is not necessary for most programs and, furthermore, it is the program rather than the machine that does the teaching. The machine simply provides convenient ways of presenting the material and some form of secondary reinforcement, which for the adult is knowledge of the correct answer and for the child is sometimes a light or buzzer as well (Figure 11-5).

The material in programmed instruction appears in a sequence of separate items or tasks, each of which is called a *frame.* The learner responds to each one, checks to see if his or her answer is correct, and then moves to the next frame. The chief advantages to programmed instruction are that the information is presented in small steps, the learner must be active in responding to the material, and the learner receives immediate knowledge of his or her results. In a *linear program* the frames are arranged in one continuous sequence, and the average student does all of them, although provisions are made for

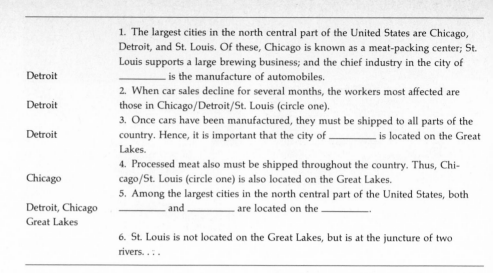

Figure 11-6   A Linear Program.
Conceal the answers and then uncover them one-by-one as you answer each frame.

1. The largest cities in the north central part of the United States are Chicago, Detroit, and St. Louis. Of these, Chicago is known as a meat-packing center; St. Louis supports a large brewing business; and the chief industry in the city of

Detroit   _____ is the manufacture of automobiles.

2. When car sales decline for several months, the workers most affected are

Detroit   those in Chicago/Detroit/St. Louis (circle one).

3. Once cars have been manufactured, they must be shipped to all parts of the

Detroit   country. Hence, it is important that the city of _____ is located on the Great Lakes.

4. Processed meat also must be shipped throughout the country. Thus, Chi-

Chicago   cago/St. Louis (circle one) is also located on the Great Lakes.

5. Among the largest cities in the north central part of the United States, both

Detroit, Chicago   _____ and _____ are located on the _____.
Great Lakes

6. St. Louis is not located on the Great Lakes, but is at the juncture of two rivers. . . .

---

the more advanced student to skip certain frames by passing intermittent diagnostic tests (Figure 11-6). Within a *branching program* there are occasional sequences of extra frames for those who need practice or remedial instruction, and there are short cuts for those who can take them.

Considerable research has been directed towards evaluating programmed instruction. Linear and branching programs have been compared; the optimal error rate has been studied; and the effects of frame size have been considered (Floyd & Lumsden, 1973). Programs involving an integration of visual, auditory, and motor responses also have been evaluated (Argyros & Rusch, 1974). In addition, much attention has been given to the *pall effect,* which refers to the boredom that may be experienced when programmed materials are used extensively. The frequent repetition, low error rate, and controlled sequence of steps are significant factors in the pall effect.

A unit of instruction.   In a unit on geography, programmed instruction might or might not be used, but in either case the instructor following this general approach would begin by identifying all the responses he or she expected the students to make. Then, the instructor would use the method of approximations and appropriate schedules of reinforcement for presenting the necessary learning activities and properly arranged reinforcements. In addition, series of progress tests would be included to ensure that the stated objectives were being achieved.

In a geography unit on the North Central states of the United States, for example, a secondary school instructor would assemble materials on those states and on Chicago, Detroit, and St. Louis—the three areas of greatest population density and economic importance. The assignments might include preparing maps, obtaining census data, and writing a brief history of the region, each task being arranged as a prerequisite for the next one. Units of programmed instruction might be included as well (Figure 11-6). If the learning environment is properly planned in this way and the students are capable, the expectation is that all students will succeed on all the objectives, much as behavior is successfully shaped in *Walden Two* and other planned societies.

Learning and Symbolic Activity

The Discovery Approach

In contrast to the programmed approach, Jean Piaget once said: "As soon as you teach a child something, you deny him the opportunity of discovering it for himself." The premise in the discovery approach is that the educational setting can be and usually is too directive. The student is led through a carefully structured sequence of material with the result that he or she does not develop the capacity to think independently. The implication for education is that the curriculum should be designed with Piaget's concept of development in mind; in *discovery learning* the focus is on the student's own discovery of meaningful patterns of thought, rather than on the acquisition of basic habits and facts.

Cognitive principles. The emphasis in the cognitive approach is on reasoning and other forms of thinking. The relevant term in early gestalt psychology is *insight,* and today the phrase *information processing* is common. The overall significance of these concepts is that most learning, especially complex learning, involves understanding. Education should serve this purpose and, therefore, the learner should not be given the material to be mastered in its final form. Instead, the learning process should require that the learner transform it, add to it, or reorganize it in some way in order to understand it (Ausubel & Robinson, 1969).

To acquire the broadest possible understanding of concepts such as "time" and "space," the individual needs diverse experience. Environmental variety is most important and, furthermore, the learner, without the usual classroom restraints, can tell what the best, most useful environment is for him or her. Given adequate circumstances, the learner will keep moving to new learning situations following a natural rate and sequence as intellectual growth continues.

Most educators agree on the value of establishing objectives, but from the discovery viewpoint these are likely to be broader than in the programmed approach, and it is expected that the students will vary in their interest and capacity to meet them. In discovery learning, the student is more often provided with the opportunity to change foci, skip tests, and make short cuts. Finding answers, not *the* answer, is stressed, as in divergent thinking. Afterwards, the conclusions can be checked by more analytic, systematic thought (Bruner, 1960). Too much emphasis on achieving specific objectives leads to overconcern with the right answer and convergent thinking. The students become too interested in the answer the teacher has in mind, rather than arriving at their own conclusions, and this concern eventually results in anxiety for the learner (Holt, 1964).

A unit of instruction. In the discovery approach, the material in a unit on geography would be presented not as a known but as a problem in unknowns. The students would be encouraged to discover the basic principles themselves. Textbooks and other carefully prepared resources would not be employed at the beginning, for these materials yield the basic facts and principles directly. Instead, the students might be given maps showing only the rivers, lakes, and other major geographic features, and then they would be asked to decide for themselves about the probable location and characteristics of the chief cities of this region. In this way, they are led to make inferences about unstated facts.

There are large waterways among the North Central states, and perhaps the student decides that the major urban areas are located in relation to them. If so, the student develops a principle and sees relationships. Later, some reference to complete maps would be permitted, enabling the students to check

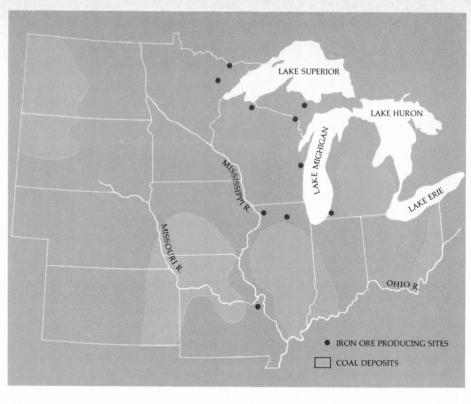

Figure 11-8 Major Cities in the North Central States. *The basic principle to be discovered by the student is that the urban areas are located near lakes and rivers, which aid transportation, and also near other natural resources. However, there is no major urban area at the juncture of the largest waterways, where Lakes Michigan, Ontario, and Huron join. The objective for another discovery unit might be to uncover reasons for this circumstance.*

their success at conceptualizing the essential geographical features that result in concentrations of population (Figure 11-7).

Also, the students would examine their failures to discover what incorrect principles were derived or how correct ones were applied wrongly. The emphasis would be on reasoning and learning to think flexibly about a topic (Bruner, 1960; Figure 11-8).

A Continuum of Structure

The teacher can serve as a model in both the programmed and discovery approaches. In the programmed approach, the model demonstrates the value of systematic methods in a carefully planned curriculum. In the discovery approach, the model emphasizes flexibility of thought and a willingness to speculate and diverge from planned objectives. The perceived consequences of the model's behavior can have a powerful influence on the learners in each approach (Bandura, 1971).

Advantages and disadvantages. The chief advantage in the programmed approach is that the learner knows the objectives, and the methods of attaining them are readily available. Therefore, learning can be achieved rapidly. This method is especially efficient for developing basic skills and enabling students to gain knowledge quickly in a new field (Ausubel & Robinson, 1969).

The main asset in the discovery approach is that the student is more likely to develop his or her own ways of thinking about problems and perhaps will encounter new ways of dealing with them. Problems as well as solutions must be identified. In choosing his or her own approach, the learner in the discovery method is likely to be highly motivated and, therefore, the learning is likely to be remembered.

But both approaches also have drawbacks. Constant exposure to the highly structured environment of programmed instruction may make the learner overly dependent on procedures established by others, rather than on his or her own capacity for learning. On the other hand, the student in the discovery method may spend a great deal of time finding a focus for learning, and eventually he or she may discover incorrect or relatively useless principles. Altogether, the decision concerning which method to use in a given instance depends partly on the goals of the instruction, since each method is especially useful for certain purposes, and partly on the learners' capabilities and past experiences. In particular, the discovery approach requires time and a certain level of ability to be employed profitably.

A range of possibilities. Neither the programmed nor the discovery approach totally excludes the other. There is some programming in discovery learning in the sense that some context and materials must be established, and there is an element of discovery in programmed instruction, not only when the learner finds out if his or her answers are correct but also when he or she arrives at the answers. The issue in instruction is, therefore, one of *degree* of guidedness or directedness, as illustrated in the following possibilities in geography:

Students are given complete or blank maps and are allowed to do whatever they wish.

Students are given maps, pencils, and rulers and are asked to consider the ways in which geographical features influence human living conditions.

Students are asked to select reading materials on the development of urban areas and are told to be ready to discuss their conclusions from these readings.

Students are assigned reading materials on the major midwestern cities and are asked to answer a prepared list of questions.

Students are given complete sets of programmed instruction on the settlement and development of Chicago, Detroit, and St. Louis and are requested to complete all the programs.

Altogether, most learning environments approximate conditions near the middle of this *continuum of structure.* As a rule, neither pure discovery nor pure programming is employed for long. Some learners prefer one method; some prefer the other. Some procedures are useful for certain objectives and others are useful for attaining different objectives, as already illustrated. Finally, it is important to remember student motivation, which sometimes can be maintained at a high level partly by intermittent changes in the mode of instruction.

Transfer of Training

Although the programmed and discovery approaches differ in the structure of the learning environment and in the types of objectives that are set, both are ultimately concerned with the transfer of training. The term *transfer of training* means that learning acquired in one situation influences learning acquired in another. Advocates of discovery learning claim that transfer is likely because the learners have discovered the principles by themselves. In the programmed approach, the learners are often given direct instruction in how to use the principles in other situations.

Studies in Education

In the previous century it was assumed by some teachers, lay people, and also scientists that a person's mental capacity could be described in terms of specific faculties. The human mind included a memory faculty, a reasoning faculty, a habit faculty, and so forth, including personality faculties. According to this view, called *phrenology,* these faculties were localized in various areas of the brain, perhaps numbering 40 or more (Figure 11-9).

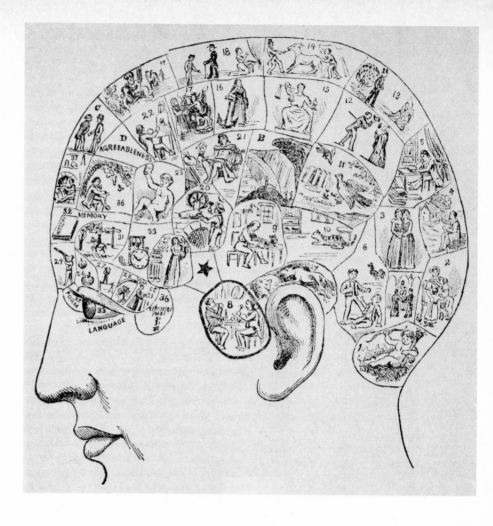

Figure 11-9 Phrenology. *In the last century, there was a craze over phrenology, which claimed that an individual's mental functions and personality could be understood by inspecting the bumps on his or her head. Phrenological examinations became widespread until it was gradually realized that practitioners did little more than relieve the client of some of his or her money. (The Bettmann Archive)*

Doctrine of formal discipline. Phrenology disappeared as soon as scientists gained greater knowledge of the brain, but another false idea arose concerning transfer. Certain mental capacities could be strengthened by studying certain academic subjects. According to the *doctrine of formal discipline*, the study of Latin, Greek, and mathematics, in particular, would strengthen one's power of reasoning. Other subjects were perhaps appropriate for developing other faculties, but the classics and mathematics were especially useful in giving "elasticity" to mental functions (Figure 11-10). Support for this doctrine arose when some school officials examined the overall academic performances of dif-ferent groups of students and found that those taking Latin and geometry had better records than those in other curricula.

Afterwards, a psychologist undertook a large-scale investigation of this issue, involving 8,564 high school students in various cities on the East Coast. Each student took a battery of mental tests and then, after following the curriculum of his or her choice for one year, the student took the same tests again. In conducting this research, the student's basic intellectual ability, which was ignored in the school officials' observations, was taken into account, and then the results were analyzed for 25 different subjects, from physics to sewing.

Learning and Symbolic Activity

Overall, no significant advantage was found for studying any particular subject. When the "good thinkers" pursued Latin and Greek, these subjects seemed to produce good thinking. When the best students studied physical education and drama, these studies appeared to make good thinkers. In fact, it was argued that drama and physical education were the basic curricula for the best thinkers produced in the world to date—the Athenian Greeks. The chief reason why one's mental functions seemed to be developed especially through the study of the classics and mathematics was because the most capable students commonly enrolled in these subjects and because there is an inherent tendency for a capable student to gain more than a less capable student from any course of study (Thorndike, 1924).

When this investigation was followed by similar studies with the same findings, the public began to favor a more practical curriculum in high school. It was decided that the student should be prepared for the "real world," since no specific course of study was highly advantageous in achieving broad mental development. Thus, changes were made to include more social studies and understanding of world problems, many of which are still in existence today.

Teaching for transfer. The study of Latin serves primarily to increase one's understanding of Latin. If one desires to improve one's English vocabulary, English should be studied, not Latin. However, Latin can be learned in various ways, and there will be some transfer to English vocabulary if word roots are stressed. If the conjugations are emphasized, transfer should occur in the learning of French, and if the cultural background is stressed, there should be some transfer to history. Transfer does not occur automatically; it is significantly influenced by the way in which the original task is learned. When certain relationships are emphasized, that type of transfer is more likely (Reed et al., 1974).

Bases of Transfer

Since everything cannot be taught in the schools, transfer of training is probably the single most significant practical issue in education. The learning objectives established for school should reflect not only in-school needs but the facilitation of later learning outside of school.

Types of transfer. When learning in one instance facilitates learning in another, we speak of *positive transfer.* It occurs when a student learns to drive a car with automatic shift and later more easily masters a standard shift. It is involved when a skilled tennis player readily learns squash. In arranging the geography lesson, the instructor should aim for positive transfer. Learning the principles of geography from studying the North Central states should enable the student more readily to master the geography of New England, the West Coast, or some other region.

■ *The other day I had to borrow a friend's bike, and there was one big difference between the one on which I learned to ride and this one—the brakes. On my own, I pedal backwards to stop, but on this one I was supposed to press handle brakes. I had quite a time at first. Every time I wanted to stop I'd find myself pedaling backwards and going right ahead, and then I'd realize that I was supposed to press the handle brakes.*

Figure 11-11 Transfer in Language. *Read the Spanish words and guess their English meanings. Then read the English equivalents on page 282.*

Spanish	English
ordinario	
ignorante	
universidad	
constipado	
embarazada	
simpático	

In other instances there may be *negative transfer* or habit interference, in which earlier learning interferes with later learning. Backing up a car with a trailer attached can result in distinct negative transfer because the results of turning the steering wheel are just the opposite of what one normally encounters. Turning the wheel to the right turns the trailer to the left, rather than the right. Learning to operate a typewriter by the touch system may be more difficult after one has developed an efficient hunt-and-peck method. ■

Sometimes, however, practicing one task makes no difference in performing another, and the transfer is negligible. In still other instances, previous experience constitutes a mix of both useful and hindering elements. The tennis player learning squash finds some similarity in the rules of the games and the importance of footwork and good position, but the scoring is different, the ball bounces differently, and the stroke is more from the wrist. There is positive *and* negative transfer (Figure 11-11).

Learning to learn. A series of studies, primarily with monkeys, illustrates both the procedures for studying transfer and some relevant outcomes. A chimpanzee, for example, is confronted with a cup on the right and a dish on the left; under the dish is a raisin. If the animal lifts the cup, it receives nothing, but if it lifts the dish, it obtains the raisin. On the next trial, the positions of the cup and the dish might or might not be interchanged and, thus, the monkey must consider both the nature of the object and its position when making the next guess. Each time the reward is under the dish, and eventually the subject "catches on"—always lifting the dish.

Next, the monkey is presented with two entirely different objects, such as a jar and a box, and on the first trial the subject can only guess which one always contains the reward. The second trial is the test for transfer. Will the monkey lift the same object if it was correct on the first trial, and will it lift the other object if the first one was incorrect? If so, the monkey has formed a *learning set* or has learned to learn (Harlow, 1949; Figure 11-12).

Probably the monkey does not perform with perfect accuracy right away, but the animal learns to solve this problem more rapidly than the previous one. When presented with still another problem, such as a large cube and a small cube, with the small cube always correct, the monkey solves it even more readily. Successively, new pairs of objects are presented until finally the monkey needs only one trial to learn the correct object. After approximately 300 such trials, monkeys perform at about 95 percent accuracy (Warrren, 1965).

Cats perform at only 70 percent accuracy, and rodents need more than 1,000 trials to score 55 percent correct, which is not much above chance. College students usually are 100 percent correct after just a few trials (Warren, 1965).

Factors influencing transfer. Outcomes such as these are described as the formation of a learning set because the organism has developed a generalized approach to the problem, bringing its prior experience to bear in the new stimulus situation. According to cognitive psychologists, such mastery is dependent on the understanding of a principle. Not all theorists agree, however, that highly abstract thought processes are involved (Medin, 1972). The two test stimuli are novel, but the context of learning and the basic principle remain the same.

These studies show that the basic factor in determining the amount of transfer is the degree of similarity between the two learning situations. When the stimulus conditions are similar and similar responses are required, high positive transfer will usually result. When the conditions are similar but different responses are required, high negative

Figure 11-12 A Learning-to-Learn Task. *The two objects are attached to strings and pulled away after the animal has made a choice. Following many such tests, with various stimuli, the subject needs only one trial to discover the correct choice, which contains the food. (Experiment courtesy of Mahut & Zola, Northeastern University; Sheila A. Farr photo)*

transfer occurs. When the stimulus conditions are quite different, it is unlikely that any transfer will occur. In the last circumstance, the teacher can best promote positive transfer by pointing out subtle response similarities in the two learning situations.

Practice and Motivation

In mastering complex tasks, the learner also must engage in a good deal of practice, apart from direct instruction and transfer. Some Olympic champions practice for four years between their successes. At the start of his career, George Bernard Shaw wrote three novels in five years and never published any of them because he felt that they were inadequate. Teachers of creative writing are now studying these materials to understand the development of his writing style and ability.

Conditions of Practice

Success in learning often involves *much* practice. There is generally no substitute for it, but there are some general rules for arranging practice sessions most effectively. ■

Distributed versus massed practice. When short practice periods are used, separated by rest intervals, the procedure is known as *distributed practice* or distributed learning. When the individual works continually for long periods of time or until the task is mastered, the procedure is called *massed practice*. Research with a wide variety of tasks and rest intervals has shown that, as a rule, there is an advantage to distributed practice, for several reasons.

If the work unit is prolonged, fatigue occurs, which limits one's performance. A short work unit, moreover, usually produces higher motivation because a goal is reached more often. Furthermore, once a person stops work there may be perseveration of the neural processes aroused by the former activity,

■ *During the past 13 years, I have spent a considerable amount of time at the piano keyboard, often tucked away in a practice room, communing with some long-extinct composer. . . . Before embarking on a new piece, one of the main concerns of my teachers has always been how well I like it—no one wants to practice or listen to a student who is learning a piece that he or she cannot stand. Consequently, from the start, I am usually fairly motivated to learn the piece. I often survey the task before beginning by listening to a recording of the piece, and proceed to a question phase, in which I might try to analyze the piece musically, looking at the form, the key modulations, etc. Then, after sight-reading the piece all of the way through, I start the actual grind of practicing.*

without specific effort and rehearsal on his or her part. This perseveration "consolidates" what has been learned. Also, during a rest period some incorrect responses may be weakened to the point at which they are forgotten. In summary, three general factors—less fatigue, higher motivation, and better recall of correct responses—all contribute to the efficiency of distributed as compared to massed practice.

Sometimes, however, a practical situation arises in which massed practice, despite its low efficiency, is necessary. For example, skilled workers might be trained in 80 hours if 2-hour practice sessions are used daily, but if the workers are needed immediately, 4-hour sessions might be used for a total of 120 instructional hours. With this massed practice, the instructional hours are 50 percent more, but the workers are ready 10 days earlier. A similar situation arises when students "cram" for an examination, but learning by this means, if not followed by further practice, is more readily forgotten.

Importance of recitation. When learning a verbal task, the value of recitation versus mere reading should be recognized. *Recitation* here does not mean reading aloud but rather actively trying to recall what has been learned. In one investigation, for example, groups of students memorized nonsense syllables and historical information. Some of them spent 100 percent of the time reading; others spent 80 percent of the time reading and 20 percent reciting what they had read; another group spent 60 percent reading and 40 percent reciting; and so forth, down to a group that spent only 20 percent of the time reading and 80 percent reciting. The final outcome was quite clear: the larger the proportion of time spent in recitation, the greater the efficiency of learning (Gates, 1917).

In another instance, students memorized arithmetical facts, vocabulary words, and spelling. Almost all the various approaches that included both

reading and recitation were more efficient than those with just reading (Forlano, 1936).

The reasons for the advantages of recitation are fairly obvious. Reading with the knowledge that one must soon recite usually raises motivation to learn and recitation tells one how well one is progressing. Most important, the person who recites during learning is practicing the performance he or she aims to achieve (Gates, 1917). In learning the geography of the North Central states, simply studying a normal map would be far inferior to obtaining also an outline map with many details missing, and then intermittently trying to determine the location of the urban areas and other geographic features.

Whole versus part learning. Another question concerns the size of the task to be mastered. Would it be more efficient to learn the geography of this region as a whole, or would it be best to break it up into parts, approaching the problem state by state? This issue is called *whole versus part learning,* and the findings are task-specific. That is, the results found for one task may or may not apply to another task.

Since the geography materials can be readily divided by states, the part approach would have special merit here, but in other instances putting the parts together requires much additional work. In most cases, it seems best to use a flexible plan, starting with the whole but subdividing it as necessary, when difficult aspects require special attention (Woodworth & Schlosberg, 1954).

Knowledge of results. Verbal and motor skills are never readily acquired unless the learner has some *knowledge of results* or information feedback. Performance curves for subjects with or without knowledge of results show marked differences in progress. The improved performance with feedback may

Answer to problem in Figure 11–11: For the first three words, positive transfer probably occurred. In the last three, however, negative transfer is likely because the meanings are not what one would expect on the basis of a knowledge of English.

Spanish	*English*
ordinario	ordinary
ignorante	ignorant
universidad	university
constipado	head cold
embarazada	pregnant
simpático	fun to be with

Learning and Symbolic Activity

be attributed to three circumstances: (1) repetition of responses known to be successful; (2) attempts to correct responses known to be inadequate; and (3) enhanced motivation in the sense that people working with knowledge of results find the task more interesting and try harder to improve their performance (Figure 11-13).

An example of the use of knowledge of results is found in *computer-assisted instruction* (CAI), in which the computer is used to present programmed learning directly to the student. The chief advantage is that the student's prior responses can be stored in the computer's tremendous memory system and the computer then can utilize this information in deciding what material the student should receive next and what degree of prompting and knowledge of results is appropriate. An illustration follows, where *C* refers to the computer and *S* designates a student:

C. Today we would like to have you figure out why the snow in the picture seemed to be melting even though the thermometer in the picture shows 28. Which of the following would you like to do?

    A. Ask some questions.
    B. Examine the picture some more.
    C. Try giving an answer.
    D. Run an experiment in varying the temperature.

S. D.

C. O.K., tell me what to do in the experiment.

S. *Decrease* the temperature to 10.

C. When the temperature is decreased to 10, the snow continues to melt.

S. *Decrease* temperature to 0.

C. When the temperature is decreased to 0, the snow stops melting.

S. A.

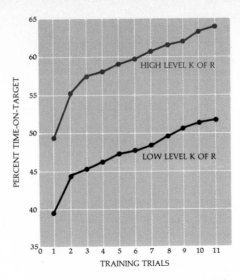

Figure 11-13　Knowledge of Results.　*In a tracking task, the low knowledge-of-results group was off the target longer than the high knowledge-of-results group, which received auditory and visual feedback. (After Smode, 1958)*

C. Now you wish to ask questions. Which one of the following would you like to ask?

    1. Is it a fahrenheit thermometer?
    2. Is it a centigrade thermometer?
    3. Is it real snow?
    4. What is the atmospheric pressure?

S. 1.

C. No, it is not.

S. C.

C. Now you want to try giving an answer. Go ahead.

S. *The thermometer in the picture is a centigrade thermometer.*

C. That is correct but you need to explain more.

S. *The freezing point on the centigrade scale is 0.*

C. Correct. You have done very well.
        (Klausmeier and Ripple, 1971)

Despite its high potential, the limitations of CAI should be recognized. At present, the cost of the equipment is extremely high, and well-constructed computer programs require a tremendous amount of time to develop. In addition, this mode of instruction has been criticized for taking the human quality idea of learning while asleep. If it is possible, the sleeping student could have a recorded lecture in history, a list of geographic features, or any other material played during a period that, from an academic viewpoint at least, is wasted. Several early studies indicated promising results, and the mass media publicized promising claims. But later investigations showed an important shortcoming in the early work: the sleepers were not fully asleep. They were partially awakened by the recordings. In studies designed to correct this defect, the recording remained on only when electroencephalograms (EEGs) showed that the subjects were truly sleeping. Whenever the subject began to wake up, as indicated by an aroused EEG pattern, the record was promptly turned off until the sleep pattern returned. Under these conditions, the sleepers showed no evidence of learning (Emmons & Simon, 1956).

The tentative, specific conclusion to be drawn from these investigations is that learning while asleep is not possible. Recent Soviet studies have stimulated further interest in this question, but they do not permit ready comparisons since the EEG commonly is not used as a major variable in these studies (Aarons, 1976).

A more general conclusion is that practicing without effort and activity will not result in significant learning. Complex learning usually requires concentration. Usually, practice will not improve performance noticeably unless the learner is motivated to do so. *Motivation,* in this context, refers to an internal state, a desire to achieve a certain goal. It can be promoted *partly* by the use of rewards and punishments, as we saw earlier in connection with conditioning.

Extrinsic and intrinsic rewards. With animals, the value of using reward is well summarized in a study in which four groups of rats learned a maze. The first group was hungry and received food; the second group was hungry but received

Figure 11-14   Computer-Assisted Instruction. *The computer, in contrast to a "teaching machine," provides variable feedback, depending on the learner's prior responses. Here, instructions are given by a tape recording and the learner notes if he has typed the correct response. (Photo Researchers, Inc.)*

out of education, although studies have shown that lack of interpersonal contact does not necessarily decrease the effectiveness of computerized instruction (Mathis et al., 1970; Figure 11-14).

Use of Reward and Punishment

Because practice sessions can be both fatiguing and time consuming, considerable speculation has surrounded the

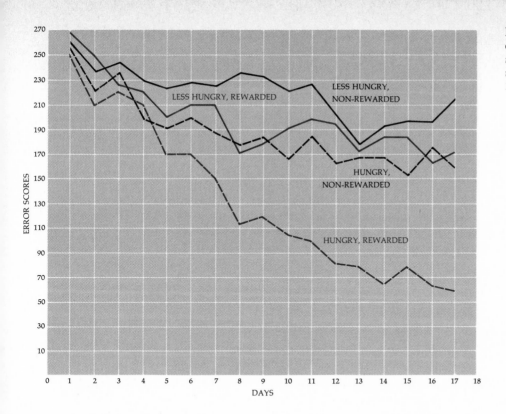

Figure 11-15 Facilitating Effect of Reward. *Performance is influenced by both motivation and reward. (After Tolman & Honzik, 1930)*

The chart labels read: LESS HUNGRY, REWARDED; LESS HUNGRY, NON-REWARDED; HUNGRY, NON-REWARDED; HUNGRY, REWARDED. The vertical axis is ERROR SCORES (10–270) and the horizontal axis is DAYS (0–18).

no food; the third group was not hungry but received food; and the fourth group was not hungry and received no food. The results showed that the hungry, rewarded group made steady progress towards mastery of the maze, while the other groups exhibited little progress. When a food reward was introduced for the unrewarded rats later, after several nonreinforced trials, they demonstrated the correct performance rapidly (Figure 11-15).

This experiment illustrates the use of an *extrinsic reward,* which is not integral to the performance of the task itself. It is something arbitrarily assigned to successful performance, such as money, a place on the dean's list or, in this case, food. An *intrinsic reward* is inherent in the task itself. It is a natural outcome of the learning, as in the satisfaction one derives from painting, without selling the product as an art object.

One advantage of discovery learning, according to its advocates, is that the discovery process itself is an intrinsic

reward. In programmed instruction, a light or buzzer used as an *additional* signal of a correct response constitutes an extrinsic reward.

With human learners, the value of extrinsic rewards is obvious, but they can be overused or used too blatantly. When perceived as bribes, extrinsic rewards generally retard learning. Even monkeys will manipulate mechanical devices when no extrinsic reward is involved, but when one is introduced, they seem to become less interested in the task per se (Harlow et al., 1950).

Praise and personality factors. At the human level especially, the effective use of reward and punishment varies also with personality. In one study, children were assessed on an introversion-extraversion scale and then received either praise or blame for their efforts on a perceptual-motor task, regardless of their

Learning and Instruction

actual performance. The results indicated that receiving either praise or blame was more effective than the absence of any reinforcement. They also showed that praise tended to be more effective with the introverts while mild blame was more effective with extraverts (Thompson & Hunnicut, 1944). Individual variations were observed, of course, and it is unwise to generalize broadly from one study.

In fact, with extremely low underachievers, praise was not found to be particularly effective (Kennedy & Willicutt, 1964). When using rewards, one should remember that different events function as different reinforcers for different individuals.

Facilitating effects of punishment. The effects of using punishment are even less predictable than those of using reward, but it is generally agreed that punishment can facilitate learning in at least two ways. Commonly, it suppresses the undesired behavior at least temporarily, which provides greater opportunity for the desired response to become established. During the suppression period, the desired response may be reinforced to such an extent that it is stronger than the undesired response. Punishment for incorrect responses, when used with reward for correct behavior, has been described as a useful procedure by many investigators (Campbell & Church, 1969; Solomon, 1964).

Second, punishment may provide the learner with knowledge of results. The child who eats too much candy and becomes ill may not do so again. Experienced cooks seldom burn themselves while taking hot pans from the oven. Here, punishment is informative rather than retaliatory.

Negative outcomes with punishment. The case for punishment is more doubtful on other bases. Once a common adjunct to education, its use is declining partly for humanitarian reasons and also because some experiments have shown that it may not be as effective as it was

thought to be. Even if effective, punishment does not teach which behavior is desired.

The meaning of *punishment* here is any outcome or consequence of behavior that has a negative value, resulting in pain or other discomfort for the performer. The adverse effects of punishment have been demonstrated with animals, but clinical investigations also support this view (Hill, 1973). The authors are not aware of any research at the human level that supports the use of severe punishment as a remedial measure with normal individuals. Electric shock has been used successfully in some exceptional cases, such as eliminating self-destructive responses in schizophrenic persons and in infants.

In general, the punished child learns to dislike the punitive parent or teacher and also the activity with which the punishment is associated. Such *negative attitudes* are a common and highly undesirable outcome of punishment, and they remain for long periods, even through the individual's lifetime (Zipf, 1960).

Punishment of various kinds, especially when coupled with conflict, also can produce *neurotic behavior,* which is a state of anxiety sometimes accompanied by lethargy, hyperactivity, or the apparently useless repetition of certain acts. Pigs, cats, and other animals have shown these reactions following punishment. Rats, for example, eventually refused to cross a simple barrier in order to solve a problem; instead, they trembled, became rigid, lay on the floor and/or remained immobile in a corner (Maier, 1949). Clinical observations of severely punished children provide further evidence.

In addition, punishment may *sustain incorrect behavior.* In one experiment, dogs learned to jump a barrier when a signal was sounded in order to avoid punishment. Later, punishment did not follow the signal. It was given on the other side if the dog jumped the barrier, but the animals continued to jump, even more quickly, after the buzzer sounded. One dog jumped for 490 trials before this investigation was discontinued. Later, an obstruction was put up to prevent the dogs from jumping, thus teaching them that it was safe to remain in the original compartment. When the obstruction was removed, however, the dogs resumed the jumping response (Solomon et al., 1953). Many such studies suggest that, under certain conditions, punishment, or fear of it, may sustain rather than eliminate behavior.

Factors influencing punishment outcomes. While the outcomes of punishment are less predictable than those of reward, one important factor in both cases is the immediacy with which reinforcement follows the response. In our legal system, for example, infractions of the law are punished not just days, weeks, or months but often years after the alleged misbehavior. This delayed punishment, of whatever strength, appears to be less effective than weaker punishment administered earlier (Figure 11-16). In an analysis of skyjacking, for instance, the certainty of punishment appeared a greater deterrent than the severity (Chauncey, 1975).

An often overlooked factor is the origin of the punished response. The effectiveness of punishment depends partly on whether the undesired behavior was established under punitive or rewarding conditions. For example, a student's poor school performance is punished by low grades and parental disappointment, and eventually he or she develops a negative attitude towards school. This attitude results in still poorer performance, for which there is further punishment by low grades and parental disapproval. Punishment then serves to reinforce the negative attitude towards school, and a phenomenon called *vicious-circle behavior* is established (Tarpy, 1975). In such instances, punishment may increase the probability of

the incorrect response, as noted previously in the study of jumping responses in dogs.

Punishment is an exceedingly complex topic, even if we confine our attention to its effectiveness under experimental conditions, but the following principles seem generally applicable. Severe punishment may fixate behavior or result in undesirable side effects. Mild punishment can be effective when it is informative and when it is combined with reward for desirable behavior. In some cases, psychological punishment,

Figure 11-16 Delayed Punishment. *The extensive reference library being used by this lawyer suggests the amount of time-consuming research and paperwork involved in today's legal proceedings. The result is that there is often a considerable delay between illegal behavior and the receipt of punishment. The eventually prescribed penalty may therefore be less effective in changing the earlier behavior than would immediate punishment. A dilemma arises, however, because hasty and possibly ill-founded decisions are obviously undesirable. (Bodin from Stock, Boston)*

■ *The parents of a high school friend used punishment in an attempt to influence their son's actions. For example, it was not uncommon for them to spend a night at home drinking or to drink when they went out, but when Steve began to drink with his friends, they became very upset and immediately put him on at least one month's restriction.*

Steve learned to dislike his parents extremely for their punishment, which was often severe, especially when he saw them doing the same thing. His drinking stopped for a month, but as soon as the month was over, he was back at it again. Soon he had to get drunk every weekend, and when he tried marijuana he had to be stoned every day. He became very distant from his parents and no longer told them his feelings on anything. As he began to take more drugs, the slightest word of reprimand from them would send him running from the house, sometimes not to return for days or weeks.

Now they say that Steve is severely disturbed. I don't know . . . but I believe that his parents' form of punishment was one of the influencing factors in his problems today.

such as verbal reprimands, may be as effective as physical punishment in deterring an unwanted act, but it also may produce considerably greater anxiety. ■

In clinical studies, Freud noted the unexpected reinforcing properties of punishment, suggesting that capital punishment may even be a stimulus to crime by providing relief from guilt feelings (Reik, 1959). Investigations have shown no significant difference in homicide rates between states in which the law prohibits capital punishment and those in which it does not (Sellin, 1959). On this basis it is difficult to say whether bombing a country, jailing individuals for the use of drugs, or even scowling at a misbehaving youngster will be a deterrent to the behavior in question. As indicated, the origin of the punished response and the perceptions of the subject receiving the punishment are important factors in determining the outcome.

Summary

Components of Instruction

1. From the viewpoint of instruction, the three major components of the learning situation are learning objectives, instructional methods, and then evaluation. Objectives identify what the student should be able to do as a result of the learning experience. They can be specified at various levels of difficulty and can concern verbal learning, motor skills, and learning in the affective domain.

2. According to social learning theory, the most effective instructional method occurs when the student observes the teacher's behavior. Intentionally or otherwise, the teacher serves as a model. Studies have shown that modeling is effective even when there is no immediate reinforcement for the observer. Social learning theory also has numerous applications outside formal instruction.

3. Learning is a construct; it must be inferred from the subject's performance. Performance is evaluated by administering various types of tests, and the cumulative results are commonly displayed as performance curves. They must be interpreted with caution, however; a decline in performance or an intermediate plateau does not necessarily reflect a lack of learning.

Applications of Learning Principles

4. In the programmed approach to education, learning is structured in a step-by-step sequence, called the method of approximations, and various schedules of reinforcement are used. The objectives are clearly specified and the learner usually receives immediate reinforcement for each successful increment of progress.

5. In the discovery method, the learners generally uncover the basic facts and principles themselves. Learning with understanding and divergent thinking are stressed. It is said that this method of learning develops creativity and critical thinking.

6. Both approaches have advantages and disadvantages, and they represent extreme positions in a continuum of directedness. Completely undirected learning sometimes places the student in an ambiguous situation, not knowing what to do or how to do it. Completely directed learning may make the learner overly dependent on procedures established by others and does not reflect the conditions of daily life. Commonly, both procedures are used for diverse purposes in the instructional process.

Transfer of Training

7. The doctrine of formal discipline stated that studying certain subjects, such as Latin and mathematics, strengthened particular mental functions, but investigations of transfer have failed to support this view. Transfer is most likely to occur when the aim of learning includes applying the new skills in a particular situation.

8. When learning in one instance facilitates learning in another, positive transfer has occurred. When earlier learning interferes with later learning, negative transfer has occurred. In general, the amount of transfer is determined by the degree of stimulus similarity in the two situations, and whether the transfer is positive or negative depends on whether the required responses are similar or dissimilar.

Practice and Motivation

9. Certain conditions of practice have been established as generally useful. Distributed learning commonly is more efficient than massed learning because a rest period decreases fatigue, raises motivation, and improves recall. Recitation is more efficient than merely reading what is to be learned because it requires active participation and provides knowledge of how well or how poorly one is doing. In using whole or part learning, the nature of the task is an important factor, and a flexible plan, beginning with the whole, may be most appropriate. Knowledge of results adds to the efficiency of learning because it tends to motivate the learner and facilitates the repetition of the correct response.

10. Both reward and punishment are used for motivating the learner. The facilitating effect of reward is widely acknowledged, although it varies with personality factors and the way in which the reward is perceived. The effects of punishment are much less predictable; they vary with several factors, including the immediacy with which punishment is applied and the origin of the punished response. Severe or unpredictable punishment can lead to unstable behavior and even fixation of the punished response. Punishment is most effective when it is immediate, used in combination with reward, and informative.

Suggested Readings

Bolles, R. C. *Learning theory*. New York: Holt, 1975. A readable volume that emphasizes theory and contributions in this century.

Bugelski, B. R. *Empirical studies in the psychology of learning*. New York: Crowell, 1975. Presents abstracts of more than one hundred significant studies in the psychology of learning.

Cronbach, L. J. *Educational psychology* (3rd ed.). New York: Harcourt Brace Jovanovich, 1977. A lengthy, well-respected text in this field.

Neill, A. S. *Summerhill: A radical approach to child rearing*. New York: Hart, 1960. A highly readable description of an unstructured approach to education in a British school.

Skinner, B. F. *Walden Two*. New York: Macmillan, 1948. A novel that depicts a utopian society based on the programmed approach, called cultural engineering.

PART FIVE

Motivation and Emotional Behavior

Chapter 12

Fundamentals of Motivation

Why does someone want to sail around the world alone? Why do people sit on flagpoles, climb mountains, or live in caves for long periods of time? Charles Lindbergh made a transatlantic flight to demonstrate the future of aviation, and Admiral Byrd apparently explored the potential of Antarctica for his country, but many solo voyagers can have no such practical goal. In the past five years, five people have died in separate attempts simply to be the first balloonist to cross the Atlantic Ocean (Hamilton & Rickwine, 1975).

When 16-year-old Robin Graham sailed alone out of San Pedro, California in a 24-foot boat, he planned to circle the globe by himself. He was asked "What makes you do it?" (Graham, 1970).

This question concerns motivation, a topic of considerable interest to laypersons and psychologists. *Motivation* is a construct, since it cannot be observed directly, but generally it is defined as a condition of need or desire within the individual that the individual attempts to satisfy in some way. Although based on an inner state, factors in the external environment are also involved.

Motivation activates and directs the organism, and this chapter is primarily concerned with those motives that prompt and direct the organism to survive biologically and maintain the survival of its species. Towards the end of this chapter and in the next one, the emphasis shifts from these physiological motives to those grounded more exclusively in one's culture and personal experience.

The Concept of Instinct

One possible explanation for Robin Graham's behavior is that it was instinctive. He had an instinct for the sea, which prompted him to undertake the trip and also helped him respond properly in times of danger. Such explanations of human behavior are common. A woman claims her husband has an instinctive love of the outdoors; a man says his wife is instinctively drawn to cocktail parties; a sports announcer refers to a football player as running instinctively through the other team. When asked about a future project, a business person replies "My instincts tell me it will not work."

What are instincts? Is this concept an appropriate explanation for human behavior? Human beings certainly are motivated, as Robin's trip illustrates, but on what basis?

Internal Factors

To find the basis for human motivation, we begin with the animal kingdom. Consider what happens when a female rat gives birth to her first litter. As soon as the little ones appear, the mother shows a very clear pattern of behavior, even when she has never observed maternal behavior in other rats. Immediately, she bites off the umbilical cord, licks the newborns clean, and then eats the placenta. She builds a nest out of grass, twigs, and other materials and then retrieves the young, places them in the nest one by one, and crouches over them. Upon birth of their first litter, all female rats show this intricate pattern of behavior, which is said to be instinctive. An *instinct* is a relatively complex behavior pattern that occurs in all normal members of the same sex of a given species and is essentially unlearned.

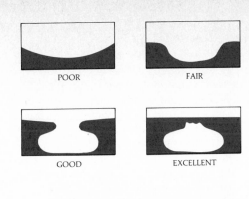

POOR FAIR GOOD EXCELLENT

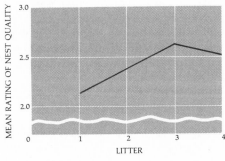

A similar pattern is found in the female rabbit. The mother-to-be collects straw and other building materials and just before the birth she pulls hair from her own body and adds it to the nest, making a soft, warm home for the newborn. Since this complex pattern of behavior occurs in all pregnant female rabbits, with no opportunity for learning, we speak of a maternal or nest-building instinct in the rabbit (Figure 12-1).

What is behind these automatic reactions? It almost seems as if a string were pulled to make them occur.

A most important factor lies within the animal in a chemical substance known as a hormone. One particular hormone, *prolactin*, which is secreted by the anterior pituitary gland, plays a crucial role in the maternal instinct. Any normal adult female rat, even a virgin, that is injected with this substance displays an intricate pattern of maternal behavior in the presence of pups (Wiesner & Sheard, 1933). In female rabbits, injections of prolactin or of a substance that causes false pregnancy both prompt nest-building (Zarrow et al., 1962).

Figure 12-1　Nest-building in Rabbits. *The drawings show that nests vary in quality. However, the graph shows that when the successive nests of 84 females were studied, a gradual improvement in quality was found over the first three litters. (Nest drawings after Swain & Crary, 1953; graph from Ross et al., 1956. Photo from Photo Researchers, Inc.)*

Sex behavior occurs on a similar basis. All male rats mate in the same way, whether or not they have observed mating in others, and female rats have a standard mating pattern also (Beach, 1942a). A necessary internal stimulus to this behavior is the secretion of hormones from the sex glands, called *androgens* in the male and *estrogens* in the female. The latter hormone also plays a role in releasing maternal behavior in rats (Siegel & Rosenblatt, 1975).

When these glands have been removed, as in castrated guinea pigs, sex behavior occurs infrequently. If the hormone is injected, sex behavior promptly returns to its original frequency (Figure 12-2). However, a fourfold increase in the injection, well beyond that required for reinstatement of the original sex behavior, produces no further increase in sexual activity (Grunt & Young, 1953). Apparently, the organism is able to utilize only a certain amount of this hormone. These same relationships also have been demonstrated with castrated rats (Luttge et al., 1975).

Considering the role of internal factors in instinct, is there evidence that Robin Graham's ocean-going behavior was instinctive? The answer is clearly negative. No hormonal secretions or other internal conditions that prompt someone to take to the sea have been identified. But there is also another consideration in instinctive behavior, as indicated through experimental work with animals.

Role of the Environment

The mother rat not only smells and licks the newborn pups, but prior to the birth she licks herself extensively, especially in the vaginal region. One scientist observing this action wondered whether it had any significance for the maternal instinct.

Prior experience. To test this hypothesis, some female rats were fitted with collars like Elizabethan ruffs, which were large enough to prevent self-licking of the vaginal region. Each rat in another group wore a collar of the same weight and size but with a carefully placed notch that enabled the animal to engage in the usual self-licking. Mating occurred normally in both groups, and all the collars were removed one to two hours before litters were produced. All litters appeared normal at birth, and 95 percent of the pups of the control mothers survived weaning. However, the experimental mothers ate most of their pups. The few that survived initially were either not retrieved to the nest, were retrieved and then eaten, or were badly suckled. None survived the usual nursing period (Birch, 1956). It appeared that self-licking prior to the birth was an important factor in the appearance of the maternal instinct.

Among ring doves, both the mother and father feed their newborns in the same way, using "crop milk," a substance developed in their own crops and regurgitated for the offspring. This behavior is partly under the influence of prolactin, as studies with the injection of this substance have shown, but crop-feeding does not occur in these birds if there has been no previous mating behavior. When ring doves are injected with prolactin, only those with prior breeding experience make any attempt at crop-feeding (Bates et al., 1937). Even the appearance of prolactin, so important in this behavior, is stimulated partly by the previous experience of sitting on and incubating ring-dove eggs (Patel, 1936).

In another study, two groups of male guinea pigs were reared under different conditions. Some were allowed to associate with peers, while the others were kept in isolation. Later, all the animals were tested for sex behavior, and significant differences were found in favor of the animals with a social history. Even when their earlier cage mates were of the same sex, normal heterosexual behavior occurred later (Valenstein et al., 1955). When young male and female monkeys are not given early experiences with other monkeys, essentially the same results are found with regard to sexual behavior (Harlow, 1965; Harlow & Harlow, 1966).

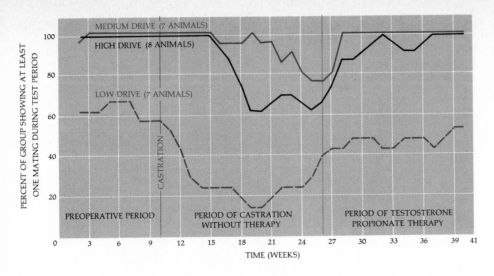

Figure 12-2 Replacement Therapy. *When testosterone is administered to castrated male guinea pigs, sexual behavior returns, but it is lower in animals with an originally low sex drive. (From Grunt & Young, 1953. Copyright 1953 by the American Psychological Association. Reprinted by permission.)*

Thus, the role of experience in instinct is demonstrated. Self-licking in female rats and mating in ring doves are essential preludes to instinctive parental behavior. Similarly, social experience is a prerequisite for successful sexual behavior in guinea pigs and monkeys. Even these behaviors, widely accepted as instinctive and therefore automatic, are partly under the control of external factors.

Releasers. In addition to past experience, a certain type of present stimulation is necessary. The intricate pattern of maternal behavior displayed by the female rat injected with prolactin occurs in the presence of pups. The nest-building behavior of the injected female rabbit occurs in the presence of nest-building materials. The internal secretions are a necessary condition, but there must be appropriate external stimulation. The external stimulus that serves to initiate the instinctive behavior is called a *releaser* or sign stimulus.

In the mating season, the male three-spined stickleback exhibits a complicated behavior pattern during which it constructs a nest and then induces the female to enter it and deposit its eggs. This elaborate "dancing" pattern is alike in all these fish, and investigators wanted to know what specific aspect of the environment served to release it. They obtained the answer by presenting the male with various models of a female about to lay eggs. By emphasizing various aspects of the female they found that the male responds to the female's swollen abdomen; other characteristics are relatively unimportant (Figure 12-3).

Figure 12-3 A Releaser. *A model that looks much like the fish is ineffective, but a poorer replica that has a swelling in approximately the correct place can set off the characteristic mating pattern. (Adapted from Tinbergen, 1951, 1953)*

This involvement of the environment does not require a revision in our definition of instinct, however. The behavior is still unlearned, although certain conditions are necessary to "release" it. Instinctive behavior may improve with practice, but the basic pattern occurs on the first trial, provided it has been preceded by an internal readiness and by appropriate stimulation in the external environment.

Instincts and Human Behavior

If your grandfather had read a psychology textbook in the 1920s, he would have read that human beings possessed dozens of instincts. One leading psychologist listed 52, another cited 110, and another expert recognized even more. Good workmanship was described as an instinct, as were disgust, retaliation, and its near opposite, altruism. Cleanliness was said to be an instinct in human beings, an idea that many parents must have questioned. The list finally became so long and cumbersome that a social psychologist published a book describing 5,648 usages of the concept (Bernard, 1924). It almost seemed that people had an instinct for

calling things instincts, but after this publication, the whole idea suddenly collapsed. People realized that there are essentially no behaviors at the human level that fit the definition. Human beings possess many reflexes, but most psychologists today have strong reservations about attributing instincts to human beings.

A reflex is also an automatic act, but it is simple and restricted. A sudden puff of air to the eye causes an eyeblink, and being doused with cold water creates goose pimples. Undoubtedly, these reflexes occurred in Robin Graham during his voyage, especially in reacting to danger, but these responses are too simple and brief to be called instincts.

Furthermore, learning was clearly involved in Robin's ocean-going behavior, both in his ability to sail and in his acquired interest in doing so. His father bought him his first boat when he was 10 years old and took him on an 11,000-mile voyage when he was 13. Robin said that during the trip he learned to handle himself like "a veteran sailor" (Graham, 1972; Figure 12-4).

Motivation and Emotional Behavior

There were probably some instinctive reactions in Robin's cats, such as mating and catching a mouse, but even at the animal level the term *instinct* is not considered particularly useful because it does not add anything to our understanding of the behavior. We say that the mother rat has a maternal instinct and therefore takes care of her babies, but we also say that she takes care of the babies because she has a maternal instinct. This reasoning is circular and, therefore, use of the term *instinct* accomplishes little.

Instead, many contemporary psychologists and ethologists prefer to speak of fixed-action patterns or species-specific behavior. Thus, *species-specific behavior* merely indicates that some complex behaviors are found only in certain animals. A *fixed-action pattern* refers to any response that is relatively fixed or "wired into" certain organisms. Current research interest focuses on the energizing aspects of these various reactions (Burghardt, 1973).

In contrast to earlier days, we are now less likely to speak of instincts and more likely to view certain behaviors as arising partly through physiological stimulation and partly on the basis of learned cues in the environment, which guide and shape the response. Heredity and physiology, on the one hand, and the environment on the other, both play a role in an interactive fashion. As we discover more about these factors, there will be less and less need to invoke some magical explanation of behavior, such as our earlier use of the term *instinct*.

Species Survival

In the animal kingdom, the degree of evolution of any given species sets limits on its behavior. In general, the lower the organism on the evolutionary scale, the narrower is its behavioral repertoire. Furthermore, the limits that do exist are usually related to survival motives (Breger, 1974). In each species, the organism's most fixed responses concern food, drink, and shelter, necessary for in-

dividual survival, or sex and parental behavior, necessary for the survival of the species.

Basics of Sex

Among apes and human beings, the behavorial limits are so broad that it is doubtful whether a mating instinct exists. In the chimpanzee, there is no universal, stereotyped mating behavior such as that in the rat. The pattern that finally emerges in the individual adult chimpanzee is largely learned (Figure 12-5). The element of learning is greatest in human beings, although here, too, certain reflexes are involved, such as erection of the nipples in the female and ejaculation in the male.

Androgens are the sex hormones in the male. The *testes* secrete this hormone, and when they are removed from a boy before puberty, normal sexual development is commonly disrupted. After puberty, castration usually does not result in a cessation of sexual behavior. Sexual interests and activities may continue for years, although at a reduced rate (Morgan, 1965). In lower animals

Figure 12-5   Chimpanzee Mating. *Although certain mating patterns are preferred by adult chimpanzees, there is also variety. Here the male adult combines mating with feeding, while a young chimp observes the feeding aspect with interest. (From* In the Shadow of Man *by Jane van Lawick-Goodall, published by William Collins Sons and Co., London. Copyright Hugo van Lawick.)*

of any age, withdrawal of androgen hormones distinctly alters not only sexual but also aggressive and scent-marking behavior (Hart, 1974). Clearly, the hormonal factor is more important in lower animals than in human beings.

A topic of considerable interest concerns the role of these hormones in newborn animals. When androgen is administered to young female rats or guinea pigs, as adults they behave like males, demonstrating mounting behavior instead of the customary bending response. When newborn and even prenatal males are deprived of androgenic hormones, their sexual behavior in adulthood is like that of females. These and other findings indicate that the genetic constitution of young mammals is highly susceptible to early hormonal influences, and they suggest that such hormones predispose the young organism to acquire certain sex-specific behavior patterns (Goy, 1970). They also raise numerous questions about the ultimate basis of the distinction between the sexes.

In the human female, the hormones called estrogens come from the *ovaries*, and the effects of removing these organs are difficult to predict. Generally, there is some decrease of sexual interests, but again the result is not as significant as in lower animals.

Both men and women whose gonads have degenerated late in life may continue to participate in sexual activities, and some women who have passed through menopause actually increase their sexual activity. In the male, contrary to popular thought, sexual activity can occur even into the seventh and eighth decades. In fact, the more regular and frequent sexual intercourse has been in earlier years, the greater is the likelihood of a sustained responsiveness in later life (Masters & Johnson, 1966).

At the human level, sexual behavior clearly illustrates the relationship between inborn and acquired factors in motivation. A readiness for sexual activity is provided by hormonal secretions from the gonads, but the various expressions of sexual behavior are molded by our environment and early learning.

Maternal Motivation

Maternal motivation also is affected by hormones, the environment, and early learning. Prolactin provides the basic condition for this behavior in lower animals, and we have seen that this behavior is highly stereotyped. Investigations with the rat, for example, indicate that prolactin, estrogen, and perhaps two other hormones play a combined role in initiating maternal behavior (Lamb, 1975).

Monkey mothering. Studies of maternal behavior in monkeys have shown three stages. First is *attachment and protection,* in which the newborn receives unconditional love and care. The mother constantly satisfies the infant's nutritional and temperature needs, provides it with security through physical contact, and protects it from dangers. For approximately three months, a "good" mother monkey shows a steady and total devotion to its infant.

During the stage of *transition,* the mother occasionally dissociates herself from the infant, disciplines it with increasing frequency, and relaxes her restraints on its exploratory behavior. These responses presumably aid the infant in achieving an emancipation from the mother. The infant is prompted to venture into a wider world partly to escape punishment.

The third stage, *separation or rejection,* may appear suddenly, and it is often precipitated by the arrival of another baby. The newborn becomes a love object in the first stage of maternal care, and the older baby is more obviously rejected. Commonly, the care of this anxious infant is taken over by an adult male, who is often the father (Figure 12-6).

ATTACHMENT

TRANSITION

SEPARATION

Human parental behavior. Among human beings, intellectual and cultural differences provide a wide variety of maternal responses; there is no fixed pattern of mothering. In fact, in some human societies there is such involvement of the father in the childrearing process that research emphasizes *parental* motivation (Lynn, 1974).

Also, at the human level a time arises at which the child is ready to leave the parents, although this readiness is more obvious in animals, among which the environment and behaviors are simpler than in our complex society. If kept too long under parental protection, the child may never develop an adequate sense of independence and self-worth. If forced or permitted to leave too soon, the child may encounter dangers that he or she cannot handle or may never develop certain skills.

When should the child, as he or she moves from infancy through adolescence, be allowed to do what? This is the universal parental dilemma. The question can be answered only in terms

of the individual child and a specific environment. The most important concept here is readiness for the given task.

This decision was particularly difficult for Robin Lee Graham's parents, for their only child wanted to circle the globe by himself at age 16 years. When Robin was allowed to do so, his parents received so much criticism that Mr. Graham wrote a letter to his wife and published it in several newspapers. A portion of this letter is as follows:

Dearest Norma:

Our work is done and Lee has sailed. I watched the boat until it was out of sight in the morning mist. I returned to the slip to pick up some things. All the farewell wishers were gone. The slip was empty.

As I drove home without him sitting beside me as we had done for so many days I had a great big empty feeling. We have been so close and so busy, and now there is nothing. I feel Lee has sailed out of my life. I have lost his boyhood companionship. When I see him again he will be a man,

Figure 12-6 Maternal Stages. *A sharp increase in the mother's punitive responses marks the transition stage, but after five months, the infant learns to escape them. (After Harlow & Harlow, 1966. Reprinted by permission,* **American Scientist,** *journal of Sigma Xi, The Scientific Research Society of North America. Photos by Leonard A. Rosenblum, SUNY Downstate Medical Center.)*

looking for a life of his own with other friends and other interests where you and I are not included.

It happens to all parents, but it is so hard to take when it happens all of a sudden as it did to me, as he moved out of his slip and down the channel. I don't think I would ever have let him go if I didn't love him so much. It would have been easier on me to have kept him at home.

In my heart I know it is the right thing to let him go.*

Individual Survival

Robin Graham's parents obviously were concerned about his survival. His father was "really worried" when he left, and for good reason. At various times during the voyage, Robin was washed overboard, bitten by poisonous animals, battered by a storm off the African coast, threatened by sharks, and nearly crushed when his 20-foot boat narrowly missed being struck by a freighter passing in the night.

He also risked the satisfaction of physiological needs because he never could be certain that his supplies would hold out for the next long leg of his trip. The term *physiological need* refers to any biochemical condition that is necessary for the maintenance of life in the organism. These conditions are established by the need for food, water, air, rest, and so forth.

The Thirst Drive

The human organism can survive for only a few days without fresh water. When this need is not met, it gives rise to a state of arousal known as a drive. The driven organism is ready to respond to stimuli related to its aroused state—that is, to the satisfaction of its needs. Thus, we speak of the thirst drive, hunger drive, and the drive to escape painful stimulation (Figure 12-7).

* From *Dove* by Robin Lee Graham with Derek L. T. Gill. Copyright © 1972 by Robin Lee Graham and Derek L. T. Gill. Reprinted by permission of Harper & Row, Publishers, Inc., and Angus and Robertson Publishers.

Goal-directed behavior. Sometimes psychologists find it convenient to consider motivation such as the thirst drive, hunger drive, and so forth as involving this sequence: need, drive, incentive, and reward. A *need* arises within the organism when a biochemical imbalance occurs. As already stated, it gives rise to a state of arousal known as a *drive*, in which the organism is ready to respond to relevant stimuli. These stimuli are called *incentives*, and they can provide satisfaction or *reward* for the behaving organism.

It should be noted that incentives are not goals. The organism's goal is to satisfy its need, and the incentive is an appropriate object or event for doing so. In thirst, water is the incentive, consuming it is a reward, and the whole sequence is referred to as *goal-directed behavior* (Figure 12-8).

The organism does not remain fully adjusted or satisfied for long, however. Needs occur in cyclic fashion, and sooner or later another sequence is required. In fact, one of the most recurring needs among human beings, besides the needs for air and rest, is for the intake and elimination of water.

Dryness in the mouth. When someone needs water, the most obvious symptom is dryness of the mouth and throat. For most people this feeling is the definition of thirst, but other physiological aspects are involved. For example, when dogs are subjected to different degrees of water deprivation, they drink amounts of water directly proportional to the deficits. This accurate estimation is hard to explain in terms of the dryness of the mouth and throat alone because the dog's first mouthful wets these areas, removing the condition that might provide a guide to the amount needed.

Wetting the mouth merely temporarily allays thirst. To be effective in removing thirst, apparently water must enter tissue in other regions (Adolph, 1941).

Motivation and Emotional Behavior

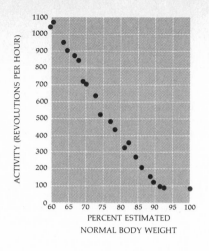

Figure 12-7 Measurement of Drive. *The animal is housed in the rectangular cage, occasionally deprived of food or water, and allowed to run in the drum, which records revolutions on a meter. In this experiment, the more the animal was deprived of food, as indicated by weight loss, the greater was its activity. (After Moskowitz, 1959. Copyright 1959 by the American Psychological Association. Reprinted by permission. Sheila A. Farr photo.)*

To test this hypothesis, dogs were deprived of water for varying periods, and then water was placed directly into the stomach of each animal via a fistula. Then some of the animals were permitted to drink water immediately, and they showed no reaction to the water already received in the stomach. The amount of water consumed was related to the previous deprivation. Other animals were required to wait several minutes before drinking, thus permitting the water to enter the tissues of the stomach and other regions. In these instances, they drank little or nothing (Adolph, 1941).

Cellular dehydration in the system. More basic than dryness of the mouth and throat in thirst is *cellular dehydration* in various parts of the organism, which occurs because we are constantly losing body fluids through urination, excretion, perspiration, and other processes. This loss prompts water inside the cells to pass outside, replacing the necessary fluids formerly surrounding the cells, but the interior of the cells is then left without water. Thus, the cells are dehydrated, and both intracellular and extracellular fluid level become factors in regulating water intake.

Figure 12-8 A Motivational Sequence. *The sequence recurs regularly for cyclic needs, such as thirst and hunger, and intermittently for others, such as the avoidance of pain.*

In contemporary studies, cellular dehydration has been investigated by injections of saline solutions, which raise the salt content of the body, prompting extensive dehydration. In such cases a most important organ is the hypothalamus, which is at the base of the brain. Both salt injections and electrical stimulation here induced drinking in experimental animals. Thus, these cells of the hypothalamus have been designated *osmoreceptors,* meaning that they are cells that signal the passage of fluids through membranes, which is a process called osmosis. Saline injections in various parts of the hypothalamus elicit drinking, but injections of plain water stop drinking only when they are placed in the anterior hypothalamus; hence, this area is most related to drinking (Thompson, 1975).

As in the case of instinct, however, physiological drives are not prompted solely by internal circumstances. Environmental factors are also important, as illustrated by the person who goes to a party and consumes more than his or her required intake of beverages. The environment can influence water consumption, even among rats in a Skinner box (Collier, 1962).

The Hunger Drive

Just as dryness of the throat and mouth is the most readily apparent aspect of thirst, hunger pangs are the most obvious aspect of food deprivation. Consequently, some years ago investigators of the hunger drive began by studying these aching and gnawing feelings.

Stomach contractions and blood sugar level. A human subject was trained to swallow a small balloon with an attached tube. When the balloon was inflated, it fit the lining of the stomach and when the tube was connected with appropriate apparatus, it gave indications of changes in air pressure within the balloon. Thus, contractions of the stomach, presumed to be a basis of hunger,

could be accurately recorded. The immediate finding was that stomach contractions coincided with the gnawing feelings, as reported by the subject, who sometimes was tested when hungry and at other times after a more recent meal (Cannon, 1934).

In later studies, however, it was found that the stomach could be removed and the nerves between it and the brain could be severed without destroying the hunger drive (Bash, 1939; Tsang, 1938). Furthermore, it was demonstrated that both stomach contractions and hunger pangs cease with the administration of dextrose, a substance that raises the blood sugar level (Quigley et al., 1929). It now appears that stomach contractions are not a necessary or sufficient condition for hunger. Indeed, some persons who have not eaten for considerable periods do not even report experiences described as hunger pangs, and when other research methods are used, there is little evidence for stomach contractions. Seemingly, they occur largely in the presence of the balloon.

The relationship between blood sugar level and hunger was investigated when blood from a starved dog was injected into a normal dog. The stomach of the injected animal showed the kind of contractions *sometimes* found in hunger, but injection of blood from a well-fed animal stopped the contractions (Luckhardt & Carlson, 1915). Such experiments and some others, involving the administration of insulin for lowering blood sugar level, provide support for the idea that blood sugar level is closely related to hunger but stomach contractions are relatively unimportant.

Hunger and the brain. More recent studies have led experts to consider other biochemical conditions, such as the function of the liver and involvement of the brain, including the hypothalamus. Electrical stimulation to certain regions of this organ, called the *lateral area of the hypothalamus,* activates and sustains eating in animals, even in those presumably satiated earlier. On the other hand, when this area is damaged or removed, experimental animals stop eating before their normal needs have been satisfied. They cease eating despite the availability of food, unless forced feeding is used (Miller et al., 1950; Anand & Brobeck, 1951).

Another area of the hypothalamus, called the *ventromedial nucleus,* provides a different picture. Electrical stimulation here prompts a cessation of eating in experimental subjects, including those previously placed on a food-deprivation schedule. Injury to this brain region causes pronounced overeating; in human beings it sometimes results in obesity. When the ventromedial nucleus is absent in experimental animals, they eat to the point where they become three times their normal size. Consequently, these brain areas have been called "the satiety cells," meaning that they indicate when the organism has consumed sufficient nutrients. Without the function of this brain area, animals simply do not know when to stop eating (Figure 12-9).

These results seem less incompatible when it is postulated that the different regions of the hypothalamus serve different functions in hunger. The lateral area seems to prompt eating behavior and the ventromedial nucleus apparently is responsible for its cessation. The ventromedial nucleus should not be considered a *center,* however, but rather a region of interconnections for many neural tracts involved in the cessation of eating (Thompson, 1975).

Even with further support for this view, we then want to know why the animal stops and starts eating under the various conditions. Overeating and undereating may not reflect different conditions of the hunger drive per se but rather greater or lesser sensitivity to food-related stimuli. Rats with lesions in the lateral area will eat when exposed to

Figure 12-9 **Destruction of the Hypothalamus.** *This animal, with a hypothalamic lesion, has eaten far beyond its need for food. (From "Experiments on motivation" by N. E. Miller,* Science, *Vol. 126, 20 December 1957. Photo by Stevenson.)*

especially strong stimuli, such as chocolate, and those with ventromedial lesions will consume almost any ingestible substance. Whatever the outcome of such research, it now seems clear that the hypothalamus plays a central role in eating and that it can be involved in obesity (Nisbet, 1972). It also regulates hormones important in body weight, insulin, and growth (Woods et al., 1974).

To add further complexity, it has been discovered that when the temperature of the hypothalamus is elevated, eating decreases, and when it is lowered, the opposite result occurs. This finding has led to the thermostatic theory of food consumption, meaning that it is based on temperature regulation. While changes in body temperature do regulate eating in this way, experimental work with animals has not given support to the importance of temperature changes in the hypothalamus per se. Another viewpoint, the gluostatic theory, focuses on a proper balance of glucose, which is related to blood sugar level. Earlier we saw that this condition is important in hunger but is not the sole explanation. Clearly, diverse research strategies are essential in discovering the bodily changes that produce hunger and eating (Figure 12-10).

Figure 12-10 Study of Hunger. *Several approaches are necessary to investigate the various factors. In the oral method of food intake, the subject sucks on a steel straw, sometimes while immersed in a tank of water in which the temperature can be regulated. In the intragastric method, he swallows a flexible tube and pumps the liquid directly into his stomach, thus eliminating the influence of the mouth and throat factors. In the intravenous mode, solutions are delivered directly into the veins. In the intracranial mode, used only with animals, chemicals are introduced directly into the brain cells that are thought to be responsible for hunger (Stellar & Jordan, 1970). (Drawing from "Hunger in man: comparative and physiological studies" by E. Stellar,* American Psychologist, 22, *105–117. Copyright 1967 by the American Psychological Association. Reprinted by permission. Sheila A. Farr photos.)*

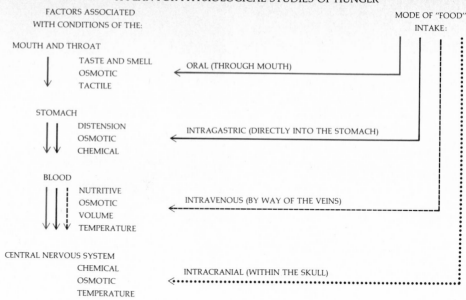

A PLAN FOR PHYSIOLOGICAL STUDIES OF HUNGER

FACTORS ASSOCIATED WITH CONDITIONS OF THE:

MOUTH AND THROAT
TASTE AND SMELL
OSMOTIC
TACTILE
— ORAL (THROUGH MOUTH)

STOMACH
DISTENSION
OSMOTIC
CHEMICAL
— INTRAGASTRIC (DIRECTLY INTO THE STOMACH)

BLOOD
NUTRITIVE
OSMOTIC
VOLUME
TEMPERATURE
— INTRAVENOUS (BY WAY OF THE VEINS)

CENTRAL NERVOUS SYSTEM
CHEMICAL
OSMOTIC
TEMPERATURE
— INTRACRANIAL (WITHIN THE SKULL)

MODE OF "FOOD" INTAKE:

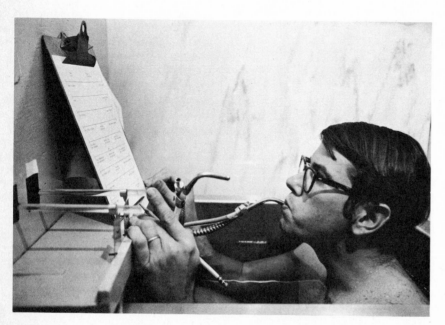

Specific hungers. Often, we want to eat not just food but a particular kind of food—that is, we have a *specific hunger*. In cafeteria feeding experiments, where many different foods are available, rats that were fed either a sugar-free or fat-free diet demonstrated a marked preference for either sugar or fat, respectively (Young, 1936, 1961). Human infants who were allowed to choose their own foods for a period of one year selected a balanced diet (Davis, 1928). One of the subjects, suffering from rickets, selected large amounts of cod liver oil, a substance that tends to counteract the vitamin deficiency that causes this disease. It is important to note, however, that *non*nutritious food choices were not offered to the infants, and clearly harmful products were not made available either.

When left alone, animals and young children *may* select foods that restore a specific deficiency, but more evidence is needed. As human beings grow older, some of them obviously acquire less healthy eating habits.

Psychological aspects. The environment often is a factor in unhealthy eating habits, including overeating. Experiments have demonstrated that external or nonvisceral cues seem to play a significant role in the total food consumption of chronically obese persons. ■ Compared with people of normal weight, their eating is more influenced by the smell of food, the time of day, and the sight of other people eating, and is less influenced by actual hunger (Schachter, 1969).

The environment also influences how and what we eat. Spaniards consume sandwiches and doughnuts with a fork and knife; Chinese use chopsticks; and some Africans use small spears. Certain French and Arab groups eat birds whole; Australian aborigines devour ants; and in some Indian societies cow urine in milk is considered delectable. The wide variety of human learning is behind the old saying: "There is no accounting for tastes." Robin Graham was impressed with these cultural differences, sampling octopus in the Tonga Islands, kava roots in the Solomons, and roast goat in the Galapagos.

Sleep and Rest

A more difficult problem than hunger for Robin Graham, the young sailor, was that of obtaining sufficient sleep. Enroute to New Guinea, he struggled continuously against a hurricane for 48 hours. He stayed awake every night in the sea lanes to Australia after his lamp broke, and he was nearly run down by a vessel in darkness. With waves of 30 to 40 feet, he remained at the helm for two consecutive days off Madagascar.

Sleep deprivation. Modern research indicates that sleep is the basic state of most living organisms; only at the highest phylogenetic levels is there more wakefulness than sleep. The human adult's extended daily wakefulness is a particularly significant evolutionary accomplishment.

When people stay awake for long periods of time, schizophrenic-like disorientations occur, including depression, extreme elation, and anxiety. In extensive studies with military personnel, psychological tests administered after 40, 65, and 90 sleepless hours showed increasingly severe perceptual disturbances and loss of emotional control, as well as disrupted intellectual functioning (Morris & Singer, 1961). When contestants in a talkathon contest went 88 consecutive hours without sleep, they gradually became irritable and withdrawn, showed marked emotional disturbances after 64 sleepless hours, and then became intensely concerned about their own mental health (Cappon & Banks, 1960). Whether these symptoms arose from deprivation of sleep, deprivation of dreams, or both is not fully clear.

■ *"You're not leaving this table until your plate is clean!" the mother said sharply, putting her child in a most unpleasant situation. The little girl had the choice of eating everything immediately to please her mother, dragging out the meal in hopes of eventual escape, or holding ground at the risk of possible punishment.*

The clean-plate conditioning of my childhood was traumatic, but I eventually learned. My response became the required one. I gobbled whatever I was expected to consume, receiving praise or dessert from my parents as a reward. Unfortunately, my behavior from that point on became less and less discriminating when it came to what I ate. Today, I'll eat anything and everything, hardly stopping to enjoy flavor or company at the table. I finish rapidly and escape. I usually can't tell when I'm full. I don't stop eating now until my plate's empty.

My parents seem to be clean-plate trained themselves. They help each other prevent leftovers and both of them are overweight. I'm a little heavy and probably will get heavier unless I can escape from the path they've showed me.

Figure 12-11 Sleeping and Dreaming. *As the night proceeds, the individual spends more time dreaming. This record shows the instances of waking (W), sleep (S), and dreaming (D) during one night for a young adult, as an average from many all-night recordings. The Xs stand for rapid eye movements, and the colored bars indicate periods of dreaming.* (From **The Biology of Dreaming** *by Ernest Hartmann, M.D., published by Charles C. Thomas, Springfield, Ill., 1967.)*

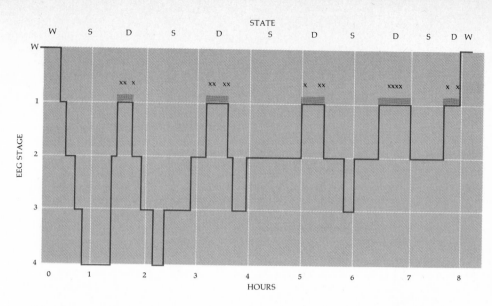

Physiological aspects. Until rather recently, most people regarded sleep as a passive state, and it is true that breathing rate, muscle tension, blood pressure, and rate of heartbeat all decrease during sleep. However, for two reasons we can no longer dismiss sleep as a passive, unchanging state.

First, brain mechanisms are actively involved, some of which apparently help to produce sleep. For example, activation of the thalamus seems to induce quiescence or sleep. In experiments with animals, sleep has been produced by electrical stimulation of this area (Hess, 1929; Akert, 1952). In other words, sleep appears to be partly a consequence of excitation in this brain region, and aspects of the brain stem and cortex also seem to constitute a sleep-inducing system (Murray, 1965).

Second, the condition of our sleep varies during the night. Four to six different stages have been identified, and one of these, in which dreaming occurs, involves considerable physiological activity. Extremely rapid eye movements (REMs) occur, breathing is heavy and irregular, there is increased blood pressure, some muscles begin twitching, and the electrical activity of the brain is at a very high level. Brain recordings have shown that this stage and the others are repeated approximately every one and one-half to two hours each night (Figure 12-11).

The study of dreaming was greatly advanced when rapid eye movements were found to be related to this state, and recently it has been found that certain respiratory patterns are associated with the brain waves of the *hypnagogic state,* which is the interval of drowsiness between waking and sleeping (Timmons et al., 1972). This finding may be similarly useful in investigations of hypnagogy, which is of growing interest to researchers because of the vivid imagery found in this state of just falling asleep and just awakening (Schachter, 1976).

Lack of rest. Human beings also have a periodic need for rest, apart from sleep, but uninterrupted performance on the job or in school generally does not decline significantly if motivation remains high. The individual simply expends greater effort to achieve the same level of success, usually by altering the ways in which he or she accomplishes the task, until the fatigue becomes more pronounced. Eventually, the worker develops a physiological need for rest, even if motivation continues at a high level.

Motivation and Emotional Behavior

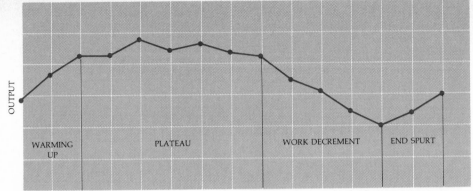

OUTPUT

WARMING UP   PLATEAU   WORK DECREMENT   END SPURT

TIME

Figure 12-12   Hypothetical Work Curve. *Fatigue, boredom, or both may be responsible for the work decrement. (Graph from* Fields of Applied Psychology *by A. Anastasi. Copyright © 1964 by McGraw-Hill, Inc. Used with permission of McGraw-Hill Book Company. Photo by Holland from Stock, Boston.)*

■ *If the reader is not familiar with the superburger, it consists of a large hamburger with pickles, catsup, onions, mayonnaise, lettuce, and tomato. When one first begins working at the Hamburger Palace, he or she is assigned the task of making superburgers. Being unusually klutzy, I remained on superburgers for most of my career at the H. P.*

When I arrived at 5:00, I would immediately head for the back board and begin making up the superburgers. All the ingredients are set up in the order just mentioned. As the job was hardly an intellectual challenge, by 5:20 or so I would be feeling quite bored and start moving into stage one—variations. This would usually mean starting at the other end, that is, with the lettuce and tomatoes, instead of the pickles and catsup. This stage would last perhaps until 6:00 or so. Then, I would advance to stage two—reduced quality. I would become very sloppy and just throw things on the burger in a hit-or-miss fashion. Depending on how long I worked in this way, I would either move into stage three—inability to perform, in which I would clean up the mess I'd already made—or look up and realize that I only had a short time left and begin to work rapidly and well until I had to leave.

The fatigue that I experienced was obviously subjective, because right after leaving the superburgers I was able to use the same muscles for doing something else.

Research workers in industry have established a *hypothetical average work curve*, in which there is an initial warm-up period, followed by a plateau, and then a work decrement. The importance of motivational factors is illustrated in the end spurt, in which the subject improves his or her performance when the end of the work period is near (Figure 12-12).

In jobs that are highly repetitive or too simple for the worker, the individual's reaction is a feeling of boredom or *subjective fatigue*. This fatigue is recognized as psychological rather than physiological when the worker immediately is able to perform a different task efficiently using the same muscles. ■

Fundamentals of Motivation

Motivation for Stimulation

Besides the periodic need for rest, food, and drink, the human organism's other physiological requirements include the elimination of wastes, intake of oxygen, and reduction of pain. Onset of pain does not necessarily occur at periodic intervals but serves as a warning signal. All of these needs arose for Robin Graham, but they did not constitute his greatest difficulty.

Robin's biggest problem at sea was extreme boredom and loneliness, which more than once made him consider abandoning his goal. In the doldrums, he said: "The calm began to get to me . . . I wanted to keep moving so I wouldn't go crazy."* Often, he talked to himself and felt such behavior would have interested "the head shrinkers."

Sensory Variation

Charles Lindbergh also experienced boredom and loneliness when crossing the Atlantic alone, at times singing, asking himself riddles, and engaging in other mental exercises to keep his mind on the trip, but he still found himself flying upside down at one point, just a few feet above the water. Admiral Byrd, after months alone at the South Pole surrounded only by the wind, snow, and Antarctic darkness, projected himself by means of hallucinations into a world of sunlight, full of green and growing things, surrounded by peaceful, easygoing, kind persons. The constancy of his external environment was the most difficult aspect of his solitary winter (Byrd, 1938).

Sensory constancy as aversive. The motivation for change in stimulation, or the *sensory variation* motive, has been studied experimentally by immersing adult human subjects in a tank of slowly flowing water. In complete darkness and

at a constant temperature, they were almost in a suspended position. They could hear only their own breathing and some faint sounds from the piping, and they reported the environment to be the most even and monotonous that they had ever experienced. The tension that developed after an hour or two was described as "hunger for stimulus action." Muscle twitches occurred at an increasing rate and the subjects developed methods of self-stimulation, such as performing slow swimming movements and stroking their fingers against one another. Longer periods in this environment eventually brought intense concentration on a single aspect of the situation, such as the slight noises, or reveries, or visual hallucinations (Lilly, 1956).

In another investigation, college students volunteered to lie individually in small rooms with coverings over their eyes, ears, and skin, which greatly limited their visual, auditory, and tactile experiences. Stimulation, or rather *changes in stimulation* in the external environment, was lacking, and at first the subjects slept a great deal. Later, they became bored and eager to be stimulated; they sang, whistled, and talked to themselves. Constant random movements and restlessness were noted. Still later, they tried to complete self-initiated problems to relieve the boredom, but instead they lapsed into daydreaming and reported "blank" periods when they could not think of anything, despite efforts at self-stimulation (Bexton et al., 1954; Figure 12-13).

Alone for days and weeks at a time, exposed to little more than the sky, the sea, and the sounds of his boat, Robin Graham also tried various methods of gaining increased stimulation from his environment. The lack of change in his environment, he said, drove him "to within a breath of madness" (Graham, 1972).

He dealt with this problem in two ways. Sometimes he made extra work of

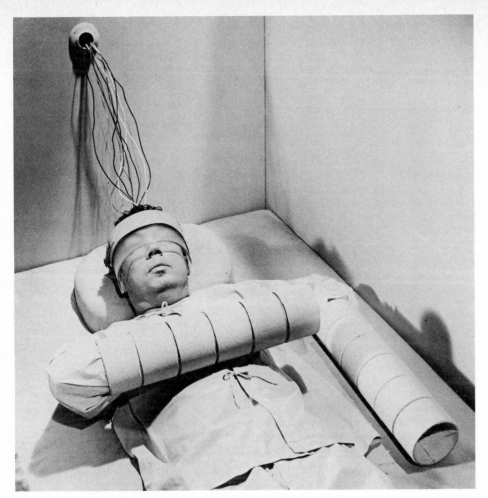

Figure 12-13 Environmental Restriction. *The subject, lying on a rubber bed, wears translucent goggles, has on gloves that permit free movement of joints but limit tactual perception, and has his head on a foam pillow containing earphones. A constant hum from fans, an air-conditioner, and an amplifier leading to the earphones masks all other sounds. (From the Bell System's Science Series Film "Gateways to the Mind")*

the daily chores, taking longer than necessary to obtain a fix on the stars or becoming overly concerned in preparing a simple meal. He also used his tape recorder extensively, speaking into it, recording other sounds, and then replaying what he had just heard; however, lack of stimulus change still remained a problem for him.

Exploration and manipulation. Need for change in stimulation can be considered from a different viewpoint, stressing not the avoidance of sensory constancy but rather the seeking of *novel* stimuli. Here the emphasis is on exploration, manipulation, and curiosity, especially among the upper primates.

Monkeys, for example, are notorious for their curiosity, staring at one another, sniffing and grooming, and picking each other's hair and skin. When a new object is presented, they approach it tentatively, and if there is no danger, they investigate thoroughly. When interest in a particular object is satiated, the introduction of new objects prompts further exploratory activity (Van Lawick-Goodall, 1967; Welker, 1956). Rats choose one alley of a T-maze even though that choice brings only the opportunity to explore more mazes (Montgomery & Segall, 1955). Monkeys perform discrimination tasks for the opportunity to look into an empty room,

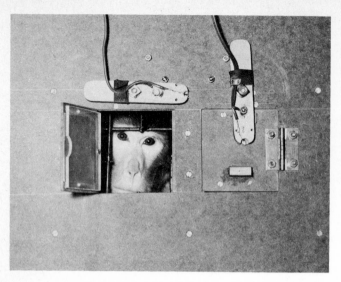

Figure 12-14 Exploratory Behavior. *If the monkey presses a lever several times, this window will open, allowing the animal to see into the next room, which has nothing in it. Monkeys will perform this task repeatedly, but human beings also expend effort to find out about their world. (Left photo from Harry F. Harlow, University of Wisconsin Primate Laboratory; right photo by Alberto Rodríguez Rey)*

and they persist when rewarded only by the sound of other monkeys heard through a microphone (Butler & Harlow, 1954; Figure 12-14).

Regarding human beings, a social psychologist emphasizes our efforts at investigating our surroundings:

The human organism expends considerable energy just finding out about the world in which he lives. He explores, he tries things out, or is just curious about things. (Festinger, 1954b)

This kind of motivation may have been a most significant factor in Robin Graham's decision to undertake his voyage. Although bored at sea, he found considerable new stimulation ashore. In the South Seas, he participated in ritualistic ceremonies with kava, a slightly narcotic drink. In the traffic jams in New Guinea, he experienced some of that country's problems in the transition from a primitive era to the twentieth century. Remote parts of Africa gave him the feeling of seeing our planet before the arrival of the human species. As Robin said himself, he wanted to find out about the world (Graham, 1972).

Affectional Stimulation

There is also motivation for affectional stimulation in human beings and certain lower animals. Like variation in sensory stimulation, it is not necessary for life but is apparently necessary for a "full and happy existence" within the limits of one's natural endowments. The puzzling part of this need for affectional stimulation, like the need for sensory variation, is that it appears rooted in the organism's biological inheritance, yet no physiological basis has been established in either case. Altogether, this *affectional stimulation* is comprised of fondling, rocking, warmth, touching, and other aspects of parental attention, sometimes called *contact comfort* (Figure 12-15).

Studies of monkeys. Research in which infant monkeys have been provided with mechanical mother substitutes is relevant to the issue of affectional stimulation. One substitute consisted of a piece of wood covered with sponge rubber and terry cloth; the other was similar in size and shape but was constructed with wire mesh, so that it lacked warmth, softness, and cuddliness. Although both "mothers" provided nourishment through a nipple, the baby monkeys demonstrated a clear

Figure 12-15 Surrogate Mother. *In play and stress, infant monkeys prefer this cuddly model to a comparable "mother" made only of wire mesh. (Harry F. Harlow, University of Wisconsin Primate Laboratory)*

Figure 12-16 Security in Exploration. *The infant explores its environment, provided it can maintain contact with the cloth mother, for example, by touching it with a hind leg. (Harry F. Harlow, University of Wisconsin Primate Laboratory)*

preference for the soft one. In times of stress, they ran and clung to it as monkeys normally do to their real mothers, and when strange stimuli suddenly appeared, they were calmer with this "mother" present. Without it, the infants remained motionless on the floor or huddled in a corner, or they moved rapidly around the room, uttering intermittent cries and shrieks (Figure 12-16).

The infants also preferred a rocking mother to one that was stationary, and other significant features included warmth and a body shape that enabled the infant to hug it. But cuddliness or contact comfort was clearly the most crucial factor. Even the features of the mother's face were quite unimportant (Harlow & Zimmerman, 1959; Harlow & Suomi, 1970).

Further studies indicated that infant monkeys not only prefer these types of stimulation—cuddliness, warmth, rocking, and hugging—but that they *need* such affectional stimulation for normal development. Without it, they display deviant behavior as adults. Infants reared with the wire mothers eventually showed inadequate social and sexual development; those reared with cloth-sponge mothers were much better adjusted in both ways, but even this model was not a completely satisfactory mother substitute as far as later adjustment was concerned (Harlow & Harlow, 1966).

Figure 12-17 Affectional Stimulation. *The mother stimulates the child, but the child's presence is also stimulating to the mother. Thus, there is a reciprocity in the system. (Miller from Magnum)*

Human infants. The question of whether human infants require comparable types of affectional stimulation to arrive at normal development cannot be answered readily, although experienced researchers report a high degree of similarity between monkey and human mothering. In fact, the desire for affectional stimulation is readily observed in both normal human adults and children (Figure 12-17).

Studies of hospitalization and wartime orphans indicate an apparently inborn need for affectional stimulation, and infants reared in a large institution where they receive only minimal adult attention are often retarded physically, intellectually, and emotionally, although their nutritional and cleanliness needs are well met. Evidence for this view also comes from the Skeels-Skodak study, in which it was found that early attention from older women had a decidedly favorable influence on the mental and physical development of a group of orphaned children. As adults, these people, compared to a control group, were more often employed, more often with family or friends, and more advanced in their education (Skeels, 1966).

Theory and Perspectives

At this point it is useful to look for some way of organizing this knowledge of the physiological basis of motivation. One helpful concept is *homeostasis,* which is the tendency of the body to maintain a balanced internal environment, chiefly in its chemical composition. Maintaining this delicate balance is one of the most remarkable features of physiology. Even in a few moments in which the circulatory or respiratory mechanisms do not function there is a disequilibrium endangering the entire organism; hence, there must be constant restorative functions.

Homeostatic Activity

Some restorative actions, called homeostatic activities, are physiologically produced; in this sense they are automatic. Satisfactory body temperature is automatically influenced by tiny neural mechanisms that control perspiration. The maintenance of an adequate oxygen supply is achieved by complex reflexes that increase respiration when there is an oxygen deficiency in the blood. The removal of damaged body cells occurs as a result of the action of white blood cells. We do not understand all the stabilizing factors, but it is clear that the automatic control of temperature, oxygen supply, and certain nutritive functions gives the organism greater freedom to engage in higher-level activities. Human beings can write books, maintain friendships, and travel to distant parts of the world because their vital organs are maintained in a relatively constant environment.

Drive reduction Some compensatory activities of homeostasis are not automatic; they require relevant motivated behavior on the part of the organism. In hunger and thirst, the organism must react to restore its equilibrium. Optimal amounts of sugar, salt, fat, and proteins in the blood are achieved by finding and .consuming appropriate amounts of food

Motivation and Emotional Behavior

and water, as we have seen in the motivational sequence. Similarly, a satisfactory body temperature is achieved by engaging in vigorous activity in cold weather and avoiding strenuous activity in warm weather. The behavior of any organism is periodically concerned with re-establishing a balanced physiological condition.

This sequence of events, also known as *drive reduction*, at one time was thought to account for all types of physiological motivation. It is still regarded as especially relevant to the motives for individual survival, but there are inadequacies in this interpretation of the motivation for species survival and for affectional stimulation and sensory variation. It is difficult, for example, to understand how copulation might be considered a homeostatic response. An individual who does not engage in this activity does not perish from its absence, and it is not necessarily true that prolonged sexual inactivity generates sexual urges.

Pain. The condition of pain is also a motivating circumstance and it fits into the homeostatic model because it is based on a change in tissue state. Reactions to pain are automatic physiological activities within the organism and also behavioral responses. Individual survival is clearly based on both types of activities.

Pain differs from the motivations discussed earlier, however, because it does not involve appetitive or *adient behavior*, in which the organism seeks stimulation. Pain induces aversive or *abient behavior;* the organism seeks to escape stimulation. Thus, pain is the basis for the learned drive of fear or anxiety. Even when a stimulus is merely perceived as painful, the organism is highly motivated to avoid it, which shows again the influence of external factors, or cognition, in motivation.

Acquired motives. Finally, the concept of homeostasis also has been applied to the organism's efforts to maintain a balanced psychological state, apart from physiological considerations. In addition to inborn needs, the individual develops *acquired motives,* which are those learned during a lifetime, rather than inborn. In attempts to satisfy these motives, the individual strives to achieve a psychological equilibrium. An intense fear of elevators, for example, prompts an individual to avoid them; staying away from them is the means of maintaining or achieving equilibrium.

Acquired motives are sometimes called *secondary motivation* because it is hypothesized by some that they develop from the individual's efforts to satisfy physiological or *primary motivation.* We shall consider these conditions in the next chapter, restricting the following comments to a possible relationship between these two sets of motives.

A Motivational Hierarchy

The basic premise in a *motivational hierarchy* is that for a given species motives exist according to a certain order or rank. For the unsatisfied individual, the most fundamental or important motives are at the bottom and those of less potency appear nearer the top. According to their motives, individuals are concerned with different levels in the hierarchy. One such hierarchy was developed by Abraham Maslow, who was particularly interested in the motives at the upper levels (Maslow, 1954, 1970).

Maslow's hierarchy. At the first level of Maslow's motivational hierarchy are the *physiological* aspects of human motivation, pertaining to thirst, hunger, sleep, and other drives necessary to the maintenance of life. When motives at all levels are unsatisfied in the organism, these are the strongest.

If the physiological requirements are minimally satisfied, then *safety* needs emerge, such as the need for security, protection, and freedom from danger.

Here the organism is concerned with being in a reasonably stable, secure environment.

In our complex human environment, complete satisfaction of all needs at each level is not expected, but if the safety needs are reasonably satisfied, the individual moves up to another position in the hierarchy, in which the acquired or social motives begin. At this level, we find the need for *love and belonging,* which includes having friends, a family, heterosexual relationships, and membership in a group.

When satisfaction of this need is achieved, the individual is prompted to another level, *self-esteem.* This motivation is not concerned with gaining membership in a group but rather with achieving a significant status there. The person desires the respect, confidence, and admiration of others. In this view, the human being is characterized as a perpetually "wanting" animal and, thus, the individual, if satisfied in terms of self-esteem, strives at an even higher level.

At the highest level of this hierarchy is the need for *self-actualization,* in which the individual is essentially concerned about doing what he or she is best suited or intended to do. Self-actualization is the desire to realize one's potential, whatever it may be, to the fullest. Like the other levels, it is not a permanent condition (Figure 12-18).

Thomas Jefferson, Albert Einstein, and Eleanor Roosevelt have been described as self-actualizing. Abraham Lincoln was considered so in the late stages of his life (Maslow, 1970). A person certainly need not be famous to be self-actualizing, as illustrated by a truly devoted parent, an artist immersed in painting, or simply a spontaneous, unrestrained individual with clearcut goals that are acceptable to society. A person who is not encumbered by the superficial restrictions of his or her culture or at odds with its basic prohibitions is most likely to achieve self-actualization, providing he or she can establish meaningful goals.

Response to the hierarchy. Maslow's hierarchy, including the concept of self-actualization, has proven controversial, however. It has been challenged, defended, and frequently reformulated. It is stated by some that there is a lack of precision, especially in the definition of self-actualization, and a lack of supporting research. Besides, there seem to be numerous examples of individuals who do not conform to the model; they bypass one or more levels of the hierarchy. The painter on the Left Bank of the Seine River in Paris does not have enough to eat, yet he or she continues an unprofitable artist's career. A soldier risks his or her life to capture an enemy position, ignoring safety needs while satisfying self-esteem. A food-deprived rat placed in a new maze will engage in considerable exploratory behavior before eating. Robin Graham jeopardized physiological and safety needs and sacrificed love and belonging to complete his voyage. The loneliness, he said, was extremely difficult—a constant problem for a thousand days and through the longest nights (Graham, 1972).

Advocates of the hierarchy view such cases as exceptions to the general hypothesis, which is still considered to have validity. It is explained that if the lower needs are regularly satisfied in childhood, a temporary lack of satisfaction can be more readily tolerated later.

Figure 12-18   A Motivational Hierarchy. *Successive steps indicate the sequential aspect, but it is not implied that persons necessarily progress to the highest level. (Adapted from Maslow, 1943. Copyright 1943 by the American Psychological Association. Reprinted by permission.)*

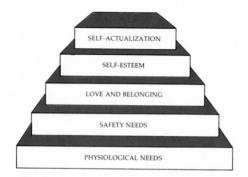

SELF-ACTUALIZATION

SELF-ESTEEM

LOVE AND BELONGING

SAFETY NEEDS

PHYSIOLOGICAL NEEDS

Motivation and Emotional Behavior

Still another interpretation is that when satisfactions are not regularly achieved at the lower levels, a person can reach higher levels but performs there in a less effective and less satisfying manner (Maddi & Costa, 1972).

Possibly Robin Graham, by one means or another, reached some level of self-actualization in moments of his voyage. As his father wrote when he set sail: "Success or failure, he is fulfilling his destiny." This idea cannot be supported or refuted, but at the conclusion of his five-year saga, Robin thought about his purpose in the trip and wondered how he could explain it: "I felt . . . it had something to do with fate and destiny. How could I phrase that? How could I tell these newsmen that I sailed across the world because I had to do so—because that was what I was meant to do?"* (Figure 12-19).

Role of Early Experience

A more pragmatic view focuses on Robin Graham's earlier experiences. It stresses the role of early learning in the reasons for his trip. When Robin was age 10 years, he was given his first boat, and he spent every day after school with it. When Robin was age 13, his father took him on an 11,000-mile sailing trip. Looking back, Robin said: "It is hard to believe that my parents, having allowed me to sail the South Seas at a most impressionable age, could ever have expected me to be a typical American school kid, to go to college and graduate to a walnut office desk. . . ."* Recognizing the importance of early learning, certain psychologists would be inclined to agree. Robin's later behavior undoubtedly was influenced by early well-formed habits.

In addition, he apparently had a long-standing aversion for school, disliking the subjects and resenting homework.

Figure 12-19   Returning Home. *Robin approaches the California coast at the end of his long, lonely voyage. Enroute he often photographed himself with an automatic timing apparatus. (From* Dove *by Robin Lee Graham with Derek L. T. Gill. Copyright © 1972 by Robin Lee Graham and Derek L. T. Gill. Reprinted by permission of Harper & Row, Publishers, Inc.)*

At one point, he described school as "almost unbearable." Even at age ten, sailing "was the chance to escape from blackboards . . . from addition and subtraction sums which were never the same as the teacher's answers, from spelling words like 'seize' and 'fulfill'. . . ."*

Further, Robin played and worked by himself for most of his youth, and apparently he liked being by himself or at least became accustomed to it. Sailing "was the chance to be alone and to be free. . . ," although his mother worried about his being "such a loner." His first boat gave him the chance for "getting away from people," and *Dove,* his round-the-world boat, gave him the same chance later. Making friends could have been a problem; Robin had attended six different schools by his sophomore year in high school.

In any case, when he reached his sixteenth year and began the trip, Robin clearly had learned to love the sea, to dislike school, to be self-reliant, and to be alone a great deal, and this constellation of traits fits the requirements for such a voyage. Habits, once formed, continue to persist. Behavior that had been found previously satisfying was repeated.

* From *Dove* by Robin Lee Graham with Derek L. T. Gill. Copyright © 1972 by Robin Lee Graham and Derek L. T. Gill. Reprinted by permission of Harper & Row, Publishers, Inc.

In addition, one might speculate about the trip on the basis of the father-son relationship. Robin's father purchased the sloop, helped him prepare for the trip, and hoped all along that Robin "would come up with just such a scheme." From the beginning, according to Robin, his father lived Robin's voyage and life vicariously. After the trip, the son promptly sold his boat and moved to Montana, where his nearest neighbor was three miles away. One wonders to what extent Robin's trip was a fulfillment of the father's ambition, perhaps more than the son's, especially since the parent long ago had decided that the trip was not possible for himself.

In summary the desire to learn more about the world, the role of self-actualization, his early learning experiences, parental influence, or some combination of these factors all may have played a role in motivating Robin to make the trip. In deciding on *the* reason among such possibilities, the reader is reminded again of the fallacy of the single cause. In all likelihood, no single factor can be identified. Motivation has a multiple basis; any given behavior probably occurs for several reasons.

Summary

The Concept of Instinct

1. Motivation is a condition of need or desire that the organism attempts to satisfy in some way. It involves activation and direction. An example of motivation is found in instinct, which is a complex, unlearned pattern of behavior occurring in all same-sexed members of a given species. Instincts are prompted by internal factors called hormones.

2. The appearance of a given instinct in lower animals, such as mating and nest-building, is not as automatic and exclusively related to internal factors as was once thought. Certain stimuli in the environment are important in releasing these behaviors.

3. As one proceeds up the evolutionary scale, there is decreasing evidence for instinctive behavior. Generally, the term is not applied to human beings, and with animals investigators now speak of species-specific behavior and fixed-action patterns instead.

Species Survival

4. At the human level, sexual behavior clearly illustrates the relationship between inborn and acquired factors in motivation. Sexual motivation is prompted by secretions of androgen in the male and estrogen in the female, but it has an extremely important basis in learning.

5. Maternal motivation is related to the secretion of prolactin in animals, but among human beings culture again plays a very large role in the development and modes of satisfaction of this form of motivation.

Individual Survival

6. For motives that are essential to the individual's survival, a sequence is often identified: a physiological need or biochemical imbalance occurs in the organism; it produces a state of arousal known as drive; the driven organism is ready to respond to incentives, which are stimuli related to its aroused state; and these incentives can serve as rewards for the organism that acquires them. In the need for water, the most obvious symptom is dryness of the mouth and throat, but to be effective in reducing thirst, water must alleviate cellular dehydration in other areas, including the hypothalamus.

7. The biochemical basis of hunger involves not only the blood sugar level and conditions of the stomach but also the hypothalamus. The lateral area of this organ seems to play an important role in initiating eating while the ventromedial nucleus is involved in its cessation. The specific ways in which the hunger drive is satisfied are significantly influenced by learning.

8. Prolonged lack of sleep leads to perceptual disturbances, loss of emotional control, and decreased intellectual functioning, but sleep is not a totally passive state. It is induced by activities in certain brain regions, especially the thalamus, and various levels of activity occur at the different stages of sleep. During dreaming, breathing is heavy and irregular, blood pressure is increased, and the electrical activity of the brain is at a very high level.

Motivation for Stimulation

9. Many organisms seek types of stimulation for which no physiological bases have been established, although the motives appear to be part of our biological inheritance. Most higher organisms desire variation in sensory stimulation, sometimes referred to as sensory variation motives. The extensive exploratory and manipulatory behaviors of primates, including human beings, illustrate the associated behaviors. For most human beings, sensory constancy is an aversive state.

10. Animal and human infants also desire affectional stimulation, sometimes called contact comfort. This type of stimulation includes warmth, cuddliness, rocking, and hugging, and studies with animals indicate that it is essential for adequate social and sexual development. Observations of human beings suggest that it plays an important role in ensuring normal human development.

Theory and Perspectives

11. The tendency to maintain a balanced physiological state is known as homeostasis. Some homeostatic activities are automatic, such as those in reflexes; others require a relevant series of behaviors, as in satisfying the hunger drive. The concept of drive reduction, while useful in understanding the basis of individual survival motives and the avoidance of pain, is not readily applied to motives for species survival and for affectional stimulation and sensory variation. Sometimes acquired motives are considered from the viewpoint of establishing a psychological homeostasis.

12. In one motivational hierarchy, the physiological and safety needs appear first in order of importance. If these needs are satisfied, the individual becomes concerned with love and belonging, then self-esteem, and perhaps self-actualization, in that order. The theory is controversial because it lacks empirical support, the vital concept of self-actualization is not well defined, and there seem to be significant exceptions to the sequence.

13. Early learning experiences can influence motivation, impelling us to continue accustomed ways of satisfying desires. Altogether, several different factors may be involved in the motivation to perform any complex act.

Suggested Readings

Bolles, R. C. *Theory of motivation* (2nd ed.). New York: Harper & Row, 1975. The concept of motivation is viewed in historical perspective and in terms of current issues.

Chiang, H-M., & Maslow, A. H. *The healthy personality* (2nd ed.). New York: Van Nostrand, Reinhold, 1977. A book of 21 readings, 2 of which concern Maslow's views on motivation and personality.

Klopfer, P. H., & Hailman, J. P. (Eds.). *Control and development of behavior: An historical sample from the pens of ethologists.* Reading, Mass.: Addison-Wesley, 1972. A series of research papers, uneven in length and reading level, on classic studies in animal behavior, including the instinct question.

Miller, N. E. (Ed.). *Neal E. Miller: Selected papers.* Chicago: Aldine, 1971. More than 60 articles by a leading experimental psychologist, several of which pertain to the physiological aspects of motivation.

Nevin, J. A. (Ed.). *The study of behavior: Learning, motivation, emotion and instinct.* Glenview, Ill.: Scott Foresman, 1973. Five authors contribute to a readable, well-documented volume.

Chapter 13

Acquired Motivation and Emotion

The poet Hölty wrote:

Giving kisses, snatching kisses,
Keeps the busy world employed.

Kissing, however, is partly a matter of culture. The Eskimos, for example, engage in nose-kissing, as do the natives of Tierra del Fuego. Upon greeting one another, they rub noses. The nose kiss is also found in tropical climates—among Polynesians, Malays, and certain African cultures.

Mouth-kissing is prevalent elsewhere. The alleged advantage of this form of kissing is that it provides a more intimate knowledge of another human being. One can smell, touch, see, hear, and also taste the other person.

Even the practice of mouth-kissing varies from culture to culture, however. In some societies it is considered acceptable only between two people of opposite sex; in others, it occurs among members of the same sex.

Not long ago, a male friend of the authors was greeted with hugs and kisses by a man from the Middle East. The American regarded the incident as embarrassing, but for the Middle Easterner it was normal and enjoyable. Later, the American recalled a similar event that had occurred 15 years earlier, when a man from Beirut had held his hand as they walked the streets together. The American's discomfort and the Middle Easterner's pleasure were largely a matter of culture. One man had been molded by his society to want to shake a man's hand but not to hold it; the other man had been molded in just the opposite manner.

Culture and Motivation

These examples illustrate that motivations can vary widely from individual to individual. All human beings have essentially the same physiological needs, but they live in different societies, with different personal endowments, different family environments, and different opportunities in life, and these conditions give rise to different acquired motivations. *Acquired motivations* are not inborn; they are learned. They develop during the individual's lifetime although they may have early origins in the individual's efforts to satisfy physiological needs.

In considering our learned motives and emotional states, the theme in this chapter is one of synthesis and integration. We see how various forms of learning and thinking combine in the development of acquired motivation and how emotion itself can be motivating.

The Need for Affiliation

Some apparently acquired motivations are found in most, if not all, normal human beings. The desire to maintain contact with other people, called *gregariousness* or the *need for affiliation*, is such a motive. It is so nearly universal in human beings that some people have considered it inborn, especially in the context of the need for affectional stimulation or contact comfort in human babies. However, the extended period of infantile helplessness, in which we are completely dependent on the presence of others for survival, could lead to the acquisition of this motive.

Anxiety and affiliation. During the period of infantile dependency, which is longer than that of any other species, the bonds of attachment can become strong indeed. By adulthood, our desire for affiliation may be partly a vestige of childhood fears of abandonment. With this possibility in mind, an experimental hypothesis was formed: when we are anxious as adults, we desire others' company, even when they cannot give us aid or protection.

To test this hypothesis, college students served as subjects in an experiment in which they were exposed to different degrees of anxiety. Some of them were shown electrical apparatus and told that later they would receive intense shock. Others were shown the same apparatus but were told that the experiment would be enjoyable. Then each subject was asked to indicate a preference for waiting alone or with someone else before the research procedures began. Analysis of the results of this experiment, which required no actual shocks for anyone, showed that the persons who were highly anxious wanted to be with other people, while those who were made less anxious were indifferent about affiliation. This outcome has been confirmed in several instances, but it is found most specifically in first-born and only children (Figure 13-1).

These figures prompted the investigators to wonder about the kind of affiliation that was desired by the anxious subjects. Did they just want to be with someone, or did they have a preference for certain people? To answer this question, a similar experimental procedure

Figure 13-1 Anxiety and Desire for Affiliation. *The theory of social comparison has been used to explain the results of this experiment. The anxious subjects wished to be together so that they could compare their feelings with those of others in the same situation. If others had the same feelings, then presumably those feelings were appropriate to the situation, and in that sense "correct." (Adapted from* The Psychology of Affiliation, *by Stanley Schachter, with the permission of the publisher, Stanford University Press. © 1959 by the Board of Trustees of the Leland Stanford Junior University.)*

	Subjects' Preferences		
Condition	Together	Don't Care	Alone
High Anxiety	63%	28%	9%
Low Anxiety	33%	60%	7%

Motivation and Emotional Behavior

Figure 13-2   Tendency to Compare.   *Comparison of ourselves with others is a way of testing our abilities, perceptions, and opinions, especially when objective standards are lacking. For example, this girl's reading ability can be assessed by objective tests, but she may wish to assess her jumping ability through contests with other girls her age. She also tests her perceptions and opinions through comparisons with others who are different from her. These comparisons contribute much to her self-knowledge. (Albertson from Stock, Boston)*

was used with other subjects, except that they were given the choice of being with someone undergoing the same experience or being in a room full of people anticipating different experiences. Again the results were decisive; the anxious subjects preferred to be with other people who were anxious. The old saying appears to be in need of refinement: Misery does not love just company; it loves miserable company (Schachter, 1959).

To recapitulate briefly, we can say that our desire for others' company relates to early experiences, that it increases when we become anxious, and that when we are anxious our preferences are strongest for relationships with people in similar circumstances. When certain persons are the source of our anxiety, of course we will want to avoid them.

Social comparison.   Especially after the early years, people also desire to be with others in order to evaluate themselves, a circumstance called *social comparison.*

We obtain guidance for present and future behavior by observing what others do, and we reduce uncertainty about ourselves by information gained in interaction with other people (Figure 13-2).

According to the concept of social comparison, the more information one has about other people who are in the same situation as one finds oneself, the less one's desire for affiliation should be. This hypothesis was tested by arranging three groups of people. Some subjects were placed in an anxiety-provoking situation and received no information about themselves or others; other subjects in the same situation received information only about their own reactions; and still others received information about their own reactions and about others' reactions. The prediction was that those receiving little or no information would have the strongest desire for affiliation, and the evidence clearly favored this interpretation (Gerard & Robbie, 1961).

As T. S. Eliot said in *The Cocktail Party,* human beings are "absorbed in the endless struggle to think well of themselves."* The social comparison process is a constant one, which helps us to find out about ourselves and also to learn new ways of behaving.

Sexual and Maternal Motivation

Developing in the context of our relations with others are various cultural motives. By *cultural motives* we mean those shared motives that are essentially acquired, yet their expression varies from one culture to another, or from one era to another, depending on the customs of that society. Different social forces, for example, have brought about considerable variation in human sexuality, especially nonprocreative sex. A *nonprocreative sex act* is one that does not have the possibility of leading to further propagation of the species (Figure 13-3).

Nonprocreative sex. Among the ancient Greeks, the practice of *homosexuality,* which is the tendency to find sexual gratification with persons of one's own sex, was widely accepted. In fact, there is evidence that it was even encouraged. Centuries later, especially beginning in the 1700s, this practice became much suppressed in the Western world. All forms of sexuality were seen as medical issues, and nonprocreative sex of any type was regarded as diseased or abnormal. Earlier in the present century, it was found that slightly more than one out of every three males studied in the Kinsey Report had experienced orgasm by some type of homosexual contact, a figure considerably higher than was expected, despite a possible bias among the volunteers in the sample (Kinsey et al., 1948; Kinsey, 1953). In the 1970s, the American Psychiatric Association decided that homosexuality is not a mental disorder and

* From *The Cocktail Party* by T. S. Eliot (New York: Harcourt Brace Jovanovich, Inc., 1959). Reprinted by permission of Harcourt Brace Jovanovich, Inc., and Faber & Faber Ltd.

classified it as a sexual disturbance only if the individual is in conflict about it (Ferlemann, 1974).

Clearly, the practice of homosexuality is influenced by social forces. In some subcultures of the United States today it is regarded as "biological play," which has no more to do with species survival than does painting or any other activity (Smith, 1975). In others, it continues to be seen as a major form of social deviance, regardless of the stand taken by the medical profession (Pattison, 1974). Amid these cultural differences, incidentally, the possible role of genetic factors in individual cases remains puzzling (Margolese, 1970; Tourney et al., 1975).

Another form of nonprocreative sexual activity that has shown the influence of social forces is *masturbation,* which is satisfaction obtained from stimulation of the genitals, usually self-stimulation. During the first half of this century, masturbation was strongly discouraged in many parts of the United States. Children were told that this practice was sinful and that it would cause blotches on the skin, damage the nervous system, and make them unfit for business activities. Still worse, physicians erroneously stated: "Masturbation is one of the great causes of insanity; to ascertain this fact it is only necessary to look over the reports of any of the insane asylums of the land" (Whitehead & Hoff, 1929).

At this same time in the United States, masturbation was encouraged in certain Indian subcultures, along with the other childhood accomplishments of standing up, building things, and walking. Such activities were considered to promote the child's feelings of self-confidence, and the gratification from masturbation was assumed to add to the child's decision that he or she could obtain pleasure from himself or herself and thus be less dependent on the parents (Kardiner, 1939; Leighton & Kluckhohn, 1947).

Motivation and Emotional Behavior

Figure 13-3 **Nonprocreative Sexual Behaviors.** *The extent to which these behaviors are regarded as abnormal depends on their strength and persistence, especially in the absence of more common modes of satisfaction.*

A male entertainer dressed in woman's clothes for a nightclub act. Such entertainers are not necessarily transvestites, and transvestism is not necessarily abnormal behavior. (Herwig from Stock, Boston)

Exhibitionism—obtaining sexual satisfaction through display of one's own sexual organs under inappropriate circumstances.

Fetishism—deriving sexual pleasure through contact with some inanimate object more than through the sexual organs of another person.

Masochism—seeking sexual excitement from being subjected to painful circumstances.

Sadism—seeking sexual excitement from subjecting someone else to painful circumstances.

Transvestism—seeking sexual gratification by dressing in and wearing the clothes of the opposite sex.

Voyeurism—obtaining sexual pleasure by observing others' sexual organs and sexual behavior; a "peeping Tom."

Maternal motivation. Despite the physiological component in sexual motivation, we see that the expression of this drive varies from culture to culture, and there is a similar variability in maternal motivation. Inborn factors are also present, but they are not highly influential for human beings. At the human level there is no worldwide pattern of mothering, unless it is feeding the child at the breast. Even breast-feeding is not universal and there are marked differences in weaning, both of which also indicate the role of learning.

North American mothers usually wean their children gradually, while some mothers in the South Pacific do so abruptly, putting hot red pepper on their nipples. In areas of Poland it has been the custom to wean suddenly, on a day selected in advance, when the child becomes approximately 18 months old (Benedict, 1949).

An example of childrearing patterns quite different from those in most of the Western world occurs in the kibbutz of Israel. In Hebrew, *kibbutz* refers to ''group,'' and kibbutz children are raised in a group, in the context of peers rather than the biological parents. The children learn, play, eat, and sleep together, under the supervision of a person called the *metapelet*, who is highly trained for this work. The metapelet has total responsibility for the children the whole day, including discipline. The parents' role varies from kibbutz to kibbutz but it is minimal. Commonly the parents play with the children in the evening after work, but they live in separate quarters from the children. The origin of this system lies partly in the economic advantage to the community, where the women and men work in similar roles, and partly in the woman's desire to live without the usual childrearing restraints.

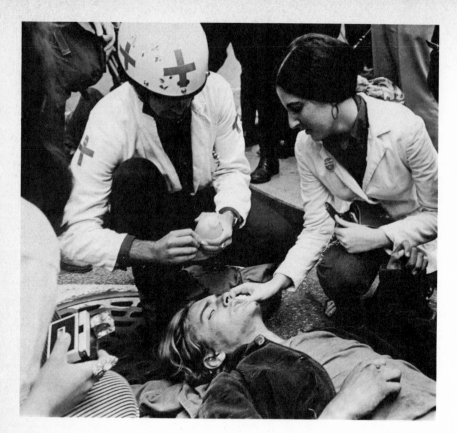

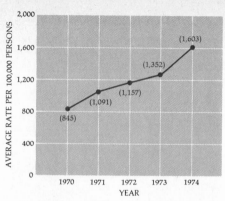

Figure 13-4 Criminal Aggression. *The graph shows a steady increase in Boston in crimes "against the person," which include murder, rape, robbery, and aggravated assault (data from Uniform Crime Reports prepared for the Department of Justice). (Photo by Carlson from Stock, Boston)*

Behavioral scientists are extremely interested in the kibbutz because it offers excellent opportunities for testing long-standing hypotheses about childrearing practices and the adult personality (Spiro, 1965). One psychiatrist speculates that the kibbutz may be difficult for a child in the early years, when he or she does not experience the closeness and constant parental attention found in the nuclear family. Later, in elementary school and in adolescence, the child may pass through identity crises more easily because he or she is in the context of peers coping with the same problem. This psychiatrist suggests that we might try to achieve the best of both worlds—continue with our present system in the child's early life and then, by developing many more community resources, shift to a greater peer orientation in the later childhood years (Blaine, 1973).

The Problem of Aggression

One of the most obvious problems in childrearing is managing the child's aggression. Here again we see the role of learning, but the problem of aggression is so extremely prevalent in many societies, including our own, that one wonders whether this motivation is inborn. In fact, there has been an ever upward trend in criminal behavior in many different parts of the world in recent years (Figure 13-4).

Aggression as inborn. At one time aggressiveness was thought to be universal, and today there are scientists who believe that the human inclination to aggression is inherited. In general, they have investigated this question from backgrounds of zoology and ethology (Lorenz, 1963; Morris, 1967). Freud, much influenced by World War I and subsequent economic depression, also maintained that the aggressive urge was inborn.

Motivation and Emotional Behavior

Aggressiveness in this context is considered in terms of our animal origins, and animals have been thought to fight for one of two reasons: to establish a position in the social hierarchy and to maintain territorial rights. Human beings, it is claimed, have both these concerns (Morris, 1967).

However, experimental studies have shown that many animals also can be prompted to aggression by a painful stimulus, such as an electric shock received through the floor of a cage. Animals were tested in a variety of circumstances: when they were alone, with a cage mate, with a member of another species, and with only a toy or similar object in the cage. In virtually all instances, the mouse, cat, monkey, snake, turtle, or other animal attacked immediately after receiving the shock, aggressing against an object when another living being was unavailable. The same outcome was observed with a variety of painful stimuli, and when no target was available for attack, the animal learned to find one by activating a simple apparatus. Since the style of the attack varied according to the circumstances, it did not appear to be a reflexive startle pattern (Azrin, 1967).

Extending these findings to human beings is risky, however. In the first place, several species did not show the reaction and, secondly, if the finding does apply at the human level, it should account for only a small portion of aggressive behavior. Human beings become aggressive under a wide variety of circumstances, including nonpainful ones.

For some people, a more compelling finding at the human level has been the disproportionately high number of criminals apparently possessing the extra Y chromosome. Rather than XY, some men are XYY, and they are generally taller and heavier than average. The incidence of such cases has been observed to be 1 in 2,000 in the general population, but it was found to be 1 in 11 among criminal males in Pennsylvania prisons (Telfer et al., 1968). In Great Britain, it has been stated that XYY individuals constitute a small but significant proportion of the population of criminal males (Lancet, 1966).

Reviews of many such studies strongly question the validity of the XYY-criminality hypothesis, however, both on the grounds of inadequacies in the research design and because the researchers have concentrated on selected populations, especially institutionalized persons (Beckwith & Miller, 1976; Owen, 1972) The XYY syndrome also is a relatively rare event, occurring in only 1 percent to 2 percent of the inmates in institutions for the criminally insane and less than .1 percent in the general population (Davis, 1976). Even if true, which now appears less likely, the XYY-aggression syndrome cannot account for a great deal of aggression in our society.

Aggression as acquired. Other investigators have searched for environmental factors, and in one early series of studies a major hypothesis was that ''aggressive behavior always presupposes the existence of frustration'' (Dollard et al., 1939). Some evidence was found to support the role of frustration in the appearance of aggression, but today we regard the idea of *always* as too sweeping. Aggression can occur without frustration, on the basis of other factors. Previously, we noted in studies of social learning theory that aggression can develop through imitation. Children who watched a movie showing an aggressive adult displayed significantly more aggression themselves than control subjects, and their aggressive responses resembled the behavior of the adult in the film (Bandura, 1965). A child may imitate aggressive behavior even when the model receives no reward for such behavior. ■

■ *On my block there is a family with two little girls about ages four and nine. They are left to fend for themselves a great deal of the time, and the oldest sister, Ann, has assumed something of a mother-role over Joanie, the little one. She often says: "If you don't go home right now, I'm going to spank you out here in front of all the kids." She always uses threats—always an order is accompanied by a threat. It wasn't until I was rather well acquainted with Ann and Joanie that I had a chance to see their mother in action. She was calling both of the girls in at bedtime and they weren't responding fast enough. Then out comes: "If you don't come in right now, I'm going to spank you out here in front of all the other kids!"*

■ *Last Saturday I was at a carnival and noticed about 25 young teenagers wandering around, calling from group to group. The topic of conversation seemed to be football. Suddenly the groups came together and a fight materialized. Two guys grappled, rolling all over the ground. The rest of the group moved immediately to surround the fight, until there was a whole crowd of teenagers around the fighters. This went on and on until the crowd was broken up and the fight ended.*

This past summer I taught reading in an elementary school in the North Philadelphia ghetto area. The students' ages ranged from 6 to 13. When teaching the older students, discipline was a major problem. Fights seemed to always spring up out of name-calling and baiting. During the arguments, the other uninvolved kids remained silent. However, as soon as the fists began to fly, crowds of kids surrounded the fighters. The staff of the program experimented with several techniques of trying to discipline the fights, but by far the most successful method was to remove the fighters to another room, away from the other kids, shut the door, and tell them to go ahead and fight. **Then** *the fight ended. Are physical fights promoted by an audience of observers?*

Early cross-cultural studies also show the learned aspects of aggression. In New Guinea, the Arapesh were seen as a peaceful people who discouraged displays of anger and aggression, regarding self-assertion and aggressiveness as abnormal (Mead, 1939). The Mundugumor, on the other hand, had fostered aggressiveness, even from infancy, and trained young boys for survival in battle.

Animals also have been trained for aggression in situations in which they otherwise might be peaceful. Through operant conditioning, rats learned to fight each other in order to avoid an electric shock. When no opponent was available, they attacked an innocent object (Miller, 1948b). Human beings, it is claimed, are constantly conditioned to aggressive behavior.

Some evidence suggests that such behavior is increased by the presence of objects typically employed for aggressive purposes, such as guns and clubs, whether or not they are actually used (Berkowitz & LePage, 1967). In Iran, for example, there are far fewer violent crimes than in the United States, and it *may* be significant that guns are generally unavailable there. Support for this view is not yet convincing, however, as partly reflected in the current controversy concerning gun control laws.

Control of aggression. The argument over the role of inborn and learned factors in aggressive behavior arises in part because the two viewpoints define aggression differently. One writer, favoring the hereditary view, describes aggressiveness as a vigorous pursuit of self-preservation (Ardrey, 1970). On this basis, all organisms are potentially aggressive and the motive can be said to be present at birth, as all of us have an innate desire to satisfy our own physiological needs.

Other people define aggression as direct attempts to inflict harm on another person or object, even when there is no obvious gain for the aggressive individual. For those people who accept this definition, aggression appears to be learned; violence and intentionally harming others are behaviors not found in all or even most human beings. Thus, researchers and theorists need to be specific about their definition of aggression (Tedeschi & Smith, 1974; Van Hemel, 1975).

The important issue is not whether aggression is inborn or acquired. Both factors are probably involved in intricate ways. Instead, we should ask: How does the environment influence whatever aggressive predispositions exist in human beings? At present we can do little about whatever hereditary aspect may exist; *eugenics,* the application of genetic principles for selective breeding, is not an accepted practice with human beings.

One of the most pressing problems today is to find ways of diminishing international, interneighborhood, and even interfamilial aggression by changing the environment. We know some of the environmental factors involved, such as the presence of aggressive models, a high drive state, and crowdedness, all of which can lead to impulsive aggression (Berkowitz, 1974). We also know that certain cultural patterns can mold us into aggressive, aggression-prone, or peaceful individuals, regardless of the ways in which our needs are satisfied (Munn, 1971). The problem is to take advantage of our present understanding, as well as to gain further knowledge. ■

Finally, the different views on the origins of aggression have different implications about how an individual should handle aggressive feelings. If the tendency towards aggression is inborn, its expression or release, called *catharsis,* should reduce the drive, just as eating something reduces the hunger drive. If it is learned, the expression of aggression may be reinforced, leading to still further aggression. There is evidence on both sides, but generally the overall weight of the evidence seems to be somewhat against the cathartic view. Opportunities for aggression have been found to stimulate rather than decrease further

Figure 13-5 Athletics and Aggression. *As a form of recreation, athletics occupy persons, both participants and fans, who otherwise might engage in less constructive activities. (Foto diario gráfico deportivo "AS," Madrid)*

aggression. On the other hand, catharsis sometimes may make the individual feel better. Therefore, another problem is to arrange an environment so that the opportunities for release of tension are constructive, rather than destructive, as in beating a rug, crushing cartons for recycling, or combating the forces of nature in the aid of needy persons (Figure 13-5).

Achievement Motivation

Besides aggressiveness, another mark of contemporary American society is the restless urge to achieve, perhaps related to our competitiveness. In a light vein, it was illustrated more than 30 years ago in this hypothetical conversation between an Indian and a missionary who was bent on improving the Indian's social and financial status:

Missionary: Brother, why don't you go to the big city and get a job in a factory?

Indian: Suppose I get a job, what then?

Missionary: If you get a job, you will get money and you can have many things.

Indian: What then?

Missionary: Well, if you do your work well, you will be promoted, become a foreman, and have more money.

Indian: What then?

Missionary: Oh, then you may become the superintendent of the factory if you work hard enough.

Indian: What then?

Missionary: If you study all about the business and work harder, you may be the manager of the whole business.

Indian: Suppose I become the manager, how would that benefit me?

Missionary: If you are an able manager, you can start a business of your own and have more money than ever.

Indian: What then?

Missionary: Oh, eventually, you will have so much money that you won't need to work at all.

Indian: That, paleface, is what I'm doing now. Why go to so much trouble to gain what I already have? (Hepner, 1941)

Developmental factors. The achievement motive is not limited to economic considerations. In the United States, even the preschool child is carefully prepared for success in formal education. Soon he or she becomes concerned with grades and prizes in school and later with promotions and possessions. From interviews with parents and children, it appears that much of this motivation is related to parental expectation (Moss & Kagan, 1961). Too much pressure, however, or too much *perceived* pressure may result in low achievement motivation (Rosen, 1962; Strodtbeck, 1958).

A most important factor in the development of achievement motivation concerns the amount of independence training the child receives. Children who are permitted to explore and find out things for themselves, especially at the early ages, and who are encouraged to use their abilities constructively and on their own are most likely to be high in achievement motivation in later years. Other influential factors are the occupational levels of the parents and the child's birth order. The first-born child generally spends his or her earliest months with relatively less peer interaction than later siblings and with greater opportunities for instruction and encouragement by adults. In many studies, but not all, the first-born child has been found to have a higher need for achievement than his or her brothers and sisters (Breland, 1973; Schooler, 1972).

The *achievement motive* is said to be present when a person's reaction to his or her own activity is not concerned solely with the outcome—success or failure. Instead, the individual is concerned with some sort of standard set by that individual, so that he or she is pleased by competence and disappointed with incompetence (Heckhausen, 1967; Kagan & Moss, 1962). In other words, there is a desire for attaining some degree of excellence.

The concern with a standard requires a certain level of mental development, which occurs at age three to three-and-one-half years in normal children. Studies of mentally retarded adults add confirmation. Signs of achievement motivation have been observed first among these older people at a mental age of approximately 36 months (Heckhausen & Wasner, in Heckhausen, 1967).

Measurement and theory. One of the most popular methods for measuring achievement motivation has been the use of *projective techniques*, in which ambiguous pictures are presented to the subject, who tells what might be happening in the picture and what the persons in the pictures might be thinking. The subject's story is then analyzed for responses involving achievement imagery. In one investigation, each subject saw a card showing a young man standing near a building. The italicized words in the following response by one subject suggest achievement motivation:

The boy is a college student. He is trying to recall a pertinent fact. He did not study this particular point enough for an examination he has to take. He is trying to recall that point. He can almost get it but not quite. It's almost on the tip of his tongue. Either he will recall it or he won't. If he recalls it, he will write it down. *If he doesn't, he will be mad.*

The boy is a thinker. . . . He has faith in his capabilities and *wants to get started on the job he has lined up, dreaming of advancements.*

The boy is *thinking about a career as a doctor. He sees himself as a great surgeon performing an operation.* (McClelland et al., 1953)

Studies in many parts of the world have indicated some value in this method. When the results for more than two dozen nations were analyzed, a positive relationship was found between the amount of achievement imagery in children's stories and folktales and the subsequent economic development of the countries involved. The sample included not only free-enterprise Western countries but also communist countries and relatively primitive societies just commencing contact with modern technological society (McClelland, 1961).

One theory of achievement motivation, not yet substantiated, concerns the heredity-environment issue. It suggests that the *desire* to achieve success is a relatively stable, inborn motivation not significantly amenable to change. However, the effort to achieve, which provides evidence for this motivation, is alterable; it is influenced by the incentives and expectancy of success in a given environment (Atkinson, 1964; Atkinson & Raynor, 1974).

Early evidence for this view came from studies of Pueblo Indians in Arizona and New Mexico, especially the Hopi. Naturalistic observations suggested a minimum of overt rivalry, a low incidence of aggressiveness, and comparatively little competition for prestige in this culture (Dennis, 1940b). However, in controlled situations, in which the subject's response was not visible to other members of the group, the achievement motive was elicited. In some respects, the Hopi children were more competitive than non-Indian subjects of comparable age living in Virginia (Dennis, 1955b). Overt competition was not encouraged among the Hopi, but it would be erroneous to conclude that the achievement motive was absent. What we can say is that the *expression* of this motive may vary from culture to culture.

Motivation to avoid success. With different social conditions, however, the achievement motive will be expressed differently. This condition has been evident for years in the United States and other countries. High achievement often has been synonymous with masculinity while it seemed incompatible with femininity. As a result, some women have learned to underplay their abilities, especially in the company of men, and to downgrade their career goals. It is hypothesized that there existed instead a *motivation to avoid success* and that the primary goal of many women has been affiliation (Stein & Bailey, 1973).

This view was stimulated initially in a study of college men and women concerning probable success in medical school. Fear of failure was prevalent in both sexes, but fear of success was regarded differently. Less than 10 percent of the men reacted in a manner that suggested that they might feel alienated from others by achieving a top rank in the class or by having a position of authority over others. Among the women, however, 65 percent displayed this concern. Such success would represent failure in the traditional female role (Horner, 1969, 1970).

The incentives for women are changing, however, and so are the findings, some of which have indicated no reliable differences. New methods of research have been suggested, which may resolve the ambiguities (Zuckerman & Wheeler, 1975). In any case, in the United States and other countries today there is an increasing tendency for women to aspire towards achievement for themselves, not just for their male offspring (Figure 13-6).

Figure 13-6 Changing Sex Roles. *In June of 1974 the first two women enrolled for training as Massachusetts State Police troopers. (The Boston Globe)*

Development of Individual Motives

Some motives, instead of being shared within a culture, are more or less specific to certain individuals. They are variations from cultural norms, sometimes mild and sometimes pronounced. We speak of these as *individual motives*.

How do these acquired motives, individual and cultural, develop? It is virtually impossible to trace their origins in anyone's life circumstances and, therefore, we must be satisfied to examine experimental analogues and speculate whether any or all the learning processes discussed earlier may be involved.

Role of Learning and Cognition

In this context, we encounter concepts from motivation, conditioning, and the cognitive processes, as well as some from Freudian psychology. Learning, motivation, perception, and cognition are sometimes referred to as the *basic psychological processes*, meaning that they are the building blocks of behavior. From a psychological standpoint, they are the components from which human behavior emerges. Let us consider some examples of the ways in which they interact in the development of individual motives.

Conditioning processes. Some individuals are motivated to sexual behavior in connection with a particular object. When this attachment is so strong that the presence of the object is essential for sexual gratification, we speak of a *fetish*. Shoes, gloves, beads, and underwear are commonly involved in fetishes, and it is believed that the attachment is acquired through learning experiences in the early years. One woman owned more than one hundred pairs of shoes, one of which she always had to wear during coitus. In subsequent analysis it appeared that this behavior stemmed from her childhood years, when she wore her mother's shoes around the house. Whenever she squatted and moved her body, the backs of the shoes

rubbed against erogenous zones, providing a pleasurable sensation. With repetitions of this and similar acts, an exceptionally strong sexual attachment to shoes was formed (Simon & Freudel, 1970).

Clinical reports may not be accurate because they depend on childhood memories; hence, a similar reaction was studied in the laboratory. Male subjects observed a pair of women's boots, not present but shown on a slide, and physiological measures indicated no sexual arousal. Then conditioning trials commenced, with the image of the boots followed every time by slides of attractive, naked females. After 30 to 65 trials, all three subjects, tested separately, showed sexual arousal to the sight of the boots alone (Rachman, 1966). This "fetish" perhaps is different from a naturally acquired one, however. How strong it is and how long it will last is open to question.

Because of the importance of learning, certain modes of sexual satisfaction, whether they are common or infrequent in the general population, may become significant for an individual. ■ One young man reported that the odor of fish has been especially stimulating for him since his first satisfying sexual encounter, involving the odorous wife of a fishmonger (Greenwald & Greenwald, 1972). While some such reports may be legendary, it is certainly true that the sight of old shoes, the sound of a marching band, the smell of dead fish, or even the taste of a certain mouthwash can be sexually motivating for some people.

Functional autonomy. According to some psychologists, any learned behavior can acquire the status of a motive. That is, a habit can become independent of its origins and eventually be motivating in itself. This principle is known as *functional autonomy*, since the habit functions apart from its original motives (Allport, 1937). Examples are cited in the case of vocational habits that persist

■ *On one of my first days at college, a friend and I became lost. Instead of taking the path that goes between the dorms, we were on the path that goes by the observatory. On our way we passed some bushes and heard someone say, "Hey, come here a minute."*

"Who are you?" Patty asked.

"A friend," came the response, as we, rather slowly, caught on and began to run.

We heard him call, "Wait!" and saw him climb on his bike and start to follow us.

After running about one hundred yards, we were tired and our bare feet hurt, and he had caught up with us. At this point we didn't see any difference between running and walking, so we began to walk to keep a better eye on him.

We kept walking and each time he passed us he asked if we would like to see him "whack-off," as he masturbated happily(?).

Why did this young man act in this way?

after retirement, such as the retired fisherman who goes to the pier each day to observe the boats and work there if possible, even without pay. Other examples are suggested in the persistence of personal habits in circumstances in which they are no longer appropriate, such as extreme frugality in someone who once was poverty stricken but is now wealthy.

But down at the pier, a person sometimes meets interesting people, which may involve the affiliation motive. The formerly poor boy who now has an adequate income may wish to acquire greater wealth than his neighbors, a behavior that pertains to the achievement motive. Hence, certain psychologists regard the concept of functional autonomy with skepticism, stating that the behavior in question is simply sustained by different reinforcements.

Cognitive factors. The wide variety of individual motives in human beings also arises through our most significant endowment over the other species—the capacity to think. We can imagine, understand, and interpret the world in a way that apparently is not possible for other organisms.

Cognitive processes, especially thinking about what is possible and impossible, can influence the achievement motivation a great deal, as shown in studies of level of aspiration. The goal that an individual sets as his or her expectation of accomplishment is known as the *level of aspiration.* Laboratory studies show that this level remains close to our actual performance and that motivation is highest when we decide that the task is just at or slightly above our previous performance. Our motivation decreases when we think of the task as far above or far below what we normally can accomplish (Lewin, 1936; Atkinson, 1965).

The self-concept. The key factor, therefore, in a realistic level of aspiration is one's *self-concept,* which is the way a person thinks about himself or herself in a global sense. The self-concept includes the most important feelings and attitudes that one has about oneself. In our culture, achievement is one of the most common ways of attempting to enhance the self-concept, but persons also strive to think well of themselves by being charitable, social, creative, beautiful, or just different from others. ∎

One of the clearest examples of the importance of the self-concept in motivation and performance occurred unexpectedly in industrial psychology. A series of investigations was carried out at a factory known as the Hawthorne Works of the Western Electric Company, and the earliest findings showed that higher pay and shorter hours induced workers to increase their output of assembled electrical relays. In order to study other factors influencing work output, still further changes were introduced, such as improved lighting, better ventilation, rest pauses, and refreshment periods. Many of these had beneficial effects. In other words, when an environmental change was introduced, production usually improved. Eventually, the investigators began to wonder what was happening, and so they restored the original conditions, even turning down the lighting gradually, so the workers did not notice it. However, output continued to improve. Finally, the conclusion forced on the investigators was that the workers were motivated to increase production not so much by the specific environmental improvements as by their increased feelings of importance. They had been selected for an investigation and the company apparently was interested in them *as individuals,* rather than as cogs in an industrial machine (Roethlisberger & Dickson, 1939).

Since that time, in the late 1930s, this experiment has been an object lesson to subsequent investigators. The

∎ *We all walked into the bathroom to watch. He sat down on the window sill, loosened his belt, unbuttoned his shirt, and after this ceremony was over, began to drink. Someone filled a cup of water and gave it to him, during which another cup of water would be filled and waiting for him. It was all planned so that he would be drinking continuously. "Twenty glasses at eight ounces a glass—four quarts—five quarts. Impossible, he'll never do it. No . . . he's getting there."*

Sam quietly sat, drank, and enjoyed his attention. He was over halfway through and seeming to feel all right. He had sat down on the toilet hoping his body could act like a pump, letting liquid out at the same rate he was taking it in. At the fourteenth or fifteenth glass, as he continued without signs of weakening, the people who made a bet with him began to worry about the security of their money. "Let's go, Sammy, that's not fast enough. There, you spilled some. That's not fair," they shouted to protect their investment. Every extra breath he took seemed to bother them. He knew this and stalled even more because of it.

Soon he began to shake without control and repeat, "I can't do it. I can't do it." He had to continue. His whole reputation depended on it. He was now shaking more and more and drinking slower and slower. We began to worry that he would hurt himself, but we knew he wouldn't stop. He finally reached for his last glass and just as he took it into his hands he spilled some of it. As a gesture of his perfection, he offered it to be refilled and drank it down in one long gulp.

He got up and could hardly walk. He couldn't straighten up, but walked back to his room by himself, muttering about the exam he had the next day.

Figure 13-7 Motivation and Group Dynamics. *In one factory, 8 women worked unhappily together, painting objects that they said came by too fast on the assembly line. Morale was low, absenteeism was high, and personnel turnover was a problem. After discussions with the foreman, the women were allowed to adjust the speed of the delivery belt themselves, which pleased them. Satisfaction and success at work increased greatly, and within 3 weeks they were performing at 30 percent to 50 percent above the level expected under the original arrangement, in which management controlled the speed.*

However, this condition caused dissatisfaction in other parts of the factory; the women were too happy with their work and earning too many bonuses in comparison with others. Consequently, the superintendent revoked their self-pacing and extra pay. The special treatment, while successsful in the smaller context, created a problem in the context of the factory as a whole. (Photo, not taken in connection with this research, by Hurn from Magnum)

■ *A young man has taken up game hunting as a very avid pastime. He is a trophy hunter, and it should be noted that he only hunts the male of a species. He also has the habit of cleaning his guns every day without fail whether he has used them or not. In the process he always takes one and aims it at a picture of his father to check the sight of the gun.*

The man did not acquire his deep interest in hunting until shortly after his father became seriously ill and was hospitalized. His father was expected to die but recovered from the illness. It seems that the trophy hunter is not consciously aware of any hostile attitudes towards his father.

term *Hawthorne effect* now refers to any improvement in motivation and performance that occurs essentially because the people involved are receiving special attention. Successful teachers, coaches, and businessmen often show considerable respect for the Hawthorne effect, providing the members of their groups with as much support and sense of importance as possible (Figure 13-7).

The protagonist in Henley's poem *Invictus* apparently has a strong self-concept; at the same time he sums up the importance of cognition in motivation when he says:

I am the master of my fate;
I am the captain of my soul.

Whether or not it is true that one is master of one's fate, the belief itself is motivating, and thereby it has an important influence on the individual's conduct.

Unconscious Processes

Earlier in this century Sigmund Freud decided that we are not masters of our fate, at least not to the extent that we would like to believe. Lurking within each of us are desires and urges of which we are unaware, called *unconscious motivation*, which can propel us in inexplicable ways. In particular, we

tend to be unaware of long-standing forbidden wishes concerning sex and aggression. ■

The sequence. Having considered basic psychoanalytic theory previously, it is sufficient here to outline the sequence by which we allegedly become subject to unconscious urges. According to Freud's description, three steps or stages are involved.

First, the individual encounters some stressful situation. Often, there is a conflict in which there appears to be no apparent solution. Because the individual cannot deal with the problem directly, the second step involves repression. In this process, threatening thoughts are unconsciously excluded from awareness. In the third step, the unconscious material, denied direct expression, reappears in disguised or symbolic form. In other words, our earlier, repressed conflicts are expressed in dream images, neurotic behavior, and "Freudian slips." A so-called *Freudian slip* today is any mistake in speech, writing, or other action that presumably reveals an unconscious motive. But not all slips of the tongue involve unconscious thoughts or feelings. ■

Examples from daily life. A man or woman contemplating a diet asks the physician for "a good seducing plan." A radio announcer introduces a singer as a "charming young sinner." These misspoken words perhaps reveal unconscious feelings. Freud himself used the term *parapraxis* to refer to any such apparently revealing error (Figure 13-8).

Freud regarded bungled actions in much the same way. One of his colleagues reported:

I entered a house and offered my right hand to my hostess. In a most curious way I contrived in doing so to undo the bow that held her loose morning-gown together. I was conscious of no dishonourable intention; yet I carried out this clumsy movement with the dexterity of a conjurer.*

Concerning forgetting, Freud reported that among his patients to be visited in a given day, he was most likely to forget those who had not yet paid their bills. To contend with this problem, he adopted the procedure of writing special notes to himself (Freud, 1914). □

Unconscious motives are not necessarily confined to relatively small behaviors, however. Presumably they can also influence our personality, choice of a career, marriage partner, avocation, or other significant events.

Examples from posthypnotic suggestion. In addition to the uncontrolled observations from daily life, psychologists have sought to study unconscious motivation through controlled methods—that is, by manipulating the subject's awareness of a particular experience. One of the most widely used methods is hypnosis.

* Reprinted from *The Psychopathology of Everyday Life* by Sigmund Freud. Translated from the German by Alan Tyson. Edited by James Strachey. By permission of W. W. Norton & Company, Inc., and Ernest Benn Limited. Translation copyright © 1960 by Alan Tyson. Editorial matter copyright © 1965, 1960 by James Strachey.

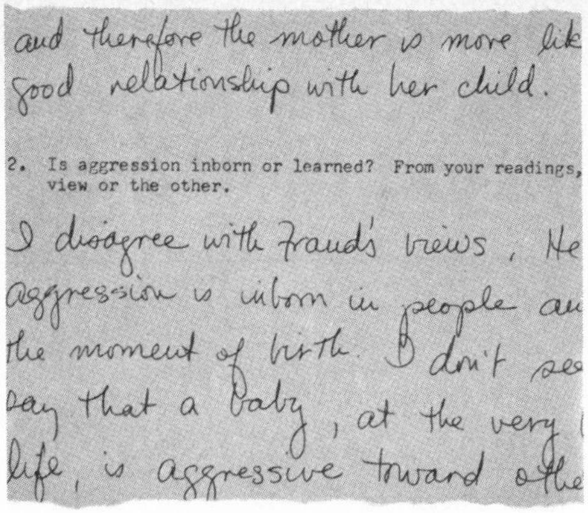
and therefore the mother is more lik
good relationship with her child.

2. Is aggression inborn or learned? From your readings,
view or the other.

I disagree with Fraud's views. He
aggression is inborn in people an
the moment of birth. I don't se
say that a baby, at the very
life, is aggressive toward othe

Figure 13-8 Slip of the Pen. *In Freudian psychology spelling errors sometimes are regarded as expressing underlying feelings, as suggested in this student's answer to an examination question.*

In the usual procedure, subjects are hypnotized and told that when they wake up they will remember nothing of what happened. They are also told that after waking they will perform a certain act in response to a signal from the hypnotist or following some specific event. This arrangement concerning the signal is referred to as a *posthypnotic suggestion.* After they have awakened, the subjects feel a compulsion to carry out the suggested act at the signal but do not know why they want to do so. An example from a psychology class illustrates this procedure:

After the subject (S) had been hypnotized and tests had demonstrated that she was in a deep trance, the hypnotist (H) said, "After I have counted to ten, you will wake up. You will return to your seat and be wide awake. When I scratch my head during the course of the lecture, you will get up from your seat and go to my office, where you will find a laboratory coat hanging behind the door. You will bring the coat here, into the classroom, and put it on me. I may not want to put it on, but you must get it on me." H then awakened S from the trance. She opened her eyes, looked a little embarrassed, and returned to her seat. When asked, she said that she remembered nothing that had happened from the time she felt her eyes getting tired until she woke up. H continued with the lecture and, several minutes later, scratched his head. The subject sat still but looked a little uneasy. However,

■ *I hadn't ever met Brian before but I spent the entire day with him—going to two hockey games, a Christmas party for a bunch of little kids, then dinner, a movie, and dancing. It was really a full day, and Brian seemed like a nice guy so everything went pretty well. At one point that night, though, we were outside walking and I was getting really cold and tired and so when he said that because it was so nice out he could walk over to the Prudential and back, I quickly retorted and just as quickly regretted saying, "Well, why don't you?" I guess it was the type of thing that I'd been feeling inside all day and had finally slipped out; I then tried to cover it up but found I couldn't and so I just listened to it echo for the rest of the night.*

□ *When extricating myself from a painfully prolonged relationship at 3:30 A.M. last Sunday morning, I was very careful not to leave any of my possessions behind in the guy's dormitory suite. I spent at least 15 minutes making sure I had remembered to take everything, as I had decided that my leaving would be the end of the relationship. Upon my arrival back at school I found I had forgotten not one but several things, including two very valuable rings, a toothbrush, and toothpaste. Perhaps subconsciously I wanted. . .*

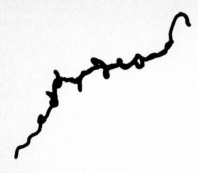

Figure 13-9 Underlying Conflict. *Under the influence of posthypnotic suggestion, Freddy, a college student who was engaged to be married, was induced to write on a piece of paper. Later, when the posthypnotic suggestion had been removed, he became extremely embarrassed and disclosed that the scrawl said "Freddy-Jean." Further analysis indicated that he was strongly attracted to this girl, Jean, but was reluctant to terminate his present engagement to another woman for fear of distressing her and his parents. (From Harriman, 1942. Copyright © 1942 by The William Alanson White Psychiatric Foundation, Inc. Reprinted by permission of the William Alanson White Psychiatric Foundation from* Psychiatry 5 *(1942):181.)*

the lecture continued. A minute or so later, S, with a great deal of hesitation, left the room. Shortly she returned with the laboratory coat. She said to H, "You had better put this on." H said that he didn't need it. S insisted, saying. "It is rather cold in here and this will keep you warm." H insisted that he did not need it, that the room wasn't cold enough to put it on. S now became very insistent. She tried to get H's arm in the sleeve, insisting that chalk might get on his clothes if he didn't put on his coat. After a few minutes, S began to plead with H to put on the coat. He finally did, and S then seemed greatly relieved and returned to her seat.

When asked why she had done what she did, S said that she did not know. She said that the idea had occurred to her when the instructor scratched his head, but, realizing how silly it was, she had decided not to do it. Finally, she could not resist. S said she knew she would feel better if she followed the impulse. The reasons she gave for wanting to perform the act constitute examples of rationalization, which is an unconsciously motivated means of finding reasons to justify one's own behavior.

In other studies, unconscious processes have been suggested in casual conversation, ambivalent feelings, artificial complexes, and rationalization, as well as slips of the tongue. Studies with writing have been used for this same purpose (Figure 13-9).

Components of Emotional Motivation

In the previous discussions we noted the interplay among various psychological processes, especially between learning and motivation. Learning clearly influences the goals for which we strive, and motivation, in turn, also influences

learning. As we now turn to look more closely at the latter influence, we encounter the topic of emotion.

Affective Reactions

Both motivation and emotion refer to complex conditions and both are derived from the Latin verb *movere,* which means "to excite," "to agitate," "to stir up," or "to move." When someone is stirred up or moved, that person is in an emotional state. When one stirs oneself up or moves oneself, we think of that person as motivated. Emotion refers primarily but not exclusively to the feeling state, while motivation refers chiefly to the goal-directed activity, which may involve gaining or dispelling a feeling state. To the extent that goal-directed activity is prompted by feelings, as opposed to cognitive processes and routine habits, we may speak of emotional motivation.

Emotional motivation and learning. In an experiment with lower animals, rats were exposed to a black compartment and a white compartment and showed no evidence of fear. Since the inner state cannot be observed directly, it was measured in behavioral terms, by noting the incidence of running back and forth rapidly, urinating, defecating, trembling, and crouching. Later, the rats received electric shocks in the white compartment and several of these signs were displayed. After a series of such shocks followed by escape responses to the black compartment, the animals showed fear reactions in response to the white compartment alone, even when no electric shocks were administered.

The question then to be answered was: Given this emotional state, what would the rat do about it? A wheel was made available in the white compartment which, if turned, would allow the animal to go into the black compartment, and all the animals, without receiving any shocks, learned to operate the wheel in this manner. The conclusion was that the animals' motivation to reduce fear prompted the new learning (Miller, 1948a). This paradigm illustrates the development of a learned *abient* or *aversive drive.*

We can describe the same process at the human level, this time illustrating an *adient* or *appetitive drive*—the seeking of human attention. The infant's need for food is satisfied when it receives milk, but the mother is continually associated with this satisfaction and gradually becomes a cherished object herself, as do other persons who are associated with the feeding. This process is basically classical conditioning. An operant component is added when the baby seeks the mother's warmth, stimulation, and other events and develops various responses in order to attain them. The reader perhaps will recognize this learning as based in two-factor conditioning. The feeling aspect is developed through classical conditioning, and the overt response towards one goal or another develops on the basis of the operant model.

Common affective states. To the emotionally aroused individual, the most obvious aspect of emotion is his or her feeling—the person has ''butterflies in his stomach'' or perhaps ''her heart in her mouth.'' One feels excited, happy, angry, or anxious. These *feelings* are just one aspect of emotion, however, and thus they are referred to as the *affective reaction.* The other aspects, to be considered later, include physiological reactions and behavioral reactions.

Certain feelings stand out in daily life, one of which unfortunately is anxiety. In fact, anxiety perhaps has been the most thoroughly studied of all human feelings. While *fear* generally is focused on some specific situation, as illustrated in the previous experiment with rats, the term *anxiety* refers to a diffuse emotional state. An individual feels a threat but cannot specify its source. In brief, anxiety seems to be precipitated by some feeling of being unable to deal with an impending situation. It can be transient or enduring.

Another common feeling is *anger,* which often seems to be precipitated by the thwarting of drive satisfaction. In instances of extreme anger, a person seems to ''leave his senses'' and may commit aggression against someone else. Here there is some temporary loss of cerebral control, which may be produced by changes in blood chemistry or it may have some other basis. A temporary shutting off or reduction of the blood supply to certain areas of the cortex might be responsible for the tendency of many old people to become unreasonably belligerent at times (Scott, 1958).

The most primitive basis of *affection* is doubtless the pleasure associated with stimulation of the erogenous zones and, especially in early maturity, the sexual factor plays a most important role in affection. But affection among adults also has a foundation in the exchanges of reinforcement that they provide for one another. More than a century ago the English philosopher-psychologist James Mill emphasized this learned aspect of family affection, although prevailing sentiment at the time pointed to the influence of biological factors. Mill pointed out that strong family ties are least likely to be found in extreme poverty, where the family cannot provide for many of the members' needs, and in very great wealth, where the family members can readily find affection and other satisfactions outside the home.

Many other affective states might be noted, such as joy, excitement, and apprehension, but we do not know a great deal about them. The subjective nature of feelings has been a major obstacle to scientific investigation since the days of Wilhelm Wundt. The anxious individual repeats the same phrases over and over again; the angry person may become speechless; and the lover says there are no words to express one's feelings.

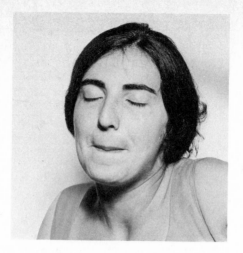
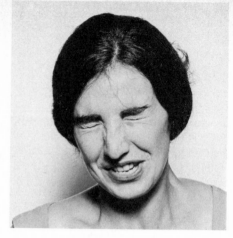

Figure 13-10 Emotion and Facial Expression. *You may be successful in judging the pleasant/unpleasant dimension in each case, but it is difficult to specify the feeling more exactly. The circumstance that prompted each reaction is indicated on page 340. (John T. Urban photos)*

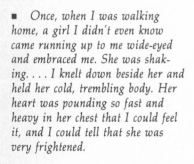

■ *Once, when I was walking home, a girl I didn't even know came running up to me wide-eyed and embraced me. She was shaking. . . . I knelt down beside her and held her cold, trembling body. Her heart was pounding so fast and heavy in her chest that I could feel it, and I could tell that she was very frightened.*

Judgment of others' feelings. Historically, the first approach to understanding another person's affect was simply to ask the person to describe what he or she felt. These *self-descriptions* were usually brief, however, and they varied widely from one individual to another. One reason is that under stress we often show a narrowing of attention (Bruner et al., 1955). The chief result, as has been found in more recent investigations, is that the pleasant/unpleasant dimension of our feelings receives the major emphasis (Izard & Nunnally, 1965).

Another approach to studying affective states is to examine the person's *facial expressions,* rather than verbal reports. We note a smile, frown, or some other reaction and try to identify the feeling with which it is connected. But when the beauty queen bursts into tears upon being selected, we realize that this method is limited also. Facial expression alone gives us little idea of what another person is feeling, apart from pleasantness or unpleasantness (Figure 13-10).

Still another approach in judging another person's affect is to consider the *circumstances,* rather than the individual's response. Here environmental cues are used, and they have been found to be more helpful than facial expression alone in telling us how the person feels.

It is because of the setting that we decide that a person is surprised, revolted, or afraid (Figure 13-11).

In daily life, the observer does not look at one set of cues or another. Clearly, there are complex interactions among the face and context ratings, and the observer attempts to integrate both sets of data into one interpretation. This viewpoint is commonly accepted and now represents the basic approach in modern research on judgments of the affective state (Ekman et al., 1971; Watson, 1972).

Physiological Bases

Earlier it was pointed out that emotion also includes physiological and behavioral reactions. In broad terms, *emotion* is defined as a complex feeling-state accompanied by glandular and muscular activities. These physiological or glandular activities have been described in connection with the widespread excitatory and inhibitory reactions that occur with the activation of the sympathetic branch of the autonomic nervous system. In an emergency, the individual's heart pounds, the palms become damp, the flow of blood to the intestine is restricted, adrenalin is secreted, and so forth. ■ Hence, a question of much interest in the context of emotion is whether the various affective states can be distinguished solely on the basis of these changes.

Motivation and Emotional Behavior

Identifying emotions physiologically.
In one study of this research question, human adults were made either fearful or angry, depending on how the experimenter introduced the idea of using electric shock in the investigation. Then the activities of the heart, muscles, skin, and breathing apparatus were studied in these subjects. When combinations of these physiological factors were analyzed, a total of 14 different measurements were available. In subsequent analyses, it was found that half of these measurements showed no significant differences between the two states—fear and anger. When the complete patterns were analyzed, the difference was more noticeable but still not highly significant (Ax, 1953).

In another investigation, people were exposed to various types of stress, and continuous records were made of heart activity and blood pressure. While attempting to solve mental problems, they were criticized, given defective equipment, and even received mild electric shocks. After the session, each subject reported his or her experience according to one of four categories: anxiety, anger directed inward, anger directed outward—towards the experimenter, or a reaction lacking in intense feeling. When these reports and the physiological records were compared, it was found that physiological responses of low intensity and the secretion of noradrenalin occurred in anger directed outward and in the few instances of no intense feeling. Physiological responses of high intensity occurred with anxiety and anger directed inward. The subjects reporting these feelings appeared to respond as if they were in an emergency, while the others did not react physiologically in an emergency manner (Funkenstein et al., 1957).

The overall results, nevertheless, are not convincing, especially in the absence of successful blind analyses. In a convincing demonstration, emotional feelings must be *predicted* on the basis of physiological responses alone, without knowledge of the type of stimulation.

The evidence for different physiological patterns for the different emotions is "disappointingly slight," despite the use of sophisticated equipment (Strongman, 1973). So far, there has been "little success" in finding such patterns (Cofer, 1972).

Psychosomatic reactions. One explanation for the lack of success in finding different patterns for different emotions is that the exact physiological changes vary sharply from one person to another. One individual may respond to a fearful situation primarily with increased heart activity, while another experiences the most pronounced changes in breathing and stomach functions. There is some evidence for this view in the study of *psychosomatic reactions,* in which disorders of the body (soma) arise through psychological causes. Somatic disorders attributed *partly* to emotional factors include asthma, sinus problems, high blood pressure, adverse skin conditions, and even the common cold.

Figure 13-11 Emotion and Context. *The woman is a subject in an experiment concerned with eliminating fear of rats. She was reluctant to touch the animal, even with her gloved hand, yet her facial expression alone does not suggest fear. If the lower portion of the photograph is removed, as below, an observer is not likely to decide that the woman is afraid of something (Mullare & Fernald, 1971). (Sheila A. Farr photo)*

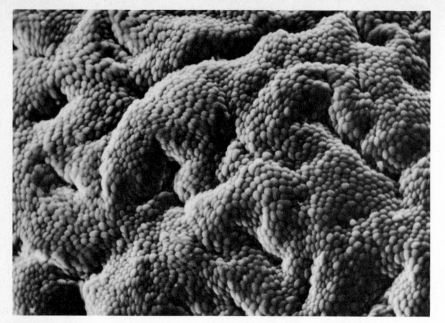

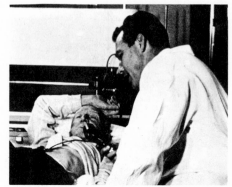

SERENITY STRESS SERENITY

Figure 13-12 Emotion and the Stomach. *The photo above shows the inner lining of the stomach, including the gastric pits, enlarged 500 diameters. Anxiety can produce overactivity in the stomach, resulting in hemorrhaging and perforation, as the stomach tries to digest itself, which produces ulcers (Davenport, 1972).*

In one case, an opening was made in a man's stomach, required by accidental injury, and the contents became accessible to direct observation. The tracing shows that changes in stomach activity occurred when the subject was under the stress. (Wolf & Wolff, 1943) His stomach became red and turgid, the production of acid sharply increased, and the beginnings of a peptic ulcer developed. (Left photo courtesy of Dr. Jeanne Riddle, Wayne State University; right photo by Sturgis Grant Productions, Inc., courtesy of Smith, Kline and French Laboratories and Cornell University.)

Gastric ulcers are widely assumed to be due partly to prolonged stress (Figure 13-12).

The reasons for an individual developing one disorder rather than another are far from completely understood, but it is clear that people show *different* physiological responses during stress. Some people experience sharp cardiovascular changes while others undergo severe muscle tensions. If the stress is prolonged, heart problems appear most likely in the first instance, and backaches and headaches, produced by sustained contraction of the neck and scalp muscles, seem a likely outcome in the second instance (Lacey, 1967; Bakal, 1975).

Practice of meditation. A practice that *may* help to prevent physiological reactions during stress includes various forms of meditation, especially as developed in Eastern cultures. Here again we encounter emotional motivation, for one of the aims of meditation is to achieve relaxation, tranquility, or calmness of mind. This condition is commonly sought by concentrating on a single object, thought, or sound for an extended period. In one method, called transcendental meditation, the alleged result is that the meditator eventually can expand his or her awareness, develop greater creativity, and make greater use of personal abilities (Figure 13-13).

It is extremely difficult to measure awareness and creativity, but the physiological conditions accompanying transcendental meditation often can be measured. Decreased heart rate, respiration, and blood lactate concentration have been observed to accompany the state of transcendental meditation, but the evidence for slow alpha brain waves, observed when an individual is resting, is mixed. An increase from the frontal area of the cortex is reported, but the patterns vary considerably with different subjects (Wallace, 1970; Wallace & Benson, 1972). Altogether, it is not yet clear that meditation has a specific therapeutic outcome, apart from the benefits that might be obtained from the expectation of improvement or from resting on a regular basis (Smith, 1975).

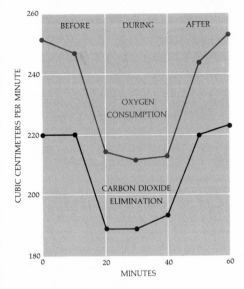

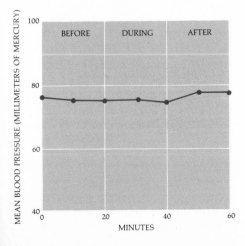

Behavioral Aspects

When we turn to behavior, the third major component of emotion, the evidence is directly available. In fact, studies of the origin of emotion within the individual have been made essentially on this basis.

When newborns are observed in the first hours of life, initially they are either calm or show *general excitement*. There are no other emotional expressions; the others develop gradually. In one instance, infants were studied for several months, and at age 3 months two basic behavior patterns were identified as developing from general excitement—*distress* and *delight*. Within the next three months, the expressions of distress became differentiated; thus, *anger, disgust,* and *fear* were inferred. At about age 12 months, delight also was differentiated, adding *elation* and *affection* to the child's repertoire (Figure 13-14).

Of course, the problem of interpretation exists throughout this study. Observers do not necessarily agree on how various emotional behaviors should be labeled, as we saw earlier. Especially with infants, it is difficult to avoid "reading into" the behavior more than may be actually present.

Origins of emotional expression. As the infant develops, crying, laughing, and smiling appear, even when there has been no opportunity to learn these expressions. Furthermore, they appear at about the same age in all children, almost regardless of the stimulation provided by adults. Hence, they seem due primarily to heredity. As in the case of instinct, however, certain environmental

Figure 13-14 Emotional Development in Infancy. *The graph represents one view of the early development of emotional expressions. (Adapted from Bridges, 1930)*

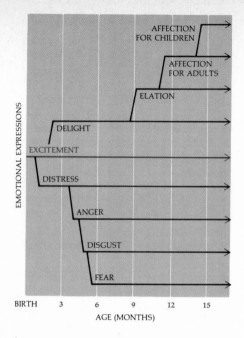

The expressions in Figure 13-10 occurred in response to: (A) the unexpected arrival of a close friend not seen for several weeks, (B) a sharp reprimand for not behaving in accordance with instructions, and (C) the sudden awareness that a raw egg has been dropped in her hand. Some answers given by people judging these photographs were: (A) receiving a compliment; seeing something she liked; (B) being stuck by a pin; feeling something dropped down her back; (C) receiving an electric shock; touching a frog.

circumstances may be necessary to evoke them.

Further evidence for the inborn nature of simple emotional expressions comes from observations of individuals born blind and deaf, who have little if any opportunity to acquire emotional behavior by imitating other people. They cannot hear the sound of laughter or observe how it is produced, and they cannot see people clench their fists in rage. The only way such expressions can be known to them is through touch, but even when deaf-blind people receive no such tactile training, they exhibit certain emotional reactions like those of normal people.

One instance involves a ten-year-old girl who was blind and deaf from birth and had not learned to speak. A small toy was unexpectedly dropped down her dress. Immediately her mouth opened, her eyes bulged, her eyebrows rose, and her neck and shoulder muscles became tense, showing the usual *startle pattern*. Later, after she was successful in removing the toy, she raised her arms, apparently in delight, laughed loudly, and then smiled (Goodenough, 1932).

These emotional expressions are relatively simple and brief, and upon them are superimposed many learned emotional reactions. The role of imitation in other responses is evident when we consider the expressions that characterize a particular culture. Scratching the ears and cheeks has been a sign of happiness among certain Chinese, but it may be a sign of indecision among Caucasian Americans. In turn, clapping generally is a sign of happiness or approval in the United States, but for Chinese people it shows worry or disappointment (Klineberg, 1938).

Other emotional behaviors differ from one person to another within the same culture, and these differences arise on the basis of individual learning experiences. One child may have temper tantrums when frustrated, another may learn to withdraw, and still another may become aggressive physically and verbally, depending on the reaction of other people to this behavior. Similarly, an anxious person may learn to cope with his or her feelings by excessive eating, drinking, or talking, again depending on how people in the environment respond to these behaviors.

We may conclude that the behavioral aspects of emotions have some heredity component and are significantly influenced by culture. Furthermore, they may vary from one individual to another within the same culture (Fantino, 1973). In this sense, the origins of emotion within each person can be considered on much the same basis as sexual and maternal motivation. There are inborn factors, but cultural influences account for a wide variety of expressions.

Arousal level. When we consider emotional behavior from the viewpoint of arousal level, again we see its motivational significance. An individual may perform well because he or she is sufficiently aroused, up to a point, but further arousal may become disruptive. If arousal is extremely high, the person may "go to pieces," reacting as if he or

Motivation and Emotional Behavior

she had lost cerebral control over his or her behavior (Figure 13-15). Some animals are paralyzed by sudden, threatening stimuli, but this reaction also has survival value. Many predatory animals, such as the frog, have generally poor vision but are quick to detect the slightest movement.

It has been suggested that the optimal level of arousal for human performance depends on the complexity of the task involved. Thus, in American football, a tackle on a line plunge should be more highly aroused than a place-kicker on a difficult field-goal try. This idea is called the *Yerkes-Dodson law,* which states that high arousal is appropriate for best performance on a relatively simple task. Lower arousal is more facilitating when the task is complex. The idea is an interesting one and it seems reasonable, but it has not yet been convincingly supported.

Conceptions of Emotion

Emotion is a complex state, so much so that some psychologists have advocated abandonment of the term, for much the same reasons that the concept of instinct fell into disuse (Fantino, 1973). The term is employed too often to explain too much with too little precision.

Classical Viewpoints

What is needed is a theory of emotion that would integrate our knowledge of the diverse components and guide and stimulate research. Some theories have been suggested, with varying degrees of success.

James-Lange theory. The first modern attempt to develop a theory of emotion was made by William James, just before the beginning of this century. James was not alone in working on this problem, however. At the same time, a Danish scientist, Carl Lange, developed almost the same viewpoint, and so their work is known as the James-Lange theory.

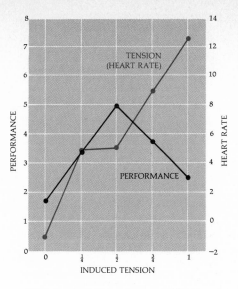

Figure 13-15 Tension and Performance. *On an intelligence test, performance improved up to a point as tension increased, but with still further tension it dropped almost to the initial level. (After Wood & Hokanson, 1965. Copyright 1965 by the American Psychological Association. Reprinted by permission.)*

James hypothesized, contrary to what one would expect, that the behavior and physiological reactions in emotion occur first, arousing the feelings. "We feel sorry because we cry, angry because we strike, afraid because we tremble . . ." and not the other way around (James, 1890). In other words, feelings are a consequence of the other reactions.

James argued for this view largely on the basis of everyday situations. Suppose someone is standing in the path of an oncoming car and quickly steps to the curb. The subjective state, called fear, is experienced after the individual has retreated to the curb and after the onset of such physiological responses as rapid heartbeat, trembling, and increased rate of breathing. When the results of our emotional behavior and physiology, such as jumping away and perspiring, reach the cerebral cortex, then we experience the feeling aspect of emotion. The earlier activities lead to the subjective state. ∎

Several objections to this viewpoint have been raised. It is said that feelings sometimes continue even after the bodily response has disappeared. It is emphasized that certain physiological changes do not take place immediately, yet our feelings appear rapidly. It is also

■ *Last summer my girlfriend and I were in an accident that completely totaled her car. The car skidded, we went over the banking and into the woods. The car was smoking and we had to get out fast. When I tried the door, it was jammed. I crawled out the window and climbed up the banking. It wasn't until we were safely on the other side of the street that I felt myself shaking and got really scared. The escape occurred first, followed by the emotion—I got out of the car, then I got scared.*

emphasized, as pointed out earlier, that little success has been met in establishing different physiological patterns for the various emotions. Thus, how can they give rise to the different feelings? James and Lange attempted to answer these criticisms but without much success. Nevertheless, their theory has served as a springboard for almost all modern theories of emotion and has stimulated much research (Strongman, 1973).

Cannon-Bard theory. One of those who took issue with the James-Lange theory was Walter Cannon, whose viewpoint was later extended by Philip Bard, producing the Cannon-Bard theory. It emphasized the role of the thalamus in emotional activity and therefore is sometimes called the thalamic theory. This brain area, just above the hypothalamus, plays a key role in activating the muscles and glands in emotion-arousing situations, in relaying impulses to the brain, and in stimulating the cerebral cortex, all of which results in much of the emotional experience. The thalamus therefore was said to activate the feelings in emotion; only when it is involved, according to the theory, do we experience emotion (Cannon, 1929).

This theory was helpful in showing the importance of the lower brain centers, not considered in James's approach, but the neuroanatomy of emotion is far more complicated than the Cannon-Bard theory suggests. Many other interrelated physiological structures and systems are involved, including the cerebral cortex.

Arousal and Cognition

James and Lange focused on bodily reactions, behavioral and physiological, but they ignored the role of the human brain. Had they placed greater stress on the aroused person's interpretation of the situation, their early views would have been quite close to a modern viewpoint, called the cognitive-physiological theory.

Cognitive-physiological theory. The cognitive-physiological theory is most readily illustrated in an experiment in which college students were injected with epinephrin, an adrenal hormone that induces an aroused state. The subjects were then divided into three groups. Some, called the informed group, were correctly informed that they would experience trembling hands, a pounding heart, and a flushed face. Others, called the uninformed group, were told that they received a vitamin compound and were led to expect no immediate effect. The members of the third group, called the misinformed group, were led to expect symptoms that would not appear, such as numbness and itching.

The subjects in each group then were exposed to one of two circumstances. In the euphoric or happy condition they were placed in a waiting room with an accomplice of the experimenter who acted in an extremely jovial manner as he too, supposedly, awaited his turn to participate as a subject in the experiment. He flew paper airplanes, pretended to be playing basketball, made jokes, and generally behaved in a happy fashion. In the anger condition, the subjects were placed individually with a person who acted in a very irritated manner, complaining harshly as he completed an insulting questionnaire. He made counterinsults and derisive comments and finally tore up the questionnaire and stomped from the room. All subjects in both circumstances were observed through a one-way mirror and later were questioned about their feelings (Figure 13-16).

It was correctly predicted that the misinformed and uninformed subjects would be most susceptible to the mood in the environment. Having no explanation for their bodily state, which was readily apparent to them, these subjects reported their emotional condition in accordance with the happy or angry circumstances. In other words, they

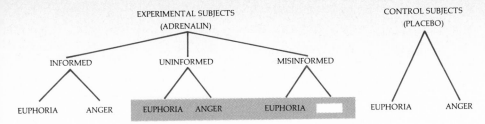

EXPERIMENTAL SUBJECTS (ADRENALIN)

INFORMED
EUPHORIA   ANGER

UNINFORMED
EUPHORIA   ANGER

MISINFORMED
EUPHORIA

CONTROL SUBJECTS (PLACEBO)
EUPHORIA   ANGER

Figure 13-16   Study of Cognition and Emotional State. *The control subjects were injected with a saline solution that had no effect. Because of research limitations, no anger condition was included with the misinformed subjects. The subjects who were aroused and did not know why are indicated in the shaded area.*

defined their feelings in terms of what was going on around them (Schachter & Singer, 1962).

According to this evidence, external circumstances determine what kind of feelings we experience, while physiological changes apparently determine how strong they seem to be. This approach is called the *cognitive-physiological theory* of emotion because the experience is said to be the joint product of the individual's understanding, or cognition, and his or her physiological arousal (Schachter, 1971).

This study has been of considerable significance in bringing attention to the role of cognition in determining emotional states. ■ Cognition can be influential in inducing, sustaining, and dispelling an emotional condition, although typically it is not considered a component of emotion. Its absence in extreme emotional states is indicated in familiar terms such as: "Sorry! I got excited and just lost my head," and "I was so upset I couldn't think."

There are also limitations in this study, and to date it has not been repeated with the same results. It seems that our emotional state is a function of cognition and emotional arousal, but it is not necessarily true that all emotional states are the same physiologically and differ *only* in cognitive factors (Plutchik & Ax, 1967). We need to know more about the underlying emotional arousal in such studies (Harris & Katkin, 1975). We also do not know in what ways the cognitive factors are influential, since the experimental subjects were never asked to give their interpretations of the situation. We only know that they were exposed to different stimulating conditions.

Emotion as an integrated response. In summary, emotion is an *integrated response,* involving the whole organism, although the components are necessarily considered separately in discussions. In the following report, a college woman tells us in detail how she interpreted or perceived a trivial incident. Her experience shows the integration of the various components of emotion:

If I leave the library now and walk past Morrill, then diagonally across the quad on that dirt path, I should see him coming this way from Goldwin Smith—middle door, probably—Oh no, here comes a girl I know—don't talk to me, please, or I won't be able to concentrate on that door—Oh well—"Just fine, how are you?" "Yes, I really have to study for that too—Yeah, see you." That was bad—hope I didn't miss him—Better cross the quad now—Oh, oh—was that him coming this way on the next path? He usually wears a white or light blue shirt, but this one was beige—I won't look, it'll be too obvious—I can't let him find out I'm looking for him—He's behind me now, facing the other way—he can't see me if I turn and look—slowly, slowly—Oh, God, he's looking right at me! He's waving! (God, this is funny!) He knows everything I've been thinking! I'm turning all red—I've got to laugh, I can't keep it inside me any longer—I wonder what I looked like when I saw him looking at me? I can't stand still—I think I'll run all the way to French. (Bishop et al., 1963)

Whether she was correct or incorrect, this woman's interpretation of the situation illustrates that cognition can induce or sustain emotional processes. She said to herself, "He knows everything I've been thinking!" A person can imagine a certain event, remember past

■ This little incident took place a few weeks ago as a friend and I were studying at the student center. Our moods were that of typical female students resigned to an evening with the books.

Then, lo and behold, who should appear but a certain gentleman in whom my friend had been exhibiting quite an interest recently. There ensued quite a spirited conversation, as both my friend and the gentleman commented on the pleasantness of life in general; to listen to them you'd think you were hearing of Utopia. It was almost enough to make you sick.

Enter frustration, in the person of another undergrad, who as it turned out, was the young gentleman's date and up till now had been busy in the restroom. Introductions and farewells were quickly exchanged, and the pair soon left. I returned to my book, as did my friend (or so I thought).

The silence was quickly broken by intermittent groans, sighs, and other nondescript sounds coming from my friend's general direction. Finally, perceptive as I am, I realized that something was probably wrong with her, so I inquired as to what it could be. This set off quite a prolonged series of complaints, laments, and pessimistic observations on studies, weather, and the generally bleak atmosphere of the university. The change in her general emotional state was so amazing that I wondered if it were actually the same person sitting there in front of me.

Acquired Motivation and Emotion

events, and anticipate future events, all of which can influence one's emotional state.

Upon being discovered, the woman reported, "I'm turning all red." Changes in blood circulation had produced blushing, which is a physiological component. Then she said, "I can't keep it inside me any longer," referring to the tension, anxiety, and other aroused feelings. She exclaimed, "I think I'll run all the way to French," reflecting an inability to stand still, which is the behavioral component.

Had someone seen her running to the French class, that person might have wondered why she was doing so. She was emotionally motivated. Apparently she was trying to escape an anxiety-producing event, the basis for which may have been only in her imagination in the first place.

Summary

Culture and Motivation

1. Acquired motivation develops during the individual's lifetime and is influenced by cultural factors. The need for affiliation is so nearly universal in all cultures that it may be based in inborn factors, but the extended period of helplessness in human infancy also could lead to the desire to be with other people. In adulthood, this desire for affiliation is most manifest when people become anxious, at which time they prefer to be with others who are in the same anxiety-provoking situation. Thus, it may be a vestige of childhood fears of abandonment. It is also prompted by social comparison, through which an individual obtains guidance for present and future behavior.

2. Human beings possess biological foundations of the sex drive and unlearned sexual reflexes, but culture plays a most important role in the development of various sexual motivations, including forms of nonprocreative sexual activities. Cultural motives are also ap-

parent in maternal motivation, especially in different methods of weaning throughout the world and in a comparison of traditional Western mothers and mothers of kibbutz children.

3. Aggression, once thought to be universal, apparently depends on both training and unsatisfied physiological needs. Whether it is regarded as inborn or acquired in human beings depends partly on the way it is defined and on the behaviors that are emphasized. Whatever its origin, the important issue in aggression is to discover the ways in which the environment influences whatever aggressive predispositions exist in human beings.

4. Parental expectations and early independence training appear to be important factors in the expression of the achievement motive. One theory of achievement motivation suggests that the desire to achieve success is relatively stable and inborn, but the effort towards achievement is alterable, influenced by incentives and the expectancy of success. Among some women, high achievement and femininity may be viewed as incompatible, prompting a motivation to avoid success.

Development of Individual Motives

5. While cultural motives are determined by common social forces, a person's unique experiences within a given society give rise to individual motives. The conditioning processes appear influential in this regard. Also, it is speculated that a habit itself can be motivating, apart from its origin, in which case it is said to be functionally autonomous. Among the cognitive factors, a person's self-concept is most important; it influences not only the kind and level of goals that a person sets for himself or herself, but also the ways in which he or she goes about achieving them.

6. Behavior may be motivated by cognitive factors of which the person is unaware. The evidence for unconscious

motivation is derived from slips of the tongue, bungled actions, and forgetting, as well as more global behavior. It is postulated that unconscious motivation is most likely to occur with regard to culturally restricted behaviors, such as sex and aggression.

Components of Emotional Motivation

7. For the individual, the most obvious aspect of emotion is his or her feeling. The individual is stirred up or moved; this affective reaction can have motivational significance in the sense that it is an activating or energizing experience. Commonly described affective states include anxiety, anger, and affection, but it is difficult to judge another person's feelings without environmental cues.

8. The physiological components of emotion include widespread excitatory and inhibitory reactions, which occur through arousal of the sympathetic nervous system, but there has been little success in differentiating emotional feeling-states on the basis of physiological conditions alone. Chronic emotional states of high tension can result in psychosomatic disorders, such as ulcers, asthma, and adverse skin conditions, in which the reaction may be due partly to psychological factors.

9. Within the first year of life a variety of emotional expressions suggests that several different emotional states have developed. Some of these behaviors, such as crying, laughing, and smiling, appear even without learning opportunities, which indicates that they are due primarily to heredity. This possibility is supported by observations of blind-deaf children. Other aspects of emotional expression are clearly learned, as is evident in comparisons of the expressions for joy, happiness, disappointment, and other feelings in different cultures.

Conceptions of Emotion

10. Theories of emotion have been only partially successful in integrating the basic components. The oldest theory of emotion in psychology, the James-Lange theory, indicates that subjective states are the result of bodily responses and behavior. The Cannon-Bard theory emphasizes the role of lower brain centers, especially the thalamus, in emotional arousal.

11. The more modern cognitive-physiological theory indicates that a person interprets a general state of arousal in terms of the situational factors that are present. Physiological changes determine the strength of the feelings, and our interpretation of environmental factors determines what kind of feelings we experience. Regardless of which viewpoints are most productive, it is clear that emotion is an integrated reaction, involving a coordination of feelings, physiology, and behavior—prompted, supplemented, or sustained by cognitive input.

Suggested Readings

Brecher, R. & Brecher, E. *An analysis of human sexual response*. New York: American Library, 1966. A readable paperback that describes significant research on sex, including the Masters and Johnson laboratory studies and Kinsey reports.

Cofer, C. N. *Motivation and emotion*. Glenview, Ill.: Scott, Foresman, 1972. A brief paperback that discusses the basic concepts of motivation and emotion.

London, H. & Nisbett, R. E. (Eds.). *Thought and feeling: Cognitive alteration of feeling states*. Chicago: Aldine, 1974. Diverse papers by well-known persons in the field.

Steers, R. M. & Porter, L. W. *Motivation and work behavior*. New York: McGraw-Hill, 1975. A text that assumes some knowledge of organizational behavior.

Trowill, J. A. *Motivation and emotion*. St. Louis: C. V. Mosby, 1976. Presents in detail topics discussed in this and the previous chapter.

PART SIX

Individual Differences

Chapter 14

Tests and Measurement

Testing in one form or another is now a large enterprise in the United States. Each year more than two hundred million standardized tests are administered in the schools, while others are used in business, industry, government, clinics and colleges. But the use of tests has been criticized often, partly on the ground that when the results are used for admissions purposes they constitute a barrier to equal opportunity for employment and schooling, discriminating unfairly against certain individuals or groups. Hence, in some areas of the country, legislation has been proposed to prevent their use.

The Testing Movement

If tests are eliminated, what would be the result? None of us would experience test-taking anxiety, and no one would be denied admission to any institution on the basis of test scores. ■ On the other hand, we might find that the truck driver was color blind, that the dentist had poor finger dexterity, and that the city accountant was inept with numbers. In short, the need for the assessment of individual differences would not disappear. School administrators, teachers, coaches, business persons, government officials, and countless others would still have to decide, from among many applicants, which ones should be selected to fill which positions.

Alternatives to Testing

Instead of testing, one might employ letters of reference, a practice widely used in business and education. However, this method also may constitute a barrier to some persons, depending on the prejudices of the letter-writer, and it may not even provide accurate information. In one study of skilled workers, letters of reference proved to be of little value. The descriptions in the letters showed only a low relationship to the individual's performance on the job, as indicated in ratings by the supervisor (Mosel & Goheen, 1958).

Another alternative might be to use the interview, and the merits of this method also have been investigated. In one instance, all the research for 15 years on the value of the selection interview was examined. The overall finding was that as the interview becomes more structured in format and more limited in purpose, its value as a selection device increases (Ulrich & Trumbo, 1965). But as the interview becomes more structured and specific, it comes closer and closer to being a formal test, which is what the opponents of testing are trying to avoid.

These alternatives are no more immune to bias than are the formal tests. According to the Equal Opportunity Employment Commission, any alternative to testing must be assessed by the same general procedures outlined for evaluating psychological tests, and the results must be expressed in quantitative form (Schmidt & Hunter, 1974).

The letter of reference and the interview are similar in certain ways to psychological tests, but behind almost any well-developed test lies the cooperation of a large number of people who have been assessed only for purposes of evaluating the test. Their participation is designed to determine the validity of the test, as we shall see later, and to make it appropriate for use with certain groups

of people. A good psychological test incorporates the contributions of hundreds or thousands of people who have served as research subjects, as well as the efforts of the test designers (American Psychological Association, 1970).

Testing is not a perfect procedure, but it probably should be understood in the same way that Winston Churchill described democracy: "It is the worst form of government there is—except for all the others."

Government and testing have something else in common. In complex societies, some form of government and some form of testing seem absolutely essential. The more accurately individual differences can be assessed, the more closely intricate needs of the individual and society can be met.

Group and Individual Tests

In this chapter, we look first at the various classifications of tests, then at how they are constructed, and finally at how they might be improved. One way to classify tests is on the basis of whether they are administered to groups or to individuals.

Group tests. The reader undoubtedly is familiar with *group tests,* which can be administered to hundreds of people at the same time and are constructed so that the administration and scoring can be accomplished by persons without extensive training. The enormous advantage in group tests lies in this efficiency. They are also called *pencil-and-paper tests* because the answers usually are indicated by writing or making pencil marks on a printed form.

The need for group testing became especially evident during the world wars, when millions of persons were assessed for military service and related work. Eventually, two group intelligence tests were developed, known as the Army Alpha and Army Beta, and the value of these tests as a screening device became so apparent that similar tests appeared for school use. The Lorge-Thorndike Intelligence Tests are

■ *In my country every examination requires a review of several years of work. Questions that ask for a four-paged answer within a period of 20 minutes plague the students and tension is high. Two years ago I remembered that I finished answering all the questions with some time left for checking during a math examination that covered five years' work. While checking, I discovered that I drew a wrong graph. The thought that I had only five minutes left sent a chill into the marrow of my bones.*

My heart sank. It began to beat violently against my ribs. I started breathing heavily; blood came surging into my face; I began to perspire. My limb muscles were tensed and I had a great desire to urinate. Only with great effort was I able to control the trembling of my hands and continue with the exam.

Vocabulary — Choose the word that has the same meaning or most nearly the same meaning as the word in dark type at the beginning of the line.

benevolent   A lordly B stingy C kindly D poor E evil

A B C D E

Figure Analogies — The first two drawings go together in a certain way. Find the drawing at the right that goes with the third drawing in the same way that the second goes with the first.

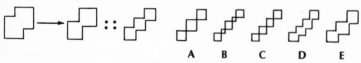

A   B   C   D   E

A B C D E

Figure 14-1 A Group Test.
These items are not part of the Lorge-Thorndike Intelligence Test, but they indicate its general nature. (Courtesy of Irving Lorge, Robert Thorndike, and Houghton Mifflin Company)

relatively modern versions of these earlier tests and are available for use with students from kindergarten through high school (Figure 14-1).

Most group tests have two significant limitations, however. The first concerns the test items. A *test item* is some stimulus situation that is designed to elicit a certain measurable response. In a group test, the items usually are written questions, which can be read and answered by examinees without individual attention from the test administrator. Hence, the content of the test items is largely *verbal*, meaning that a heavy emphasis is placed on the use of words. In some cases, however, one's mental ability is not adequately reflected in his or her use of words.

In the second place, the examiner in a group test cannot be sure that each subject has understood the instructions properly, is trying to do his or her best, or is in a fit condition to be taking the test. The problem was readily illustrated in one instance in which a boy with a very high intelligence obtained a low score on a group test. Later, it was found that the teacher had emphasized the importance of blackening carefully the space between the lines indicating the correct answers. This child was especially conscientious, marking the spaces with minute care. As a result, he completed relatively few items.

A simple rule can be set forth for the interpretation of results on group tests.

High scores probably represent a high level of ability. It is unlikely that the test results show a greater capacity than the person actually possesses. Low scores must be considered with more skepticism. For various reasons, a person may perform far below his or her capacity.

Individual tests. Individual tests are less familiar than group tests because they are time-consuming and expensive to administer. Here the examiner generally must be highly trained and administers the test to only one person at a time, watching carefully as the subject responds. The subject, in turn, answers by speaking to the examiner or by performing some other overt act; only rarely does he or she respond in writing. The advantages of individual tests relate to the drawbacks of group tests: a wide variety of test items can be used and the examiner can observe the subject closely, asking for additional information whenever necessary.

In individual testing, the examiner notes the efficiency of the subject's responses, the conviction with which he or she responds, and the methods by which he or she arrives at a conclusion. The examiner observes *behavior*, not just a pencil mark in column C of a computer-coded answer sheet. Thus, it may be discovered that the subject is correct but without confidence, brashly incorrect, or correct for the wrong reasons. This information is helpful to the examiner in understanding how the individual uses his or her abilities.

Individual Differences

Individual tests include many *nonverbal* or *performance* items, in which actions, rather than words, are required. The subject must manipulate puzzles, blocks, pictures, and other objects. These procedures permit the testing of persons who are deficient in language, and they allow further observations of the individual's behavior.

The administration of an individual test is an exacting task. The examiner must adhere strictly to the directions in order to allow comparison of the individual's performance with that of others who have taken the same test under the same conditions. To understand the qualitative nature of the person's thinking, however, the examiner also must be able to discover why the person answered in a certain way. Thus, additional questions might be asked that are not part of the standard procedure, probing further into the subject's perception of the task and style of thinking. To the extent that the examiner uses the test to *understand* the subject, apart from arriving at a test score, the individual test provides more information than a group test. A greater investment is required but the potential return is also far greater.

Categories of Tests

New tests appear so rapidly that some publication is needed merely to catalogue those currently available. One such compendium is the *Mental Measurements Yearbook,* now in its seventh edition (Buros, 1972). Descriptions of tests appear in several categories, including intelligence, achievement, aptitude, interest, and personality.

Intelligence tests. Intelligence tests are intended to measure the individual's ability to reason, think, and understand. Just as there are many definitions of intelligence, there are many types of intelligence tests, and they vary considerably in content and quality.

The oldest and one of the most respected intelligence tests is the *Stanford-Binet Intelligence Scale,* which is an individual test that includes many performance and verbal items. The first American form appeared in 1916, and since then there have been several revisions. It has been translated into many languages and adapted for use throughout the world.

Another widely used individual intelligence test is the Wechsler, which includes two widely used forms— the *Wechsler Adult Intelligence Scale* (WAIS) and the *Wechsler Intelligence Scale for Children* (WISC). Each of these tests includes several subtests for measuring different intellectual functions, such as memory, comprehension, and problem solving. They provide measures of mental ability for both verbal and nonverbal behavior, and they too have been translated into many languages (Figure 14-2).

Figure 14-2   Adaptation of a Test. *Changes in format were made when an American picture arrangement test was used in a different culture. A Japanese child should be familiar with this sequence. (Adapted from the Wechsler Intelligence Scale for Children, Revised. Copyright © 1971, 1974 by the Psychological Corporation, New York, N.Y. All rights reserved. Photo by Becky Young.)*

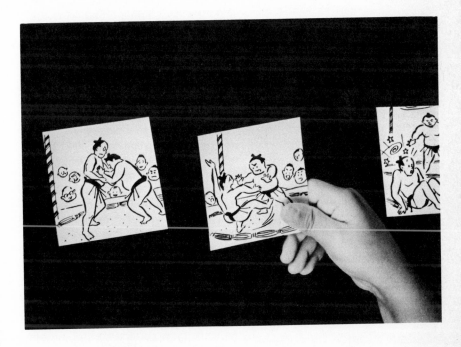

Figure 14-3   A Test of Clerical Aptitude. *On the dotted line, after each name in a long list, the examinee indicates the number of the drawer in which the records should be filed. Speed is an important aspect in this test.* (Reproduced by permission. Copyright © 1944 by The Psychological Corporation, New York, N.Y. All rights reserved.)

Kuczma, H. G. ....
Davidson, C. H. ....

Achievement tests. All students are aware of the use of achievement tests for assessing school progress. These tests are sometimes prepared by teachers and used on a local basis, and other times they are prepared for national use, as achievement tests for college admissions, civil service employment, and licensing and certification in many professional fields.

Certain methods must be used in test construction, especially when a test is intended for use on a broad basis. Data must be collected that permit the comparison of scores among a large number of subjects, and the value of the test as a measuring instrument must be carefully assessed. These issues, which concern all tests, are considered in detail later in this chapter.

Aptitude tests. The capacity to learn is known as *aptitude;* it refers to probable accomplishment at some future date, following training. A test of clerical aptitude is used to predict how well an unskilled person will perform clerical skills after being trained. Achievement, on the other hand, refers to the individual's current level of accomplishment. It is used to discover how well the person performs at the present moment. But this distinction between aptitude and achievement is not always maintained, for sometimes performance on an aptitude test improves after training, which suggests that elements of achievement are involved in the test.

Aptitude tests are used chiefly for guidance and selection in school and industry. Since workers in occupations involving mechanical and clerical skills comprise two of the largest groups in the United States labor force, tests of these aptitudes are common (Figure 14-3). Other common aptitude tests measure artistic and musical ability, but here the vocational opportunities are extremely limited. Unless persons demonstrate unusually high potential for success in these fields, they are usually encouraged to consider them as avocations instead of careers.

Interest tests. Other tests concerned with vocational choice are *interest inventories.* They are known as inventories or checklists because the individual is not tested in a formal sense. There are no correct or incorrect answers and, therefore, a person cannot do "well" or "poorly." The individual simply indicates his or her preferences or vocational interests in response to a series of questions.

One well-known interest inventory is the Strong-Campbell Interest Inventory, in which a person indicates "like," "indifferent," or "dislike" for a wide range of occupations, amusements, school subjects, and other undertakings. The pattern of the subject's responses is then related to six general occupational themes and to 124 different occupational scales. The results do not indicate that the subject should enter a particular field, however. They merely show the extent to which the person's scores are

Individual Differences

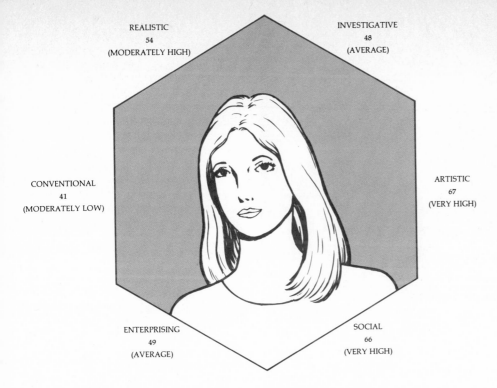

REALISTIC
54
(MODERATELY HIGH)

INVESTIGATIVE
48
(AVERAGE)

CONVENTIONAL
41
(MODERATELY LOW)

ARTISTIC
67
(VERY HIGH)

ENTERPRISING
49
(AVERAGE)

SOCIAL
66
(VERY HIGH)

Figure 14-4 An Interest Test.
On the Strong-Campbell Interest Inventory the "realistic" theme suggests a practical, robust outlook with an interest in dealing with things, often outdoors, rather than with ideas and people. The "investigative" theme centers on scientific activities; persons scoring high in this area are often more task-oriented than person-oriented. Occupations associated with the "artistic" theme are those in music, art, and literature; persons scoring high in this area generally have greater interest in self-expression than in dealing with highly structured problems. Sociable, responsible, and humanistic are the adjectives generally associated with the "social" theme, and the related work often involves arranging or changing interpersonal behaviors. The "enterprising" theme involves an interest in using words and other forms of persuasion, as in selling, other business work, and administrative positions. The "conventional" theme reflects an interest in working within a well-structured environment without necessarily seeking a leadership position, as in bookkeeping, banking, and other aspects of business. The scores shown represent the profile of a female college student (Campbell, 1974).

similar to those of people in certain occupations who have completed this same inventory. In vocational counseling, interest test results are used only in the context of a great deal of other information about the individual (Figure 14-4).

Personality tests. The term *personality* implies a broad description of an individual. It generally refers to the characteristic integration of an individual's behavior, interests, attitudes, abilities, and other qualities. Hence, most of the tests mentioned previously involve some selected aspect of personality; conversely, personality tests, like the concept itself, tend to be diverse and broad in scope.

These tests range from multiple-choice questions to inkblots, and they focus on both readily observable characteristics and the so-called depth factors in personality. Literally hundreds of such devices are currently available, and they are best discussed in the context of personality theory.

Preparation of a Test

For anyone to maintain a well-informed position in the current controversy over testing, a knowledge of how tests are made is essential. The test functions in accordance with its construction, like most other objects. The *basic* procedures in test construction are the same for all types of tests and, therefore, one illustration will serve our purposes here. The problem we have selected is that of creating a test for selecting spacecraft pilots. The development of tests for selecting flying personnel is a continuous project (Miller, 1974).

Development of Test Items

The first step in preparing a test, after one has decided on the goals and general purposes, is to make a careful search in the relevant literature and currently existing tests for suitable test items. Invariably, there are some items already available that can be used in the first draft of any new test. To achieve the greatest efficiency and highest chance

Figure 14-5 Measurement of Physiological Responses. *In a study of stress and heart functions, these firemen wear a portable recorder of heart activities at all times during their 12-hour shift. (Rick Stafford photo)*

of success, modern test construction begins with what has already been accomplished.

Task analysis.   When more items are needed, the test constructor uses a practical approach, as illustrated by military psychologists during World War II. At that time, test items were needed for selecting successful pilots, navigators, and other flying personnel, but few tests then were available. The psychologists, therefore, went aboard the aircraft and observed successful flying personnel in their roles. Then they converted the acquired information into test items. Some psychologists even went through the pilot training program themselves, paying particular attention to the kinds of abilities they were called on to use.

These psychologists performed a *job* or *task analysis,* gathering data on the requirements of the job without any preconceived idea or theory about flying ability. They made a detailed study of the psychological processes and physical skills required in performing the task in question. Then test items were prepared to reflect these processes and skills.

In addition to the use of existing tests and task analyses, test items can also be developed on the basis of theory. The test constructor prepares items based on his or her own ideas about the characteristic in question. Tests of personality and intelligence, in which the construct is broad and difficult to define, are often approached on this basis, as illustrated in the use of inkblots to assess the so-called depth factors in personality and motivation. The procedure for item selection and construction in any test can be partly empirical and partly rational.

An item pool.   The requirements for space pilot seem to involve several characteristics, including general intelligence, mechanical aptitude, and emotional stability. Hence, it is necessary to find or prepare a large *pool of items* concerning these traits. A large supply is needed for two reasons—many of the items will prove to be relatively worthless and must be discarded, and best results will be achieved when a *test battery* is developed, in which many test items are combined into several subtests or clusters of items. A test battery, with several subtests providing measures of intelligence, aptitude, and emotional stability, is more likely to be successful than a test with just a few items or one that measures just one trait. Each subtest, with its special assets and limitations, pertains to the general purpose of the test, but each makes its own unique contribution to the full score.

The items for a test battery can be constructed using software and hardware. *Software* means that the materials are disposable and nonmechanical in nature, such as pencils and paper. *Hardware* usually implies that complex and expensive apparatus is involved, such as electronic timers, rulers, and counters. Hardware is often used in modern methods of measuring emotional responses (Figure 14-5).

64	16	48	12	36	9	A. $2\frac{1}{4}$
						B. $6\frac{3}{4}$
						C. $9\frac{1}{4}$
						D. 27
						E. 81

Figure 14-6 Test Items for General Intelligence. *Picture arrangement (above): Arrange the pictures in a meaningful sequence. (Drawing by Alain; © 1943, 1971 The New Yorker Magazine, Inc.)*

Number series (left): The numbers at the left are in a certain order. Find the number in the column at the right that should come next. (Courtesy of Irving Lorge, Robert Thorndike, and Houghton Mifflin Company)

For purposes of illustration in our spaceflight test battery, suppose that six test items are available for use. There are two items for testing intelligence. One is nonverbal and concerns *reasoning;* the other concerns *number* ability (Figure 14-6).

There are also two items for the sub-test on mechanical aptitude. Both of these concern the ability to discover the underlying principles of mechanical operations (Figure 14-7).

The items for measuring emotional stability are found by looking back into the history of testing. Fortunately, there are two tests of this nature that were

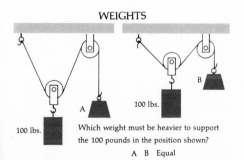

WEIGHTS

100 lbs.   Which weight must be heavier to support the 100 pounds in the position shown?

A   B   Equal

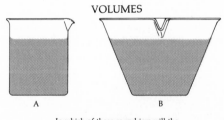

VOLUMES

In which of these round jars will the liquid press harder on the bottom?

A   B   Equal

Figure 14-7 Test Items: Mechanical Comprehension. *(Reproduced by permission. Copyright © 1941 by The Psychological Corporation, New York, N.Y. All rights reserved.)*

Figure 14-8 Test Items: Emotional Stability. *In the pistol-shot test, the gun was suddenly fired and the candidate's responses were measured. A cold-cloth test, in which a wet cloth was thrown into the candidate's face, was also used for the same purpose. (The Bettmann Archive)*

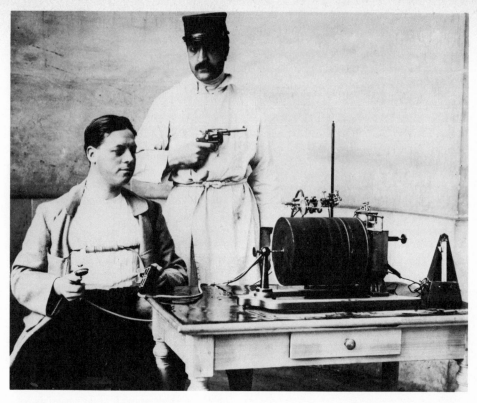

used in the selection of pilots during World War I. They involve some hardware and are a bit old but perhaps worth a try (Figure 14-8).

Thus, the first draft of the full test contains these six items, organized into three subtests. In actual fact, there would be hundreds of items, but these suffice for moving to the next step. We are now ready to test the adequacy of these materials. The aim here is to discover the quality of the tentatively prepared items by trying them on a group of subjects and then to improve the items by making whatever changes are necessary.

The Field-Test Procedure

Usually a small group of subjects is selected for this first trial, and then the test is administered, scored, and interpreted according to the established procedures. Since this *field test* or *field trial* primarily serves the examiners' interests,

the sample of subjects is often selected for convenience and willingness to co-operate. But representativeness must be considered too. If the sample is not reasonably close to the target population in the characteristic being measured, much of the value of the field test is lost.

Test administration. The test administration carefully follows specified procedures, and there are detailed guidelines for recording and scoring each response. Then the results are analyzed and evaluated. Occasionally the subjects may have reactions to the sequence of items, the contents, or the way in which the items are presented, which makes them less valuable or less agreeable for use. In most field trials, however, the answers are not reviewed with the subjects (Figure 14-9).

General intelligence (Figure 14-6)
1. Picture arrangement: D, F, C, A, E, B
2. Numbers: D

Mechanical comprehension (Figure 14-7)
3. Weights: B
4. Volumes: equal

Emotional stability (Figure 14-8)
5. Pistol shot: little/no startle pattern
6. Cold cloth: little/no startle pattern

Figure 14-9   Scoring the SPACE Battery.   *These are the correct answers for this test. When the subject has a chance of simply guessing the correct alternative, as in the items on mechanical comprehension, a correction for guessing is made.*

The second phase of the field trial, after the test administration, involves identification and correction of the defective test items. Also, changes may be made in the way the test is administered. Invariably, many alterations are required.

Revisions of the test.   The testing procedures must be changed whenever it is obvious that many of the subjects misunderstood the directions. Field-test subjects are sometimes asked to make special comments in this regard. Revisions in the test items or in the scoring are made largely on the basis of statistical analyses (Figure 14-10).

Statistical procedures used for detecting unsatisfactory items are called *item analysis.* They are used to identify those items that are not serving the purposes of the test as a whole. Basically, item analysis involves a study of how often an item is answered incorrectly and which subjects are unsuccessful. If no one in the group is successful or if everyone is successful, then the item has no value for the purpose of identifying individual differences. The candidates undoubtedly are different in various ways, but from this particular test item we learn nothing about which ones may be superior or inferior in which aspects of flying ability. All subjects have performed alike; for detecting differences in ability, the test item is effectively useless.

An item has much greater value when the difficulty level is in the vicinity of 50 percent, meaning that about half the subjects answer correctly and, furthermore, when that 50 percent of the subjects who answer correctly are the very candidates with the greatest aptitude for flying spacecraft. The ideal selection item elicits one type of response from those with much flying ability and a different response from those with little flying ability. In other words, it has high power for discriminating among potentially good and poor flyers.

Suppose that one of the items on mechanical comprehension was answered correctly by about half the subjects. Is it a valuable item for selecting persons for pilot training? Not necessarily. For each item, those answering correctly and those answering incorrectly must be compared on some external criterion, such as past successes in similar training programs (Fossum, 1973). If the candidates with the most success are the ones who answered correctly, and those with the least success answered incorrectly, then we would feel that the item discriminated successfully.

Often, no external criteria are available. Perhaps there has been no previous space program, or it was distinctly different in nature. Then the examiner's only recourse in evaluating the worth of a test item is to use the total test score as the criterion of flying ability. The premise here is that the test as a whole, even in the first draft, is a better measure of individual differences for flying aptitude than any one of its items considered alone. Thus, the subjects are considered to be high or low in flying ability according to their total scores on the test. Any item that is answered correctly by those in the high group and

Figure 14-10   Assigning Partial Credit.   *In the picture arrangement item (Figure 14-6), a subject might arrange the pictures as follows: F, C, A, E, B, D. Thus, picture D is incorrectly placed at the end of the sequence instead of the beginning. Some subjects explain that the man's dinner has been stolen and now he wants to leave the restaurant before losing anything else. Hence, they describe him as taking his hat and coat off the hook rather than placing them there before eating. This line of reasoning greatly lessens the joke and makes a less concise story, but it is not clearly contradicted by evidence in the drawing. Hence, this sequence might receive partial credit, or a change could be made in the test materials. (Drawing by Alain; © 1943, 1971 The New Yorker Magazine, Inc.)*

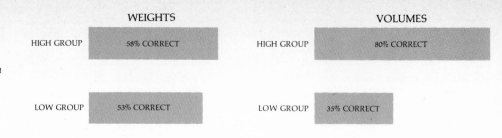

Figure 14-11 Analyzing Test Items. *In the items for mechanical comprehension, both questions were answered correctly by about half the subjects altogether, but the question on volumes proved more discriminating. People who are high in mechanical comprehension tend to answer it correctly, while those who are low generally respond incorrectly. (Reproduced by permission. Copyright © 1941 by The Psychological Corporation, New York, N.Y. All rights reserved.)*

incorrectly by those in the low group is considered an effective item (Figure 14-11).

When the testing procedures have been changed, as necessary, and the items have been revised on the basis of item analysis, a final version of the test is prepared. Actually, the test is never in final form; it can alway be revised and improved, but eventually a point is reached at which it must be evaluated and used.

Evaluation of the Test

In evaluating the test, we identify a new sample of subjects and collect a whole new set of data. The subjects used in the field-test procedure cannot be used again, for they were the people employed for refining and selecting the items in the first place. To use them again, in evaluating these same items, perhaps would give us an overestimate of the value of the test.

Assessment of Reliability

Even the simplest tests can have significant defects. A tape measure can sag or deviate in some way from a straight course, thereby giving an incorrect result. The wooden ruler must be repositioned over and over in measuring long distances, increasing the potential error each time. The metal ruler expands in hot weather and contracts in cold, giving slightly different results at different temperatures. An important characteristic of any test is its consistency of measurement, which is known as *reliability*.

There are various kinds of reliability, but in general the term refers to the degree of agreement between scores each time the test is used. Provided the characteristic being measured does not change, the result should be the same in each instance.

Inter-judge reliability. Suppose we are selecting people for further training in graphic arts, in which job opportunities are relatively scarce and training is expensive. Since we want to select the people with the highest potential, we administer a battery of tests, including the Horn Art Aptitude Test. On this test, each subject makes several different sketches, including drawings developed from a few given lines as a "starter" (Figure 14-12).

How do we score the response? What is a good drawing? The answer is not right or wrong and, therefore, we must have a number of judges rate it according to certain guidelines.

In this instance, we are concerned with *inter-judge reliability* or inter-judge agreement. The basic question is this: Do two or more judges score the same answer in the same way? If so, there is high inter-judge agreement. Research has shown that when detailed scoring procedures are used, inter-judge reliability on the Horn test is fairly high (Horn, 1953; Figure 14-13).

Individual Differences

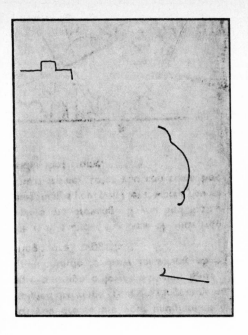
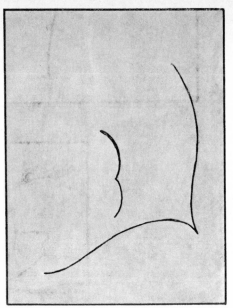

Figure 14-12   Measuring Art Aptitude.   *In the Horn Art Aptitude Test, the subject is required to make a complete sketch, using the indicated lines in any manner he or she wishes. A wide variety of such tasks is included in this test (Horn & Smith, 1945). (Courtesy of Stoelting Company)*

Figure 14-13   Inter-Judge Reliability.   *How would you score these pictures, one drawn by one of the authors and the other by a professional illustrator? To determine the inter-judge reliability, several judges would score each drawing, using a carefully constructed rating scale, and then their scores would be compared.*

Indicate the next number in the series:

45 15 30 10 20 ?

A. 5
B. $6\frac{2}{3}$
C. 0
D. $2\frac{1}{2}$
E. 8

Figure 14-14 Equivalent-Form Reliability. *This test item measures the same capacity as the number series in the test battery but the contents and correct answer (B) are different.*

Test-retest reliability. Another problem in reliability concerns this question: When the same subject is tested on two or more occasions, are the results in agreement? This type of consistency, called *test-retest reliability,* is determined by administering the test to a group of subjects, repeating the procedure with them later, and then comparing the two sets of scores. The test is reliable to the extent that each subject makes a similar score on both occasions. If the test of numerical ability in our battery for spacecraft pilots is reliable, the candidates should answer it in the same way in September and May.

In some instances, the subject may recall his or her earlier answers. Hence, a different set of test items, equivalent in structure and similar in content, is administered instead. This measure of consistency is called *equivalent-form* reliability (Figure 14-14).

Standardized procedures. Reliability depends on not only how the test is constructed but also how it is used. A watch, compass, or ruler, when used carelessly, will yield unreliable results. All well-constructed tests involve carefully specified instructions so that each subject is evaluated in the same way, involving a *standardized procedure.*

Even the influence of different test administrators has been demonstrated. When two different examiners tested the intelligence of a group of Puerto Rican children, the marked differences in scores seemed to reflect differences in examiner style (Thomas et al., 1971). Careful examiner selection and training are also essential to high reliability.

Interpretation of reliability data. When a test is evaluated for reliability, each subject's score in one case is compared with his or her score in another, or two judges' ratings for the same response are compared. Then, the relationship between the pairs of scores for the whole group is expressed as the degree of correlation or agreement between the two sets of data (Figure 14-15).

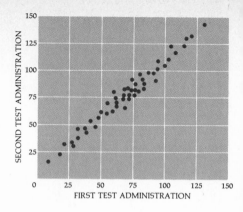

Figure 14-15 Scattergram of Reliability. *Scattergrams show the degree of correlation between two sets of scores. In test-retest reliability, the results of two administrations of the same test to the same subjects usually show a high correlation.*

Perfect reliability for psychological tests is very seldom found, but in general, the longer the test, the higher the reliability. As more items are included, provided they are of comparable value, the less likely it is that the final score will be disrupted by one or two test items that the subject has misunderstood or otherwise answered in uncharacteristic fashion. On the other hand, as the time interval between testings increases, the test-retest reliability becomes lower, since the subject's responses may be influenced by changes in mood, setting, age, and various cultural factors.

Potentially, the reliability coefficient can range anywhere from .00 to 1.00, and it is not uncommon to have reliability coefficients for aptitude tests, such as the battery for testing spacecraft pilots, in the vicinity of .90. Reliability coefficients for personality tests are lower because the results are more likely to be influenced by temporary states, such as mood. Thus, adequate test-retest coefficients for such tests range as high as the 70s and 80s (Hay & Stewart, 1974; LoPiccolo & Stegar, 1974).

Individual Differences

Assessment of Validity

One wonders whether a particular test score will be the same on the next testing, but one also wonders whether that score measures what it is supposed to measure. In other words, the scores may be reliable, but are they also valid? A test has *validity* when it measures the qualities it is intended to measure.

Reliability and validity are the two most important characteristics of any psychological test, and of these, validity is the more critical. Reliability simply places an upper limit on validity. A test that is not reliable—does not yield the same scores consistently under the same conditions—cannot be valid. A test that is reliable might or might not be valid, depending on whether it measures the *intended* trait. For example, a test of running speed may give highly reliable results, but it is not a valid measure of intelligence.

On the other hand, a test that has high validity, accurately measuring the intended trait, must be reliable. It does not give different results from one time to the next, unless of course the characteristic being measured is itself unstable, perhaps depending on environmental conditions.

In determining validity and reliability, we use a sample of subjects, but we cannot include those people who were employed in the field trials. To stress the point again, any errors inherent in that process, especially a sampling bias, would give us a falsely high estimate of validity. We would be deciding that our test items are valid or worthwhile by judging them against the same criteria used to select them originally (Anastasi, 1976). To emphasize the need for a new sample, this assessment of validity is formally known as *cross-validation*. Test validity is convincing only when it is based on such an independent assessment.

Face validity. As one approach to validation, consider the two items in the battery for spacecraft pilots pertaining to emotional stability. During World War I, several of the Allied countries used both of these tests to select candidates for pilot training. If the young man failed to show a certain reaction time after the pistol was fired or after being slapped with the cold cloth, or if his breathing and hand tremor changed more than a certain amount, he was rejected as a candidate. On this basis, hundreds of men were told that their reactions were too slow or that their emotional responses were too strong for them to succeed as pilots.

Later, investigators evaluated the relationship between these reactions and skill as a pilot, and the correlation was found to be negligible. There was no significant association between these test scores and ability as a pilot. Those in charge of selecting pilots would have done just as well without the pistol-shot and cold-cloth tests; these procedures had no validity for the specified purpose (National Research Council, 1943a).

When a test merely seems to be appropriate for its avowed purpose by its appearance, as in the pistol-shot and cold-cloth tests, it is said to have *face validity*, but it may not have any actual value, as demonstrated through statistical analysis. In fact, it is questionable whether face validity, based on superficial qualities, should even be considered in this context. ■

Types of validity. In selecting space pilots, we are interested in *predictive validity*, which is the extent to which the test scores indicate the subject's later success on the job or in a training program. While the pistol-shot and cold-cloth tests were useless, a pilot selection battery developed later, during World War II, did have predictive validity. This test was constructed through the rationale of a careful task analysis, rather than on the basis of face validity, and items were retained in the test on the basis of their discrimination power.

■ *Knowingly or not, the principle of "face validity" is practiced by everyone. People are often judged on outward appearance or on other qualities that may not be valid at all in indicating real character.*

I think my parents are two of the most avid believers in this principle—especially when it involves me and my "gentlemen callers." As soon as the innocent young man sets his foot in the house he is given a quick once-over accompanied by a rapid third degree. If he is neat and has short hair, they decide that he is OK—they think he has a good personality too. On the other hand, if his appearance is a bit antiestablishment, they immediately feel he is a "defective character" of some sort.

Figure 14-16 Value of a Pilot Selection Battery. *The graph shows the percent eliminated at each of the nine ratings. Candidates who received the highest scores were least likely to be eliminated for flying deficiencies. (Staff, Psychological Selection, AAF. 1945; photo by Capa from Magnum)*

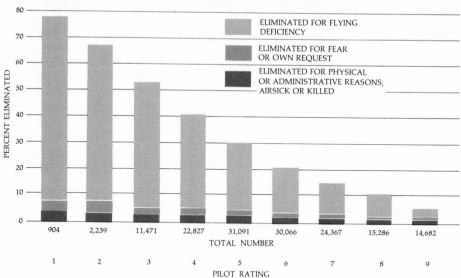

Those with little or no value were discarded, others were revised, and eventually a useful test was prepared (Figure 14-16).

Generally, the best predictor of future behavior is a sample of that behavior.

Thus, the test for selecting persons for dangerous secret service assignments during World War II consisted of three days in which they adopted a disguise and false background and tried to prevent the examiners from learning their

Individual Differences

true identity (OSS, 1948). In school and job situations, tests of predictability often employ work samples (Massengill et al., 1975; McClelland, 1973).

The purpose of some tests is to indicate those individuals best suited for the job right away rather than to predict future performance. A test that successfully predicts an individual's present level of functioning on another task is said to have *concurrent validity*. Such a test also contains items similar to the requirements of the job, and sometimes a work sample is included. Tests of concurrent validity are most valuable when workers are needed immediately, rather than after a training program. The National Teachers' Examinations are analyzed for both concurrent and predictive validity (Quirk et al., 1973).

The issue in *content validity* is the representativeness of the test items. A test of ability to pilot a spacecraft should be representative of all the skills that a good pilot needs. A test designed to assess knowledge in a college geology course should contain items representing all aspects of that course—lectures, discussions, films, readings, field trips, and laboratory work. Students, quite understandably, sometimes become irritated when an examination does not have content validity.

Still another type of validity, more theoretical in nature, is involved whenever a test is evaluated against a construct. This measure of validity is thus called *construct validity*. Several terms in our present discussion, such as mechanical aptitude, anxiety, and intelligence, have referred to constructs. These are inferred; they are not directly observable entities or processes. Thus, a test is said to have high construct validity whenever it accurately measures the diverse phenomena that are presumably associated with that construct. In a test of anxiety, behavior such as sweating, tremors, forgetfulness, and word repetition would be considered. Due to the abstract and usually amorphous nature of constructs, convincing evidence for this type of validity is obtained only through a broad accumulation of research results (American Psychological Association et al., 1974).

Interpretation of validity data. To determine validity, it is always necessary to have a *criterion*, which is a standard for judging the value of something. The test scores must be measured against some acceptable standard to see how closely the scores and the standard are related. For assessing concurrent validity, the test might be administered to experienced and inexperienced pilots with known performance records, and then the test results would be compared with the pilots' records. For predictive validity, the test scores might be compared with the time required to complete the training program, final grades in the training program, or ratings of independent judges at the end of the course. In assessing validity, sometimes several criteria are combined and treated as a composite standard against which the success of the test is judged (Figure 14-17).

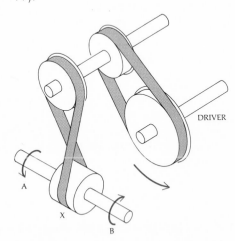

Figure 14-17 Determining Validity. *To assess the validity of this test item as a measure of mechanical comprehension we must find out whether successful mechanics, or some other group known to be high in mechanical ability, answer it correctly and others answer it incorrectly.*

Tests and Measurement

Again, correlations are obtained, but validity coefficients, although they constitute the most crucial measure of any test, tend to be lower than reliability coefficients. It is more difficult to show that a test actually measures what it purports to measure than it is to show that it gives comparable results on two different occasions (Figure 14-18). Hence, predictive validity often shows a coefficient around .50. In one review of aptitude tests for personnel selection, the average predictive validity obtained in a number of studies was only .39 (Ghiselli, 1973).

Clearly, tests that are valid for some purposes are not necessarily valid for others. For example, the Purdue Pegboard Test of finger and hand dexterity is a reasonably valid indicator of certain brain malfunctions. It discriminates between essentially normal people and brain-damaged individuals. However, the test is not successful in differentiating between psychotic and brain-damaged persons (Fernald et al., 1966). The validity of the test depends in part on the types of subjects involved.

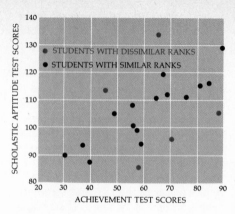

Figure 14-18   Scattergram of Validity.   *The scores are rather widely scattered, indicating only a moderate coefficient of correlation, in this case for predictive validity. The colored dots indicate students for whom the aptitude test was an especially poor predictor of later achievement.*

The Normative Study

Suppose that you took the first four items in the battery for spacecraft pilots, excluding the pair on emotional stability. Furthermore, suppose that you answered two of them correctly. What does your score mean? Is a raw score of two correct items a high, low, or average result? Here the problem of norms arises. Test scores that serve as guidelines for interpreting other scores are called *norms*. They are obtained by giving the test to a large number of subjects who are similar to people who will be taking the test later. Their scores are used as reference points to determine what is normal, above normal, and below normal for the subsequent subjects. The procedure of collecting the data from norm groups is known as a *normative study*.

Establishing Norms

Norms cannot be developed until the instructions and specific test items have been firmly established. Hence, the results of the earlier field trials are also unsuitable here, but we can obtain some norms from data collected while determining reliability and validity. If these data are scores of male and female college graduates, for example, then we have some norms for college graduates. Afterwards, we might want to collect scores from high school graduates to have norms for this group, or we might want to collect norms for specified age groups.

An appropriate norm.   Since norms are used for judging a person's performance on a test, it is essential that the norm groups be similar to those persons for whom the test is intended. A math test that has norms only for fourth graders is of little use with eleventh graders studying mathematics. Even norms that simply refer to "the general population" are often inadequate.

Usually, a test is administered for selection and placement purposes, in order to compare an individual with some specific group, such as licensed plumbers, professional musicians, or undergraduate students majoring in history. Thus, there are separate norms for experienced and inexperienced workers, for older people and younger people, for high school graduates and nongraduates, and so forth. Even geographic area of residence is important in some communities with unequal educational opportunities (Seisdedos, 1972).

Local norms.   In some instances it may be best to develop *local norms*, which are scores that apply only in a particular setting and thus are even more narrowly specified. A certain high school may develop its own norms for admitting people to language classes, regardless of how they score on state or national examinations. The United States Air Force, in selecting pilots, may employ norms developed only from previous applicants for this same training. These highly specific standards permit even more accurate prediction than would be possible with norms derived simply from the population in general (Anastasi, 1976).

In this context, it is sometimes helpful to employ a *critical score*, or a critical range of scores, which is used as a reference point for selection decisions. Persons at or above the score are selected; those below it are rejected. This procedure can result in a high percentage of successful predictions with the screening test (Anastasi, 1976).

Use of Norms

Norms are most important whenever the number of applicants exceeds the number of vacancies and there is a need to select the best candidates. The score of each subject is judged against the norms, and the test is called a *norm-referenced test*. Its aim is to indicate differences among individuals.

In a recent study, norms and a critical score were studied for jet pilots undergoing training for specific missions with the fleet. Using the norms before the course would have eliminated approximately 41 percent of the unsuccessful aviators, while less than 7 percent of the successful ones would have been excluded. Hence, employment of the norms in this case is an effective procedure (Figure 14-19).

One caution in the use of norm-referenced tests is that they may be unfair to persons who have had little opportunity to learn the skills reflected in the norm group. To administer an intelligence test in English to a minority group member who speaks little English may give a grossly incorrect idea of that person's intellectual ability. A more reasonable testing method would be to use nonverbal or performance items, in which the subject is asked to respond to pictures, puzzles, blocks, and other apparatus in a problem-solving manner. Furthermore, a test is unfair whenever it includes any type of items that are not related to job performance and in which minority groups score below average. This problem is a matter of validity, and it reflects poor test construction.

Figure 14-19   Using Norms. *Here, 850 serves as a useful critical score. When it is employed, many potentially unsuccessful pilots are eliminated and only a few potentially successful ones are excluded. (After Bale et al., 1973)*

Score	Percent Unsuccessful	Percent Successful
550	3.4	0.5
655	10.3	2.1
760	41.4	6.9
850	65.5	19.0
955	79.0	33.3
1,060	89.7	60.8
1,150	93.7	81.5
1,210	100.0	89.9

The recent outcry against normative testing has occurred on these bases. Despite the efforts at constructing tests that are free from cultural influences, distinct racial and ethnic biases exist in many norm-referenced tests. Culture-free tests have been more of a hope than a reality. Advances have been made, but no satisfactory solution to this problem has been developed as yet (Schmidt & Hunter, 1974).

Improving Tests and Test Usage

In view of these limitations and the apparent need for testing in our complex society, the mandate for psychology is to improve current tests and test usage as much as possible and discover additional methods of psychological measurement. In recent years, one response to this demand has occurred in the context of educational technology, in which new developments and efforts at educational reform have led to greater opportunities for individualized instruction and self-paced learning.

Criterion-Referenced Tests

Individualized instruction, just as any other instructional method, requires compatible methods of assessment. In individualized instruction the students are not being compared with one another, and therefore norm-referenced tests are inappropriate. Instead, there is a need to measure growth or change within one individual, as he or she proceeds through the instructional process. Thus, the scores for such a test are measured against a specific, established criterion, and the tests are called *criterion-referenced tests*. In these tests, a certain criterion or standard is set as the passing level, and if the student meets this criterion, he or she passes the course regardless of the performance of others.

In education, these tests generally focus on the amount learned. In therapy, they focus on the amount of personality change. To measure the amount of change within an individual in any context, the test construction must be somewhat different from that used for norm-referenced tests.

Suppose we want to develop a criterion-referenced test for determining the progress of student pilots in a training program. In selecting the test items following a field trial of the test, we would not retain those that are at a 50 percent level of difficulty because we are not interested in discriminating among individuals. Instead, we would retain those items that show close to 0 percent success when used as a *pretest*, given before the course, and close to 100 percent success when used as a *posttest*, at the end of the course. In other words, the same test items would be employed in both testings, and those items that are most sensitive to individual improvement would be the best items for measuring the acquisition of flying skills.

Insofar as reliability is concerned, we are interested in the consistency of scores at different times of testing, but in criterion-referenced testing we are especially interested in the consistency of the *change* between the two test administrations, before and after the course. Thus, to evaluate reliability we might administer two different forms of the test before the pilot-training course and two other forms afterwards. The agreement or constancy of the change in this pair of pre- and post-course scores would be our measure of reliability.

For validity, the chief requirement is still that the test measures what it purports to measure, but in this case it is supposed to measure gain or improvement. Hence, rather than comparing the individuals against some established criterion, as in determining the validity of a norm-referenced test, we would administer the test before and after any situation in which we know how much gain has occurred. The degree to which the change in test scores reflects the actual gain in skill, as determined by some other measure, provides an estimate of

Figure 14-20   Norm-Referenced
and Criterion-Referenced Tests

Characteristic	Norm-referenced	Criterion-referenced
The chief concern is with . . .	selection, based on differences among individuals. How does Mary's performance compare with that of others taking the test?	growth, based on differences within individuals. Has Mary's performance improved over the course of instruction?
The individual's test score is expressed as a . . .	percentile. Mary ranks second among all 20 students who took the test, placing her at the 95 percentile.	percentage. Having answered 16 out of 20 questions correctly, Mary's percentage is 80.

the validity of the criterion-referenced test.

In short, the two types of tests have different purposes. Norm-referenced tests reveal differences among individuals; criterion-referenced tests reveal differences within individuals. Norm-referenced tests indicate the individual's percentile or standing in comparison with others; criterion-referenced tests indicate the percentage of the material that the individual has learned (Figure 14-20).

Occasionally, a norm-referenced test may include a cut-off score for passing a course, regardless of the performance of other group members or members of the norming population. Thus, a criterion is added if it appears advantageous in the testing situation. Similarly, a criterion-referenced test can be constructed through data collected with a normative group. But if the instruments are properly constructed, and the different goals are kept in mind, most tests are more suitable for one purpose than for the other (Carver, 1974).

Testing Standards

The concept behind criterion-referenced tests is far from new, but what is new is the greatly increased interest and research concerning such instruments. High-speed computer technology now allows for self-paced instruction and the large-scale criterion-referenced testing that must accompany these procedures.

Within this context, there is reason to be optimistic about future research in mental measurement (Holtzman, 1971). One circumstance to be avoided, therefore, would seem to be a prohibition against the use of tests.

Instead, two conditions of the testing situation must be kept in mind. In the first place, one sometimes hears psychological tests described as either "good" or "bad," perhaps depending on the speaker's general attitude toward psychology or one's experience in a particular testing situation. Instead, it seems more appropriate to consider the *potential of a test*. A well-constructed test developed by a knowledgeable person probably has a higher potential for measuring intelligence, if that is the aim of the test, than one developed by an inexperienced person who does not evaluate the test or carefully analyze the purpose for which it is to be used. In short, a test with high validity and an adequate set of norms has a high potential for success in certain situations.

In the second place, we must consider the *person who uses the test*. All human instruments can be used in many ways. A high-powered microscope, a knife, or a new law can be handled by someone who is capable and experienced or by someone who is careless and without scruples. The knife can be employed skillfully in peeling an orange, or it can be used to inflict injury on another human being. Tests are also tools, and whether the result is beneficial or harmful or a particular potential is achieved depends partly on who uses them.

As in all fields, instances of malpractice occur. For this reason, the American Psychological Association has established explicit ethical standards and specific procedures governing the use of psychological tests (American Psychological Association et al., 1974). The privacy of each individual always should be protected. All persons must continue to have the right to decline to be assessed by any test and to refuse to answer any questions that seem improper, impertinent, or an unnecessary intrusion. In any testing situation, these rights prevail and should be pointed out to the examinee (American Psychological Association, 1970).

Furthermore, tests should be used only when the desired information is not already available from other sources involving less effort. Overtesting continues to be a problem today, especially by those not sensitive to the limitations of tests. Again, it should be pointed out that the use of most tests assumes that the individual's behavior is largely the result of personal dispositions and attributes, rather than the context in which the individual is engaged.

The use of psychological tests increases and probably will continue to increase unless better alternatives are offered. For the future of psychology, as well as the field of tests and measurement in particular, it is incumbent upon those who develop and employ tests to ensure that the highest possible standards are maintained.

Summary

The Testing Movement

1. In a complex society, there is a need to assess individual differences, and psychological tests have been used for this purpose. Because of limitations and misuse of tests and a misunderstanding of their purpose and function, the testing movement has become controversial. However, no clearly superior methods are available.

2. Group tests are administered to a large number of subjects at the same time. The advantage is efficiency in administration and scoring, but these tests often are limited to verbal items and sometimes the results are markedly inaccurate. Individual tests, administered to one person at a time, usually include a wide variety of items and the subject can be observed closely. These tests generally provide more information about the individual than do group tests.

3. There are many categories of psychological tests. Intelligence tests measure an individual's ability for reasoning, thinking, and understanding. Achievement tests evaluate an individual's level of accomplishment. Aptitude tests indicate a person's probable accomplishment after a specific training period and the capacity to profit from training. There is no concern with ability in interest inventories; they merely indicate preferences in work and related areas. Personality tests include a wide variety of materials and testing procedures; some are concerned with readily observable traits and others are concerned with the deeper aspects of an individual's mental makeup.

Preparation of a Test

4. The first step in constructing a psychological test is to prepare tentative test items. These can be developed through a survey of the literature, a task analysis, and on the basis of some theory.

5. After the tentatively selected items have been assembled, together with the instructions for administration and scoring, a field trial is made, using a sample of subjects. The results from this field trial are then analyzed and used for revising the test items, improving the directions for administration and scoring, and developing new items.

Evaluation of the Test

6. The new version of the test is then evaluated for reliability and validity. Reliability is the degree to which a test gives similar results when used with the same subjects on different occasions. It concerns the consistency of measurement. Correlations are determined for test-retest and equivalent-form reliability. When judges are involved in scoring, inter-judge reliability also becomes an important issue.

7. Validity concerns the extent to which the test measures what it is intended to measure. Face validity is not a true measure of validity, since it involves no empirical assessment, as determined by the correlation between the test scores and some criterion. Predictive and concurrent validity pertain to future and present performance, respectively. Content validity concerns whether or not the test is representative of all the knowledge and skills in question. Construct validity, more theoretical in nature, is concerned with measuring those observable reactions that define the construct in question.

The Normative Study

8. For tests of individual differences, the final step in the preparation of the test is the development of norms, which are standards obtained by administering the test to large groups of subjects and determining their scores. Commonly, subgroup norms and even local norms are established.

9. Norm-referenced tests indicate a person's standing with respect to others who have taken the test. They are used for revealing differences among individuals, as in selecting or classifying the most suitable people for certain educational programs or work opportunities. Whenever such a test requires skills or knowledge not related to the position sought, the test is partly invalid.

Improving Tests and Test Usage

10. Criterion-referenced tests measure change within a single individual, rather than differences among several individuals. The aim is to assess a person's progress in school, on the job, or in therapy, apart from the performance of others. A criterion is established and the person's progress is measured only against this criterion.

11. Despite limitations, psychological tests probably will continue to be widely employed. As with any human tool, success depends not only on how well the test is constructed but also on the user's concern and skill. Since psychological tests appear to be an integral aspect of highly developed societies, the constant goal of measurement research is to find ways of improving them.

Suggested Readings

American Psychological Association et al. *Standards for educational and psychological tests.* Washington, D.C.: American Psychological Association, 1974. This 70-page pamphlet serves as a basic guide for those interested in evaluating or constructing mental tests.

Anastasi, A. *Psychological testing* (4th ed.). New York: Macmillan, 1976. A comprehensive discussion of the most common psychological tests.

Buros, O. K. *Seventh mental measurements yearbook.* Highland Park, N.J.: Gryphon Press, 1972. A comprehensive reference source that describes the background, purpose, and chief characteristics of hundreds of tests.

Cronboch, L. J. *Essentials of psychological testing* (3rd ed.). New York: Harper & Row, 1970. A thorough introduction; includes discussion of theoretical and practical issues.

Tyler, L. E. *Tests and measurements* (2nd ed.). Englewood Cliffs, N.J.: Prentice-Hall, 1971. Describes in brief form basic statistical techniques and methods of psychological measurement.

Chapter 15

Intelligence

Figure 15-1   Galton's Weights.
These weights, about which the subject made judgments, ranged from an ounce to more than a pound. Altogether, 9,337 people passed through Galton's laboratory to take such tests.

Sir Francis Galton was a highly versatile Englishman with no financial worries, and he entertained himself by making important discoveries in diverse fields, ranging from biology to statistics to anthropology. In psychology, Galton inaugurated the modern testing movement, largely through the founding of his famous Anthropometric Laboratory in South Kensington, London. Beginning in 1882, one could come here, for a slight fee, to be measured for head size, reaction time, hearing, strength of grip, sensitivity to visual movement, and other characteristics. Galton's records constitute the first significant collection of data from tests of individual differences.

At one point, Galton decided to measure intelligence, and he thought that the senses should be the key factor. He reasoned that the only information we have comes to us through our senses. Thus, "the more perceptive the senses are of difference, the larger is the field upon which our judgment and intelligence can act" (Galton, 1883).

One test that he devised was a carefully graded series of weights presented to a blindfolded subject in a random order. The idea was that the more capable subject should be able to make finer discriminations, indicating whether any given weight was heavier or lighter than the one preceding it (Figure 15–1). Thus, he tested people known to be of exceptionally high or very low mental ability, and he discovered that they were also high or low, respectively, in sensory discrimination. But aside from work with these extreme populations, his tests were of little value. They showed little capacity to indicate intellectual differences among more typical people (Peterson, 1926).

Galton's method was crude, and part of the problem lay in his conception of intelligence. In fact, he created some confusion with his focus on sensory abilities, but even in the intervening years we have found it difficult to define intelligence. In this chapter, we intermittently trace the history of this concept, focusing on measurement, theory, and differences in intelligence, for this background is of significance in our understanding of mental ability today.

Measurement and Theory

In one respect, Galton was in agreement with current views. Intelligence tests for infants are necessarily limited to sensory and motor responses. When tested today, the infant is stimulated to identify certain objects, follow their movement, or assemble them in some fashion. For the first 18 months of postnatal life, the only significant responses are sensory-motor activities, and therefore these reactions are tested. However, Galton measured only the sensory aspect and he erroneously used this method with adults too (Figure 15–2).

The principal concern in most contemporary tests of adult intelligence is with thought processes. At all levels, but especially in adulthood, intelligence is broadly defined as the capacity to learn from experience and adapt to new situations. This definition has the advantage of being applicable at various phylogenetic stages as well, but it does not show the complexity of our current view of intelligence, as indicated in subsequent discussions.

Tests of Intelligence

The earliest modern conception of intelligence is reflected in the work of Alfred Binet, a French psychologist who in the late 1890s was asked to serve on a commission for Paris's public schools. His task was to discover which children had insufficient ability to learn in the usual classroom setting. It would be inappropriate to make such decisions solely on the basis of teachers' judgments and, therefore, a set of objective tests was needed. These tests would measure the intelligence of all children on a comparable basis.

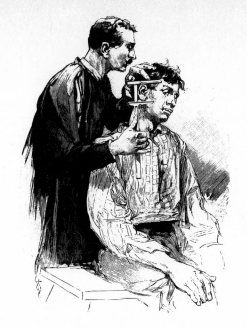

Figure 15-2   Measuring Individual Differences.   *The work in Galton's laboratory focused on physical as well as psychological characteristics. Among the numerous devices that he developed is the high-frequency Galton whistle (not shown here), which he used for testing the upper limits of hearing among animals in the zoo. (The Bettmann Archive)*

Early tests.   Binet felt that a graded series of psychological tests could be devised that would indicate the various levels of children's intelligence. He and his collaborator, Theophile Simon, devised a number of different tasks involving attention, memory, and also visual discrimination. By experimenting with children who were making normal progress in school, they determined which tasks could be performed by average individuals of various age levels. This tentative collection of items was known as the Measuring Scale of Intelligence and more popularly was referred to as the Binet-Simon test.

There were many   defects in their original work, and Binet and Simon eventually devised an improved scale in which they attempted to eliminate all poorly constructed items and those that could be performed only after special schooling. In addition, the items of the new scale were arranged more systematically, according to age groupings. A certain item was included at the five-year level because the average five-year-old child could pass it. It was too difficult for the average four-year-old and too easy for the average six-year-old. In this

Figure 15-3 Stanford-Binet Intelligence Scale. *Young children are asked to point to certain parts of the body, make constructions with blocks, string beads in a certain fashion, and accomplish tasks with other equipment. Verbal materials, not shown here, are used with older children and adults. (Sheila A. Farr photo)*

The difficulty in defining intelligence continues today, but fortunately a concept still can be quite useful even without a universally accepted definition—beyond that of versatility in adaptation, in this case. Our most important concepts, such as justice, life, and beauty, inevitably are the most difficult to define.

Stanford-Binet Scale. Eventually, psychologists at Stanford University devised an American version of the Binet-Simon test, called the Stanford-Binet. It has appeared in several editions and includes tests of reasoning, numerical ability, vocabulary, and general information. In addition, the subject is asked to perform nonverbal tasks, such as constructing bridges, assembling puzzles, detecting flaws in pictures, and manipulating symbols and designs. With this broad range of tasks, the examiner obtains a better idea of the subject's versatility, which is part of adapting to one's environment (Figure 15–3).

As a consequence of arranging the items into age groupings, Binet developed the concept of mental age. A child who can pass all the items at the five-year level but none at any higher level is credited with a *mental age* (MA) of five years. Furthermore, the child with a *chronological age* (CA) of five who achieves an MA of five is regarded as having average intelligence. If a child has a chronological age of eight and a mental age of five, he or she is regarded as dull; if a child is only three years old with this same mental age, he or she appears to be of extremely high intelligence.

An *intelligence quotient* (IQ) can be derived by dividing MA by CA and multiplying by 100 to remove the decimal point. This quotient shows the MA in relation to the CA. A 10-year-old with an MA of 10 has an IQ of 100; a 10-year-old with an MA of 6 has an IQ of 60; and a 10-year-old with an MA of 14, has an IQ of 140 (Figure 15-4).

$$IQ = \frac{MA}{CA} \times 100$$
$$= \frac{10}{10} \times 100 = 100$$
$$= \frac{6}{10} \times 100 = 60$$
$$= \frac{14}{10} \times 100 = 140$$

Figure 15-4 Computation of the IQ. *The conventional formula is MA/CA × 100, but this procedure has been modified to provide a deviation IQ, which is obtained from reading prepared tables. Since the difference between the conventional and deviation IQ is usually small, the older method is still recognized as yielding a rapid, close approximation.*

way, they demonstrated that a person's intelligence could be measured in a precise and scientific manner.

Binet, incidentally, like Jean Piaget, began his study of intelligence through observations of his own children. Eventually, he formulated a definition of intelligence which focused upon three characteristics: the capacity to (1) take and sustain a definite direction, (2) make adaptations for achieving a desired goal, and (3) criticize one's own behavior (Terman, 1916). Most modern conceptions of intelligence, like Binet's, refer to some flexibility in achieving adjustment and, on this basis, intelligence is more than thinking. Memory, general knowledge, perceptual quickness, and motor skills are other capacities that seem important in our adjustment to the environment.

This method of obtaining the IQ is called the *conventional method*. In 1960, it was replaced by the *deviation method*, which indicates the deviation of the individual's score from the mean in relation to the deviations of all the scores in the norm group. It is obtained by consulting prepared tables, and it usually differs from an IQ obtained by the conventional method by less than three points.

Wechsler scores. In the 1930s, a group of psychologists under the direction of David Wechsler of Bellevue Psychiatric Hospital began to develop a test for measuring adult intelligence. The Wechsler-Bellevue, as the first test was called, was later revised as the Wechsler Adult Intelligence Scale (WAIS), which is now a popular individual test for persons from age 16 to age 74. Its counterpart, the Wechsler Intelligence Scale for Children (WISC), measures intelligence in persons from age 5 to age 15. A recent revision of the children's scale is the WISC-R, in which new test items have been added and some old items have been changed; also the test has been re-evaluated for use in contemporary society (Doppelt & Kaufman, 1977).

In contrast to the Stanford-Binet, the items on the Wechsler scales are grouped according to type rather than age level. That is, all the items on general information or hand-eye coordination, for example, are together in a subtest, arranged in order of increasing difficulty. Each subject starts on the simpler items of a given type and goes on to more difficult ones until his or her limit for that subtest is reached. Then, another subtest is administered.

Since each subtest measures a different function, different persons can receive the same overall intelligence score on the Wechsler, yet they may have quite different intellectual styles or profiles. A person with a strong background in school might perform well on the subtests of general information, vocabulary, and numerical ability; another person,

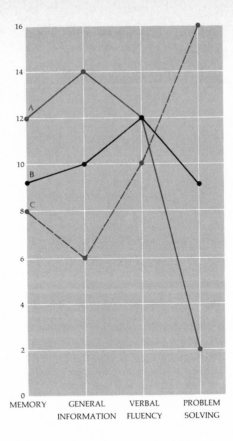

Figure 15-5 Differences in Intellectual Ability. *These profiles of intellectual ability all show an average score of ten, but the results on the various subtests are quite different. Such data indicate that persons with the same general level of IQ may have quite different mental abilities.*

with much practical experience, might succeed best in the areas of problem solving and comprehension; and another person might score highest in memory, perceptual tasks and tasks requiring rapid motor coordination. These distinct patterns of abilities indicate that each of these persons has a different kind of intelligence, although all three may be said to function at the same overall level. The capacity to understand these differences is a most important characteristic of the successful psychological examiner (Figure 15-5).

One subtest alone, such as memory, is not a good measure of intelligence. One of the authors once encountered a young man in a mental institution who was then called an *idiot-savant*, meaning that he was mentally retarded but very skillful in certain ways. He could recall all the names, addresses and birth dates of the many patients who had resided in this facility during the 15 or more preceding years and he could do various mathematical problems easily in his head, but he could not manage to get his clothes on properly or maintain a conversation.

The purpose of including a variety of tasks in an intelligence test is to sample as many aspects of the individual's adjustment or versatility as possible. An intelligence test is basically a way of obtaining a sample of behavior. We could follow a person around for several days or weeks to find out about his or her intelligence, as Piaget did with his children, but that procedure would be even more time consuming, more expensive, and perhaps less accurate than a formal test.

Models of the Intellect

These newer tests emphasize that intelligence in the modern conception is not considered a unitary or one-dimensional function but rather is regarded as multifaceted. It is viewed by most psychologists as a composite of abilities required for adjustment or survival in a given society.

The g *factor.* The recent history of the "composite" view of intelligence goes back to the 1920s, when 17 specialists in the testing of mental ability were called together for the purpose of defining intelligence and suggesting the most promising areas of further research (Thorndike, 1921). At this time, it had been observed that subtests of intelligence tests are correlated and that subtests of aptitude tests also have similarities. On this basis, an English psychologist, Charles Spearman, hypothesized that the different items in different tests measure some common factor, which he called *general intelligence,* or *g,* and that many different skills involve this common factor. Mechanical ability, musical ability, mathematical ability, and others show a correlation with each other because certain amounts of *g* are required in all instances.

In addition to *g,* Spearman argued that each skill called for a specific ability, or *s.* Thus, facility in mathematics, besides requiring a certain amount of *g,* would require specific mathematical abilities, such as facility with numbers, ability to factor, ability to multiply, and so forth, which would be the *s*'s in mathematical performance. Similarly, mechanical skill would require mechanical *s*'s, as well as a certain amount of *g* (Lovell, 1965; Spearman, 1927).

The s *factors.* Following Spearman's reasoning, a pair of American psychologists, Louis and Thelma Thurstone, eventually defined seven *primary mental abilities,* verbal and nonverbal, that could be measured readily by group tests. These tests emphasized a few basic components of intelligence, rather than a *g* factor. The components were word fluency, number ability, verbal comprehension, memory, reasoning, spatial relations, and perceptual speed (Thurstone & Thurstone, 1941; Figure 15-6).

These components or factors were identified by a statistical method for finding the most basic elements in psychological processes. The procedure, called *factor analysis,* reduces many data to a few basic factors, essentially through a statistical analysis of the intercorrelations among test data. Test scores that cluster together belong to the same factor. Following the Thurstones's first work, a great many factor analyses of intelligence were accomplished with varying results. Recently, British psychologists surveyed these findings and decided to construct an intelligence test using six basic factors: verbal, reasoning, spatial, number, fluency/creativity, and memory (Ward & Fitzpatrick, 1970).

The problem in all these analyses, however, is that there are still intercorrelations among the different factors, which means that the method is not entirely satisfactory or that some *g* factor remains. In any case, this approach, which began with high hopes 40 years

Word Fluency. Name the pictures below; each name must begin with the letter P:

Spatial Relations. Mark the figure which is like the first figure in the row. Do not mark those which are made backwards:

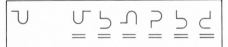

Perceptual Speed. Mark the two which are exactly alike:

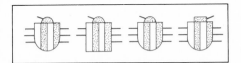

ago, has failed to yield *the* specific factors. We do not as yet know the most basic components of intelligence, and estimates of their number have ranged increasingly upwards in recent years. All we can say is that Spearman's concept of the broad *g* factor appears much over-simplified.

Reasoning. Find the way in which three of the pictures are alike, and then mark the one which is different from these three:

The SI model. The most comprehensive multifactor theory to date has been offered by J. P. Guilford, who hypothesized that intellectual ability should be considered in terms of these dimensions: what information is being dealt with, called *content;* how it is processed, called *operation;* and the result, called *product.* These three dimensions define his *structure-of-intellect* (SI) model. Each of these dimensions, in turn, is subdivided into 4, 5, and 6 parts, respectively, making a cubic model with 120 potential intellectual abilities (Figure 15-7).

Memory. Learn the names, so that when the last name is given you can write the first name. On the next page the last names are listed in a different order. You will be asked to write the first names.

First name	Last name
Mary	Brown
John	Davis

Number Ability. Mark every number below that is exactly three more than the number just before it. Work as fast as you can:

15 19 21 26 29 22 25 5 8 7 11 4

Verbal Comprehension. Underline the word in each line which means the same as the first word in that line:

FETID   amusing   feverish   putrid contagious

FRANK popular queer brutal open

Figure 15-6 Tests of Specific Abilities. *Some of these tests are for children; all of them are timed.*

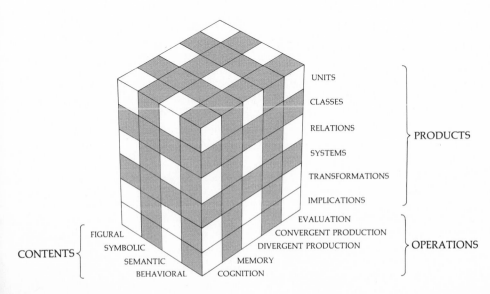

Figure 15-7 The Structure-of-Intellect Model. *Each cell in the cube represents a certain mental ability in terms of contents, operations, and products. Some aspects of the shaded areas are described in the text. (Adapted by permission from J. P. Guilford, "Creativity: A Quarter Century of Progress," in Irving A. Taylor and J. W. Getzels (Eds.),* Perspectives in Creativity. *Chicago: Aldine Publishing Company. Copyright © 1975 by Aldine Publishing Company.)*

PRODUCTS: UNITS, CLASSES, RELATIONS, SYSTEMS, TRANSFORMATIONS, IMPLICATIONS

OPERATIONS: EVALUATION, CONVERGENT PRODUCTION, DIVERGENT PRODUCTION, MEMORY, COGNITION

CONTENTS: FIGURAL, SYMBOLIC, SEMANTIC, BEHAVIORAL

Some examples illustrate this approach. On the content dimension, intellectual ability might involve the use of *symbolic* information, such as letters or numbers. This information is readily evident in mathematics. Another kind of information is *behavioral*, in which an individual's reactions are studied to understand his or her feelings. These contents are colloquially called "body language." All behavioral contents are sometimes said to concern social intelligence. A very bright mathematician is not necessarily astute with people.

Aspects of the operation dimension have been discussed in earlier chapters. *Memory*, for example, involves the perception and retention of information. *Convergent thinking* requires the retrieval and use of stored information in a focused search for one particular answer to a problem. In the product dimension, one construct is *classes*, in which two or more things are simply grouped together, as in concept formation; another is *systems*, in which two or more things are organized together, such as words in a sentence or postulates in a scientific theory. Theoretically, all intellectual abilities required in any sort of problem should be found somewhere in the model.

This model is still in the speculative stage, although a number of the components now have empirical support. These studies, which have concerned adult intelligence for the most part, emphasize that intelligence is not a constant, singular trait. Also, they prompt the hypothesis that mental ability, like personality, shows increasing differentiation from birth through the most formative years. There appears to be a proportionately greater *g* factor in infancy and more *s*'s in adulthood, just as there is general excitement in the emotional expression of the infant, which later becomes differentiated into distress, delight, anger, elation, affection, and so forth in adulthood.

Nonintellectual factors. Most recently, it has been suggested that intelligence should not be equated solely with mental operations. Nonintellectual factors, such as persistence, goal awareness, and the concern with social values seem important. Motivation and goals are seen as part of one's intellectual functioning, as well as ability to learn, reason, and solve problems.

According to this view, intelligent behavior is that which is rational, purposeful, and worthwhile. In short, a value judgment is fundamentally involved in any definition or view of intelligence (Wechsler, 1975). Indeed, a value judgment is involved in our definition of almost any abstract concept.

By way of summary, we might say that psychologists, even after eighty years, struggle to define intelligence more precisely. Thus, while some measuring instruments are considered far superior to others, this problem in definition clearly limits the interpretation of any test designed to measure intelligence.

Exceptional Intelligence

More than a century before Binet began his work, a young soldier from the American Revolution began a line of descendants that eventually prompted the study of intelligence from a different viewpoint. He stopped at a tavern for a few hours away from the war, and nine months later a "feeble minded" woman he met there gave birth to a baby boy. When Martin Kallikak, Jr. grew up, he too went on to help populate the world. According to historians, his descendants numbered 480 in 1912. Meanwhile, his father, Martin, Sr., had married another woman and produced another line of descendants. In 1912 there were 496 members on this side of the family tree.

The name "Kallikak" is fictitious. It comes from the Greek *kalos,* meaning "good" and *kakos* meaning "bad," suggesting that each Kallikak line showed one of these qualities. On the nonmarital side, traced through five generations, 143 people were judged to be retarded, 46 were reported as normal, and the rest were of doubtful or unknown status. Allegedly included in this group were horse-thieves, paupers, convicts, prostitutes, and many illegitimate children. On the marital side, all 496 descendants were judged to be of at least normal intelligence, although one was "sexually loose" and two succumbed to an "appetite for strong drink." With these exceptions, they became landholders, traders, and educators and they married "into the best of families" (Goddard, 1912; Figure 15-8).

It is not our purpose to debate the morality of this issue or the work of Dr. Henry Goddard, who brought to light these two different lines. Undoubtedly, he had some preconceived ideas in this research, as we shall see later. Our concern at the moment is to examine extreme differences in intellectual ability.

The Mentally Retarded

In Martin Kallikak's time, intelligence was believed to be determined essentially by the parents' genetic background. A person of low mental level was referred to as an idiot, imbecile, or moron, depending on whether the IQ was below 25, below 50, or below 70, respectively. The case of Deborah, a fifth-generation descendant on the nonmarital side, was presented as that of a moron (Goddard, 1912).

Eventually, these terms acquired a distinctly unfavorable connotation. In contemporary clinical language, the retarded individual is now described as having a handicap that is mild, moderate, severe, or profound. The focus of treatment also has changed from custodial care to training for practical skills, social confidence, and independence,

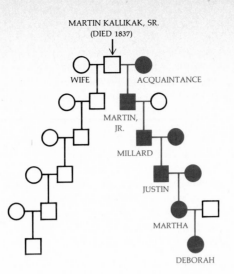

MARTIN KALLIKAK, SR.
(DIED 1837)

WIFE — ACQUAINTANCE

MARTIN, JR.

MILLARD

JUSTIN

MARTHA

DEBORAH

Figure 15-8 Descendants of Martin Kallikak. *Five generations of descendants were traced through the line of the eldest son, except in the fourth generation of the nonmarital line, where there were no sons. The shaded figures indicate apparent mental retardation; the circles and squares indicate males and females, respectively.*

since it is now clear that some gains can be made by almost all retarded persons. Furthermore, such people are also commonly classified in educational terms, according to potential level of behavioral development—totally dependent, trainable, and educable.

Inheritance. When mental retardation occurs extensively along family lines, as among the nonmarital Kallikaks, it *seems* due to inheritance. In some instances, parents, children, and even grandchildren have received custodial care in the same institution. Another story of inherited retardation is reported in the history of the Juke family, traced before the Kallikaks (Dugdale, 1877). ■

There is no doubt that inheritance can be an important factor in mental retardation. Whether it is the total factor among the Jukes and the Kallikaks is quite another matter. Today, it appears that these early studies completely overlooked the possibility of important environmental factors.

In some cases, the inheritance leaves a defective brain at birth, as in the unusually small brain of the *microcephalic* person. Here, the development of the cerebrum stops at an early age, and the retardation can be profound. *Down's*

■ *Three children in the neighborhood were much slower than the others. I don't know what was wrong with them, but they were brothers and attended a school for very slow learners. The eldest was 13 and was easily mistaken for an 8 year old. One day he and his brothers mistook the garbage truck, which was big and white, for the big white ice cream truck.*

syndrome also involves congenital retardation. In this case the defect presumably is due to inheritance of an extra chromosome. One of Martin Kallikak's descendants on the nonmarital side was diagnosed as a "mongolian type," an earlier term referring to Down's syndrome.

Illness and disease. In other cases, low intelligence is caused by acquired health problems, such as infection, intoxication, brain injury, and malnutrition (Kaplan, 1973). These cases often include psychological components, but when a treatment is available, it is essentially medical. Malnutrition can be prevented by a proper diet; drugs are available for use against many types of infectious diseases; and defective metabolism sometimes can be altered.

If the thyroid glands are severely underactive at birth, it may lead to a disorder known as *cretinism,* in which the individual is characteristically dwarfed, overweight, and also lethargic. The IQ usually does not exceed 50, but if this disorder is diagnosed early and thyroxin is administered, it too can be alleviated (Figure 15-9).

Another medical problem in mental retardation that can be treated is *phenylketonuria,* or PKU, in which an important liver enzyme is either missing or ineffective. Consequently, phenylpyruvic acid accumulates in the body and interferes with brain functioning, producing mental "sluggishness." This disorder, estimated to afflict more than six thousand persons in the United States, is now diagnosed early by testing the urine of all newborn babies for the presence of phenylpyruvic acid, and a special diet is administered when necessary. A similar program is now being implemented in India, where it is estimated that there are over 16 million mentally retarded persons (Banerji, 1973).

Emotional factors. Another factor in mental retardation can occur in an individual's emotional condition. With severe adjustment problems, intellectual functioning may be markedly disrupted. Sometimes the individual is so disturbed that he or she cannot even speak, read, or do simple numerical calculations. More commonly, minor emotional intrusions simply prevent a person from achieving his or her full intellectual potential.

Many individuals who are retarded in other ways also experience an emotional problem. The original handicap leads to frustration, which causes emotional upset, which in turn engenders a further mental handicap. Retarded students, for example, overwhelmingly reject their placement in special classes because of the stigma attached. Apart from this aspect, their attitudes towards school have been found generally comparable to those of nonretarded students (Jones, 1974).

The importance of emotional factors in lowering intelligence test performance was illustrated when an investigator used a modified procedure for administering the Stanford-Binet Intelligence Scale, inserting an easy test item in the sequence whenever a child failed to answer a question correctly. This procedure raised the IQ of disturbed children by more than ten points, whereas it increased the performance of the normal children only slightly (Hutt, 1947). The lower performance of the disturbed children under the usual test conditions was judged to be due partly to their strong emotional reactions to failure.

Cultural deprivation. Today we know that lack of early learning experiences also can contribute to mental retardation. This *cultural deprivation* was not understood in earlier days and, therefore, it was assumed that the "bad side" Kallikaks developed solely on the basis of heredity. But that line of descendants could have remained dull because each dull parent was unable to

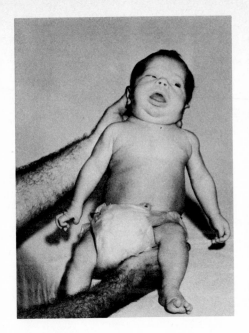 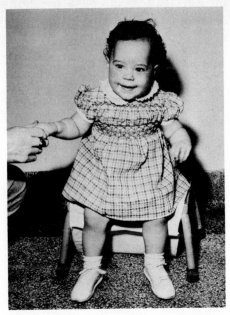

Figure 15-9 **Treatment of Cretinism.** *With early administration of thyroxin, the disordered child develops normally, both mentally and physically. (Wide World Photos)*

provide appropriate learning opportunities for his or her children, especially regarding the acquisition of verbal skills so often included on tests of intelligence.

Previously, we saw the influence of environmental factors in the Skeels-Skodak cases. A group of children who received considerable attention and stimulation early in life showed significantly greater mental development in later years than did those in a control group, who were left isolated and unattended much of the time in their early years (Skeels, 1966).

Altogether, early environmental handicaps are extremely detrimental because early in life one learns how to learn. Each accomplishment prepares the way for others, in a cumulative manner. The child who masters a language uses it to learn more about language and about other aspects of the world, and the child's capacity grows accordingly. It has been suggested that even the brain's physical development is influenced by the activities of its possessor (Hunt, 1969). The child who is deprived of learning experiences not only fails to acquire the skill itself—or the conjectured brain development—but also is deprived of the intellectual tools by which he or she can develop further skills. Recognition of this "snowball effect" has prompted educational programs such as Headstart, in which the aim has been to provide improved learning experiences for underprivileged children so that they can take advantage of later educational opportunities.

Our conception of intelligence has changed markedly on the basis of such observations. The conclusion drawn today by most investigators is that intelligence is not fixed at birth, as was believed in the days of the Kallikaks. In the past, intelligence perhaps seemed more stable because most people remained in the same environment most of their lives. Environmental changes can influence mental ability at most levels of functioning. Intelligence is now regarded as more fluid than fixed, although there are clear limits on the development that anyone can make, especially in extreme cases.

Education of the retarded. Since the formation of the President's Commission on Mental Retardation in 1963, there have been steady improvements in the diagnosis, treatment, and care of retarded persons. The argument over labeling continues, as it does in the case of mental illness, since there is as yet no way of identifying these persons that does not eventually have detrimental aspects (Guskin, 1974; MacMillan et al., 1974). But the idea that retarded persons can be assisted in many ways has grown more rapidly in the last two decades than at any time since Samuel Howe's plea to the state legislature in 1848 "on the condition of idiots in the Commonwealth of Massachusetts" (Figure 15-10).

In educating the retarded, the trend is moving away from complete separation of these special children towards the provision of extra resources for the typical classroom teacher in arranging an appropriate educational environment. The main procedures are: a slower rate of presentation of new material, greater structure in the learning tasks, and the use of concrete rather than abstract materials.

There is also a trend in training parents in better ways of helping the retarded to control their own behavior at home. Several of these approaches involve applications of operant conditioning (Das, 1973; Pulvermacher, 1974). Usually, the aim is to enable the retarded person to function on his or her own in some community residence program rather than in an institutional setting (Rodman & Collins, 1974).

The Mentally Gifted

Mentally gifted persons are also a minority, and funds available for the education of exceptional children are usually spent for the retarded. *Exceptional* children are those at either end of the intelligence continuum, comprising the upper and lower 2 percent of the general population. Persons with an IQ below 70 are generally regarded as mentally retarded while those above 130 are known as mentally gifted, but school performance is also used as a basis for such decisions (Figure 15-11).

IQ Range	Classification	Percent	Cumulative Percent
130 and above	Very superior	2.2	100.0
120 to 129	Superior	6.7	97.8
110 to 119	Bright normal	16.1	91.1
90 to 109	Average	50.0	75.0
80 to 89	Dull normal	16.1	25.0
70 to 79	Borderline	6.7	8.9
Below 70	Defective	2.2	2.2

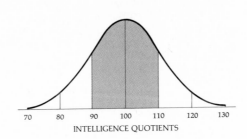

INTELLIGENCE QUOTIENTS

Figure 15-11 Distribution of IQ. *Intelligence scores in the general population are distributed according to the normal curve. The tests are usually constructed so that the average IQ is 100, and the cases decline at similar rates as the ends of the continuum are approached. Approximately two-thirds of the population falls between an IQ of 90 and 110. (Table adapted from* The Measurement and Appraisal of Adult Intelligence, *4th ed., by David Wechsler. Baltimore: The Williams & Wilkins Co., Baltimore.)*

One argument raised against special education for the gifted is that these children will learn on their own, which is true to a large degree, but if society is to make best use of its human resources, the gifted require special education programs. Furthermore, it is argued that special provision for the gifted is in keeping with the basic American premise: every student has the right to an education that is appropriate to his or her abilities (Trezise, 1976).

Problems of the gifted. Sometimes the traditional learning environment also creates a hardship for gifted persons. One investigator, herself a gifted person, talked with a 10-year-old "problem child" with an IQ of 165. This child was considered impudent, a liar, and without academic interests:

What seems to be your main problem at school?

Several of them.

Name one.

Well, I will name the teachers. Oh boy! It is bad enough when the pupils make mistakes, but when the teachers make mistakes, oh boy!

Mention a few mistakes the teachers make.

For instance, I was sitting in 5A and the teacher was teaching 5B . . . telling those children that the Germans discovered printing, that Gutenberg was the first discoverer of it, mind you. After a few minutes I couldn't stand it. I am not supposed to recite in that class, you see, but I got up. I said, "No; the Chinese invented, not discovered printing, before the time of Gutenberg—while the Germans were still barbarians." Then the teacher said, "Sit down. You are entirely too fresh" . . . [and] gave me a raking-over before the whole class. Oh, boy! What teaching . . . .

N__, that teacher is foolish, but one of the very first things to learn in the world is to suffer fools gladly. The child was . . . filled with resentment . . . [and] heard only the word "suffer."

Yes, that's it. That's what I say! Make 'em suffer. Roll a rock on 'em. (Hollingworth, 1942)

My parents had three daughters. The first two finished high school, but had neither the ability nor the time to go further. They were both well balanced, popular students, and while at their academic best, produced average work. I came out very differently, from a very early age, to the amazement of family and friends, who wondered how "Buss and Marsie" could have produced such a child. I read avidly, had a wild imagination and, at age 11, was using words my parents did not understand.

John Stuart Mill, the famous English philosopher, began to study Greek at age 3, geometry and algebra at age 8, and philosophy at age 12 (Cox, 1926). Mary Baker Eddy perceived the basic tenets of Christian Science as a healing doctrine when she was age 12. Einstein, at age 16, discovered the paradox from which his theory of relativity was developed (Polanyi, 1955). ■ The gifted child must develop some tolerance for more typical learning and teaching rates. The teacher, on the other hand, must develop a tolerance for certain characteristics generally found in the gifted, such as quickness, independence, and sometimes outspokenness (Pankove, 1974).

Study of the gifted. One longitudinal study of gifted persons, begun in 1921, involved over a thousand children with IQ's ranging from about 140 to 200. Most of them, referred to as "termites" in recognition of the original project director, L. N. Terman, have been interviewed and tested several times over the years, and it has been found that their early level of intelligence has been retained. When tested at an average age of 30 years, the group's performance again placed it higher than the upper 2 percent of the population. It was as much above the general adult level as it had been above the general child level and its success in education and employment was 10 to 30 times greater than what would be expected in a random sample of persons of the same age (Terman, 1954).

Furthermore, the physical and mental health of the gifted group remained at or above the average of the general population. In this study there are no grounds for the commonly held view that brightness is offset by poor physical condition and poor personal adjustment. The stereotype of the gifted intellectual as weak and undernourished has not been supported. On the contrary, intellectually gifted persons seem more likely to have good health and adequate personal adjustment, even in disadvantaged environments (Gruber & Kirkendall, 1973).

The most recent follow-up investigation occurred when the males in the group, at an average age of 62, were approaching partial or complete retirement. By means of questionnaires, they were asked to evaluate their satisfaction in life with respect to occupation, family, friendships, service to the community, and other factors, and generally they rated themselves as highly satisfied. The high vocational satisfaction may arise partly because they have the capacities that permit considerable autonomy in occupational activities, but in spite of their apparent occupational success, the subjects placed a greater emphasis on achieving satisfaction through family life (Sears, 1977).

Education of the gifted. It must be remembered that giftedness, like intelligence, involves several dimensions. A student may be quite advanced in certain mental abilities and not at all in others, or well ahead intellectually but not physically or emotionally. These different developmental rates make placement in a single grade difficult (Meyers et al., 1974; Figure 15-12).

As a rule, school programs for the gifted are faster in pace and less structured than those for the average child, and behavior modification techniques are less likely to be used. Instead, the students are given greater encouragement in developing research skills on their own. The emphasis is on how knowledge is acquired, and originality is stimulated by attempting to sensitize the student to problems as well as to solutions (Kirk, 1972).

Situations requiring creativity are encouraged, just as they should be emphasized in the normal classroom. In one procedure, called *brainstorming*, which can be used at all ability levels, the idea is to develop as many unique solutions as possible to a given problem. For example, the teacher might pass a tube of lipstick around the classroom

Individual Differences

Figure 15-12   Education of Gifted Children. *When special programs are not available, the question arises as to whether the gifted person should receive acceleration, being placed at a higher grade level, or enrichment, in which additional topics are studied at the usual grade level. Neither solution is entirely satisfactory because the accelerated student is no longer with age peers for social activities, and the busy classroom teacher usually cannot provide an adequate enrichment program for each gifted student. (Siteman from Stock, Boston)*

and ask: "How can we improve the container?" In the first place, no evaluation or criticism of any idea is permitted by anyone. Each individual alone or in a group setting contributes as many ideas as possible, regardless of how irrelevant or preposterous they may appear at first glance. The participants are also encouraged to build on the ideas of others, if possible, without criticizing them. Then, in the second stage the thinking is more systematic and objective. All the ideas are evaluated to discover how they might be used, if at all, and how they might be improved.

Programs for the gifted often require extra resources and special training on the part of the teacher. Hence, many specialists agree that of all the arrangements that can be made, there is no substitute for allowing gifted students to work together with others of similar ability some of the time (Trezise, 1976). This temporary grouping commonly occurs on a multigrade basis, in which students may differ by two or three years in chronological age yet possess comparable special abilities.

Determinants of Intelligence

Ideas on the origins of the differences in intelligence have prompted a long history of public controversy. In fact, the beginnings date back to Sir Francis Galton, who not only founded the first laboratory for studying individual differences but also coined the phrase *nature-nurture question*. This expression refers to the speculated contributions of heredity and environment, respectively, in the origin of intelligence.

Nature-Nurture Controversy

The nature-nurture controversy was evident even in the days of Alfred Binet. Although he succeeded where Galton failed by developing the first widely used intelligence test, his work was much criticized, especially in his native land (Wolf, 1973). The unrest has continued for 75 years.

National differences.   Shortly after the appearance of Binet's test, adaptations of his method were used in the United States to develop group tests of intelligence, which were needed for the assessment and placement of more than 100,000 draftees in World War I. After the war, statistical analyses of the scores showed some startling figures. Those immigrants to the United States who had served in the armed forces and had come from the northern and western European countries had significantly higher scores than did those from southern and eastern Europe. More specifically, Nordic males showed greater intellectual ability than men from the Mediterranean countries, and it was concluded that these national differences were inborn. In the early decades of our present century, this result was used partly for political purposes, to support the stricter immigration laws that were then in progress.

While the differences were undeniable, the reasons for them remained speculative. Doubters called for further analyses, which showed that performance on the tests also was related to length of residence in the United States. Recent immigrants achieved low scores; those who had been here 20 years achieved scores comparable to native Americans, regardless of national background. Hence, the environmentalists cited exposure to the American culture as the crucial factor.

Hereditarians had another explanation. There had been a steady decline in the natural endowment of immigrants coming to this country in successive generations. Each generation that arrived had a lower potential than the preceding one; the difference was not due to the new environment (Brigham, 1923 in Kamin, 1974).

Racial and class differences. In subsequent years, the nature-nurture focus changed from national to racial differences. In the 1930s and 1940s many comparisons of intellectual performance were made among American Indians, Negroes, and Caucasians, and consistent differences were found in favor of the third group (Garth, 1931; Klineberg, 1944). But once more, the issue concerned the interpretation: What was the source of these differences? Thus, the nature-nurture controversy continued.

In 1969, the Jensen Report was published, which cited the "uniform failure" of compensatory programs of education, such as Headstart and similar projects. The implication was that if such early and intensive educational projects could not alter intellectual performance, it must be largely inherited. Furthermore, the report revived the racial issue, stating that "the possible importance of genetic factors in racial behavior differences has been greatly ignored" (Jensen, 1969).

Two years later, intelligence was considered in the context of social class differences. The basic thesis was that inheritance is a considerable factor in intelligence and that as societies throughout the world achieve equality in opportunity for learning and employment, "social standing . . . will be based to some extent on inherited differences among people" (Herrnstein, 1973). There is little room for argument against this position; it is a fairly guarded statement about human affairs (Cronbach, 1975). Nevertheless, the viewpoint was given distinct racial overtones by the press, and considerable turmoil followed again.

Limitations of the data. All the research on the nature-nurture issue indicates that the measurement of national, racial, social, or other group differences in mental ability is beset with enormous difficulties. In the first place, there is the virtual impossibility of constructing a *culture-free test,* in which the items do not come from any particular culture. Clearly, language cannot be used, but even in the most carefully constructed nonverbal items, some cultural factors become involved. Geometric figures have been used, but squares and rectangles are the basic designs in some cultures and circles are the characteristic pattern in others, such as the Zulu. Hence, there have been attempts to eliminate all items that are influenced more by one culture than another, in a *culture-fair test,* but this work has not been successful either. Almost always, some subjects are at a disadvantage.

In this context, we must remember once again that intelligence does not appear to be a simple, unitary trait. Even if we could prepare culture-fair items, it is not clear what contents should be included in any test allegedly measuring group differences.

Another, seemingly inescapable, problem in the measurement of racial and national differences concerns the definition of any particular national origin or racial stock. From a genetic viewpoint, an American Indian, for example, is a person whose chromosomes all came from Indian ancestors, yet many Indians in this country have chromosomes from Caucasian and Negro predecessors. The same mixed conditions apply to almost all national and racial groups. Hence, it is exceedingly difficult to establish appropriately homogeneous subgroups for study.

To add to the complexity, comparative investigations have shown that results on intelligence tests are partly a function of the examiner's ethnic or national origin. The subject performs best with an examiner of his or her own background (Figure 15-13).

One conclusion seems clear at this point. It is impossible to study the *genetic basis* of group differences in intelligence. Performance differences exist, but there is no way of establishing sufficiently controlled conditions to determine the role of genetic factors in producing them. Fortunately, the question is of little practical significance. Furthermore, it is essentially incompatible with the concept of intelligence as a multifaceted ability.

Interaction in Intelligence

Instead, there is more interest today in the role of genetic and environmental factors in the development of intelligence within the individual. The issue of individual differences not only has greater potential significance but is also more feasible to study. Since identical

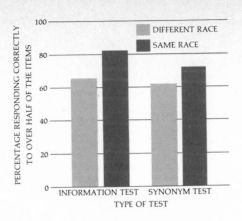

Figure 15-13 Race and Test Performance. *Results of studies with two different tests show that the subject performs best when examined by a member of his or her own race. (Adapted from* A Profile of the American Negro, *T. F. Pettigrew. Copyright 1964 by D. Van Nostrand Company. Reprinted by permission.)*

twins have the same genetic makeup, they provide a controlled context for some investigations.

Identical twin studies.   The psychological literature contains data from a great many twin studies in many parts of the world. Commonly, the results are reported as correlation coefficients, showing the degree of relationship between two factors; the result can vary from 0, in the case of no relationship, to ± 1.00, indicating perfect agreement. Overall, the correlations for numerous sets of identical twins are in the vicinity of .70, even when the two people have been reared apart. In other words, the members of each pair are rather similar in intelligence. Correlations among fraternal twins and other brothers and sisters are in the range of .40 to .50 (Burt, 1970).

This result seems to support the hereditarian viewpoint, but there are two general objections. First, the correlation of .70 is less than perfect, thus demonstrating environmental influence as well. In fact, in magnitude it is almost equally distant between the .40 to .50 correlation of ordinary siblings and a perfect 1.00 correlation, which would occur if heredity were the only influence.

In the second place, when identical twins have been reared apart, generally their environments have not been very different, largely because agencies try to place children with adoptive parents who have comparable IQs (Kamin,

1974). Instances in which one member of the pair has been reared as the proverbial prince and the other as a pauper are rare. In a notable exception, one twin was raised in the home of wealthy, well-educated people and the other was raised under conditions of low income and isolation from educational opportunities, which resulted in IQs that differed by 24 points, the largest reported difference between identical twins reared apart (Newman et al., 1937). ■ The average difference is around 8 points, about 2 points more than for identical twins reared together.

The identical twins studies are of considerable interest and show a mark of progress, but they are not yet conclusive. They can be interpreted as favoring heredity when one focuses on the generally high correlations for identical twins, even when reared apart. On the other hand, they can be interpreted as favoring environment when one notes the differences even among identical twins, especially in extreme cases. On this basis, we still cannot identify the relative contributions of heredity and environment with any certainty.

Assessment of compensatory education. Another approach to the heredity-environment issue has been through assessment of programs of compensatory education, in which disadvantaged children are given special learning opportunities, both within and outside school. Despite the Jensen Report, it is generally considered that these studies have not been an adequate test of the hereditary and environmental influences either, chiefly because many of the children did not receive the anticipated educational advantages. In the early days of Headstart, the teacher aides came from the same deprived communities as the children and, thus, could offer their students only the same interaction styles to which they were accustomed at home. The classrooms were often inadequate because so many were needed in such a short time, and the same limitation was involved in the in-service teacher-training programs. Because of budgetary considerations, new materials and equipment apparently became less available as the program proceeded (Katz, 1969).

Many experts feel that the programs gave too little too late. Most of them involved children from three to five years of age, yet postnatal environmental influences begin in the very first day of life, and in most respects the first years are the most important. It would be unwise to conclude from these efforts, in which perhaps there was a failure to marshal sufficient environmental opportunities, that the premise is incorrect.

The interaction principle. Even the Kallikak saga is a poor test. When it appeared, Dr. Goddard pointed out that it was "a natural experiment in heredity." There was the "defective" branch on one side and, for comparison purposes, a normal branch on the other. He exulted: "The biologist could hardly plan and carry out a more rigid experiment or one from which the conclusions would follow more inevitably."

Today, we realize that the "bad side" Kallikaks had very different life circumstances than the favored ones. We know that children can appear retarded and, in fact, can become retarded from being reared in deprived circumstances. We know that the environment is exceedingly important and that Goddard was decidedly biased towards the hereditarian viewpoint.

Considering all these efforts, what can we say about the contributions of heredity and environment to the intelligence of a given individual? Most psychologists probably would answer: The range of potential intelligence appears to be largely inherited, but the actual level obtained within this range seems to depend on environmental factors. Apart from this view, we do not know. At this time we have neither the research techniques nor the opportunities to make such an assessment. Furthermore, it is inappropriate to consider the question as an either/or issue.

Both factors are always present and influential for any individual. The influences of any particular heredity or any particular environment inevitably occur within the context of the other, and the contemporary view stresses that intelligence is the product of the *interaction* between them. The outcomes from each source are interdependent, as emphasized in prior discussions.

Thus, our concern should be refocused, just as in the debate over the origins of aggression. There we saw that the most useful question is not whether aggression is inborn or learned but rather: How can aggression, regardless of its origin, be diminished? We should use the same question again, except in reverse form: How can intelligence, regardless of its origin, be augmented? This question is one to which the efforts of psychologists are now being devoted.

As for the controversy, the reader is reminded that the journalist, probably more than anyone else, controls what the public thinks about psychology. At any given moment, the field contains numerous potentially controversial findings (Cronbach, 1975). Whether a controversy occurs is usually determined not by the actual data but by the way they are presented in the mass media.

Intelligence and Employment

Data concerning the testing of intelligence and group differences in intelligence are more readily transformed into public controversy than those in many other areas of psychology because the role of intelligence in modern society is so widely recognized. Mental capacity is regarded as a most significant factor in achieving success in work and other aspects of public and private life.

Occupational Differences

People in all societies have jobs, but the size and diversity of the labor force in modern industrialized nations is especially impressive. A study of the work force is made regularly in the United States by the government, in the form of surveys, and in recent years more than 20,000 separate occupations have been listed.

To investigate efficiently the role of intelligence and other factors in this broad spectrum of jobs, psychologists have sought readily available groups of people in which the occupations are extremely mixed. One such group is the armed forces, in which, during wartime, many thousands of individuals from different vocations are gathered together. On entering the service, each individual is administered a battery of tests, including a group test of general intelligence, and the results are used for the practical purposes of selection and placement. In addition, they can be made available for research.

Intelligence and occupations. During World War II, over ten million people from all backgrounds and modes of employment in the United States were tested in various ways in military service. In one extensive study of these data, representative of several in this area, a steady increase in the mean score for *general* intelligence was observed as one ascends the occupational scale, from unskilled labor to professional work. The scores of almost 19,000 men indicated a hierarchy of occupations according to general intellectual capacity. This result is not surprising, however.

A second and more impressive characteristic is the wide range of scores at every level. Among all 74 occupations represented in the sample, there was a distinct overlap of scores. That is, a significant minority of persons in the lowest-ranking occupations, according to the mean intelligence scores, attained higher scores than did some of the persons in the highest-scoring fields (Harrell & Harrell, 1945). In other words, in these studies, which are now more than 30 years old, a significant number of truck drivers, plumbers, and miners made higher scores than did the

Figure 15-14 Mean AGCT Scores
and Range of Scores for Various
Occupations. *The Army General
Classification Test (AGCT) is a group
test of intelligence involving both verbal
and performance items (Harrell and
Harrell, 1945).*

Occupation	Mean Score	Range of Scores
Lawyer	127.6	96–157
Engineer	126.6	100–151
Teacher	122.8	76–155
Bookkeeper	120.0	70–157
Radio repairman	115.3	56–151
Salesman	115.1	60–153
Machinist	110.1	38–153
Mechanic	106.3	60–155
Plumber	102.7	56–139
General painter	98.3	38–147
Truck driver	96.2	16–149
Farmer	92.7	24–147
Miner	90.6	42–139

lawyers and engineers, at the top of the distribution (Figure 15-14).

One conclusion that can be drawn from these data is that it is difficult to specify the upper limits of *general* intelligence for any given occupation. High test scores are found among some workers in all fields. On the other hand, in selecting individuals for certain jobs, a minimum or critical score is sometimes established, although this procedure may exclude individuals who might have succeeded despite a low score. Consequently, a range of scores is used in conjunction with other factors. In any case, the results emphasize that many occupations are not sharply defined according to general intellectual ability, as demonstrated by test scores.

Sex differences and occupations. Particularly since the 1940s, when countless women entered jobs vacated by men who went to war, the percentage of females in the paid labor force of the United States has been growing steadily. Increased urban living has resulted in

more work opportunities and has provided household conveniences that enable women and men to be gainfully employed outside the home. Most important, a factor that may be both a cause and an effect of this trend, is the changing attitude of both sexes towards family life (Figure 15-15).

In the early 1950s, almost two-thirds of all the women in the paid U.S. labor force were employed as clerical workers, service workers, or machine operators. This distribution partly reflects sex differences in tested abilities. In comparison with males, females tend to be higher in perceptual speed and manual dexterity, and these skills are involved in many clerical and operative tasks. However, women in general are superior in verbal fluency and in certain types of memory (Tyler, 1965). These capacities are not reflected in their employment. Also, there is no substantial evidence of an overall difference in intellectual capacity between men and women, but the proportion of women holding jobs in occupations demonstrating the higher mean intelligence scores is much smaller than that for men.

The field of dentistry shows this sex difference sharply. Surveys in the 1970s indicate that 97.8 percent of all practicing dentists were men, at the top of the hierarchy in this occupational group (Coombs, 1975). A step down the scale, 99 percent of the 16,000 dental assistants who are members of the national association are women (American Dental Assistant Association, 1977).

These different distributions apparently are not based on differences in ability. In fact, women, with intelligence comparable to that of men yet with generally more nimble fingers and greater interest in cosmetics, might be expected to perform better than men in the dentist's role. The determining factors seem to be precedent and current attitudes. Similar circumstances occur for diverse minority groups.

Figure 15-15 Male and Female
Employment. *The figures show the
percentage of the labor force composed
of males and females in the last
decades. (Adapted from Isaacson, 1966;
U. S. Department of Labor, 1970)*

Sex	1940	1950	1960	1970
Male	75.2	72.0	67.0	62.1
Female	24.8	28.0	33.0	37.9

Vocational Adjustment

For years, differences in intelligence were regarded as the only significant concern in the study of individual differences. Because intelligence was assumed to be a more global capacity than it is today, investigations in this area were assumed to hold promise for solutions to a wide variety of problems. But gradually, prompted partly by the Thurstones' work in intelligence, psychologists became interested in aptitudes, interests, and personality. When these findings were considered collectively and put to practical use they became an integral part of a movement called *vocational guidance,* which is the process of assisting a person in career planning and development.

The guidance movement. Inauguration of the vocational guidance movement is generally credited to Frank Parsons, a Boston philanthropist who organized The Vocational Bureau in 1908 and also wrote books on choosing a vocation that contain principles still applicable today. This movement and certain parallel developments, such as educational guidance programs and mental health institutes, have been attributed to two broad factors: (1) near the turn of the century people were beginning to accept the principle of societal responsibility for the welfare of individual citizens, and (2) at the same time, psychologists were developing procedures for identifying and appraising individual differences (Nelson, 1954b).

When an individual comes to a vocational counselor for guidance, the process usually involves an intake interview, collection and analysis of test data and case history information, and one or more counseling interviews. The test data usually pertain to general intelligence, aptitudes, vocational interests, and personality factors. The counselor's primary function is to help individuals help themselves, using whatever relevant information is available.

The adjustment process. If the authors were to offer a bit of vocational guidance to the reader who has not yet entered the labor market on a permanent basis, it would be to emphasize that one's vocational problems are never fully solved; the adjustment process continues throughout the adult life of virtually all individuals. Sometimes college students feel that the vocational issue would be resolved if only they could make a correct vocational choice, but this view ignores two important facts. First, we are all developing organisms and our changing physical and intellectual makeups require constant adjustments and readjustments during our working lives. Making an occupational choice is just the beginning of the process. Second, especially in modern times, jobs themselves often change rapidly, or they disappear. Thus, vocational development demands regular evaluation of changes in oneself and in the environment (Figure 15-16).

One theory of occupational behavior reflects this steady adjustment process. It is based on the viewpoint of successive life stages or changes in the life cycle. In the *exploratory stage,* which lasts from approximately age 15 to age 25, the individual attempts to attain greater understanding of himself or herself in relation to the world of work and makes a tentative vocational

Figure 15-16 Vocational Development. *New skills often must be learned in order to find desirable or better employment or to improve one's prospects in a chosen field. This challenge may present itself to newcomers to a particular country or region, to young people whose education has trained them for occupations where jobs currently are not available, or to older people faced with technological changes in their occupational field. (Wollinsky from Stock, Boston)*

choice. The individual tries to discover the type of person he or she wants to become and, insofar as possible, makes a choice in accordance with this self-concept. Several initial choices may be made at this stage.

In the *establishment stage,* which may last for the next 10 to 20 years, the trial process is finished and the individual concentrates on advancing in his or her chosen field. Here the person is often faced with the problem of working long hours and forgoing pleasures in order to rise nearer the top of the work hierarchy or giving up business opportunities and possible advancement in favor of leisure time with family and friends. These choices, when available, influence the level of achievement.

In the *maintenance stage,* which begins around mid-life, the individual continues the activities in which he or she is now established, generally without trying to make further advancements. Here the person is faced with the difficulty of maintaining his or her status in the face of diminishing energy and abilities and against the pressure of younger, often better-educated people rising through the establishment stage. The years of *decline,* usually beginning in the 60s and typically involving retirement, require adjustment to a new way of life, as well as acceptance of the physical and mental ailments of old age (Super, 1957).

Vocational choice is particularly difficult in the United States, where a diversity of occupations exists and freedom of choice and upward mobility are so commonly stressed. These factors, coupled with our extended period of formal education and varying economic conditions, mean that it is not unusual to be undecided about a career—and thus in the exploratory stage—well into the third decade of life.

Summary

Measurement and Theory

1. Intelligence is an extremely difficult concept to define, but most definitions generally refer to some aspect of flexibility or versatility of adjustment. Its measurement is often accomplished by using individual intelligence tests such as the Stanford-Binet, from which the concepts of mental age (MA) and intelligence quotient (IQ) developed, and the Wechsler scales, which feature a wide variety of subtests with both verbal and performance items.

2. Intelligence is now considered to be a composite of specific abilities rather than a unitary function. This view is reflected in factor analysis, a statistical procedure that is used to discover the irreducible components of mental ability. These efforts have been only partially successful. They have been guided by various theories of intelligence, such as the structure-of-intellect model, which postulates many distinct intellectual abilities.

Exceptional Intelligence

3. The mentally retarded, comprising the lower 2 percent of the population in measured intelligence, are classed as totally dependent, educable, or trainable. Causal factors in mental retardation include inheritance, in which a defective brain or defective biochemisry is inherited; illness and disease, involving conditions such as malnutrition, infection, intoxication, and brain injury; emotional factors, which can accompany any sort of retardation; and cultural deprivation, in which there is an absence of the usual early learning and social experiences. At all levels, intelligence is regarded as fluid rather than fixed, in the sense that environmental factors can influence mental ability.

4. The mentally gifted comprise the upper 2 percent of the population in mental intelligence. Both the gifted and

retarded can be assisted by special educational and training programs. As a rule, the programs for the gifted are less structured and proceed more rapidly than those for other children. They also stress research skills and originality, and the goals are achieved partly by permitting such students to work together occasionally, on a multigrade basis.

Determinants of Intelligence

5. The nature-nurture controversy in intelligence has a long history, extending through many studies of national and racial differences. The question of the genetic basis of group differences is impossible to answer because of the absence of satisfactory tests and the difficulty in establishing appropriate samples of subjects.

6. The most promising research on inherited and environmental influences in the intelligence of individuals involves comparisons of identical twins reared apart, but even these investigations afford diverse interpretations. The influences of heredity and environment are always present and they depend on one another; the significant issue is to understand their interaction in the production of intelligence.

Intelligence and Employment

7. Surveys have shown a hierarchical structure of occupations according to intellectual capacity, from unskilled labor to professional work, but equally significant is the broad range of scores at every level, which overlap among all occupations. There is no evidence to support employment differences between the sexes on the basis of general intelligence.

8. The problem of vocational adjustment involves not only intelligence but also consideration of other factors as well, especially interests, aptitudes, and personality. Sometimes these factors are assessed through tests and interviews, in a procedure called vocational guidance. The process of vocational adjustment is life-long, beginning with the exploratory stage in young adulthood and continuing through the individual's life cycle.

Suggested Readings

Bindra, D. *A theory of intelligent behavior*. New York: Wiley, 1976. A broad perspective based on the fundamental psychological processes and neurological research.

Browning, P. L. *Mental retardation: Rehabilitation and counseling*. Springfield, Ill.: Charles C Thomas, 1974. A collection of papers on the origins, classification, and treatments of mental retardation.

Herrnstein, R. J. *I.Q. in the meritocracy*. Boston: Little, Brown, 1973. A well-referenced, readable statement largely from the viewpoint of heredity.

Kamin, L. J. *The science and politics of I.Q.* Potomac, Md.: Lawrence Erlbaum, 1974. A well-documented work presenting the environmentalist position.

Kirk, S. A. *Educating exceptional children* (2nd ed.). Boston: Houghton Mifflin, 1972. A textbook with emphasis on the retarded and an extensive chapter on the gifted.

PART SEVEN

Integration of Behavior

Chapter 16

Personality

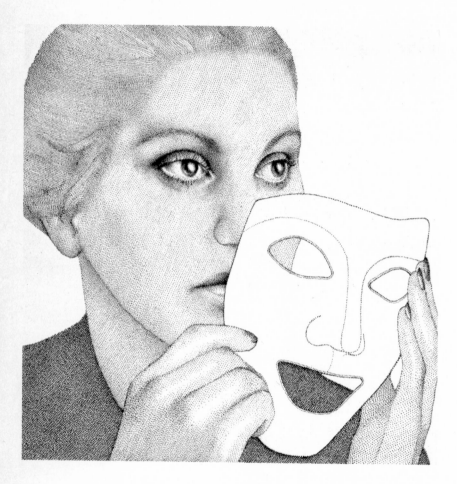

It has been a favorite pastime of human beings to try to describe and understand other people. Most of us do this frequently, analyzing the faults and strengths of our friends or colleagues and speculating about the actual nature of individuals with whom we work or go to the movies. What we are doing is trying to comprehend others' personality. Some people are apparently much easier to understand than are others; one might say that they reveal their personality more readily. Others may seem to be hiding behind masks. In early Greek drama the actors wore masks, but for quite the opposite reason. The masks worn in Greek drama were intended to show the audience what kind of personality the actor was portraying, usually a hero or villain. In fact, our word ''personality'' comes from *persona*, the Latin word for the masks used in classical drama.

Study of Personality

In studying personality, we are concerned with the whole person. The focus is not on a selected aspect of the individual, as in most of the previous chapters, but on the overall organization of the diverse components. In this respect, the present chapter marks a transition point in this book, for most of the subsequent chapters are also concerned primarily with the individual in a global sense, as seen in personal adjustment, therapy, and social behavior.

Definition of Personality

As a rule, *personality* is defined as the unique and characteristic ways in which an individual reacts to his or her surroundings. It is a convergence of all the important factors that influence one's behavior and experience, resulting in some relatively consistent patterns of behavior. The uniqueness is stressed because all of us have some characteristics in common with other persons, but in each individual these are combined in special ways and unite with less common characteristics to form a personality that is distinct from all others. An example illustrates this uniqueness.

Jenny. Tall and sturdy, with gray-green eyes and jet black hair, Jenny Masterson's features suggest an Irish ancestry. In her late 50s, her skin is unwrinkled and physically she is a striking woman. Her appearance is immaculate, conservative, perhaps slightly masculine, and a bit old-fashioned (Figure 16-1).

At the age of 58, without family except for her son, Jenny has moved from Chicago to New York to Montreal and back to New York City within a year, searching each time for a more suitable home and job. She always seems ready to try something new, if she thinks it would improve her situation, and when she encounters a circumstance not to her liking, she readily speaks her mind. In New York City, after searching endlessly, she found a job caring for children but left within a month, announcing that she disliked the institution's ways of handling the children.

Jenny is outspoken in other ways, criticizing ethnic groups and constantly making uncomplimentary remarks about the girl friends of her son, Ross. She calls them "she-dog," "beast," "prostitute-woman," and other names.

The oldest of seven children, Jenny's father died when she was 18, and she supported the family for nine years by working in a telegraph office. As soon as her brothers and sisters left home, she married a divorced railroad inspector, thereby alienating herself from her family, who did not approve of either the man or his divorce. Following a bitter quarrel, she broke off relations with her family completely, moving to Chicago with her husband.

Two years later, just a month before their son Ross was born, her husband died. In many respects, Jenny's life from age 29 to 58 has been the story of her endless efforts to give Ross the best possible care and schooling (Allport, 1965).

A lover of books, she sent him to an expensive private school by working as a librarian and living a frugal existence. Her home was a windowless linen room in an apartment building, where she ate chiefly milk and cereal. When he grew older, Ross referred to her as a "swallow who lives in a flue," but no self-denial was too great for Jenny if it gave her son the best education and the most gentlemanly comportment possible. Upon graduation, he was admitted to an excellent university on the East Coast, but he left after two years to go to war.

After returning from the war, Ross spent less time with his mother, more with his girl friends, and much money entertaining them, despite his mother's protestations. When Jenny finally decided that her beloved son was being deceitful in these regards, she broke off relations with him too, despite the fact that she was otherwise alone, nearing old age, almost penniless, and without a home for herself.

Figure 16-1 Jenny. *As usual, Jenny is wearing black, with a choker round her neck and a gold pin on her blouse, the pin a wedding-day gift from her husband. (From* Letters from Jenny *edited by Gordon W. Allport, © 1965 by Harcourt Brace Jovanovich, Inc. and reproduced with their permission.)*

Characteristics of Theories

How do we go about understanding this whole individual, this personality called Jenny Masterson? In psychology, there are four major personality theories, each of which can be used in our efforts to explain and predict an individual's behavior. These are psychoanalytic theory, trait theory, learning theory, and the humanistic viewpoint.

Different contents. In most influential personality theories there is consistent recognition of the basic psychological processes, but different theories give emphasis to different processes. Motivation, for example, is an important theme in psychoanalytic theory; conditioning processes are commonly fundamental in the learning theories; and perception and cognition are stressed in the humanistic viewpoint.

In addition, the theories differ in the attention given to past and present events in shaping an individual's life. All of the theories recognize that both sets of events are important and interrelated, but psychoanalysis, more than the others, stresses a person's earliest experiences. Learning theory also emphasizes past events, but not the distant past. The other theories are more centrally concerned with the individual's current circumstances and ways of perceiving them.

Different methods. Since contents have relevance for methods, and vice versa, personality theories also differ in the methods used to assemble the relevant data. Some theorists rely heavily on a *clinical approach,* in which professional judgment and opinion play an important role. The theory is constructed from data collected in working with individual clients or patients, as in a therapist's private practice, or from observations in the normal routines of daily life. Quantitative data generally are not sought and, if available, are interpreted in terms of the clinical experience.

Other theorists rely on a more quantitative or *statistical approach.* The data for developing or supporting a theory are obtained through research conducted explicitly for this purpose, and the results are analyzed in the most objective manner possible. Experimental methods, formulas, and computers are employed, and the information is collected from large groups of subjects who have agreed to participate in psychological research. These data are more objective than those from the clinical approach, but they are collected under less natural circumstances.

Of the four theories, psychoanalysis and the humanistic approach tend to be more clinical; trait and learning theories have a stronger statistical basis. These differences and similarities will become more evident as we examine each approach in detail.

Psychoanalytic Theory

Sigmund Freud developed his theory of psychoanalysis near the beginning of this century from self-analysis and intensive work with a few cases in his private practice. Emphasizing motivation, he saw the human personality as the derivative of two basic forces—sex and aggression—which are constantly seeking expression in the individual. These impulses are part of our inborn nature and, therefore, denial of their expression, as often required by the demands of society, does not result in their disappearance. Instead, they find release in a disguised form, called *unconscious motivation.* Conflicts concerning these motives, especially those from childhood, when the personality is being formed, can have a significant influence on adult behavior.

This viewpoint was strongly resisted in the early post-Victorian era, but slowly gained increasing acceptance. Aspects of this theory now occupy an important position in the social sciences and public thought, although since Freud's day many concepts have been clarified or made more useful than they were initially (Figure 16-2).

Systems and Stages

In psychoanalytic theory, the building blocks of personality, apart from the unconscious, consist of three systems—the id, ego, and superego. In a very general sense they represent biological, psychological, and social forces, respectively.

Id, ego, and superego.   The newborn is activated purely by inborn impulses. It strives for physical satisfaction and nothing more, and these biological urges, found in all human beings, are collectively referred to as the *id.* The id includes not only reflexes but also two classes of drives or "instincts." One of these, the *life instinct,* concerns the survival of the individual and the species and, thus, the organism needs food, drink, protection, sleep, and sex. The other, the *death instinct,* operates in a more subtle fashion. It leads away from life, towards the destruction of the organism, and is manifest chiefly in aggressive behavior, directed towards the self and also outward towards others. It should be noted here that Freud used the term *instinct* essentially to refer to strong motivational and emotional impulses; he did not use it in the conventional sense.

According to the psychoanalytic theory, life in the newborn occurs essentially without environmental concerns. The newborn is "all id," wanting food right away when hungry and urinating without consideration of time or place. In short, the id follows the *pleasure principle,* which requires the immediate satisfaction of needs, regardless of the circumstance. ■

Figure 16-2 Freud in His Later Years. *Freud had several dogs, and one of them, Jofi, was said to be an astute judge of human character. (Photo by H. G. Casparis)*

While the biological drives of the id continue throughout life, the growing infant soon learns to react to his or her outer environment as well and, thus, the expression of the id becomes modified. Gradually, the *ego* emerges. It is speculated that this force develops partly out of the energy provided by the id and partly from the environment. Eventually, the ego becomes the executive or problem-solving dimension of the personality. The Latin word ego means "I" or "self."

■ *One day while my aunt was busy doing something else, my four-year-old cousin asked her to unzip her dress, but my aunt ignored her. A couple of minutes later, my cousin walked into the room with a pair of scissors in her hand. She had cut her dress all the way up in front.*

■ *As I sit here chewing my gum, I'm beginning to realize that some of my personality traits fall into a pattern. Not only can a piece of Trident generally be found between my jaws, but I'm usually also talking. I love to talk. I talk a great deal and very fast.*

If I think a bit further, I remark on other traits of mine that center around my mouth. My fiance has often commented about how much I enjoy kissing him. Hmm, I remember a guy I dated in high school also noticed that I liked kissing.

For years, I was constantly putting things in my mouth—pencils, buttons, almost anything I picked up. I now remember my parents, greatly annoyed by such behavior, continually nagging, "Sue, take that out of your mouth," or, "Sue, that's dirty. . . . How can you . . . ?"

I have used my mouth, not only for a receptacle for objects, but as a tool—to cut thread, to open wrappers, to unscrew container tops, to trim my nails.

However, of all things, my thumb found its way into my mouth most frequently. I continued to suck my thumb in school through fourth grade. The orthodontist said thumb sucking was giving me an overbite, and he tried everything to keep my thumb out of my mouth—bad tasting goo, strings around it, covers over it—to no avail. Only when I went to overnight camp did I stop.

All these traits fall into the pattern of an oral incorporative personality. What caused it? Did my mother wean me too soon? Was I deprived of adequate sucking as a baby because my brother, only a year younger than I, came along, wanting a nipple to suck?

Well—I've got to go brush my teeth now.

The ego develops in the service of the id but follows the *reality principle,* which often requires a suspension of the pleasure principle according to the conditions of the environment. The infant discovers that sucking on clothes does not satisfy his or her hunger and that wet diapers are uncomfortable. Thus, the infant seeks to alter these conditions, perhaps by calling for his or her mother. As the infant finds ways to solve such problems, the ego emerges. Behavior becomes less blind and more adaptive through psychological processes such as perceiving, learning, remembering, and reasoning, which are aspects of the ego. Under the influence of the ego, the child gradually refrains from acting solely according to biological impulses.

One might compare the relation of the ego to the id with that between a rider and his horse. The horse provides the locomotive energy, and the rider has the prerogative of determining the goal and of guiding the movements of his powerful mount towards it. But all too often in the relations between the ego and the id we find a picture of the less ideal situation in which the rider is obliged to guide his horse in the direction in which it itself wants to go. (Freud, 1933)

Throughout life, the ego usually is confronted with another force in the personality, which develops through the social aspects of the environment. The child acquires certain values and standards of behavior from others, and this system is known as the *superego,* which has two divisions. One part, the *conscience,* discourages the expression of behavior that is deemed socially undesirable by parents and elders, and it develops primarily under the influence of scorn and threats of punishment. The parents may say to a dishonest girl, "You are bad." If the child internalizes the parents' standards, the next time she lies or thinks about lying, she says to herself, "I am bad," or "I am ashamed of myself." In acquiring this aspect of the superego, the child controls her behavior much as the parent would control it.

The *ego-ideal,* on the other hand, arises largely through encouragement. Rewards, privileges, and praise are given to the child when he or she behaves in a certain manner or achieves certain goals desired by the parents. Also, the ego-ideal develops as the child tries to imitate some older person. Together, the conscience and ego-ideal, formed early in life, can exert profound influences on the ego.

Early psychosexual stages. As the child matures, basic changes in personality are due to the growth of the ego and superego, since the id remains constant throughout life. The most important of these emerging systems is the ego, which, in the child's early years, develops as the child copes with his or her energy related to three erogenous or sexual zones—the mouth, the anus, and the genitals, respectively. For Freud, these early periods, called *psychosexual stages,* have much significance for the developing personality (Figure 16-3).

The first task for any infant is to obtain food, and thus the first period is called the *oral stage.* If the breast or bottle is readily available at this time, it is speculated that the child is likely to develop trusting and basically optimistic attitudes. The basic requirements of human existence are regularly satisfied and a benign view of life emerges. On the other hand, if food is not available, feelings of uncertainty, mistrust, and pessimism are hypothesized as the likely outcomes. Furthermore, these early deprivations and conflicts are likely to be reflected later in the adult personality through the processes of unconscious motivation. ■

In the second year of life, the *anal stage* occurs, in which the child is confronted with the first real task for which little assistance can be given—toilet training. Here again, the ego must obey the reality principle, not the pleasure principle. According to Freud, if this training is too harsh or too lenient, the resulting conflicts again are likely to

Figure 16-3 Psychosexual Stages. *After passing through the oral and anal stages, the child enters the phallic stage. In psychoanalytic theory, these stages of psychosexual development are important in the growth of the ego. (Bodin from Stock, Boston)*

Figure 16-4 Identification. *According to Freud, this process has more depth than imitation, which is simply copying someone else. Through identification, another person's ways of thinking and behaving are incorporated by the child as his or her own. (Zimbel from Monkmeyer)*

have consequences later in life. Still coping with this particular problem, perhaps in symbolic fashion, someone may be excessively prompt, neat, and clean or, on the other hand, unusually messy and disorderly, depending on the management of the earlier training. Again unconscious motivation is involved.

The period from three to six years of age is the *phallic stage,* a term applied to both boys and girls despite its reference to the penis. In this stage the child discovers sexual pleasures associated with the genitalia and subsequently develops behaviors such as stroking, rocking, and forms of masturbation. Far more important for personality development, however, is an increasing awareness of the different sex roles of the parents and an emerging interest in the parent of the opposite sex. Freud called this reaction the *Oedipal complex* in boys and the *Electra complex* in girls. Both names are

derived from early Greek drama in which an offspring sought relations with the parent of the opposite sex and regarded the like-sexed parent as a rival. ■

It is hypothesized that the normally developing child eventually handles the Oedipus (Electra) problem by reversing his (her) outlook. In the *process of identification,* the child adopts the manner, attitudes, and interests of the like-sexed parent, thus attempting to win the love and respect of the other parent. This identification process is assumed to be particularly important for developing an appropriate sex role in later life, and it is the primary way in which the superego is established (Figure 16-4).

Later stages. Following the early psychosexual periods, there is a stage characterized by the apparent absence of

■ *During the period of age four to four and one half years, my sister, who had always been very affectionate with both parents, began to exhibit a definite predilection for my father. She was always climbing onto his lap, hopping into his bed in the morning, kissing him goodnight at least a dozen times per evening, combing his hair, picking out a favorite sweater of his for him to wear, asking him if she looked pretty in her new dress, waiting excitedly for him to return home every night and racing down the block to meet him, and generally craving his attention in numerous other ways. Perhaps the most blatant expression of my sister's Electra Complex occurred when she occasionally declared that, just as soon as she was old enough, she was going to "marry Daddy."*

sexual interests. The interests are still present, claimed Freud, but he called this period the *latency stage* because they are submerged. This stage is said to occur from age six to the onset of adolescence, but there is some suggestion that it is a cultural artifact. In certain primitive societies the late childhood years are not characterized by a diminution in sexual interests.

With the beginning of adolescence, the *genital stage* appears, which involves a reawakening of sexual interests and the seeking of other persons to provide sexual satisfaction. The individual becomes other-oriented as well as self-oriented; he or she must combine self concerns with those of other people. If handicaps acquired at earlier stages are not insurmountable, the person settles into the tasks of establishing mature relationships with other individuals and developing personal independence, a stage that lasts throughout the mature years.

Unconscious Motivation

The reason that the early stages can have such a lasting influence, Freud emphasized, is that the unresolved problems in early life do not simply go away—they only *seem* to disappear, being dismissed to the realm of the unconscious by the process of *repression*, as we have seen previously. Unconscious conflicts, and the motivations associated with them, consequently are considered the most important determinants of the adult personality.

Unconscious symbolism. As described by Freud, mental life is like an iceberg. The most significant aspects lie below the surface in the unconscious, which is generally inaccessible to the individual (Figure 16-5).

When these contents reappear, they do so in disguised or symbolic form, as in Freudian slips, dreams, defense mechanisms, and neurotic behavior, as well as in our choices of occupations, hobbies, and other basic interests. The "oral character," for example, presumably relates to conflict and frustration in the first stage of development. This personality type develops from unconscious efforts to work out unresolved oral problems, as seen in someone who engages in excessive eating and drinking, is extremely gullible, is prone to sarcasm and arguing, or is inclined to depression and pessimism when not receiving personal attention. In the psychoanalytic view, this person may have a *fixation*, which means that psychological growth is temporarily or permanently arrested at a given point.

Similarly, it is speculated that the adult "anal character" has a symbolic link, through the unconscious, to problems in the second stage of childhood. The anal personality may be overly concerned about collecting things and saving them, becoming miserly about money until "rolling in it," or else the individual may be inclined to go on binges instead, "letting it all go at once." More symbolically, the anal adult may be scrupulously clean, conforming, prompt, and precise in all phases of adult life or else incurably sloppy, unruly, messy and disobedient. It is these opposed reactions to the same presumably unresolved problems at the anal level that are a source of humor in the well-known play *The Odd Couple*. ■

The reader, however, should not focus on these stereotyped descriptions of personality, which are regarded with skepticism by many psychologists. The important point to remember is not a given cluster of personality traits but rather that Freud saw all of us as the product of early childhood experiences. In adult life each of us has our own reenactment of these problems. In bringing attention to the role of early childhood experience in adult behavior, Freud made a most significant contribution to the study of human personality development.

■ *I can distinctly remember often withholding my bowel movements when I was a toddler—I now realize that I must have been afraid of making a mess. To this day I remain an extremely neat and orderly person, and I budget my money down to the last penny, although I'm not sure it all relates back to my toilet training.*

Jenny's unconscious. When we look at Jenny Masterson in her 50s, we are struck by her excessive attentions and interest in her only son, her aggressive reactions towards women of any age, and perhaps by her attractive and also slightly masculine appearance. How can we understand these aspects of Jenny in terms of psychoanalytic principles?

It is hypothesized that Jenny's most basic motivations are known neither to her nor directly to us and, furthermore, that their origins lie in childhood problems. Jenny's orderliness, fastidiousness, and obstinacy, for example, are typical of the anal character. However, there are no facts on her toilet training (Allport, 1965).

A most significant aspect of any personality is the social dimension, involving one's relations with others, and here the phallic stage seems relevant. It could be speculated that Jenny never was able to resolve the Electra struggle in the usual manner, by identifying with the like-sexed parent. We know little of her early relationship with her father, to whom she should have been attracted, but her adult anger towards all women could have developed from latent hostility towards her mother. In letters to Ross's friends, by which we know of Jenny's life, she describes her antagonism towards other women and her abrupt discontinuation of relations with them. We know that later, during the genital stage, Jenny experienced few opportunities for relationships with girls her age, which facilitate a feminine identification. Instead, in her teens, she became the financial head of a large family, assuming a traditionally masculine role.

Her own marriage, which was brief and impoverished, did not resolve this confusion in sexual identity, but the birth of Ross offered a partial answer. She could continue the masculine role as she strove to support the helpless child and at the same time, this new male figure in her life gave partial satisfaction to the frustrated Electra strivings, curtailed by the early deaths of both her father and

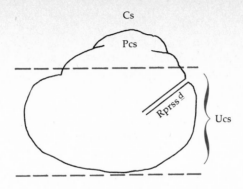

Figure 16-5 Levels of Consciousness. *Freud used the abbreviations Cs, Pcs, and Ucs to refer to the conscious, preconscious, and unconscious, respectively. The conscious consists of our current thoughts and experiences. Below this level, the preconscious includes information that is available following some direct effort at recall. For example, "Who was your schoolteacher ten years ago?" The contents of the unconscious are repressed (Rprss^d) and, therefore, not so readily accessible. (Reproduced by permission of Sigmund Freud copyrights, The Institute of Psycho-Analysis, The Hogarth Press Ltd., and W. W. Norton & Company, Inc., from* The Ego and the Id *in Volume XIX of the* Standard Edition of the Complete Psychological Works of Sigmund Freud, *translated and edited by James Strachey. Copyright © 1960 by James Strachey.)*

husband. In short, Jenny's furious, unprovoked attacks on Ross's girl friends suggest that she is extremely jealous of them and that she has more than the usual maternal impulses towards her son. With much feeling, almost incestuously, she describes trips with Ross, dining out together, and going to the theater. As Jenny wrote in one of her letters, following a Broadway play they "kissed goodnight under the stars" (Figure 16-6).

In psychoanalytic theory, the story of personality is that of the ego's struggle to maintain a balance among the intrapsychic systems. In Jenny, as in all of us, the id impulses continued throughout life, but reared in a strict Victorian manner, she also had a strong superego. Amid these pressures from the id and the superego, as well as the constraints of the environment, her ego's first line of

Figure 16-6 An Intense Mother-Son Relationship. *Constantly rivalrous with Ross's girl friends, Jenny said after his death that he was finally "safe from other women." (From* Letters from Jenny *edited by Gordon W. Allport, © 1965 by Harcourt Brace Jovanovich, Inc. and reproduced with their permission.)*

defense was repression. Afterwards, the unconscious sexual and aggressive impulses gave rise to behavior that was otherwise inexplicable—Jenny became a "smother mother"; she found other women too coarse, ugly, or sexy; her appearance was "slightly mannish"; and she had no insight into her extremely domineering, authoritarian manner.

Modified Psychoanalysis

Under Freud's leadership, psychoanalysis was a unified system of psychology, but eventually psychoanalysts separated into a variety of groups. Now there are several distinct systems. All are concerned with the deeper aspects of personality, but in other respects they differ markedly.

Analytic psychology. The first heir-apparent to Freud's work was Carl Gustav Jung, who after a few years rejected Freud's emphasis on sex as the primary energizing force in personality. The two men also differed in their conception of the unconscious. Freud postulated an *individual unconscious,* containing the unknown fears, desires, and conflicts of a particular individual, while Jung in addition hypothesized a *collective unconscious,* which is the "deposit of ancestral experiences from untold millions of years . . . to which each century adds an infinitesimally small amount of variation . . ." (Jung, 1928). In this realm are all of humanity's past experiences, not only in human history but also in the earlier evolutionary stages of animal life. The collective unconscious is said to be potentially inherited by all human beings, and the underlying similarities among different cultures are regarded as support for this idea. Hence, Jung's *analytic psychology* is of interest in anthropology too (D'Aquili, 1975).

One aspect of the collective unconscious is the feminine side of the male personality, called the *anima,* and the masculine side of the female personality, called the *animus.* While these conditions are due partly to hormones and

other aspects of human physiology, they are also shaped in all people by the experiences of men and women living together through countless centuries. As men associate with women they become feminized in outlook and values, and as females share life and work with males, they become masculinized. In Jenny's case, it would be speculated, the animus was overdeveloped, prompting not only her somewhat masculine ways but also her inability to understand and relate successfully to those of her own sex. Freud, incidentally, emphasized that each sex possessed both male and female hormones, even though at the time there was no known way to verify this viewpoint.

Individual psychology. Another early analyst who diverged from Freud was Alfred Adler, who was significant in turning Freud's attention to the issue of aggression. Adler did not view sex as the basic motivating force in life and placed little emphasis on unconscious processes.

His *individual psychology* was reformulated on several occasions. At one time the idea of striving for superiority played an important role; later, the concept of social interest became more significant. Today, *sibling rivalry,* which refers to a child's competition among brothers and sisters for the parents' love and attention, is one of Adler's most influential ideas. ■ Another is *inferiority complex,* referring to an individual's feelings of being less competent than others. Both concepts imply an effort to overcome personal deficiencies, real or imagined.

In Jenny's early life with six brothers and sisters, there was a high possibility for sibling rivalry. As the oldest child, she once had her parents to herself, but then she was displaced by more and more children while she, in turn, was given increasing responsibility for their care and survival. These conditions undoubtedly led to increased resentment, exemplified later in Jenny's poor relations with almost everyone of either sex. In a

■ Shortly after my birth, my mother took me to my grandparents' home to show me to the family and to introduce me to my two-year-old cousin Eunice. Until that time she had been the only child in the family and had received constant attention, so when I arrived and "took a piece of her action" Eunice was very jealous. She was interested in me at first but later became angry with me when she discovered my incompetence as a playmate. After that, my mother decided to keep me in a laundry basket with sides too high for her to reach in and poke at me.

One afternoon, my mother put me in my laundry basket on top of the dining room table where she thought I would be safe, and left to work in the kitchen. A few minutes later responding to a banging around she ran into the other room to find Eunice under one end of the table wielding a broom and trying to push the basket over the edge.

Integration of Behavior

symbolic sense, Jenny perhaps became a sibling among Ross's girl friends, fighting with them for his love and attention.

This emphasis in Adlerian psychology on the cultural determinants of behavior is found among many contemporary psychoanalysts. Altogether, most modern analysts show more interest in social forces and less concern with sexual repressions than was the case in Freud's earlier work.

Assessment and Research

In science, formulation of a theory is preceded or followed by empirical study, which involves careful observation and measurement. Some psychologists interested in personality theory, therefore, have developed tests of personality. Other tests have been developed for practical purposes, as in the diagnosis of mental disorders. Sigmund Freud relied on the interview, rather than formal tests, but many psychologists who approach personality from the psychoanalytic viewpoint are inclined to use projective techniques, involving inkblots, ambiguous pictures, and incomplete sentences.

Projective techniques. When a person perceives his or her own characteristics in another stimulus, animate or inanimate, we generally say that *projection* has occurred. ■ In a projective test, the subject is given some ambiguous stimulus and asked to describe it, and it is assumed that this description reveals the person's inner feelings, desires, and fears. Consider this sentence fragment: "On rainy days, I carry a(n)_____." When asked to complete it, Jenny might respond with the word "umbrella" or "raincoat," which tells us little about her except that she, like most of us, is interested in shielding herself from the rain. This incomplete sentence has too much structure to elicit a projective response.

Consider this shorter fragment: "On rainy days, I _____." Here Jenny might

answer "worry about my son." Ross might reply, "think about my girl friend." A certain girl friend, in turn, might say," . . . I can't answer this one." This less-complete sentence is more projective. Even when a person refuses to answer, the response probably tells us more about that person than a stereotyped answer to the first item. The same sort of rationale is present when we ask people to describe what they see in inkblots or to tell stories based on ambiguous pictures.

In the test called the *Rorschach inkblots,* after the young Swiss psychiatrist who developed the technique, there are ten cards, each containing a smudged black or colored inkblot. The person taking the test is asked to state whatever he or she sees in these blots or whatever they bring to mind. Thus, if a man asks, "What am I supposed to see?" or "Can you see more than one thing?" he is informed that he may do as he wishes. Similar to Freud's notion that unconscious thoughts can be revealed when one is in a relaxed position and says whatever comes to mind, it is assumed that the predominant aspects of one's personality are revealed when the person associates freely to the inkblots. Thus, this stage of the Rorschach testing is called the free-association phase (Figure 16-7).

Figure 16-7 A Rorschach-type Inkblot. *In response to this inkblot, one person said:*

"Well, this part here [points to upper center] might be sort of a monk or someone like that with his hands raised up in the air. You can see his hood and cloak. He might be giving somebody a blessing or something."

"These things on the sides might be crabs fighting, but they are not very clear. [Pause.] Actually, the whole thing looks like a strange bug."

"Right here you have a woman's private parts. That definitely looks like a human female to me—but you have to use your imagination."

This man, in his 40s, reported that he had been in constant conflict with his wife for the past five years and was contemplating a divorce. At the same time, he was worried about his wife's future should they become separated. This indecision apparently is what brought him to the clinic, but further study suggested that there were other complicating factors.

■ *Last year, on the day his father left to go hunting, five-year-old Bruce did not cry or pout as he had in the past. In fact, he seemed unconcerned about his father's absence. Shortly after he went to bed that night, a neighbor stopped in to see his mother. As the two women were chatting, I walked past his room and saw him sitting bolt upright in bed. He called me in and motioned for me to sit down. His face was very serious as he asked, "Sal, why is Mrs. Senden here? I know it's because Mommy is scared 'cause Daddy's not home!"*

Later, during the inquiry phase, the subject is asked to describe his or her earlier responses more fully. The subject is asked to indicate where and why he or she perceived a certain object in a certain inkblot. This phase of the test may seem puzzling to the subject, but it is usually regarded as an essential part of the test procedure, allowing the examiner to probe into the subject's manner of thinking and perceiving the world. The proper administration of this test requires considerable training and experience.

When a person is asked to tell a story about an ambiguous picture, we have a similar situation, as in the *Thematic Apperception Test* (TAT). The term *apperception,* no longer used in psychology, refers to the final stage of perception, in which something is prominently in the perceiver's awareness. In this test, there are 20 pictures, any one of which may reveal a prominent theme in the subject's thinking (Figure 16-8).

All projective tests are controversial, especially the Rorschach and TAT. Those psychologists who use them feel that they are uniquely helpful in understanding the deeper aspects of personality. According to Freud, the projective response to any stimulus represents energy, sexual or aggressive, pressing for discharge. For other psychologists, however, the concepts of repression and projective testing are considered too speculative to be of any value. Research on this issue continues unabated (Klopfer & Taulbee, 1976).

Illustrative research. In one experiment illustrating research on psychoanalytic theory, four different pictures were shown on a screen at a shutter speed of .03 seconds, which is much too fast for the image to be consciously recognized or identified. Thus, these stimuli were analogous to ambiguous drawings or inkblots. The subjects could not even guess what the pictures involved, but when asked to indicate which pattern was the most attention-getting, approximately 80 percent chose a picture involving sexual stimulation, such as symbolic masturbation. They were most attentive to this ambiguous stimulus, rather than the other neutral pictures, even when they could not consciously perceive its meaning (Blum, 1954).

In further study, the investigator tested a contrasting hypothesis: when the psychosexual stimulus was not below the level of awareness, the subjects would seek various ways of denying it. This time the four pictures were exposed at a shutter speed of .20 seconds, which enables familiar pictures to be recognized; 85 percent of the subjects were less successful in identifying the psychosexual stimulus, in comparison to neutral stimuli. Results of the previous testing were virtually reversed. The psychosexual stimulus was responded to most frequently in the vigilance series, when it was below the level of awareness, and it was reported least often during the defense series, when it was theoretically well within awareness (Blum, 1954). In the latter instance, however, it is quite possible that the subjects did perceive the picture but were simply reluctant to tell the experimenter what they thought they had seen.

Figure 16-8   TAT-type Picture. *What sort of story does it bring to mind for you? Analyses of TAT stories pertain to the symbolic as well as manifest content of the subject's responses. (Reprinted by permission of the publishers from Henry A. Murray,* Thematic Apperception Test, *Cambridge, Mass.: Harvard University Press. Copyright © 1943 by the President and Fellows of Harvard College; renewed 1971 by Henry A. Murray.)*

Integration of Behavior

Trait Theory

Most people, when asked to describe Jenny Masterson's personality, probably would not refer to her unconscious life. They would follow a more popular viewpoint, referring to her as a certain personality type or describing her in terms of personality traits.

A Personality Typology

A *typology* is a system for classifying people according to certain basic, pervasive characteristics, an approach to personality that has been common since the days of Hippocrates, an early Greek physician. Hippocrates described four personality types on the basis of the four fluids or "humors" of the body assumed to be present in people at that time. Persons with an excess of black bile, called *melancholic,* were depressed and pessimistic. The *choleric,* possessing excess yellow bile, were quick-tempered and irritable. People with a predominance of blood were *sanguine,* as reflected in their cheerful, optimistic manner. And the *phlegmatic,* with excess phlegm, were slow, impassive, and uninvolved with the world. While the theory has long been discarded, the meanings of some of the terms persist.

Even Shakespeare referred to people as types. He had Caesar say:

Let me have men about me that are fat;
Sleek-headed men, and such as sleep
  o'nights;
Yond Cassius has a lean and hungry look;
He thinks too much: such men are
  dangerous.
  Julius Caesar, Act 1, Scene 2

Somatotyping. The most ambitious attempt at establishing a typology occurred in the 1940s when a group of researchers studied approximately four thousand male college students with respect to body type and personality. This procedure was called somatotyping, coming from the Greek root *soma,* which means "body." In the first phase of this work, analyses of photos of the nude young men indicated three basic dimensions of physique, each of which could be rated on a seven-point scale: the fleshy *endomorph,* the muscular *mesomorph,* and the thin *ectomorph.* Thus, Jackie Gleason would rate high on endomorphy; Muhammed Ali would be a mesomorph; and Abraham Lincoln would be an ectomorph (Figure 16-9).

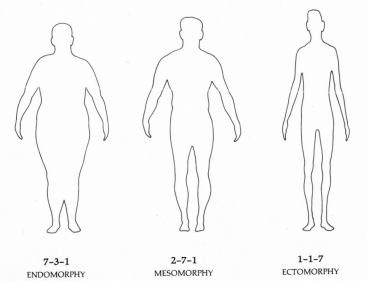

Figure 16-9 Somatotypes. *Each subject is rated on a scale from 1 to 7 and then described in terms of his or her dominant feature. (Adapted from Sheldon & Stevens, 1942)*

7–3–1	2–7–1	1–1–7
ENDOMORPHY	MESOMORPHY	ECTOMORPHY

In the next step, the subjects were rated for temperament, which refers to the emotional aspect of personality; again, three types emerged—*viscerotonia,* in which the individual is jovial. relaxed, and enjoys bodily comforts; *somatotonia,* in which the person is energetic, competitive, and perhaps rather aggressive; and *cerebrotonia,* in which the individual is thoughtful, restrained, and sensitive. Again a 7-point scale was used; an extremely energetic subject was rated 2-7-1, while a thoughtful and apprehensive person received a 1-3-7 rating.

The final step was to look at the relationship between body type and temperament for each subject, and this correlation was found to be quite high ($r = .80$). It indicated that, in general, subjects rated as endomorphic also were rated as viscerotonic; those seen as mesomorphic appeared to be somatotonic; and those who were ectomorphic were rated as cerebrotonic (Sheldon et al., 1940). The results seemed to provide some confirmation for Shakespeare's view that fat people are happy and relaxed, while thin people think too much.

Interpretation. There is some degree of association between body structure and behavior, particularly in the extremes. A person who is very short in stature and weighs over three hundred pounds cannot be extremely active. A person who is emaciated cannot be a boxer. Also, muscular people look strong, and so perhaps other people tend to behave towards them as though they were strong and aggressive. Our personalities are determined in part by others' reactions to us. The social aspect of this theory must be given recognition. ■

Despite these considerations, the theory has little support. A major weakness in the original study is that the same investigators made both the physique and temperament ratings, thus permitting a possible experimental bias.

Moreover, both dimensions involved a three-fold classification judged on seven-step scales, a condition that increases the likelihood of a high correlation. What is needed is fully independent body typing and personality typing; indeed, when such procedures were used with 300 college men, a decidedly smaller relationship ($r = .20$) was obtained (Hood, 1963). Other studies, with adults and children, also have shown a much lower correlation (Rees, 1961; Walker, 1962). Altogether, somatotyping has stimulated a moderate amount of research, and invariably some association between body type and personality is found, but within the general population, it is not of large significance.

Traits and Personality

The overall problem with the type approach is that it is too simple to express the uniqueness and complexity of personality that is found in each individual. People are far more differentiated from one another and far more complicated than can be indicated in a three-dimensional approach.

A personality type is actually a broad category, involving a pattern of personal traits. The cerebrotonic, for example, is said to be thoughtful, restrained, and sensitive, all of which are traits. Second, a type is considered to endure for the individual's lifetime, while a trait is regarded as long-standing but not necessarily permanent (Cartwright, 1974). Third, and most important, a type implies a discrete category, such as male or female, while a trait is assumed to be a continuous dimension within which individuals vary in degree, as in aggressiveness, joviality, and independence. Thus, the trait approach offers greater potential than the type approach for describing an individual's uniqueness.

■ *From earliest childhood my sister had been overweight, yet she was not even remotely "jovial and relaxed." Indeed, she was strongly introverted. As a result of not being able to compete adequately with her classmates and their constant teasing, she became more moody, self-conscious, and unhappy. As a result, she tended to overeat to console herself, and the situation was a vicious circle. This is not to say that there is no relation between her physique and personality. On the contrary, I believe that there was a very definite one in my sister's case—but it was backwards from what the popular view leads you to expect.*

Integration of Behavior

Identifying basic traits. The idea behind the trait approach is relatively straightforward. Individuals differ from one another, yet they behave consistently in a wide variety of situations. One individual acts in an aggressive manner at home, in school, on the athletic field, and elsewhere; another is jovial in most situations. This consistency is the key aspect of the trait approach. A *trait* is a persistent tendency or characteristic, and an individual's personality is fundamentally composed of a unique set of these persistent tendencies. A study of sky divers, for example, showed distinct individual differences, but the group as a whole was characterized as self-confident, socially deviant, impulsive, hedonistic, and relatively free from worries about health (Delk, 1973).

The chief goal in most trait research has been to find those traits or elements that are common to all individuals. These are called the primary or basic traits. The next problem is to understand the ways in which they are arranged, modified, or augmented from individual to individual (Cattell et al., 1970, Cattell, 1973).

The task of finding primary traits appears impossible at first glance because of the complexity of personality, but as a preliminary effort one could catalogue all the pertinent adjectives used in literature and everyday life. Indeed, two investigators following this procedure found almost 18,000 terms referring to personality. Some of these terms had similar meanings, such as *fearful, apprehensive, troubled,* and *worried,* and thus one term, such as *anxious,* might represent many of them. Analysis along similar lines for the thousands of remaining words suggested that most of them could be represented by relatively few key terms or traits (Allport & Odbert, 1936).

Some years later, the statistical procedure known as *factor analysis* came into wide use. According to some trait theorists, this procedure would identify the primary or irreducible traits by indicating which traits correlate with one another and, thus, one investigation revealed seven basic traits—general activity, masculinity-femininity, impulsiveness, dominance-submission, emotional stability, sociability, and reflectiveness (Thurstone, 1950). As more studies were made, however, it became evident that we cannot say how many different personality traits exist. The investigations give different results, the traits overlap, and they fall into different categories. Some of those in the list of 7, for example, can be regarded as aspects or combinations of those appearing in a later list of 16 primary traits (Figure 16-10).

In these findings, a distinction should be made between easily observed traits and those that are "deeper" and perhaps more central to the personality. The readily observed characteristics are described as *surface* traits and the deeper ones as *source* traits, meaning that they are more basic influences, pertaining to physical as well as psychological factors. The traits obtained by factor analysis are usually considered source traits, but there are still differences among these findings (Guilford, 1975).

Reserved versus Outgoing
Low intelligence versus High intelligence
Easily upset versus Emotionally stable
Mild versus Assertive
Serious versus Happy-go-lucky
Expedient versus Conscientious
Timid versus Uninhibited
Tough-minded versus Tender-minded
Trusting versus Suspicious
Practical versus Imaginative
Unpretentious versus Polished
Self-assured versus Apprehensive
Conservative versus Liberal
Group-dependent versus Self-sufficient
Undisciplined versus Controlled
Relaxed versus Tense

Figure 16-10 Sixteen Personality Traits. *The adjective pairs represent opposite ends of a continuum. (Copyright 1970 by the Institute for Personality and Ability Testing. Reproduced by permission.)*

Jenny's traits. On several occasions, Jenny Masterson's personality has been studied through the trait approach. In one instance, selections from more than 300 letters written by her were examined by 36 people in an effort to identify her most significant traits (Figure 16-11). These judges used a total of 198 terms, but many of them were synonymous or closely related. Further analysis showed that nearly all the terms could be represented by just 8 trait names, and almost all the judges basically described Jenny's traits according to the first 3 of the following:

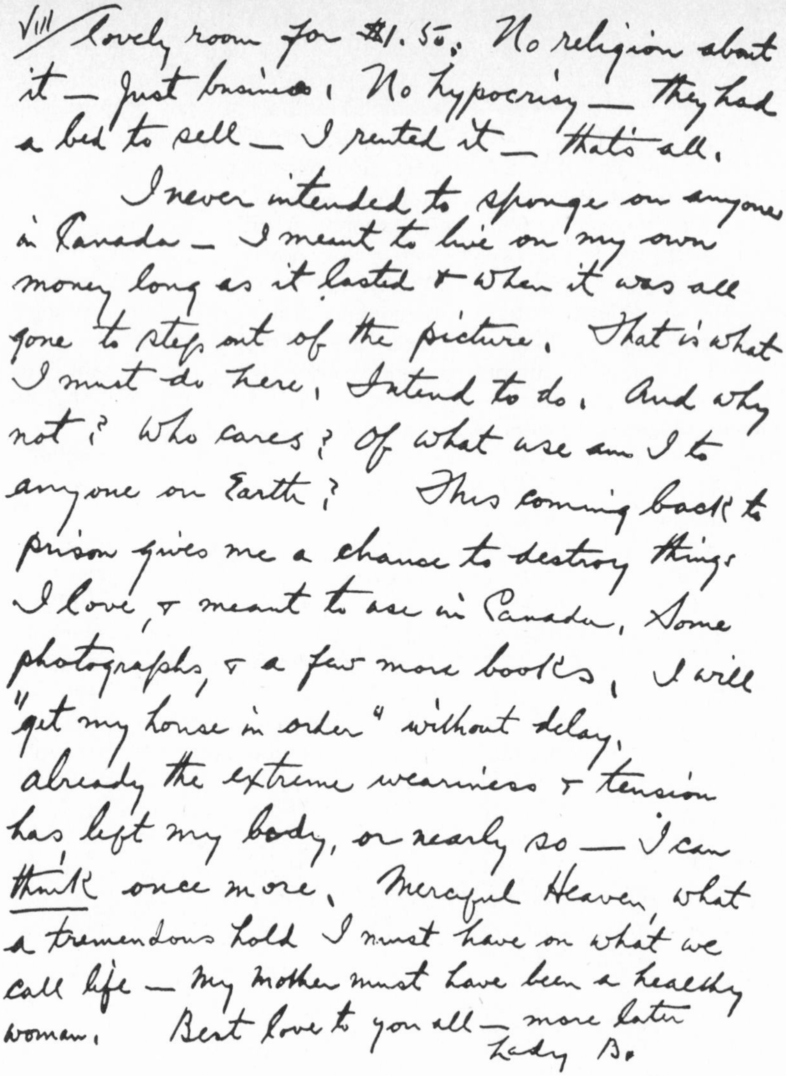

suspicious	artistic
self-centered	aggressive
independent	morbid
intense	sentimental
	(Allport, 1965)

Another analysis, by high-speed computer, yielded eight basic traits quite similar to those on the first list. The most significant deviation was the inclusion of a trait labeled *sexuality*, and further analyses showed that Jenny's attitudes towards sex were consistently strong and negative. In the first list, this aspect of her personality most likely was included as part of suspiciousness and morbidity (Allport, 1965).

A most important question, however, concerns the ways in which these traits are combined or clustered. Another individual might show these same eight characteristics, or the same basic three traits, yet have a different personality because these components are organized and related differently. It has been suggested that Jenny's suspiciousness and aggressiveness are closely associated, as well as her sentimentality and artistic nature. But attempts to find an organizing theme, a conception that would give coherence to trait clusters, have not been convincing. This difficulty is one of the weaknesses in the trait approach.

Assessment and Research

No single method of assessment can embrace all of personality. Thus, tests used in connection with trait theory are generally designed to measure specific, manifest behaviors, rather than underlying themes in a personality.

Inventories. A printed form containing statements, questions, or adjectives that apply to human behavior is called a personality *inventory*. The subject indicates his or her reactions to each of the various items and then, when the form has been scored, there is an indication of the person's self-rating, usually according to several traits.

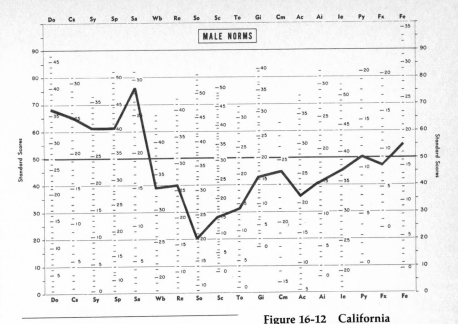

Sample items:
I liked *Alice in Wonderland* by Lewis Carroll.
I would never play cards (poker) with a stranger.

Trait scales:

Dominance	Good impression
Capacity for status	Communality
Sociability	Achievement via
Social presence	comformity
Self-acceptance	Achievement via
Well-being	independence
Responsibility	Intellectual efficiency
Socialization	Psychological mindedness
Self-control	Flexibility
Tolerance	Femininity

Figure 16-12   California Personality Inventory. *In completing this inventory, the subject answers true or false to a large number of items such as those shown as sample items. After the subject completes the test, a profile can be made showing his or her results for each of the 18 traits measured by the inventory. (Reproduced by special permission from the California Psychological Inventory by Harrison G. Gough, Ph.D. Copyright 1957. Published by Consulting Psychologists Press, Inc.)*

One widely employed instrument of this type is the *California Personality Inventory* (CPI), intended for use with normal individuals. It is designed to yield information on 18 traits, such as dominance, tolerance, and intellectual efficiency, and the results are presented in the form of a profile. On this inventory, based on what we know about Jenny, we would expect her to score high on dominance, responsibility, and achievement via independence and to score relatively low on tolerance, sociability, and femininity (Figure 16-12).

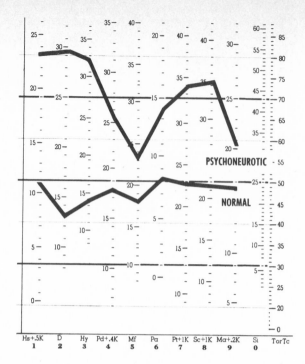

PSYCHONEUROTIC

NORMAL

Hs+.5K	D	Hy	Pd+.4K	Mf	Pa	Pt+1K	Sc+1K	Ma+.2K	Si	TorTc
1	2	3	4	5	6	7	8	9	0	

Figure 16-13 MMPI Profiles.
These profiles were generated by two groups of men in the armed services, one being routinely re-evaluated and the other experiencing adjustment difficulties and diagnosed as severely neurotic. The K factor included in some of the scales is not of psychiatric significance; it is a correction factor designed to improve the discrimination of certain scores. (Adapted from Schmidt, 1945, p. 119. Profile blank reproduced by permission. Copyright © 1948 by The Psychological Corporation, New York, N.Y. All rights reserved.)

Key

Hs Hypochondriasis
D   Depression
Hy Hysteria
Pd Psychopathic deviation
Mf Masculinity-femininity
Pa Paranoia
Pt Psychasthenia
Sc Schizophrenia
Ma Hypomania

Another widely used inventory is the *Minnesota Multiphasic Personality Inventory* (MMPI), in which the emphasis is decidedly psychiatric. This inventory shows the degree to which the subject's pattern of responses resembles that of schizophrenic patients, depressed patients, and so forth, and these scores also are presented in the form of a profile (Figure 16-13).

One objection to both the CPI and MMPI is their length. There are approximately 500 items in each, requiring considerable time to complete. Thus, efforts have been made to develop shorter forms (Dean, 1972). Since the subject completes the inventory by himself or herself, it is easy to administer and not time consuming from the examiner's viewpoint. But, as with most inventories, the subject sometimes can create a false impression, if he or she wishes to do so.

Illustrative research. Inventories and judges' ratings can be used to measure currently existing traits, but there is little consideration in trait theory of how personality develops. Thus, the few studies of source traits from childhood into adulthood have generated considerable interest. In general, they show that relatively few traits emerge in the early years but some of them seem to remain constant (Cattell, 1957, 1973).

In one investigation, 25 babies were observed during their first 2 years of life, and it was found that at least a "personality nucleus" exists from the start (Shirley, 1933). Many of these subjects were studied again 15 years later, when they were 17 years old; then a panel of judges compared personality sketches of them at this time with the trait descriptions from infancy. The judges were considerably more successful in matching trait descriptions and personality sketches than would be expected on a chance basis, suggesting that some traits are of long-standing duration (Figure 16-14).

Learning Theory

The trait approach, which dominated personality research in earlier years, is challenged by theorists who focus on the role of the environment in the organism's behavior. This viewpoint stresses learning and emphasizes that people acquire certain behaviors according to the conditions of the situation.

Sketch at age 17	Sketch at Infancy					
	Winnie	Virginia	Sibyl	Patty	Judy	Carol
Winnie	10					
Virginia		9				1
Sibyl			7		3	
Patty*				6	3	
Judy			2	3	0	5

* Only nine matches were indicated for Patty's 17-year sketch.

Figure 16-14 **Matching Infant and Adolescent Personality Sketches.** *The numbers indicate successful matches out of 10. Since there were only five girls in the sample, a hypothetical infant description, labeled Carol, was included to make the task more difficult for the ten judges. One judge omitted the matching for Patty, but out of the 49 remaining matches, 33 (65 percent) were correct. (Table 4 from "Shirley's babies after fifteen years: a personality study" by Patricia Neilon, in* The Journal of Genetic Psychology, *1948, 73, 175–186.)*

Social Learning Theory

There are two general approaches to learning as it relates to personality, both of which have been considered previously, but in other contexts. The reinforcement of selected responses is still a basic concept, but in the more liberal view, called *social learning,* the fundamental principles have been extended to include learning that occurs through symbolic processes without direct reinforcement.

Situations versus traits. In this view, the defect in the trait approach is best demonstrated when personality is measured in different situations. In one instance, hundreds of school children were placed in diverse situations that were designed to assess honesty and self-control, in which there were numerous possibilities for lying, stealing, and cheating. The investigators had special means of detecting these behaviors and, thus, it was found that the children were not highly consistent from one situation to another. A child who lied at home did not do so at school; another cheated at a club meeting but not in church. The median correlation for honesty in two different situations was relatively low (r = .23). On this basis the investigators concluded that honesty is a situational response, rather than a general personality trait (Figure 16-15).

One reason that the trait view persists, according to learning theorists, is that we tend to see people only in selected situations—going to work, in the classroom, in church, or on the athletic field. Since there is regularity in each of these conditions, we infer that certain traits are responsible for the individual's consistency. Instead, one should look more closely at the way in which the situation is interpreted by the individual—as an occasion for truth, dishonesty, or some other behavior, and at the environmental support for these behaviors. ∎

Modeling and cognitive processes. When learning occurs without direct reinforcement, as in social learning theory, it is called observational learning or *modeling.* It involves *cognitive* processes, such as thinking and reasoning. These terms stress that the organism can acquire new knowledge and potential behavior without making the observed response. Learning is facilitated by reinforcement, but it also can occur through the internal manipulation of symbols, when a person merely observes a model, interprets the situation, and behaves accordingly.

This approach makes an important distinction between learning and performance. *Learning* is what an individual *can* do at any given time, and it depends on the skills and information that the person has acquired. *Performance* is the

∎ *I've seen a girl be intellectual and sophisticated with one guy and crude and fun-loving with another. It's not that the girl is artificial or hypocritical, but people, perhaps females more than males, try to get along as best they can with other people. If rowdy behavior is expected and accepted, then we will display rowdy behavior. People's traits seem to vary a lot that way.*

Figure 16-15 A Test Measuring Honesty. *This coin test illustrates one of many situations used to study deceit. In a parlor game, children were asked to identify coins and other small objects without looking at them and afterwards to place these objects in a box in the next room where they were being collected for later use with other people. The box appeared solid when viewed from the front, and there was a small slit at the top through which the objects could be dropped. But unknown to the children it was open on the side towards the observer, who could record the behavior of each child and note which items were not returned (Hartshorne & May, 1928).*

act itself, which depends on the reinforcements immediately available in the environment. Many people know how to punch, kick, scratch, and pull hair, but this behavior is not emitted by most of us because it is not reinforced, or supported, by the environment (Mischel, 1976).

In an experiment demonstrating this viewpoint, children observed a film in which an adult was aggressive towards a large doll, with different consequences. After the film, those who had seen the model's aggressive behavior resulting in rewards were aggressive in a test with the doll. Those who saw no consequences for the model's aggression displayed fewer aggressive responses. And those who saw the aggressive model receiving punishment showed the least aggression. Still later, when the children were reinforced for reproducing the model's behavior, all groups behaved as the model did. In other words, the behavior was learned through *vicarious* or symbolic reinforcement, in terms of what happened to someone else, but it

was performed on the basis of the actual reinforcement available to the individual (Bandura, 1965).

According to social learning theory, the individual's behavior is a function of symbolic learning and the support that it receives in the environment. A person may be aggressive in one context, passive in another, jovial in a third, and tense in a fourth, all depending on prior models and available reinforcements.

Operant Learning

According to Skinner, it is the environment that controls behavior; reinforcement is the *primary* basis upon which learning occurs. Cognition, motivation, emotion, conflict, and other postulated inner states are not necessarily denied, but they are not part of this system of thought. Instead, an effort is made to discover whether scientific progress can be made by studying human behavior exclusively in terms of directly observable, external circumstances and consequences.

Responses and reinforcement. Personality, in the operant conditioning view, is composed of S-R connections, which occur when responses are reinforced. As the reinforcement continues, the associated response increases in strength and then becomes attached to a stimulus that signals an appropriate moment to emit it. Even when a response has not been reinforced on several occasions, it may be repeated on the basis of the intermittent reinforcement principle. In short, all the principles of operant conditioning considered previously are central concepts in this approach to personality.

Like the psychoanalysts, these learning theorists stress the early years, although to a lesser degree. A person's personality arises from the ways in which he or she is treated by the environment, especially by the parents and siblings during the most helpless years. ■ If the mother reinforces aggressiveness, the child will soon display this behavior when with the mother and, through generalization, perhaps with other females too. If aggressive behavior is ignored or punished by the father, it will be extinguished in this context, and friendly behavior will occur if it is reinforced. According to Skinner, operant conditioning shapes behavior in just as convincing a manner as the sculptor shapes the clay.

Conditioning occurs in early toilet training, the feeding situation, and relations with peers at home and in school. A child who receives extra attention for being disruptive in class may continue his or her acting-out behavior. The approach to understanding any behavior, neurotic or otherwise, is to try to discover what reinforcement in the environment maintains it. In learning theory, there is no deep-seated symbolic connection between adult behavior and the earlier years; if reinforcement from the environment is totally discontinued, the response eventually will disappear.

Jenny's reinforced responses. At age 18, when her father died, Jenny was left as the financial head of a large family. In her 20s, after her husband's death, she found herself in the same situation, this time with her own child to support. The learning theorist would point to the consequences of Jenny's hard-working behavior in both instances. Not only did she obtain food and drink for herself but also respect and recognition from six brothers and sisters, and later she received the affection and growing responsiveness of her baby.

When her husand was alive, Jenny said she felt like a ''kept woman,'' having been requested to remain at home rather than seek employment. Immediately after her husband died, Jenny took a job in a telegraph office and then in a library to support herself and Ross, whom she had all to herself. This self-sufficiency and independence, learned early in life, thus were further rewarded in her new circumstances. But these efforts left little time for other people, which diminished Jenny's social skills (Figure 16-16).

As Jenny became less sociable, others perhaps were inclined to be less friendly to her, interpreting her reaction as hostile, yet she continued to receive reinforcement, financial and intellectual, from her work. Thus, she became more socially isolated and came to depend more and more on combativeness to make a place for herself and her son (Allport, 1965).

If Jenny was a bit masculine, it was because masculine responses were reinforced. If she was overly attentive to Ross, it was because attentive behaviors were the most regularly reinforced of all, especially in the early maternal years. Hence, these responses continued throughout long periods of intermittent reinforcement later, when Ross neglected her in favor of girl friends.

■ *I remember an anecdote told to me by a friend, Alicia, about the somewhat malicious pleasure that she used to take from teasing her tiny brother. She started to call him a ''baby,'' which many small children seem to resent highly and he would cry, so that his mother would punish Alicia and give him comfort and attention. After a time, she began to sing the song ''Yes, Sir, That's My Baby!'' to infuriate him still more. Finally, all that she had to do was to hum the song, without any words, and he would immediately make the connection between the tune of the song and the teasing word ''baby'' and begin to bawl. Alicia was delighted at the success of this tactic, for her brother was too young to explain his unhappiness to anyone, and her mother, misunderstanding, would say to him, ''She's just humming, Richie. She's not hurting you. Now hush!'' At this point, she might even punish him if he continued to cry.*

Figure 16-16 Jenny's Habits. *Early in life, according to the conditioning viewpoint, Jenny was reinforced for independence, assertiveness, and later solitary behavior, and these behaviors became her way of life. (From* Letters from Jenny *edited by Gordon W. Allport, © 1965 by Harcourt Brace Jovanovich, Inc. and reproduced with their permission.)*

Assessment and Research

With their emphasis on external circumstances, learning theorists are not inclined to use projective tests or even personality inventories. The former are intended to reveal inner states, which are of little interest to the learning theorist, and the latter indicate only what subjects say about themselves, not what they actually do. No one method is used exclusively in learning theory, but situational tests illustrate the general viewpoint with regard to personality measurement.

Situational tests. To decide how an individual will react in a given situation, we might try to observe the person in that situation or, when such observations are impossible, to observe the person in a similar context. When careful records are kept of the subject's behavior, the procedure is called a *situational test.*

Years ago, a situational test called the Brook Test was used to select young men for difficult wartime missions. They were taken in small groups to a brook that was to be regarded as a raging torrent, so fast and deep that nothing could be rested on the bottom; their task was to transport heavy equipment across it. To solve this problem, the men had to cooperate in building a bridge, an overhead cable, or some other device, while the observers looked for signs of leadership, initiative, cooperation, and related behaviors (Figure 16-17).

An example of a situation test in the natural environment occurred when adolescent boys were observed living together for six weeks in a residential cottage for juvenile offenders. Gradually, different boys laid claims to different portions of the cottage as their domain. When other information about the boys was obtained, it was confirmed that the most desirable areas of the cottage were controlled by the strongest and most aggressive. In other words, one could identify the dominant and submissive boys by their exclusive use of the more and less desirable areas, respectively (Figure 16-18).

Figure 16-17 The Brook Test. *Four to seven men were assigned to this problem, but no leader was designated. The observers studied emerging leadership and also shifts in leadership when a particular approach proved ineffective (OSS Assessment Staff, 1948).*

Integration of Behavior

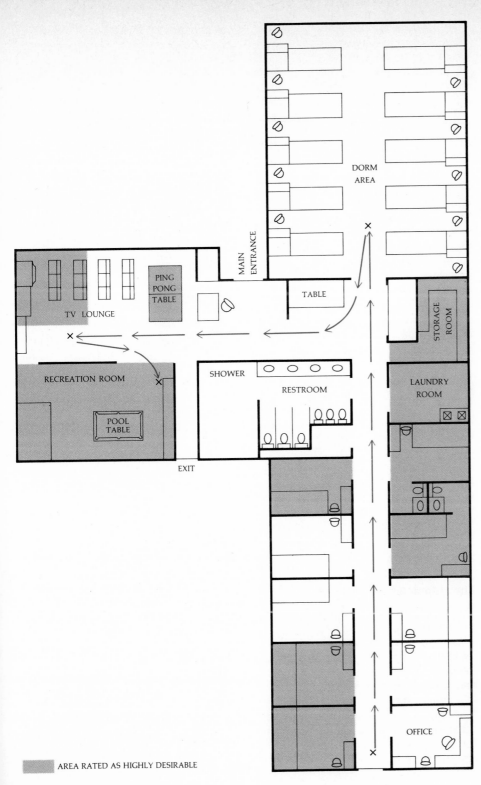

Figure 16-18 Situational Test.
The observer's path is shown by arrows and the boys were informed that he was studying how the cottage was used. The shaded areas in the cottage floor plan were deemed the most desirable. (From Sundstrom & Altman, 1974. Copyright 1974 by the American Psychological Association. Reprinted by permission.)

DORM AREA

MAIN ENTRANCE

TV LOUNGE

PING PONG TABLE

TABLE

STORAGE ROOM

RECREATION ROOM

SHOWER

RESTROOM

LAUNDRY ROOM

POOL TABLE

EXIT

OFFICE

AREA RATED AS HIGHLY DESIRABLE

The advantage of situational or behavioral tests is that they involve fewer assumptions about the applicability of the findings and are potentially more useful in making predictions about human behavior (Goldfried & Kent, 1972). The great disadvantage is that they are extremely time consuming to construct and administer, since the subject must be observed continuously.

Illustrative research. The role of the environment in supporting certain behaviors was illustrated in an experiment on conformity and deviance. In a series of group conferences, some college subjects were told "Good, that is right," whenever they agreed with what others had said. Thus, they became more conforming in the group situation as the experiment progressed, tending to agree on later occasions. Other subjects were reinforced with the same expression only when they disagreed with the group. In this way, they became more deviant, tending to disagree more and more as the group sessions continued. Furthermore, both groups differed from a neutral group, in which no reinforcement occurred (Endler, 1965).

This experiment illustrates only a temporary behavior change in a laboratory setting. According to learning theory, when the reinforcing conditions persist for long periods of time, as in a family or school setting, the behavior involved will appear regularly in these settings, too.

The Humanistic Viewpoint

Any theory of personality is based on certain conceptions of human nature. According to psychoanalysis, personality emerges as we are acted upon by internal forces in the form of id impulses and unconscious conflicts. In operant learning theory, personality emerges from the ways in which we are acted upon by external forces through reinforcement in the environment. Both these views involve *determinism*, which states that any action is the inevitable result of certain antecedent conditions. Psychoanalysis is essentially a biological determinism and operant learning is an environmental determinism. Free will and choice are not part of these approaches to human behavior.

Conceptions and Directions

In opposition to the psychoanalytic and operant learning views, which have been dominant forces in personality theory for years, a new outlook has arisen, which states that human beings *do* have the capacity for self-direction and the potential for change. This approach, based on a more optimistic or exalted view of humanity, is called the *humanistic viewpoint*.

Basic conceptions. Humanism stresses the *complexity and uniqueness* of human beings. They are not simply at a higher level of evolution than the lower animals but are a unique species, with extraordinary capacities and complexities. In view of this complexity, humanists emphasize that people cannot be studied in segments. Laboratory experiments focusing on isolated aspects of behavior are helpful, but reliance solely on *reductionism*, in which a complex whole is analyzed in terms of its basic parts, is insufficient. The premise of gestalt psychology, that the whole is greater than the sum of its parts, applies particularly to humanity.

There is also emphasis on one aspect of this uniqueness—our experiencing. We think, decide, and feel; we are *subjective* creatures, doing more than responding to the environment in an overt manner. We are shocked when we read in the newspaper that a certain person has committed murder or suicide, acts that do not typically occur among the lower animals. We are shocked because we make the wrong inferences from this person's behavior, not knowing his or her thoughts and feelings: "Externals don't portray insides; Jekylls may be masking Hydes" (Jourard, 1964). This aspect of humanity, according to the humanistic viewpoint, should receive more emphasis.

A third characteristic emphasized in this approach is a person's capacity for *growth*, fulfillment, and happiness. These capacities have been overlooked in a psychology that developed partly out of concern with maladjustment, as in the psychoanalytic tradition. Humanists stress that human beings seek expression, achieve goals, and maintain value systems that are important to them. Earlier, we mentioned the idea of self-actualization, in which the individual's life is expressed in terms of values and goals that are important to him or her, apart from strivings for food, safety, love, and the admiration of others.

Directions and trends. Based on these premises, certain trends have emerged within the humanistic movement. Some of them, at the moment, are merely expressions of dissatisfaction; others have been translated into action.

Regarding human complexity, the humanistic psychologists advocate a broader, more imaginative approach in psychological inquiry. Current research is recognized for its value, but humanists feel that the emphasis on precision, control, and lack of error has decreased creativity in research. Analogy is made to the man who lost his wallet in a dark alley but searched for it under a street light where he could see better. In its

sharpest form, the criticism is that many psychologists concentrate on less significant questions for which there are adequate research methods rather than attacking more significant issues with less precision (Maslow, 1957).

Concerning the second point, our subjective nature, humanists believe that Western psychology has largely ignored private experience. It is suggested that we have much to learn from Eastern societies that emphasize meditation and introspection. Abandonment of the introspective method, as inaugurated by Wundt, is considered a limitation in contemporary psychology, and recently there has been an increase of research interest in this general area.

When we turn to the concept of personal growth, we find one of the most obvious products of the humanistic movement—an extension of therapy into daily life. The effort to foster personal development and awareness of interpersonal relations among laypersons has led to several forms of therapy, including the encounter-sensitivity-training group practices, to be considered shortly.

Self Theory

The humanistic viewpoint is evident in *self theory*, which focuses on the role of the individual in shaping his or her own destiny. The *self* is the sum total of any individual's physical, mental, and behavioral characteristics. According to William James, it also includes a person's material possessions, family, friends, work, and recreation. Thus, a person's *self-concept* is that individual's organized, consistent perception of himself or herself in these regards (Rogers, 1959, 1961).

A helpful term in understanding self theory is *phenomenology*, which emphasizes that behavior is determined by the way one experiences the world, rather than by objective reality. From the phenomenological viewpoint, it is not the external stimulus but the experienced stimulus that is important in behavior. It is not the actual environment and a student's actual ability that determine whether that student enrolls in advanced mathematics. Rather, it is the student's view of his or her ability in that situation that is important. Again, the emphasis is on the subjective side of humanity.

Sources of incongruence. The leading advocate of self theory, Carl Rogers, stresses that maladjustment occurs when the self-concept or perceived self is not in accordance with the self as it exists in *external reality*—that is, as experienced by the individual. When a person's self-perceptions and personal experiences are not in agreement, that individual becomes defensive, rigid, and constricted. Similarly, there is personal dissatisfaction when there is a disparity between the self-concept and the *ideal self,* which is what a person wants to become. The ideal self is that self-concept that an individual wants to achieve. The goal of everyone, according to self theory, is to reduce the personal dissatisfaction stemming from these two sources of incongruence (Figure 16-19).

Figure 16-19   Congruence and Self Theory. *The upper diagram indicates that an individual evaluates his or her self-concept in relation to experience and in relation to the ideal self. The lower figure shows greater congruence; the self-concept is more in accordance with external reality and with the ideal self.*

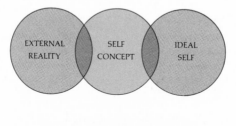

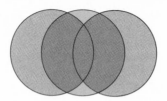

As in other theories, early experiences are considered most significant for personality development. It is postulated that in any growing infant there is an *actualizing tendency,* which is the inborn tendency to develop all one's capacities in the fullest ways to serve, maintain, and enhance the organism. Inevitably, the growing child encounters restrictions on his or her behavior and thus the key issue is how the child comes to perceive these circumstances. If a boy is punished for breaking something, he can take a look at himself and say "I *ought* to be so-and-so." Or the child might say, "I am ashamed of myself;" "My parents do not love me any more;" "The spanking did not hurt." All these responses involve some distortion, and incongruence develops to the extent that the child ignores, rejects, or otherwise avoids true feelings. Thus, the perceived self moves away from external reality and, at the same time, becomes more distant from the ideal self.

The process by which this incongruity can be reduced is allegedly found in some encounter-sensitivity-training group practices. It is also said to occur in client-centered counseling, in which the individual, in nonthreatening circumstances, will feel sufficiently safe to explore his or her self-concept, experiences in reality, and ideal self, thereby diminishing incongruence. This approach is significantly based on another premise concerning human behavior that was emphasized earlier—the capacity for personal growth. In contrast to psychoanalysis, it is assumed in self-theory counseling that the client, by himself or herself can achieve the most significant insights into personal dissatisfaction, if he or she is provided with an appropriately warm atmosphere in which to make the effort at self-discovery.

Jenny's incongruence. Jenny, in many respects, appears to be an unhappy person, often saying or writing that life "isn't worth living." She finds fault with everyone—her mother, her brothers and

Integration of Behavior

sisters, her son, his friends, and her acquaintances, a condition apparently brought about by her insensitivity to her own shortcomings. Jenny, in fact, is commonly abrasive, domineering, and self-centered (Allport, 1965).

The chief problem, then, is that the way Jenny perceives herself is not in accordance with her experience; there is considerable incongruence. Her self-concept is that of a good, honest, hardworking person who even starves to help others, but she finds herself rebuffed and rejected by nearly everyone, including Ross.

A nonthreatening situation, such as that provided in an appropriate counseling relationship, would allow her possibility for greater self-understanding and openness to experience. This greater self-awareness then would enable her to make more appropriate reactions to others. In the hypothetical individual completely open to experience, self-awareness is totally congruent with experience, and there can be no psychological threat. Jenny, by contrast, is readily threatened and therefore continues to deny and distort reality.

Assessment and Research

Self theory developed from clinical work, primarily through Carl Rogers's counseling with college students. The assessment procedures involve the inventories and self-reports commonly used in this context. The subject, or someone rating the subject, describes that person's actual self, self-concept, or ideal self.

Q-Sort. In one method, called the *Q-sort,* many statements or questions have been printed on cards, one statement to a card, and then the whole deck is sorted according to the way each card describes a given aspect of some person. Specific categories must be used, following the normal distribution, so that relatively few statements can be placed in the "most like" and "least like" categories, while many appear in the intermediate positions. If several judges performed a Q-sort for their perceptions of Jenny, for example, the most characteristic statements probably would include: "Is basically distrustful of people . . . ," "Keeps people at a distance . . . ," and "Is moralistic." Statements considered least like her would be: "Has insight into own motives and behavior," "Has warmth," and "Tends to arouse liking and acceptance in people" (Block, 1961).

In sorting the same one hundred statements, Jenny probably would reveal a self-concept quite different from the judges' descriptions. Since each statement is assigned a score according to its placement in that arrangement, the differences between any two arrangements can be determined statistically. Thus the overall incongruence is stated in precise terms.

Illustrative research. According to the self theory, incongruence should decrease during therapy and there should be less incongruence among well adjusted than among poorly adjusted persons. In one instance involving the Q-sort, college students were studied for incongruence between the self-concept and ideal self, and it was found that those for whom the incongruence was least were those encountering the most academic success, participating in the most extracurricular activities, receiving the highest personal-social ratings by fellow students, and scoring the highest in adjustment on other personality tests (Turner & Vanderlippe, 1958).

However, some therapies associated with self theory have not received sufficient research attention, as shown in the encounter-sensitivity-training group movement, in which people are stimulated in various ways to look at themselves and their interpersonal relations critically and openly. This movement, which became extremely popular a few years ago, dates back to the late 1940s, when psychologists were interested in improving interpersonal relations in industry and established training sessions, called *T-groups*, for this purpose. The main goal in an authentic group is to help persons gain greater self-awareness in a controlled setting. Later, it is hypothesized, this increased self-awareness can be used in interpersonal relations in society at large. Unqualified individuals have seen opportunities for financial profit in leading T-groups, however, and consequently there has been a wide variety of groups with different outcomes, favorable and unfavorable (Giff, 1971; Hartley et al., 1976). Owing to this diversity and the difficulty of measuring the alleged changes, we simply do not know yet the long-run impact of these procedures (Figure 16-20).

Eclecticism in Theory and Assessment

When the various theories are assessed, it appears that psychoanalysis offers the broadest and most penetrating approach to understanding personality. Perhaps more than any other, this theory attempts to consider the whole individual, and thus it still implicitly guides much research (Carlsen, 1975). But it has also drawn the most criticism, primarily because of the extensive emphasis on unconscious processes and sexual determinants of behavior, which have not yet been demonstrated to have scientific validity. In other words, the theory is difficult to test.

Trait theory provides a ready characterization of almost anyone and is popular among many psychologists and laypersons for this reason. The approach is also parsimonious and objective, and it is especially useful for describing individual differences. In many respects, however, it is more descriptive than theoretical, since a trait is essentially a label. When Jenny abruptly leaves the woman with whom she has been living, we say she does so because she is independent, but we have decided that she is independent partly on this basis. We have not explained her behavior. At the present time, the trait approach is unclear not only in identifying the basic traits but also in how they are organized and in how they develop in the growing individual.

Learning theory, as presented by Skinner, is probably the most precise, practical, and parsimonious of all. No guesses are made about what goes on inside a person or how a person feels. Behavior is considered entirely from the viewpoint of observable events and, therefore, the theory is more testable than others. But not everyone agrees that the whole individual is no greater than the sum of the parts. This approach may be adequate for studying simpler responses, but perhaps it is inadequate for understanding the entire range of complexity found among human beings.

Humanistic psychology focuses attention on human uniqueness, the whole person, and the role of an individual's own perceptions in determining behavior. Self theory, in particular, has stressed the human potential for change and growth. But the theory depends heavily on subjective data, as in self-reports, and it is generally considered less comprehensive than psychoanalysis, which also comes from the clinical tradition.

Thus, no one theory of personality is adequate to explain all aspects of human behavior. Each makes its own contribution and each has its limitations (Figure 16-21).

On this basis, many psychologists concerned with personality theory have become eclectic in their position. The word "eclectic," of Greek origin, means to "pick out" or "to select." The essential characteristic of an eclectic person is that he or she selects whatever approach seems most appropriate in a given circumstance. The individual does not abandon theory but rather works apart from any exclusive system and tries to use the advantages of all approaches.

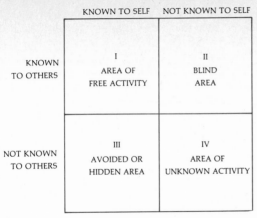

KNOWN TO SELF   NOT KNOWN TO SELF

	KNOWN TO SELF	NOT KNOWN TO SELF
KNOWN TO OTHERS	I AREA OF FREE ACTIVITY	II BLIND AREA
NOT KNOWN TO OTHERS	III AVOIDED OR HIDDEN AREA	IV AREA OF UNKNOWN ACTIVITY

AREAS OF AWARENESS

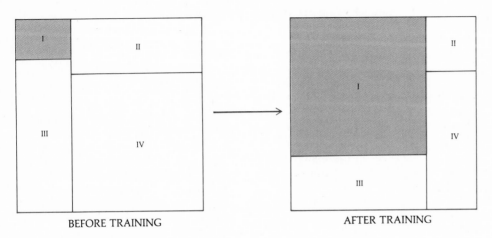

BEFORE TRAINING   AFTER TRAINING

Figure 16-20 Awareness in Interpersonal Relations. *In quadrant I are the behaviors and feelings known to an individual and also to other people. In quadrant II, called the blind area, are aspects of the individual of which he or she is not aware but which are known to other people. The avoided or hidden area, quadrant III, involves personal characteristics that the individual knows about but does not wish to reveal to others. In quadrant IV, the area of unknown activity, are aspects of behavior and motivation unknown to the individual and to others. One aim of sensitivity training is to enlarge quadrant I by decreasing the areas not known to the self or others. (After Luft, 1963)*

When studying a certain individual, the eclectic psychologist might employ the concept of unconscious motivation, especially if the behavior in question seemed to involve some symbolic expression. In another instance, the concept of reinforcement might appear most adequate, and an interpretation would be made on this basis. In still another context, the idea of the self-concept might seem most relevant. In short, any approach that seems of the greatest potential value is used, regardless of its origin or association with a certain viewpoint.

PSYCHOANALYTIC
In marrying an older man, Jenny was attempting to fulfill unresolved Electra strivings.

TRAIT
Jenny is a totally independent person who does not want to be dominated by anyone, especially her family.

LEARNING
In the past, Jenny has been reinforced for depending on her own resources, and marrying this man offered an escape from an aversive family situation.

SELF
Jenny's feelings about herself are congruent with her self-concept when she is with this man.

Figure 16-21 Interpretations of Jenny's Behavior. *Jenny married against her family's wishes. Also, her husband was much older than she, from another country, another religion, divorced, and otherwise not part of her family's conservative expectations. Four interpretations of Jenny's behavior are offered.*

A similar circumstance occurs in personality assessment. Many psychologists use *several* of the tests mentioned previously. In fact, test batteries commonly include a projective test and a personality inventory, such as the Rorschach and MMPI. Situational tests are less often used in this way because they are so time consuming, but they are not incompatible with the others. Some psychologists even regard the situational test as a type of projective technique.

In addition, the interview can be employed in various ways as a test of personality. It may surprise the reader to find the interview discussed as a test, but it can be used for this purpose. The questions, instead of being written, are spoken, and the advantage is that no fixed pattern must be followed. The questions can be changed at any given moment and observations can be made continuously. Perhaps the greatest single advantage of the interview is the flexibility it affords in personality assessment.

At one extreme on the continuum of flexibility, the interviewer can leave the situation largely unstructured, saying and doing little. After a greeting, the interviewer might wait several minutes to see how the other person handles the situation or might ask a very general question, such as, "What do you have to say about yourself?" In these instances, the interview is being used as a projective technique. The subject does whatever he or she wishes in an ambiguous situation and the interviewer attempts to understand the personality in this context.

At the other end of the continuum, there can be a highly structured interview, in which an established sequence of questions is followed precisely, with the same phrasing and voice inflections insofar as possible. These interviews are more analogous to personality inventories and self-rating scales, except that the subject speaks the answers. The test questions concern those aspects of the interviewee that are regarded as most important. To increase the reliability of the scores, the interviewer may use rating scales (Figure 16-22).

The interview also can be changed into a situational test. The interviewer may spill an ashtray, ask the subject to answer the telephone, not provide a chair, or accuse the interviewee of taking something that is missing from the office. This approach sometimes has the advantage of placing the interviewee in a situation that is analogous to that for which he or she is being tested. To the extent that this condition is achieved, the prediction of future behavior is improved.

Altogether, most practicing psychologists do not adhere exclusively to one approach or the other, in theory or practice. The issue, ultimately, is one of usefulness, and as yet no one approach has incorporated all that is beneficial in the other viewpoints.

Figure 16-22 Sample Rating Scales. *Instructions to the rater might be—Indicate your opinion by checking the appropriate place on the scale.*

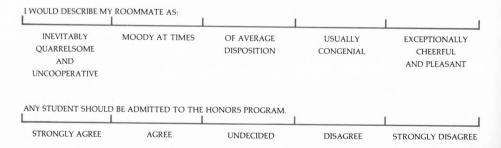

I WOULD DESCRIBE MY ROOMMATE AS:

| INEVITABLY QUARRELSOME AND UNCOOPERATIVE | MOODY AT TIMES | OF AVERAGE DISPOSITION | USUALLY CONGENIAL | EXCEPTIONALLY CHEERFUL AND PLEASANT |

ANY STUDENT SHOULD BE ADMITTED TO THE HONORS PROGRAM.

| STRONGLY AGREE | AGREE | UNDECIDED | DISAGREE | STRONGLY DISAGREE |

Integration of Behavior

Summary

Study of Personality

1. Personality is generally defined as the unique and characteristic ways in which an individual reacts to his or her surroundings. It is composed of relatively consistent patterns of behavior, some being common to other individuals and others being distinct from all other individuals.

2. Personality theories have been devised to explain and predict these individual patterns. Since no one theory can encompass all of human behavior, each theory usually focuses on selected psychological processes, such as motivation, learning, or perception. Theories of personality also differ in origin. Some have developed through clinical work, in which professional judgment and opinion play an important role, and others have come from a research background, based on experimental procedures and statistical methods.

Psychoanalytic Theory

3. The basic elements of personality in psychoanalytic theory are the id, ego, and superego, which represent biological, psychological, and social dimensions of personality, respectively. In personality development, early experiences are emphasized, particularly the psychosexual stages—oral, anal, and phallic. The phallic stage involves the Oedipal / Electra complex, which is normally resolved by identification with the like-sexed parent.

4. A most important aspect of psychoanalytic theory is its emphasis on unconscious processes, which concern repressed impulses, usually sexual and aggressive in nature. Early conflicts and frustrations often result in repression, and later they reappear in symbolic form, as seen in fixations and other aspects of personality.

5. There are various systems of psychoanalysis, most of which differ from the traditional approach by placing less emphasis on the role of sexual impulses in the organization of the personality. Analytic psychology postulates a collective unconscious, containing the past experiences of all humanity as well as those of our predecessors in earlier evolutionary development. Individual psychology stresses one's desire for competence, especially in the social environment and, thus, has contributed concepts such as sibling rivalry and inferiority complex.

6. Projective techniques are assumed to be especially useful for measuring the subject's underlying motives and attitudes. They are based on the principle that responses to unstructured stimuli must come largely from within the subject. These tests involve inkblots, ambiguous pictures, incomplete sentences, and similarly nebulous stimuli.

Trait Theory

7. A popular approach to the study of personality involves classifying people according to types. One such method, called somatotyping, assumes a relationship between physique and temperament, but as yet it has received little empirical support.

8. According to trait theory, the basic elements of personality are a cluster of primary or source traits. Factor analysis has been used to identify these traits, but no final agreement on the basic traits has been reached. This theory offers an objective approach to the study of personality and has been useful in describing individual differences.

9. Personality inventories are printed forms containing questions and statements about human behavior that the examinees answer about themselves. These instruments, used to assess both normal and psychiatric characteristics, are easily administered, but commonly the subject can create a false impression of his or her personality.

Learning Theory

10. Social learning theory states that behavior is acquired not only through direct reinforcement but also on the basis of symbolic processes, as illustrated in modeling, in which another person is observed. Under appropriate conditions of reinforcement, often the model's behavior is reproduced later by the observer.

11. According to operant learning theory, the basic elements of personality are reinforced responses, and these are to be understood exclusively on the basis of environmental factors. The acquisition of such responses involves principles such as intermittent reinforcement, generalization, and extinction. Operant theory notes the vulnerability of the child in the early stages of life to the various reinforcement contingencies in the environment.

12. In situational tests, the subject is observed in a certain context, rather than asked a series of questions. The person might be observed interacting with others, solving a problem, or exploring a new environment. The aim is to study the person in a situation comparable to the one for which assessment is being made.

The Humanistic Viewpoint

13. The humanistic viewpoint stresses the complexity and uniqueness of human beings, their capacity for experiencing, and their potential for growth. These conceptions suggest the need for certain changes in contemporary psychology: a more creative approach to research, more interest in subjective states, and better methods for developing personal awareness.

14. Self theory emphasizes the role of the individual in shaping his or her own destiny, in contrast to a deterministic outlook. Maladjustment and dissatisfaction occur when one's self-concept is at odds with one's experiences in the environment or when the self-concept and ideal self lack congruence. These discrepancies can be diminished when an individual is provided with a nonthreatening environment in which to make efforts at self-discovery.

15. Assessment procedures in humanistic psychology usually involve inventories and rating scales, employed by the subject or an observer. In the Q-sort, the individual's self concept and ideal self are indicated, and then the degree of incongruence is established statistically.

Eclecticism in Theory and Assessment

16. All theories and tests of personality have assets and limitations. The eclectic psychologist selects whatever approaches seem most appropriate at a given moment.

Suggested Readings

Freud. S. *The basic writings of Sigmund Freud* (A. A. Brill, trans.). New York: Random House, 1938. A compendium of Freud's most significant writings.

Hall, C. S., & Lindzey, G. *Theories of personality* (2nd ed.). New York: Wiley, 1970. Reviews 13 major theories or approaches to personality, including those discussed in this chapter.

Jourard, S. M. *Healthy personality: An approach from the viewpoint of humanistic psychology.* New York: Macmillan, 1974. A small but comprehensive volume surveying the concept of the healthy personality.

Mischel, W. *Introduction to personality* (2nd ed.). New York: Holt, 1976. This book presents personality from two viewpoints—the major theories and the roles of the basic processes in personality development.

Semeonoff, B. *Projective techniques.* New York: Wiley, 1976. This book places emphasis on the Rorschach Test and Thematic Apperception Test but includes other topics also.

Chapter 17

Adjustment

Adjustment is an elusive concept. Consider the words of an expert:

When I entered the field . . . nearly half a century ago . . . I assumed that abnormal people were in . . . hospitals and normal people were outside. I never put this assumption into words; I never even formulated it in my mind. But it was there.

Now the matter is not so clearcut. To mention just one side of my education, I have seen a surprising amount of normality in patients with severe mental diseases, in spite of overwhelming swings of mood in some and delusions and hallucinations in others. . . .

A second side of that learning process was the observation of abnormality in people assumed to be in mental health—in everyday people carrying on the work of the world, in leaders in all aspects of our civilization.

An early experience was to leave a logical and cooperative patient to meet an unreasonable and confused relative. Were both the patient and the relative on the wrong side of the hospital entrance? (Bond, 1958)

Progress has been made in the past 20 years since the preceding excerpt was written but it still expresses the modern viewpoint: adjustment exists *on a continuum*. There is no clear distinction between well adjusted and poorly adjusted. This concept is emphasized throughout this chapter, as we examine various points on the continuum and consider the underlying factors.

The Adjusted Individual

Adjustment not only exists on a continuum, but also is a continuous process. In fact, *adjustment* is defined as the continuous process of satisfying one's desires. It is not a fixed or static state, and it involves many aspects of the individual's behavior. No one achieves a complete adjustment—at least not for long. Shortly, one need or another, physiological or psychological, arises, and the individual must find ways of satisfying his or her needs again.

Adjustment as a Process

If adjustment is a process and it exists on a continuum, then the extremes of the continuum are also processes. At one end there is the mentally healthy person, who is seen as ever-changing and ever-adapting rather than as possessing a set of enduring traits. At the other end is the mentally ill person, who is less adaptive and responds in much the same way regardless of the circumstances. Hence, this person's behavior is often inappropriate.

Conceptions of mental health. Already we have encountered several views of mentally healthy behavior. Thus, Freud described it as expressing oneself in love and work. Although more interested in the maladjustment end of the continuum, Freud saw the mentally healthy person as constantly fulfilling himself or herself in both these respects.

Erik Erikson emphasized the life-long process of adjustment as a succession of crises that occur in the full life cycle. The sequential mastery of these crises is the basis of mental health, although mastery of even the first step is never permanently accomplished.

Abraham Maslow has described the mentally healthy person in terms of self-actualization. Here again, a process is stressed. Human beings are characterized as continually wanting creatures, and some, who at a given moment are developing and utilizing their capacities to the fullest, are said to be self-actualizing.

Carl Rogers has cited two aspects of the adjustment process: openness to experience and trust in oneself. Regarding the former, rather than shutting himself or herself off from certain feelings, the individual acknowledges feelings of fear, pleasure, and anger. With this openness, rather than defensiveness, the fully functioning person, as Rogers calls this type of individual, shows increasing self-trust as a basis for action. This person trusts his or her own experience and self-knowledge to do what seems appropriate (Figure 17-1).

Characteristics of mentally healthy persons. College students, drawing on such conceptions and their own experience, have described the "optimally adjusted" person. In the course of a longer essay, one woman states that such a person" . . . does not resort to work as a means of escape . . . is not embarrassed to conform nor afraid to differ . . . can accept criticism and appreciation and is also objective in . . . evaluation of others." This student recognizes the process aspect of adjustment, stating that the mentally healthy person "is not free from problems because (s)he is actively engaged in life." Instead, this person "recognizes problems and tries to understand them" (Block, 1961).

These descriptions and views can be summarized in the following points, pertaining to the basic psychological processes considered throughout this text.

1. Perception. As a rule, the mentally healthy person perceives reality efficiently and accurately; in particular, this person perceives himself or herself realistically.

2. Learning. As a rule, the mentally healthy individual is capable of forming close relationships with a few people yet is able to be independent when necessary, even enjoying solitude; this person also can work productively and creatively alone or with others.

3. *Motivation.* As a rule, the mentally healthy person is concerned with problems affecting society as well as those of personal concern, attempts to improve society in addition to his own condition, and in a nonhostile way enjoys the humor in our common human predicament. Altogether, this person feels reasonably comfortable about his or her work, relations with others, and personal assets and shortcomings.

Criteria for a definition. For years, mental health was defined only as the absence of mental illness. Today, more positive statements are made, as indicated in the previous descriptions. Also, in most societies two criteria—personal discomfort and disruptive social behavior—are used for making decisions regarding any point on the adjustment continuum, from mental health to so-called mental illness.

In *personal discomfort,* the individual is unhappy with himself or herself, is often unable to relate to others, and is unable to work well. The person is tense and unhappy, sometimes despite an appearance of confidence and satisfaction. In casual conversation and the routine of daily life the inner turmoil often is not evident to others. ∎ The poem of Richard Cory is suggestive:

He was a gentleman from sole to crown,
Clean favored, and imperially slim.
       * * *
And he was rich—yes, richer than a king—
And admirably schooled in every grace;
       * * *
And Richard Cory, one calm summer night,
Went home and put a bullet through his head.
        (Robinson, 1948)
        By permission of the publisher

In socially *disruptive behavior,* a person fails to conform to social norms to the point at which he or she is constantly

	SOCIAL ASPECTS	INDIVIDUAL ASPECTS
FREUD	LOVE	WORK
ERIKSON	GENERATIVITY INTIMACY IDENTITY INDUSTRY TRUST	INTEGRITY INITIATIVE AUTONOMY
MASLOW	SELF-ACTUALIZATION LOVE AND BELONGING	SELF-ESTEEM
ROGERS	OPENNESS TO EXPERIENCE	TRUST IN SELF

Figure 17-1 **Conceptions of Mental Health.** *All four viewpoints are based on the idea that social behavior is a highly significant dimension of human adjustment. However, some of the concepts differ in the degree to which social responsiveness is involved.*

damaging other persons. These reactions are sometimes known as psychopathic behavior, and they include juvenile delinquency and criminal actions. Such persons are not necessarily discontent with their behavior; they are judged to be maladjusted on the basis of their actions, despite the lack of personal discomfort.

Since most of us have committed misdemeanors at one time or another and all of us have experienced discomfort, it is the intensity and persistence of these conditions that define any point on the continuum. And the position of any given individual on the continuum varies from time to time as that person seeks to readjust to almost everpresent needs and desires.

A coping sequence. When someone is prevented from satisfying a need or desire, we say that frustration has occurred. Some sort of *barrier* is present, internal or external, which restricts the individual's action. Weakness, lack of skill, or low intelligence, all of which can stand in the way of achieving our goals, are internal barriers, and often they are

∎ *Mr. Smith, a respectable neighbor of mine, jumped off a ten-story building last year. No one knew why since he had "everything to live for"—a wonderful family, security, nice home. His family was sad but they seemed to understand. He was so interested in birds. He used to say he was a bird and I thought he was kidding.*

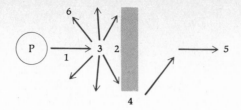

quite lasting. External barriers can be nonsocial, as illustrated in floods and poor weather, or social, when someone else prevents the achievement of our goal. These occur whenever parents force a child to refrain from sex play, to remain in a certain place, or to go to bed without watching television. In either case, internal or external, the barrier leads to a state of unsatisfied motives called *frustration*.

The process of dealing with the barrier and seeking readjustment has been described as a *coping sequence*. The motivated individual (1) pursues a course of action and (2) encounters a barrier that prevents further progress. In all likelihood, the person (3) engages in exploratory behavior and perhaps (4) discovers that a particular response is sufficient to overcome the obstacle. In this case, the person (5) reaches the goal and is temporarily adjusted again. If the barrier cannot be overcome, the person (6) makes some other, less effective adjustive reaction. The individual may withdraw from the situation, pursue a substitute goal, or find some means of denying that some frustration has occurred, by retreating into a world of his or her own creation, in which no barriers are encountered (Figure 17-2).

This sequence is readily illustrated in the experience reported by the college student at the end of the discussion of emotion (Chap. 13). Let us reconsider it. This woman was frustrated in a minor way when she attempted to encounter a male friend unobtrusively. As she walked across the campus, she (1) watched for him to emerge from the building, but her effort to concentrate on the middle doorway (2) was thwarted when she met a classmate and became engaged in

conversation. Then, directly or symbolically, she (3) tried several courses of action—deciding whether or not she had missed him, changing her route across the quadrangle, and thinking about the color of his shirt. Finally, she (4) decided to turn around, and then she (5) was able to find him. But she was frustrated again in the sense that she was unable to do so without being caught, so she (6) ran all the way to French class, perhaps releasing the accumulated tension.

In all cases, the adjustment reaction in the final stage can be integrative, nonintegrative, or somewhere between the extremes. In this mild example, the reaction appears largely integrative; the student responds to the frustration by hurrying to the next class, rather than becoming distraught, missing it altogether.

Conflict and Adjustment

On further examination, another aspect of this ordinary situation is evident. The young woman was frustrated by the crowds and conversation, which distracted her attention, but she was also in conflict. A *conflict* occurs when a motive is opposed by an incompatible motive, rather than blocked by a barrier. The woman wanted to look for her friend but did not want to be seen searching for him. To look or not to look, that was the conflict. In one sense, all conflicts involve frustration, since one motive serves as a barrier to the other.

Types of conflict.   The legendary donkey, flanked by equally enticing and distant bales of hay, is said to have starved in the midst of plenty. When there are two equally attractive alternatives, such as choosing between two invitations to dinner, the situation is called an *approach-approach* conflict.

Sometimes two or more alternatives are equally unattractive or repellent, in which case there is an *avoidance-avoidance* conflict. A student with financial problems must sell the car or leave college; a man must have remedial surgery or run the risk of later illness.

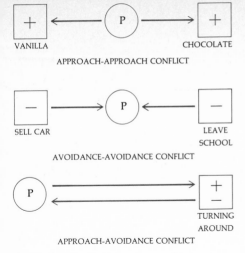

VANILLA   CHOCOLATE

APPROACH-APPROACH CONFLICT

SELL CAR   LEAVE SCHOOL

AVOIDANCE-AVOIDANCE CONFLICT

TURNING AROUND

APPROACH-AVOIDANCE CONFLICT

The college woman mentioned earlier was not faced with two attractive or two unattractive alternatives but rather with a *single* possibility having both positive and negative aspects. The question of turning around or not turning around to look for her friend involved a mild *approach-avoidance* conflict. Similarly, a child starts to pat a dog but is afraid and pulls back his or her hand. A person picks up the telephone and dials a number, but fearing the other person's response, puts the receiver back on the hook. All these examples illustrate the approach-avoidance type of conflict (Figure 17-3).

What are the outcomes of such situations? The most immediate consequence is an increase in drive or tension, but how is this condition manifest in behavior?

Conflict outcomes. To study the behavioral results of conflict under highly controlled conditions, a group of rats was used in a laboratory setting. Each animal was trained to run down an alley to obtain food, while being attached to a noninterfering harness that measured the amount of pull the rat exerted. One by one, each rat was placed at either 30 cm or 170 cm from the food, and it was

observed that the amount of pull was stronger when the rat was closer to the goal. This difference in force is called a *gradient,* and it was found that the approach gradient increases as the distance from the goal decreases. In other words, the tendency to approach a positive goal grows stronger as one draws closer to it (Figure 17-4).

Figure 17-3 Conflicts. *The diagrams illustrate basic conflict situations, and the photograph suggests a conflict of the approach-approach type. (Photo by Wollinksy from Stock, Boston)*

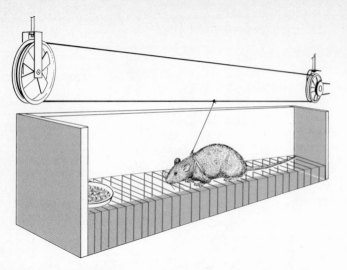

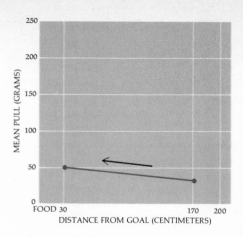

Figure 17-4 Approach Gradient. *As the subject approaches a goal, greater effort is exerted to reach it.*

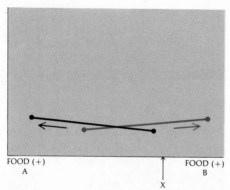

FOOD (+)
A

X

FOOD (+)
B

Figure 17-5 Approach-Approach Conflict. *A subject placed at position X would move towards the closer goal, which is B.*

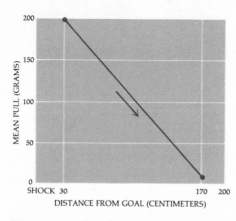

Figure 17-6 Avoidance Gradient. *The subject exerts greater effort to avoid the shock (goal) region when close to it.*

Compared to the others, approach-approach conflicts are easily resolved. Even if the two goals are equal, the individual eventually moves towards one of them; then the motivation for that goal increases and the conflict is resolved. The legendary donkey, in the course of making a decision, no doubt turned its head closer to one bale, and this movement would have been enough to resolve the conflict. In short, the animal should not have starved in this situation (Figure 17-5).

In the experiment with the rats, the food later was changed to an electrical shock, and when the amount of pull was measured at both distances, it was found that the avoidance gradient also increases as the distance from the goal decreases. The closer the subject is to the negative goal, the stronger is the effort to avoid it (Figure 17-6).*

In the avoidance-avoidance situation, the subject eventually is prompted to abandon whatever solution it attempts, and so the problem is insoluble. The organism advances in one direction, finds itself repelled, advances in another, is

*Figures 17-4 through 17-8 from J. S. Brown, 1958. Copyright 1958 by the American Psychological Association. Reprinted by permission.

Integration of Behavior

repelled again, and so forth. In the experiment with the rats, sooner or later they jumped out of the alley, and in daily life people also try to choose a third alternative, which is some form of escape (Figure 17-7).

Now what will happen if the rat is in an alley that contains both food and electric shock in the same area? Since the avoidance gradient is steeper than the approach gradient, the point of conflict and the animal's behavior can be estimated. The conflict should occur at the intersection of the two gradients, and the animal should spend most of its time here, vacillating between the alternatives. The animal will be drawn into the conflict by the larger approach gradient, but after passing the intersection, the individual will be repelled by the steeper avoidance gradient, as demonstrated by experimental tests (Miller, 1948; Figure 17-8).

Because of these properties, the approach-avoidance conflict generally is more enduring than the other two, but even these conflicts do not necessarily continue for long periods. A new element is usually introduced, raising the approach gradient or lowering the avoidance gradient, thus ending the conflict. The dog begins to wag its tail and reduces the child's fear of patting it. A friend urges the person to make the telephone call. With the new elements, the gradients shift.

We should add that approach-avoidance conflicts also can have two or more alternatives, each with both positive and negative features. This situation is called *multiple approach-avoidance*. ■ All approach-avoidance situations, whether they involve one or multiple alternatives, are characterized by *ambivalence* within the individual, meaning that he or she experiences opposed feelings, such as love and hate for the same person. In fact, one reason that decisions are so difficult in life is that we are ambivalent about so many things (Figure 17-9).

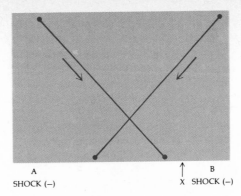

A SHOCK (−)   X SHOCK (−) B

Figure 17-7 Avoidance-Avoidance Conflict. *A subject at point X would retreat from B until he or she had passed the point of intersection of the two gradients. Then he or she would retreat from A until passing the intersection again, and so forth. Eventually, the subject might try to resolve the dilemma by escaping from the situation.*

■ *Two guys asked me to go on a date on the same night. One wanted to take me to a nightclub where there was a group that I had always wanted to see in person. However, the other guy, who I really wanted to date, had asked me to go to a movie that I really didn't want to go to because I had already seen it before and really didn't like it.*

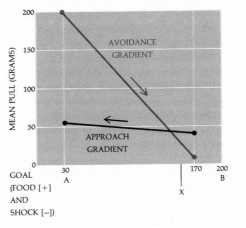

GOAL
(FOOD [+]
AND
SHOCK [−])

Figure 17-8 Approach-Avoidance Conflict. *At point X, where the approach gradient is stronger than the avoidance gradient, the subject moves toward A, but after passing the point of intersection, he or she retreats towards B, because of the stronger avoidance gradient. The subject's behavior at any moment depends on the comparative strengths of the gradients.*

Figure 17-9 Types of Conflict

Type of Conflict	Number of Alternatives	Resolution	Duration
Approach-approach	2	Choice of one or the other	Short
Avoidance-avoidance	2	Indecision or choice of a third alternative	Long if a third alternative is not chosen
Approach-avoidance	1	Indecision	Long
Multiple approach-avoidance	2 or more	Indecision	Long

Figure 17-10   Physiological Reactions in Emotion.   *Under persistent stress, the stomach wall begins to show ulcerations, as shown in the photograph on the right. (From* The Stress of Life, *2nd ed., by Hans Selye. Copyright 1976 by McGraw-Hill Book Company. Used by permission of McGraw-Hill Book Company.)*

Common Reactions to Stress

Suppose that the individual cannot overcome the frustrating barrier or resolve the conflict. What is the likely outcome? One possibility is that the individual experiences inexplicable aches and pains, tissue damage, or organ malfunctions (Figure 17-10). Earlier, we noted these possible psychosomatic reactions as potential outcomes of prolonged psychological stress. In the present context we focus on behavioral and thinking reactions, rather than physical disorders, beginning with those usually less severe.

Decreased Responsiveness

Years ago an experimenter placed a pig in an approach-avoidance situation. The pig learned to lift the lid of a foodbox to receive an apple, and later it encountered a shock. Still later, both the shock and an apple appeared when the lid was lifted. Eventually the animal seemed torn in both directions, became sulky, ignored the foodbox completely, and went into a sleeplike trance (Curtis, 1937).

Lethargy.   A lethargic reaction such as that demonstrated by the pig is a frequent response to stress. In more recent research, dogs were placed in a suspension harness that allowed them some freedom of movement, and in this circumstance they received a mild shock for a few seconds. Some of them could not terminate it, but others were allowed to stop the shock by turning the head and pressing a nearby panel. Then all the subjects were placed individually in an open compartment without a harness, and there another electric shock occurred. The dogs that had previously learned to escape by turning the head readily learned to jump a barrier and thereby escape the shock in the new situation. The others, although they could move about freely also, usually whined and then settled into a certain position to endure the shock, making no escape movements. The previously *learned helplessness,* in which they could do nothing about a stressful situation, apparently induced these subjects to become lethargic under stress in a later situation (Seligman & Maier, 1967; Seligman, 1975). This reaction appears parallel to what is described as depression in human beings.

If one is inclined to *speculate,* we might say that at times we are like the pig, caught between opposing response tendencies, and at times like the dog, listless and unresponsive because it seems that nothing we do makes any difference. In the former case, there is a conflict; in the latter case, there is a sense of helplessness. In both cases, there is decreased responsiveness to the environment.

The concept of laziness. Suppose that a young man is offered an attractive but demanding job and is asked to inform the prospective employer of his decision within a week. He does not do so, and then the employer decides not to hire a man who is "too lazy even to write a letter." But in fact the man is not lazy at all; he has been thinking and worrying about the job constantly but is unable to make the decision. As happened with the pig, competing responses can result in behavior that, at a distance, looks like lack of interest and laziness. If we saw the pig without knowing what happened, we would think it was too lazy to lift the lid or move around in its pen. In terms of our earlier discussion, we might speculate that the animal is in an approach-avoidance situation and has become immobilized at the point of intersection of the gradients.

The learned helplessness of the dogs, on the other hand, has its analogy in ghetto conditions. Persons sometimes express the view that poverty-stricken people are simply too lazy to do anything about their situation, but possibly, like the dogs in harness, ghetto persons have learned—rightly or wrongly—that there is nothing they can do to change the situation. Therefore, they have stopped trying. Even when there are alternatives, it may be difficult to see them, after years of "learned helplessness."

Fantasy. Inaction does not mean that the individual has not thought about the problem. Sometimes when we are under stress, problems in the outer world are "resolved" inwardly, by wishful thinking and dreams, called *fantasy* (Figure 17-11). The person who cannot cope with the real world creates one of his or her

Figure 17-11 Fantasy. *Children's play activities are often suggestive of fantasy; they seem to be trying out roles that are not otherwise available to them at their age. In this respect, fantasy represents a constructive force in the child's personality development, provided it is not overused. (Wollinsky from Stock, Boston)*

My third grade teacher was the source of several educational handicaps. Although I tried as hard as the others, I could not write neatly and clearly. Yet this old bitch would continually hold my best efforts up in front of the class and come out with something like "Now isn't this just disgusting?" or "Guess who this mess belongs to?" I was quickly lowered to the "dumb row," a fact which she continually reminded me of. I spent the next five years in the "dumb row" before I was finally able to prove myself.

I often think about going back there to wave my 3.4 high school average and 3.2 college cum in her face and then give her a good swift kick.

own, temporarily. In one's mind unfulfilled goals such as extreme revenge and unusual love affairs can be accomplished readily. ■

Everyone engages in some form of fantasy, and such activities are not necessarily deviant. In talking openly with other persons, it is always surprising to find out how much their private thoughts are like our own. Fantasy is a sign of maladjustment only when it becomes a *persistent* substitute for dealing directly with problems.

Aggression and Regression

Interestingly, stress can also result in the opposite reaction. As we saw in the case of extreme emotion, the individual under stress may show frustration openly, behaving in an uncontrolled manner.

Aggression. Some years ago, the *frustration-aggression* hypothesis was formulated, which states that "the occurrence of aggressive behavior always presupposes the existence of frustration and, contrariwise, that the existence of frustration always leads to some form of aggression." This aggression is expressed towards the frustrating barrier, or if that is too dangerous, towards some less threatening object or towards oneself (Dollard et al., 1939).

A sales manager notes that income is down and berates a worker who has nothing to do with the decrement. During economic depression, aggressive crimes increase, even those not involving robbery. When food is unavailable, experimental animals are more likely to fight and to aggress against their cages. These examples illustrate *displaced aggression,* in which the tension from frustration is discharged onto a less threatening object, rather than towards the source of frustration, which may be dangerous or impossible to confront.

The frustration-aggression hypothesis has considerable support but also has limitations. Regarding the first part of the hypothesis, that aggression always indicates frustration, we have already

noted that aggressive behavior also can be the product of imitation and operant conditioning. Frustration is not the only source of aggression. Concerning the second part, that frustration always leads to aggression, we have seen that frustration may result in fantasy, fantasied aggression, or running off to French class, and shortly we shall see other possibilities. Thus, aggression is only one outcome of frustration. Altogether, the hypothesis is a good working assumption, but it is clearly not supported in every instance (Berkowitz, 1974).

Regression. When other responses to stress prove inadequate, sometimes we *regress,* meaning that we move backwards, repeating behavior that was satisfying and more appropriate at an earlier stage of development. Following the birth of a new brother or sister, an older child may revert to actions that obtained satisfaction in the past, such as crying, baby talk, and bedwetting. □ According to one viewpoint, this behavior may represent an effort to regain parental attention.

Such behavior is not limited to children. Husbands sometimes attempt to dominate their wives, and wives their husbands, by fits of sulking, weeping, and threats that they will "do away with themselves" if they do not get their own way. Loosely, regression might be considered to be a form of childish behavior.

Defense Mechanisms

In response to stress, individuals behave in subdued, aggressive, and regressive ways; they also behave in ways unknown to them. Actually, the behaviors themselves are not unknown, but the reasons for them apparently are not evident to the individual concerned. These reactions are called *defense mechanisms,* a Freudian term referring to the various subtle methods by which a person denies thoughts that arouse anxiety. The basic mechanism, upon which all others are presumably based, is *repression,* which is the unconscious process of excluding unpleasant thoughts from awareness. It clearly differs from *suppression,* which is a conscious attempt to avoid certain thoughts or actions.

Types of defense mechanisms. Sometimes repression is aided by other processes, such as *rationalization,* in which an individual is not only unaware of the repressed thoughts but also substitutes false reasons for real ones. A man not admitted to law school decided that he did not want to become an attorney because there was too much work involved. A three-year-old boy wanted to take his teddy bear to school, but he also wanted to be considered a ''big boy,'' so he decided not to take the bear. His reason: the bear might catch cold.

It is often difficult to determine when someone is using false reasons. Sometimes the distinction can be made by observing the individual's willingness to examine his or her thinking. If the person becomes upset, perhaps the real reasons are not being acknowledged; the person becomes anxious upon being brought closer to awareness.

Repression also can be used in another defense mechanism, called *reaction formation,* which involves attitudes and overt behaviors that are exactly opposite to those that the individual has judged unacceptable and consequently repressed. In this circumstance, it is hypothesized, the expression of attitudes opposed to the repressed thoughts serves to aid the repression. For example, after a narrow escape on one of his missions, a wartime flyer reported that he was eager to return to combat, and during an interview he declared that he never feared anything. He fainted, however, after each of his next two flights. Later, following administration of sodium pentothal, the ''truth drug,'' he revealed his more basic feelings. He said: ''I was scared. Me scared! I didn't think I'd ever be scared'' (White, 1964).

A father, finding childrearing an arduous task, may try to conceal this resentment from himself by being overly solicitous of the child's welfare. An overly ''sweet'' person indicated what she did when she became angry with other people: ''I kill 'em with kindness.''

Rather than adopting a false reason or one that is the opposite of our underlying feelings, we sometimes attribute the problem to someone else, in which case we are engaging in *projection.* Again, there are two general aspects: repressing unacceptable thoughts and then, in this case, ascribing them to others. In a general sense, whenever an individual attributes his or her own characteristics to another source, he or she is projecting. In the context of defense mechanisms, however, projection has a more restricted meaning, referring only to unknowingly attributing one's *unwanted* traits to others.

In an early study of projection as a defense mechanism, college men rated themselves, and each man rated all the others on four socially undesirable traits: stinginess, obstinacy, disorderliness, and bashfulness. Some students apparently were aware of their undesirable traits, giving themselves high ratings on the same traits for which they received high ratings from their friends. Others

□ *After living with them for over 18 years, it is relatively easy to predict the way that members of my family will react to certain situations. My younger brother, for example, exhibits a certain habit whenever he encounters a situation that he cannot deal with effectively or that causes him great distress.*

If Paul has such a problem, he will go into his room and take out a small baseball glove, put it on, and walk around the room punching in it. After this, he will pull down the shades, turn off the light, shut the door and lie on his bed in a prone position and begin to snap his fingers. He will not pay any attention to anyone or anything.

Since Paul was his only son, frequently my father would take him to the usual places that a father takes his son. He bought Paul this glove after they had gone to a Yankee baseball game. Exhausted after the outing, my father decided to take a nap but Paul was wide awake. My father decided to keep him busy by showing him how to snap his fingers. While Paul practiced this, my father fell asleep. When Paul woke up the next morning he learned that my father was going to be admitted to the hospital. While he was waiting for the ambulance to come, my father told eight-year-old Paul that he would be back home before Paul could snap his fingers a hundred times. My father died three days later.

For over a year, Paul would lie in bed with the glove tightly clasped in his hand and gently snap his fingers until he fell asleep. As he got older he didn't do this all the time, but I notice that he still does it occasionally when he encounters a difficult situation.

■ *Ophelia and Delilah were in the dining room eating lunch. The menu for that day listed gingerbread as the dessert. Ophelia, who liked gingerbread very much, was quite pleased, and while in line to get her food, thought about getting two servings but then decided against it and only took one. Finishing her meal, Ophelia turned to eat her gingerbread only to discover she had no milk to drink with it. She got up to get some more and asked Delilah if she also would like some milk. Delilah declined. When Ophelia returned she had not only a glass of milk, but another serving of gingerbread which she set down in front of Delilah. The following conversation took place.*

Delilah: What's that for?

Ophelia: You asked me to get you some gingerbread.

Delilah: No, I didn't.

Ophelia: Yes you did. Why did you think I asked you if you wanted more milk?

Delilah: I thought you were just being nice. And I didn't ask for any gingerbread.

Ophelia: You didn't? Could have sworn you did. Couldn't figure out why you didn't want any milk to eat with your gingerbread. Makes sense now since you never asked for it in the first place. Guess I'll have to eat it then.

Is Ophelia mad, or is there method in her madness? Methinks a little projection is at play here. Wanting two desserts, how easy it would be to hear someone else asking for another dessert.

gave themselves low ratings on traits for which they received high ratings from others and, furthermore, they rated other people higher on these undesirable traits than did the rest of the group (Sears, 1936). They lacked insight into their own undesirable qualities and falsely saw these traits in others instead. ■

Use of defense mechanisms. One must recognize that the use of defense mechanisms is not *necessarily* disadvantageous to adjustment. When a disappointment is forgotten or denied via repression, the individual may become more readily involved in new activities. As a result of reaction formation, the fearful flyer continued his assignments awhile. On the other hand, repression requires ''psychic energy'' in keeping unwanted thoughts from awareness and, therefore, the individual may find it difficult to give concerted attention to other matters. Again, we must remember that there are *integrative,* or successful, forms of adjustment as well as *nonintegrative* ones.

Defense mechanisms, therefore, can be helpful in two respects. Through repression, we forget some of our most difficult problems, and through the other types of reactions we sometimes find partially effective ways of dealing with them. But the best adjustment is made when we can drop our defenses and cope with life's problems directly.

Neurotic Disorders

The distinction between direct and indirect coping is an important one. In general, coping directly with a problem, by exerting extra effort or finding alternative solutions, constitutes the more satisfying reaction, and it falls towards the mentally healthy end of the continuum. Indirect solutions, as illustrated in fantasy and displaced aggression, generally are not as satisfying. As we turn to neurotic behavior, we see clearly less-direct problem solving and evidence that the individual is towards the discomfort end of the adjustment continuum.

Concepts and Labels

These more extreme reactions to stress have been conceptualized in many ways in the course of psychiatric history. They are generally referred to today as *neuroses* and *psychoses,* and a brief look at the background of these concepts and terms is helpful in understanding the current situation.

History of the problem. As recently as the early twentieth century, people with deviant behavior were thought to be possessed by the devil and thus were described as ''mad'' (Figure 17-12). With advancements, milder terms were used, first ''insane'' and then ''abnormal,'' but these too came to have negative connotations and eventually were considered detrimental to the individual. In the 1950s, the concept of ''mental illness'' was introduced, suggesting that emotionally disturbed persons have some type of disease, analogous to physical illness. Viewed in this manner, deviant behavior seemed still more acceptable to the individual and to society.

Within a decade, however, mental illness was called a myth. The new term was criticized because it implied that psychological problems are no different from physical disorders, and as a result the disturbed individual is encouraged to take little responsibility for his or her condition. This criticism is provocative

"TAKE ME AWAY"

Figure 17-12 "Mad" Person in the Nineteenth Century. *Both the description of madness and the treatment of "mad" persons were harsh. (The Bettmann Archive)*

and has been widely respected, but the suggested replacement, "problems in living," has not been adopted (Szasz, 1960). The concept may be more accurate but perhaps the term is too nonspecific.

As this history suggests, any term applied to this set of behaviors eventually becomes derogatory. Even if we focused more on determinants of the patient's problems, rather than on symptoms, these descriptions would become "labels" too. The problem will continue, unfortunately, because no science is possible without some kind of nomenclature.

Current criticisms. At least three defects are pointed out in our present system of labeling mental conditions. First, any labels oversimplify the concept by not adequately representing the currently understood differences among and within the various disorders. Second, they continue to stigmatize the individual, branding that person as a deviant, social misfit, or malcontent, which is largely due to the lack of acceptance and understanding of emotional disturbance on the part of the general public. ■

Third, psychiatric labels are inconsistent with the clinical approach, which should emphasize personal and causal aspects of the condition, rather than symptoms. In the present system, stating that an individual has an obsessive-compulsive neurosis does not indicate why this particular response appeared, how it serves the individual, or the nature of the individual's feelings. In fact, in the more severe disorders, the patient's prior history is more useful in predicting the outcome of treatment than are his or her symptoms (Cromwell, 1975).

Nevertheless, such terms persist because they are useful in organizing clinical knowledge and in treating some patients, but now they are used with greater sensitivity for the individual's needs and progress in science. Improvements in terminology are being made, although not at an acceptable rate (Braginsky et al., 1969; Rosenhan, 1973). With this discussion as a background, it is hoped that the reader will be cautious in describing any behavior as neurotic, psychotic, or even a defense mechanism.

Characteristics of Neurosis

The term *neurosis*, coming from *psychoneurosis*, indicates a persistent and ineffective way of dealing with a personal problem, usually accompanied by anxiety. But the so-called neurotic person does not abandon reality, becoming "crazy" or "insane." Instead, the individual is quite aware of our world and much worried about it. This *anxiety*, a strongly unpleasant emotional state, is a chief feature of neurosis. The neurotic person experiences feelings of unhappiness, guilt, and inferiority, and there is often difficulty in interpersonal relationships. Besides being upset, the person sometimes has inexplicable physical ailments, and for these reasons out-patient assistance, but not hospitalization, is often required.

■ *Within my mother's circle of friends, the ideas of mental illness and psychiatric help are considered absurd. The attitudes these ladies exhibit are so discouraging to me. I wonder if they have ever had any feelings of compassion.*

My mother often speaks of Mrs. Kaltenborne, a neighbor who had a "nervous breakdown" a few years ago. She's home now, and apparently healthy, but my mother always lowers her voice when she mentions her. "I saw Mary Alice out gardening today," leaving out an unspoken "She looks almost normal." It seems impossible for her to accept the fact that all sorts of people seek psychiatric help.

An illustrative case. The following case demonstrates some typical symptoms. It also shows that the neurotic individual usually has little insight into the nature of the problem:

Ms. L. was a deeply depressed woman of thirty-two—"in constant pain." Her pain was a muscular tension around the lower part of her back. She described it as a "burning, tearing, fiery-tongue-like, torturing" sensation. Neurologists, internists, surgeons, were of no avail. . . .

"My whole life is concentrated on my back, and believe me, my pains are real. When I get my attacks, I scream like a wounded or tortured animal, and mind you, this goes on for hours at a time."

She was deeply offended when someone voiced the suspicion that she was "acting up" to torture her husband. "I don't believe that: I started having my attacks before my marriage. Too bad that marriage didn't cure the pain." (Bergler, 1974)

In response to questioning, Ms. L. indicated that she was not satisfied with her marriage. She also stated that she was sexually unsatisfied but did not consider her marriage to be the source of her difficulties. When she entered treatment, it was discovered that these symptoms first became severe after her marriage had proven unsatisfactory, but other factors seemed to be involved as well.

Interpretations. Psychoanalysts have long emphasized the role of underlying or unconscious conflict in neurosis, commonly stemming from childhood. In this view, neurosis is described as both a denial and an expression of this unconscious conflict. It is a denial in the sense that the symptoms hide the real problem, both from the individual and from others. It is an expression in the sense that the symptoms are not random but rather pertain to that underlying problem. As a child, this woman had been punished specifically by receiving a beating on her lower back and buttocks, which is the locus of her pains in adulthood.

According to the theory, if the patient expressed her marriage and punishment problems directly, rather than in the *symbolic* form of neurotic symptoms, she might lose further self-respect and her anxiety would increase. Neurotic symptoms relieve anxiety by offering a "focus" for the patient's concern and directing attention away from the real problem(s).

The traditional behaviorist views the problem differently. Neurotic behavior does not suggest that something *else* is wrong with the individual; the behavior itself is of primary interest. Somehow, the neurotic responses are being supported or reinforced by the environment, partly to the subject's advantage. Inconsistent stimuli and incompatible responses also may be involved, but in any case it is the therapist's task to identify the relevant behavior-reinforcement relationships and then alter them in such a way that the undesired behavior no longer occurs. With Ms. L., the husband's behavior appears particularly significant.

From most viewpoints, two aspects of the neurotic condition are recognized— the *primary gain,* which is the basic reason for the behavior, such as controlling the person's anxiety, and some other advantage, the *secondary gain,* which concerns the sympathy and assistance thereby elicited from others. The benefits in secondary gain apparently can cause ailments to persist long after the original reason for their development has passed.

Neurotic Styles

In deference to tradition and still-current usage, various *types of neuroses* are described in this section, based on categories established by early psychoanalytic workers; however, in an effort to promote the newer emphasis, they are referred to here as *neurotic styles.* This expression more readily acknowledges that the basis for classification is merely the symptoms or behavior patterns, rather than causal factors.

Anxiety neurosis. When anxiety is experienced directly, without being channeled into specific symptoms, it is referred to as *free-floating anxiety* or *anxiety neurosis.* In severe cases, the individual may feel as if he or she is about to "go to pieces." The person may say, "Doctor, I'm worried, but I don't know why. I'm just worried. I have no reason to be, but I am."

Sometimes the anxiety is chronic; in other cases there are periodic attacks, lasting anywhere from a few minutes to an hour or more. The individual also may experience depression, insomnia, and inability to concentrate. In severe instances, there may be pronounced physiological reactions, such as perspiring, trembling, and pounding of the heart.

Phobic neurosis. When anxiety involves extreme fear of some harmless object or event and is highly focused on that event, the reaction is called a *phobia.* Unlike the individual with free-floating anxiety, the phobic individual "knows" what he or she fears and therefore believes that something can be done about it. By avoiding the harmless something, the person avoids much anxiety. After studying the case of Little Hans, a five-year-old boy who feared horses, Freud decided that this fear partially relieved the child of anxiety concerning his father. Since horses were relatively easy to avoid, in Freud's view the phobia could be managed more readily than the generalized anxiety. ■

There are other phobias that develop from a single traumatic experience and do *not* involve redirected anxiety. A person may be fearful of horses after having been trampled and bitten by one that was enraged. Such a fear develops from a truly fearful incident. As such, it constitutes an isolated aspect of the individual's functioning and is therefore more amenable to brief treatment. It is only when a phobic response is an integral part of the personality that the pattern is said to be neurotic.

Conversion neurosis. While anxiety can be free-floating in some instances and attached to an object in the external environment in others, it is "converted" into a bodily symptom in *conversion neuroses.* Hand tremors and uncontrollable body movements, skin problems, losses in hearing, vision, and other sensory capacities are possible conversion symptoms. By definition, there is no known neurophysiological basis for the physical ailment in these reactions (Figure 17-13).

■ *I know a respectable lawyer who seems able to function competently in most every situation except when he must drive his car across a bridge. The actual causes or sources of the fear are not known to me but he simply cannot drive over a bridge. If there is a passenger in the car, the passenger must drive while he shuts his eyes until the bridge is passed.*

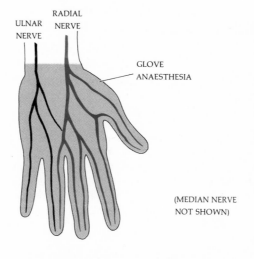

ULNAR NERVE

RADIAL NERVE

GLOVE ANAESTHESIA

(MEDIAN NERVE NOT SHOWN)

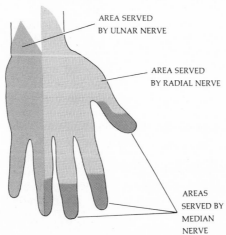

AREA SERVED BY ULNAR NERVE

AREA SERVED BY RADIAL NERVE

AREAS SERVED BY MEDIAN NERVE

Figure 17-13 Glove Anaesthesia. *In this reaction there is a loss of skin sensitivity on the entire hand up to the wrist, but this pattern does not conform to the locations of nerve pathways in the hand and lower arm. Hence, glove anaesthesia usually is considered to be due to psychological rather than physical factors.*

If physical damage occurred in the ulnar nerve, for example, there would be insensitivity only in the ring finger and little finger and partway up the arm. If both the ulnar and radial nerves were damaged, there still might be sensitivity in the tips of the fingers, which are served by the median nerve. (After Gray, 1959)

Dissociative neurosis.
When part of one's personality is separated from the rest of the personality, the condition is called a *dissociative neurosis*. The two aspects of the personality seem to function independently, yet they coexist.

Extensive loss of memory, called *amnesia*, together with a sudden departure from home are the major characteristics of one type of dissociative neurosis known as a *fugue*. In a fugue state, a man engaged to a woman he no longer loved was found wandering hundreds of miles from home, having forgotten his name, the woman, and everything that would identify his past. In this case, the individual does what many of us may wish to do occasionally—forget everything and get away for awhile. Upon recovery, earlier events are often well remembered but those that occurred during the fugue are forgotten.

A more dramatic and popularized aspect of the dissociative neurosis is the alternating or *multiple personality*. The dual personality, such as that represented fictionally in *Dr. Jekyll and Mr. Hyde*, falls within this general classification. Here the individual may be adventurous and assertive in one "self" and conservative and self-effacing in another. Sometimes several alternating personalities appear in the same individual, as in the case study *Three Faces of Eve* (Thigpen & Cleckley, 1957).

Obsessive-compulsive neurosis.
Most fugues and multiple personalities are rare events, but most of us experience certain thoughts and actions of a recurring nature. We may repeat a telephone number over and over or be unable to forget an embarrassing experience. When such behavior is unusually persistent and severe, so that it *greatly* disrupts normal functioning, it is considered to be a neurotic pattern. The unwanted thoughts are traditionally regarded as *obsessions;* the recurring acts, such as washing one's hands continually through the day, are described as *compulsions*.

Frances P. was an unmarried typist, aged twenty-four. She was trying to control erotic fantasies which she could not repress. Her counter-measures put into practice, in a compulsive way, the advice often given to adolescents who are struggling with sex problems. "Think of something else!" Walking to work was an activity that permitted erotic fantasies to emerge easily. So each time Frances stepped on or off the curb at a corner she made herself think of a different person. This kept her mind busy preparing for the next intersection. If she ran out of persons she allowed herself to change streets and start the list over again. (Cameron, 1963)

This case illustrates that compulsive behavior may be used to "crowd out" anxiety-provoking ideas, as well as to give focus to one's underlying problems. The important part of this behavior, however, and what differentiates it from the recurring thoughts and acts that we all have from time to time, is its pervasiveness. It disrupted Frances's life to a considerable extent:

As it became entrenched, it made her shun company to avoid having to explain her preoccupations and her zigzag course as she changed streets. She needed to concentrate upon the task of having names ready in time for the next block. The device failed, however, and kept her from the benefits and pleasures of sharing in the company of others. (Cameron, 1963)

This obsessive countermeasure was not only inefficient but even increased Frances's anxiety, since it required her to alienate herself from other people and eventually dominated most of her life.

Psychotic Disorders

Frances is still in "our world." Within her neurosis she is aware of reality, as we conceive it, enough so that she knows her zigzagging would seem strange to other persons and therefore avoids people when she is out walking.

■ *About a year ago a close friend of mine "cracked up." No one really knows what happened, but apparently for about ten days, he was wandering around without really knowing what he was doing. He tried to get in touch with me, but each time I was out, and he was never at his apartment when I tried to reach him. He was finally found by his landlady sleeping in her bed, having broken into her house. The police took him to a hospital where he stayed for five months.*

Integration of Behavior

The chief characteristic in a *psychosis* is that the individual is essentially out of contact with reality, although there may be intermittent periods of normality, as well (Plate 7).

The psychotic individual may experience false perceptions, called *hallucinations,* such as seeing visions or hearing voices that have no objective basis. A psychotic person also may have *delusions,* which are false beliefs. The delusional person may think that he is Napoleon, that he is the head of the institution in which he is a patient, that some mysterious force is giving him vital energy, or that he has detected ground glass and poison in his food.

Psychosis is clearly at the maladjustment end of the adjustment continuum. This disturbance is severe. In fact, for many psychotic people adjustment is no longer a process; they are static or "stuck," unable to make the necessary adaptations to their environment and, therefore, they need assistance. When someone says that a man goes berserk or a woman is crazy, usually a psychotic reaction is implied, which almost inevitably requires some period of hospitalization. The less specific term "nervous breakdown" is also used in this way. ∎

Schizophrenic Conditions

Among the various psychotic disorders, the most common condition is known as *schizophrenia,* in which severely disturbed thought processes are involved. In this withdrawal from reality, there is usually a distinct impairment in abstract thinking (Wright, 1975). Extreme emotional responses also may appear, however, because the individual is often upset with himself or herself and the environment.

Process and reactive schizophrenia. In a recent effort to surmount some of the labeling problems here, many professionals now speak of schizophrenia in terms of only two conditions. *Process schizophrenia* refers to a condition that has been developing over a long period.

For years, the individual's maladjustment has been obvious, and eventually it is recognized as sufficiently severe to be considered schizophrenic. *Reactive schizophrenia,* on the other hand, refers to a sudden condition, apparently in response to acute environmental stress. It might appear in an individual who suddenly has lost his or her job or has suffered the death of a spouse. Numerous studies have demonstrated behavioral differences between long-term and short-term psychoses, but it is not known yet whether they represent two essentially different processes (Strauss, 1973). In any case, the prospects for recovery are significantly greater in the reactive condition, in which the major stress factors might be removed or spontaneously disappear.

The advantage of these newer designations is not only that they are more respectful but also that they focus on the origin rather than the symptoms of the disorder. Since the traditional terms have not yet been abandoned, however, and since they illustrate the behaviors involved, they are worth noting.

Behavior patterns. Rather than the highly dramatic reactions described in the popular press, individuals in the *simple* schizophrenic condition live a secluded, generally irresponsible life, lacking personal interests and social relationships. Introverted and preoccupied, they are almost the complete opposite of the popular notion of psychosis. Except for occasional signs of irritability, they show little emotion and are uninvolved with the world around them. Many of them, by depending on their families or a highly structured environment, are able to maintain a marginal adjustment without institutional care. ▯

▯ *My first contact with mental illness was when I went to see my great-uncle in a nursing home. He has been diagnosed as a schizophrenic and has been ill since he was a teenager. He is now practically 80 years old. Throughout the years he has received all kinds of treatment including electric shock, but he has remained constantly within his own little world. I often wonder whether with today's knowledge he would get better if he were young again.*

His illness began with an aversion to being with other people but then it grew to the point where he refused to go to school one day. He was an excellent student. He knew three languages fluently when he was a sophomore in high school, but he used his studies as an escape from people. After he refused to go to school any longer, his mother and father took care of him for years and years until his mother was in her late 70s. Most of the time he sat calmly in the rocker by the stove, dreaming his own little dreams, sometimes moving his hands to accompany his thoughts. He talked very little and usually was not at all violent although he could become so when crossed or forced to do something he did not want to.

Of course when I first went to see him I did not know any of this. I knew only that I was going to see my sick uncle. Therefore, in the typical child's way I treated him completely normally and jabbered quite constantly to him and of course expected an answer. He did say a few words to me which is a lot more than he does with most people.

The *hebephrenic* state involves greater emotional display, such as inappropriate laughter, giggling, and crying, but the most pronounced aspect is illogical thinking. A patient who is considered to be hebephrenic said:

No, I never was crazy, a little nervous. Look at my teeth. I came here to have my teeth fixed. We're going to have a strawberry party now. Yesterday I heard voices. They said ''I ran to the drugstore and I am going home tomorrow.'' I heard J. B. Scott's voice and it came from up here in the air. We've got 39 banks on Market Street. We've got 39 banks on Market Street. We've got lots of property. Say, take me home and I'll give you three laundry bags. I'm 29 and a half, 29 and a half. Now I want you to get me ten apples. . . .'' (Zax & Stricker, 1963)

Other schizophrenic individuals may go for weeks or months rigidly resisting any change in bodily position, simply staring into space, sometimes refusing even to eat or walk. In the past, they have been tube-fed whenever necessary. When not completely immobile, the *catatonic* patient may endlessly repeat certain gestures, grimaces, or stereotyped acts, or may permit his or her body to be molded in any way, a state called ''waxy flexibility.'' Regardless of the posture, comfortable or uncomfortable, the individual maintains it for long periods of time (Figure 17-14).

In certain respects, the most difficult psychotic behavior to detect, and the one that sometimes seems most ''normal,'' is *paranoid* schizophrenia. Here the thought processes initially are more systematized; the individual commonly speaks quite lucidly and convincingly, often about a central theme. On closer inspection, it becomes clear that the theme is based on irrational premises, such as delusions of persecution, in which the person wrongly believes that people are ''out to get him,'' or delusions of grandeur, in which the person believes that he or she is some famous figure.

■ *A patient in the hospital where I work believed he was G-O-D, busied himself with arrangements for a trip to the Vatican, and generally attempted to operate as a supreme being. One of the aides grew increasingly frustrated with the patient's insistence and decided to tell him that he was the ninth Christ he had met in two years. He also allowed a second patient, who had at one time believed himself to be God, to tell the new patient how crazy an idea it was. But nothing denied the delusions of this patient. With each confrontation he became increasingly angry and irrational.*

At the Ypsilanti State Hospital in Michigan, three paranoid male patients each claimed to be Jesus Christ, and it was thought that they might more readily abandon their delusions of grandeur if they regularly encountered conflicting evidence. Consequently, they were assigned to sleep in adjacent hospital beds, to eat together in the same dining area, to work together in the hospital laundry, and to be interviewed together regularly by a social psychologist. But even these continuous, direct confrontations did not result in the disappearance of the delusions, not a surprising outcome since they had been experiencing daily confrontations in other aspects of their lives. The two older men remained essentially unchanged, while the third, a man less than 40, showed some decrease in his delusional thinking (Rokeach, 1964). The chances of responsiveness to special stimulation are greater in younger patients. ■

Affective Conditions

Schizophrenic conditions are often regarded as primarily thinking disorders, while other psychotic states are considered chiefly mood disorders. Actually, alterations in thinking and mood are present in virtually all cases of psychosis, but in the *affective disorders* inappropriate emotions are the most obvious characteristic.

Manic-depressive reaction. The psychotic condition characterized by extreme fluctuations of feeling, up and down, is called the *manic-depressive* reaction. In the manic state, the individual may be extremely happy, singing at the top of his or her voice, dancing in an unrestrained fashion, and working on enterprises that he or she is certain will change the world. Sometimes there is a ''flight of ideas''; the individual goes off rapidly on one tangent, then another, and then another, as each idea occurs. In the depressive state, the person may engage in coarse language, curses, and sexual displays. Some individuals in this state refuse to eat or drink because ''it

Integration of Behavior

would be a sin to keep this evil body alive." Others commit self-destructive acts, including suicide.

The manic and depressive conditions alternate in a variety of ways, and normally each state lasts for several days. Often, patients go into only one state, usually the depressive one, with periods of normality between the depressions. Today, extreme mania and depression are seldom seen in mental hospitals, as a consequence of the use of various psychotropic drugs.

Depression. As individuals reach late middle life, feelings of dissatisfaction and depression may begin to increase or become more intense. In women between age 40 and age 55 and in men approximately 10 years older, usually several readjustments are required because of declining ability, retirement, and the fact that their children, to whom they may have devoted much of their lives, are leaving and becoming self-sufficient. In addition, there may be biochemical factors that prompt men and women at this stage of life to experience feelings of uselessness, frustration, and disappointments. When these feelings become particularly intense, they are referred to as *involutional melancholia.* This condition is illustrated in the following remarks of a depressed person, who sat immobile in the initial interview in a clinic and finally said, in a barely audible voice:

I wish I'd died—nobody cares—All against me—all—everybody . . . don't want to talk—let me alone. (Strange, 1965)

Many involutional conditions are milder, and the range of symptoms is so wide that the term *involutional* seems to do no more today than indicate that the condition occurred for the first time during middle life. The disorder often disappears without treatment, but the period before recovery may be several years.

**Figure 17-14 Catatonic Reaction.** *Some recent treatments of these persons who maintain rigid postures have placed the responsibility for eating and sleeping on the patient instead of hospital attendants. After missed meals, some patients have shown a change in behavior, which has been the beginning of a beneficial treatment program. In other cases, this procedure has not been successful. (Larry Keighley,* The Saturday Evening Post*)*

The Search for Causes

What makes a person suddenly leave the world of accepted reality and enter one of his or her own making? The frank answer is that we do not yet know. In fact, we do not even know whether psychosis and neurosis are qualitatively different problems or whether they *only* represent different points on the same continuum (Figure 17-15). Almost invariably, psychosis is considered the more extreme reaction, and at this point we can only emphasize that both environmental and physiological factors appear to be involved.

AS A SINGLE CONTINUUM

NORMAL ⟵——— NEUROTIC ———⟶ PSYCHOTIC

AS TWO SEPARATE CONTINUA

NORMAL ⟵————————⟶ NEUROTIC
NORMAL ⟵————————⟶ PSYCHOTIC

Figure 17-15 Views of Neurosis and Psychosis. *Some psychologists regard psychosis as an extension of neurosis; others suggest that the two reactions are unrelated. According to the latter view, an individual under stress might become neurotic or psychotic but not neurotic and then psychotic.*

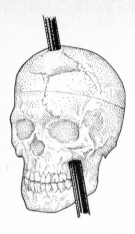

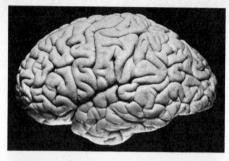

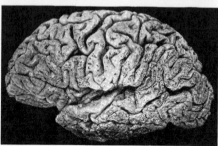

Figure 17-16 Normal and Paretic Brains. *The cortical destruction in advanced paresis is due to syphilis of the brain, but only a small proportion of people who contract syphilis become paretic. If treated early, as it now can be with penicillin, general paresis does not occur. (Photo of normal brain from Gardner, Ernest:* Fundamentals of Neurology, *6th ed. © 1975 by the W. B. Saunders Company, Philadelphia, Pa. Photo of paretic brain from Jelliffe and White's* Diseases of the Nervous System, *6th ed. Philadelphia: Lea & Febiger, 1935.)*

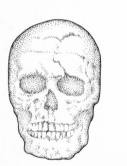

Figure 17-17 Brain Damage and Psychotic Behavior. *On the unlucky 13th of September, 1848, Phineas P. Gage, a railroad foreman in Vermont, was injured in an explosion that sent a 13-pound, 4-foot iron crowbar completely through his head. Miraculously, he recovered physically from the accident, but afterwards he was profane, extremely obstinate, unrealistic, and, at times, wildly emotional. His friends, who had known him before as a well-controlled, successful man, said simply that he was "no longer Gage" (Harlow, 1869). The drawing depicts the size of the skull in relation to the size of the crowbar, as displayed in the Harvard Medical Museum, and shows the way in which the bar passed through the skull.*

Organic and functional psychoses. Some psychotic disorders are related to impairment of body organs, particularly the brain, and therefore they are described as *organic.* The psychotic condition resulting from structural changes that are induced by syphilitic infection of the brain is clearly an organic disorder; it is called *paresis* (Figure 17-16). A brain tumor, head injury, or deterioration of the central nervous system through disease also can produce an organic psychosis (Figure 17-17).

In *functional* psychosis, there are no known physical defects, yet the person behaves in a psychotic manner. These disorders are thought to be the result of maladaptive learning, but this view is not consistent with the idea that all human functioning is based on organic factors. For persons who make the organic-functional distinction, and most psychologists do, the label "functional" simply indicates a lack of knowledge about the underlying physiological conditions. This long-standing differentiation eventually may turn out to be artificial.

Hereditary factors. The evidence that heredity plays a role in psychotic reactions, especially schizophrenia, is chiefly borne out by studies of identical and fraternal twins. Since identical twins have the same heredity, schizophrenic reactions, if based on inheritance, should show a higher correspondence in them than in fraternal twins, and a number of studies support this conclusion. When one twin is schizophrenic, the chances of the other twin also being schizophrenic are approximately five times greater for identical than for fraternal twins (Figure 17-18).

Further support for heredity factors comes from the study of foster children adopted shortly after birth, some having a biological parent diagnosed as schizophrenic and others with apparently normal parents. In these cases the rate of schizophrenia or borderline schizophrenia is significantly higher for the children having a biological parent diagnosed as schizophrenic. Since both groups had

Country	Identical Twins N	Identical Twins %	Fraternal Twins N	Fraternal Twins %	Investigators
United States	174	69	296	11	Kallman, 1946
United Kingdom	37	65	60	13	Slater, 1953
Sweden	11	64	27	15	Essen-Möller, 1941
United States	41	61	53	13	Rosanoff et al., 1934
Japan	55	60	11	18	Inouye, 1961
Germany	19	58	13	0	Luxemburger, 1928
United Kingdom	24	42	33	9	Gottesman & Shields, 1966a
Denmark	7	29	31	6	Harvard & Hague, 1965
Norway	8	25	12	17	Kringlen, 1964
Weighted average		62		12	

Figure 17-18   Schizophrenia: Studies of Twins. *Note the very large differences in percentages between identical and fraternal twins for all countries. (Adapted from Gottesman & Shields, 1966b)*

Diagnosis of Biological Parents	Diagnosis of Children Schizophrenic or Borderline Schizophrenic	Nonschizophrenic	Total Number of Children
Schizophrenic	26(30%)	60(70%)	86
Nonschizophrenic	6(6%)	91(94%)	97

Figure 17-19   Incidence of Schizophrenia among Adopted Children. *(Adapted from Wender, 1969. Reprinted, with permission, from the* American Journal of Orthopsychiatry; *copyright 1969 by the American Orthopsychiatric Association, Inc.)*

foster parents with apparently comparable childrearing methods, the difference among the children seems to reflect differences inherited from the biological parents (Figure 17-19).

Other investigations do not necessarily imply a heredity factor, but they do suggest a biochemical basis for psychosis. For example, blood plasma and urine extracts from persons diagnosed as psychotic, when injected into lower animals, produced behavior disorders. Serum obtained from schizophrenic patients and injected into volunteer human subjects has resulted in schizophrenic symptoms, including catatonic and paranoid conditions (Heath et al. 1958). Further, schizophrenic individuals have been found with glandular defects, disturbed body metabolism, and chemical malfunctions of various kinds, as well as deviant electrodermal activity (Jordan, 1974).

Environmental factors. Investigators interested in environmental influences regard the evidence from the twin studies differently, emphasizing that when one twin is schizophrenic, the other is not inevitably schizophrenic, although their inherited structures are exactly the same. In the foster-children studies, some of the children from normal parents have borderline schizophrenic reactions. Thus schizophrenia cannot occur solely on the basis of heredity. The childrearing practices of the parents or adoptive parents could be most significant.

Even the biochemical studies, most of which involve institutionalized patients, can be interpreted from an environmental viewpoint. Compared with nonhospitalized persons, schizophrenic patients with institutional history have had greater exposure to infectious diseases, less exposure to varied diets, and a more or less steady administration of drugs, all of which may play an important role in the biochemical differences (Kety, 1960). Furthermore, if a biochemical factor is found that inevitably accompanies schizophrenia, it is still necessary to prove that it is a cause of the disorder rather than a result of it.

One environmental factor often cited as influential in schizophrenia is the *double bind* situation, in which a parent makes contradictory demands on the child, expecting full obedience, for example, yet berating the little one for not being more self-assertive. Circumstances of this type can be difficult for the child who cannot recognize the conflict, much less describe it. The evidence for this theory is not yet substantial, however. Conflict between the parents and inadequate communication between them now seem to be the most prominent environmental factors (Fontana, 1966).

It is widely known also that psychiatric disorders are more prevalent in the lower socioeconomic levels. According to the *social conditions* viewpoint, low-income communities engender schizophrenia through frustrations, cultural conflicts, minority group tensions, and social disorganization. In a different view, called *drift* theory, it is assumed that schizophrenic individuals migrate to impoverished urban areas by a process of social selection. Unable to make an adequate adjustment in other subcultures, they eventually move to one in which there are others like them, and they are able to achieve at least a marginal adjustment (Dunham, 1965). While the results of a large-scale investigation do not clearly reject one view or the other, even the drift theory recognizes that environmental factors are conducive to schizophrenic conditions.

Predisposing and precipitating factors. As the reader now realizes, a psychotic condition arising only from a single incident is unlikely but not impossible. Usually, several *predisposing factors* have set the stage for a disorder,

making it more probable or hastening its occurrence. These factors could include a certain inheritance, a difficult childhood, marital conflict, or physical illness. Perhaps a person has maintained a marginal adjustment despite these circumstances, becoming only mildly upset from time to time. Suppose the individual then loses his or her job or reaches a difficult stage in life, such as retirement, and a psychotic condition occurs. If so, that immediately preceding event would be referred to as the *precipitating factor;* it is the most obviously disrupting circumstance prior to the "breakdown."

As a rule, no single event becomes a precipitating factor unless there have been predisposing conditions earlier. Furthermore, any predisposing factor might have been the precipitating one if the sequence of events had been reversed. "Well, he was normal before *that* happened." "It's the divorce that did it." Such statements usually reflect the fallacy of the single cause—and a lack of awareness of predisposing factors. Even in reactive schizophrenia, there are commonly predisposing conditions.

In summary, it appears that both environment and heredity can be influential in the onset of schizophrenia. Even when neither factor alone is significant, they can combine in various ways to induce a psychotic condition. One current view is that genetic factors may play a significant predisposing role, while environmental or biological stress can serve as precipitating events.

Society and Adjustment

Not long ago, a psychologist wished to demonstrate the elusiveness of the criteria for deciding whether or not a person is psychotic, and so eight presumably normal accomplices individually went to the admitting offices of several different mental hospitals and claimed to hear voices that said "empty," "hollow," and "thud." After these false claims of symptoms, each malingerer was admitted to one hospital or another with some diagnosis of psychosis. While in these mental institutions some of these persons made copious notes on their environments, which showed that the hospital treatment was deplorable in many instances (Rosenhan, 1973).

The results of this deception received considerable attention in the popular press but prompted a mixed reaction in the scientific community. Several objections were raised by psychiatrists, for whom the results of the study appeared most damaging. Inadequacies in patient care were revealed once again, but the study did not necessarily demonstrate the impossibility of diagnosing psychosis per se (Millan, 1975). It did emphasize that what the patient says is the most important single factor in determining the diagnosis, just as it is in the diagnosis of physical problems. Almost anyone can fool a physician about physical ailments if he or she wishes to do so, feigning lower back pains, headaches, or any other problem (Liberman, 1973). Some physical and mental difficulties are obvious, but many are known largely through patient reports.

Once in the hospital, all these ''patients'' ceased feigning the symptoms, and all were discharged, usually within two weeks, which suggests accuracy in detecting the absence of psychosis. Unfortunately, however, all were dismissed with the diagnosis of *schizophrenia in remission,* which simply means that the symptoms have disappeared. Lamentably, *none* of the physicians managed the problem in the opposite manner, deciding that the initial diagnosis might have been in error. Had these persons been true patients, they would have gone forth with all the difficulties of a harsh, even inappropriate label.

Sociopathic Disorders

In this research, the concern was with each patient's personal disturbance or discomfort, but earlier in this chapter it was pointed out that socially disruptive behavior is also a criterion by which

Figure 17-20 Sociopathic Behavior. *"I get a feeling of superiority," says C.W.H. when asked why he has stolen scores of automobiles. He has done so for an evening's drive to a distant state, upon which he has abandoned the car, stolen another, and returned home. At age 18, he has sold stolen merchandise, including drugs and guns, and reports that he learned the technique of auto theft in state institutions. (The Boston Globe)*

maladjustment is measured. So far, our focus has been exclusively on personal discomfort, and we have followed the continuum from common adjustment reactions through neurosis and psychosis. Now we turn to socially disruptive behavior, which also exists on a continuum. The mentally healthy person can live within the general restraints of his or her society, but the sociopathic personality cannot seem to do so.

Chronic lack of conformity to social standards and legal regulations is referred to as a *sociopathic* or *psychopathic disorder.* Both terms refer to aggressive behavior that tends to destroy society, whether it is the product of an individual or of a deviant subgroup (Figure 17-20). When such behavior is a symptom of another problem, however, such as psychosis or brain damage, the individual is not regarded as sociopathic.

Individuals and groups. The term *antisocial reaction* refers to an individual who is chronically in difficulty with school, home, work, or legal authorities. Such persons can be charming and witty, possessing likeable surface traits, and, thus, they sometimes can continue antisocial behavior for extended periods before others become aware of their transgressions and unfulfilled promises. Underneath, they are generally selfish and intolerant of the daily frustrations that most persons take for granted, and they have little concern for others. In psychoanalytic terms, they are ''all id,'' seeking immediate gratification.

When apprehended for an offense against society, even a violent crime, the sociopathic individual may show little or no remorse for the act itself. The only concern is with the fact of being apprehended and thus facing possible punishment. Basically, this individual is much alone in the world, with no personal attachment to other people and no significant sense of guilt for wrongdoing.

Another kind of sociopathic disorder does involve personal ties and loyalties, but these are engendered in a deviant subculture. In the *dyssocial reaction,* there is no prolonged individual variation from subculture norms, but the subculture itself is deviant from society. The individual group members sanction and support one another, while their actions as a group are hostile towards the larger society. Underworld gangs, with constant transgression against the larger culture, illustrate the dyssocial personality, as do certain groups of delinquent adolescents.

Theory and research. As a rule, the dyssocial reaction is assumed to represent inappropriate earlier learning. The group members simply regard the larger population as a hostile force or ''fair game'' for predatory behavior. The personal ties are to the subgroup, within which there is some social code, as ''honor even among thieves.'' The full context of this inadequate character development needs to be explored further, however.

The antisocial reaction, in contrast, seems to pose a more complex problem.

Again, predisposing factors may involve the family structure, in which no adequate social attachments are available to the developing personality. It is hypothesized that the parents or others are rejecting, aloof, or neglecting and, thus, the individual uses antisocial behavior to gain attention. Another possibility is that the child is unable to make an appropriate identification with any adequately functioning adult. In any case, this disorder is usually found in males and among those with a history of low school achievement (Robbins, 1974).

Another set of factors may lie in the individual's genetic endowment. Adopted children born to female antisocial personalities, in comparison with adopted control children, have shown a significantly higher rate of antisocial behavior, despite leaving the mother in infancy (Crowe, 1974). Thus, one view of antisocial behavior postulates an underactivity of the nervous system. According to this view, the sociopath, in terms of brain function, simply does not become aroused as readily or markedly as more normal individuals. The behavioral result of this lower cortical excitability is that such persons engage in actions that yield more than normal excitation (Hare, 1970).

One experiment that points towards this lower arousal involved a comparison of reaction times among eight male clinically diagnosed sociopaths and eight employees in the same hospital, who served as control subjects. Each person was instructed to press a response key as soon as possible after a light appeared, and warning signals were given anywhere from 1 to 16 seconds in advance of the light. With several different methods and many trials, the sociopathic subjects were uniformly slower in all conditions (Pfeiffer & Maltzman, 1974; Figure 17-21). It is possible, however, that this difference in excitability is a result or correlate of the sociopathic condition, rather than a cause. Altogether, a heredity-environment interaction is likely.

With this lack of knowledge, treatment of the sociopathic personality has not been effective. One difficulty is that, because of the individual's lack of conscience, institutional rules have little significance, except insofar as punishment is involved. Further, the apprehended individual often must be segregated from society, which may (1) increase that person's feelings of being ignored and inconsequential, (2) expose him or her to a deviant and aggressive subculture, and (3) decrease opportunities for alternative kinds of interesting stimulation. For these reasons, many current methods of managing early antisocial behavior may lead to further antisocial behavior. The problem is not readily resolved.

Cultural Relativism

All societies must deal with members who act against the accepted social code, and certain behaviors are deemed unacceptable in most cultures. There are clear prohibitions against homicide, rape, theft, arson, treason, and assault and battery in every major society in the

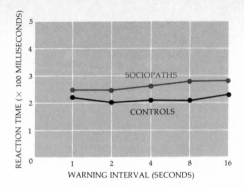

Figure 17-21 Reaction Time in Sociopathic Disorders. *Compared with matched control subjects, the sociopaths respond more slowly in reaction-time studies. Other data indicate that this difference is not due to lesser attention and interest in the task but rather to lower arousability in sociopaths. (From K. Pfeiffer and I. Maltzman, "Warned reaction times in sociopaths,"* Journal of Research in Personality, *8, 64-75, 1974.)*

world. These actions are destructive to social order. However, other behaviors, especially those of a less aggressive nature, are regarded quite differently in different societies. Forms of polygamy have been the custom in Middle Eastern societies; nakedness has been accepted in several cultures; and homosexuality and prostitution are practiced openly in diverse societies. However, in contemporary Western society, these behaviors are considered deviant, if not illegal (Figure 17-22).

Figure 17-22 Cultural Relativism. *Nudity may be commonplace in one culture but unacceptable in another. The setting is therefore an important factor in deciding whether a certain behavior is deviant. (Photo on left by N. R. Farbman, Life Magazine, © Time Inc.; photo on right from Photo Trends)*

■ *Every summer I go with my family to the extreme northern coast of _____, where there is a small fishing village. This village contains about 300 people, comprised of 30 families. Thus, the average number of people in a family is about 10. The ideas of people in this village about intermarriage between members of one family, or incest, are quite different from the American view of the subject. Mr. R married a girl from the K family. Several years later Mr. R's oldest son married the youngest K sister, thus marrying his aunt. The natives considered it wise that the young boy marry someone he knew well instead of a stranger from a neighboring town. And this goes on in every family. In fact, by now, all 30 families are related . . . and the situation is looked on as quite moral and legal.*

The term *cultural relativism* reflects this difference among societies. It means that acceptable behavior, virtue, beauty, and similar concepts are culture-bound; they have meaning only in relation to a particular environment. The standards of a given group cannot be applied to others because they are not absolute. Anthropologists, sociologists, and others have continually pointed out that behavior that is considered acceptable in one society may be regarded as disruptive in another. ■

Even within one society there are sharp subcultural differences, as illustrated by a man from the Ozark Mountains who received a revelation from God and a "call" to preach to his community. His work was enthusiastically received and later he was "called" to preach to neighboring communities. Again he was successful, and eventually he gained the reputation of a prophet and spiritual leader. His fame was quickly tarnished, however, when he accepted a "call" to go to St. Louis, where he was arrested for preaching in traffic during rush hour. Lauded and encouraged in a rural environment, he was considered a nuisance and apprehended for disturbing the peace in an urban society (Skotkin, 1955).

Such incidents emphasize varying cultural standards. In this respect, there can be no universal definition of mental health and mental illness that is applicable across all cultures. Any specific definition simply favors a particular social or ethical order (Szasz, 1956, 1970). The continua exist but, to a significant degree, they are defined differently in different cultures.

Summary

The Adjusted Individual

1. Adjustment exists on a continuum; there is no adjustment in the absolute sense. Adjustment is also a continuous process, in which the individual strives to satisfy physiological or psychological motives; it is never achieved for an extended period. When satisfaction is thwarted by a barrier, external or internal, the condition is described as frustration.

2. Conflict occurs whenever incompatible motives are present in the same individual. Three types of conflict are: approach-approach, which is the most readily resolved; avoidance-avoidance, usually resulting in tension and the selection of a third alternative; and approach-avoidance, which is the most difficult to resolve and often accompanied by vacillation and other anxiety reactions.

Common Reactions to Stress

3. Under stress, lethargy and other forms of decreased responsiveness may occur. This outcome is produced by approach-avoidance conflicts and by uncontrollable circumstances, in which feelings of helplessness are engendered.

4. Another common reaction to stress is aggression against oneself, against aspects of the situation, or against innocent persons. In regression, a person resorts to emitting responses that are characteristic of an earlier stage of development.

5. Defense mechanisms are presumed to be unconscious means by which the individual protects himself or herself from anxiety. Repression, in which unpleasant thoughts and feelings are forgotten or excluded from awareness, is the basic defense mechanism. Other defense mechanisms, based on repression, include: rationalization, in which false reasons are adopted; reaction formation, in which the opposite attitude is assumed; and projection, in which an undesirable characteristic is attributed

to another person. The contribution of these reactions to the individual's adjustment depends on how often and in what situations they occur.

Neurotic Disorders

6. The labels attached to persons considered to be mentally ill in one form or another have changed considerably with the passage of time, reflecting greater acceptance of the problem, but eventually any label becomes derogatory. Criticisms of the contemporary system of classifying maladjustment are that it is oversimplified, that it continues to stigmatize the individual as a misfit, and that it reflects symptoms rather than the origin of the problem.

7. A neurosis is a persistent, ineffective way of dealing with a personal problem, usually accompanied by considerable anxiety, but there is no significant departure from reality. According to psychoanalytic theory, neurosis involves a repressed conflict, usually from early childhood, which reappears in symbolic form as inexplicable neurotic behavior. From the viewpoint of behaviorism, neurotic behaviors are simply reinforced responses; to understand them, one must discover the environmental conditions that support them.

8. The different neurotic reactions or styles include: anxiety neurosis, which consists chiefly of free-floating anxiety; phobic neurosis, which is an irrational fear; conversion neurosis, in which anxiety is transformed into a bodily symptom that has no physiological basis; dissociative neurosis, in which parts of one's personality are unconsciously forgotten, as in fugue states and multiple personalities; and obsessive-compulsive neurosis, in which seemingly meaningless thoughts and acts persist.

Psychotic Disorders

9. Psychotic individuals are usually out of contact with reality, experiencing hallucinations and delusions and usually requiring hospitalization. The most common psychosis is schizophrenia, characterized chiefly by irrational thought. Process schizophrenia has a long history of development, while the reactive condition involves a sudden onset. Characteristic schizophrenic behavior patterns include: simple, in which there is a secluded, irresponsible, asocial existence; hebephrenic, in which there are obviously inappropriate emotional reactions; catatonic, in which the individual endlessly repeats certain words or actions or remains in the same position for long periods of time; and paranoid, in which there are systematized delusions of persecution and grandeur.

10. Psychoses also involve primarily affective disorders, as in manic-depressive illness and involutional melancholia. The former is characterized by alternating periods of extreme elation and depression. Depression occurs by itself in melancholia, which usually occurs during late middle age and apparently relates to adjustment problems at that time of life.

11. Both hereditary and environmental factors seem to be involved in psychotic disorders, but the importance of either factor alone has not been convincingly demonstrated. Again, an interaction effect seems most likely.

Society and Adjustment

12. Adjustment exists on a continuum of socially disruptive behavior as well as personal discomfort. Individuals who cannot reasonably conform to the established social and legal standards are considered to be sociopathic persons. One form is the antisocial reaction, in which there is no significant allegiance to other human beings. In another form, the dyssocial reaction, there is allegiance to a deviant subculture. Either reaction may be due to defective early learning, in which there is extreme neglect or rejection in the family. Also, genetic factors may be involved, perhaps

relating to the arousability of the individual. As yet, little is known about this problem.

13. Cultural relativism indicates that certain abstract concepts have meaning only in relation to the standards of a given culture. Any specific definition of adjustment or maladjustment indicates a preference for a certain social or ethical order.

Suggested Readings

Bateson, G. *Steps to an ecology of the mind.* New York: Ballantine, 1972. For the advanced reader, this book considers possible environmental origins of neurosis and psychosis, especially in terms of human communication.

Rimm, D. C. & Somervill, J. W. *Abnormal psychology.* New York: Academic Press, 1977. A comprehensive text that surveys the major disorders and treatments.

Seligman, M. E. P. *Helplessness: On depression, development and death.* San Francisco: W. H. Freeman, 1975. Presents a theory, research data, and examples from daily life on organisms' reactions when exposed to uncontrollable events.

Szasz, T. S. *The manufacture of madness.* New York: Harper & Row, 1970. Compares "the belief in witchcraft and the persecution of witches with the belief in mental illness and the persecution of mental patients."

Zax, M. & Stricker, G. *The study of abnormal behavior: Selected readings* (3rd ed.). New York: Macmillan, 1974. This book comprises 44 papers focusing on one of four topics: issues in abnormal behavior, approaches to psychotherapy, methods of psychotherapy, and recent trends.

Chapter 18

Therapy

All of us have problems and try to deal with them. To the extent that we have given or received assistance, we have been involved in *therapy*, which is any procedure designed to alleviate a disordered condition. The purpose of this chapter is to examine instances of formal therapy, in which the persons consulted for assistance are professionally trained, such as the clinical psychologist and psychiatrist.

Methods of Psychotherapy

At the age of 29, G, an unmarried young man with professional aspirations, found his career in jeopardy, primarily because he perspired excessively in the company of others. This condition prompted him to avoid contact with people, including those in his work. The sweat appeared first on his forehead, then on his temples, hands, and face, and when it began to drip, he wiped it with a handkerchief; thus, he felt that he attracted further attention to the problem. Consequently, he ate alone in unfrequented restaurants, shunned public meeting places, and attended movies because he could not be seen in the darkness. When by himself, G did not sweat, nor did sweating occur when he was with friends, but the problem was acute with other persons, especially if they were important to him. If someone inquired about his condition, it immediately worsened.

453

Traditional Psychoanalysis

From the viewpoint of psychoanalysis, any significant adult emotional problem, such as G's sweating, is traceable at least in part to some conflict or trauma from childhood, presumably buried in the unconscious. Accordingly, psychoanalysis is an attempt to help the patient discover these disrupting earlier experiences and then deal with them more appropriately. There are three basic techniques by which this goal is accomplished.

Free association. In the traditional method of psychoanalysis, the person to be analyzed, such as G, lies on a couch while the therapist, called an *analyst,* remains unobtrusively nearby, encouraging the patient to say anything that comes to mind, just as it occurs to him or her. This unrestrained flow of ideas is called *free association;* in this procedure the person attempts to express all thoughts, no matter how trivial, absurd, embarrassing, disrespectful, or illogical (Figure 18-1).

The task of lying on a couch and saying anything that comes to mind sounds easy, but actually the person is hard at work against himself or herself, attempting to uncover the very thoughts that are most painful. In daily life G was a fastidious person, but eventually he talked at length about unclean toilets, dirty underclothes, and lice. At one point he suddenly recalled awakening at age five with the fear of having defecated; instead, he discovered the black object in his bed was a shoe. Soiling himself was a constant fear for him as a child, even when he was five years old.

Transference. In addition to encouraging free association, the analyst permits or encourages *transference,* which means that the patient temporarily reacts to the analyst as though he or she were someone else, displacing onto the analyst behavior appropriate to that other person. The patient may become angry or disappointed with the analyst,

Figure 18-1 Freud's Consulting Room. *This room was used by Sigmund Freud during most of his psychoanalytic investigations. Note the stuffed chair, in which he was usually seated, at the head of the couch. (From* Berggasse 19: Sigmund Freud's Home and Offices, Vienna 1938, The Photographs of Edmund Engelman, *Basic Books, Inc., Publishers, New York, 1976. By permission of Basic Books, Inc., and Edmund Engelman.)*

At this time G's parents were living in a distant city with his sister, who was two years younger than G. He had enjoyed generally good health until two years earlier, when his fiancée abruptly left him for another man. Afterwards, he became gloomy and troubled. He left the city in which they both lived and then returned there to work six months later, at which time he first noticed the excessive sweating. In G's case an emotional difficulty *apparently* had been converted into a physical symptom and, therefore, his problem might be called a conversion neurosis.

In appearance, G was always neat and clean and therefore especially concerned that his sweating might be accompanied by some repulsive odor. The only remedy he had encountered was drinking alcohol; three glasses of beer or some vodka prevented the problem.

although the latter has done nothing to provoke this reaction; these feelings perhaps pertain to the patient's earlier relationship with someone else, such as parents, aunts and uncles, or grandparents. G became extremely anxious and perspired a great deal in the presence of a friendly publisher whom he wanted to impress; later, it appeared that he had reacted to this older man as though he were his father.

In therapy, the patient may react to the analyst in this way, thus gaining insight into his or her relations with others. The analyst facilitates this outcome by remaining neutral, avoiding personal biases and interests as much as possible. Hence, the analyst can be more readily used by the patient in working out problems of personal relations (Figure 18-2).

Interpretation. A third technique of psychoanalysis, and one in which the analyst is more actively involved, is *interpretation*, in which the analyst leads and stimulates the paient to consider the significance of his or her thoughts and actions. Contrary to popular opinion, the analyst does not tell the person what is wrong or give the patient an answer to his or her problems, but rather assists by making interpretations occasionally and by leading the patient to self-discovery.

Of all the behavior available for interpretation, Freud was most interested in the *interpretation of dreams*. Here the contents of one's dreams, together with free association to these contents, are considered in the light of psychoanalytic theory and the patient's total life history. The actual events of the dream, as they occurred to the dreamer, are called the *manifest content*, and they are considered relatively unimportant. This content is influenced by recent happenings in the dreamer's waking life and is significant only as a disguise to protect the individual from the anxiety associated with the true meaning, which is unconscious and known as the *latent content*. The aim of dream interpretation is to discover this latent meaning. ■

P (Patient)   I feel like I should say something important. It's wrong for me to just say nothing or to talk about something insignificant. After all I shouldn't take up your time and do nothing.

T (Therapist)   You feel you are taking up my time unnecessrily.

P   Yes, I sure do. After all you have a doctor's degree. I should say what I've got to say and get out of here. I shouldn't be taking up your time. I feel like you couldn't be interested in me if I don't have something important to say. I become very anxious when I can't say something important. I figure you're probably angry with me when I don't keep you interested.

T   But I'm not angry with you for not keeping me interested, and although I'm busy, I enjoy spending the hour with you.

P   Well . . . Well, why do I feel this way then? It's the way I always feel . . . like no one is interested in me. I'm always afraid to talk with my teachers for fear that they aren't interested in what I have to say. That's the way it always was with my father. Being a doctor he was continually on call. If we ever started talking, which was seldom, the phone would always ring and he would have to leave.

T   Then you are reacting to me and your teachers as if we were like your father?

P   I guess that's so . . . you know, that's just what I'm doing.

G had the same brief dream on several occasions—"Someone in grey says that a Cesarian section will have to be performed." In analysis, it appeared that this dream perhaps was related to incidents of punishment by his father, represented as the surgeon, and to the Oedipus complex. Castration anxiety was suggested in the surgical operation. Later it appeared that G's sweating also might concern the Oedipus complex, as perhaps symbolic of his earlier bedwetting. In bedwetting, he constantly disappointed his mother and thereby lost her

Figure 18-2   Transference.
Consider this case of a student whose father was a busy physician.

■ *One very vivid dream that I can remember occurred when I was about seven years old. At the time, my mother was my girl scout leader and my Sunday school teacher. It seemed that I was always living under her rule, which I must have resented. During this dream I was in the part of a girl scout (do-gooder) but was taking great pleasure in wildly steering a little old lady around in a wheel chair.*

love; in sweating, he expressed the loss of his fiancée's love and there was considerable shame in both instances.

Sometimes, in moments of discovery or self-revelation, the patient breaks down emotionally—weeping, cursing, and so forth. This emotional release of anxiety and tension, called *catharsis*, is considered essential to the therapeutic process. The patient must do more than intellectually discover the sources of his or her difficulty; he or she must re-experience them emotionally, and so the analyst accepts these instances as part of the therapeutic process. Afterwards, the person may be able to understand the problem in a new light, one that is more rational and appropriate to adulthood. In short, the recovery of early memories and consequent "working through" of their emotional significance form the basis of the psychoanalytic treatment.

Status of psychoanalysis. The procedure of traditional psychoanalysis is long and expensive, sometimes requiring three to five one-hour sessions per week for several years. It is usually accomplished only by physicians, who have gone through training in medicine, in psychiatry, and then in the methods of psychoanalysis. Freud emphasized that a medical background is not necessary for the practice of psychoanalysis but the tradition continues, and both the training and the therapy are costly.

However, many people view the process of psychoanalysis as the only appropriate means for bringing about a thorough personality reorganization. Adherents state that it is the only psychotherapy concerned with unraveling the individual's defenses and thereby making available to that person the energies attached to earlier conflicts. Thus, a number of modern analysts adhere to the procedures outlined by Freud.

An even larger number of therapists today subscribe to the basic tenets of the system but adopt a modified approach. Among them, there has been a movement towards short-term psychoanalysis, in which the time-span is

briefer, the fee commensurately lower, and the focus somewhat changed. In view of the less-restrained childrearing practices since Freud's day, there is often less interest in the patient's early sexual and aggressive impulses and greater concern with the current social environment. There are constant reappraisals of the Freudian tenets in an effort to keep the approach relevant to modern society (Wallace, 1976).

Still other therapists, including some former patients and trained analysts, testify to the ineffectiveness of psychoanalysis (Ellis, 1962; Wheelis, 1958). It is said that the procedure is not only too costly in time and money but also that the outcomes are questionable and the fundamental principle of unconscious processes is untestable. We shall turn to this problem of evaluating therapy later, after considering the other methods that are available.

Client-Centered Therapy

If G decided instead to consult a client-centered therapist, the approach would be different in several respects. He would sit in a comfortable chair, rather than recline on a couch; he would be considered a client, rather than a patient; and, most important, the therapist would place greater reliance on G's own capacity to solve his problems.

Empathy and positive regard. As the name suggests, the therapy hour in *client-centered therapy* is used in ways determined by the client. The therapist makes no effort to encourage free association, transference, or dream interpretation, although if these things happen they are accepted as potentially useful to the client. The counselor does not offer advice nor prompt the discussion of any particular topic. If the client remains silent, the therapist accepts this behavior. The focus is on the client's *current* life experiences and the extent to which they are in harmony with the self-concept and the kind of person that individual wishes to become. The goal is to

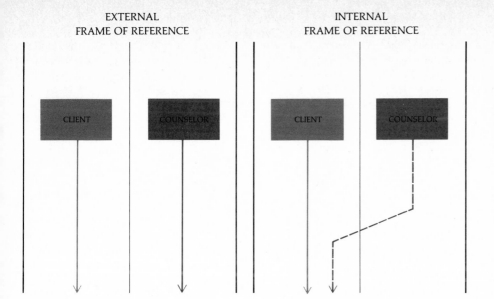

EXTERNAL
FRAME OF REFERENCE

CLIENT   COUNSELOR

INTERNAL
FRAME OF REFERENCE

CLIENT   COUNSELOR

Figure 18-3   Internal Frame of Reference. *In ordinary social interaction, each person listens and speaks from his or her own viewpoint. In the internal frame of reference, the counselor tries to put himself and his own interests aside and enter the world of the client. He attempts to think* **with** *the client rather than* **about** *her. (Photo by Franken from Stock, Boston)*

enable the client to achieve congruence in these respects

According to client-centered therapy, developed by the clinical psychologist Carl Rogers, it is the client who can achieve the most meaningful insights into his or her personality imbalance. The necessary atmosphere is provided by a therapist who can act with genuineness towards the client, demonstrating two important characteristics: empathy and unconditional positive regard for the client. In *empathy*, the therapist comprehends and accepts the client's mental and emotional states, seeing them from the client's viewpoint. That is, the therapist adopts the client's frame of reference, thinking *with* that person rather than about him or her. Empathy is apprehending the state of mind of another but, unlike sympathy, without necessarily feeling as the other person feels (Figure 18-3).

The other important therapist characteristic is an *unconditional positive regard* for the client, which means that the client is totally accepted by the therapist, regardless of the client's actions, thoughts, or experiences. No aspect of the client's behavior is regarded as more worthy or less worthy than any other;

instead, the therapist communicates full acceptance of the total individual. Gradually, in an atmosphere of unconditional positive regard, the client can achieve greater acceptance of his or her own experiences, which enables the client to become more of a whole person, functioning effectively as a congruent individual (Rogers, 1951, 1959, 1967).

Therapeutic techniques.   When it was first developed, client-centered therapy was referred to as *non-directive counseling,* meaning that the counselor did not influence the direction of the client's thoughts or expressions. This term was discarded, however, when it was realized that the counselor, merely by his or her presence, clothes, or some facial characteristic, exerts at least some influence on the direction of the interview. Nonverbal signals and subtle reinforcements are almost inevitable. However, there are several techniques by which the therapist attempts to let the client lead the session.

One method is for the therapist to restrict his or her responses to what the client has already said, especially to the feelings expressed. The therapist acts as a sort of mirror, by which clients can see themselves more clearly. This *reflection of feelings* is illustrated in the following therapy session, in which a 28-year-old man, called C, considers himself an outcast. Like G, he feels that no one wants his company:

C. No, I just ain't no good to anybody, never was, and never will be.

T. Feeling that now, hm? That you're just no good to yourself, no good to anybody . . . .

C. Yeah. (muttering in low, discouraged voice) That's what this guy I went to town with just the other day told me.

T. This guy that you went to town with really told you that you were no good? Is that what you're saying? Did I get that right?

C. M-hm.

T. I guess the meaning of that if I get it right is that here's somebody that—meant something to you and what does he think of you? Why, he's told you that he thinks you're no good at all. And that just really knocks the props out from under you. (C weeps quietly.). It just brings the tears. (silence of 20 seconds)

C. (rather defiantly) I don't care though.

T. You tell yourself you don't care at all, but somehow I guess some part of you cares because some part of you weeps over it. (Rogers, 1967)

Here the therapist has reflected the client's feeling of worthlessness and also, at the end of the excerpt, has noted that the client is weeping. No interpretation is made, other than the fact that the client feels both worthless and sad.

The therapist also uses *silences* to show acceptance of the client and the therapy process. There are significant periods during this therapy in which nothing is said. Further, the therapist uses "vocalized pauses," uttering almost inaudible expressions such as "umm-hmm" and "m-hm," indicating that all is understood and that the therapist is thinking *with* the client. ■ These conditions were evident in the following therapy session, when C returned, expressing the wish that he would die:

C. I wish it more'n anything else I've ever wished around here.

T. M-hm, m-hm, m-hm. I guess you've wished for lots of things but boy! It seems as though this wish to not live is deeper and stronger than anything you ever wished before.

(silence of 1 minute, 36 seconds)

T. Can't help but wonder whether it's still true that some things this friend said to you—are those still part of the thing that makes you feel so awful?

C. In general, yes.

T. M-hm.

(silence of 47 seconds)

T. The way I'm understanding that is that in a general way the fact that he felt you were no good has just set off a whole flood of feeling in you that makes you really wish, *wish* you weren't alive. Is that—somewhere near it?

C. I ain't no good to nobody, or I ain't no good for nothin', so what's the use of living?

T. M-hm. . . . (Rogers, 1967)

We can assume that similar procedures would be used in client-centered therapy with G. The therapist would decide that the young man himself had the best potential for solving his problems and would try to create an atmosphere in which this potential was released. Interpretation would not be used for that would suggest that the young man did not have the capacity to find his own

■ *This past summer I worked for one of the telephone hot-line services that have been set up around the country in an attempt to help people who call with their problems. We did help people with severe problems by referring them to the appropriate agency. More often the caller just wanted to talk over a problem. The direction of the call was always determined by the caller. Silences were welcomed rather than being broken as rapidly as possible. Our reactions took the form of simply trying to understand the person's thoughts and ideas. We had a high percentage of second- and third-time callers.*

Integration of Behavior

solutions. Instead, G would feel completely free to express his concerns about sweating, the loss of his fiancée, and the damage to his career, and then he would struggle with these problems himself. It is hypothesized that in the context of a fully accepting therapist, G could consider these aspects of his experience more completely, especially the injury of being rejected by his fiancée. Eventually, he would be able to regard this loss with greater awareness, without feeling so personally damaged, and without regarding it as something shameful, against which he had to defend himself.

Status of client-centered therapy. More than any other, client-centered therapy has prompted investigations of the therapeutic process. This approach, under the leadership of Carl Rogers, inaugurated the first large-scale studies of therapy, developed methods for rating the conditions and procedures of therapy, and emphasized the use of audio recordings. Obtained with the client's permission, these records serve as a basis for evaluating the therapeutic relationship (Figure 18-4). Such studies are continuing, and they are essential for further progress in therapy.

Opponents of the client-centered viewpoint suggest that perhaps each individual does not have the capacity to solve his or her own problems and, furthermore, that if such a capacity does exist, the permissiveness of client-centered counseling may not bring it about any more readily than another method. Instead, the therapist, by virtue of more training, broader experience, and greater objectivity, should be more assertive with the client (Ellis, 1959). In response, Rogers emphasizes that the client-centered approach was developed through counseling and psychotherapy with clients for more than 30 years. It was not anticipated; it grew from experience on the basis of what was successful. Today, Rogers's followers testify to its effectiveness.

1. The individual does not talk about problems such as wrongs, difficulties, confusions, and conflicts.
2. The individual talks about problems or problem situations.
3. The individual talks about his or her direct involvement in a problem situation or event.
4. The individual talks about his or her own reaction to the problem situation.
5. The individual talks about the contribution of his or her own reactions to the problem.
6. The individual talks about his or her understanding of these feelings, experiences, or attitudes.
7. The individual talks about a resolution of the problem in terms of changes in his or her feelings, experiences, or attitudes.

Figure 18-4   Rating Scale for Problem Expression. *This abbreviated scale does not indicate mental health or mental illness, but rather is used to indicate the ways in which someone talks about personal adjustment. At position 1, the individual ignores or avoids discussing problems, while at the other end of the continuum, problems and their possible resolutions are considered in a highly personal manner (van der Veen & Tomlinson, in Rogers, 1967).*

Rational-Emotive Therapy

In rational-emotive therapy, G's despair and excessive sweating would be approached in still another way. In fact, this therapy affords a sharp contrast with the two previous approaches. The basic premise is the opposite of psychoanalysis, and the basic method is contrary to client-centered therapy.

Thoughts and feelings.   Both psychoanalysis and rational-emotive therapy recognize the interaction between thoughts and feelings. Thinking can influence the way we feel, and feelings, in turn, can influence our thoughts. However, psychoanalysis approaches the problem of therapy primarily through dealing with feelings, attempting to uncover early emotional experiences that disrupt thoughts and behavior in adult life. Rational-emotive therapy, in contrast, aims at uncovering illogical adult thinking, which causes us to feel upset and behave emotionally. In short, both therapies deal with both aspects of human functioning, but each has a different starting point. The name *rational-emotive* indicates that the departure point in this therapy is that thinking is a significant determinant of one's feelings.

Suppose that you are standing on a crowded bus on a rainy day and suddenly experience a sharp pain in your back. Thinking an inconsiderate passenger has poked an umbrella into your ribs, you turn around enraged. To your surprise, you discover a small blind boy who says, "Please, pardon me." With this observation would you remain outraged, or would your anger subside and possibly turn to sympathy?

Silent sentences. Rational-emotive therapists claim that our emotions can change if we think differently about the circumstances. We feel as we think, and the role of the therapist is to induce us to think differently about the problem. For example, a man came to therapy complaining that some other people did not like him, but the therapist insisted that he was not unhappy for this reason:

P (Patient). Well, why was I unhappy then?

T (Therapist). It's very simple—simple as A, B, C, I might say. A, in this case, is the fact that these men didn't like you. Let's assume that you observed their attitude correctly and were not merely imagining they didn't like you.

P. I assure you that they didn't. I could see that very clearly.

T. Very well, let's assume they didn't like you and call that A. Now C is your unhappiness—which we'll definitely have to assume is a fact, since you felt it.

P. Damn right I did!

T. All right then; A is the fact that the men didn't like you, C is your unhappiness. You see A and C and you assume that A, their not liking you, caused your unhappiness, C. But it didn't.

P. It didn't? What did, then?

T. B did.

P. What's B?

T. B is what you said to yourself while you were . . . with those men.

P. What I said to myself? But I didn't say anything . . . .

T. You did. You must have. Now think back to your being with these men; think what you said to yourself; and tell me what it was.

P. Well . . . I . . . .

T. Yes?

P. Well, I guess I did say something.

T. I'm sure you did. Now what did you tell yourself when you were with those men?

P. I . . . well, I told myself that it was awful that they didn't like me, and why didn't they like me, and how could they not like me, and . . . you know, things like that.

T. Exactly. And that, what you told yourself, was B. And it's always B that makes you unhappy in situations like this. Except as I said before, when A is a brick falling on your head. That, or any physical object, might cause you real pain. But any mental or emotional onslaught against you—any word, gesture, attitude or feeling directed against you—can hurt you only if *you* let it. And your letting such a word, gesture, attitude, or feeling hurt you, your *telling yourself* that it's awful, horrible, terrible—that's B. And that's what *you* do to *you*.*

Questioning "needs." In the example just cited, we can see how the method is different from client-centered therapy. The therapist questions and sometimes even contradicts the patient's ideas, hoping to persuade him to a more rational view of the situations that disturb him. According to Albert Ellis, spokesperson for this point of view, the rational-emotive therapist "believes wholeheartedly in a most rigorous application of the rules of logic, of straight thinking, and of scientific method to everyday life. He ruthlessly uncovers the most important elements of irrational

*From "Reason and Emotion in Psychotherapy" by Albert Ellis, Ph.D. Copyright © 1962 by the Institute for Rational Living, Inc. Published by arrangement with Lyle Stuart.

thinking in his patient's experience and energetically urges this patient into more reasonable channels of behaving'' (Ellis, 1962).

To rid himself of emotional disturbance, the patient is told that he must question his silent sentences. He is instructed to ask himself ''Why must I be liked? ''What would be so awful about so-and-so not liking me?'' This questioning process leads him to distinguish between *desires* and *needs*. Needs, such as hunger and thirst, are necessary for life. A desire, on the other hand, is not essential to life, but its fulfillment may make life more pleasant. It is the therapist's job to help the patient see that it is not essential, only desirable, to have others like him and not to make mistakes. To expect more is irrational (Figure 18-5).

Thus, if G, coping with his problems, had gone to a rational-emotive therapist, he would have been informed that it was not his fiancée's departure that made him unhappy but rather the way he thought about that event. He would be instructed to ask himself, ''Does her not caring make the whole world change?'' ''Or does it just make my life somewhat less pleasant for awhile?'' To dissuade patients from irrational ways, the therapist sometimes points out the humor in their problems, trying to make them laugh at themselves. Thus, G might be told, ''It's impossible to be loved or approved by everyone. Don't sweat it so much!''

Status of rational-emotive therapy. As suggested earlier, Albert Ellis is largely responsible for the interest in and practice of rational-emotive therapy. A former psychoanalyst, Ellis decided that psychoanalysis was too time consuming and client-centered therapy depended too much on the client. Hence, rational-emotive therapy is basically a teaching process. The therapist, with a broad perspective, educates the patient about rational and irrational living. The therapist-patient relationship is an instructional one, and some people make good

1. It is a dire necessity for an adult to be loved or approved by almost everyone for virtually everything he or she does.
2. One should be competent and achieving in all possible respects.
3. Human unhappiness is externally caused. People have little or no ability to control their sorrows or rid themselves of their negative feelings.
4. If something is dangerous or fearsome, one should be terribly occupied with and upset about it.
5. People and things should be different from the way they are. It is catastrophic if perfect solutions to the grim realities of life are not immediately found.
6. Maximum human happiness can be achieved by inertia and inaction or by passively and uncommittedly "enjoying oneself."

Figure 18-5 Irrational Ideas. *Rational-emotive therapists sometimes state that they are simply helping their patients discover how to live rationally in an irrational world. They try to dissuade people from these viewpoints, as well as others. (From the book* A New Guide to Rational Living *by Albert Ellis, Ph.D. and Robert A. Harper, Ph.D. © 1975, 1961 by Institute for Rational Living, Inc.)*

students, according to Ellis. These persons are usually young, intelligent, and not too rigid or naïve.

Opponents of rational therapy point out that even if the therapist does know what to prescribe, the patient probably will not follow his or her ideas. Good advice is available everywhere, from Ben Franklin's rules for decision making to books on winning friends and influencing people, but people cannot seem to follow it. A significant factor in Ellis's success may be the personal relationship he is able to develop with the patient (Patterson, 1973).

The Existential Approach

A group of therapists who are more philosophical and less scientific than those discussed previously tend to reject the previous approaches as being too involved with theory and, therefore, disruptive to the authenticity of the patient-therapist relationship. *Existentialists* stress human existence as emerging or becoming, not as essence, which is a static concept. Humanity is constantly in transition, partly because human beings have the capacity for self-direction; thus, the therapist should focus on what the individual is becoming rather than on how past problems arose or how they can be solved. The past and the future are relevant only to the extent that they affect the person's immediate existing.

Problem of meaning.   According to existential therapists, most patients' problem is experiencing meaning in their existing. *Existential neurosis* is the condition of finding little, if any, meaning in life, and it comes about for several reasons. First, it occurs when one's values are severely challenged, as happens in our fast-changing society. When one must abandon cherished ways, there is anxiety, despair, and a lack of zest for life. Second, each human being is aware that he or she exists and will no longer exist at some future time, and this understanding causes anxiety and despair. Third, most of us realize that we have the potential to accomplish many things in life, but we must choose. In choosing what we want to become, we simultaneously choose not to be something else, and this awareness also brings about anxiety. Has one chosen correctly to find the fullest meaning in life?

In the existential viewpoint especially, there is freedom and choice. Heredity and environment are recognized as influential factors in life, but they are not totally decisive—each individual is responsible for his or her own becoming. Human beings are viewed as determining as well as determined. In therapy, another aim is to help individuals understand the ways in which they are determined and yet have some control over their lives.

Therapy techniques.   The obvious goal of therapy is to help the patient find meaning, as expressed in Nietzsche's dictum, "Whoever has a reason for living endures almost any mode of life." The goal of existential therapy is not to eliminate anxiety altogether, which is impossible, but rather to give it meaning or to help the patient deal with it more

constructively in the process of becoming. Years ago, Viktor Frankl, a prominent existential therapist, noted that persons who most readily endured the hardships of concentration camps and prison during World War II were those who had found meaning in their suffering (Figure 18-6).

One problem, however, is that existentialists are not clear on the techniques to be used in achieving this goal. For the most part, they employ the methods of other therapies, especially psychoanalytic ones (Patterson, 1966). Frankl, with his form of existential treatment, called logotherapy, is an exception. In *logotherapy* it is assumed that

Figure 18-6   Origins of Existentialism.   *Viktor Frankl, an early leader in existentialism, was a prisoner of war, and most of his family perished under these conditions. Here, he encountered an important principle of existentialism: the most basic of all human freedoms is the capacity to "choose one's attitude in a given set of circumstances." (Photo by G. D. Hackett)*

the patient's problem stems from a confusion in feelings or in his or her value system. The therapist's aim is to help the individual achieve a readjustment by examining his or her feelings, attitudes, and values in a systematic fashion.

One procedure in logotherapy is called *paradoxical intention;* here the patient is encouraged to assume, as strongly as possible, the very attitude or feeling that is troublesome. By confronting the feeling directly and regularly in this way, in a controlled setting, the patient gradually gains increased control over it. Thus, in logotherapy, young G, rather than struggling against his symptoms of sweating, would give the fullest possible expression to these feelings, which eventually should bring about a change of attitude towards this problem. Like blushing, when he ceased to fear the symptom, he could detach himself from it and it would disappear.

Status of existentialism. Existentialism is the product of a loosely organized group of European therapists; it is more a philosophy than a specific therapeutic method. Many followers of existentialism have been trained in psychoanalysis, but they have their own viewpoints and thus there is no overall systematic approach. The unifying principle among these therapists is a resistance to the extreme rationalism of most other therapies.

In America, existentialist concepts are most readily encountered in client-centered therapy, and perhaps the reader noted some of the similarities. There is the common focus on the person's immediate experience, the idea of development or becoming, and also the stress on not imposing one's own standards and values on another person. There are two reasons for the fact that existentialism has not become a more dominant force in American psychotherapy—the popularity of client-centered therapy and the existentialists' lack of concern with methods.

Behavior Modification

Instead of dealing with a person's thoughts and feelings in an interview, some approaches to therapy are primarily concerned with the individual's overt responses or behaviors. In this type of therapy, known as *behavior modification,* it is assumed that understanding and insight are not essential in solving maladjustment problems. This therapeutic method has developed largely within the last two decades, but the basic viewpoint was demonstrated more than 50 years ago in an experiment that was never completed.

A normal 11-month-old baby named Albert was chosen for study partly because he showed no fear when confronted with various animals, a hairy mask, burning newspapers, and other objects. After these tests, a rat was placed in front of Albert and then a steel bar was struck with a hammer, just as he reached to touch the animal. He was startled and fell forward. The next day, when he reached for the rat again, the bar was struck once more, and this time Albert fell forward and began to whimper. After five more daily pairings of the rat and noise, the boy began to cry as soon as the rat appeared. Classical conditioning had occurred; the child had become fearful of the rat, which was previously a neutral stimulus (Figure 18-7).

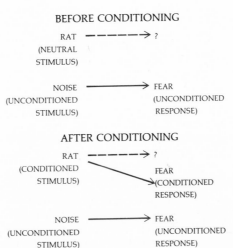

Figure 18-7 Albert's Conditioning. *The rat, initially a neutral stimulus, became a conditioned stimulus.*

Figure 18-8 Generalization of a Fear. *Little Albert had never seen Santa Claus previously, but he scuttled away from the white, bearded face as fast as possible. (Adapted from* Psychological Care of Infant and Child *by John B. Watson, by permission of W. W. Norton & Company, Inc. Copyright renewed 1955 by John B. Watson.)*

Would the new fear be generalized to similar objects? A white rabbit, cotton, a dog, and a bearded mask, all previously neutral stimuli, were introduced one at a time, and all of them evoked the fear response to some extent. Wooden blocks, bearing no similarity to the rat, did not induce the response. Thus, the investigators decided that an irrational fear could be acquired directly through conditioning or indirectly through stimulus generalization (Watson & Rayner, 1920; Figure 18-8).

When Little Albert was tested again 13 months later, the fear was less intense but still present. The researchers were about to undertake the next step, removal of the conditioned emotional reaction, but unfortunately they were unable to do so. Little Albert and his mother moved from the vicinity, and we know nothing more about him, not even his last name. The researchers have been criticized for doing this experiment, but it must be remembered that they were denied the opportunity to see it through to completion, for which they had made careful plans. With hindsight, we can say that a favorable outcome would have been likely. The "reconditioning" techniques they proposed are widely accepted today.

Classical Conditioning Methods

Later, a student of the investigators accidentally discovered a three-year-old boy who seemed to be "Albert grown a bit older." The boy was afraid of small, furry animals such as a rat and rabbit, as well as a fur coat, cotton, and feathers. Here was a chance to test the proposed removal procedure. The experimenter had no way of knowing how the fear originated in this boy, but that is not an important issue in conditioning therapies. Instead, she began to remove this fear by "reconditioning" it out of existence.

Whenever the boy was seated in his high chair, a rabbit was brought into the room, *immediately* followed by something very pleasant, such as food or his friends. Gradually, as the rabbit was paired with these favorable circumstances, the fear was replaced by a positive emotional response. Eventually the boy enjoyed having the animal in his lap and said, "I like the rabbit" (Jones, 1924, 1974).

The fear was removed by classical conditioning procedures, a process now called *counterconditioning* when used in therapy; however, here the therapist must proceed carefully. If the food were only mildly positive and the rabbit induced an intense negative reaction,

Integration of Behavior

then through backward conditioning we might have a fearful boy who also had an eating problem. He would learn to fear the food rather than love the animal. For this reason, counterconditioning must be a gradual process.

Another caution is in order. The child behaved like Albert and had a similar fear, but it does not necessarily follow that the two boys arrived at this similar condition by the same process. Furthermore, a successful treatment does not demonstrate that the fear developed by the reverse process. Fears are acquired in various ways, and there is evidence that classical conditioning is more powerful in some instances than others.

Systematic desensitization. Since the time of the experiments with Little Albert, behavior therapists have developed additional techniques for use with counterconditioning, one of which is called *covert conditioning.* For example, suppose that a person is extremely fearful about something, such as taking a college examination. The test or final exam usually cannot be brought into the therapist's office, and it would be inappropriate to conduct therapy sessions in the classroom. Hence, counterconditioning occurs by having the patient *imagine,* in a systematic fashion, those aspects of the examination that are most feared. Then the therapist applies conditioning procedures to each imagined aspect. The procedure is called *covert* because the conditioned stimulus is not immediately present. In order to make the procedure thorough, an *anxiety hierarchy* is constructed, which is an ordered list of all the things about the examination, job, or whatever, that the patient finds disturbing. The items in this list are carefully ranked from most anxiety-provoking to least anxiety-provoking (Figure 18-9).

Also, just as the feared stimulus need not be transported to the therapist's office, the attractive stimulus need not be brought there either. Rather than using food, candy, or the patient's friends as a favorable stimulus, the therapist teaches

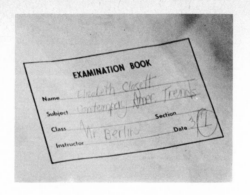

Figure 18-9   Anxiety Hierarchy. *The therapist and client constructed this hierarchy concerning fear of college examinations. (After Wolpe, 1969; John A. DeCindis photo)*

Examination hierarchy
1. On the way to the university on the day of an examination.
2. In the process of answering an examination paper.
3. Before the unopened doors of the examination room.
4. Awaiting the distribution of examination papers.
5. The examination paper lies face down before her.
6. The night before an examination.
7. The day before an examination.
8. Two days before an examination.
9. Three days before an examination.
10. Four days before an examination.
11. Five days before an examination.
12. A week before an examination.
13. Two weeks before an examination.
14. A month before an examination.

the patient how to relax. The person receives training in *deep muscle relaxation,* a state that is incompatible with anxiety. In this training, the patient tightens the fist and then loosens it, and does the same with the forearm and other body parts, gradually learning the location and better control of all the various muscle groups in the body and what it feels like to have them relax. The muscles in the neck and head are especially important, and sometimes hypnosis is used to aid the relaxation procedure (Wolpe, 1961).

With the anxiety-arousing stimulus well identified in the person's mind and the incompatible response well established, the counterconditioning begins.

I am now going to ask you to imagine a number of scenes. You will imagine them clearly. . . . If, however, at any time you feel disturbed or worried and want to attract my attention, you will be able to do so by raising your left index finger. First I want you to imagine that you are standing at a familiar street corner on a pleasant morning watching the traffic go by. You see cars, motorcycles, trucks, bicycles, people and traffic lights; and you can hear the sounds associated with all these things. *(Pause of about 15 sec.)* . . . Now imagine that you are at home studying in the evening. It is the 20th of May, exactly a month before your examination. *(Pause of 5 sec.)* . . . Now again imagine that you are studying at home a month before your examination. *(Pause of 5 sec.)* . . . If you felt any disturbance whatsoever to the last scene raise your left index finger now. *(Patient raises finger.)* If the amount of disturbance decreased from the first presentation . . . again raise your finger. *(Patient does not raise finger.)* Just keep on relaxing. *(Pause of 15 sec.)* Imagine that you are sitting on a bench at a bus stop. . . .

With the eyes closed, the patient leans back and becomes fully relaxed; then the therapist instructs him or her to visualize the least disturbing item in the list of anxiety-provoking events. If this image produces no anxiety, the therapist and patient move to subsequent items on the list, until anxiety is encountered, at which point progress is temporarily discontinued or the direction is reversed. Further training occurs, relaxation is encouraged, and in later sessions forward progress begins again. Always, the method is to approach anxiety-producing images gradually when fully relaxed (Figure 18-10).

At this point, a word about terminology is in order. This therapy is based on counterconditioning, but when the covert technique and muscle relaxation are also employed, the whole process is called *systematic desensitization*. It means that a person's emotional response to some stimulus is systematically lessened or desensitized. This ap-proach is commonly used with problems of anxiety and phobia (Bergin & Suinn, 1975).

Aversion therapy. While systematic desensitization refers to the elimination of unwanted negative emotional responses, *aversive* therapy can be used to eliminate unwanted positive emotional responses. The procedure is the same, except that punishment is used, and the personal problems usually concern behaviors such as consuming alcohol, consuming drugs, having sexual relations with persons of the same sex, and wearing the clothes of the opposite sex. When persons wish to rid themselves of these impulses, they often request aversive therapy.

In one instance, nine males, age 19 to age 43, underwent aversive therapy for homosexual tendencies. Stimuli concerning homosexuality, depicted by means of photographic slides, were followed by mild electric shock. After a number of presentations in therapy sessions for one year, sexual arousal to such stimuli decreased markedly in most subjects, as measured by self-report inventories and by responses such as penile erection and orgasm. In this study, other therapy procedures also were used, and follow-up investigations 18 months later showed no homosexual interests in seven of the nine cases (Freeman & Meyer, 1975).

In alcoholism, a negative reaction is induced by pairing the taste of alcohol with an electric shock or with a drug that immediately produces nausea. However, merely creating a negative reaction towards an undesirable stimulus is not the most efficient or effective solution to the problem. In addition, it is desirable to develop positive feelings towards more appropriate stimuli, which also can be accomplished by classical conditioning procedures. Furthermore, these procedures can be used in conjunction with operant techniques, as we shall see shortly.

Operant Conditioning Methods

Suppose that Little Albert, rather than fearing a white rat or something else, displayed an inappropriate response of a more voluntary nature, such as refusing to eat, refusing to dress himself, or stealing things. These behaviors also can be dealt with through conditioning, but rather than the classical model, which involves reflexes and emotional reactions, operant methods are used, which involve the development and maintenance of desirable habits and the elimination of undesirable ones. Actions, not feelings, are the focus of the operant methods. The term *behavior modification,* while used with reference to all conditioning therapies, is most appropriately applied in this context.

Using an operant method, the therapist looks carefully at the circumstances surrounding the undesirable behavior with the assumption that something in the environment sustains it. It might be helpful to know what caused the problem in the first place, but the original factors may be different from the current ones, and so the important issue is to find out what kinds of rewarding consequences are currently maintaining the undesirable behavior. Suppose Little Albert refuses to eat. It might be found that he eats rather well for the baby sitter, who puts his meal on the table and then watches TV, although he makes quite a fuss with his parents. Perhaps the extra attention he receives from them when not eating is more satisfying than the food itself. Or maybe he dislikes a certain food that is usually served, or perhaps he has obtained between-meal snacks. These factors, singly or together, make it more profitable for Little Albert not to eat his meal.

After this analysis, the therapist changes the environment accordingly. At mealtime, Little Albert receives attention only when he is actually in the process of eating. As soon as he begins just sitting and looking at his food, the parents immediately leave the room.

Also, Albert is served the most appetizing food possible and is not allowed between-meal snacks. If he sits longer than a specified time without eating, his meal is removed. In brief, the environment is carefully arranged to promote the desired behavior and to extinguish undesired behaviors.

Contingency management. The procedures with Albert are relatively simple, but in other cases they can be quite complicated and concern life or death. In anorexia nervosa, otherwise normal people refuse to eat to the point at which they become extremely emaciated and sometimes die of starvation. To treat this problem, *contingency management* is used, which simply means that operant methods are employed on a carefully planned basis by one or several persons, all aimed at changing a specific response. The change is brought about because the whole environment is carefully managed; rewards and punishment are always contingent on the presence and absence of the response, respectively.

In one instance of anorexia nervosa, which is most prevalent in adolescent females, an 18-year-old newly married woman who was 5 feet 4 inches tall lost weight steadily for several years, until she went from 120 pounds to 47 pounds and could hardly stand without assistance. When she arrived at the clinic, she was put in a typical hospital room, in which the experimenters analyzed her behavior carefully. They could not discover what events in the environment seemed to be maintaining this behavior, established over many years, but they did discover which things she apparently enjoyed, such as flowers, radio, television, and visitors, and these could be used for reinforcement.

She was then transferred to a barren room with only a bed, sink, night stand, and chair and, with the aid of the hospital staff, contingency management procedures were applied by everyone in contact with her. A person was in her room only at mealtime and talked with

■ *There was a small house on the park grounds where I worked last summer in which we stored games and sporting equipment overnight. This place was off-limits to the general park population.*

Ricky, who was six years old, knew the shed was restricted; consequently it held a tremendous attraction for him. He did everything imaginable to get into this shed. His tactics included feigning "sunstroke," telling us that he had been hired by the Parks Department and therefore had legal access to the shed, claiming that his Dad had bought the house the previous night, and telling us that he had to escape from "communisms" who were chasing him.

Finally, in exasperation, we decided to try what we called "reverse psychology." We approached Ricky and told him that we were in need of someone to sit in the shed during the day to keep an eye on things, and would he please do it for us? He very enthusiastically accepted. He arrived at 9:00 sharp the next morning and took his post. He spent his first day on the job exploring the place to his satisfaction. The next day, however, he could be seen at the window watching the other kids play from time to time. Each day he returned somewhat less enthusiastically until at last he asked if he could quit. After a little hesitation (for his benefit) we agreed. He didn't even come near the shed for the remainder of the summer.

her only when she began to eat. The more she ate, the more the other person talked, and after the meal, if she had eaten more than previously, she was given the use of a radio, TV, or phonograph. Gradually, progress was made. Eventually, she was required to eat everything on her plate, and slowly her health improved. When she weighed over 60 pounds, she was discharged from the hospital.

The problem then was to avoid any relapse at home and also to make further gains. Thus, the family members were instructed in contingency management; they were to avoid reinforcing any invalid behavior, discussing unpleasant topics at mealtime, and preparing any special diet for her. On the other hand, they were to follow a rigid schedule for meals, use an alarm clock and a purple table cloth to indicate mealtime, compliment her on weight gain without overreacting, and be with her whenever she ate. Her weight rose to 88 pounds before the study was concluded, but she still experienced intermittent gains and losses (Bachrach et al., 1965).

Token economies. Sometimes the concept of contingency management is used to manage the routine but diverse responses of a large number of subjects. In this case the program is called a *token economy* because tokens are used to bridge the gap between the subjects' responses and reinforcement. In a large mental hospital, for example, each patient cannot be taken to the movies after brushing his or her teeth, but each patient immediately can be given a ticket, points, or some other credit that later can be exchanged for some desirable event.

In one mental hospital, considerable difficulty was experienced in prompting the patients to habits of personal grooming, cleansing, and exercising; also, the patients were grossly negligent in the performance of their hospital jobs, such as washing dishes, mopping floors, and serving in the dining room. Thus, the first task in arranging a token economy

for a group of 40 patients was to discover what sort of reinforcements might elicit the desired behaviors. The patients were observed for several weeks, and it was discovered that they often sought to gain privacy, go to the store, talk with the staff, and go for walks. Consequently, it was decided that they should no longer have free access to these events but could obtain them in exchange for metal tokens earned by doing the previously neglected tasks. Under these conditions, it was found that the patients took better care of their personal health, reported more promptly for work, and missed far fewer work days than under the earlier free-access system (Ayllon & Azrin, 1965; Figure 18-11).

The investigators also kept detailed records of how the tokens were earned and spent, and it was discovered that certain tasks, such as dishwashing, were not sought after, and therefore the number of tokens to be earned for these jobs was increased. Similarly, it was discovered that the patients spent the tokens more readily to gain privacy and to leave the ward than to talk with the staff or go to movies and dances. In establishing another token economy program, the tokens to be earned for each task would be assigned according to these data (Figure 18-12).

Use of punishment. In some cases, the nature of the problem and condition of the subject make the use of rewards impossible. In these instances, after careful consideration, punishment is sometimes employed. For example, an infant less than one year old had been unable to maintain food in its stomach in spite of various therapeutic measures. The baby always vomited within ten minutes after eating, and medical investigation revealed no organic basis for the problem. Since the infant's health was in jeopardy and there was no indication that the difficulty would disappear spontaneously, the medical staff decided to try behavior modification techniques.

The infant was given a brief electric shock on the legs as soon as vomiting commenced and at regular intervals during the vomiting. After the fifth conditioning period, this behavior disappeared; the infant then gained weight and showed an increased interest in its surroundings (Lang & Melamed, 1969).

A milder form of punishment is simply *satiation*, in which the individual is provided with a certain object or event in such excess that it loses its desirability and in fact becomes aversive. For example, a patient in a mental hospital always kept 19 to 29 towels in her room even though the staff continually recovered the supply. Using behavior modification, during the first week of treatment the patient was given 7 towels daily. By the third week the staff was putting 60 towels in her room daily. Finally, the patient had 624 towels, and then she removed a few. Later, she was given no more towels, and eventually the mean number of towels found in her room declined to 1.5, and this level was maintained for the next 12 months.

Remarks made by the patient during the treatment procedure illustrate how the towels changed from a positive to a negative reinforcer. During the first week, as the nurse entered the patient's room carrying a towel, the patient would smile and say, "Oh, you found it for me, thank you." In the second week, when the number of towels given to the patient was increasing rapidly, she told the nurses, "Don't give me no more towels, I've got enough." In the third week she said, "Take them towels away. . . . I can't sit here all night and fold towels." And in the fourth and fifth weeks she said, "Get these dirty towels out of here." Finally, in the sixth week, after she had started taking the towels out of her room, she remarked to the nurse, "I can't drag any more of these towels, I just can't do it." These remarks suggest that the initial effect of giving towels to the patient was reinforcing, but as the towels increased in number, they ceased to be reinforcing and became aversive (Ayllon, 1963). ■

Average Number of Tokens Received for Successful Completion of Different Tasks

On-ward jobs	217
Off-ward jobs	186
Self-care jobs	73

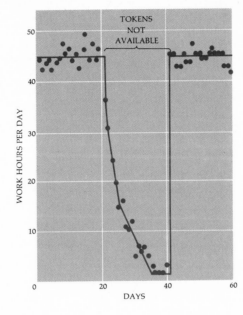

Goal	Number of Exchanges
Gain privacy	1,352
Go to the store	970
Leave the ward	616
Interact with the staff	4
Have recreational opportunities	2

Combinations of procedures. Earlier, in describing classical conditioning procedures, it was indicated that suppression of undesirable reactions accompanied by support for desirable ones is usually the most effective method for inducing attitude change. The same

Figure 18-11 Behavior in a Token Economy. *The table shows that the patients worked at jobs on and off the ward and at self-care when they received tokens. These behaviors disappeared as soon as the token economy was removed, after 20 to 40 days, but reappeared when it was restored. (From T. Ayllon and N. H. Azrin "The measurement and reinforcement of behavior of psychotics,"* Journal of the Experimental Analysis of Behavior, 8, *357–383. Copyright 1965 by the Society for the Experimental Analysis of Behavior, Inc.)*

Figure 18-12 Token Exchange in a Token Economy. *The table shows that the subjects often emitted the desired behavior to gain more privacy. (Abbreviated from Ayllon & Azrin, 1965)*

condition holds true for the operant methods; that is, reward for correct responses and punishment for undesirable responses typically produces the most permanent and significant result. Moreover, both the classical and operant procedures can be used together in many instances, including school phobia, eating problems, transvestism, and many others. People can be trained to certain attitudes and emotional reactions through classical conditioning methods, and operant methods can then be used to support the relevant behaviors per se, as in two-factor conditioning.

Further, the process of *modeling* can be included. The basic concept here, it may be remembered, is that a great deal of learning takes place on a social basis, through observing what others do and noting the consequences of their behavior. In this technique, the therapist demonstrates the correct response and the patient attempts to imitate this behavior. This type of learning can be rapid, as when an adult demonstrates that a certain animal is harmless, and a child immediately begins to play with it. The modeling procedure is particularly helpful in overcoming phobias, developing an increased identity in a child, and learning certain heterosexual behaviors (Birk, 1974; Mullare & Fernald, 1971).

Ultimately, the aim in all operant methods is to place the individual on a *self-reinforcement schedule,* in which the person administers his or her own support for desirable responses and removes the support for undesirable ones. In one study of alcoholism, self-administered electric shock appeared as effective as punishment administered by the experimenters (Wilson et al., 1975). This goal is not always achieved, however; the treatment of alcoholism, in particular, is very difficult. Usually, social support is necessary, as attested by the continuing popularity of Alcoholics Anonymous among those with this problem.

Somatic Therapies

In earlier days, emotionally disturbed people were thought to be possessed by the devil or by evil spirits, and they were treated accordingly. They were beaten, whipped, or dunked in hot liquids in the hope of "driving the devil" out of them. In presumably more advanced treatment, individuals so afflicted were spun rapidly in circles on huge wheels, rendered immobile, or branded with a hot iron (Figure 18-13).

Today we have different ideas about the cause of mental disorders and, consequently, different treatments. We no longer think that the devil is inside a disordered individual, but in many cases it is believed that something may be wrong with that person's body. Hence, certain treatments are carried out by medically trained individuals. These treatments are collectively called *somatic therapy,* which means that some condition of the body is manipulated in an effort to alleviate mental disturbance.

Shock and Surgery

Among the many important differences between the earlier and current practices is the assumption about the location of the difficulty. Since the devil could be in any place, earlier treatment was applied to the whole body or to any part at random, from the forehead to the toes. Based on what we now know about the role of the central nervous system in virtually all behavior, this part of the body, especially the brain, is the focus of somatic therapy.

Types of shock. Several decades ago it was discovered that when a coma or convulsion is induced in a patient, sometimes the individual shows an improvement in adjustment afterwards. Today there are two basic methods for achieving this condition, one of which is called *electroconvulsive therapy* or ECT because the convulsion is induced by passing a weak electric current through the brain. A period of unconsciousness follows, but recovery is rapid and today

Integration of Behavior

the patient usually leaves the psychiatrist's office within an hour after arrival. This method is used mainly in cases of depression. It produces less favorable outcomes with persons experiencing schizophrenic disorders and sometimes has been found to impair memory. Usually, patients receive a series of 6 to 12 treatments, spaced days or weeks apart, apparently without a great deal of discomfort during the actual treatment (Figure 18-14).

In *insulin shock therapy*, the patient receives injections of insulin, which lower blood sugar level to the point at which a coma, convulsions, or both are produced; then, if the patient does not regain consciousness spontaneously, carbohydrates are injected to return the blood sugar level to normal. The procedure usually is repeated at intervals of days or weeks, but because it is less efficient than ECT, insulin shock is rapidly falling into disuse.

There are wide differences of opinion regarding the use of shock therapies today. They are dramatically effective in some instances, but little is known about what actually happens in the brain as a result of the treatments. In fact, the psychiatrist's use of shock treatment has been compared to a radio operator's shaking or hitting the radio to eliminate static. The procedure *sometimes* works, yet there is no knowledge of the changes that produce the outcome.

Psychosurgery. Still another procedure that is falling into disuse is *psychosurgery*, meaning that surgery is performed on the brain for purposes of alleviating mental disorders. Originally, two methods were employed: *lobectomy*, in which parts of the frontal lobe are actually removed, and *lobotomy*, in which the connections between this lobe and other parts of the brain are destroyed. Later, lobotomy became the preferred approach because of its greater simplicity and precision (Freeman & Watts, 1950).

Figure 18-13 Eighteenth-Century Treatment. *One method of therapy was to starve "the mad ones" and place them in a basket in which they could watch others banqueting. Thus, they would be brought back to their senses. (The Bettmann Archive)*

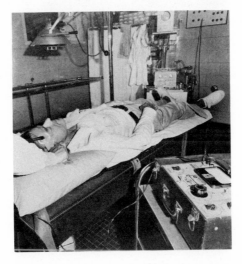

Figure 18-14 Electroconvulsive Therapy. *This treatment still remains controversial, but the use of drugs in preparing the patient has greatly improved the technique. In the foreground is an electrical stimulator used in this method. (Photo by Walter Dawn)*

The operation is still extremely serious however and has given rise to debate. Fatalities have not been high, compared with those encountered in equally difficult brain operations, but the change in the patient is irreparable. Furthermore,

Figure 18-15 Boxing and Brain Injury. *As suggested by the x-ray, a strong blow displaces the brain and can cause permanent brain damage. Traumas of this sort apparently are involved in certain kinds of psychotic behavior. In addition, JW received a head injury in an automobile accident just before the onset of his emotional disturbance. (Photo by Howard Sochurek)*

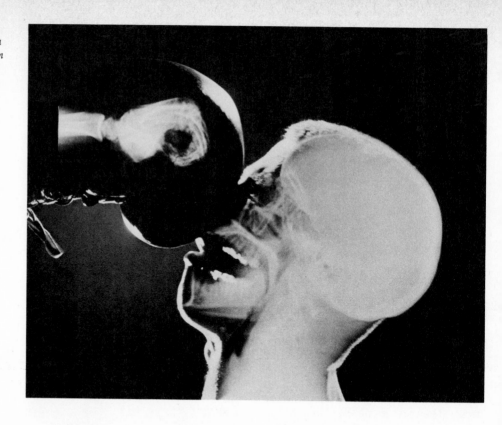

should the surgeon err in the measurements, cutting away too much tissue or the wrong part of the brain, the patient becomes grossly incapacitated and is unable to engage in any higher-level thought processes. According to critics, intentionally inducing brain damage, which is the basis of lobotomy, is highly questionable even in the most desperate cases.

Even when the operation is a success, in the sense that the paient becomes less depressed, there is an emotional loss. The lobotomized person is often less interested in the environment and less capable of thinking about his or her role in the world. The depression is gone but so is some of the zest for life. For these reasons, and because drug treatments appear much more efficient and effective, psychosurgery now is largely of historical interest.

Drug Treatments

In his younger days, J W was a boxer and, like others in this activity, he occasionally suffered a concussion. Following a career in the British Royal Navy, he did civilian work, in which he was cheerful, punctual, and friendly. His marriage apparently was happy until 1955, when he showed a distinct personality change (Figure 18-15).

For 24 hours, J W was extremely active, elated, talkative, and aggressive, if resisted; then, for the next 24 hours he became lethargic and depressed. Every two days this cycle was repeated, and it persisted for 11 years. For example, one day at work he would fill the entire suggestion box with ideas for improving the engineering industry, the next day he would apologize, and two days later he would make still more suggestions. Not surprisingly, he was often fired and his family found him barely tolerable at home. He would put together a piece of firewood, a pencil, and handkerchief and

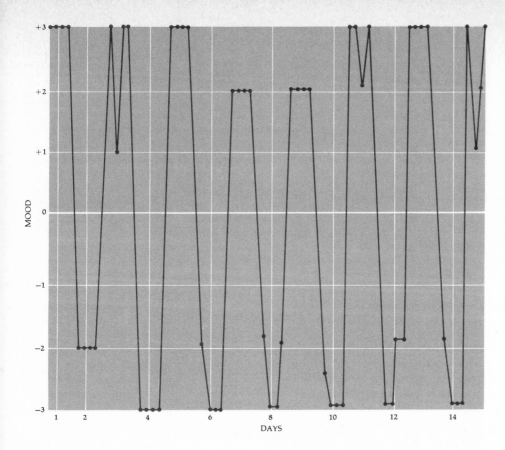

Figure 18-16 JW's Mood Changes. *This record was made from nurses' ratings on a scale +3, +2, +1, 0, -1, -2, -3. The patient was rated +3 when he was almost constantly abusive, shouting, and quarrelsome, and -3 when he was almost totally inactive and despondent. Intermediate ratings were also carefully specified. Note the regularity of the results. (Adapted from Jenner et al. Copyright by The British Journal of Psychiatry.)*

describe the apparatus as a perpetual motion machine. A piece of wood with a few lines on it became a revolutionary approach to chess, darts, and cards. The next day the "inventions" would be disowned. When J W came to medical attention, his condition was diagnosed as manic-depressive psychosis, and his therapy illustrates the use of drugs in treating mental disorders.

Analysis of the situation. The first phase in any drug treatment is to investigate the nature and extent of the problem. In the case of J W it was found that the mood change almost invariably occurred while he was asleep, between 2 and 3 A.M. If he was kept awake all night, the change still occurred. Furthermore, when he was placed in an altered day-night cycle of 22 hours, living in a special room in the hospital, the full pattern

occurred every 44 hours, rather than every 48 (Jenner et al., 1968).

In 11 years, there were only seven or eight occasions on which J W "missed a day." In a few instances the mood change occurred a few hours later than usual, but otherwise the cycle was highly predictable (Jenner et al., 1967; Figure 18-16).

A Treatment. Then J W received a medication known as lithium for his manic-depressive condition, and it appeared helpful. But the reaction of any therapeutic drug with any patient is partly unpredictable. The person's diet, general state of health, and constitutional factors all influence the reaction, and soon it was discovered that the lithium was not effective under certain circumstances. After further study, the problem was identified. A high salt diet

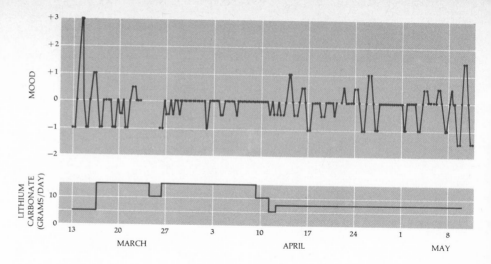

Figure 18-17 Lithium Treatment. *The higher the dosage of lithium that JW received, the steadier and more normal was his mood. (Adapted from Jenner et al. Copyright by The British Journal of Psychiatry.)*

was interfering with J W's response to the lithium (Hanna et al., 1972). The patient therefore was instructed to continue taking 500 mg of lithium carbonate twice daily and also follow a low salt diet. After some time in the clinic, he was sent home again, remained well, and worked regularly on his new job (Figure 18-17).

Three years later he became listless, apathetic, and complained of deafness and dryness of skin. Clinical examination revealed a hypothyroid condition, apparently produced by the lithium. When it was corrected by administration of thyroxin, the patient's health returned. During this period the effects of the lithium were tested by giving J W a salt pill without medicinal properties, rather than the lithium. Then the thyroid problem disappeared and the periodic psychosis returned. Hence, the patient was discharged from the hospital, this time with prescriptions for lithium and thyroxin, and he went home to more normal health. Except for one minor disruption, when his dosage was incorrect, this satisfactory condition has continued.

This case history emphasizes two points. First, a man who essentially was unemployable for 18 years and "impossible" at home has worked regularly for 4 years and has led a normal life while receiving lithium treatments. Drug treatments can be extremely valuable. Second, it emphasizes that arriving at a proper prescription of therapeutic drugs for any individual can be a complex, time-consuming task. The result can be influenced by diet; it can include unwanted outcomes; and it can vary decidedly with the dosage (Hanna et al., 1972).

Types of therapeutic drugs. Scientific understanding of the value of drugs in treating mental disorders has just begun, although their influence on psychological functioning has been recognized for centuries. Today, the major tranquilizers, such as Thorazine and Stelazine, are recognized as being especially effective in reducing hallucinations and delusions and therefore are considered *antipsychotic* medication. They diminish agitation to the point at which potentially aggressive patients can benefit from other treatment procedures, such as occupational therapy, recreational activity, and psychotherapy. They are also administered in cases of incomplete recovery from LSD ingestion.

Minor tranquilizers are used in less severe cases. They induce feelings of relaxation and serenity and are sometimes called *anti-anxiety* drugs.

Type of Drug	Generic Names	Indications for Use	Possible Side Effects
Antipsychotic	Chlorpromazine Trifluoperazine	Psychotic or severe neurotic symptoms	Dizziness, sleepiness, dry mouth, blurred vision, jaundice, liver damage
Minor tranquilizers	Meprobamate Chlordiazepoxide	Mild neurotic symptoms	Initial dizziness, possible addiction
Antidepressants	Imipramine Amitriptyline	Anxiety, agitation, and insomnia	Anxiety, trembling, sleep problems, overt psychosis

Figure 18-18 Psychiatric Drugs.
The usage of these drugs has increased precipitously in the past generation.

In case of depression, there are drugs known as *antidepressant* or mood-elevating drugs. Some of them require 10 to 21 days before they begin to have an effect, but when they work they stimulate the individual to increased activity and more interest in the world around him or her (Figure 18-18).

Unquestionably, drugs have been a significant asset in the treatment of mental illness, so much so that the field now is called *chemotherapy*, referring to the use of any chemicals for treating mental disorder. According to many psychotherapists, however, drugs generally do not eliminate a mental problem but merely reduce or suppress the symptoms. Others argue that the symptoms are the problem. In either case, a psychotic person taking drugs may not appear to be in a psychosis, but if the drugs are withdrawn the delusions and inappropriate emotional reactions may reappear. For this reason, therapeutic drugs are commonly regarded as agents for dealing with crises and for making patients more suitable for other treatments, rather than as cures for emotional disorders.

Furthermore, drugs and indeed all somatic therapies can produce *side effects*, which are undesirable symptoms, such as insomnia, dry mouth, or liver damage in the case of drug treatments. J W's hypothyroid condition was a side effect. Another disadvantage of drug treatment is that long-term chemotherapy is expensive, can induce psychological or physiological dependencies, and can interfere with a person's learning (Tobias & MacDonald, 1974).

Despite the promise of chemotherapy, there are clear limitations in this procedure.

Innovation and Evaluation

If the reader is surprised at the diverse treatments available today for psychological disturbance, he or she only has to look around to know that adjustment problems are experienced by persons of any age, sex, race, or national origin. Many of these problems are not readily resolved, even by the current methods, and therefore new forms of treatment appear regularly.

The Group Context

Thus, some psychotherapies occur in a group context. There are several participants; there can be more than one therapist; and the structure of the group can vary from one approach to another. These group procedures are economical in terms of time and money, and sometimes the social context appears helpful for therapy.

Role playing and acting out. In *transactional analysis*, as the name implies, the focus is on the transactions or interactions between people. These take place largely as planned exercises and activities for pairs or triads of people. In such groups, people solve problems and have a relationship while other members of the therapy session, together with the therapist, analyze and interpret what happens in this role playing. Commonly,

One memorable experience that I had with intense group interaction came during a 14-hour marathon sensitivity group session. I, as well as most of the others, had never been in a group such as this before and came to it out of curiosity—12 of us met one morning in a small living room that had no furniture.

Sitting around on the floor in a circle the group leader told us to give our name and describe who we were, refraining from using the usual labels such as a sophomore from such and such college.

The members of the group started off hesitantly, some skeptical and fairly unresponsive. We went through attempts at role playing, group confidence-building games, nonverbal communication, and giving first impressions of each other. After a few hours there had developed a fixed pattern of interaction with one boy always being the loud one, one usually the quiet one, and so forth.

When it was my turn in the period in which the whole group focused on each individual separately, I felt defensive. I was asked questions that I didn't really want to answer and I felt that these people didn't really want to hear the answers. Of course I had the option of not answering. Some of the questions that the leader asked showed great perception and were thought-provoking. I still feel, however, that someone who was unstable might have reacted in an unhealthy manner. I feel fairly stable and this 14-hour session did shake me up and drain me emotionally for a while.

At 1:00 A.M. after it was all over, I walked down the quiet streets of Cambridge with gentle snow falling, feeling very alone. I was just thinking, how can one be completely open with other people when there are so many things about which one is not even open with oneself?

there is emphasis on undesirable aspects of the communication process, as in subtle or "hidden" meanings (Berne, 1961).

Much of the theory in transactional analysis shows a debt to psychoanalysis and a recognition of the principles of learning. One of the main contributions of this approach, and a reason for its popularity, is that some of these basic, important psychological concepts are presented in a more readily comprehensible style for the layperson.

Another therapy that takes place in a group setting and stresses personal expression and the acting out of thoughts and feelings is *gestalt therapy*. According to its founder, Fritz Perls, this method is a type of existential therapy, devoted to the principle that "awareness *per se*—by and of itself—can be curative" (Perls, 1969). Each therapy session includes a number of participants, who make contributions to the therapy process, but the therapist works primarily on an individual basis, with one member at a time. Within this interview context, role playing is stressed, as the individual acts out fears, fantasies, and feelings. Otherwise, each gestalt therapist works much in his or her own way, attempting to develop and maintain a strong creative relationship with each individual (Rosenblatt, 1975).

Less-structured groups. In some other group approaches, the interactions are less planned and the leader works less intensively with one individual. Hence, the group members exert a more powerful influence on the progress of therapy. The basic concept in this traditional *group therapy*, in which a number of people participate more or less freely in each group session, is expressed in the early dictum, "By the crowd they have been broken and by the crowd they shall be healed."

This method is popular partly because it permits people to benefit from the experiences of others who have had similar problems. Alcoholics Anonymous and Synanon operate somewhat in this manner. Apart from these long-established programs, there is considerable interest today in the whole encounter-sensitivity-training group approach, in which people attempt to relate to each other on the basis of feelings, rather than primarily in a rational, problem-solving style. One such approach is the *marathon group*, which lasts two to four days, based on the premise that the typical 50-minute session does not provide enough time for people to take off their "social masks" and experience more fundamental aspects of the other individual's personality. ■

Problems in Evaluation

A group therapy called *psychodrama* was popular with the previous generation of young adults. Here, the emphasis also is on acting out one's problems, and several group members are assigned roles, almost as an unrehearsed play, while other members assist by observing and responding as the audience. The claims for the success of this technique were legion 25 years ago, but now they are less common. The problem is that it is very difficult to know the long-term benefits of *any* therapy, especially if it is a new one. One is reminded of the psychiatric adage that almost any new method obtains positive outcomes until it is no longer new.

Why is it difficult to evaluate the outcomes of therapy? What are the limitations, even in assessing a well-established therapeutic procedure?

Measuring change in therapy. The first problem in deciding whether or not a particular therapy is effective lies in choosing the criteria. What does "effective" mean? What constitutes "improvement," a "cure," or "better adjustment?" Should the criterion be the client's opinion, the therapist's opinion, or the opinions of both? In one instance, it may be the disappearance of symptoms; in another, perhaps the patient should accept his or her problems and simply try to deal with them more constructively. Discharge from the hospital, going to work, or meeting stangers may each be considered improvement, depending on the context in which they occur. Defining valid criteria for deciding on the effectiveness of therapy poses difficulties, but they are not insurmountable (Garfield et al., 1971).

A second problem is that, regardless of what criteria are selected, the investigator can never be certain of the patient's future condition. Will any improvements be lasting? If changes have not taken place, will they occur at some future date? Even if improvements appear several years after therapy, the treatment procedures may have played a vital role in this outcome (Nelson, 1954a). For this reason, follow-up studies are absolutely essential in any effort to evaluate the effectiveness of therapy.

The question of *symptom substitution*, which is the appearance of new symptoms as a replacement for those that were removed by therapy, has come up in this context. In the psychoanalytic view, the underlying conflict must be resolved; if merely the symptoms are removed, new defenses will arise later. According to behaviorism, the problem is essentially the symptoms, and if they are removed, there will be no substitution. In fact, other maladaptive responses also may disappear because the individual's overall adjustment has improved (Bandura, 1969). Thus arguments and data still appear on both sides of this issue, but the overall evidence now seems to favor the view that replacement symptoms do not appear (Grossberg, 1964; Rachman, 1967). This controversy emphasizes the need for follow-up studies in therapy, despite the fact that the question of symptom substitution may be nearing resolution.

Spontaneous remission. A third difficulty in deciding whether or not a particular therapy is effective was well illustrated 25 years ago when an English psychologist found that the rate of recovery or distinct improvement in the treatment of neurosis was about 67 percent. Approximately the same rates have been reported recently (Bergin & Suinn, 1975). This finding presented no problem except in comparison with the rate for *spontaneous remission,* which refers to recovery without formal treatment. Sometimes people get better without any special attention, and this figure must be weighed against whatever gains are achieved through therapy. Since the rates of spontaneous remission also were reported to be 67 percent, the same as those for clinical treatment, psychotherapy appeared useless (Eysenck, 1952, 1965).

These results prompted a closer look at the data for spontaneous remission, which came chiefly from two studies in the United States. One involved allegedly untreated psychoneurotic patients in state mental hospitals; the other concerned insurance disability cases. Both were criticized as not meeting the essential standards for demonstrating spontaneous remission rates (Denker, 1947; Landis, 1937). In the insurance study, the prospect of disability income may have induced the subjects to develop or maintain symptoms, which might readily have disappeared when financial gain was no longer a possibility. Hence, these disorders may be very different from the well-established neurotic behaviors encountered in psychotherapy. Furthermore, the patients in both groups may have received some form of therapeutic attention. The insurance patients regularly consulted physicians and were given medications, and it seems unlikely that the hospitalized neurotic patients received no form of treatment, particularly when mental institutions are populated largely by psychotic people. The hospital staff is likely to work with the most promising patients, which would be the neurotic cases.

Some psychologists believe that the rates for spontaneous remission are still approximately 67 percent. Others believe that they have yet to be demonstrated. Still others believe the rates are well below 50 percent (Lambert, 1976; Rachman, 1973; Subotnik, 1972).

In any case, the problem of establishing the incidence of spontaneous remission is obvious. Only in rare cases does an individual arrive at a clinic and refuse *all* forms of treatment. When the individual does not go to a clinic, it is unlikely that the problem will be detected and studied by a field worker. Hence, the problem of finding an adequate control group for comparison purposes is exceedingly difficult (Eysenck, 1972).

Effectiveness of Therapy

Despite the obstacles in ascertaining the effectiveness of therapy, evaluation studies have been accomplished. Patients have been located and examined years after treatment has been terminated. Multiple criteria have been established as measures of effectiveness. Control groups have been used, comparing patients on the clinic waiting list with those currently in treatment. In comparative studies of this nature, involving behavior therapy and psychoanalysis in one series of studies and combinations of rational-emotive therapy, client-centered therapy, and systematic desensitization in others, all therapy groups were found to be significantly more improved than the control groups (Devine & Fernald, 1973; DiLoreto, 1971; Sloane, et al., 1974).

Factors in therapy. In research involving the effectiveness of therapy, three factors emerge as obviously important: the patient, the therapist, and the method. Each accounts for some of the success or failure in therapy (Bergin & Suinn, 1975).

Concerning the patient, several conditions influence the *prognosis,* which is the predicted outcome of any therapy. Generally speaking, success is more likely when the patient is young, when symptoms involve neurosis rather than psychosis, and when previous adjustment has been satisfactory. In addition, it is important that the patient desire treatment, rather than being coerced into it by some authority, and also that he or she expect to benefit from it. The importance of the subject's expectation has been widely demonstrated (Figure 18-19).

Figure 18-19 Expectation and Successful Treatment. *University women were measured for fear of rats in a situational test. Low scores indicated much fear, high scores little fear. Treatment consisted of 20-minute modeling sessions in which each subject was encouraged to approach and handle the animal. The subjects in Group A were told that successful treatment required three sessions, and they improved about two points each session. Those in Group B were informed that successful treatment required only one session, and they improved about six points in the single session. The subjects in Group C, receiving no treatment, showed slight but insignificant improvement. (From Mullare & Fernald, 1971; Sheila A. Farr photo)*

		Average Fear Scores			
Group	Pretreatment	After Session 1	After Session 2	After Session 3	Post-Treatment
A	6.9	8.9	10.1	12.3	12.3
B	5.4	11.6	—	—	11.6
C	6.5	—	—	—	6.9

For years, the only characteristics of the therapist that were assumed to be important were his or her training and experience, especially in psychoanalysis, but eventually investigators studied the therapist's personality too. It was found that the capacity to express personal concerns and to evaluate the motives of others are characteristics of highly competent beginning psychiatrists (Knupfer et al., 1959). On the other hand, when therapists have conflicts similar to those of their patients, they are less adequate in helping them with these conflicts (Butler, 1958). Certain traits of the therapist unquestionably are important in helping the patient with personal issues. When asked about the most beneficial aspect of the therapeutic process, patients in a large-scale study most commonly mentioned the therapists' personal characteristics (Sloane et al., 1974).

The findings with regard to method illustrate the inter-relations between these three sets of factors. Method is important, certainly, but no method is satisfactory when it is inappropriate to the patient's problem. That is, the value of any therapeutic procedure can be determined only in relation to some patient who is treated and, to a lesser extent, some therapist who uses it. An adult might undergo psychoanalysis and the process could be evaluated on this basis, but a child would enter play therapy, which provides an opportunity for "playing out" one's problems, rather than talking about them.

Similarly, different methods may be appropriate depending on the severity of the person's problem. A man who consulted a hypnotherapist about nail-biting proved to be an excellent subject, and he was relieved of this habit in six sessions (Brownfain, 1967). However, such treatments may be totally ineffective with other problems. One possible explanation is that the behaviors in question are deep-seated aspects of the individual's personality, rather than more superficial characteristics, as was determined beforehand in treating the nail-biting problem. It is speculated by some that an integral aspect of the personality is not likely to be readily eliminated by brief treatment. (Figure 18-20).

The interaction effect. In short, certain methods are most effective with individuals who have certain types of problems. But the method does not operate independently of the therapist either, as emphasized in the following comment:

Therapists can no longer be regarded as interchangeable units who administer a clearly definable treatment, even if they subscribe to similar theoretical assumptions . . . different therapists, depending on variables in their personality, training, experience, outlook on life, and personal values, exert different effects on a patient regardless of the particular therapeutic techniques they may employ. (Strupp, 1971)

Thus, we must conclude that the important aspect of any therapeutic situation is the *interaction effect* among the various patient, therapist, and method

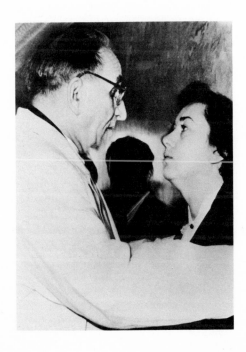

Figure 18-20   Hypnotherapy. *This woman is being hypnotized by a physician in the Soviet Union to cure stuttering. Many claims are made for hypnotherapy, and some have been substantiated; however, the results of this method of therapy are unpredictable. (United Press International)*

factors. The extent to which any particular therapy is effective depends on the ways in which these different factors influence one another. The outcome of therapy does not depend on a single circumstance, such as client-centered therapy or the use of a certain drug, but also on the therapist's skill and the patient's personal characteristics. The research problem in therapy is not merely to discover the value of new techniques, which are usually overestimated, but to discover why certain techniques when used by certain therapists are most effective with certain kinds of patient problems. The complexities of the interaction effect are no doubt partly responsible for the proliferation of therapies that we have today.

In reference to our earlier cases, J W, for example, probably would not have improved a great deal through psychotherapy or behavior modification; his difficulty apparently was based in some physiological condition. Little Albert and his "replacement" both had a specific fear, for which the use of drugs would have been unnecessary and severe; furthermore, since this fear was not an integral part of the personality, the case for long-term psychotherapy seems less convincing. Finally, G might have undergone some form of chemotherapy, using decreased dosages as he learned to cope with the problem. But the decision is not easy, for he might have been an excellent candidate for systematic desensitization.

Some problems seem more amenable to certain types of treatments—not a surprising circumstance. As a result, many therapists today are *eclectic,* meaning that they choose from the various approaches the one that seems the most appropriate for a given patient and problem. Eclecticism is a common position in both theory and practice, as seen earlier in connection with personality theory and assessment (Figure 18-21).

Approach	Weighted Score
Eclecticism	161
Freudian psychoanalysis	94
Client-centered therapy	68
Behavior therapy	39
Rational psychotherapy	13
Existential approach	12

Figure 18-21   Preferences for Therapy Methods. *A survey of clinical psychologists showed eclecticism to be the most popular orientation. The ranking of the other approaches cannot be considered reliable because of the limited return of questionnaires. (After Wildman & Wildman, 1967)*

Because of the complexity of the patient, method, and therapist variables, however, outcome predictions are still very difficult to make. At this point, the best we can say is that some treatments seem helpful to certain therapists working with certain kinds of patients—some of the time.

Preventive Mental Health Care

Any approach to therapy is usually based on some conception or model of what makes an individual maladjusted. Years ago, the *devil model* suggested that emotional disorder was caused by the devil residing in the body and, therefore, the most appropriate treatment would be some physical punishment that would cause the devil to leave.

In our century, the *medical model* has been often followed; it suggests that mental illness, like physical illness, reflects a diseased or injured condition of the body. Some psychological disturbances certainly are of this nature, and this assumption is the basis of the various somatic therapies, which have been effective in certain instances. But for the majority of cases this model does not yet seem appropriate, as evident in the enormous interest in the various psychotherapies and behavior modification.

Integration of Behavior

At present, the *sociocultural model* is becoming more popular, emphasizing the role of the environment in contributing to maladjustment. The value of this model lies not only in its implications for certain psychotherapies and behavior modification techniques, already in vigorous development, but also in its relevance for preventive mental health care. If social and cultural conditions can bring about mental disorder, then this outcome can be partly prevented by appropriate attention to environmental factors.

Facilities. The concept of preventive mental health care is relatively new and is based on the premise that an ounce of prevention is worth a pound of cure. One aim of this movement is to provide assistance for people when they are beginning to experience maladjustment, before the problem grows worse. Partly for this purpose, *mental health centers* have been established in many states; they are not located in remote areas, like the old asylums, but in crowded, low-income urban areas, where the incidence of mental disorders is often highest. In addition to drug and supportive therapy, these centers offer nursing services, social and recreational programs, evening clinics, and halfway houses, for persons trying to make a readjustment in the community after a period of hospital residence. Sometimes there are also "night centers" that serve anyone during the night hours, which are particularly difficult for many troubled persons.

To solve the problem of finding sufficient personnel for such facilities, a number of *paraprofessional persons* have been trained; these are people without extensive education and preparation but who have learned the rudiments of a selected aspect of mental health care. These nonprofessional workers can expedite programs in many ways by intervening temporarily in critical home and work situations, bridging the gap between client and professional service, developing meaningful relationships with disturbed persons, and in some cases offering minimal therapy. They can also increase the effectiveness of the center by performing tasks that are often handled by psychologists and physicians even though they do not require special training.

Public education. The other major dimension of the preventive mental health movement is educating the public about the nature of mental disorders and how they are believed to be developed or augmented. Part of this task lies in obtaining answers to the numerous important questions that remain, but another part lies in communicating to the layperson what is already known about this complex topic. Direct contact with mental patients also seems to promote understanding and accepting attitudes towards mental disorders. Communities that have open-ward mental hospitals have more accepting attitudes towards mental patients than those with locked-ward hospitals (Wright & Shrader, 1965). Significant attitude changes also have been observed among college students who have had weekly contact with chronic mental patients during an academic year (Holzberg & Knapp, 1965). ∎

Even the capacity to recognize psychological problems when they first occur is not common. One investigation revealed that two or three years usually elapse between the onset of schizophrenic symptoms and the decision of relatives, friends, or the patient to seek treatment (Dunham, 1965). Consumer awareness of available treatment methods has increased significantly in recent years, partly because of the efforts of the mass media. But much remains to be accomplished.

∎ *The first night at the hospital was rather scary. The patients were having a birthday party and when we first arrived all the patients were just sitting neatly against the walls of the ward. After a while they began to get up and dance and I was petrified that one of the "crazy" guys would ask me to dance. I thought that the humiliation would be more than I could bear. As the evening progressed I became more at ease and began to enjoy myself.*

The first few times that I went to the hospital, I still felt a bit uneasy when I got there but after a few minutes I would warm up. Now I arrive there feeling at ease and I really enjoy talking to the patients and doing things with them. I don't think of them as mere "crazy" people anymore and I truly think that I am helping them in some way.

Summary

Methods of Psychotherapy

1. Psychotherapy involves a series of interviews between a person seeking assistance and a therapist who listens, questions, or otherwise creates an atmosphere conducive to dealing with emotional problems. In psychoanalysis, three techniques are emphasized: free association, in which the person tries to uncover hidden thoughts and feelings by saying whatever comes to mind; transference, in which the person achieves emotional release and insight by responding as though the therapist were someone else; and dream interpretation, in which the person, with the aid of the analyst, tries to determine the deeper, underlying meanings of his or her behavior, including dreams.

2. In client-centered therapy, the emphasis is on the client's ability to solve his or her own problems, provided that person is given sufficient understanding and acceptance to concentrate on himself or herself. The therapist's responsibilities lie in creating an unconditional positive regard and in reflecting the client's feelings and ideas, thus letting the client lead the way.

3. Rational-emotive therapists take the view that the therapist should control the therapy sessions and try to demonstrate to the patient the source of the problem. The basic assumptions are that the therapist usually knows best and that irrational ideas are behind many emotional problems; therefore, it is the person's thinking and reasoning that must be changed.

4. In existential therapy, it is assumed that anxiety is an inevitable aspect of human life and, therefore, people must learn to accept it and deal with it more effectively. The goal is to help emotionally disturbed people find greater meaning in life.

Behavior Modification

5. The behavior therapies are based on principles from the psychological laboratory. Those arising from classical conditioning methods are of two types: systematic desensitization, which is concerned with reducing negative emotional responding, as in anxiety and phobia; and aversive therapy, which is concerned with reducing positive emotional responding, as in homosexuality and alcoholism.

6. The operant methods are based on the systematic use of rewards and sometimes mild punishment as well. When these procedures are used on a large scale for the management of routine behaviors, a token economy is sometimes established. Often, operant and classical conditioning procedures are used in various combinations in behavior modification.

Somatic Therapies

7. Somatic therapies attempt to change mental functioning by altering body conditions. In shock therapy, most commonly used with depression, a coma or convulsion is produced by injection of insulin or by electric shock. Psychosurgery involves cutting some nerve pathways in the frontal area of the brain, after which some patients seem more adjusted. Except for electroconvulsive shock, these procedures have been largely discontinued.

8. With the advent of psychotherapeutic drugs, persons who formerly would have been institutionalized are able to maintain their jobs and appear at the clinic on an out-patient basis. The use of drugs generally suppresses rather than eliminates symptoms and is therefore commonly considered a prelude to other treatment.

Innovation and Evaluation

9. Today, many new psychotherapies take place in a group setting. Transactional analysis focuses on the interactions between people, and gestalt

therapy, which is not of recent origin, is aimed at developing greater self-awareness by providing each individual with an opportunity for acting out in a group setting. Other socially based approaches are simply called group therapy because the procedures are less structured and thus the members exert a stronger influence on the progress of therapy.

10. The chief problems in evaluating the effectiveness of therapy are: the difficulty in establishing adequate criteria for cure or improvement; the difficulties in maintaining continuous, long-term, follow-up studies to detect changes in adjustment; and the absence of accurate data on the incidence of spontaneous remission within the general population.

11. Research has indicated three categories of significant factors in the effectiveness of therapy: patient variables, among which age, type of symptoms, prior adjustment, and motivation for change appear most important; therapist variables, in which training and experience were formerly stressed and personality characteristics are now considered important; and method variables, in which certain techniques are sometimes most appropriate for a certain problem and certain therapist. Research suggests that an interaction among these factors determines the effectiveness of therapy.

12. The burden of mental disorder for the individual and community and the limitations of available treatment methods have resulted in increased emphasis on preventive mental health care. The chief preventive measures are the immediate ·availability of facilities in high incidence areas, employment of paraprofessionals for providing greater service, and the efforts to educate the public concerning the conditions and treatment of mental disorders.

Suggested Readings

Frank, J. D. Persuasion and healing (rev. ed.). Baltimore: Johns Hopkins University Press, 1973. A comparative study of cures and healings in a broad perspective, including the role of suggestion, expectation, and faith in treatment results.

Freud, S. An outline of psychoanalysis. New York: Norton, 1949. Presents the fundamentals of orthodox psychoanalysis as a therapeutic system and a theory of human behavior.

Honigfeld, G., & Howard, A. Psychiatric drugs: A desk reference. New York: Academic Press, 1973. A handy, brief guide on the clinical uses of psychiatric drugs, including appendixes on the trade and generic drug names and identification of drugs.

Thompson, T., & Dockens, W. S. (Eds.). Applications of behavior modification. New York: Academic Press, 1975. Almost thirty papers on a wide range of topics, including theoretical and ethical issues and the training of behavior therapists.

Wexler, D A., & Rice, L. N. (Eds.). Innovations in client-centered therapy. New York: Wiley, 1974. Papers of varying length and focus, prepared especially for this volume, by persons who worked with Carl Rogers at the University of Chicago.

PART EIGHT

The Individual in Society

Chapter 19

Language and Communication

Communication is the essential fabric of society. It occurs whenever the behavior of one organism acts as a stimulus that influences the behavior of another organism. It may indicate that danger is approaching, that food is available at a particular place or, at a much greater level of complexity, that a friend is due to arrive in New York next Wednesday. There is no social behavior without some type of communication.

In this chapter we consider both personal communication and the mass media, with an emphasis on the acquisition and use of human language. There are two schools of thought in this area of research. Some investigators believe that the study of language among non-human primates eventually will increase our understanding of our own language, while others perceive little value in this approach. In any case, chimpanzees, our closest relatives from the standpoint of evolution, biochemical makeup, and neurological development, have been studied extensively in recent years.

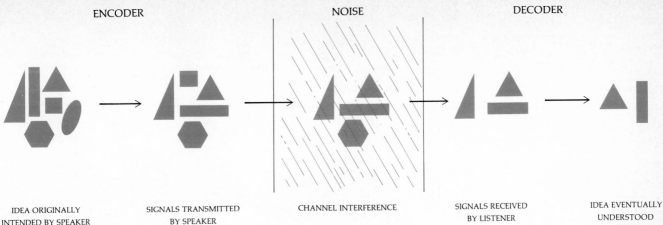

ENCODER	NOISE	DECODER

IDEA ORIGINALLY
INTENDED BY SPEAKER

SIGNALS TRANSMITTED
BY SPEAKER

CHANNEL INTERFERENCE

SIGNALS RECEIVED
BY LISTENER

IDEA EVENTUALLY
UNDERSTOOD
BY LISTENER

Figure 19-1   A Communication Model. *In communication theory, noise interferes with the transmission of a message. It can involve interfering signals from another communication or interference within the same channel, as in radio transmission static.*

Basic Elements in Communication

Mr. Worzle is an elderly chimpanzee, living on the shores of Lake Tanganyika, the longest lake in Africa. He appears more nervous than other males in his community, perhaps because of his low rank in the dominance hierarchy. Like the pecking order of chickens, social status among these males is determined by battles between pairs of chimpanzees, with the victor rising up the social ladder and the vanquished falling closer to the bottom. Mr. Worzle apparently has lost many such encounters.

The Communication Process

On this particular day, the highest-ranking member, called Goliath, has just caught and killed a baby baboon, and he is up in a tree apparently preparing to eat it. Mr. Worzle is there too, whimpering, and every few moments Goliath retreats to another branch. After each move, Mr. Worzle follows, reaches out his hand, and whimpers again. When Goliath pushes his hand away for perhaps the tenth time, Mr. Worzle suddenly throws himself off the branch and out of the tree. On the ground he begins to strike wildly at the trees and leaves and cries louder. Finally, Goliath yanks apart his small prey and tosses one half to Mr. Worzle. Then he enjoys the rest of it in peace (van Lawick-Goodall, 1971).

The basic model.   Obviously, communication took place between the two chimpanzees. At the simplest level, *communication* involves the transmission of information from a source to a receiver. In the broadest sense, communication can occur between inanimate objects, as when the thermostat sends a "turn on" signal to the furnace. In the present context we are concerned only with information exchange between living organisms.

The major components of the communication process are sometimes described as: encoder, signals, a channel, and a decoder. The *encoder* sends a message by selecting and transmitting various signals. These *signals* may be gestures, dots and dashes, words, or some other representation. They are any signs or symbols that have meaning, and they are transmitted to someone else via a communication *channel*, such as sound waves, wires, or printed pages. The *decoder* receives the signals and interprets them, thus obtaining the message. A deaf person decodes gestures; as you read this page you decode the letter arrangement. The process is not a simple one, however, because the same signals can have different meanings for different people, and outside influences can distort the communication (Figure 19-1).

Figure 19-2 Kissing Chimpanzees. *In addition to mouth kissing, the male chimp has been known to greet the female by grasping her hand, drawing it towards him, and kissing it with his lips.* (*From* In the Shadow of Man *by Jane van Lawick-Goodall, published by William Collins Sons and Co., London. Copyright Hugo van Lawick and National Geographic Society.*)

With gestures, Mr. Worzle apparently told Goliath that he wanted some food. Receiving none, he resorted to more dramatic signals—throwing himself out of the tree and pounding on surrounding objects. He also whimpered and emitted various cries, which are called *vocal* signals, since they pertain to the voice but do not include words.

Limits of animal communication. On another day, Mr. Worzle was sitting alone when a female baboon passed close by and startled him. He barked and raised his arm, and she immediately crouched down and turned her rump in his direction. Then old Mr. Worzle reached out and touched her on the rump, and she relaxed her posture and sat down beside him.

Through investigations by Jane van Lawick-Goodall, who spent more than a decade studying the habits of this chimpanzee colony, we have a verbal decoding of this scene. Each animal knows its status within the social structure and demonstrates this knowledge by the way

it greets other chimpanzees. In the submissive gesture, the animal requests reassurance from a more dominant individual. By crouching and turning her back, which leaves her defenseless, the baboon is saying something comparable to "I know you are dominant. I admit it." By touching her lightly on the rump, Mr. Worzle replies, "I acknowledge your respect; I shall not attack you just now" (van Lawick-Goodall, 1971).

Such research suggests that certain primates show striking similarities to human beings in gestural and postural communication. Chimpanzees, in particular, communicate by bowing, grinning, holding hands, kissing and hugging, touching and patting. But they have developed few vocal signals, such as calls and grunts, and apparently no language (Figure 19-2).

Human communication is accomplished chiefly but not exclusively by *language,* which is a system of signals used according to certain rules, allowing *wide flexibility* in the content of the communication. All but the simplest animals communicate to others of their kind. A chirping cricket induces others to chirp, and a croaking frog initiates this same activity in other frogs, but these acts are largely reflexive and alone certainly do not qualify as language.

Structure of Language

Studies have indicated at least three basic aspects of language—phonemes, morphemes, and syntax. These are found in all human languages, and an understanding of these components enables us to examine more thoroughly the process of language acquisition.

Phonemes. The various sounds found in all languages are surprisingly similar, considering the wide variety of noises that human beings are capable of making. In English there are 46 basic sounds, called *phonemes;* some languages use considerably fewer, while others have almost twice as many. Phonemes are the meaningful sound units that can be distinguished in a language. For example, the word "cat" has three phonemes—*k, a,* and *t,* using phonetic notation. "Sat" also has three—*s, a,* and *t.* "Scat" has four—*s, k, a,* and *t,* but "seat" only has three— *s, ē,* and *t.*

Generally speaking, we might say that phonemes of English are the different pronunciations for the vowel, consonant, and diphthong sounds in our language. It should be emphasized again, however, that phonemes are features of language only as it is heard. They bear no consistent relation to the written language that one sees.

Morphemes. Phonemes can be combined in various ways to form *morphemes,* which are the smallest language units having distinct and separate meanings. Each morpheme has a meaning, and its presence in a word gives the word a distinctive meaning. For example, "booklet" contains two morphemes—"book" and "let." The root meaning of "book" is modified by the addition of the morpheme "let," which signifies something small.

An idiom, which is an expression that cannot be fully understood merely by knowing the meanings of the separate words of which it is composed, is also a morpheme. The idiom "penny pincher" is a morpheme, but if "penny" and "pincher" are used separately, each is then a morpheme. Altogether, we can say that morphemes are often but not exclusively words.

Syntax. Morphemes, in turn, are arranged in certain ways to form phrases, clauses, and sentences. The set of rules for forming such arrangements usually is known as *syntax. Grammar,* of which syntax is a part, is a broader term, being concerned not only with the arrangement of words but also with their pronunciation and meaning; thus, grammar concerns phonemes and morphemes as well, and it implies the correctness or incorrectness of various constructions.

The importance of syntax is illustrated in this example: "Furiously sleep ideas green colorless" and "Colorless green ideas sleep furiously." Both of these expressions are improbable English. "Furiously" is unlikely to be followed by "sleep," which is unlikely to be followed by "ideas," and so forth. Similarly, in the second sequence "colorless" is unlikely to be followed by "green," which is unlikely to be followed by "ideas," and so on (Chomsky, 1957). Yet, due to syntax, which is the ordering of words in an appropriate sequence, the second expression is considerably closer to a meaningful English statement than is the first. Thus, we see that the organization among a group of words, or syntax, also contributes significantly to the overall meaning that they convey.

To summarize, the basic elements of any language are the classes of single sounds, called phonemes, which are combined to form units of meaning, known as morphemes. These units are used together according to certain rules, or syntax, to form still larger, more specific expressions.

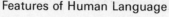

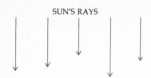

SUN'S RAYS

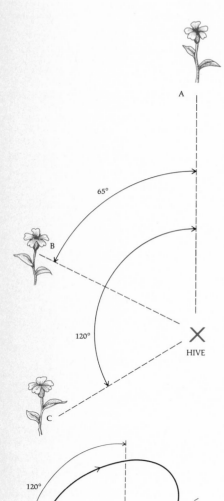

Features of Human Language

Constructed in this way, human language allows far greater flexibility in communication than is found in lower animals. In all human languages, immense flexibility has been demonstrated.

Interchangeability. The flexibility in human language is achieved partly because the roles of the encoder and decoder are interchangeable. Both the sources can transmit and receive the same message. This requirement seems simple enough, but it is not met in many elaborate communication rituals among animals. The male three-spined stickleback fish exhibits an almost frenzied, zigzag pattern of movements when it perceives the swollen abdomen of the female of the species, and this "dance" stimulates the female to deposit its eggs in the nest. Communication is involved but not language; neither the male nor female can reproduce the signals transmitted by the other.

Chimpanzee calls, which include emotional cries and a few other vocalizations, are essentially interchangeable, and for the most part their gestures and communicative postures can be used by any member of the species. In this limited sense, their communication resembles ours.

Displacement. Another feature of human language is *displacement*, which means that the encoder and decoder can communicate about things that are remote in time or space. This capacity is important in any society, especially a highly developed one, for thereby we

Figure 19-3 Communication among Bees. *In this dance, the size of the angle from the vertical shows the direction with respect to the sun. This bee is communicating that the source is at flower C. (From "Dialects in the Language of Bees" by K. von Frisch. Copyright © 1962 by Scientific American, Inc. All rights reserved.)*

can transmit our education, history, art, science, and technology from one generation or culture to the next.

Among bees, a certain communicative act so elaborate that it has been called the "language of the bees" seems to involve displacement. When a bee returns to its hive from a successful foraging trip, it brings with it nectar and pollen, which may signal the kind of flower the bee has visited, but much more information is conveyed by a special "dance" that the bee then performs. In one type of dance, the direction of the food is indicated by the direction of the "run" between pirouettes, and the distance is indicated by the rapidity of the tail-wagging during the run. Afterwards, the spectator bees perform the same dance, no doubt instinctively, and then they fly off unerringly to the site, even one that they have never visited previously (von Frisch, 1955; Figure 19-3).

This remarkable capacity for displacement is present in the communication of only a few other species. There is no solid evidence for it in the communications of wild chimpanzees, and it also seems to be absent in the gibbon, a close relation of the chimp.

Productivity. In human language new expressions can be formed from combinations of familiar signals. Thus, the system is open or *productive* and the response repertoire is essentially infinite.

When a chimpanzee finds food, it barks loudly and other chimps hurry to the scene. When threatened, it gives a soft pant-bark, and when attacked, it screams. Confronted with a potentially dangerous situation, the chimpanzee utters a spine-tingling "wraaa," and to maintain contact with others of its kind while out of sight, the animal emits "hooo" sounds interspersed with audible inspirations of air. It is believed that most chimpanzees in a colony can recognize one another by their distinctive "hooo" sounds (van Lawick-Goodall, 1971). But that is all. The chimpanzee call system contains only a small, finite

The Individual in Society

Design Features	Stickleback Courtship	Bee Dancing	Chimpanzee Calls
1. The vocal-auditory channel	No	No	Yes
2. Broadcast transmission and directional reception	Yes	Yes	Yes
3. Rapid fading (transitoriness)	?	?	Yes
4. Interchangeability	No	Limited	Yes
5. Total feedback	No	?	Yes
6. Specialization	In part	?	Yes
7. Semanticity	No	Yes	Yes
8. Arbitrariness	—	No	Yes
9. Discreteness	?	No	Yes
10. Displacement	—	Yes	No
11. Productivity	No	Yes	No
12. Traditional transmission	No	No	?
13. Duality of patterning	—	No	No

Figure 19-4 Systems of Communication. *A full description of all the design features of human language appears in "The Origin of Speech." (From "The Origin of Speech" by Charles F. Hockett. Copyright © 1960 by Scientific American, Inc. All rights reserved.)*

number of signals, which are not combined into new expressions. It is a closed system, with no evidence of productivity.

On the basis of these criteria and others, we cannot credit the wild chimpanzee or any other animal with a communication system that approaches the complexity of our language. Chimpanzee calls and gestures convey some very basic information about the immediate circumstances but not much more (Figure 19-4).

Acquisition of Language

One wonders, nevertheless, what Mr. Worzle might be able to accomplish in a special environment. The capacity for language might emerge with appropriate learning opportunities. We turn to this possibility after considering the normal course of language development in human beings.

Vocalizations and Word Recognition

Like other aspects of human development, the acquisition of language can be roughly characterized in terms of stages. Certain predictable changes occur in every normal child as he or she matures. While the rate at which these changes appear is not universal, the sequence of stages is essentially the same for all normal children.

Cooing. The first vocalizations of human infants are unpatterned sounds. They consist of crying, gurgling, a few other noises, and *cooing,* particularly when contented. During this early period, the infant's speech mechanisms continue to mature, perhaps partly as a result of this vocal activity. Some of these sounds also have reward value, bringing the caretaker to tend to the infant's needs.

The infant hears the sounds that he or she makes and, through muscular involvement, probably senses the motor aspects as well. This auditory and kinesthetic feedback may be further reinforcing, as a form of self-stimulation.

Babbling. There is a gradual transition from cooing to *babbling,* in which a particular sound pattern is repeated consistently, as occurs in "da-da-da" and "lal-lal-lal-lal." This behavior becomes prevalent in about the fifth month and clearly represents greater control over the speech mechanisms than the earlier unpatterned cooing, which is simply a reflex emission of air through the vocal cords, with little apparent relation to human language. In babbling, the baby's noises include many of the important sounds found in adult speech.

These babbling sounds are similar in all normal babies. Research has demonstrated that European, American, Asiatic, and other babies cannot be distinguished from one another on the basis of their vocalizations at this stage.

Word recognition. Around the eighth to eleventh month the typical baby begins to distinguish the meaningful phonemes in the language that he or she hears. Since these phonemes almost always appear in words, this stage is known as *word recognition*, and it consistently appears before word usage. Gradually, the baby shows an understanding of intonations, words, and phrases, although of course this learning continues for several years.

The test of an infant's word recognition is to observe his or her response in a given situation. At this age, for example, the infant clearly learns to avoid things said to be *hot*, although the child has no special sound to represent hotness.

Early Use of Words

The infant's first word, usually indistinguishable from babbling except by fond parents, is almost invariably a name of some sort. Hence, this next stage is called *naming* or the *first words*, and it generally appears around the twelfth month. When something is hot, the infant now gives it a name. Most likely he or she says ''ta'' because the front consonants, explosives such as *p* and *t*, and nasals such as *m* and *n*, are more readily produced than those from the back of the throat. However, the back vowels, such as *a* in ''mama,'' are the first to appear. Hence, it is no accident that ''mama'' and ''papa'' are such universal names for parents around the globe (Greenfield, 1973; McNeill, 1970).

Holophrastic expressions. The first words are used principally to designate persons or objects, but the exact meaning varies with the situation. Thus, ''mama'' might mean ''That's mama,'' or ''Mama come here,'' or ''I'm hungry'' (Slobin, 1971). In many ways,

the successful communicator in these instances is the parent, who decodes the message, not the child, who transmits signals that are both limited and ambiguous. Such expressions are sometimes called *holophrastic*, meaning that a single word is intended to convey a more complex idea.

The beginning of language ability in the child, according to many experts, is not the child's first word. It occurs when he or she first puts words together. Prior to this event, we cannot speak of an active grammar or language system (Brown, 1973a; Crystal, 1973).

Stage I expressions. Sometime between the first and second year, the normal human child achieves the developmental landmark of using words in combinations. This point is called the beginning of Stage I of language development. More specifically, Stage I begins when the mean length of utterance (MLU), measured in terms of morphemes, first rises above 1.0, and it continues until the MLU is 2.0. Longer combinations of morphemes sometimes occur within this first stage, but the average is less than 2.0.

These first word combinations are known as *telegraphic utterances* because, like telegrams, they are highly abbreviated but contain the most important elements. Thus, the mother says ''Now your toy is lost.'' The child responds, ''Toy lost.'' The father says ''Let's go to the tennis court.'' The child replies, ''Go tennis.''

These early combinations have been analyzed extensively in several languages in order to determine the relationships being expressed, and in general the results agree fairly well with the developmental concepts of Jean Piaget. Within his or her limited language, the child just over one year old is talking about a sensory-motor world. The infant is primarily concerned with experiencing things and with actions directed towards them, and the infant's expressions reflect this sensory-motor orientation.

In terms of semantic relations, or meanings, 75 percent of the child's expressions fit into one of 10 to 12 simple categories. Commonly, the expression is nominative, or naming, as when the child says "That ball." Sometimes it indicates recurrence, as in "More ball." Often it shows possession, such as "Daddy chair." Virtually all of the child's expressions can be accounted for in terms of 18 such semantic relations (Figure 19-5).

Word Combination	Relation
That ball	Naming
More ball	Recurrence
All gone ball	Disappearance
Daddy chair	Possession
Go store	Location
Big house	Attribution
Daddy hit	Agent-action
Hit ball	Action-object

Figure 19-5   Relations in Stage I Word Combinations. *(After Brown, 1973a)*

Forming Complex Constructions

After mastering phonemes and combinations of morphemes, the next problem is syntax. Language almost always requires a certain sequence. For example, there is a very important difference between "Tom hit Sally" and "Sally hit Tom."

Word order. Consider Kathryn, an American girl 21 months old. Her MLU is 1.32, which is expected at this age, and she has seen her mother's stockings lying on the floor. She points to them and says "Mommy's sock." From the context, this expression seems to mean "Mother's socks," and the word order is correct. The child did not say "Socks' Mommy." In instances of this type, in which two orders should occur equally on a chance basis, normal children of Kathryn's age commonly use the correct one. Apparently they have some understanding of word sequence (Brown, 1973a).

Children's efforts to master word order are seen in *grammatical transformations,* which require changes in word forms and sentence construction with various expressions. Children learn, for example, that in simple statements the subject generally appears before the verb. They also learn that the "wh" words, such as "what," "why," and "when," always come first in questions. Thus, their first "wh" questions become, "Where I should put it?" and "What he can ride in?" Only gradually does the child learn to change the positions of the subject and auxiliary verb in these instances, asking "What can he ride in?," and so forth. Interestingly, when the "wh" word is not involved, the child readily reverses the subject and auxiliary verb to form a question, for example, "Can he ride in it?" Apparently the child can master one change, the inclusion of the "wh" word *or* the change in sequence, but not both together when first learning to form questions.

Language units.   Eventually, the MLU reaches 2.0, and then the child has begun Stage II. Three more stages are identified, each accompanied by an increase of .50 in the MLU, up to Stage V at 3.5, but none of them has been studied as carefully as Stage I.

The content of these stages is extremely useful in studying language acquisition. Two children with the same MLU are much more likely to show the same language constructions than are two children who are simply of the same chronological age. There is variation in the individual rate of development, but at all stages the order of occurrence of new constructions is essentially constant, even for different languages (Figure 19-6).

Figure 19-6 Combining Words. *The mean length of utterance rises consistently with age, although a given child may be consistently ahead of or behind most others of his or her age. The one decrement in Eve's progress, at about age two years, occurred when she had a cold (Brown, 1973a).*

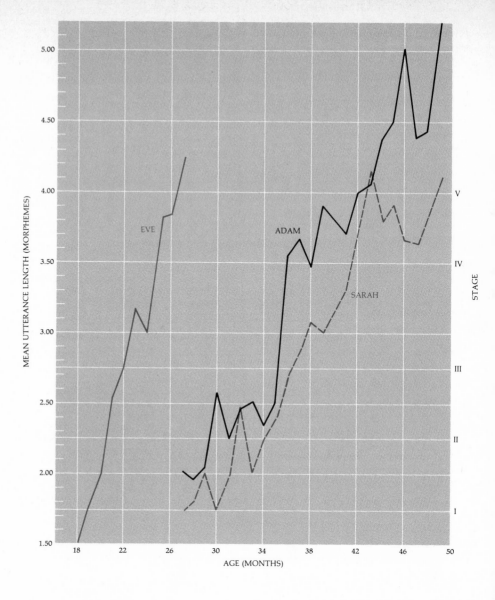

Figure 19-7 Language Tree. *At some indeterminate level, Susan understands this diagram in the sense that her language reflects the two main branches of the tree.*

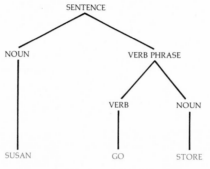

In Stage II, the child's utterances not only become longer but they become organized into units and subunits. This development is evident in Susan's expression, "Go store," which she later expanded into the three-word sentence, "Susan go store." In the child's thinking, the word "Susan" apparently was one unit and the phrase "go store" another, and the two eventually were combined (Figure 19-7).

As the sentences grow still more complicated, they further reflect the hierarchical structure of language. Even the child's speech hesitations reflect a comprehension of linguistic units. The child says, "Put . . . the red hat . . . on"; the verb comes first, then the complete noun phrase, and then the isolated preposition. Careful studies show that the average child does not say, "Put the . . . red hat on," or even "Put the red . . . hat on." The verb and the noun phrase are recognized as distinct linguistic units. The speaker somehow perceives the underlying grammatical elements (Brown & Bellugi, 1964). On the basis of such studies, psychologists and linguists have been much impressed by the similarity of language acquisition in all normal children, even beyond the first few years (Palermo & Molfese, 1972).

A Comparative Study

Some years ago, Winthrop and Luella Kellogg decided to study the similarities and differences in language acquisition not among normal children but between their ten-month-old son Donald and a chimpanzee of approximately the same age. Accordingly, Gua, a seven and one-half month-old female chimpanzee was adopted into their household, to be treated in the same fashion as Donald. Both infants wore diapers, were dressed alike, and were fed in the same way. They were allowed equal play opportunities, slept at the same times, and the parents tried hard to give them equal affection. In going to the park, going to bed, or being toilet trained, both had essentially similar experiences (Figure 19-8).

At this time, in the early 1930s, no one had reared a young chimpanzee just like a human infant for purposes of research. The Kelloggs were interested in all facets of the chimp's development—physical, emotional, social, intellectual, and communicative.

Figure 19-8 Gua and Donald. *The chimpanzee and the child followed the same daily schedule (Kellogg and Kellogg, 1933).*

A.M.

7:00	Reveille.
7:30	Breakfast.
8:00 to 8:30	Sit in high chair while adults breakfast.
9:00 to 11:30	One or more of the following:

    Ride in perambulator.
    Physiological measures.
    Observation of special behavior.
    Automobile ride to Experiment Station (for weighing.)
    Photographs.
    Outdoor or indoor play.
    Experiments, tests, or measurements.

12:00	Lunch.

P.M.

12:15 to 1:30	Nap.
1:30 to 2:00	Walk or play out-of-doors for Gua. (Donald still sleeps.)
2:00 to 2:30	Bath.
3:00	6 to 8 oz. milk.
3:30 to 4:00	One or more of the following:

    Outdoor or indoor play.
    Observation.
    Photographs.
    Experiments, tests, or measurements.

6:00	Supper.
6:30	Retire.

Figure 19-9 Word Comprehension. *For example, the command addressed to Donald was "Take Gua's hand," but at first the chimpanzee responded more readily (Kellogg & Kellogg, 1967).*

Months of Training	Distinctive Responses	
	Ape	Child
2	7	2
4	14	8
5	21	20
6	28	32
9	58	68

Word recognition. Shortly after the experiment began, Gua became slightly superior to Donald in word recognition. "No, no" was the first command she learned, followed by "Kiss, kiss," both of which were understood in the first month of training. In the next weeks, the animal continued to surpass the child.

Donald's early inferiority might be explained on the basis of less physical ability, however. The ape was more agile and therefore could respond more readily to requests such as, "Get up on the chair." Also, the animal was generally more cooperative than the boy. In any given instance it was difficult to tell whether the child's inferior response was due to his lesser comprehension of language or to his lesser cooperation (Figure 19-9).

As time passed, the child gained rapidly on the chimpanzee, and he was significantly ahead by the end of the research. In fact, the investigators suggest that their data do not do full justice to Donald's superiority at the conclusion of the nine-month period of investigation (Kellogg & Kellogg, 1933; Kellogg, 1968).

Use of words. In using morphemes, Donald showed much more progress than Gua, although he lagged behind human babies of his age, perhaps because he rarely played with other children during the months of research. Neighbors generally did not extend to him opportunities to play with their children because Gua would have to come along too, according to the research plan.

Gua remained nonverbal throughout the experiment, although her communication included some gestures; she threw herself on the floor when sleepy and wiggled her lips in the direction of apples when she wanted to eat them. At age 16 months, she had only four vocalizations, and she never progressed to the use of words. Her loud bark seemed to say "Get away from me," or "Let me alone"; a softer bark was emitted in anticipation of food; she uttered a screech in times of fear or pain; and finally her "oo-oo" cry indicated uncertainty, anxiety, and minor excitement.

Donald had passed through the normal sequence of cooing and babbling, practicing consonants and vowels along the way, and by the end of the research period he spoke a few words. He said "ba," meaning "boo," "da" for "down," and "bow-wow" to indicate the dog, but he did not use words in combination. His parents concluded that neither infant had learned to use language during the experimental study (Kellogg & Kellogg, 1933). The child had not approached Stage I, while the chimpanzee had made almost no progress whatsoever.

In other areas, such as toilet training, the ape's performance more closely resembled that of the child. In physical skills, furthermore, she developed rapidly. In fact, her increasing strength and enormous agility around the house prompted discontinuation of the research.

Theories of Language Learning

How does Donald or any other child learn language? When asked, the casual observer will generally say that imitation is the crucial factor. The child copies what he or she hears, in a process called modeling.

One child learns the Portuguese language; another learns English. Within English, an Australian acquires one accent and the Texan another. To indicate half past ten, the Irish child says "half ten" while the American says "ten thirty." Examples in support of imitation are endless, but there is more involved.

If children learn only by mimicking, how do we account for their predictable errors, not found in adult language? Further, how do we explain the fact that deaf children learn to speak? Helen Keller lost her capacity for vision and hearing at age 18 months, yet she mastered English not as a series of mechanical signals but as an instrument of thought (Figure 19-10).

The Conditioning Viewpoint

Adult speakers in the environment are certainly important, for they serve to help children sort out which of the many possible human sounds are relevant in their own particular language community. According to the conditioning viewpoint, they also serve to shape the understanding and use of morphemes.

Operant and classical processes. The most important aspect of language learning in this theory is the reinforcement that the child receives for making the sounds that approximate the words of his or her language. The infant's first vocalizations are reinforced by parents, who cuddle and smile when the baby begins cooing and babbling. They also imitate the sounds made by the infant, and gradually infants become aware of their own capacity for stimulating and satisfying themselves in this way. As attention, food, and other attractive outcomes are gained through these vocalizations, they become closer and closer approximations to adult speech. This aspect, the performance of verbal behavior, illustrates operant conditioning.

Classical conditioning is also involved. Someone says "daddy" and the father appears; after several pairings of this nature, "daddy" comes to signify the father. Eventually the child says "da-da," for which he or she usually receives considerable reinforcement. In the same way the child masters "mama,"

"milk," and thousands of other words. Shaping, extinction, secondary reinforcement, and stimulus generalization are the chief conditioning principles by which words are acquired (Garcia & De-Haven 1974).

Emphasis on functions. The analysis described in the preceding section, as originally presented by B. F. Skinner, also distinguishes between mands and tacts. The term *mand* designates words, phrases, or sentences that have an element of demand or request, such as "Up," meaning "Lift me up," or "Go!" A word that names, symbolizes, or represents some object or event in the environment, such as "ball," is called a *tact,* suggesting the idea of making contact with something. Both types of responses are reinforced by what follows, such as the cooperation of the other person, praise, fondling, and so forth. Today, this distinction is not considered important except to indicate that this approach to language learning emphasizes the function of the child's responses, rather than their grammatical classifications.

Figure 19-10   Helen Keller's Ability. *The reasoning process is especially important in true language acquisition, as demonstrated by the blind-deaf Helen Keller, who suddenly discovered in a flash that everything can have a name. One morning during her seventh year, Helen patted the hand of Miss Sullivan, her teacher, and pointed to running water, signifying that she wanted to know its name. At this time Helen knew a few words, but only in a rote manner; she did not know how to use the words or that everything could be named.*

The word "water" was spelled out on her hand in the manual alphabet, and later, while she was filling a cup at the pump, it was spelled for her again. This time the cold water was overflowing on her free hand, and the spelling of the word at the same time had a remarkable effect, which Miss Sullivan describes in the following way:

"The word, coming so close upon the sensation of cold water rushing over her hand seemed to startle her. She dropped the mug and stood as one transfixed. A new light came into her face. She spelled water several times. Then she dropped to the ground and asked for its name and pointed to the pump and the trellis, and suddenly turning round she asked for my name. I spelled 'Teacher.' Just then the nurse brought Helen's little sister into the pump-house and Helen spelled 'baby' and pointed to the nurse. All the way back to the house she was highly excited, and learned the name of every object she touched, so that in a few hours she had added 30 new words to her vocabulary" (Keller, 1903). (Culver Pictures)

Later, two-word combinations, three-word combinations, and eventually whole sentences develop. At first the child says "Daddy"—a tact. Later, the child says "Daddy up"—a tact and a mand. At a later stage, the child requests, "Daddy me up high," in which formerly separate responses have been linked together. If the child is lifted on these occasions and finds it pleasurable, the phrase is repeated and expanded on later occasions. As such reinforcement continues, together with chaining and response hierarchies, the child's expressions appear in successively larger and more complex units. And as intermittent reinforcement becomes more significant, saying a whole sentence is reinforced merely by hearing a response from someone else. Largely through these extensions of conditioning principles, the child becomes increasingly more capable in language.

The training of Viki. In the 1950s, a test of the conditioning approach to language learning was begun when Viki, a six-week-old chimpanzee, was introduced into the household of Cathy and Keith Hayes. The idea was to give this animal more direct and intensive language training than that provided for any previous chimpanzee, including Gua, and thereby to discover whether she might achieve a significantly higher level of verbal ability.

Since Viki showed no cooing or babbling, the first problem was to induce her to make nonemotional sounds. At first it seemed hopeless, but once when her food was about to be taken away, she became concerned and emitted little "oo-oo" sounds. For such reflex vocalizations, she was immediately given reinforcement, in this case a sip of milk. Later, when she made some reflex barking sounds, she was given more milk.

Viki was not "speaking" spontaneously, however. For five weeks, such noises were "tricked" out of her and then on one notable day, with face contorted and much obvious effort, she

Figure 19-11   Teaching Viki to Say "Mama."   *At first, Viki's lips were moved for her; later, touching her lips with a finger prompted her to say "Mama." Afterwards, she needed no help at all. (From* The Ape in our House *by C. Hayes, published by McIntosh and Otis, Inc., 1951. Used with permission of McIntosh and Otis, Inc.)*

began to make a sound like "ahhh" and reached for the milk. At long last, Viki apparently was vocalizing intentionally, and she was immediately reinforced. Later she went "ahhh" when she was requested to speak, and she made this same sound when "asking" for things.

In addition to these typical operant techniques, the Hayeses increased Viki's chances of speaking by manipulating her lips directly. They pressed her lips together and moved them as she said "ahhh," and eventually the animal learned to say a word approximating "mama." Finally, she made this vocalization without aid, under obviously relevant circumstances, as when it would bring food. "Papa" was similarly acquired after Viki had learned to imitate close approximations. Later the word "cup" was learned, as combinations of the sounds "k" and "p," one quickly following the other (Hayes, 1951; Figure 19-11).

Viki also learned to click her teeth when she wanted to go for a ride, but her record as a speaker of the English language is not very impressive. It consisted of no more than these three or four "words," never combined in the form of a Stage I utterance, despite several years of intensive training. In no way

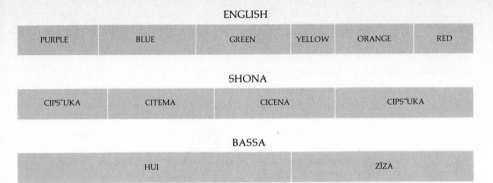

ENGLISH

| PURPLE | BLUE | GREEN | YELLOW | ORANGE | RED |

SHONA

| CIPS"UKA | CITEMA | CICENA | CIPS"UKA |

BASSA

| HUI | ZÌZA |

Figure 19-12 Color Spectrum in Three Languages. *The results reflect differences in the classification of colors rather than in color vision. (From* An Introduction to Descriptive Linguistics, *Revised Edition by H. A. Gleason. Copyright © 1955, 1961 by Holt, Rinehart and Winston, Inc. Reprinted by permission of Holt, Rinehart and Winston.)*

does her achievement meet our criteria for human language.

If we assume that Viki's training was adequate, then there are two possible explanations for her lack of success. Operant conditioning perhaps is not the basic process or the only process in language acquisition, or the animal's limitations in speech mechanisms and mental ability may have been too severe. No other primate has ever demonstrated the fine coordination of lips, tongue, and throat mechanisms displayed by a young child in speaking (Canning & Rose, 1974; Lenneberg, 1964).

The Information Processing Approach

However, another view of language acquisition was presented by Noam Chomsky in the 1950s. It described language as an exceedingly complex skill, argued that conditioning models cannot readily account for a listener's ability to understand complicated sentences never heard previously, and emphasized the role of the human mind as an information processing system (Chomsky, 1957).

A genetic predisposition. Chomsky argued that human beings inherit a deeply ingrained predisposition for using specific language structures. We are, so to speak, "wired" to speak; we are born with a specific aptitude for acquiring the rules of grammar. This capacity is part of our biological inheritance, although the particular language we learn—English, Shona, or Bassa—as well as our dialect and accent, of course, are influenced by the environment (Figure 19-12).

Similarities in languages throughout the world are cited by some linguists as evidence for this inborn predisposition. For example, the vocalizations in all the world's languages use only a fraction of the sounds that human beings are capable of making. In addition, there is a similarity in hierarchical structure, in which word symbols are juxtaposed to form larger units, such as phrases, sentences, and the grammar of full discourse. Not all linguists accept the similarity-in-language hypothesis, but it is also stressed that there is no cultural group that does not have a fully developed language. The languages of primitive African and Australian tribes are comparable in morphemes and syntax to those of the most advanced European communities. In fact, "the earliest reconstructable stage for any language shows all the complexities and flexibility of the languages of today" (Hockett, 1960).

A creative process. Perhaps most important of all is the remarkable rapidity with which all normal children acquire essentially the same complex grammar. This outcome, it is speculated, must be due to some internal capacity of the organism for processing immense amounts of verbal information. This idea underscores the *information processing* viewpoint. The chief contributions in language learning come not from the environment, as the conditioning approach would have it, but rather from the interaction of environmental influence with the unique information processing characteristics of the human organism.

In other words, in learning language, children are thinking about the words and sentences that they hear and are trying to make some sense out of them, as shown in their errors. A girl says "hisself," although she rarely if ever hears this expression, and generally she is not reinforced for using it. She arrives at the idea, apparently, from analyzing language.

In English, reflexive pronouns are made by combining the possessive pronoun—your, my, her, and so forth—with "self," and, thus, "hisself" is a logical derivation. Similarly, children create expressions such as "digged" and "goed," which would be correct if the verbs were not irregular: When these overgeneralizations occur regularly, children show that they are acquiring the rules of grammar (Brown, 1973b). On such bases, language is regarded as a creative activity on the part of the child, not a "stamping in" process on the part of the environment.

Deep and surface structure.   Thus, this "creative" approach to language focuses more on syntax and grammar than does the conditioning model. It is concerned with how human beings process or understand an infinite number of possible sentences, and it is postulated that any given sentence reflects two kinds of structure. The *deep structure* refers to the underlying meaning, thought, or intent of the sentence, while *surface structure* refers to the order in which the words actually occur. Furthermore, the operations that relate surface structure to deep structure are known as *transformations* or transformational rules.

A sentence that closely represents deep structure might be a simple declarative sentence—The boy caught the dog. Other sentences, more complex in nature, are understood by using appropriate rules to transform surface structures into the deep structure. Among these transformations are those for the passive voice—The dog was caught by the boy; negation—The boy has not caught the dog; and interrogation—Has the boy caught the dog? Note that the relations among the key words, "boy" and "dog," remain unchanged despite the different surface structures. In all instances, the boy is the agent and the dog is the object of his action. Thus, transformational rules enable the language user to deal with variations in surface structure as related to the deep structure, or meaning, of the sentence.

A Combined Perspective

Viewed broadly, the two basic requirements for any language are signals, composed of phonemes and morphemes, and a system for assembling these signals into phrases and sentences, known as syntax. When we consider these two aspects of language separately, a tentative resolution can be achieved between Skinner's conditioning approach and Chomsky's information processing orientation.

Language habits.   When one is learning the basic signals of his or her language, such as vocabulary and tonal expressions, the conditioning principles seem most important. The child is learning to attach certain meanings to certain symbols, and often the relationship is arbitrary. He or she learns the word "book" in connection with this thing you are now reading, but it might have been called "desk," "cloud," "bag," or anything else, as far as the child is concerned. In the classical conditioning tradition the learning process takes place as the word "book" is spoken or written on several occasions when the object is present. After many such associations, the child recognizes the word as a substitute for the thing (Stemmer, 1973).

Later, in operant fashion, the child says the word "book" and other words and receives some sort of reinforcement; thus, the child uses words more and more (Garcia & DeHaven, 1974). In terms of two-factor theory, it appears that word meanings are acquired essentially through classical conditioning, and word usage is acquired through the operant process. These results are referred to as language habits.

Language rules. Eventually the child's language becomes more complex and vocabulary grows markedly. Since there is no evidence that the conditioning process changes sharply at this time, how can we explain the extremely rapid increase in vocabulary in the third and subsequent years? One answer is that the child is using words to acquire new words. The child asks, using an incorrect grammatical construction, "But what means 'bucket'?" The parent replies that a bucket is essentially a pail, and thus the child has increased his or her vocabulary not so much by conditioning as by understanding words, using them, and thinking about them.

The conditioning process appears even more inadequate as an explanation of language learning when the child begins combining words and intonations in such a systematic way that they become sentences, not random words, and permit the enormous nuances of meaning that are characteristic of a true language. The child often makes basically correct grammatical constructions, with or without minor elements, even though he or she has never previously heard the particular sequence of sounds. At some underlying level, at which he or she is unable to articulate to an adult, the child is formulating and following "rules" about how the language works. Even the child's incorrect grammatical constructions, as in "teached" and "hitted," suggest that the speaker is following some rule.

In recent years, studies of language acquisition in older children have clearly moved away from the conditioning approach towards the more creative aspects of language postulated in the information processing approach (Lewis, 1971). The process of reasoning by analogy, in which the child knows "wait-waited" and therefore says "teach-teached," has received a great deal of attention.

A synthesis. The environment, it is agreed, is a necessary condition for language development. The child must have the opportunity to learn the sounds, words, and meanings of his or her language. But beyond this aspect, the child must learn a well-constructed system for using these basic ingredients; that is, the child must learn language rules. The relatively short time within which an implicit understanding of these rules is mastered suggests to some linguists that there is an innate predisposition towards this aspect of language competence. In short, conditioning may best explain the learning of words, sounds, and meanings, known as language habits, while the information processing capacities of the human organism may best explain the learning of word constructions and syntax, known as language rules.

In passing, we should note that there are also two competing theories regarding the origin of language in the human species, rather than the individual. According to one view, our language had its earliest beginnings in the vocalizations of our animal ancestors, such as the reflex "oo-oo" sounds made by Gua when she was in pain and by Viki when she was about to lose her dinner. Thus, human language eventually evolved from the call systems of our predecessors, as illustrated in the "wraaa," "hooo," bark, and other emotional animal sounds (Hockett, 1960).

■ I'd like to pose a question that I've considered off and on a great deal—If two babies were isolated from any verbal contact with adults, would they develop their own language in order to communicate with each other? The experiment could never be performed because it would ruin the lives of two human beings, but speculation on whether they would develop a language and the form that the language would take is inviting.

More recently, it has been argued that a pre-existing system of gestures seems the more likely stepping-stone to human language. The tool-using behavior of chimpanzees, in which they are observed to imitate one another and make signals regarding the use of instruments, and the continuing role of gestures in human language are presented in support of this view (Hewes, 1973). Both views, however, lack convincing evidence. We simply do not know any answer to this question about the origin of language in human beings, and there is no compelling reason to believe that we shall discover one soon. ■

Language, Communication, and Culture

To find out whether the chimpanzee is capable of learning language habits, and perhaps even basic language rules, the problem of the animal's limited speech mechanisms must be resolved. For this purpose, Allen and Beatrice Gardner

raised a wild-born, one-year-old female chimpanzee named Washoe, and spoke not a word in her presence. As soon as Washoe arrived, she was exposed only to American Sign Language (ASL), the gestural form of communication employed by the deaf in North America. In this system, hand gestures, or signs, are used instead of words. The sign for "listen" is made by touching the ear with the index finger, and "dog" is signed by slapping oneself on the thigh (Figure 19-13).

A Test of Animal Capacity

During the four years of the experiment with Washoe, the ASL gestures were taught to her through modeling, operant conditioning, and, in some cases, direct manipulation of the hands. Whenever Washoe imitated a sign that was modeled by one of her experimenters, she was immediately tickled, an experience that she obviously enjoyed. Once, when Washoe brought her hands together at the tickled region in a pattern crudely

Figure 19-13   Learning Sign Language. *The American Sign Language sign for "drink" is made by placing the thumb between the lips. This drawing shows a chimpanzee learning to make this sign.*

The Individual in Society

resembling the ASL sign for "more," she was tickled again. When she made still another such gesture, even more tickling occurred. Gradually, in this operant conditioning, closer approximations were required before each reinforcement, and finally an acceptable ASL sign for "more" was established.

The sign for "tree" was taught to Washoe by manipulating her arm, bending it at the elbow, and making her grasp the elbow with her free hand. If she did not do so, sometimes the experimenter grasped it himself, thus teaching partly through manipulation and partly through modeling (Fouts, 1972).

In these ways, Washoe acquired a larger and larger vocabulary, learning at a more rapid rate as the experiment progressed. Like a normal child, rather than becoming more confused as more words were added, she seemed to learn them more easily and had a vocabulary of 160 signs at the end of the four-year experiment (Fleming, 1974; Figure 19-14).

Word combinations. Washoe has used more than one hundred signs during just one meal, and she has employed them in several contexts. The sign for "more" has been used for more pushing, more swinging, and more food. "Funny" has been signed in diverse humorous situations. "Dog," "flower," and other signs have been used with pictures, as well as for the objects themselves. As indicated earlier, however, the beginning of language ability is not the child's first use of words but first success in putting them together.

After three years, Washoe had made 294 different two-sign combinations. When comparisons are made with Stage I language in human beings, 228 of Washoe's combinations, which is 78 percent, were similar to the earliest two-word combinations of children (Figure 19-15). This finding suggests that 4-year-old Washoe, who began training at age 1 year, has been using language much like a child approximately 16 to 27 months old (Brown, 1973a). On this basis, Washoe's attainment is noteworthy, despite the fact that she lags behind a human child. She "speaks" ASL, which may have a slower developmental rate than English, and her teachers were not native signers, which also may have influenced her progress.

Word order. When any language user reaches an MLU greater than 1.00, the next task is that of word order. Unfortunately, the evidence for word order has not yet been made available in Washoe's case. Washoe uses many correct sequences, but she also makes mistakes, such as signing "Drink you" instead of "You drink." Despite their importance, we simply do not know the exact frequencies of her appropriate and inappropriate word orders or how they compare with those of human babies, especially deaf children using ASL as a first language (Brown, 1973a).

Washoe apparently has achieved Stage I of human language development, but just how far she or others like her will progress remains to be observed. Educated human beings use language in highly abstract and complex ways, far in advance of Washoe's level of communication, as illustrated even in

Months of Training	Total Signs Used
7	4
14	13
27	34
36	85
48	160

Figure 19-14 Acquisition of Signs by Washoe. *The table shows the increasingly rapid rate of learning. (From Gardner & Gardner, 1969)*

Word Combination	Significance
In hat	Location
Dirty monkey	Attribution
Roger tickle	Agent-action
Gimme key	Action-object

Figure 19-15 Washoe's Word Combinations

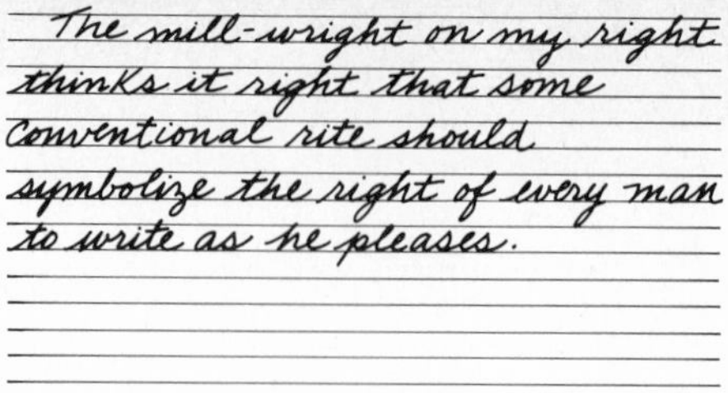

Figure 19-16 Complexity of Language. *Here, one sound is spelled four different ways, used as four different parts of speech, and has more than four different meanings. (From Lashley, 1951. Used by permission of the California Institute of Technology.)*

The mill-wright on my right thinks it right that some conventional rite should symbolize the right of every man to write as he pleases.

Franklin Roosevelt's simple wartime slogan for the American people, "All we have to fear is fear itself" (Figure 19-16).

Intraspecies communication. Today there are perhaps two dozen chimpanzees similar to Washoe, currently being schooled in one way or another. One chimpanzee is acquiring language on a vertical keyboard console that communicates with a computer and keeps records of all the conversations. After six months of training, this chimpanzee was able to "read" word symbols corresponding to those on her keyboard (Rumbaugh et al., 1973). Another chimpanzee, using ASL, has progressed to the point at which she called a radish "food" until she experienced the bitter taste. With no sign for this flavor, she immediately called it "cry hurt food" (Fleming, 1974). Still another chimpanzee, acquiring language by using plastic chips as word-symbols, apparently can respond correctly to compound sentences, even those involving two different commands (Premack, 1970, 1971).

Suppose that Washoe or one of these other chimpanzees progresses to Stage V of language development. Better yet, suppose that two or three chimps do so. What then? Has the chimpanzee achieved our level of communication?

Language learning in chimpanzees will be most impressive not when one or two or more animals can communicate with human beings through cleverly arranged human systems but when they use language to cooperate with and instruct each other. Hence, some young male chimpanzees are currently being

prepared for such an experiment. They are being taught a specified and intentionally limited number of ASL signs. Then, when they know the rudiments of this language well and the time is right, they will be exposed to Washoe. With this start, will the more learned chimpanzee be capable of and interested in tutoring the youngsters in a fuller use of language? If so, only then can we say that the species, through language, is perhaps headed towards a cultural evolution—that is, to a significantly higher level of social organization than it now displays.

Forms of Human Communication

Washoe's language is *nonverbal*, meaning that it does not involve words. Except for sign languages, such as ASL, this type of communication may seem of small importance, until we look at it closely. Then we discover that it is extremely prevalent, often efficient, and sometimes quite subtle. In many cases, a nonverbal communication can express one's intention more adequately than words. ▪

Nonverbal signals. Every society employs *gestures* in order to communicate, such as facial expressions, head-shaking, and nose-thumbing, but these actions may have different meanings in different cultures. The Spanish hand signals for beckoning someone are almost the opposite of those used in the United States. An American boy in Madrid was chastised by his Spanish teacher for responding improperly to her signal. To him, it meant that he should move further away.

One's *posture* constitutes another category of nonverbal signals. A man may stand firmly erect, as though he is "master of all he surveys" or he may walk in a stooped manner, indicating utter despair. Much has been written about "reading" another person's thoughts by decoding his or her different postures, especially in a business conference. These findings are suggestive, but they are not well documented.

▪ *Recently, a friend of mine died in a tragic accident. His close friends, also close friends of mine, were extremely emotionally upset by this event and I felt I should try to help. But what can one say? I have never known anyone to know the right words to say or how to say them in a situation such as this. Finally, I approached one of my friends, and grasped his hand tightly and held it. Nothing was said, but I think he knew what I meant.*

Figure 19-17 Nonverbal Communication. *Choosing to sit together on the bag rather than farther apart in the available space is an instance of nonverbal communication between the two young men. Nonverbal communication is also apparently taking place between them and the photographer. (Prelutsky from Stock, Boston)*

Less obvious than gestures or postures, but still with communicative significance, are the *objects* that a person possesses, such as clothes, car, books, and bathing suit. A barrier across the road tells us that we should go no farther; the junk lying by the roadside tells us that someone has been careless, if not malicious. The reader need only look around to discover the many subtle and obvious instances of nonverbal communication and appreciate their significance in human behavior (Figure 19-17).

Verbal meanings. The powerful influence of *verbal* communication is known to all of us. In many respects, words are the binding force in society. This form of communication has been considered in many instances throughout this book, but so far we have focused only on denotative meanings. The *denotative meaning* of a word or other symbol points to something; it denotes something specific and generally does not cause much confusion. The denotative meaning of the word ''pencil'' is much the same for all of us—an elongated object containing graphite that is used for writing.

On the other hand, *connotative meaning* concerns abstract qualities or properties, often with emotional implications. The denotative meaning of the word ''pig'' is a four-legged mammal with coarse bristles, but when this word is applied to a human being, the connotative meaning suggests that this person is unclean, greedy, or obese, since the denotation clearly does not apply. This example gives the merest hint of the nuances that are added to language by connotative meanings. Such meanings give the skillful writer or speaker a powerful expressive tool, but at the same time they increase the possibilities of misunderstanding.

In a single communication, both connotative and denotative meanings can be used, with verbal and nonverbal signals. In fact, human communication typically involves *multiple signals,* in which several messages are sent and received

simultaneously (Figure 19-18). Psychological research on communication is concerned with not only spoken but also unspoken messages whenever people interact (Miller, 1974).

Communication and Persuasion

Whenever people interact, persuasion is commonly involved. Even when two friends talk together, one often tries to persuade the other to accept a certain viewpoint. Persuasion is also the aim in many public speeches and television broadcasts. Campaigns to persuade people to buckle seat belts, stop smoking, and go to church are familiar to all of us, and certain principles have emerged from research on this aspect of communication.

Lecture versus discussion. During World War II, choice cuts of meat were scarce; hence, attempts were made to persuade people to use less-preferred meat products. In one approach, some subjects listened to a lecture on using these products, while others were involved in group discussion about the problems they might experience in using such foods and how they might overcome them. At a later date, the investigators checked to discover the effectiveness of the two presentations and found that the discussion method was much superior in precipitating a change in attitude and behavior (Lewin, 1947).

In an industrial setting, factory workers showed markedly decreased work output whenever new production procedures were introduced, but after group discussions, attitudes towards job changes and work output improved considerably (Coch & French, 1948; Figure 19-19). The superiority of group discussion is attributed to individual involvement, as compared with the relative passivity of lectures (Conte et al., 1974). However, such studies do not indicate that discussion necessarily should replace lectures in a classroom, even if this were practical. The lecture method is considerably more efficient for simply providing detailed or technical information to large groups of people.

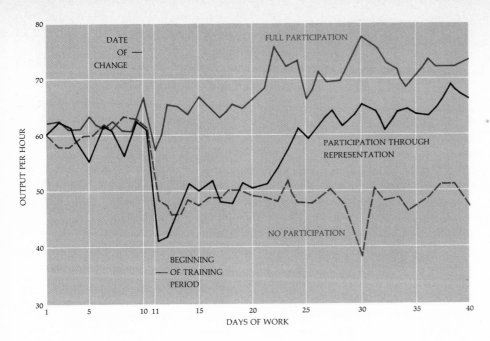

OUTPUT PER HOUR

DATE OF CHANGE

FULL PARTICIPATION

PARTICIPATION THROUGH REPRESENTATION

NO PARTICIPATION

BEGINNING OF TRAINING PERIOD

DAYS OF WORK

Figure 19-19   Participation and Motivation.   *The graphs show a difference in production when the employees were allowed no participation in work plans, participation through an elected representative, and direct discussions with supervisors. (From L. Coch and J. R. P. French, "Overcoming resistance to change,"* Human Relations, *1, 512-532, 1948, by permission of Plenum Publishing Corporation.)*

One-sided versus two-sided presentation.   Suppose that a speaker wishes to persuade an audience to adopt and maintain viewpoint A. Should viewpoint B be ignored completely or should it be acknowledged? In general, the findings indicate that a communicator, to achieve the most lasting effect, should also present the opposing viewpoint and counterarguments. In this way, the audience has been prepared against future propaganda on behalf of viewpoint B. It seems that people can be inoculated against psychological as well as physical conditions.

In other words, we can say that a two-sided presentation, in which the speaker discusses both the pros and the cons of an issue, can provide "immunization" against later exposure to opposing viewpoints (McGuire, 1964). This approach appears particularly important for audiences of high intelligence.

Perceived intention.   Another factor in the persuasiveness of a communication is its perceived intention. In one instance, some college students touring a psychology laboratory "overheard" a private conversation concerning misconceptions on smoking. Actually, it was intended that they hear it. Other students were permitted to listen directly to the conversation, which was the same recording in both instances, while control subjects were not exposed to the recording. Analysis of the subjects' attitudes one week later showed that both communications were persuasive, but the difference was clearly in favor of the "overheard" conversation (Walster & Festinger, 1962; Figure 19-20). It appears from these and other studies that a communication may be more effective when the subject does not perceive the speaker as having the intention of persuading someone.

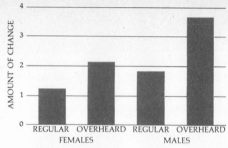

Figure 19-20 Influence of Overheard Communication. *The graph shows the amount of attitude change following the direct and overheard communications. (Photo by Harbutt from Magnum)*

This finding suggests a way in which parents might impart information to children who are reluctant listeners. Particularly during adolescence, children seem quite attentive to "overheard" conversations between adults about sex, money, and interpersonal relations, but they are not particularly inclined to attend to formal discourse on these matters.

Credibility of the source. When speaking on politics, economics, and the future of European civilization, Winston Churchill had enormous credibility. If he were alive today and speaking on computer techniques, his message presumably would be less persuasive, since he was a trustworthy person but not an expert in the computer field. The crucial elements of credibility are *trust* and *expertise* in a given context.

A convincing demonstration of the importance of credibility occurred when students were exposed to communications on several different issues, such as the sale of antihistamines and the potential of atomic-powered submarines. Each communication was attributed either to a high-prestige source or a low-prestige source. A typical high-prestige source was a professional journal of biology, and a low-prestige source was a

popular picture magazine. After the subjects read the identical articles in one context or the other, analyses of the results showed that the changes in attitude were significantly related to the subjects' opinions of the source (Hovland & Weiss, 1951).

It has been almost 20 centuries since Aristotle wrote in his *Rhetoric* that the *ethos* or credibility of the communicator is the most important single factor in the persuasiveness of the communication, and most modern research still supports this view. The audience's trust in the communicator even accounts for discrepant results obtained in various studies (Touhey, 1975). When a communicator is judged to be an expert and also of good will, he or she may be able to persuade people who are unmotivated, "immunized," or otherwise disposed to ignore the message.

Influence of the Mass Media

For this reason, advertisers in any mass medium—TV, newspapers, magazines, or radio—seek celebrities to endorse their products. With the phenomenal growth of all these media today, combined with a credible source, the persuasive effect can be enormous. In the *mass media*, a single source communicates to a large audience, and much research in psychology has been devoted to analyzing the results of these efforts at communication and persuasion.

Attention and the mass media. One consistent finding, whether the communication is designed to inform or persuade, is that people who pay attention to a particular message are those who are already favorably disposed initially. For example, individuals who were most attentive to a campaign concerning the United Nations, conducted by means of mailed circulars, radio broadcasts, public speeches, and newspaper articles, were essentially those who were in agreement with the issue before the campaigning started (Star & Hughes, 1950). Despite huge investments of time and money in political campaigns, there is no substantial evidence that a significant number of voters *change* their political preference as a result of the mass communications (Weiss, 1970). Similar results have been reported in England (Becker, 1967).

Altogether, it appears that existing attitudes and opinions are merely strengthened, a result that is not surprising when we recall the selectivity of attention and perception. If the media are effective in persuasion, it is perhaps because they induce the persons in the ''undecided'' and ''don't know'' categories to adopt one view or the other.

Television and aggression. One of the most hotly debated issues concerning the mass media is the influence of television violence on viewers, especially young children. In the interval between age 5 and age 15, the average child observes the violent destruction of almost 13,500 people on television programs (Liebert et al., 1973). Earlier, we noted that in one form of learning, called modeling or observational learning, an observer's behavior often changes after watching a model. It seems likely that this learning can occur through TV as well.

One reviewer examined the results of over 50 investigations on this topic, involving more than 10,000 children, and concluded that there is a socially significant relationship between watching TV violence and aggressive behavior in the observing child (Liebert, 1974). Other reviews support this conclusion, indicating that this relationship does not occur simply because aggressive people like to watch aggression on TV; instead, it appears that observing TV violence tends to lead to aggressive habits (Lefkowitz et al., 1972).

As in most broad, complex issues, the numerous experiments and field studies are not without flaws. In all these investigations there is the virtual impossibility of finding control subjects, who do not watch TV at all; hence, many investigations last only a few weeks, during which period the children are assigned to watch certain programs or the TV is available only at certain times, rather than on a more spontaneous basis. In one illustrative experiment with 395 teenaged boys, no increase in aggression was observed among those exposed to violent TV programs, as measured by a teacher's rating scale and personality inventories (Feshback & Singer, 1971). This study, however, did not include young children, lasted only six weeks, was conducted in an institutional setting, and required only a minimum of six TV hours per week per subject. On the average, American television sets are turned on more than six hours per day (Lesser, 1970). The effect of viewing aggressive stimuli on television may not have been well tested in this study.

Also, it is well to remember the distinction between learning and performance. The TV subjects might not become aggressive soon after viewing violence, but the constant exposure, over thousands of hours, may increase the probability of aggression when provoked in the future. Without this exposure, an aggressive reaction might be less likely. In other words, learning may occur by watching TV violence, although it is not immediately evident in performance (Bandura, 1973).

Use of television. It is the authors' view that the overall evidence, while mixed, is now sufficiently convincing to warrant a distinct change in TV programming. The solution to the problem obviously is not the elimination of television but rather a redirection of this medium towards more socially constructive purposes. "Sesame Street," an educational television program for children, apparently has been an advance in this direction (Minton, 1975). But unfortunately the popularity of this program has not been followed by a general improvement in the quality of the television shows (Lesser, 1974). Further, a change in TV programming would not mean that children would be unexposed to violence, which is constantly illustrated in newspapers, magazines, and other media.

Studies have shown the potential of television in shaping behavior in desirable directions. Among groups of preschool children fearful of animals, those exposed to TV models playing with these animals and enjoying them overcame their fear more readily and completely than did those not exposed to the TV program. Similarly, children fearful of dental treatment, after viewing a TV program on oral hygiene, showed greater willingness to visit the dentist than did control subjects (Liebert, 1974). Television is clearly a powerful tool for influencing human thought and action. Our great need is for a less violent world, and one way for helping to achieve such a society may be through the development of programs, especially children's programs, that show a less destructive, more cooperative way of life.

Summary

Basic Elements in Communication

1. Communication occurs whenever the behavior of one organism acts as a stimulus and influences the behavior of another organism. There is no interaction between organisms that does not involve some type of communication. A basic model of this process includes an encoder, signals, a channel, and a decoder. The most common channels of human communication are sound waves and printed pages carrying signals called words.

2. Human languages are constructed of at least three basic elements. These are phonemes, which are classes of basic sounds; morphemes, which are the smallest language units having separate meanings; and syntax, which is a system of rules for organizing morphemes into conventional sequences, such as phrases, clauses, and sentences.

3. The use of human language permits interchangeability, which means that both the encoder and decoder can send and receive the same message; displacement, meaning that the communication can concern things that are remote in time and space; and productivity, in which new expressions can be formed from combinations of familiar signals.

Acquisition of Language

4. A sequence of language development has been observed in normal human beings, provided they receive appropriate environmental stimulation. It begins with cooing, followed by babbling and, before the end of the first year, there are signs of word recognition.

5. The infant's earliest words appear around age 12 months as the child gives names to things in the environment. The beginning of language, called Stage I, is said to occur when the child's mean length of utterance (MLU), measured in

morphemes, exceeds 1.0. These first combinations of words are sometimes known as telegraphic utterances.

6. After mastering phonemes and combinations of morphemes, the next task is that of syntax, or word order. Here the child must deal with grammatical transformations, which require changes in word order with various expressions. As the child's linguistic expressions increase in length, he or she approaches Stage V in language development, in which the MLU exceeds 3.5.

7. When given an environment as comparable as possible to that of a human child and brought up with a human playmate, a chimpanzee showed some word recognition. However, word usage was not achieved in any way and the chimpanzee never approached Stage I of language development.

Theories of Language Learning

8. From the conditioning viewpoint, language acquisition occurs primarily on the basis of reinforcement, and it is influenced by principles such as shaping, extinction, and stimulus generalization. Apparently, word meanings are learned through classical conditioning, and word usage is learned through operant conditioning.

9. From the information processing viewpoint, the structure of the organism is the primary concern in language acquisition. The capacity for processing and utilizing large amounts of verbal information is especially evident in the child's attempts to discover the grammatical constructions of his or her language.

10. A combined viewpoint postulates that conditioning pertains to the learning of language habits and that information processing pertains to the learning of language rules. Both processes appear to be essential in language acquisition, but before such issues can be settled further, we must also know more about the nature of language itself.

Language, Communication, and Culture

11. To discover the upper limit of a chimpanzee's capacity for language acquisition, a system of language usage must be employed that does not require the use of the animal's inferior speech mechanisms. Under these conditions, several chimpanzees apparently have reached Stage I of language development, but the extent of further progress and the use of language for interspecies communication remain to be observed.

12. Much human communication is nonverbal, involving gestures, posture, and objects; this form of communication is prevalent and can be subtle. Verbal communication can involve denotative meaning, in which a word clearly indicates some object or event, and connotative meaning, which pertains to abstract qualities and has emotional implications, thus providing many nuances in human language. As a rule, human communication involves multiple signals, in which several verbal and nonverbal messages are transmitted and received simultaneously.

13. Studies of persuasion have indicated that group discussion generally is more effective than lectures, that a two-sided presentation may provide immunization against later counterattacks, and that the perceived intention of the communication is also important. Most crucial of all, however, is the communicator's credibility, which depends chiefly on his or her expertise and trustworthiness.

14. Mass media involve communication by a single source to a large audience. The showing of considerable violence on television programs is a controversial issue, but in general the evidence suggests that such programs foster aggressive behavior. In any case, television appears to be a powerful tool for influencing human thought and action and, therefore, means should be developed for using it in socially constructive ways.

Suggested Readings

Brown, R. *A first language: The early stages*. Cambridge, Mass.: Harvard University Press, 1973. A readable but detailed account of language development in children, based on a longitudinal research program.

Franklin, V. & Rodman, R. *An introduction to language*. New York: Holt, 1974. An introductory text directed to both linguistics and nonlinguistics students.

Glucksberg, S. & Danks, J. H. *Experimental psycholinguistics: An introduction*. Hillsdale, N. J.: Erlbaum, 1975. Describes the contemporary issues, problems, and findings in research on the psychology of language.

van Lawick-Goodall, J. *In the shadow of man*. New York: Dell, 1971. An entertaining story of an extensive series of field studies of the chimpanzee.

Williams, F. *Language and speech: Introductory perspectives*. Englewood Cliffs, N. J.: Prentice-Hall, 1972. Diverse perspectives briefly presented, from physics to sociology.

Chapter 20

Social Behavior

Human beings are inescapably social beings, so much so that we find it exceedingly difficult to live in isolation from one another. Our responsiveness to others of our kind is perhaps the most obvious aspect of human experience. Simply defined, *social psychology* is the social problems that confront human society.

In this chapter we first review the origins and bases of social behavior in the individual, then turn to the controversial question of attitudes and, for most of the chapter, consider modern research on human behavior in a social setting. We are interested in those research methods that facilitate investigations in the community as well as in the laboratory, for one aim of social psychology is to contribute to the solution of practical social problems that confront human society.

In particular, we consider a series of studies on altruism—designed to discover the circumstances under which people will and will not come to the aid of someone apparently in distress. This research of course must be carried out under conditions of everyday life.

Socialization of the Individual

The influence towards social behavior begins at birth, when we are completely dependent on others for survival. As others take care of our physical needs in the postnatal years, we gradually learn the rudiments of acceptable social behavior in our culture, and we develop

■ *Watching a baby come into the cafeteria in yellow pajamas reminds me of one time when my parents had gone out for the evening and left me lying in my crib. I must have been about three and felt lonely. My brothers came in and they stretched the arms and legs of my pajamas and tied them to the crib. All I can really remember was how excited I was while lying there because my brothers had come to play with me.*

□ *When I was about seven years old, I had a friend, Nik, who lived on a farm in the country. It was Nik's job to give bread to the geese at the little pond, and we both found this an excuse to remove ourselves from the summer heat and feed the birds from the water. We played at being geese, and though our attempts at diving were unsuccessful, our honking prospered. I remember finding some eggs hidden in the bushes near the water's edge. We checked on them every afternoon until one day we discovered that most of them had hatched, and only a few stragglers were still pecking away at their shells. The mother was, as usual, upset to see us near her offspring, so we backed away. Nik went to do the chores, but I returned and honked at one funny-looking gosling that apparently couldn't decide whether it should join the world or remain half in the egg. My raucous persuasion finally urged him out. I don't know how I had the nerve, but I started to play with him, talking softly, honking, and gently stroking his sticky fuzz. After a while I got tired, and when Nik came back to find out if I'd like to go wading, I forgot about my new friend. Luckily, Nik noticed him following us to the water, and from then on I had a constant companion. Specks wasn't unfriendly to his mother or siblings; he just didn't care much about them.*

social motives—the desire to be with other people, to have a relationship with them, and to do things with them. ■

Early Social Influences

The best examples of our attachments with others come from controlled studies of very young animals. Even here we see that the members of a species remain in groups, apart from the need for protection. And we also see the importance of the earliest social influences.

Contact and critical periods. Under normal circumstances, newborn ducklings and goslings follow their mother soon after hatching, perhaps because they are stimulated initially by her movements or vocalizations. This learned attachment of young animals to members of their own species is called *imprinting.* There is nothing especially remarkable about this following behavior, and it would receive no more than passing mention were it not for the fact that it is acquired during a certain optimal period for learning called the *critical period.* This period varies for different species, but in geese it is 13 to 16 hours after birth. Afterwards, readiness to learn to follow declines rapidly with age. Furthermore, during the critical period this following behavior can be elicited by almost any perceptible object that moves, even a human being. Here we see again the combined influence of inborn tendencies and environmental factors.

A German naturalist, Konrad Lorenz, once imprinted a group of goslings on himself by feeding the newly hatched young and ensuring that he was the first moving object observed by them in the first hours of life. They formed the attachment immediately, and thereafter followed him everywhere—around the yard, into the house, and even in swimming (Figure 20-1).

In one demonstration, Lorenz took a group of goslings that had been imprinted on him and a group that had been imprinted on their mother, permitted them to intermingle, and then placed all the goslings under a box. As

the mother moved away, Lorenz lifted the box and walked in a different direction. The goslings imprinted on Lorenz followed him, and those known to belong to the mother goose followed her. These and other examples indicate that once imprinting has occurred, the attachment is highly stable although not irreversible (Lorenz, 1935; Bateson, 1966). □

As for the possibility of such periods in human development, one investigator says that a child will not develop normally unless he or she has "a certain amount of attention and handling during a critical period of its infancy. This period is doubtless not so sharply defined as the imprinting period in birds, but it may lie within the first six months of life" (Hess, 1958). Most researchers believe that there is an early critical period for human social responsiveness, but they refuse to speculate regarding the exact interval. It is probably unwise to assume *a* critical period when there may be different critical periods for different responses (Hinde, 1963). Previously, in our discussions of affectional stimulation, intelligence, and the development of personality, we noted the profound influence that early social experience seems to have on later behavior.

Withdrawal of contact. The parent can influence the child not only by providing love, attention, and protection, but also by withdrawing affection, isolating the child from other people, and depriving the child of desired social contact. This approach to punishment is called *love-oriented* or *psychological punishment.* The other approach, called *object-oriented* or *physical punishment,* involves spanking the child or the removal of desired objects and privileges. By *punishment* we mean any event or outcome of behavior that brings pain or discomfort to the learner, usually applied in an effort to change the learner's behavior.

In general, it appears that children raised under love-oriented methods of punishment tend to develop a strong conscience. As the parent withdraws love for misbehavior, children tend to internalize the parent's standard in an effort to retain the parental love. Thus, their behavior in future situations becomes controlled by internal as well as external factors. Children raised under physical punishment, on the other hand, are more concerned with simply avoiding the punitive circumstances. Thus, their future behavior is more likely to be influenced by the presence or absence of external restrictions, such as the presence of authority figures. Expressed differently, we might say that love-oriented or psychological punishment is associated with greater internalization of adult standards than is physical punishment.

Confirmation of this view was provided in the 1930s when college students were observed through a one-way mirror as they tried to answer difficult examination questions. Each subject had been instructed not to look at the answer sheets, which were readily available, but approximately half of them violated this prohibition, and in a follow-up interview many of these violators also lied about their actions. More important, a large proportion of the violators, regardless of whether they lied, reported that their parents' childrearing practices were centered around physical punishment, whereas a majority of the nonviolators reported that their parents had used various forms of psychological punishment (MacKinnon, 1938).

The nonviolators also reported stronger feelings of guilt when they were merely asked about cheating, even though they had not done so. Ironically, the individuals who are the most guilt-ridden have the least objective grounds for feeling guilty. The apparent reason is that their conscience prevents wrongdoing and also prompts guilt feelings in even thinking about wrongdoing. ■

Figure 20-1 Imprinting. *These goslings, first exposed to Konrad Lorenz and isolated from their mother early in life, learned to follow Lorenz everywhere. (Thomas McAvoy, Life Magazine, © Time Inc.)*

Determinants of Attraction

Most of us want some form of contact with others, but what kind of contacts do we seek? In other words, what are the chief factors that determine with whom we associate outside the family, forming a couple, a three-person group, or some larger group? It is probably not surprising to discover that similarity is a most important aspect of interpersonal attraction.

Similarity. When a large, outspoken woman marries a small, quiet man, people say, "Opposites attract!" Yet this conclusion usually ignores many basic similarities between the marriage partners. Indeed, these people may even have a common concern about physical size, each finding some consolation in the other's dimensions. When one considers all the marriages and friendships one knows, and all the possible dimensions of individual differences, it is clear that the phrase "opposites attract" describes exceptions rather than the rule. If not, there would be little interest in the announcement: "80-year-old millionaire marries adolescent peasant girl."

■ *The type of punishment that marked my years 4 through 12 predominantly was the "spank her, scold her, and send her to bed without supper or TV" variety. Oh, that made me so hostile! I reacted violently against missing a favorite TV show. I cried and pleaded—anything to gain a reprieve before the show. When that failed I actively hated my parents and my brother (it was always his fault) for about a half hour. There was no regret for any of my actions, only their consequences.*

As I grew older, mother (perhaps at the utter frustration of seeing our fights continue) often cried, or at least let me know how disappointed she was that her children couldn't get along "like other kids." I saw in her a huge sense of despair. Instead of hurting me by spanking, she was hurt by our actions. It gave me the feeling of being a less lovable child, which was a totally new perspective. I felt terrible, and wished for a chance to redeem myself.

Figure 20-2   Similarity and Attraction. *The girls' fathers may be friends too, but it is unlikely that one of them is a close member of this group. (Malloch from Magnum)*

■ *Last year at my high school in Connecticut we kept a daily record of group seating patterns in the cafeteria during all lunch shifts. A plan of the table arrangement was made and filled in each period according to the "type" of student eating at each table. The types of students were denoted by color: purple for freak (the turned-on members of the suburb), red for greaser (those into shop and shorthand, not college bound), blue for jock (the muscles that ran the school and kept the bars in nearby New York State doing a brisk business), orange for cheerleaders (and all the others who held all the offices of all the organizations, all of which would impress all college admissions officers), green for freshman males (they deserved a class of their own), yellow for those involved in theater and music, and gray, for all the faceless, nameless people who always fill up the halls between classes and are never seen again.*

An amazing thing occurred. Every day the color pattern of the cafeteria was identical. Every group sat in the exact same section of the cafeteria every day. The freaks ate next to the PTA poster and the more dramatic ones ate at the opposite end, near the stage, while the whole scene revolved around the jocks, stationed in the center of the long room. A situation existed in which individual identities were immersed in the group identity, and invisible boundaries grew between tables in an innocent, simple-looking mass of chaos—the high school cafeteria.

As a rule, highly intelligent and retarded individuals do not seek one another's company; business executives do not form close relations with workers at much lower levels; and people who speak different languages are not found together. All told, it is likely that in any marriage, friendship, or even social gathering there are many. many more important similarities than differences. ■

Among the studies supporting this conclusion, one showed that people who were engaged to one another or dating steadily were similar in appearance and also in degree of attractiveness. Using photographs, the members of 99 couples were rated on physical attractiveness, and then when these same persons were paired by random matching, the couples' ratings were compared again. It was found that the attractiveness scores for each member of the true couples were in significantly greater agreement than the scores of the randomly paired couples (Murstein, 1972). In addition, the married couples were more similar in other respects, apart from physical attractiveness.

The groups that your grandmother joins are probably composed of elderly women, and your father's associates, even apart from his work, are likely to be middle-aged men. Most of your friends probably are of approximately your age, intelligence, and interests (Figure 20-2).

Proximity. Our most common associates also are nearby, as might be expected, but the importance of physical distance is probably underestimated by most people. In a study of married university students, consistent evidence of friendships was obtained between occupants of adjacent apartments, even when the living units were randomly assigned by the university administration. The further the distance between residence units, the less likely it was that friendships developed among the couples. Even differences as small as 20 to 30 feet played a part in determining friendships (Figure 20-3).

This finding has been confirmed in cities, suburbs, and college dormitories. In studying a new suburban community in which the residents were of much the same social class, investigators used news articles of social events to discover the friendship and affiliation choices, and it was found that an overwhelming number of social events were essentially "block parties." Persons living in the same areas went to the same bridge-club dances, New Year's Eve parties, and baby showers (Whyte, 1956). In a college dormitory, in which distances are shorter, the proximity factor is still evident, although weaker. Especially early in the academic year, friendship choices in residence halls are found to be highly influenced by proximity.

It should be added that the effect is due to functional distance, not physical distance per se. Installation of an elevator in a large living unit, for example, can change friendship patterns considerably.

Familiarity. Proximity and familiarity are related, but the significance of familiarity in interpersonal attraction also is probably more powerful than most persons realize. There is so much evidence that attraction increases with interpersonal contact that this relationship has been called a general law of human behavior (Homans, 1961).

In one instance, mere *anticipation* of interaction was shown to increase liking for another person. The college students in this study met in groups, expecting to work afterwards with some students and not with others. Although exposure was equal, the ratings for likability of anticipated partners were significantly higher than those for anticipated nonpartners (Darley & Bescheid, 1967). In another instance, the names of 200 public persons and 40 nonexistent "persons" were rated on a like/dislike scale, and a marked direct relationship was discovered between the familiarity of the figure and the favorability of the ratings (Harrison, 1969). This general law extends

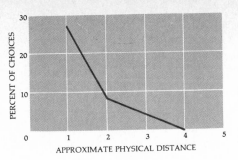

Figure 20-3 Relationship between Physical Distance and Friendship Choice. *Physical distance was measured in terms of a composite unit designed for this experiment. (Adapted from Festinger et al., 1956)*

even to inanimate objects. People exposed to certain nonsense words several times and to others less frequently rated most favorably the words to which they had been exposed most often (Zajonc, 1968).

Despite the strength of this relationship, there are other considerations. Liking for complex stimuli increases more steadily with continued exposure than does liking for simpler stimuli, for which we reach a point of satiation sooner. Another determinant of satiation, in addition to simplicity, is the length of time between exposures to the stimulus. As the time interval is lengthened, satiation occurs more slowly (Saegert & Jellison, 1970; Zajonc et al., 1974).

Measuring interpersonal attractions. One method of determining interpersonal attractions within a group is to ask the group members to nominate, confidentially, the members of the group with whom they would most like to live, go on a mission, or carry out some project. Interpersonal preferences obtained in this manner can be represented in a diagram, called a *sociogram,* which shows each member of the group in terms of his or her acceptance or rejection by the other members. Sometimes there are two people who choose one another and thus are called mutual pairs. Others, chosen by many, are "stars," and still others, not chosen at all, are isolates. Refinements of these rating procedures have been employed in a variety of interpersonal situations, such as selecting compatible team members, developing

Figure 20-4 Sociogram. *Each individual is asked to choose three people with whom he or she would like to work. Dotted arrows indicate a one-way choice, solid arrows indicate a mutual preference, and the numbers indicate the times that that individual is selected by others. (After Maier,* Psychology in Industrial Organizations, *4th ed. Copyright © 1973 by Houghton Mifflin Company.)*

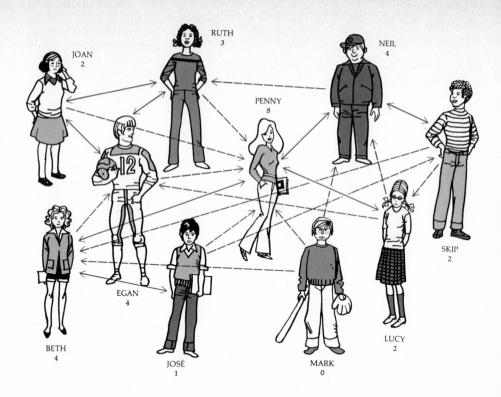

morale in industrial settings, and creating harmonious employer-employee relations (Figure 20-4).

Attitudes

According to tradition in social psychology, attitudes are precursors of behavior. They determine how one will act toward another person or in any given situation. Hence, there has been a long history of research in this area and there is now a large body of literature describing these findings.

Some social psychologists, especially those with a behavioral orientation, recently have questioned the significance of studying attitudes. The relationship between attitude and action, they claim, is still uncertain (Calder & Ross, 1973; Ehrlich, 1969). Attitudes may be important in determining what we do but since they cannot be measured precisely, it is more efficient and practical to confine one's studies to readily observable events (Abelson, 1972). These psychologists prefer to study behavior directly.

Attitude Formation and Change

The different viewpoints about attitude and behavior are partly reflected in our definitions of "attitudes" over the years. More than 40 years ago a leading social psychologist proposed that an attitude is simply "a mental . . . state of readiness" (Allport, 1935). Thus, it was widely held that an attitude was a *predisposition to behave in a certain way.* Modern psychologists who are interested in attitudes have attempted to be more specific, and they include behavior as part of an attitude, rather than merely its consequence. Thus, the three components of attitudes now have been identified as *thinking, feeling,* and *reacting.*

The first aspect involves the thoughts that a person has about any given topic, such as fluorides. Perhaps he or she believes that all fluorides are poisonous. The second aspect concerns the person's feelings. Does the individual experience attraction, repulsion, or some other feeling in connection with this thought? Presumably the individual is repelled by the thought of poison. The third element involves a reaction tendency, meaning that the thoughts and feelings may become manifest in overt behavior (Lambert & Lambert, 1964). In this case the person may try to avoid the fluoridation of drinking water. These three aspects are also described as the cognitive, emotional, and behavioral components of an attitude, respectively, and each of them can be used to illustrate a way in which attitudes presumably are formed (Kothandapani, 1971; Middlebrook, 1974).

Formation of attitudes. Sometimes attitudes are formed essentially by means of instruction. A small girl was told that she would have tapioca for lunch. She replied; "I don't like that." Then she asked, "What is it?" Later, it was discovered that she had been told by her older sister that tapioca has a disagreeable taste. This example emphasizes the role of belief, thinking, or cognition in the formation of attitudes.

Attitudes also are learned through classical conditioning, and here the focus is on the feeling dimension, especially positive and negative emotional responding. In one study, the names for various nationalities—German, Swedish, French, and Dutch—were paired with positive, negative, or neutral terms. Thus, "Dutch" was paired with "gift," "sacred," and "happy," while "Swedish" was paired with "bitter," "ugly," and "failure." For other subjects the procedure was reversed, and for still others the nationalities were paired with neutral terms. When an attitude questionnaire was administered later, the nationality was perceived as positive, negative, or neutral, depending on its previous associations (Statts & Statts, 1958). More complex investigations have followed this early experiment, and today there is abundant evidence of the classical conditioning of emotional reactions (O'Connell & Brown, 1973; Statts et al., 1972). ∎

Operant conditioning pertains to the behavioral aspect of attitude formation, and illustrations of this process have been frequent throughout this book. For example, the student who performs well in mathematics and is rewarded for this performance often wants to continue this activity. Social psychologists who find the concept of attitude useful would say that the student develops a positive attitude towards this work. Attitudes are also learned through imitation or modeling as when a child learns to like baseball because he admires his older brother, who is a ballplayer.

Considering attitude formation in a broader sense, we should add that we usually form attitudes that are consistent with our already existent attitudes. That is, we seem to seek consistency, a topic to which we shall return shortly.

Changing attitudes. When an attitude has been formed largely on an emotional basis, without unbiased consideration of the available evidence, we often say the issue has been prejudged and speak of a *prejudice,* which can be positive or negative. We can be prejudiced against a person who is accused of a crime or prejudiced in favor of a certain tax measure. If the word is used without qualification, however, it typically refers to a negative judgment based on inadequate grounds.

The changing of attitudes usually involves one or more of the processes just described in attitude formation. Direct instruction, conditioning, and modeling all have been found useful. In many respects, psychotherapy involves attitude change towards persons or events in one's life. Illustrations from therapy also are relevant to the acquisition of attitudes.

∎ *One night WBS played a lot of old (1960s) albums, and one of the ones they chose was the first album I ever owned. It has been seven years since I got it, and I have heard it many times, but still whenever I hear it I remember the first night when I heard it over and over and got to know the songs. A bunch of us were together for dinner; we had each made some sort of exotic foreign dish—I just remember the stroganoff and the Mandarin chicken. I have never been so ill after a meal; I just couldn't stand the water chestnuts. It was just before I went home—and so awful. I hate so much to be sick that to this day, hearing even one line from a song on that album, I can't keep myself from feeling sick. I just don't like that album at all any more.*

Figure 20-5 An Attitude Scale.
In this method, called a Likert scale, three to seven positions are usually established for a given statement. The subject indicates his or her attitude towards each statement by choosing one of the positions, and afterwards these responses are scored by using assigned weights. In this example, these values might range from +3 to –3, excluding 0, and this subject would receive scores of +1, –3, and +2. (After Anderson, 1965)

SA	A	(TA)	TD	D	SD	1. Public assistance to the dependent adult encourages him to become independent.
SA	A	TA	TD	D	(SD)	2. Very few dependent adults are getting something for nothing.
SA	(A)	TA	TD	D	SD	3. Most people on public assistance are needy, not greedy.

SA	strongly agree	TD	tend to disagree
A	agree	D	disagree
TA	tend to agree	SD	strongly disagree

Many attitudes are exceedingly difficult to change, however, especially those with a strong emotional component anchored in the individual's personality structure. When attitudes serve an important personality function, as do certain prejudices, they are extremely resistant to change (Adorno et al., 1950; Izzett, 1971). The *authoritarian personality,* for example, is characterized by aggression towards minority groups, cynicism, preoccupation with power, and extreme conventionalism. Archie Bunker of ''All in the Family'' has typified this personality syndrome for TV audiences in the 1970s. For him, a change in these attitudes would require a basic personality alteration.

Measurement of attitudes. In any study of attitude change, methods of measurement are necessary. Attitude scales are the most widely known measuring instruments, but they have definite shortcomings. Sometimes they are ambiguous, often they are too lengthy, and they can be faked, if a person desires to do so. Nevertheless, they are popular because they are easy to administer and efficient to score and interpret.

In the most common approach to constructing attitude scales, called the *Likert method,* many different statements concerning a certain issue are assembled, and each one is accompanied by a scale of three to seven steps, which vary from extremely negative to extremely positive. The subject indicates his or her attitude by marking a position on the scale (Figure 20-5).

The construction of an attitude scale is far more complex than this description suggests, and other procedures, such as behavioral observations, projective techniques, and physiological measures of emotion, also involve considerable effort and have various limitations. It is clear that measuring attitudes is a difficult process, no matter what method is used (Figure 20-6).

The Consistency Principle

In recent years, the field of attitude formation and change has been much concerned with the issue of consistency. ''A foolish consistency is the hobgoblin of little minds,'' according to Ralph Waldo Emerson, but consistency in our attitudes apparently is a concern for most of us. Several theories of attitude change are based on this principle.

The authoritarian personality offers one such example, in which a person's hardheadedness, prejudice, cynicism, and concern with power are consonant with one another. This cluster of attitudes, however, is not consistent with the trait of *intraception,* which is the desire for self-awareness and broad consciousness. Thus, the authoritarian personality is also characterized by an anti-intraceptive attitude, which is an attitude against subjectivity, imagination, and ''tender-minded'' phenomena.

The Individual in Society

Such awareness, presumably, is threatening to or inconsistent with the authoritarian outlook (Stanford, 1956).

Early consistency viewpoints. Among the theories of attitude consistency, the oldest has been called *balance theory* because it stresses the balanced state that exists when the important elements in a given situation are harmonious. If a husband and wife like each other and both are liberals politically, there are positive relationships in these respects and a balanced state exists. If they like each other and neither wants to live in Paris, a balanced state still exists, for they like each other and dislike the same thing. If, however, the husband favors a tax reform and the wife is against this legislation, there is imbalance. Neither partner's attitude is supported by the other, whom he or she likes. Similarly, there is imbalance if they dislike each other and both dislike federal spending. Here, each partner's attitude is supported by someone whom he or she dislikes. In the latter two situations, the individuals are likely to strive to achieve a better balance, in ways to be considered in a moment (Figure 20-7).

Another approach, the *congruity theory,* emphasizes attitude shifts, which are assumed to occur in the direction of increased congruence or agreement among a person's attitudes. Thus, if a woman is against abortion and finds that her lawyer, whom she admires, is in favor of abortion, then it is most likely

(LIBERAL POLITICS)

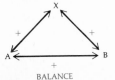

BALANCE

(LIVING IN PARIS)

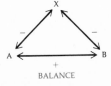

BALANCE

(TAX REFORM)

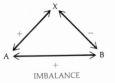

IMBALANCE

(FEDERAL SPENDING)

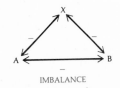

IMBALANCE

Figure 20-7 Balance Theory. *The letters A and B represent two people, and X is an object or event towards which they both have attitudes. (After Heider, 1946)*

Figure 20-8   Principle of Congruity. *In the first situation, there is incongruity because the individual's attitudes are related but of unequal strength. Hence, there is a shift to congruity, as shown in the second situation, and the element with the weaker sign shows the greater shift. (Adapted from Osgood et al., 1957)*

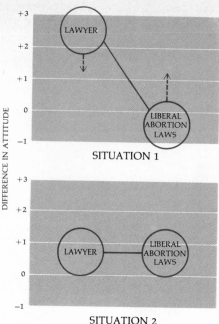

DIFFERENCE IN ATTITUDE

+3
+2
+1
0
−1

LAWYER

LIBERAL ABORTION LAWS

SITUATION 1

+3
+2
+1
0
−1

LAWYER

LIBERAL ABORTION LAWS

SITUATION 2

that her attitude towards the lawyer will become less positive and her attitude towards abortion less negative. The degree of change will not be equal, however, unless the different attitudes are of the same strength. Generally, there is a greater shift in the milder attitude. If the lady has a very high regard for her lawyer and is not particularly concerned about abortion, then her attitude towards abortion will undergo the greater change in rating (Figure 20-8).

Dissonance theory.   The third theory of attitude consistency is similar in basic ways to those already considered, but it is more recent and generated considerable research interest in the 1960s (Kiesler & Munson, 1975). More than the others, it focuses on the resolution of inconsistency in an individual's attitudes, and it emphasizes the aspect of choice in human behavior and attitude change. The inconsistency within an individual is an aversive state called *dissonance,* and the individual is motivated to dispel it in some way. The dissonance approach stresses that the individual's

cognitions are inconsistent, and therefore it is also called *cognitive dissonance* theory.

In a typical experiment, college students examined several manufactured articles, such as a radio and coffee maker, rated the desirability of these products, and then were allowed to select one as payment for their services. Some students were required to choose between two objects that they had rated as desirable, thus being placed in a high-dissonance situation. Other students chose between one product that they had rated as desirable and another rated as less desirable, thus being placed in a low-dissonance situation. It had been predicted that the subjects choosing between two highly desirable products would attempt to decrease the dissonance afterwards by re-evaluating the selected object more positively and the nonselected product more negatively, and this prediction was supported (Brehm, 1956).

As another example, consider what happened when people opposed to the use of electric shock agreed to administer shocks to others as part of a research project. Before the experiment, they experienced directly the amount of shock that the subjects would receive and rated its painfulness. After the experiment was over, in which they had shocked other people, they again rated the painfulness of the shock. The reader is asked to make a prediction based on dissonance theory—In the second rating did they increase or decrease their estimate of the painfulness of the shock? It had been anticipated that the subjects, in order to decrease the dissonance, would rate the shock as less painful after administering it to other persons, and this prediction also was supported (Brock & Buss, 1962).

According to the theory, dissonance can be reduced not only through attitude change but also through rationalizing, perceiving selectively, or seeking new information. Thus, the subjects might have decided that the persons in the experiment deserved to be shocked even more, that they showed no reaction to the shock, or that they received a considerable sum of money for participating in the experiment. However, there is no dissonance when the individual does not perceive any inconsistency. A person may engage in business practices that are fundamentally inconsistent with his or her religion, but if that person has no awareness of business on Sunday morning or of religion Monday through Saturday, there is no dissonance.

Use of Stereotypes

When attitudes have a pronounced cognitive component and involve oversimplified perceptions of certain persons or social groups we speak of a stereotype. A *stereotype* is any rigid generalization, positive or negative, about members of a particular social class, occupational group, race, or other category of people. Examples of stereotypes include, "Portuguese are passionate"; "the upper-class is snobbish"; and "librarians are prim and proper."

A great deal has been written about stereotypes, and there has been considerable reluctance among educated people to think in these categories. When a college student was asked to indicate characteristics associated with racial groups, he wrote, "I must make it clear that I think it ludicrous to attempt to classify various ethnic groups. . . . I don't believe that any people can accurately be depicted as having, in total, certain characteristics" (Karlins et al., 1969).

Need for generalizations. In spite of the resistance of some to generalize about characteristics of various racial groups, we all constantly use generalizations in dealing with people. We make a generalization at the savings bank; we

assume that the people there are careful, reliable, and honest. Otherwise, we would not trust them with our money. We also make generalizations about adolescents, used-car dealers, ministers, and kings. Without these generalizations, life would be difficult indeed; we would have to start from the zero point in each new relationship.

If you are to be a host for the weekend you want to know whether your guest-to-be is a child or an adult, male or female, a lawyer or a guide from the Maine woods, and then you will make certain assumptions about what to plan. In beginning any relationship, we look for ways of understanding the other person most readily, and therefore we use generalizations. They are essential if we are to get on with the business of understanding other people. The problem lies in finding generalizations that are accurate (Figure 20-9).

Stereotypes as facilitating. The word "stereotype" comes from the Greek *stereos*, meaning "solid" or "hard," and today it also refers to a metal plate used in printing. Things are said to be made from a stereotype when they are printed from a certain mold. Resistance to using the term in talking about people arises from this idea; it is inappropriate to think of a whole group of people, or even two, as cast from the same mold.

No two people are from the same mold, not even identical twins, once environmental influences have begun to operate. However, understanding other persons is sometimes facilitated on *first impression* by ignoring individual differences, as has been demonstrated experimentally.

Thirty persons, who served as judges of six strangers—three males and three females, were asked to predict the strangers' occupational interests as measured by a standard interest inventory. First, they made predictions without seeing the strangers, simply on the information that the person in question was a typical male or female undergraduate in a teacher-education program at a certain university. Then, predictions were made as each stranger appeared separately before the judges and completed simple tasks, such as drawing on the blackboard, building a house of cards, and describing the room. When the two sets of predictions were analyzed, it was found that accuracy based on stereotypes was significantly greater than accuracy after observing each individual's expressive behavior in completing the required tasks. Whatever clues the behavior provided were either ignored or misunderstood by the judges (Gage, 1952).

These results suggest that knowledge of a stereotype may be superior to brief observation in forming first impressions. The crucial factor, of course, is the accuracy of the stereotype.

Liabilities of stereotyping. Despite the prevalence of stereotypes and the possible advantage to which they may be used in forming first impressions, some distinct limitations must be kept in mind.

In the first place, many stereotypes are founded on insufficient evidence and, therefore, their accuracy is unknown. There is, for example, a stereotype of the genius as physically small and weak, but extensive investigation of intellectually gifted persons has not supported this generalization (Terman, 1954). In the second place, although a stereotype may have some validity for a group, the chances are considerably less that it applies to any given individual within the group. Inevitably, there are deviations from the general average. For these reasons, stereotypes must be used tentatively and flexibly.

A more important limitation and one that concerns international relations, is that sometimes stereotypes involve *ethnocentrism*, which is the tendency to judge foreign cultures on the basis of one's own ethnic standards and customs. Thus, the other cultures are regarded as inferior. It is one thing to have certain expectancies in dealing with other people and quite another to decide that they are inferior, bad, or in some way unworthy because their customs differ from one's own (Figure 20-10). The damaging consequences of such a viewpoint need not be elaborated.

For many years, people living in the United States described countries with considerably fewer technological developments as "backward." Recently, the expression has been changed to the more euphemistic term "underdeveloped," but as a native from one of these countries explained to a missionary, in a cartoon from the *New Yorker,* "It's not that my country is underdeveloped but perhaps that yours is overdeveloped." Although the term "developing" countries is now often used instead, the same point can be made concerning cleanliness, ambition, and efficiency—traits that have been highly esteemed in the United States. Countries that do not meet our standards in these respects are not inferior; they are merely different. It has been pointed out that our concept of cleanliness, with two, three, or more

Figure 20-10 Ethnocentrism. *Such groups as the American National Socialist (Nazi) party believe in the superiority of their own culture and race. Members of the party are shown here at a rally. (Berndt from Stock, Boston)*

baths per week, might be regarded as mere sensual indulgence in cultures in which people bathe less frequently (Brown, 1965).

Changing viewpoints. A long-term study of national stereotypes suggests that college students do describe various national groups by a few common adjectives, but in recent years a new trend has occurred. Fewer unfavorable traits are assigned, tolerance is more common, and hostility is less evident. Overall the tendency to generalize has decreased and the stereotyping that does occur has generally become more objective (Figure 20-11). As always, however, there is the question of reliability and faking in these scales of attitude measurement (Sigall & Page, 1971).

Interestingly, the only exception to this trend has been the students' attitudes towards themselves—that is, towards Americans, whose characterizations have become less flattering in successive generations. Recently, the trait "materialistic" was considered an American characteristic by 67 percent of all subjects. It was assigned to Americans more frequently than any other trait was assigned to any other group (Figure 20-12).

Spaniards, incidentally, refer to people from the United States as *estadosunidenses,* which means "United Statesians." It seems a noteworthy observation that our language has no adjective by which we can describe ourselves, as distinct from Brazilians, Costa Ricans, Cubans, and Canadians, all of whom are Americans. Several interpretations might be made concerning this condition. It may represent extreme nationalism in the sense that we really do not readily recognize the existence of other countries in our hemisphere. It may represent antinationalism; perhaps we are reluctant to promote ourselves as distinct from our neighbors. It may be mere habit, reflecting a lack of interest in precision in our language. The reader is left to decide.

Figure 20-11 Study of National Stereotypes. *Of the ten national groups studied, undergraduates of the same university in 1932, 1950, and 1967 selected these traits from a list of 84 possibilities. Only the Turks were not described in terms of a few salient characteristics, and all groups received more favorable ratings in the later years. ("On the fading of social stereotypes: studies in three generations of college students" by M. Karlins, T. L. Coffman, and G. Walters,* Journal of Personality and Social Psychology *13, 1969, 1-16. Copyright 1966 by the American Psychological Association. Reprinted by permission. Left photo by Ruth Block for Monkmeyer Press; middle photo by Gordon N. Converse, Christian Science Monitor; right photo by Art Sokoloff from DPI.)*

Trait	Percent Checking Trait			Trait	Percent Checking Trait		
	1932	1950	1967		1932	1950	1967
ITALIANS				**CHINESE**			
Artistic	53	28	30	Superstitious	34	18	8
Impulsive	44	19	28	Sly	29	4	6
Passionate	37	25	44	Conservative	29	14	15
Quick tempered	35	15	28	Tradition loving	26	26	32
Musical	32	22	9	Loyal to family ties	22	35	50
Imaginative	30	20	7	Industrious	18	18	23
Very religious	21	33	25	Meditative	19	—	21
Talkative	21	23	23	Reserved	17	18	15
Revengeful	17	—	0	Very religious	15	—	6
Physically dirty	13	—	4	Ignorant	15	—	7
Lazy	12	—	0	Deceitful	14	—	5
Unreliable	11	—	3	Quiet	13	19	23
Pleasure loving[a]	—	28	33	Courteous[b]	—	—	20
Loyal to family ties[b]	—	—	26	Extremely nationalistic[b]	—	—	19
Sensual[b]	—	—	23	Humorless[b]	—	—	17
Argumentative[b]	—	—	19	Artistic[b]	—	—	15

[a] Indicates additional traits reported by Gilbert (1951).
[b] Indicates new traits needed in 1967 to account for the ten most frequently selected traits today.

	Percent Checking Trait		
Trait	1932	1950	1967
Industrious	48	30	23
Intelligent	47	32	20
Materialistic	33	37	67
Ambitious	33	21	42
Progressive	27	5	17
Pleasure loving	26	27	28
Alert	23	7	7
Efficient	21	9	15
Aggressive	20	8	15
Straightforward	19	—	9
Practical	19	—	12
Sportsmanlike	19	—	9
Individualistic[a]	—	26	15
Conventional[b]	—	—	17
Scientifically minded[b]	—	—	15
Ostentatious[b]	—	—	15

[a] Indicates additional traits reported by Gilbert (1951).
[b] Indicates new traits needed in 1967 to account for the ten most frequently selected traits today.

Figure 20-12   Traits Assigned to Americans. *Note that in each successive survey, Americans assign themselves the traits "industrious" and "intelligent" with decreasing frequency. (Karlins et al., 1969; John A. DeCindis photo)*

	Percent Checking Trait		
Trait	1932	1950	1967
ENGLISH			
Sportsmanlike	53	21	22
Intelligent	46	29	23
Conventional	34	25	19
Tradition loving	31	42	21
Conservative	30	22	53
Reserved	29	39	40
Sophisticated	27	37	47
Courteous	21	17	17
Honest	20	11	17
Industrious	18	—	17
Extremely nationalistic	18	—	7
Humorless	17	—	11
Practical[b]	—	—	25

Patterns of Interaction

The basic concern of social psychology is an understanding of social interaction at any level—international, national, local, or family. In order to further knowledge of the important factors in these interactions, social psychologists are constantly looking for improved methods of investigation. One method that represents a generally new trend is illustrated in the following experiment.

A number of college students, one by one, walked through a back alley, passing a slumped figure in a doorway. This man, not moving, with his head down and eyes closed, was shabbily dressed, and he coughed and groaned as the student opened the door and passed into the building. Apparently he was in need of help, but what happened? Did the student become a good Samaritan or pass on by, continuing with personal business?

This experiment is not unique and there are many precedents, but it illustrates the *field experiment,* which is becoming increasingly popular in research in social psychology. The individual slumped in the doorway was a member of a research team, the students were subjects, and the experimental purpose was to discover some of the factors that determine when assistance will and will not be offered to a person in distress.

The field experiment differs from *naturalistic observation,* in which the investigator simply observes naturally occurring events, and from *laboratory experiments,* in which researchers cause certain events to happen in a controlled setting in order to discover which events stand in a causal relationship to which other events. The field experiment combines aspects of both approaches. A natural event occurs or is simulated, and then it is studied through controlled procedures. The advantage is that the method and data are objective, yet the study takes place in an everyday setting.

The field experiment has drawbacks, however, and it gives rise to an ethical issue. To what extent is it justifiable and moral to expose unsuspecting persons to a seemingly natural event that is really an experiment? The answer is complex, but we can express a general viewpoint held by contemporary social scientists— such a deception is acceptable provided it involves an event that would occur naturally in that context, no one is harmed physically or psychologically and, when the subject's behavior is altered, each subject has had the choice of participating or not participating in the procedure.

Altruistic Behavior

In this particular experiment, the subjects were 67 divinity students and the research concerned *prosocial behavior,* also known as *altruism,* in which one person helps another for no obvious reward. Such behavior appears sacrificial, performed as an end in itself, and it has long interested both scientists and philosophers.

The circumstances for this field experiment had been carefully arranged. Some of the divinity students were on their way to give a brief talk on the exact issue in question—the parable of the good Samaritan. Other were en route to give a short talk on divinity careers after graduation. Some subjects in each group were in a great hurry to present their speech, others were just about on time, and still others had time to spare. Of these people, 40 percent offered aid, directly or indirectly, to the person slumped in the doorway.

Personal states. Those who offered aid to a person in need were not necessarily the students with the idea of the good Samaritan in mind, and they were not necessarily those thinking about careers after graduation. Instead, the factor that made the difference was the time element. The students most likely to help were those with a few minutes to spare; those least likely to stop were in great haste; and the others, just on time, were in an intermediate position with regard to helping behavior. In later interviews, it was found that the subjects in haste experienced some emotional upset after their encounter in the alleyway, but to stop and help the "victim" would have meant a delay in proceedings that other persons had carefully arranged. Another allegiance, rather than pure callousness, seemed to be partly responsible for their failure to offer assistance (Darley & Batson, 1973).

Behavior is complex, however, and having time to spare is not the only determining factor in altruism. It has been demonstrated that being in a good mood is also important (Isen & Levin, 1972; Figure 20-13).

Situational factors. Besides the helper's internal states, factors in the altruistic situation are influential. In fact, investigators have been quite successful in identifying temporary personal states and situational factors related to altruism and notably unsuccessful in identifying long-term personality characteristics of altruistic individuals (Darley & Batson, 1973; Krebs, 1970).

Social scientists have been prompted to do these studies on bystander intervention by real-life incidents in which people have observed murders or the damage of property without making any effort at intervention. One of the most significant findings to come out of all these investigations is that when other people are present at the event, any given individual is less likely to intervene. There seems to be a perceived *diffusion of responsibility.* For example, when a college student overheard someone having an epileptic seizure, his or her effort to help was decidedly slower and less frequent when he or she believed that someone else also heard the victim's cries, although neither the victim nor anyone else was in sight. The "innocent bystander" apparently feels more innocent when others are observing too;

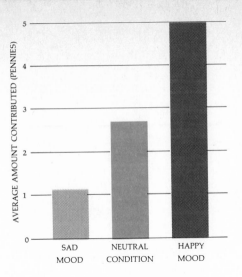

Figure 20-13   Mood and Altruism. *Children in a sad mood were found less generous in sharing their money than were children in a neutral condition. Most generous of all were children in a happy mood. (Adapted from Moore et al., 1973. Copyright 1973 by the American Psychological Association. Reprinted by permission.)*

when alone, he or she feels more personally responsible (Darley & Latane, 1968).

Another more obvious situational factor is the amount of personal risk to the helper. People are less inclined to interfere in an incident in which they may incur harm themselves (Allen, 1972).

In short, while many of us think we know people who are especially conscientious helpers in all circumstances, research has not been successful in identifying such persons in cases of bystander intervention. As one research group has said:

Some types of people are likely to be more helpful in some situations; other types will emerge as the "good guys" in other situations. *When* people help depends heavily on how the situation happens to interact with their personal dispositions at the time. There seem to be very few all-around good Samaritans among us. (Gergen et al., 1972)

Tendency towards Conformity

The presence of other persons at an emergency situation seems to retard helping behavior for another reason besides diffusion of responsibility. When others are present and do nothing, the onlooking individual tends to *define the situation as not being an emergency,* as

Figure 20-14   Conformity.
Surveys show that an important concern for people of all ages is to be accepted by others. (Shelton from Monkmeyer)

■ *Chris was the butt of a joke one afternoon as we sat around on our lunch break. As planned, George told a "joke" that was totally non-sensical:*

Q: What did one elephant say to another when the former asked for some soap?

A: No soap; radio!

Everyone who was in on this, which meant everyone except Chris, laughed hysterically. Meanwhile, we watched, and Chris was laughing as hard as everyone else, saying, "I get it."

not requiring action. If he or she intervened, it might be the wrong thing to do; it might be embarrassing or even harmful. In one experiment, each subject was in a college room in which smoke irregularly and unexpectedly came through the ventilator. The subjects responded quickly when alone and more slowly when with two other students. When in the presence of two accomplices of the experimenter, who acted normally during the whole episode, the subjects did not respond in an emergency manner until the smoke was so thick one could hardly see (Latane & Darley, 1968).

Most emergencies, at least initially, are ambiguous events from the observer's viewpoint. One risks making a fool of oneself by acting inappropriately, and so the presence of others who do not appear to be alarmed tends to produce a definition of the situation as one not requiring action. The man lying in the doorway may be in a drunken stupor, sleeping, or suffering a heart attack. The possibility of being wrong, of acting inappropriately in front of a number of other people, seems to influence one's decision about offering aid. In short,

conformity to the group standards, which may be explicit or implicit, is an enormous factor in social behavior.

Conformity as agreement. For a society to function smoothly, the members must adopt most of its norms. In most long-established social groups there is agreement on a wide variety of behaviors, including patterns of dress, style of speech, religious outlook, sexual customs, and even eating habits (Figure 20-14). Even in spontaneously formed groups, the experienced pressure towards conformity can be intense.

In a series of laboratory experiments some years ago, American college students were asked to make judgments about the length of vertical lines, selecting one line from a group of three that was equal in length to another vertical line. Seven persons made these simple judgments in a group, but the sixth person in the sequence was the only true subject; the others were the experimenters' accomplices. Unknown to the subject, on some trials all the others intentionally made the same incorrect guess. Thus, perhaps for the first time, the true subject suddenly found the evidence of his or her senses clearly contradicted by the majority (Figure 20-15).

Altogether, only about one-fourth of the subjects completely resisted the group pressure, making no errors, and even these people remained doubt-ridden throughout the investigation. Among the majority who yielded, some were influenced occasionally; others followed the incorrect but unanimous opinion on every trial, showing complete acquiescence to group pressure. In addition, it was found after the experiment that the yielding subjects grossly underestimated the degree of their compliance. They offered various reasons for their behavior, but the most common was that they became extremely anxious when faced with a unanimous and disagreeing majority (Asch, 1956). ■

The Individual in Society

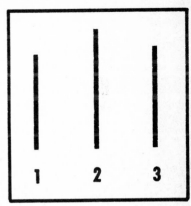

Figure 20-15   One against a Majority.   *The stimulus cards were placed 40 inches apart on a ledge, and the subjects were required to match the single line with one of the other three. Reports began with the first person on the left; the true subject (6) at times found his judgments to be in conflict with those of all the others in the group. (From "Opinions and Social Pressure" by Solomon E. Asch. Copyright © 1955 by Scientific American, Inc. All rights reserved. Copyright 1956 by the American Psychological Association. Reprinted by permission. William Vandivert photos.)*

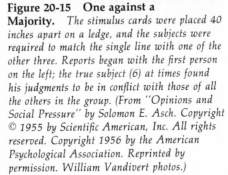

In terms of our earlier discussion of stereotypes, it is noteworthy that similar experiments have been conducted with French and Norwegian subjects, and the two groups performed quite differently. Distinctly more conformity was found among the Norwegians; many of the French even became distinctly more indignant each time their deviant response was questioned by the majority (Milgram, 1961).

These results should not prompt us to think that conformity is undesirable. People conform for various reasons, and conformity certainly leads to a greater feeling of group cohesion. Nonconformity, furthermore, does not necessarily represent independence. Some people adopt the contrary view regardless of the issue. They cannot be described as independent because their views are determined by prevailing opinion, although in the opposite direction (Willis, 1965).

Conformity as obedience. In a comparable but more controversial series of laboratory studies on conformity, each subject at a large university was told that the experimenter was studying the effects of punishment on learning, and as a participant in the study he or she would be required to punish someone else's incorrect responses by giving that person electric shocks. After a demonstration of the apparatus, during which the subject, a "teacher," experienced a slight shock, the experiment began. Because the learner made errors regularly, the experimental question was— How much shock would the subject administer before refusing to follow the experimenter's requests?

When this procedure was carried out with 40 subjects, and later with more, it was discovered that 65 percent of the "teachers" obeyed *all* of the experimenter's orders, punishing the learner with the most powerful shock available, even when the learner no longer responded to the task and therefore was being punished for the absence of a response. In the remaining 35 percent of the cases, the experiment was discontinued when the subject refused to administer a stronger shock, but no subject refrained from doing so before reaching 300 volts, labeled "intense shock." At this point in the experiment the learner pounded on the wall and then became silent (Figure 20-16).

Actually, the learner never received any shocks because the generator had been disconnected. Furthermore, he was an accomplice of the experimenter and the subject, while applying greater and greater voltage at the experimenter's request, simply heard the accomplice's curses and yells in simulation of being shocked. Thus, the findings have been seen by some as a most important experimental contribution to our understanding of conformity, indicative of the unthinking obedience of Hitler's hideously cruel SS troops during the 1930s and World War II. Others see the cruelty as residing within the experimenter, who duped his subjects and then persuaded them to perform this distasteful task (Milgram, 1964; Baumrind, 1964). In any case, it was demonstrated here that conformity is far greater than one would expect.

Research ethics. The ethical question raised by research such as the shock-administration experiment deserves further consideration. Despite extensive debriefing, in which the purposes, procedures, and rationale of the research are explained to all subjects and their questions are answered, participation in an experiment of this kind involves some loss of dignity or loss of trust in authority. For these reasons, in most research institutions all proposed experiments now must be approved by interdisciplinary ethics committees. The goal is to permit the most useful, productive research to be conducted without endangering the subjects or other persons in any way. The best solution to this problem, and the one towards which many psychologists are working, is the development of

Designation and Voltage Indication	Number of Subjects Who Administered This Shock as Maximum
Slight shock	
15	0
30	0
45	0
60	0
Moderate shock	
75	0
90	0
105	0
120	0
Strong shock	
135	0
150	0
165	0
180	0
Very strong shock	
195	0
210	0
225	0
240	0
Intense shock	
255	0
270	0
285	0
300	5
Extreme intensity shock	
315	4
330	2
345	1
360	1
Danger: severe shock	
375	1
390	0
405	0
420	0
XXX	
435	0
450	26

Figure 20-16   Maximum Shock Administered. *(From "Behavioral study of obedience" by S. Milgram.* Journal of Abnormal and Social Psychology, *1963, 67, 371-378. Copyright 1963 by the American Psychological Association. Reprinted by permission.)*

research techniques that rely on the subjects' usual behavior and naturally occurring events, rather than misleading instructions (Kelman, 1967).

In most studies in which the subject is intentionally misled, the relevance for social problems in daily life becomes questionable. In fact, the investigation on "teaching" with electric shocks may show more about the desire to be a good subject in a laboratory experiment than about adherence to a dictatorial leader in the outside world (Keisler & Munson, 1975; Orne, 1962). Similar criticisms have been made of other compliance research. In one instance, students voluntarily adopted the roles of guards and prisoners in a study of a simulated prison environment, and it appeared that within a few days the prisoners became truly depressed, passive, and confused about their identity while the guards grew more hostile and exploiting (Haney et al., 1973). Here again, another interpretation has been made of the findings. The subjects, it has been suggested, while perhaps feeling miserable in their roles, did not undergo a transformation of reality but were simply acting out their *ideas* of the roles of prisoners and guards in accordance with the experimenters' expectations (Bannazizi & Movahedi, 1975).

The problem of ethics is not unique to social psychology; it occurs in all disciplines. For some people, the whole field of nuclear physics is an ethical issue because of its capacity for developing atomic bombs. In biology, animals are constantly confined to cages and then surgery is performed solely for research purposes. In legal and psychiatric research, ethical principles arise concerning clients' rights (Foster, 1975). Even research in educational intervention for children from low-income families involves ethical considerations, for in the intervention procedure the researcher is imposing his or her own values on the subjects (Gray, 1974). For the investigator in these instances, the justification is that any possible discomfort incurred by all subjects collectively is outweighed by the potential gain in alleviation of human problems.

It has been pointed out that the ethical issue also can be considered from the opposite viewpoint. *Not* to do certain research may leave millions of human beings to cope unaided with difficult physical, psychological, and social problems (Seligman, 1975).

Cooperation and Competition

Most group situations, in addition to conformity, engender some form of striving to perform well in the task at hand. This striving may be as mild as in simply trying to talk intelligently with others, or it may involve much effort, as in attempting to win a political election.

Social facilitation. The higher degree of responsiveness and greater productivity in a group setting generally is known as *social facilitation,* and it occurs even among animals. Fish eat more in a group than when alone, ants excavate more dirt when they work in a group than when they work by themselves, and even rats show evidence of social facilitation (Chen, 1938; Harlow, 1932; Strobel, 1972; Welty, 1934).

With human beings, the facilitating effect appears to be due partly to rivalry. When individuals work in groups and are told that their results will not be compared, the facilitating effect fails to appear. On the other hand, when they are told that their performance will be compared with that of other people working at the same time in separate rooms, the amount accomplished by these subjects is comparable to that in the group situation. As in the animal studies, social facilitation seems to be the result of some competitive effort (Dashiell, 1935).

Not all psychologists would agree with this single-factor interpretation, however. Social facilitation also may be due to simple arousal in the presence of an audience, the result of "face saving," or simply trying to keep pace rather than trying to outdo others. For example, some bystander intervention studies have shown that when a few persons begin to intercede in behalf of the victim, others join the effort. They are stimulated to help but they are not necessarily trying to outperform others.

Inducing cooperation. Whether social interaction becomes competitive or cooperative depends in a large measure on how the situation is perceived, just as in the case of conformity. When the teaching-learning experiment with electric shocks is repeated in less impressive circumstances than a respected university, distinctly less obedience ensues. Even in a parlor game, cooperation can be readily increased or decreased simply by altering the rules of play (Figure 20-17).

In daily life, two basic factors stand out as engendering cooperation or competition. Extreme competition commonly involves some form of aggression, and earlier we noted the cultural influences on this behavior, which can mold us into aggressive or peaceful behavior patterns. Thus, a most important factor is early childhood experience. In the United States, childrearing generally fosters competition and individuality, especially in the school system, in which "getting ahead" is stressed. In some other cultures, such as communist China and the kibbutz in Israel, different habits are emphasized, and the child's identity is more tied to the group of which he or she is a constant member. In school, young children in these cultures are taught to clean the table *together* or to calculate the classroom budget *together,* an approach that presumably fosters cooperative behavior and attitudes that are lasting in later years.

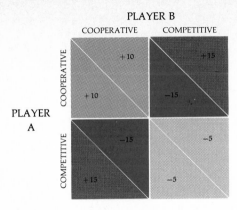

PLAYER B

	COOPERATIVE	COMPETITIVE
COOPERATIVE	+10 / +10	+15 / −15
COMPETITIVE	−15 / +15	−5 / −5

PLAYER A

Figure 20-17 Nonzero Sum Game. *In such a game, one player's gain does not inevitably occur at the other's expense. The game is so named because the players' aggregate gains and losses do not necessarily total zero, depending on whether they play cooperatively or competitively.*

Thus, players A and B each have a cooperative and a competitive choice. If both make cooperative choices, both win points. If both are competitive, both lose points. But if only one player is competitive, that player wins the maximum points while the cooperative player loses the same amount.

In a widely cited experiment of this type, called Prisoner's Dilemma, two suspects are apprehended by the police and separated, each one being aware of the fact that the other may or may not confess. If both confess, both receive major punishments; if neither confesses, both may receive minor punishments for other crimes. If one confesses and the other does not, the confessor receives freedom for assisting the police and the other receives the major penalty. The dilemma occurs because if both try to obtain the greatest personal gain, both will lose. Nevertheless, this situation is common in our society when the instructions are "neutral," not stressing one mode or the other (Deutsch, 1960).

Two men are being stopped and questioned by a policeman. Imagine that they have cooperated in committing a minor theft. If they are apprehended by the police and separated, they will be faced with the dilemma called the nonzero sum game. (Waldo from Stock, Boston)

Superordinate goals. The second basic factor, in addition to cultural influences, is illustrated in an experiment carried out in the natural setting of a boys' camp. For three different summers, 11- and 12-year-old boys who did not know one another previously were brought together for the first few days of camp. After careful measurements were made of the friendships established, the boys were separated into two groups, "best friends" being placed in different groups as much as possible. New friends were established quickly, nicknames were coined, esprit de corps grew, and favorite places and activities developed for each group.

Then, competition was introduced. A tournament of games was arranged between the two groups: touch-football, tug-of-war, baseball, and a treasure hunt. In the course of time, what commenced as good sportsmanship became extremely rivalrous; the opposing groups began name-calling, planned raids on one anothers' territory, destroyed property, and engaged in scuffles.

The experimenters then aimed to change this situation, first by following the hypothesis that pleasant social contacts would reduce the friction. Sometimes this procedure was successful, but other times it merely provided greater opportunities for conflict. In the dining hall, individuals from the two groups shoved and pushed one another, called names, and threw food and utensils with no sign of abatement in the friction.

A second hypothesis was then tested. The experimenters intentionally created a series of problems that challenged everyone in both groups, producing *superordinate goals,* which were goals that had a higher priority than any others and were shared by both groups. A solution to each problem would benefit both groups, but neither group could achieve it alone. A break in the water supply required close inspection of the terrain for one mile, and a breakdown in the truck that was to take both groups on a picnic required that everyone pull together on the same rope used previously in the tug-of-war. Eventually, hostilities eased— but not immediately. At first the old conflicts began again as soon as a superordinate goal was achieved, but gradually new relationships developed to the point at which the boys sought opportunities to mingle in the other group, had "best friends" there, held a joint campfire, had a combined party, and went home together (Sherif, 1956).

It was not simply close proximity that reduced the earlier tension but rather working together towards overriding goals that were important to all concerned. This situation is sometimes referred to as responding to *outside threat.* A nation at peace may undergo internal strife, but in wartime the increased cooperation among its citizens is readily apparent.

Group Structure

A *role* is a pattern of behavior that is expected of a group member. In some situations, as in sudden emergencies with a number of bystanders, the role of helper perhaps is not adopted, partly because it has not been assigned to anyone and partly for the reasons mentioned earlier. Observers may not define the situation as an emergency and each of them anticipates that someone else will adopt the helping role, as indicated in the concept of diffusion of responsibility.

Role, Status, and Hierarchies

Usually, a role is assigned on the basis of the person's standing or *status* in the group. A leader clearly has high status, and therefore the leadership role entails overall responsibility for the group and its endeavors. Positions of lesser status usually involve narrower roles. Moreover, people's roles are complementary; appropriate behavior for a given role depends on the roles played by the others. The role of helper cannot exist without someone who needs assistance. The role of a parent cannot be described without reference to the role of the child.

Formal and informal roles.   If a policeman or policewoman is on duty at the scene of emergency, this person's status in the social order requires that he or she immediately adopt the role of helper and later that of data collector. This role is a formally assigned one, as is that of captain and navigator on a steamship, or the role of bellhop in a hotel. However, an individual also may assume an informal role, apart from his or her official position in a group. Among a group of navigators, a humorous, lighthearted individual may become the social leader, although never elected to this position. Similarly, another member of this same group may be expected to maintain schedules and post bulletins, although he or she never has been designated to handle these tasks.

Most cultures designate sex roles, both formally and informally. Boys are supposed to play in the dirt and girls are supposed to smell flowers. Men traditionally work outside the home and women work within it. In the United States and elsewhere, some of these prescriptions are changing and thus differences are diminishing. Others perhaps will remain for some time. ∎

■ *I can remember a summer when I was either four or five years old. It was hot, and it was perfectly natural for me to take my shirt off. I usually didn't even bother to put one on; I just ran out to play. And I remember being told for the first time that I could not play outside like that any more. At first I didn't understand the prohibition, but as it was repeated every day that summer, and quite a few times since, I started acting accordingly. I am female—in case you didn't guess.*

The Individual in Society

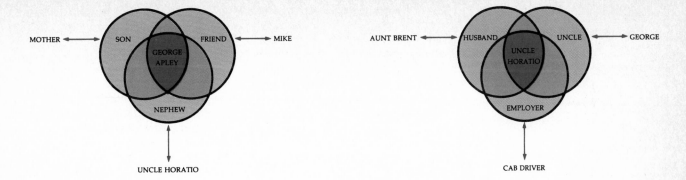

In the course of daily life, most of us assume several roles and become adept at changing from one to the other. A man assumes the role of teacher when he is conducting a class, the role of husband when he is with his wife, the role of tourist on a trip, and that of father when with his children. Social scientists say that he exhibits different ''selves'' in these various roles (Figure 20-18).

Animal hierarchies. Even in the animal world, in which there are presumably no titles, money, or politics, status and role seem to be a function of power. This condition was called to scientific attention years ago by a Norwegian investigator who carefully observed barnyard chickens. The most dominant chicken pecked all others and was pecked by none in return. Another chicken pecked all others except the most dominant, which of course pecked it. This social order extended down to the bottom of the hierarchy at which one chicken was pecked by all others and pecked none in return. A *pecking order* or *dominance hierarchy* had developed. Similar hierarchies have been observed in modern variations of these experiments (Schjelderup-Ebbe, 1935; Figure 20–19).

Figure 20-18 Multiple Roles. *Letters written by the fictional character George Apley illustrate that a person's roles depend partly on others and partly on his or her own status. The "real" George Apley and the "real" Uncle Horatio are composites of several different selves as they interact with different people in Paris. (From* The Late George Apley *by John P. Marquand, by permission of Little, Brown and Co.)*

Dear Mother: No sooner did we arrive at the hotel after a very rough channel crossing than I found again what a very small place the world is. There in the dining room were Dr. and Mrs. Jessup from Mt. Vernon Street, and Jane Silby and her aunt from Commonwealth Avenue, and the Morrows from Brookline. Aunt Brent says that the Hotel Metropole is one of the few hotels in Paris where one can be sure of meeting congenial people. . . . Uncle Horatio and our driver had great difficulty over the fare, as Uncle Horatio does not believe in giving more than the usual ten per cent fee extra. We are going with Dr. and Mrs. Jessup through the Louvre tomorrow, where I am looking forward to seeing the Mona Lisa. . . .

Dear Mike: Well, here I am in Paris and I wish you were here too. I saw Wintie over in London and we split a bottle together in a Public House and talked about the Club. . . . Uncle Horatio and Dr. Jessup and I have been out several evenings to "see the town." We have been to several shows. . . . Uncle Horatio is really quite a "sport" and once he has got Henrietta and Aunt Brent safely out of the way you would be surprised at some of his goings-on. Several evenings we have both of us been quite tight. He is very glad to have a vacation, he says, from Boston. . . .

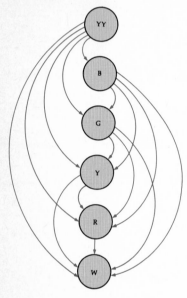

Figure 20-19   A Dominance Hierarchy. *Chicken YY pecked all the others; B pecked all others except YY; and W was pecked by every chicken in the group. This straight-line dominance developed in 36 weeks. (Photo from Animal Behavior Enterprises, Inc.)*

The introduction of a new group member requires that the established order be changed. Similarly, the order is changed when one of the lower chickens receives an injection of male hormones, for then it rises in the hierarchy. Studies of mice, dogs, and many other species show dominance relations based on fighting, but the perfect straight-line dominance seen in hens is rare.

Human hierarchies. Among human beings, it is reported that playful aggressiveness in children, if unchecked or unsupervised, should theoretically result in a dominance order based on fighting (Scott, 1958). Something approximating such a hierarchy develops in street gangs and certain primitive societies. A member of one city gang said, "Nutsy was the head of our gang once. I was his lieutenant. He was bigger than me, and he had walloped me different times before I walloped him. . . . After I walloped him, I told the boys what to do" (Whyte, 1955).

Usually, a person's status is based on something other than physical domination. Bowling performance also was closely associated with the status of the individual in this gang because it became the chief social activity of the group. Bowling was the means whereby an individual could gain, lose, or maintain prestige.

In society at large, important determinants of status are money, education, intelligence, and physical competence, as in acting and athletics. The existence of hierarchies in societies in which social mobility is possible is based on many such interacting characteristics.

Social Class and Caste

Differences in status and roles exist in all major human societies. Some of them are thrust on us at birth; others are acquired as we grow older. But in all societies, in one manner or another, the members are distributed according to some positions within the social structure.

Many large societies throughout the world are organized into a structure according to socioeconomic levels, or *social classes*. These develop whenever there is an economic surplus and certain groups or individuals gain control over it for several generations. That such a structure exists in the United States has been demonstrated in many studies, one of which involved a midwestern community given the fictitious name Elmtown, showing five class levels (Hollingshead, 1949). Other investigations have suggested slightly more or fewer levels, but some type of stratification appears to be a fundamental aspect of human groups. Some decades ago, an investigation of a northeastern community referred to as Yankee City suggested two upper, two middle, and two lower levels (Figure 20–20).

Class differences. Studies of social class structure also have indicated several behavioral differences among social classes. For example, the lower the social class, the higher is the rate of mental illness (Dohrenwend & Dohrenwend, 1974). Psychosis appears more prevalent among the lower classes and neurosis among the upper classes, or at least the psychiatric labels are assigned in this way (Hollingshead & Redlich, 1958). Comparable results have been obtained in Pakistan, Italy, and Lebanon (Ahmad, 1971; Frighi et al., 1972; Katchadourian & Churchill, 1973).

Rather sharp differences in sexual behavior were reported 20 to 30 years ago. Lower class individuals were more likely to have premarital intercourse than middle-class persons, but the latter group more commonly engaged in nonprocreative sexual activities, such as masturbation and various forms of sexual foreplay (Kinsey et al., 1948; Kinsey, 1953). With our broader sexual mores today, these class differences are gradually decreasing.

In many societies, verbal behavior is widely recognized as an index of socioeconomic class. The speech of highly educated English persons is similar in London, Manchester, and Southampton, but there is great divergence in the dialects spoken by lower-class people living in or near these cities (Hockett, 1958). Among other groups, such as the Spanish, speech is not nearly so indicative of social class.

Class differences also have been observed in methods of disciplining children. Lower-class parents have been more likely to use physical punishment, whereas middle-class parents more commonly have used withdrawal of love in controlling their children (Bronfenbrenner, 1958). This difference exists in other cultures as well (Magmer & Ipfling, 1973).

The data for juvenile delinquency do not necessarily show a distinction between social classes. The most common view is that individuals of low socioeconomic status are most likely to engage in delinquent acts, but there are exceptional circumstances (Hurry, 1974; Wax, 1972). Another view is that delinquent acts occur with about the same frequency in the middle and lower classes but arrests are more common in the lower-status category (Erickson, 1973).

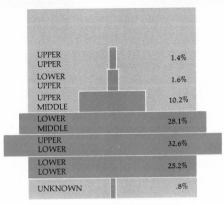

UPPER UPPER	1.4%
LOWER UPPER	1.6%
UPPER MIDDLE	10.2%
LOWER MIDDLE	28.1%
UPPER LOWER	32.6%
LOWER LOWER	25.2%
UNKNOWN	.8%

Figure 20-20   Class Structure.
Societies in the northern hemisphere, at least implicitly, have become organized into socioeconomic levels, making up a class structure, or social classes. Place of residence, occupation, and financial status were among the several criteria used in establishing the different class levels of this Massachusetts community, given the pseudonym Yankee City. (From Warner and Lunt, The Social Life of a Modern Community. *New Haven: Yale University Press, 1941. Sheila A. Farr photos.)*

Fluid and fixed structures.   Children in the United States are exposed to the idea that they can rise from the lower to higher classes. As Benjamin Franklin said, "Early to bed and early to rise/ Makes a man healthy, wealthy and wise." If a person works hard, reward will come in *this* life. One can gain increased wealth and access to some of the highest offices in the land. The United States is a highly mobile or fluid society, particularly in comparison with India; among the sources of this fluidity are the opportunities for education and the widespread changes brought by increasing urbanization.

The caste system of India is somewhat comparable to social class but is much more rigid. Altogether there are several hundred distinctions, but traditionally they comprise four major groups: the Brahman, formerly the priests; the Kshatriya, who were the warriors; the Vaisya, composed of herders and farmers; and the Sudra, who were laborers. Today, these castes are more occupationally diversified. The Vaisya, for example, are mostly tradesmen. Nevertheless, the people generally believe that their position in one of these castes is preordained, and therefore they do not expect to rise to the next higher level. In the *Bhagavad-Gita,* a widely read holy text, a most important message is that one must do his or her own job well, regardless of what it is. If a person does his or her duty, reward will come in *another* life.

When we compare the caste and class systems, we cannot conclude that all the disadvantages lie with the fixed structure and that only advantages occur in a fluid society. The avowed function of the caste system is to make the citizens content, and it constitutes a division of labor presumed to be socially optimal. Inasmuch as one's position in society cannot be changed, one's role is to do what one has to do, to enjoy it as much as possible, and to receive recompense in another life. In certain ways this condition is less frustrating and in other ways more frustrating than that in the United States, where some people "get ahead," but at great sacrifice, and where others are all the more thwarted because they cannot change their lot. But the avowed function of our fluid system also is to make the citizens content.

In the course of history, the caste system often has been eroded by social revolution or evolution and replaced by a class structure. Many writers have gone even further, describing a classless society, but today some hierarchy still exists in every large nation or social group.

Even in the Soviet Union there is a gradation of the citizens from the scientists and artists at the top, who are close to the leaders, down to two classes of peasants at the bottom (Cohen, 1970).

The Leadership Question

In the early history of psychology, studies of leadership occupied a niche of considerable importance, but the hope of depicting all the various traits essential to being an effective leader turned out to be unrealistic. It was found that different situations required different traits in a leader. More specifically, as in a typical interaction effect, the type of leadership that proves most effective depends on the condition of the group, its goals, and the characteristics of its members (Gibb, 1968).

Emergence of a leader. When the leadership is emergent, rather than imposed, the individual who assumes control is usually well above average in intelligence but not the most brilliant individual in the group. The leader must be bright although not exceptional. Secondly, he or she must be at least close to the other group members in attitudes and interests. If the members tend to be authoritarian, the leader must be moderately authoritarian as well.

Studies using a method called *interaction process analysis* have shown the close relationship between leadership and group characteristics. Using this method, interaction patterns are studied by well-trained observers who employ a system of various response categories. When the data from many sessions are analyzed, they usually indicate two general leadership styles. On the one hand, there is a *task specialist,* who is concerned with analyzing the problem, discovering methods of dealing with it, and implementing the best solution. This person is oriented to a specific obstacle or threat to the group. On the other hand, there is a *social specialist,* who emerges as the central figure in group cohesion and maintenance of group morale. This person is also called the

Figure 20-21 **Task and Social Specialists.** *Task specialists usually respond in categories 4 to 9; social specialists respond in the first three or four categories. The profile in black indicates interactions in an adult group with a nondirective leader. The profile in color represents interactions among preschool children in a play situation. (Graph from* Interaction Process Analysis *by R. F. Bales. Copyright © 1951 by University of Chicago Press. Photo by Siteman from Stock, Boston.)*

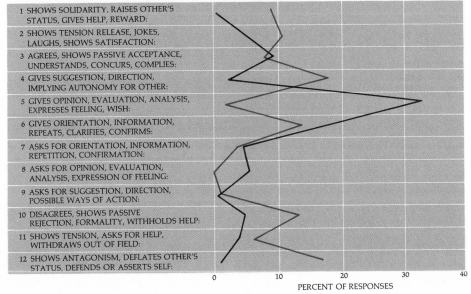

1 SHOWS SOLIDARITY, RAISES OTHER'S STATUS, GIVES HELP, REWARD:

2 SHOWS TENSION RELEASE, JOKES, LAUGHS, SHOWS SATISFACTION:

3 AGREES, SHOWS PASSIVE ACCEPTANCE, UNDERSTANDS, CONCURS, COMPLIES:

4 GIVES SUGGESTION, DIRECTION, IMPLYING AUTONOMY FOR OTHER:

5 GIVES OPINION, EVALUATION, ANALYSIS, EXPRESSES FEELING, WISH:

6 GIVES ORIENTATION, INFORMATION, REPEATS, CLARIFIES, CONFIRMS:

7 ASKS FOR ORIENTATION, INFORMATION, REPETITION, CONFIRMATION:

8 ASKS FOR OPINION, EVALUATION, ANALYSIS, EXPRESSION OF FEELING:

9 ASKS FOR SUGGESTION, DIRECTION, POSSIBLE WAYS OF ACTION:

10 DISAGREES, SHOWS PASSIVE REJECTION, FORMALITY, WITHHOLDS HELP:

11 SHOWS TENSION, ASKS FOR HELP, WITHDRAWS OUT OF FIELD:

12 SHOWS ANTAGONISM, DEFLATES OTHER'S STATUS, DEFENDS OR ASSERTS SELF:

0   10   20   30   40
PERCENT OF RESPONSES

maintenance specialist. On rare occasions, the two roles are adopted by the same individual, but especially as the group continues to function, different individuals emerge in these capacities (Figure 20–21).

An important characteristic of the social specialist seems to be humor, but unfortunately scant research has been accomplished on this topic. Without humor, it is sometimes said, there would be little point to life. Humor is part of virtually every social system, or potentially so, and it can affect that system as a "lubricant" or an "abrasive," thereby influencing the pattern of interaction (Martineau, 1972).

Figure 20-22 Churchill's Leadership. *Sir Winston Churchill, one of the great leaders in English history, occupied the highest position in the land in times of war. In peace, he was voted out of office on several occasions. (The Bettmann Archive)*

The situation. In general, a task leader is likely to be most suitable if the morale of the group is unusually good or if it has deteriorated almost to the point of disintegration. In both cases, a task-oriented, almost dictatorial leader is acceptable. When the conditions are neither extremely favorable nor extremely unfavorable, a social leader is likely to be effective for group performance, simply to maintain group solidarity and cohesion (Fiedler, 1964).

Since so few persons are found to be outstanding in both respects, investigators have reconsidered the "great man" view of leadership, in which one individual is presumed to possess all the important qualities for leadership in a wide variety of situations. As the group goals change, a leader may become a follower; the group is likely to choose a new leader, if it has this option (Figure 20–22).

Psychology and Society

Research in social psychology has extended beyond interpersonal interaction patterns and group structure to consider diverse social problems, several of which have been cited already in other contexts of this volume. These include especially the increasing aggression and crime in our society, the need for methods of mental illness prevention, the education of culturally disadvantaged persons, women's rights, the prejudices arising through ethnocentrism, and the need for more effective use of TV for everyone. Other significant issues are closer to the realms of sociology, economics, and political science, but the most effective solutions in all these instances will be achieved by interdisciplinary teams of scientific investigators, working together rather than separately, and eventually brought into closer association with national policy making (Goodwin, 1975).

A Perspective

As we summarize not only this chapter but also the preceding ones, we are reminded of the remark of the early German psychologist, Hermann Ebbinghaus, "Psychology has a long past but only a short history." The long past refers to speculations about human behavior that date back to the Renaissance, the Middle Ages, and even classical antiquity. Contemplations of human nature are as old as human beings themselves. The reference to a short history is based on the fact that scientific psychology is just a century old, if we regard the founding of Wundt's laboratory in 1879 as its birth. During this first century of psychology's existence, three major trends have occurred.

In the earliest years, both in the United States and Europe, psychologists were associated with philosophers. At the universities, psychologists held chairs of philosophy, and in the American Psychological Association, philosopher-psychologists were elected to the presidency. Productive relations between the two disciplines were praised and sought, and investigations of human behavior were often more speculative than empirical.

By the turn of the century, the influence of philosophy was lessening in favor of a new element. A prominent psychologist noted that psychological theory was being influenced to a significant and perhaps embarrassing extent by viewpoints from the physical sciences (Sanford, 1903). A growing number of psychologists were not embarrassed, however, and they continued to employ methods from the natural sciences. Empirical studies became the essence of psychological inquiry, and in 1907 members of the American Psychological Association met for their annual convention with the American Association of Naturalists, rather than with American philosophers. The president of the psychologists noted, in the grand style of his day, "An outsider might well say, we are off with our old love and on with a new . . ." (Marshall, 1908).

A third discernible trend in psychology's short history is the diversity within the discipline itself. Especially from the 1940s to the present time, psychology has been marked by the continual development of specialized branches. Today the field is so diverse that one sometimes wonders whether it will continue to function as a single whole. The enterprise now concerns almost every aspect of human society, and as new developments arise, other specialties will appear. The common aim of these diverse activities is to gain a better understanding of human behavior and experience and to provide knowledge that can be turned to the betterment of the human condition.

Summary

Socialization of the Individual

1. Human beings are inescapably social beings, perhaps because they are so completely dependent on others for survival in the early years of life. There are critical periods for social learning in lower animals, and there seem to be critical periods early in human life, during which time normal development is arrested if appropriate social stimulation is not received.

2. In seeking social interaction in later life, several factors seem influential in interpersonal attraction. These include similarity of interests, intelligence, and even physical appearance; proximity of the individuals; and their degree of familiarity with one another. Interpersonal attractions are sometimes assessed by obtaining confidential preferences and representing them in a diagram called a sociogram.

Attitudes

3. Attitudes at one time were defined simply as a predisposition to behave in a certain way, but now they are considered to have three components: thinking, feeling, and reacting. They seem to be acquired through direct instruction, classical conditioning, operant conditioning, and modeling, and the same processes are involved in attitude change. However, attitude change can be exceedingly difficult when the attitude is an important aspect of the individual's personality structure.

4. Several theories of attitudes are based on the principle that human beings try to avoid or eliminate inconsistencies. These approaches include balance theory, congruity theory, and cognitive dissonance theory, all of which stress the individual's attempts to achieve harmonious attitudes. Rationalizing, selective perception, and the seeking of new information are all used to reduce dissonance.

5. Stereotypes may be useful in forming quick first impressions of people, but it is extremely difficult to determine the accuracy of such generalizations. A more important problem with stereotypes is that some of them are negatively toned, stemming from ethnocentrism, thus leading to the highly undesirable condition of prejudice.

Patterns of Interaction

6. Incidents of altruism or prosocial behavior seem attributable not so much to a particular type of personality as to aspects of the individual's personal state, such as haste, mood, and degree of conscience. Characteristics of the situation are also important, such as the number of other bystanders and the degree of personal risk involved.

7. Conformity as agreement and obedience has been demonstrated in various laboratory studies, some of which have raised the question of research ethics. In these instances individuals have conformed to group norms even when confronted with contradictory evidence, and others have conformed to the demands of a leader requesting highly inappropriate behavior.

8. When people work in the presence of others, they often accomplish more than when working alone. This social facilitation has been attributed to some type of competitive effort, arousal, face-saving, and the presence of an audience. Two factors that seem important in inducing cooperation in natural settings are early childhood training and the existence of superordinate goals, which benefit all group members.

Group Structure

9. Formally or informally, a group member usually is assigned a role, which is a pattern of expected behavior. A person of a given status, such as a leader, generally has a fairly explicit role, and in a complex society each person usually plays several roles. Status, which is usually closely related to role, refers to a person's position in the group hierarchy.

10. All large societies distribute their members according to some social structure or hierarchy. In Western societies, there are socioeconomic levels, called social classes, which show behavior differences in several areas: severity of psychiatric disorders, sexual mores, verbal behavior, the discipline of children, and apparently juvenile delinquency. A society of social classes offers more mobility than a caste system, but it can engender special frustrations, as well.

11. Studies of leadership indicate that different groups and different situations require different traits in a leader. The emergence of a leader is dependent partly on intelligence and partly on some degree of congruence in leader-follower characteristics. Even within the same group, two prominent leadership styles may be required, one involving a task specialist and the other a social specialist, depending on the situation.

Psychology and Society

12. Research in psychology concerns a wide range of social problems, some of which are unique to this field and others that must be solved by interdisciplinary teams of scientific investigators. In its short history, psychology has moved from a position closely associated with philosophy to an emphasis on empiricism and, most recently, to a high degree of diversity and specialization concerning problems in almost every aspect of the human condition.

The Individual in Society

Suggested Readings

Altman, J. *The environment and social behavior.* Monterey, Calif.: Brooks/ Cole, 1975. Considers the need for privacy as a key concept in understanding contemporary social behavior.

Aronson, E. *The social animal.* San Francisco: W. H. Freeman, 1972. A highly readable discussion, often used as a basic text.

Baron, R. A., & Byrne, D. *Social psychology: Understanding human interaction* (2nd ed.). Boston: Allyn & Bacon, 1977. A comprehensive survey of the field.

McKee, M., & Robertson, I. *Social problems.* New York: Random House, 1975. Presents the sociology of social problems in readable, well-documented form.

Middlebrook, P. N. *Social psychology and modern life.* New York: Knopf, 1974. A comprehensive text with a research orientation and numerous citations.

Glossary

This glossary defines technical terms used in this textbook, as well as a few other words used in a special sense, but only the meanings relevant to the text appear here. For additional meanings, and for definitions of other psychological terms, the following dictionaries will prove helpful: J. P. Chaplin, *Dictionary of Psychology,* New York: Dell, 1968, and H. B. English and A. C. English, *A Comprehensive Dictionary of Psychological and Psychoanalytical Terms,* New York: David McKay, 1958.

ability   Present skill, as in riding a bicycle or reciting a poem. Contrasted with *aptitude,* It refers to what an individual can do rather than what one might do if given appropriate training.

abscissa (ab-sis'-uh) The horizontal or X axis of a graph.

absolute refractory period   See *refractory period.*

absolute threshold   See *threshold.*

abstract thinking   Thinking in terms of concepts and general principles, as contrasted with thinking of specific objects or events.

abstracting   Discerning common elements in situations which are otherwise different.

accommodation   See *visual accommodation.*

achievement motive   The desire to accomplish difficult tasks and overcome obstacles. More specifically, when an individual is not so much concerned with success or failure in a given task as with attaining a certain standard set for himself or herself.

achievement test   A test which, as distinguished from aptitude and intelligence tests, measures what has been accomplished, as in mathematics, history, or French.

acquired motivation   Motivation which is not inborn in the organism. For example, the desire for a certain set of golf clubs or to receive a passing grade in school. Also called secondary motivation. See *inborn motivation.*

ACTH   The hormone from the pituitary gland which stimulates the adrenal cortex. The full name is adrenocorticotrophic (uh-dree'-nō-kort-i-ko-trof'-ik) hormone.

action potential   The nerve impulse; changes in electrical potential along a nerve fiber which accompany the conduction of an impulse. See also *nerve impulse.*

activity cage   A cage equipped with some device to record the running or other activity of an organism.

activity cycle   Rhythmic fluctuations of activity, as in the two-hour hunger and four-day sex rhythms of rats.

adaptation   Adjustment. Sensory adaptation involves a change in the characteristics of experience as a result of prior stimulation, as when we gradually see more clearly in a darkened room or taste something as especially sour after eating sweets.

adequate stimulus   The *normal* or typical stimulation for a given receptor. For example, light waves are the normal and therefore adequate stimuli for vision, though visual experiences may be produced by other means, such as a sharp blow on the back of the head. Usually, the term *stimulus* is used alone.

adjustment The more or less continuous process of satisfying one's inborn and acquired motivations.

adolescence A period between the ages of approximately thirteen and twenty for boys and one to two years earlier for girls during which the individual acquires the secondary sex characteristics and other adult traits. The physical changes are accompanied by important psychological changes, relating particularly to the self-concept.

adrenal gland (uh-dreen'l) An endocrine gland, about the size of a pea, located above each kidney. The central part (medulla) secretes adrenalin or noradrenalin, while the outer part (cortex) secretes cortisone.

adrenalin (uh-dren'-ul-un) A secretion of the adrenal medula which plays a role in making available extra energy during emergency. See also *noradrenalin.*

aerial perspective Clearness of details under different atmospheric conditions. Objects with clear details appear nearer than hazy objects. Therefore aerial perspective is a cue for depth perception.

affective psychosis A psychiatric disorder characterized by a severe emotional reaction, often depressive in nature, usually with a disruptive effect on the person's thinking and behavior. See two common affective reactions, *manic-depressive psychosis* and *involutional melancholia.*

affective state A psychological condition which underlies or involves feeling or emotion. The feeling aspects of emotion, as opposed to behavioral and physiological aspects.

afferent Sensory; leading in. Used in describing the function of some nerve fibers. See also *efferent.*

after-image A sensory experience which appears after withdrawal of certain visual stimuli. A *negative after-image* has a color that is approximately complementary to the original stimulus. A *positive after-image* is a momentary increase in the brightness of a color experienced immediately after one ceases looking at that color.

age regression When a hypnotized person behaves as he or she allegedly did at an earlier age; regarded as a characteristic of some hypnotic behavior.

aggression Hostility which may involve actual attack, physical or verbal, upon other people.

all-or-none principle The principle that a nerve fiber responds completely if it responds at all. The principle that there is no partial nerve impulse.

ambivalence Being pulled psychologically in opposite directions, as in both loving and hating the same person.

ambivert One who has neither pronounced introvert nor extravert characteristics; a person between these extremes.

amnesia Loss of memory, as after a blow on the head or an emotional upset.

amniotic sac One of the sacs that surround the embryo.

amplitude The extent to which a vibrating body is displaced from the resting position.

anaesthesia (an-us-thee'-zhuh) Partial or total loss of sensitivity, especially in the skin, as when one's sense of pain is dull or absent.

anal character Qualities such as stubbornness and excessive orderliness, presumably relating, in the Freudian view, to early toilet training.

analgesia Insensitivity to normally painful stimuli; regarded as characteristic of some hypnotic states.

analytic psychology The approach to psychoanalysis presented by Carl Gustav Jung; a significant concept in this approach is the collective unconscious, in addition to the individual unconscious.

androgens (an'-druh-junz) Male sex hormones.

anti-social reaction The behavior disorder shown by an individual who is hostile to the laws and norms of his or her culture. See *dyssocial reaction.*

anvil Small bone in the middle ear located between the hammer and the stirrup.

anxiety Apprehension, dread, uneasiness. The feeling stems from fear, but it is more a fear of what might happen or what has happened than of an obvious, specific fear-provoking situation. An important term in psychiatry with a variety of meanings.

anxiety hierarchy A mental patient's ranking of a class of situations from least to most anxiety-producing, which is then used as a basis for a procedure called systematic desensitization.

anxiety neurosis A form of neurosis characterized by widespread anxiety without an obvious source and with no obvious defensive reaction.

aperiodic Without rhythm or cycle.

aphasia (uh-fay'-zhuh) Literally, "without speech." A disorder involving loss of linguistic meaning, such as loss of ability to understand what is heard or what is read. Motor aphasia is loss of ability to articulate.

apperceiving Perceiving a situation in terms of past experience rather than in terms of the immediately present stimuli.

appetitive behavior (a-pet'-it-iv) Movement of an organism toward a certain type of stimulation, such as food or a mate. Also called *adient behavior*. See also *aversive behavior*.

applied psychologist Psychologists who attempt to utilize or apply scientific discoveries for some practical purpose. The emphasis is upon using currently existing knowledge for the benefit of humanity rather than upon the discovery process. Compare with *research psychologist*.

approach-approach conflict A situation of indecision in which the individual is confronted with equally attractive alternatives.

approach-avoidance conflict A situation of indecision involving a single object or event which has both attractive and aversive features. When two or more such objects or events are involved, the situation is called double approach-avoidance.

approximations, method of A procedure in operant conditioning by which an organism learns a certain behavior in a step-by-step fashion, each step involving a response slightly more complex than the one preceding it. The correct behavior at each step is reinforced until that step is mastered. Then, the next step, which is still closer to the final criterion, is reinforced, and so forth.

aptitude The capacity to learn readily and to achieve a high level of skill in a specific area, such as music, mathematics, or mechanics. It refers to potential rather than actual accomplishment. See *achievement test*.

aqueous humor (ay'-kwee-us) A jellylike substance behind the cornea of the eye.

area sample A sample which includes subgroups of people or items from certain geographic areas in the same proportion as they appear in the population. In a given region, if two-thirds of the population lives in Orange County, one-sixth in Brown County, and one-sixth in White County, then the sample is composed of people from these same counties in these same ratios. Within each county, however, the sample is selected on a random basis.

assessment Evaluating an individual with respect to his or her various traits.

association area The most forward portions of the cerebral cortex, assumed to integrate previously stored and incoming information. Activation of the association area apparently adds the influence of prior learning to current stimulation.

associative processes Establishing relationships between or among events, especially through conditioning; a form of learning in which the basic elements are stimulus-response connections. The strength of the association is influenced by the frequency with which the events are presented together.

associative strength The strength of an S-R linkage as measured by the frequency with which a stimulus elicits a particular response. Thus, the stimulus word *white* brings the response *black* more often than the response *green*. We can say, therefore, that the *white-black* connection has greater associative strength than the connection *white-green*.

astereognosis Literally, "without tactile knowledge of space." A disability associated with lesions in the parietal lobe, characterized by inability to recognize objects or geometric forms by touch.

attending Readiness to perceive, as in listening or looking. Focusing of sense organs is sometimes involved.

attitude A predisposition to react in a certain way; a readiness to react, a determining tendency. Basic components of attitudes are sometimes said to be thinking, feeling and reacting in a certain manner.

attribution theory Study of the process by which people attribute characteristics to other individuals; the attempt to identify the ideas or procedures that people use in making inferences about other people's personality and behavior.

audiogenic seizure A convulsion produced by exposure to certain high-frequency sounds, demonstrated to occur on a genetic basis in certain lower animals.

auditory labyrinth Part of inner ear concerned with hearing, as opposed to balance.

auditory localization Naming or pointing to positions from which sounds emanate.

authoritarian personality A cluster of personality traits reflecting a desire for security. These traits might include a rigid, highly conventional outlook, extreme obedience, scapegoating of minority group members, and a desire for structured lines of authority. The trait pattern is assumed to develop from the child's interactions with a domineering parent.

autistic thinking Thought which is clearly removed from reality, markedly influenced by one's desires; an extreme form of fantasy sometimes characteristic of children and adults with psychiatric disturbance.

autokinetic effect (aw-tō-kuh-net'-ik) The apparent drifting of a small fixed spot of light in an otherwise completely dark room.

autonomic nervous system The relatively independent system, comprising the sympathetic and parasympathetic divisions, which regulates the various inner organs of the body, such as the heart, stomach, and glands.

aversion therapy The use of classical conditioning procedures to remove unwanted positive emotional responses, such as the desire for alcohol, smoking, and sexual relations with persons of the same sex. For example, an electric shock, nauseous drug, or some other negative stimulus is paired with alcohol on numerous trials, thereby creating an aversive reaction towards the alcohol consumption.

aversive behavior Movement of the organism away from a certain type of stimulation, such as electric shock. Also called *abient behavior*. See also *appetitive behavior*.

avoidance-avoidance conflict A situation in which the individual is caught between two unattractive alternatives.

avoidance conditioning An organism's learning to avoid punishment by making an appropriate anticipatory response. Compare with *escape conditioning*.

axon That part of the neuron which carries the nerve impulse away from the cell body and into another nerve fiber or neural structure. The axon of a motor neuron carries the nerve impulse into the muscle fiber; the axon of a sensory neuron carries impulses into synaptic connections with the dendrites of a motor or an association neuron.

backward conditioning A variation of classical conditioning in which the usual order is reversed; the unconditioned stimulus appears first, followed by the conditioned stimulus. This procedure generally is not regarded as a form of true classical conditioning, and the learning, if present, is often of short duration.

balance theory See *consistency principle.*

barrier Insurmountable obstacle which interferes with need satisfaction. It may be environmental or within the individual.

baseline A measurement of the frequency of a certain response prior to treatment by an experimenter.

basilar membrane A membrane at the base of the cochlear canal. Its movements play an important role in stimulating the auditory nerve.

behavior In its broadest sense, anything an organism does; any response made by an organism. Some psychologists prefer to limit usage of this term to responses that may be observed or measured.

behavior chain See *chaining.*

behavior genetics A field concerned with the influence of heredity on behavior.

behavior modification The use of conditioning procedures in the treatment of psychological problems. Both classical and operant methods are used. Also called behavior therapy.

behaviorism A school of psychology which stresses an objective, natural science approach to psychological questions. Observations are confined to observable behavior. Conscious experience, because of its subjectivity, is considered outside the scope of scientific psychology, according to behaviorists.

binaural Pertaining to both ears.

Binet-Simon Scale The forerunner of individual intelligence tests, particularly the Stanford-Binet; named for its originators.

binocular (bi-nok'-yuh-ler) Involving both eyes at the same time.

biofeedback A condition in which an electroencephalogram, electrocardiogram, or comparable device is used to present information to an individual about his or her bodily functioning, such as type of brain waves being emitted or rate of heartbeat. Studies have indicated that with this information some persons are able to alter the relevant bodily processes.

biosocial Involving the interplay of biological and social influences.

blind spot A small area in the retina which has no receptors and therefore provides no visual image. It is the area where the optic nerve connects with the retina.

brain The large mass of nerve tissue above the spinal cord, including the brain stem, cerebellum, and cerebral hemispheres.

brain bisection Surgical division of the brain longitudinally, between the two hemispheres. This procedure is sometimes used to alleviate epileptic seizures and also to study brain functions, in which case the term *split-brain research* may be used.

brain localization The effort to identify mental and behavioral functions related to certain areas of the brain, such as mapping the sensory and motor areas adjacent to the central fissure.

brain stem The part of the brain below the cerebral hemispheres and cerebellum.

brainstorming A group problem-solving situation in which members contribute any ideas which seem to have the slightest bearing on the problem. A central principle is that all evaluations of ideas are withheld until later, thus creating maximum opportunity for novel thoughts to emerge.

brainwashing Inducing people to modify their attitudes and behavior in certain directions through various forms of social pressure and perhaps also physical torture.

brightness The intensity aspect of light; the visual dimension represented by the black-white continuum. Also, a high level of intelligence, in contrast to dullness.

California Psychological Inventory A personality inventory used with normal persons. Emphasis is upon social interaction variables.

Cannon-Bard theory The view that the feeling aspect of emotion and the pattern of emotional behavior are controlled by the hypothalamus.

carpentered-world hypothesis The hypothesis that individuals from societies in which "carpentered" (rectangular) objects are present will be more susceptible to illusions involving rectangular patterns than will individuals from cultures which are not oriented to rectangular shapes.

case history Assembled data which reconstruct an individual's past with the aim of understanding his or her present problems and aiding in future adjustment.

catatonic (kat-uh-ton′ik) A form of schizophrenia characterized by such symptoms as extreme negativism, physical rigidity, and holding bizarre postures.

catharsis A release of tensions by expressing pent-up emotions and by reliving early traumatic events; an aspect of psychotherapy often encouraged by the therapist.

cell body The compact central portion of a neuron; the neuron exclusive of its projections, axon and dendrites.

central fissure The crevice or invagination separating the frontal and parietal lobes of the brain.

central nervous system The brain and spinal cord.

central tendency A statistical measure representative of a distribution of scores; the mode, median, and mean.

cephalocaudal development (sef-uh-lō-kawd′-l) A gradient of growth, particularly in the embryonic stage, proceeding from head to tail. In a fetus, the head is likely to be more fully developed than the trunk and lower body parts.

cerebellum (ser-uh-bell′-um) A brain structure, connected to the brain stem via the pons, which plays a central role in motor coordination throughout the body.

cerebral cortex The greatly invaginated outer layer of cerebral cells (gray matter); the region for many complex neural connections..

cerebrontia (sa-ree-bra-tō′-nee-uh) Temperament characterized by such features as restraint, shyness, hypersensitivity, reflection.

cerebrum (sa-ree′-brum) The largest portion of the human brain, consisting of two symmetrical divisions known as the cerebral hemispheres. The outer layer (cortex) is gray; the inner area is white matter. This structure plays a vital role in the versatility of human functioning.

chaining Learning related behaviors in a series, in which each response serves as a stimulus for the next response, as when a child learns to write his or her name letter by letter.

character Personality viewed from the standpoint of what is ethical or moral, such as a person's honesty; ordinarily it has reference to relatively fixed traits.

chemosensitivity The senses of smell (gaseous forms) and taste (soluble substances).

chemotherapy Treatment of mental disorders by the use of drugs and chemicals.

chlorpromazine (klor-prōm′-uh-zeen) A tranquilizing drug.

choleric A personality type suggested by Hippocrates, characterized as easily angered, ready to fight.

choroid coat (kor′-oyd) The middle, pigmented layer of the eyeball. Its primary function is to exclude light.

chromosomes (krō′-muh-sōmz) Structures within the nucleus of a cell which contain the hereditary determiners, or genes.

chronological age Actual age from birth, regardless of developmental level.

chronoscope (kron′-uh-skōp) A device which measures speed of reaction.

ciliary muscle (sil′-ee-er-ee) Muscle surrounding the lens of the eye, which regulates the curvature of the lens to focus the eye for clear vision.

circumvallate papillae (ser-kum-val′-ayt puh-pill′-ee) Structures toward the back of the tongue which contain receptors generally credited with mediating bitter tastes.

clairvoyance An aspect of extrasensory sensory perception in which someone allegedly is able to know about on-going events without the aid of currently known sensory processes.

classical conditioning A form of learning, as in the experiments of Pavlov, in which a previously neutral stimulus becomes a conditioned stimulus—capable of eliciting a given response—after being repeatedly presented with an unconditioned stimulus. The process is sometimes called stimulus substitution because a new stimulus evokes the response in question, such as salivation.

client-centered therapy A verbal therapy characterized by relatively little suggestion or direction from the therapist. Solutions to the client's problems are developed primarily by the client, while the therapist acts largely as a catalyst.

clinical psychology Concerned with diagnosis and psychotherapy of behavior disorders. Many clinical psychologists work in collaboration with psychiatrists.

closure, principle of The principle that when we view fragmentary stimuli forming a nearly complete figure, we tend to ignore the missing parts and perceive the figure as whole.

cochlea (kok′-lee-uh) A coiled structure of the inner ear which contains the receptors essential for hearing.

coefficient of correlation A numerical value which represents the degree of relationship between two variables. It ranges from zero to ± 1.00.

cognition A general term indicating knowledge and awareness; it includes perceiving, remembering, reasoning, and other means of knowing about oneself and the environment.

cognitive dissonance theory A theory of attitude formation and behavior which indicates that persons try to achieve consistency and avoid dissonance; when dissonance arises, it may be handled by changing one's attitude, rationalizing, selective perception, and other means.

cognitive-physiological theory The view that physiological arousal and an interpretation of the stimulating circumstances are the chief elements in determining the affective component of emotional experience.

cognitive processes A general term emphasizing knowledge, understanding, and awareness on the part of the organism; it includes the processes of perceiving, remembering, and reasoning. In this approach to learning, the contribution of the organism is emphasized.

collective unconscious According to Jung, a portion of the unconscious which is inherited and found in all members of a given race or species.

color blindness A weakness or defect in sensitivity to hue; for example, in red-green blindness the individual has difficulty in distinguishing red and green from grays of the same brightness.

color constancy The tendency for an object to be perceived as maintaining its basic color despite changes in illumination, as when snow is seen to be white even though in shade or at dusk it has a purple cast.

color vision Response to the wavelength properties of light, i.e., what we experience as hue.

communication The transmission of information from one source to another.

comparative psychology Often used as synonymous with animal psychology. More accurately, the comparison of behavior at different levels of development to discover development trends—as in the evolution of intelligence from amoeba to human beings.

compensation Counterbalancing some change, such as a lowering of temperature, or some defect, such as a feeling of inferiority. The term has somewhat different implications for psychologists of different schools. As a defense mechanism, it is shown when a person who falls short of his or her goal in one area strives to achieve in another area instead.

compulsion An irresistible urge to perform some act, such as to steal, to light fires, or to avoid stepping in any shadows when out for a walk.

computer-assisted instruction Use of a computer to present educational tasks to the student. Often, the tasks are prepared in the form of programmed learning, involving a step-by-step sequence. An important advantage of the computer is that its enormous memory system and immediate recall can be used to present material at the appropriate level for a given individual, in accordance with his or her prior responses.

concept An abstract idea or conclusion based on a generalization from particular instances, such as "anything burning is hot."

conception Fertilization of an ovum by a sperm.

concrete operations According to Piaget, a stage of development in thinking, occurring approximately between ages 7 and 11 years, during which the child becomes capable of reasoning about concrete situations.

concrete thinking Thinking in terms of particulars, such as pears, apples, and bananas, in contrast to thinking in terms of categories, such as fruit. The latter involves abstract or conceptual thinking.

concurrent validity The extent to which a test may be used to predict present performance on another task.

conditioned response A response aroused by some stimulus other than that which naturally produces it, such as salivation in response to a tone, or, in operant conditioning, a response that has become more frequent after being reinforced.

conditioned stimulus A previously neutral stimulus which acquires the property of eliciting a particular response through pairing with an unconditioned stimulus.

conditioning Sometimes used as synonymous with learning. More specifically, the process through which conditioned responses are developed. Two major types are often identified, classical conditioning and operant conditioning.

cone A receptor in the retina primarily for color vision.

conflict The tension or stress involved when satisfaction of needs is thwarted by equally attractive or unattractive alternatives. See *approach-approach, avoidance-avoidance,* and *approach-avoidance.*

confounding variables Extraneous factors which influence the outcome of an experiment in unknown ways; variables which, because they represent mixed and uncontrolled influences, give an experiment an uninterpretable result.

congenital Present from birth but not necessarily inherited. Congenital syphilis, for example, is not inherited but contracted through contact with the mother. A congenital mental handicap is sometimes the result of an hereditary defect in the nervous system and sometimes the result of a defective prenatal environment.

congruity theory See *consistency principle.*

connector neuron Neurons existing in the brain and spinal cord which connect sensory, motor, or other connector neurons. Also called *association neuron.*

connotative meaning The abstract, often emotional meaning of a word. The connotative meaning of the word *fox,* for example, suggests slyness and cunning. See also *denotative meaning.*

conscience An attitude assumed by the individual when he or she fails to conform to the moral or ethical ways of his or her group, or when tempted to behave in ways other than the approved ways; in Freudian psychology, part of the superego. Ideals and ideas acquired from the parents or other significant persons in one's early life.

conscious experience Experience of which the individual is currently aware, as distinguished from *past experience.* Conscious experiences may be considered as those which the individual can describe, such as sensory experiences and feelings.

consistency principle The desire of the human being to be consistent, especially with regard to attitudes and beliefs. Theories of attitude formation and change based on the consistency principle include *balance theory* and *congruity theory,* which suggest that the individual seeks to avoid imbalance (incongruity) in various attitudes. See also *cognitive dissonance theory.*

constancy phenomenon The tendency for color, size, or shape to remain relatively constant despite marked changes in stimulation.

constitutional typology A personality theory which attempts to relate body structure and personality.

construct (kon'-strukt) An hypothesized relationship concerning structures or processes underlying observable events. Motives, for example, are constructs. Many theoretical terms in science are constructs. The *engram,* the *subconscious,* and *insight* are psychological constructs.

construct validity A type of validity indicating the extent to which the items in a test reflect the constructs upon which they are presumably based. Related to content validity but more theoretical, less empirical in nature. See also *construct.*

consumer psychology A specialty which focuses upon consumer behavior of all sorts. The field began with developments in advertising and buying behavior but has been expanded to include noncommercial purposes, such as campaigns for government projects and opinion surveys for educational and environmental programs.

content validity The adequacy with which a test measures representative components of the skill in question.

context The general setting in which an event occurs; the surroundings.

contingency management The use of techniques of operant conditioning for therapeutic purposes, especially on a widespread basis. For example, an individual's environment is managed in such a way that reward is contingent upon the appearance of the desired behavior.

continuity, principle of The principle that a line or movement tends to be perceived as continuing in the direction which has already been established.

continuous reinforcement A schedule of reinforcement in which every correct response is reinforced.

control group A group of subjects comparable to the experimental group in all respects except for the condition under investigation, usually referred to as the independent variable.

controlled Varied or held constant, according to certain specifications, by the investigator in an experiment.

conventionalization In memory, the tendency to transform the original stimulus into familiar patterns.

convergence The turning inward of the eyes, as when focusing on a nearby object.

convergent thinking Thought which is directed toward obtaining a certain answer to a given problem, generally recognized as the only answer or the obvious best answer.

conversion reaction A neurotic reaction in which a psychological problem is converted into a physical one.

cornea The transparent front portion of the eyeball, which admits light.

corpus callosum The connecting structure between the two hemispheres of the brain, currently assumed to be responsible for the development of duplicate memories in both cerebral hemispheres; it apparently transmits information gained in one hemisphere to the other one.

correlation A relationship between variables such that changes in one are to some degree accompanied by changes in the other.

correlation coefficient See *coefficient of correlation.*

cortex Bark or outer layer, as in the cortex of the adrenal gland and in the cerebral cortex.

cortical Having reference to the cortex.

cortical localization Attributing a certain physical or psychological function to some particular region of the cerebral cortex, such as localizing hearing functions in the temporal lobe.

cortisone (kort'-uh-zone) One of the hormones secreted by the adrenal gland.

co-twin control The use of identical twins to make controlled studies of the hereditary contribution to behavior. One twin is subjected to experimental conditions and the other is not.

counseling psychology 'A specialty within psychology which deals with the educational, vocational, and adjustment problems of so-called normal persons.

counterbalancing A procedure for distributing unwanted influences equally among the different experimental conditions or subjects. For example, if the experiment requires learning both French and Spanish, some subjects will learn French and then Spanish; others will learn Spanish and then French. In this way, the subjects' fatigue affects the learning of both French and Spanish similarly.

counterconditioning The procedure of classical conditioning as used in therapy to remove some fear or other negative affective state. A positive stimulus is presented in such a fashion that it outweighs the patient's potential negative response to the fear-producing stimulus.

covert conditioning A procedure in counterconditioning in which the negative stimulus is not actually present but only imagined by the fearful individual. The conditioning procedures are applied to the imagined aspects, at least in the early stages of therapy. See *counterconditioning.*

cranial nerves Twelve pairs of nerves arising directly from the cerebrum and passing through an opening in the skull.

creative thinking Productive thinking, with novel rather than routine outcomes.

cretinism (kreet'-n-iz-m) An abnormality of structure and behavior which results from insufficient thyroid secretion during early growth. Involves stunted growth, protruding abdomen, and pronounced mental retardation.

cristae (kris'-tee) Small structures in the semicircular canals containing hairs which are bent by rotary motion. These structures are important in maintaining balance.

criterion A standard against which tests are validated, such as grades or sales records. Plural, *criteria.*

criterion-referenced test A test in which the person's score is compared with some previously established criterion, rather than with the performances of others; used for determining the amount of learning or amount of change within one individual, not for assessing differences among individuals.

critical period A term with special reference to imprinting. It is the period of maximum imprintability or, as sometimes used, the period before and after which imprinting is difficult or impossible to obtain. Also, in animals, a period when socialization is possible. See also *imprinting.*

critical score The minimum score a candidate must achieve to be accepted into a given program or to pass the test.

cross-sectional method A developmental method involving the comparison of groups of individuals at different age levels. Contrasted with the longitudinal method, where the same individual is observed as he or she grows older.

cross-validation Assessing the value of a test by using it with a sample of subjects other than the ones employed in its construction; testing with new subjects a set of test items already found to be of value with an earlier group.

cultural relativism The view that concepts such as beauty, normality, or virtue and standards of behavior have meaning only in relation to a particular culture.

culture Traits, implements, beliefs, and practices which characterize a certain group of people.

culture-fair test A test of general intelligence allegedly of the same difficulty for persons from different cultures; the items are presumed to be no more difficult for persons from one culture or another. Attempts to construct a test of this sort have not been notably successful.

culture-free test A test of general intelligence in which the influence of culture presumably has been eliminated; the items do not pertain to any particular culture. Attempts to construct a test of this type have been unsuccessful.

cutaneous (kyoo-tay'-nee-us) Pertaining to the skin.

cycle Rhythm; in auditory stimulation, one full periodic vibration. Often the number of such vibrations per second is recorded.

dark adaptation Increasing visual sensitivity as one remains in darkness or low illumination.

daydreaming Fantasy in the waking state.

decay theory A theory of forgetting based on the premise that the engram deteriorates during an interval when it is not activated.

defense mechanisms Behavior patterns primarily concerned with protecting the ego. Presumably the process is unconscious and the aim is to fool oneself. For examples, see *repression* and *rationalization*.

déjà vu (day'-zha voo) The feeling that a new situation is familiar—that one has "been there" before. *Déjà* experiences occur through several of the senses—visual, auditory, olfactory, and others.

delayed conditioning A method of classical conditioning in which the conditioned stimulus remains present until the appearance of the unconditioned stimulus.

delusion A false judgment or conclusion, as when a mentally ill person incorrectly believes that people are putting ground glass in his or her food.

dementia praecox (di-men'-chuh pree'coks) A name formerly given to schizophrenia. It means "youthful insanity."

dendrite Part of the neuron which carries the nerve impulse toward the cell body.

denotative meaning The specific class of objects or events to which a term refers. *Fox,* for example, refers to mammals of a certain size, shape, coloring, and other characteristics. Compare with *connotative meaning*.

deoxyribonucleic acid (DNA) The chemical substance presumed basic in the genetic code and possibly in the physiological basis of memory.

dependent variable An aspect of behavior or experience which goes with or depends upon changes in the independent variable. Example: speed of reaction is partly dependent upon the intensity of the stimulus to which the response is made.

depression A melancholy mood, a feeling of hopelessness, an attitude of dejection. In serious cases, a symptom of mental illness.

depth perception Perceiving three-dimensionality or distance.

depth factors Underlying aspects of the personality, usually revealed by probing into the motivational aspects of personality, especially those of which an individual is not aware or which are, in Freudian terminology, *unconscious*.

descriptive method See *naturalistic observation.*

descriptive statistics Numerical values which describe the chief features of a group of scores, without regard to a larger population.

determinism The doctrine that for every effect there is a cause; in psychology, the view that every aspect of behavior or experience is related to an antecedent event, external or internal to the individual.

development Continuous change, as when an organism approaches maturity. Used to represent growth of language, of understanding, or of some skill. Development resulting largely from hereditary factors is often referred to as maturation, which may be contrasted with development resulting largely from the learning process.

developmental psychology The study of changes in the organism which occur with aging.

deviation IQ A statistically derived IQ. In contrast with the conventional IQ (MA/CA X 100), it is determined by the standard deviation of the distribution of MA scores at a given age level and the deviation of the individual score from the mean of this distribution.

dexterity Skillfulness, expertness, versatility. The person who uses both hands well is said to be ambidextrous, to possess ambidexterity.

difference threshold The smallest perceptible difference between two stimuli. See also *just noticeable difference; threshold.*

differential conditioning Conditioning in which the organism discriminates between stimuli, giving a conditioned response to one stimulus and not to a similar but different one.

differential forgetting Selective forgetting, especially forgetting erroneous responses faster than correct ones.

discovery learning Learning situations in which the subject must discover the chief contents or principles and then incorporate them into his or her behavior and thinking.

discrimination Responding differentially, as when an organism makes one response to a reinforced stimulus and another response or no response to a stimulus that is not reinforced.

displaced aggression Hostility directed against some object or person other than the source of one's anger, usually a weaker person or an inanimate object, from which retaliation is unlikely.

dissociative reaction Separation of ideas or of responses normally associated. A neurotic reaction. For example, having two or more different personalities, e.g., Dr. Jekyll and Mr. Hyde.

dissonance In social psychology and attitude theory, an aversive state which arises when an individual is aware of inconsistency or conflict within himself or herself.

distal stimulus A source of stimulation as it exists apart from the stimulated individual; physical energy at its source, such as light reflected from a building. Compare with *proximal stimulus.*

distributed practice Learning with small units of work and/or interpolated rest periods. Contrasted with massed learning, where the individual works continually until the skill is mastered.

divergent thinking Thought which is directed toward finding many different answers or novel answers to a problem; the goal is to seek numerous possible solutions rather than *the* single answer.

DNA See *deoxyribonucleic acid.*

dominance In heredity, a trait which depends upon the presence of one gene (dominant) which suppresses the effects of its counterpart (recessive). Two recessive genes must be present to express the recessive trait. Cortical dominance refers to the dominance of one side or hemisphere of the brain in control of handedness and speech.

dominance hierarchy   A social situation in which one organism dominates all below it, the next all below it, and so on, down to the organism dominated by all. A pecking order in barnyard hens.

dominant gene   See *dominance*.

double alternation problem   A situation in which the organism is required to make a right, right, left, left, . . . (*rrll*) or some other comparable sequence of turns in a temporal maze.

double-bind situation   A situation in which contradictory demands or meanings are communicated in the same message or environment. The father, for example, may encourage his son to be competitive and follow the "law of the jungle" while the mother urges him to cooperate with other people and "turn the other cheek." On this basis, the son is in a double bind.

double-blind procedure   In a psychological experiment, any method which prevents both the experimenter and the subject from knowing which treatment the subject receives. Often used in drug experiments.

Down's syndrome   A condition of mental retardation and other abnormalities presumably related to the inheritance of an extra chromosome.

dream interpretation   A fundamental technique in psychoanalysis in which dreams are interpreted in terms of underlying meaning. See *latent dream content*.

drift theory   A social theory stating that schizophrenic individuals migrate to impoverished urban neighborhoods by a process of social selection.

drive   A physiological condition involving sensitivity to certain types of stimulation. Usually it impels the organism to become active. Distinguished from a motive in being initially indiscriminate, without an appropriate direction.

drive reduction   Alleviating tensions associated with drives.

dual personality   See *multiple personality*.

dyssocial reaction (di-sō'-shul)   A personality deviation from the norm of the general culture which is nevertheless in accordance with the norm of a particular subculture. The subculture as a whole represents a deviation from the broader norm, usually in the form of aggression or resistance to it. Juvenile delinquents, for example, may conform to the mores of a "street gang," but usually they are considered delinquent in the larger population.

Dvořák keyboard   The typewriter keyboard as designed by Augustine Dvořák in the early decades of the twentieth century. The vowels and most commonly used consonants are placed in the home row, making the keyboard generally more efficient than the conventional keyboard in wide usage today.

eardrum   The tympanic membrane, stretched across the inner end of the auditory canal. It vibrates in resonance with external sounds, activating mechanisms of the middle ear.

eclectic (e-klek'-tik)   Literally, "choosing." Eclecticism in therapy, for example, occurs when the therapist espouses no single approach but chooses among the viewpoints available.

ectomorphy (ek-tuh-mor'-fee)   A dimension of body build characterized by thinness and predominance of skin and neural mechanisms.

educational psychology   The field having to do with applications of psychology to the processes of education, such as teaching school subjects.

effectors   Muscles and glands. The nerves that go from the central nervous system to effectors.

efferent   Motor (muscle) functions; leading out. See also *afferent*.

ego The individual's conception of himself or herself. Also, in psychoanalysis, that part of the personality which, as an outcome of experience, restrains the expressions of the id and deals with the demands of the external environment. See also *superego* and *id.*

ego-defensive Compensatory, attempting to maintain self-esteem under conditions which threaten it.

ego-ideal The person an individual is striving to become; a positive identification. Contrasted with the conscience, which pertains to behaviors the individual wishes to avoid. See also *superego.*

ego-involvement Personal involvement in some person or situation, as when the parent feels that the child's triumphs or defeats are his or her own.

eidetic imagery (i-det'ik) Imagery of such clearness that the objects represented appear in some respects to be present.

elaboration In memory, emphasis and perhaps exaggeration of central themes, in contrast to the loss of lesser details.

Electra complex A term used by Freud to represent the erotic attachment of a daughter to her father, with accompanying jealousy of the mother. This attachment may be repressed and disguised in various ways. See also *Oedipus complex.*

electrocardiogram (i-lek-trō-kard'-ee-uh-gram) A record of the various phases of heart activity derived from electrical concomitants of this activity. Abbreviated EKG.

electroconvulsive therapy Also referred to as *electric shock therapy* and *electro-shock therapy.* Attempting to relieve such symptoms as extreme depression by passing a weak electric current through the brain from electrodes applied to the scalp, thereby producing widespread convulsions. Abbreviated ECT.

electroencephalogram (i-lek-trō-en-sef'-uh-lō-gram) A record of electrical rhythms associated with some brain activities. Recorded with an *electroencephalograph;* abbreviated EEG.

emotion A complex condition underlying such feelings, actions, and physiological changes as occur in fear, rage, excitement, and so on. In its most obvious manifestations it is an acute condition characterized by disruption of routine experiences and activities.

empathy Understanding and accepting another person's mental and emotional states, as opposed to sympathy, where the individual actually experiences the other person's feelings.

empiricism (im-peer'-uh-siz-m) Seeking evidence through direct experience rather than through reasoning or intuition.

encounter groups Meetings of interested individuals and one or more trained leaders for the purpose of relating to one another on an affective, emotional level; sometimes called *T-groups* or *sensitivity groups.*

endocrine glands Glands which pour their products (hormones) directly into the bloodstream. Ductless glands.

endolymph (en'-duh-limf) Liquid contained in the semicircular canals and vestibule of the inner ear.

endomorphy (en'-duh-mor-fee) The dimension of body build characterized by predominance of fat, especially in the abdominal region.

engineering psychology The study of human functioning in relation to the equipment which people use. The general aim is to develop machines suited to our special capacities and limitations. See *human factors psychology.*

engram An altered state of living tissue which underlies memory. A general term or construct used to explain retention in learning. Also called memory trace.

environment Everything which surrounds the units of inheritance. There is the *intracellular environment,* within the cell; the *intercellular environment,* involving the effect of cell upon cell; the *prenatal external environment,* surrounding the embryonic or fetal organism; the *internal environment,* within the organism, such as the blood; and the *external environment,* which is what we usually think of as *the environment,* and which includes the social or cultural environment as well as the purely physical environment.

epilepsy A disorder characterized by intermittent convulsions and loss of consciousness.

equilibrium, sense of Sensory information involved in maintaining balance and knowing one's body position relative to gravity through stimulation of nonauditory receptors in the inner ear.

equivalent-form reliability The consistency of measurement obtained when two comparable forms of the same test are administered to the same subjects.

equivalent groups Two or more groups which are comparable on the basis of group data, such as the average scores on specific factors. Equivalent groups differ from matched groups in that subjects are not matched on a one-to-one basis but rather on the basis of group scores.

escape conditioning The situation in which the organism learns to terminate punishment by making a certain response, e.g., pressing a lever. Compare with *avoidance conditioning.*

estrogens (es'-truh-junz) Hormones from the ovaries which play an important role in female sexual development, including development of the sex drive.

ethnocentrism The tendency to evaluate other groups according to the values and standards of one's own ethnic group.

evolution, theory of A conception of the development of the species, presented by Charles Darwin, stating that contemporary plant and animal species have developed through modifications in pre-existing forms. The process of modification and selection is called the survival of the fittest, meaning that organisms with characteristics well adapted to their environment generally survive and produce others of their kind, also with favorable modifications, while the poorly adapted perish.

exceptional child A child with an IQ above 130, called gifted, or below 70, known as retarded. Exceptional children comprise the upper and lower two percents of the population with respect to general intellectual ability.

existentialism (eg-zis-ten'-chul-iz-m) A philosophically oriented approach to personality and therapy which stresses subjectivity, the individuality of experience, and, consequently, a spontaneous approach to life.

exocrine glands Glands which are presumed to make their secretions through a duct, as in perspiration or tears, thus influencing only specific body parts or organs. Compare with *endocrine glands.*

experiment The control or manipulation of stimulus and/or organism conditions in order to determine their causal influence on aspects of experience and behavior of the organism. In the classical experiment, only one condition, called the independent variable, is manipulated at any given time in order to determine its influence on the dependent variable, which is usually some reaction of the organism. Thus, the classical experiment is sometimes called the single-factor experimental design. Compare with *multifactor study.*

experimental group A group of subjects exposed to the independent variable of the experiment, as opposed to the control group.

experimental introspection Describing one's experiences under controlled laboratory conditions. An important method in structuralism.

experimental method Control of environmental, physiological, or attitudinal factors in order to observe dependent changes in aspects of experience and/or behavior.

experimental neuroses Behavior disorders produced experimentally, as when an organism is required to make a discrimination of extreme difficulty and "breaks down" in the process.

experimental psychology Experimental investigation of psychological problems. Not limited to physiological processes.

experimenter effects The influence of the experimenter's behavior, personality traits, or expectancies on the outcomes of research.

exploratory drive The urge to find out about strange situations. Perhaps comparable, in apes and human beings, with curiosity.

external environment See *environment*.

extinction Eliminating a learned response by failing to reinforce it.

extrasensory perception (ESP) Perception which allegedly occurs without sensory awareness, such as communication between two individuals when there appear to be no channels of information exchange.

extraversion The tendency to be outwardly expressive, active, and engaging in social activities. The opposite extreme from introversion.

face validity Apparent validity, as distinguished from statistically established validity.

factor analysis A statistical procedure aimed at disnovering the constituent irreducible traits in a complex mass of data, as in the case of intelligence or personality.

factors Component or constituent parts or conditions. In intelligence or personality, the constituent aspects revealed by factor analysis.

fantasy Imagery that is more or less coherent, as in dreams and daydreams, yet without due regard for reality.

fear An emotion characterized by unpleasant feelings, tension, and, when possible, avoidance of a specific situation. There is also marked involvement of the autonomic nervous system.

feedback The return of impulses to a control center where they play a part in further control, as in the case of impulses produced by muscle activity returning to the brain, informing it of the posture of the muscles, and thus contributing to further control of these muscles.

feeling Affective experience reported by the individual as pleasantness, unpleasantness, excitement, calmness, tension, sadness, happiness, and so on.

feral child A child raised in isolation from other human beings and therefore lacking in human personality; often, a child allegedly reared by animals but also a child who has received only indirect contact with other people.

fetish Strong sexual attachment to an object.

field experiment A research method which combines aspects of naturalistic observation and the laboratory experiment. A natural event occurs or is simulated, and then it is studied through controlled procedures. The study takes place in an everyday setting, rather than the laboratory, but usually there is some manipulation of the environment for purposes of data collection.

field test Application of a newly constructed test to a group of subjects solely for the purpose of improving the test, especially by identifying such deficiencies as ambiguous instructions, inappropriate time limits, and misleading questions.

figure and ground Seeing one part of a situation as a shape with the rest of the situation as background, like seeing an airplane against the sky.

fixation A firm, stable, or inflexible aspect of behavior—like the firm acquisition of some habit. In abnormal psychology, the retention of some infantile trait.

fixed interval reinforcement See *schedule of reinforcement.*

fixed ratio reinforcement See *schedule of reinforcement.*

forced-choice test A test situation in which the subject must choose one of two or more specified alternatives.

forebrain The uppermost portion of the brain, containing the olfactory bulbs, cerebral hemispheres, and other organs. The most highly developed portion of the brain.

formal discipline, doctrine of The theory, now rather generally discredited, that the study of certain subjects, like mathematics and Greek, improves the intellect more than the study of other subjects in the curriculum. It was assumed that these subjects "discipline the mind."

formal operations The final stage of intellectual development, according to Piaget, beginning at approximately eleven years of age. The child or adult at this stage can imagine the possibilities in a given situation; reasoning can occur apart from concrete materials; hypotheses can be formed and tested in the abstract. Sometimes formal operations are simply referred to as abstract thinking.

fovea (fō′-vee-uh) A small depression in the retina which is the area of sharpest vision. It contains only cones.

fraternal twins Twins who have different hereditary characteristics, hence may also differ in sex. Twins derived from different ova, hence *binovular twins.* See also *identical twins.*

free association Allowing thoughts or words to occur spontaneously, as contrasted with various types of controlled association, where certain directive tendencies are introduced.

free-floating anxiety Anxiety without a particular focus.

free nerve endings Branching ends of afferent fibers which are not embedded in receptors. They mediate pain and some aspects of pressure sensitivity.

frequency distribution A distribution of data showing the number of times (frequency) each score occurs.

frequency polygon A graph of a frequency distribution. See *frequency distribution.*

frequency theory The theory of hearing which assumes that the frequency of nerve impulses accounts for pitch and the number of activated nerve fibers accounts for loudness. See also *volley theory.*

Freudian slip A mistake which presumably reveals some underlying motive, often sexual or aggressive in nature. Example: A woman who continually "forgets" to wear her wedding band may wish she were not married.

frontal lobes The lobes at the front of the brain, just back of the forehead.

frustration A state of the organism which results when the satisfaction of motivated behavior is rendered difficult or impossible.

frustration-aggression hypothesis The hypothesis that frustration inevitably leads to aggression and that aggression is always the result of some form of frustration.

frustration tolerance Ability to withstand frustration without developing inadequate modes of response, such as "going to pieces" emotionally or becoming neurotic.

fugue (fyoog) Literally, "a flight." Applied to neurotic behavior, it involves some episode which the individual is unable to recall after he or she recovers.

functional autonomy The tendency of habits to continue even though the motivation which led to their acquisition is no longer present. Different from habit in that the original motivation has ceased to exist.

functional disorders Disorders with no known organic basis; dependent upon past experience rather than physical defects.

functional fixedness Inflexibility in solving a problem because objects are used only in the habitual manner.

functional psychology A school of psychology which argued, against the structuralists, that psychology should concern itself with what the processes of mental life do rather than with the nature of their conscious "structures," such as sensations, images, and feelings. Also called *functionalism.*

galvanic skin reflex (GSR) Lowered resistance of the skin to passage of an electrical current following emotional and other forms of stimulation. Recorded with the psychogalvanometer.

Ganzfeld effect A form of light adaptation during which the hue in a completely uniform color field appears to fade to neutral gray.

general intelligence The term used by Spearman—as his concept *g*—to represent an alleged general ability or capacity which expresses itself through special skills, such as social, mathematical, and mechanical skills. See also *intelligence.*

generalization A general conclusion, theory, hypothesis, or concept based on certain facts or observations. See also *stimulus generalization* for a different sense of the term.

generalizing Reasoning in such a way as to arrive at a basic principle which applies to many different items. For example, after experience with red, green, blue, and so forth, the child understands the concept of color.

genes Determiners of inheritance located within the chromosomes of the cell nucleus.

genital stage The stage at which, according to Freudian theory, full maturity has been attained; in the genital stage, the individual has achieved mature relations with the opposite sex.

gestalt psychology The school of psychology which disparages the partist approach to experience and behavior and argues for emphasis upon wholes, which, gestalt psychologists say, are more than the sum of their parts. In learning, this school emphasizes insight as opposed to trial and error; in perception, it stresses primitive organizations, such as figure-ground relationships and the phi-phenomenon, which appear to be independent of past experience. The word *Gestalt* is often translated as *configuration* or *form* and the school is sometimes referred to as *configurationalist,* i.e., as emphasizing configurations rather than their constituent parts.

gifted Persons with special talents. Also, individuals with an IQ of 130 or above, such as Terman's gifted children, in the upper 2 percent of the general population.

glands Secreting organs, like the tear glands (duct) and the adrenal glands (ductless, or endocrine).

goal An event or object which the organism seeks to achieve or attain, such as reducing its hunger or winning a prize.

gonads (gō'nadz) Sex glands; ovaries in females and testes in males.

gradient A graded or gradual difference in strength of a response or response tendency, as shown by a rising or falling curve in a graph.

graph A visual representation of the results of research, in some quantified form.

group dynamics A term used to represent the study of underlying features of group behavior, such as motives, attitudes, and the like. It is concerned with group change rather than with static characteristics.

group test A test designed to be administered to more than one individual at a time.

group therapy Patients meeting with other patients and with a therapist or counselor to discuss their problems.

grouping, principles of Gestalt principles stating that objects are perceived as belonging together on the basis of *similarity, proximity, closure,* and *continuity.*

gustation The sense of taste. *Gustatory,* pertaining to taste.

habit A recurring, acquired mode of behavior, such as a motor or verbal skill, a way of doing things, or a way of thinking. The learning process is also called *habit formation.*

hallucination A false perception, generally regarded as abnormal. Hallucinations differ from one individual to another. Illusions, on the other hand, are false perceptions which are typically alike in all people and not regarded as abnormal. See also *illusion.*

hallucinogenic A term applied to drugs which commonly produce hallucinations.

hammer A small ossicle of the middle ear attached to the eardrum.

Hawthorne effect A general improvement in performance which occurs when persons receive special attention.

hebephrenia (hee-buh-free'-nee-uh) A variety of schizophrenia characterized by silliness and inappropriate feelings and mannerisms, as well as regression and delusions.

Helmholtz theory of hearing The theory of hearing which correlates pitch with the region of the basilar membrane which is maximally activated by a sound frequency. Also known as *place theory.*

heredity That which is passed on from parents to offspring biologically through the genes. *Hereditary,* dependent upon the genes.

Hering theory A theory of color vision which assumes that there are three types of opposing processes in the retina: red-green, yellow-blue, and black-white.

hierarchy An organization of habits or concepts, in which simpler components are combined to form increasingly complex integrations.

higher-order conditioning The use of previously conditioned stimuli to condition further responses, much the way unconditioned stimuli are used.

hindbrain The part of the brain composed of the pons, medulla, and cerebellum and located close to the spinal cord.

histogram A series of rectangles representing a frequency distribution. The height of each rectangle indicates the frequency of a particular score.

holophrastic expression The use of a single word to convey a more complex idea. For example, a child merely says "lake," meaning "I am going to the lake."

homeostasis (hō-mee-ō-stay'-sus) The compensatory mechanism by which a constant physical or chemical state is maintained. Physiologically exemplified by sweating and other processes which maintain a constant body temperature. *Psychological homeostasis* may be illustrated by maintaining one's self-respect through such compensatory devices as rationalizing and blaming others.

hormones Chemical products of the endocrine glands, such as adrenalin.

hue The characteristic of visual experiences related especially to the wavelength of light — e.g., red, green, yellow, and blue. *Color* in the everyday sense of the word.

human factors psychology A specialty in which the psychologist is concerned with the design of tools, machines and systems of all types best suited for human use. The field began largely with the development of tools and equipment, such as radar and sonar gear, but has expanded to include the design of administrative systems and organizations. Formerly called engineering psychology and human factors engineering.

humanistic psychology An approach to psychology which emphasizes human uniqueness, subjectivity, and capacity for psychological growth.

hypnagogic state   The condition of extreme drowsiness, just prior to the onset of sleep.

hypnosis   A trance-like state brought on through suggestion that the individual is to relax his or her muscles, sleep, and carry out various acts under the control of the hypnotist. Literally, "a nervous sleep."

hypnotherapy   Use of hypnosis in individual therapy. Occasionally this technique is used in group therapy, where a single individual is placed in a hypnotic trance.

hypothalamus (hī-pō-thal'-uh-mus)   The underside of the thalamus, containing neural mechanisms which play an important role in emotion, sleep, eating and other physiological functions.

hypothyroidism (hi-pō-thi'-royd-iz-m)   A condition in which there is a less than normal secretion of the thyroid hormone, thyroxin.

id   A Freudian term representing the primitive, animalistic urges which underlie much behavior. It is said to be "the deepest part of the psyche." See also *ego; superego.*

identical twins   Twins derived from the same ovum; hence sometimes called monozygotic. Such twins have the same hereditary characteristics.

identification   The process of modeling one's behavior after another individual, usually an older person.

identity crisis   When an individual, especially a young person, urgently seeks greater self-understanding; when a person undergoes significant turmoil attempting to formulate a self-concept and decide upon future goals, particularly career choices.

idiographic (i-dee-ō-gra'-fik)   Concerned with the behavior of a particular individual. Idiographic analyses are of special interest in clinical and counseling psychology. See also *nomothetic.*

idiot   A term formerly used to describe individuals with an IQ below 25. Mental handicaps are now described as mild, moderate, severe, or profound.

illusion   A perception considered as mistaken because it does not agree with objective measurement of the physical form or pattern, which is regarded as more fundamental.

imbecile   A term used to describe individuals with an IQ between 25 and 50. Mental handicaps are now described as mild, moderate, severe, or profound.

implicit response   An event not directly observable but inferred from relevant facts. Brain processes and thought processes are implicit because we do not observe them directly.

imprinting   A learning process observed in some birds and possibly other animals, which occurs with extreme rapidity and at an early "critical period" of development. It involves the socialization of an instinctive response, such as following a moving object, and once it has been established, it is typically not reversible.

inborn motivation   Motivation which is part of the organism's biological inheritance, such as the need for food, drink, rest and so forth. Also called primary motivation. See *acquired motivation.*

incentive   An object of motivated behavior. That which is sought — such as food, a sex object, or money.

incidental learning   Sometimes referred to as *passive learning,* i.e., learning without a direct attempt.

independent variable   The variable manipulated by the experimenter — e.g., the intensity of light, the hunger of an animal, or the presence or absence of a rest in learning. Usually some form of stimulation or some condition of the organism. See also *dependent variable.*

individual differences   Deviations of individuals from the average or from each other.

individual motives   Motives which originate in unique individual experience as contrasted with those that are inborn and those that are learned by most members of a particular culture.

individual psychology The approach to psychoanalysis presented by Alfred Adler emphasizing in human motivation the striving for superiority or power. In contrast to Freud's traditional psychoanalysis, sexual motivation receives less emphasis.

individual test A test administered to one person at a time.

industrial psychology A specialty in which the psychologist works in an industrial setting and is generally concerned with such problems as employee recruitment and selection, employee training, job analysis, and techniques for improving work efficiency.

inference Guess, hypothesis, or judgment based on certain data but not directly evident.

inferential statistics Statistics from which an inference is made about the nature of a population. The aim is to generalize (or draw an inference) from a sample to a population.

inferiority complex Feelings of worthlessness and inability to cope with situations. Real or imagined inferiority that the subject has difficulty in accepting.

information processing The storing and handling of information within a system, as in a computer or human being. In human beings, the chief processes considered to be involved include perceiving, remembering, reasoning and other forms of thinking.

inhibition The complete or partial arrest of an activity or process.

inner ear The innermost part of the ear, containing the cochlea and the semicircular canals.

insanity Legal term for mental illness of such severity that the individual cannot be held responsible for his or her acts. The psychiatric term is *psychosis,* the most common form of which is schizophrenia.

insight Sudden understanding, as when one "sees through" a situation or "gets the idea." Also, it may be inferred from sudden improvement in learning or the solution of a problem.

instinct A descriptive term for a complex, unlearned adaptive response; an unlearned pattern of reflexes appearing in all members of a species. If the adjustment were learned, the behavior pattern would be called a habit.

instrumental conditioning Conditioning in which the response is instrumental in achieving some end, such as obtaining food or escaping punishment. Often used as a synonym for *operant conditioning,* but some psychologists make distinctions in the usages of these two terms. See also *operant conditioning.*

insulin An internal secretion which is necessary for carbohydrate metabolism. An undersecretion is responsible for diabetes and the related symptoms.

insulin shock therapy Injection of insulin in sufficient quantity to produce a coma, from which the patient recovers through administration of glucose. Used in treating certain psychotic conditions.

intelligence A complex term dealing with the ability of a person or animal to adapt to novel situations. In human beings, it often involves an ability to utilize abstract concepts, and to learn and grasp novel relationships.

intelligence quotient In its original meaning, the ratio of a subject's mental age, as determined by a standard test, to actual age multiplied by 100 — i.e., MA/CA x 100. See also *deviation IQ.*

intensity The *quantitative* as contrasted with the qualitative aspect of stimulation or experience; for example, the magnitude or amplitude of a sound wave as distinguished from its frequency, and the brightness of a color as distinguished from its hue.

interaction principle The concept of reciprocal influences between or among two or more variables; the idea that the outcome of any one variable is influenced by the presence or absence of other variables. In the nature-nurture issue, the interaction principle holds that the influences of heredity and environment always depend upon one another. The result of any given inherited potential depends upon the environment with which it interacts and vice versa. Also called the *interaction effect.*

interaction process analysis Analysis of small group behavior in terms of twelve categories — e.g., shows solidarity, shows tension release, shows agreement.

interference theory The view that the forgetting of an event is caused by interference or other learning experiences, occurring before and/or after the learning in question.

inter-judge reliability The consistency of measurement obtained when different judges or examiners administer the same test to the same subjects.

intermittent reinforcement Any schedule of reinforcement in which less than 100 percent of the organism's correct responses are reinforced; noncontinuous reinforcement. See also *schedule of reinforcement.*

internal environment See *environment.*

internal stimuli Stimuli which originate inside the organism.

interposition A monocular, psychological cue in visual space perception, involving the overlapping or partial obscuring of one object by another.

intersensory perception Perception arising from the contribution of more than one sensory modality, such as seeing and smelling a freshly baked cake. Our perceptions commonly arise from several sensory processes simultaneously.

intervening variable An event inferred to occur within the organism between the stimulation and response in such a way as to determine or influence the response.

interview A conversation, with varying degrees of directedness, between one or more persons; the usual purpose is to elicit information for diagnosis, therapy or research.

introspection Looking inward, so to speak, and describing one's own experiences.

introversion A tendency to be especially concerned with one's thoughts; to be inwardly reflective rather than overtly expressive. The opposite pole from extraversion.

invagination Turning or folding inward, as on the surface of the cerebrum.

inventory A test or list of questions which is used to assess a subject's interests, attitudes, and so forth.

involutional melancholia A psychosis sometimes associated with middle age, especially the forties and early fifties in women and a decade later in men, characterized by extreme depression. The term involutional, formerly referring to the menopause in women, now signifies no more than that the depressive condition first occurred during middle life.

iris The flat circular muscle which controls the amount of light admitted to the retina. It is situated in front of the lens and gives the eye its color, such as brown or blue.

item analysis Assessing the effectiveness of a test item, especially its power to discriminate among successful and unsuccessful persons concerning the behavior in question, by making comparisons based upon statistical results.

James-Lange theory The theory that the feeling aspect of emotion is an experience of body changes, such as activities of the viscera and of the skeletal muscles.

job analysis Studying a job to discover its components and its psychological and other requisites.

just noticeable difference (j.n.d.) The smallest discriminable (or perceptible) difference between stimuli.

kibbutz A condition of communal living; commonly, the children are reared together, apart from the biological parents except for occasions of recreation.

kinesthesis (kin-us-thee'-sus) The muscle sense or movement sense, mediated by the receptors in the muscles, tendons, and joints.

knee jerk A reflex kick of the foot following a blow on the tendon just below the kneecap.

knowledge of results Information on success or failure supplied to a learner during or immediately after performance of a task. Immediate knowlege of results usually facilitates learning. Also called *feedback*.

latency The period between the time the stimulus is presented and the moment a response occurs.

latency stage A period of apparent lack of sexual interests. In Freudian theory, the stage before the genital period.

latent dream content The symbolic, hidden meaning of a dream. Contrast with *manifest dream content*.

lateral fissure The crevice or invagination separating the temporal and frontal lobes.

learning A more or less permanent modification of an individual's behavior which results from previous activity, special training, or observation.

learning objective An outcome that the learner is expected to achieve at the end of a given unit of instruction; sometimes called an instructional objective, especially from the teacher's viewpoint. Learning objectives can be established at different levels of difficulty and in three domains: the cognitive domain, usually concerned with verbal learning; the motor domain, usually concerned with physical skills; and the affective domain, involving attitudes, feelings and values. Commonly, learning objectives involve more than one domain.

learning set Learning how to learn or learning an approach to a problem, as when an organism solves each successive problem in fewer trials than earlier problems of comparable difficulty.

legal psychology A specialty concerned with the application of psychological knowledge to legal issues. Specialists in this field sometimes testify on the ways in which the basic psychological processes, such as perception and motivation, may influence recall and other behaviors; sometimes the concern is with the uses and abuses of psychological testing; psychiatric issues and the plea of insanity also are important concerns. Sometimes called *forensic psychology*.

lens A structure behind the iris of the eye which is involved in changing the focus of light on the retina. Known as the crystalline lens.

level of aspiration The level of performance which the individual desires to reach or which the individual feels he or she can reach.

lie detector A device for recording changes in respiration, blood pressure, the galvanic skin response, and other responses while the person is questioned about some crime or asked to give associations to relevant and irrelevant words. The physiological changes are presumed to be indicators of emotional reactions.

light adaptation Decreasing visual sensitivity when a person remains in a condition of bright light, such as the glare of sunlight upon a sandy beach or the water.

Likert scale An attitude scale on which the respondent indicates his or her degree of agreement or disagreement with each statement.

linear perspective Perception of the distance of objects through apparent convergence of lines toward the horizon and through decrease in size with increasing distance.

lobes The main structural divisions of the human brain: frontal, temporal, parietal, and occipital.

lobectomy A severe form of psychosurgery, no longer in use, which involved removal of a portion of the frontal lobe of the brain.

lobotomy An operation which involves cutting some nerve fibers that connect the frontal lobes with the thalamus in order to relieve psychotic symptoms; now largely replaced by chemotherapy.

loci, method of A mnemonic system in which the items to be remembered are mentally pictured as located along an accustomed route. The subject uses familiar places (loci) in remembering a less familiar sequence.

logotherapy A form of existential therapy, especially as practiced by Viktor Frankl, in which it is assumed that the patient's problem is based in a confusion of feelings and meanings. The term *logo* refers to word or thought, and the therapist's aim is to help the person examine his or her thoughts and feelings in a systematic fashion.

longitudinal fissure The deep crevice separating the two cerebral hemispheres.

longitudinal study A study which follows the same individuals from early to later age levels. Contrasted with cross-sectional studies, in which different groups represent each age level.

long-term memory (LTM) Retention which has been established for long periods, presumably involving a consolidation of the memory trace. Compare with *short-term memory*.

loudness The intensity aspect of auditory experience, scaled in decibels.

LSD Lysergic acid diethylamide; one of the group of psychotomimetic, hallucinogenic drugs.

mammals Animals that carry their young in the uterus and suckle them after birth.

mand A word used to demand or request something; coined by Skinner, from "demand."

mania An exceptionally excited, aroused state found in manic-depressive psychosis.

manic-depressive psychosis Mental illness characterized by periods of mania and depression which alternate in different ways, depending upon the person.

manifest dream content The presumably superficial aspects of the dream, as recalled and understood by the dreamer. Contrast with *latent dream content*.

marathon therapy A method of group therapy based on the premise that it takes longer than fifty minutes for the patient to discard his or her defenses. Marathon therapy may continue for several days.

marijuana Cannabis; a drug derived from hemp. Types include bhang, dagga, and Acapulco gold.

masochism (mas-uh-kiz′-m) Pleasure gained from subjecting oneself to pain. The pleasure is allegedly sexual in nature.

mass media Communications media which reach large numbers of people, such as newspapers, magazines, radio, and television.

massed practice Learning without interpolated rest peiods.

matched groups A method of experimental research control in which individuals in one group are matched on a one-to-one basis with individuals in other groups with regard to all organism variables which the experimenter deems important. For example: Subject A in Group 1 is the same age, sex, height, and weight as Subject A in Group 2.

maternal drive The urge to care for the young.

maternal instinct An unlearned stereotyped pattern of caring for the young which is found in some animals.

maturation Development depending almost solely upon biological conditions which characterize the species, as distinguished from learning, which, although it is somewhat dependent upon the level of maturation attained, requires exercise, practice, or observation of the performance of others.

maze A more or less complex pathway having blind alleys used in the study of learning.

mean, arithmetical The average score; the sum of the scores divided by the number of scores.

median The middlemost score in a series arranged in rank order.

median plane The plane which runs vertically between the ears.

melancholic A personality type suggested by Hippocrates characterized by a pessimistic outlook and sadness.

memory Retention of what has been learned. It is evidenced by later recall, recognition, or relearning with a savings. See also *engram*.

memory span The maximum number of items (words, syllables, digits) recalled after a single presentation, whether presented in an auditory or visual manner.

memory trace The neural modification inferred to underlie memory. An engram.

menopause The end of menstrual cycles in the female life. It marks the cessation of the female reproductive period.

mental In its original sense, pertaining to *the mind*. Now used with reference to the adjustments of organisms to their environment, especially those adjustments which involve symbolic functions and of which the individual is aware.

mental age (MA) The degree of intelligence exhibited by an individual in relation to the age norms established for the particular test. A boy is said to have a mental age of 8, for example, if his performance on a standardized intelligence test equals that of the average child of 8 years, according to the norms. His chronological age (CA) might be greater or less than his mental age.

mental health A mental state marked by the absence of personal discomfort and socially disruptive behavior. The emphasis is not upon an enduring set of traits but rather upon the capacity for adapting to environmental conditions, working productively with others or alone, and attempting to improve society as well as one's own personal condition.

mental illness Any psychological disorder characterized by severe maladjustment.

mental retardation See *mentally handicapped.*

mental tests A general term sometimes used for all psychological tests, especially those measuring intelligence.

mentally handicapped Persons in approximately the lower 2 percent of the general population with regard to intelligence; usually, IQ below 70. The handicap may be due to hereditary or environmental limitations, or to both factors.

mesomorphy (mez'-uh-mor-fee) A dimension of body build characterized by predominance of muscularity.

microcephalic (mī-krō-suh-fal'-ik) A person with an especially small head and therefore limited brain development; usually mentally handicapped.

midbrain The middle of three main divisions of the brain. It contains important reflex centers for vision and hearing and pathways to and from the forebrain. See also *forebrain* and *hindbrain.*

middle ear Part of the auditory mechanism between the eardrum and cochlea, containing the ossicles.

mind A general term representing all intelligent behavior, including memory, thought, and perception. Often used in older publications as synonymous with conscious experience.

Minnesota Multiphasic Personality Inventory (MMPI) An objective test used for evaluating personality in terms of psychiatric categories.

mode In statistics, the most frequent score of a series.

modeling Following the example of another person. A child or adult who acquires a new behavior pattern through imitation of someone else is said to have engaged in modeling.

monaural Involving only one ear.

monocular cues Cues that can be obtained or used with one eye, as distinguished from binocular cues.

mores (mor′-ayz) Group ways; social customs.

moron An individual of tested IQ 50-70. The term *mentally handicapped* is now used to refer to people of such low intelligence, accompanied by the description mild, moderate, severe, or profound.

morpheme The smallest language unit with a distinct and separate meaning, composed of at least one phoneme.

motivation Inner influence on behavior as represented by physiological condition, interests, attitudes, and aspirations.

motivational hierarchy A hierarchy of needs which human beings presumably fill successively in the order of lowest to highest. The five levels are physiological needs, safety, love and belonging, self-esteem, and self-actualization.

motivational sequence A series of related events involved in motivation, namely need, drive, incentive, and reinforcement.

motive An urge to attain some goal object, such as food when hungry, or some goal, such as becoming an engineer. Similar to *drive* except that drive has no clearly defined incentive.

motor Pertaining to muscular or glandular activity.

motor area The region of the cerebral cortex which controls voluntary motor activity.

motor neuron A neuron (efferent) which carries impulses to the motor organs (muscles and glands).

Müller-Lyer illusion A line of a given length appears shorter or longer by the addition of lines, such as enclosing arrowheads or arrowheads extending outward from its end.

multifactor study Experimental investigation of the influence of several variables simultaneously. These variables may be additive, meaning that their total influence is equal to the sum of the separate influences, or interactive, in which case the influence of any one variable depends upon the presence, absence or level of another variable. Multifactor studies are generally more complex than the traditional single-factor experimental design.

multiple personality A pathological condition wherein several personalities are expressed by the same person. *A dual personality* is exemplified by Dr. Jekyll and Mr. Hyde. There have been cases known to express as many as four personalities.

natural selection Darwin's view that variation naturally occurs in structure and behavior and that, in the struggle for existence, those organisms having the most adaptive characteristics will survive and reproduce their kind.

naturalistic observation Observation in the field without manipulation of the situation by an experimenter.

nature-nurture issue An issue concerned with the relative importance of heredity (nature) and environment (nurture) in various aspects of individual development.

needs Requirements for survival or for optimal adjustment to the environment, such as the need for food and water.

negative transfer Habit interference, as when learning one skill makes learning another more difficult.

neo-Freudians Psychologists and psychiatrists who espouse many aspects of psychoanalysis but differ from Freud in placing less emphasis upon sexual motivation and usually greater emphasis upon social factors.

nerve A bundle of neurons.

nerve cell The central part of a neuron; the body of the neuron from which the fibers extend.

nerve fiber A threadlike structure extending from the cell body of a neuron, which transmits the nerve impulse.

nerve impulse A successive release of energy along a nerve fiber.

nerve net A network of nerve fibers in which there are no synapses and the impulse thus goes indiscriminately through all fibers.

nervous breakdown A non-specific, layman's term referring to the onset of a severe neurosis or psychosis.

nervous system A general term referring to all neural structures and mechanisms.

neural circuits The courses followed by nerve impulses in traversing various parts of the nervous system.

neural trace See *engram.*

neuron A nerve cell and its fibers. Sometimes the terms *neuron* and *nerve* are used interchangeably.

neurosis A functional behavior disorder which, though troublesome, is seldom sufficiently severe to require institutionalization. Chronic, inefficient, partially disruptive ways of dealing with personal problems. Also referred to as a psychoneurosis.

neurotic Pertaining to neurosis; a person who has a neurosis. Neurotic behavior is behavior involving the symptoms found in a neurosis, particularly anxiety.

neutral stimulus One which does not elicit the response in question. A puff of air to the eyeball, for example, is a neutral stimulus for salivation. It does not evoke the salivary response automatically. Through repeated presentations with a stimulus such as meat, it could become a conditioned response for salivation. A puff of air is not a neutral stimulus for the eye-blink, however; it is an unconditioned stimulus in the case of the eyeblink. See also *conditioned stimulus* and *unconditioned stimulus.*

nomothetic (nō-muh-thet'-ik) Concerned with the discovery of general laws, pertaining to groups of individuals. Much of contemporary research in psychology involves nomothetic studies. See also *idiographic.*

nonauditory labyrinth The semicircular canals and vestibule.

non-directive therapy See *client-centered therapy.*

non-participant observer An investigator who studies a group of subjects engaged in certain activities but does not join them in these activities.

nonsense syllables Three or more letters which do not make a word and which have little or no meaning for the subject.

non-verbal communication Communication without words — by gestures, pictures, the wearing of certain uniforms, and so on.

non-zero sum games Games which involve choices for achieving a goal, such as winning points. Some choices require cooperation between the players; others involve competition. Called non-zero sum games becasue one player's gains are not necessarily at the expense of the other player. The final scores, for and against each player, do not necessarily add up to zero.

noradrenalin (nor-uh-dren'-ul-un) A secretion of the adrenal gland (along with adrenalin) and apparently also of nerve endings in the sympathetic nervous system. This hormone is involved in the maintenance of normal blood pressure.

norm An empirically established standard. Sometimes refers to normal, defined as average.

norm-referenced test A test in which each person's score is evaluated in the context of others' performances. Usually used for purposes of selection and for identifying individual differences.

normal probability curve The so-called chance distribution, which is symmetrical and bell-shaped, with most of the measurements clustering near the middle and the rest tapering off to the two extremes.

November boy A male child in the United States who, because of his November birthday and the age requirements for entrance to various grade levels, is one of the youngest members in his school class.

object constancy The tendency for objects to be perceived as unchanging despite variations in the conditions under which the objects are observed. A desk viewed from the top, the side, in daylight, or in twilight, is still seen as a desk.

objective test A test scored with a prescribed key and therefore usually yielding high interscorer reliability.

observation A step in all scientific research in which information is acquired by the use of the senses. In overt observation, the investigator makes no effort to conceal his or her intentions; in covert observation, the investigator attempts to hide or disguise his or her interests, so that the subjects are not aware that they are being studied.

observer A term used by experimental introspectionists to represent the person who observes and reports on his or her own experiences; the person who introspects under these circumstances. Now largely replaced by the term *subject,* which has no introspective connotations.

obsession A thought which occurs over and over again, often irrational in nature and involving anxiety.

obsessive-compulsive reaction A neurotic reaction in which the individual is beset with unwanted but recurring thoughts (obsessions) and/or ritualistic behaviors (compulsions).

occipital lobe (ok-sip'-ut-ul) The area at the back of each cerebral hemisphere, concerned primarily with vision and related perceptual and associative functions.

Oedipus complex (ed'-i-pus) A Freudian term representing the sexual attachment of a son for his mother, usually regarded as repressed and disguised in various ways. Also, it is assumed that the son will be jealous of the father because the father can have intimacies with the mother that the son is denied. See also *Electra complex.*

olfaction (ōl-fak'shun) The sense of smell.

olfactory bulbs The two small bulblike structures below the frontal lobes and immediately above the olfactory epithelium. The bulbs give rise to nerve fibers which mediate olfactory sensitivity.

olfactory epithelium (ōl-fak'-tuh-ree ep-uh-thee'-lee-um) Tissue in the nasal cavity which contains the receptors for smell.

one-trial learning The view that a habit or response pattern can be fully acquired on the first successful trial.

operant behavior Any response that produces certain consequences — such as obtaining a food reward. It "operates" on the environment. The eliciting stimulus cannot be identified precisely, as it can in respondent behavior. The operant response is said to be emitted rather than elicited.

operant conditioning A type of conditioning which involves the modification of an operant response through reinforcements. A response which the organism emits is reinforced in certain ways, in accordance with certain schedules, and resulting changes in its rate of occurrence are studied. The rat's pressing a lever and the pigeon's pecking a disk are widely studied operants. The reinforcement is usually food, although a secondary reinforcer, such as a click previously associated with food, may be used. See also *successive approximations, reinforcement,* and *schedules of reinforcement.*

operational definition A definition in terms of observable conditions or operations under which an event appears. For example, an operational definition of "good memory" might be successful recall of nineteen out of twenty names immediately after a two-minute learning period.

optic chiasma The structure in the brain which transmits visual information to both hemispheres; for each eye, it has connections with both the left and right hemispheres. See *split-brain technique*.

optic nerve The tract carrying all nerve impulses from the eye to the brain stem.

oral character Behavior traits pertaining to the mouth, such as excessive eating, smoking, and gossiping, which presumably are related to early feeding experiences; a Freudian concept.

ordinate The vertical or Y axis of a graph.

organ of Corti A structure on the basilar membrane of the inner ear where the energy of sound waves stimulates receptors and initiates nerve impulses.

organic Related to an organ such as the brain or to the physical aspects of the whole organism. Sometimes having to do with the structure or function of a known anatomical unit. For example, an organic psychosis is related to impairment in the structure of the brain, as in paresis.

organism A living creature.

organism variable A condition of the organism, which, in psychological research, is manipulated as the independent variable or controlled. These variables include such conditions of the organism as degree of hunger, set, and attitude.

orienting response Adjustments in attending; any response in relation to the reception of available stimulation, such as pupil dilation, increased heartrate, or a change in the electrical activity of the skin. See *attending*.

osmoreceptors Receptors which are sensitive to the passage of fluids through membranes; certain cells of the hypothalamus have been designated as osmoreceptors.

ossicles The three small bones in the middle ear which play a role in perception of movement and maintenance of equilibrium.

otoliths Small grains in the endolymph of the labyrinth of the ear which play a role in maintaining balance.

outer ear That portion of the ear outside the cranium and extending inward to the eardrum.

out-of-role behavior Behavior which is not expected in a given situation; a reaction not in accordance with typical roles, as when a football player deserts the team in the middle of a game.

oval window A membrane at one end of a cochlear canal, against which the ossicle know as the "stirrup" vibrates. It makes the transition from the middle to the inner ear.

overlearning Practicing beyond the point where one is able to perform according to the specified criterion.

own controls A method of experimental control in which the same subjects are used in both experimental and control conditions.

Pacinian corpuscles (Puh-sin'-ee-un kor'-pus-lz) Specialized end organs in the skin which are responsive to heavy pressure.

pall effect Boredom associated with extensive use of programmed materials.

papillae Small protrusions such as those found on the surface of the tongue.

paradoxical sleep Sleep which occurs during the REM state, so-called because records of REM sleep are more similar to records of waking states than to records of other stages of sleep, but an individual in the REM state is difficult to awaken.

paranoid (pair'-uh-noyd) Pertaining to a type of mental illness in which the person has delusions, especially delusions of reference, such as imagining that people are doing things or saying things about him or her.

parapraxis See *Freudian slip*.

parasympathetic nervous system The part of the autonomic system which is most important in quiescent states of the organism. For example, secretions of the stomach are activated by this system, but increased emotional activity, such as accelerated heartbeat, is checked. This system functions in opposition to the sympathetic system.

paresis (puh-ree′sis) An organic psychosis usually originating in syphilitic infection.

parietal lobe (puh-rī′-ut-ul) A region of the cortex situated between the central fissure and the occipital lobe. It plays a special role in somesthetic sensitivity.

participant observer An investigator who, while studying a group of subjects, also participates in their activities. Presumably, in this way, he or she is able to gain more detailed, relevant information.

pecking order See *dominance hierarchy.*

perceiving Awareness of objects, as in discriminating, differentiating, or observing.

percentile The rank position of an individual in a serial array of data, stated in terms of what percentage of the group he or she equals or exceeds.

perception The process of perceiving.

perceptual constancy See *constancy phenomenon.*

perceptual-motor response Any response involving overt reactions to perceptual cues. See also *sensorimotor response.*

performance curve A graph representing the course of learning. Time or trials are plotted on the horizontal axis; the subject's performance is shown on the vertical axis. Also called *learning curve.*

performance item A question in a psychological test which does not require the use of words on the part of the person answering it. For example, the subject may be required to assemble a puzzle or point to certain details or omissions in pictures.

periodic vibration Oscillations occurring at specific frequency rates and giving rise to tonal experiences, as distinguished from aperiodic vibrations, which give rise to noise.

peripheral nervous system The spinal and cranial nerves, including the autonomic system. The nervous system which connects the brain and spinal cord with the receptors and effectors.

persona The mask worn by an actor in ancient times to indicate his or her role; possibly also the origin of the term "personality."

personality The most characteristic integration of an individual's structures, modes of behavior, interests, attitudes, capacities, abilities, and aptitudes — the whole person as others know him or her.

personality profile See *profile.*

phallic stage (fal′-ik) The period when the child becomes interested in his or her sexual organs. This stage, according to Freudian theory, is preceded by the oral and anal stages.

phase The relations between two or more sound waves, or light waves; for example, waves are in phase when their crests coincide.

phenomenology Systematic study of immediate experience or of the world as it appears to the observer. Contrasted with behaviorism or with the analytic approach of Wundt and his followers.

phenylketonuria (fen-l-kee-tuh-noo′-ree-uh) Mental deficiency which occurs when an enzyme necessary for oxidizing a substance in protein is missing; phenylpyruvic acid accumulates in the tissues and interferes with normal functioning of the brain.

phi-phenomenon Apparent motion, as in motion pictures and certain electric signs. The appearance of motion is generated by non-moving stimuli, as when two lights are flashed at certain distances apart and one following the other by a certain time interval.

phlegmatic A personality type suggested by Hippocrates, characterized by sluggishness and lack of interest.

phobia A strong but apparently irrational fear, as when one fears a mouse or fears to stand on a high place when there is no danger of falling.

phoneme One of the basic sounds in a given language, used in communicating meaning(s). See also *morpheme*.

physiological cue A cue for space perception which is due to the organism's biological makeup, such as retinal disparity and accommodation of the lens.

physiological drive A state of arousal which stems from the biological needs of the organism, such as the need for food and the need for sleep. Also called *primary drives*.

physiological need A need determined by biological makeup.

pitch The qualitative aspect of sounds, which may be described as high or low; determined chiefly by frequency.

pituitary gland A structure at the lower end of the hypothalamus which has extremely important endocrine functions. Its anterior lobe secretes hormones which play a role in sexual and general body development. The anterior lobe also secretes hormones which play a key role in metabolic processes. Prolactin, important in motivating maternal behavior in animals, is likewise secreted by the anterior pituitary. The pituitary is generally regarded as the master gland of the whole endocrine system.

place theory The theory that the pitch of a sound is determined by the place on the basilar membrane that is maximally activated by a sound wave of a particular frequency.

placebo (pluh-see′-bō) Literally, "to please." A pill of no medicinal value given to a male patient, for example, "to please him" or to make him think that he is taking medicine. Used in drug experiments to prevent subjects from knowing whether they have been given the drug or a control substance and thereby distributing equally the suggestive effects of taking the drug.

plateau A period of little or no progress.

play therapy Play designed to help the patient, usually a child, release tensions or learn adequate adjustments to the situations which disturb him or her.

pleasure center An area of the brain, usually involving the limbic system, which apparently produces a pleasant reaction in an animal when stimulated electrically.

pleasure principle The tendency of organisms to seek satisfaction of their urges.

point estimation Estimate of a point or value, such as a population mean, on the basis of information from a sample. See *inferential statistics*.

polygraph Apparatus for recording several responses concurrently, such as a lie detector, in which changes in respiration, blood pressure, and the GSR are recorded simultaneously on a moving tape.

pons Located at the base of the medulla, a "bridge" connecting the cerebrum with the cerebellum.

population All the objects, events, or subjects in a particular class. For example, all the two-year-old babies in the United States comprise a population, and some babies from this group constitute a sample of the population.

positive transfer When learning one task facilitates the learning of another.

post-hypnotic suggestion After being awakened from a hypnotic trance, a subject follows suggestions given during hypnosis.

postnatal Period of life after birth.

preconscious Anything which may readily become conscious. Thus, a person may become aware of some obligation of which he or she was oblivious a few moments earlier. Conceived by Freudians as a region between the conscious and the unconscious.

predictive validity The extent to which a test is useful for estimating future performance, particularly the capacity to benefit from a training program and to perform successfully at some future date.

prejudice Pre-judgment; an attitude or opinion formed prior to or independent of an examination of the facts.

prenatal Period of life before birth.

pre-operational period The age from 18 months to approximately six or seven years; during this period, according to Piaget, the child's thinking tends to focus upon the most striking feature of an object or event, ignoring other aspects. The focus is upon states or conditions, rather than transformations or operations, hence the term pre-operational thought.

primary drives See *physiological drives*.

primary gain In psychosomatic medicine, the alleviation of anxiety by converting emotional concerns into bodily ailments. See also *secondary gain*.

primary mental abilities The abilities disclosed by factor analysis to be the basic components of intelligence. There are differences of opinion as to the number and nature of primary mental abilities.

primary reinforcement Satisfaction or physiological needs, such as that supplied by food or sleep.

proactive inhibition A type of interference or negative transfer observed in memory experiments and other learning situations. It occurs when something learned previously interferes with present learning or recall. Compare with *retroactive inhibition*.

problem box A device with latches, strings, or other objects which the subject must manipulate in an appropriate way in order to open the box.

problem solving Adjusting to a situation by acquiring new modes of response. Especially, learning in which a certain amount of insight or reasoning may be displayed.

process schizophrenia Chronic schizophrenia. Contrast with *reactive schizophrenia*.

product-moment correlation A statistical procedure which yields the coefficient of correlation known as *r*. It involves the actual values, rather than ranks, of the measurements. Compare with *rank-order correlation*.

profile A graph which represents an individual's scores in each of several skills or on several tests.

prognosis Prediction of an outcome, especially of an illness or a program of therapy.

programmed learning A carefully prepared sequence of study materials. Common features include introducing new information on a step-by-step basis, requiring active participation by the learner, provision for immediate knowledge of results for the learner, and many opportunities for review.

projecting The act of perceiving one's own characteristics in another. In fantasy, interpreting situations as though one is part of them and they reflect one's own situation, problems of adjustment, and so on. See also *projection*.

projection Attributing one's own motives or thoughts to others.

projective methods Those which require the subject to interpret ambiguous situations. The person's interpretation is considered as a projection of his or her personality.

prolactin (prō-lak′-tun) A hormone from the anterior pituitary gland which stimulates milk secretion and in other ways promotes maternal behavior.

proprioceptive sensitivity Sensitivity to body position and movement; more generally, sensitivity to stimuli coming from within rather than outside the body. The chief receptors are those in the semicircular canals and vestibule of the inner ear, concerned with rotary and rectilinear motion, balance, and body position in space; and those in the muscles, tendons and joints, concerned with voluntary movement of the body and body parts.

proximal stimulus Stimulation as it acts upon a receptor, such as light waves from a building as they contact the eyes, activating various mechanisms, including the retina. Compare with *distal stimulus*.

proximity, principle of A principle of perceptual organization which states that stimuli which are near one another (in time or space) tend to be grouped together.

proximodistal development (prok'-suh-mō-dist'-ul) A gradient of development in which functions near the center of the body develop before those at the extremities.

psyche An ancient Greek word meaning "soul" or "mind."

psychedelic Literally, "mind expanding;" more specifically, also refers to hallucinogenic drugs.

psychiatrist A medical doctor who specializes in the treatment of mental (or behavior) disorders.

psychiatry A branch of medicine concerned with mental (behavior) disorders.

psychoanalysis A system of understanding human behavior based on Freud's writings. Emphasis is placed upon unconscious determinants of behavior. Also, a method of psychotherapy which typically involves free association and analysis of dreams. The data made available through these procedures are usually interpreted in accordance with psychoanalytic theory.

psychoanalyst A psychologist or psychiatrist who is qualified to use psychoanalytic procedures in dealing with mental disorders.

psychodrama A method of therapy in which mental patients act out situations relevant to their difficulties.

psychogenic Literally, "having its origin in the mind."

psychological cue In space perception, a cue which becomes meaningful through previous experience in comparable situations.

psychologist Usually, an individual who has completed a program of graduate study in psychology and is engaged in research, clinical treatment, teaching, or other applications of psychology. In most states, persons in private practice who call themselves psychologists must be certified or licensed by law.

psychology The science of behavior and experience; the science of the adjustments of organisms to their environments.

psychomotor tests Tests which, although based on perceptual processes, require a motor reaction, such as pressing a key, holding a stylus steady, or manipulating controls.

psychoneurosis See *neurosis*.

psychopathic A general term often referring to unspecified psychological maladjustments. Sometimes used as synonymous with sociopathic disorder.

psychophysics Quantitative measurement of the relation between experienced aspects of stimulation, such as brightness and loudness, and the characteristics of the stimulus, such as its intensity.

psychoquack A charlatan; in psychology, someone who claims, without justification, to have special training or expertise in dealing with problems of human behavior and experience.

psychosis A serious type of mental disorder in which the individual loses contact with reality and thus becomes unable to manage the problems encountered in daily life. It is known, legally, as *insanity,* and it usually requires treatment in a mental hospital. The person is said to be *psychotic.* This disorder is characterized by disturbed thought processes, extreme emotions and, in some cases, delusions. A common form is schizophrenia.

psychosomatic reaction A branch of medicine concerned with physical disorders, such as some allergies, high blood pressure, and ulcers, which originate in or are aggravated by emotional difficulties.

psychosurgery The use of surgical methods in the treatment of psychological problems; brain surgery performed on mental patients in an effort to alleviate the disorder.

psychotherapy Any expressive procedure, usually verbal, used to alleviate behavior disorders and adjustment problems.

psychotic Deriving from a psychosis; the person who has a psychosis.

psychotomimetic A term applied to drugs producing a state similar to psychosis.

psychotropic Drugs used to alleviate mental illness; the therapeutic use of drugs.

puberty The time at which menstruation begins in girls and seminal emission begins in boys. The onset of adolescence.

punishment The appearance of negative consequences following an action. Not to be confused with negative reinforcement, which is the disappearance of negative consequences following an action, and therefore a form of reward.

pupil The opening in the iris through which light enters the eye.

pupillary response Constriction or dilation of the pupil, as when more light strikes the eye or when light is decreased.

Purkinje phenomenon (per-kin'-jee) A difference in the perceived brightness of colors at different points of the spectrum under low illumination. In twilight, for example, red hues appear dimmer than equally illuminated green hues.

Q-sort technique A method of personality assessment in which the subject sorts a large deck of statements about human behavior into categories, according to the extent to which they apply to him or her.

qualitative Having to do with certain distinguishable aspects of experience—such as sour, blue, and middle C. These are called "qualitative" aspects of experience or merely "qualities," in contrast to the intensive or "quantitative" aspects of experience, such as the sourness of what is sour, the brightness of blue, and the loudness of middle C.

quantitative Having to do with measurable intensity or degree. Psychophysics is quantitative in that it deals with measurable stimuli and measurable responses, often in terms of intensity.

quantitative ability Ability to deal with numbers, as in solving mathematical problems. Distinguished, in some tests, from so-called *verbal ability,* which is facility with words and related concepts.

quota sample A sample which includes subgroups of people or items in the same proportion as they are represented in the population. If the population is one-half red, one-fourth blue and one-fourth green, the sample is composed of subgroups in these same ratios. Within each subgroup, the members of the sample are chosen on a random basis. See *random sampling.*

random groups Groups of subjects, usually large in number, formed on a random basis, generally for purposes of research. Compare with *matched groups.*

random sampling A procedure for selecting subjects or items for research, on the basis of chance. The cases are chosen from the population in such a way that all of them presumably have the same chance of being selected.

range The difference between the highest and lowest scores in a series.

rank-order correlation Correlation between paired series of measurements, each ranked according to magnitude. It yields a coefficient known as *rho*.

rapid eye movements (REM) Quick movements of the eyes during sleep, often occurring in series, as measured by sensitive electrodes. Subjects awakened during REM periods usually report that they have been dreaming.

rational-emotive therapy Therapeutic procedures based on the premise that lack of information or illogical thought patterns are basic causes of the patient's difficulties. Furthermore, it is assumed that the individual can be assisted in overcoming his or her problems by a direct, prescriptive, advice-giving approach by the therapist.

rationalization Finding "good" but false reasons for actions. Making what is irrational appear rational. Excusing one's actions on irrational grounds.

raw scores Scores obtained directly from the measuring instrument; the results of research or of a test administration which have not yet been treated by any statistical methods.

reaction formation Excluding a desire from awareness by repressing it and assuming the opposite attitude.

reaction time Speed of reaction to a stimulus.

reactive schizophrenia A schizophrenic condition the onset of which involves an acute and sudden reaction to severe environmental pressure.

readiness The time, resulting largely from maturational factors, when the organism is first capable of responding correctly to a task.

reality principle The principle that the demands of the id usually must be adapted to actualities in the physical and social environment. Awareness of the conditions of the environment.

reality testing A term used by Freud to refer to the exploratory or probing behavior by which the individual learns about his or her environment. Basic to development of the ego.

reasoning Solving some problem implicitly, using symbols to represent objects or situations. Thinking one's way through a problem rather than engaging in overt trial and error.

recall Retrieval of past experience; remembering a past event with minimal cues. In free recall, a series of events is recalled in any order; in serial recall, a specific order is required, as well.

receptor A specialized end organ which receives stimulation. The receptors of the eyes, for example, are the rods and cones.

recessive gene See *dominance*.

recitation In learning, trying at intervals to recall and recite what one is memorizing, as opposed to merely reading it repeatedly.

recognition Perceiving something as having been experienced before, as being familiar; a method of measuring memory.

rectilinear motion Movement in a straight line.

redintegration (re-dint-uh-gray'-shun) Recalling a whole experience on the basis of some fraction of the original circumstances. For example, a man may be reminded of his childhood and experiences with his mother upon smelling cookies such as his mother used to bake. A form of recall.

reflex An unlearned response of a particular part of the body, like the knee jerk to a blow on the patellar tendon, or the contraction of the pupil in response to light.

reflex arc The essential neural mechanism involved in a reflex, i.e., the sensory, motor, and association neurons which link the stimulus, the activated receptor and the response.

refractory period The period immediately following stimulation, during which a neuron is incapable of further excitation. Following this *absolute* refractory period is the *relative* refractory period, during which only a stronger than normal stimulus can excite the neuron.

regression Going back to an earlier, usually less adequate, mode of response. In hypnosis, behaving as one did at an earlier stage of life.

reinforcement Generally, a reduction or satisfaction of a drive; a reward. In classical conditioning, any instance in which a conditioned stimulus is followed by an unconditioned stimulus. In operant conditioning, any instance in which a response is followed by favorable consequences; any event which increases the probability of a response. See also *primary reinforcement; secondary reinforcement; reinforcer, positive;* and *reinforcer, negative.*

reinforcer, negative Any object or event which, by its disappearance, increases the probability of a given response. For example, the cessation of loud noise after turning down the volume of a television set during a commercial.

reinforcer, positive Any object or event which, by its appearance, increases the probability of a given response. For example, scoring a point in tennis after hitting the ball correctly.

relative refractory period See *refractory period.*

relearning Regaining a skill that has been partially or wholly lost. The saving involved in relearning, as compared with original learning, gives an index of the degree of retention.

releaser A stimulus which serves to elicit instinctive behavior. For example, the swollen abdomen of the female stickleback fish is a releaser for a "mating dance" on the part of the male; it initiates this behavior.

reliability Consistency of measurement; dependability as a measuring instrument. Reliability may be indicated by a high correlation between test and retest scores for the same individuals. See *reliability coefficient.*

reliability coefficient An index of the consistency of measurement. Often based on the correlation between scores obtained on the initial test and a retest (test-retest reliability) or between scores on two similar forms of the same test (equivalent-form reliability).

repression Unconsciously excluding unpleasant thoughts from awareness. Preventing ego-threatening ideas from returning to consciousness. A primary defense mechanism.

research psychologist Psychologists who perform scientific investigations solely for the purpose of acquiring further knowledge, without interest in how their findings might be used. Also called pure research in psychology. Compare with *applied psychologist.*

respondent behavior Behavior in response to a specific stimulus. Usually associated with classical conditioning.

response An action, such as doing or saying something; involving the action of a muscle or a gland.

response hierarchy Alternative reactions or modes of adjustment to a given situation arranged in the probable order of prior effectiveness. A mother attempting to discipline an unruly child may first cajole, then plead, then scold, and finally ignore the child's misbehavior.

response-produced cues Successive cues in a behavior chain. Each response serves as a reinforcer for the previous response and a stimulus, or cue, for the next response.

response variable Any reaction or behavior of the organism that is of interest in psychological research. Often, the dependent variable.

retarded Unusually slow or abbreviated psychological development; individuals with an IQ below 70, comprising the lower 2% of the general population.

retention Maintaining what has been learned so that it can be utilized later, as in recall, recognition, or relearning.

reticular formation (ri-tik′-yuh-ler) A network of intricately connected nerve-cell groupings which runs through the center of the brain stem from the level of the medulla to the lower part of the thalamus. Its main function appears to be alerting the cerebral cortex for incoming information. Its lower part has an inhibitory influence on certain motor activities.

retina The innermost coat of the eye, which contains the rod and cone receptors and is thus photosensitive.

retinal disparity The slight difference between the retinal images perceived by the two eyes when a nearby object is viewed. The difference is caused by the different locations of the two eyes. An important cue in some types of stereoscopic or depth vision.

retinal image The optical image projected on the retina by light rays; roughly analogous to the picture projected on the photographic film in a camera.

retroactive inhibition The partial or complete obliteration of memory by a more recent event, particularly new learning.

reversible configuration A picture perceived alternately as one symbol, then as another.

rewards Incentives; positive consequences following an action.

ribonucleic acid (rī-bō-noo-klay′-ik) A chemical substance involved in cell functions; presumed by some investigators to play an important role in the genetic code and in the physiological basis of memory. Abbreviated RNA.

rigidity Inability to change behavior patterns, attitudes, or body postures.

RNA See *ribonucleic acid.*

rods Rod-like retinal structures serving as the receptors for black and white vision.

role The part played or the function performed by a person in a particular group situation, such as the role of teacher, president or secretary.

role playing The acting out of certain roles in simulated situations, as when a person being trained for a foreman's role in industry acts the part of foreman with others playing the parts of workers.

Rorschach test (roar′shok) A series of inkblots used as a projective personality test.

round window A round, membrane-covered, separation of the middle ear from the tympanic canal of the cochlea, located just below the oval window.

saccadic movements The jerky movement of the eyes from one fixation to another, as in reading. During saccadic movements the eye is nearly blind.

saccule A small sac-like structure making up part of the vestibule of the nonauditory labyrinth.

sadism (sā′diz-m) Deriving gratification, presumably sexual, from inflicting pain upon others.

salivary response Secretion of saliva by the glands of the mouth.

sample A portion of a given population of organisms, objects or events. In an incidental sample, convenience is the chief criterion in selecting the portion of the total population, and therefore it is usually not representative of that population. See *random sampling.*

sanguine A personality type suggested by Hippocrates which is characterized by optimism and warmth.

satiation Fulfillment of a need, desire or other motivation to the point where the organism is no longer interested in relevant stimuli. For example, an animal that has eaten all it wishes is said to be satiated; for the moment, it is not interested in food.

saturation The degree to which color of a given hue is present, i.e., the degree to which it differs from gray of the same brightness. A highly saturated red, for example, is very red and a minimally saturated red is only barely distinguishable from gray.

savings score Estimating degree of retention in terms of the reduction in time or trials to relearn as compared with those required in original learning.

scattergram A graph which illustrates the extent to which two series of paired measurements are correlated.

schedule of reinforcement An established procedure or sequence for reinforcing operant behavior. Thus, in a lever-pressing situation, every displacement of the lever may bring a pellet of food *(continuous schedule)*; the pellet may come every five seconds, regardless of how many displacements occur earlier *(fixed interval schedule)*; the pellet may come at every tenth displacement *(fixed ratio schedule)*; the pellet may appear on an *average* of every five seconds *(variable interval schedule)*; or the pellet may appear on an average of every tenth displacement *(variable ratio schedule)*.

schizophrenia (skit-suh-free'-nee-uh) Literally, "a splitting of the mind or of the personality." A form of psychosis characterized by extreme withdrawal from reality. Since it involves marked mental deterioration (dementia) and often appears relatively early in life (adolescence or early adulthood), it originally was given the name *dementia praecox.* See also *simple schizophrenia, hebephrenic, catatonic,* and *paranoid,* which are being replaced by the terms *process* and *reactive schizophrenia.*

scientific method The systematic, impersonal, search for verifiable knowledge.

sclerotic coat (skluh-rot'-ik) The outermost covering of the eyeball.

second-order conditioning In classical conditioning, the use of a conditioned stimulus as the basis for further conditioning.

secondary drives Acquired drives; drives not directly related to physiological conditions. For example, the desire for an auto or a fashionable dress.

secondary gains Assistance, sympathy, and other forms of attention gained indirectly through illness, as in the conversion reaction. See also *primary gain.*

secondary reinforcement A learned reinforcer. Reinforcement through something which, while it does not satisfy a need directly, has been associated with direct need satisfaction. Thus, a sound associated with food (primary reinforcement) may come to have reward value in itself and serve as a secondary reinforcer.

secondary sex characteristics Aspects of the mature human body which differentiate the sexes but which have no direct sexual functions, such as body build, voice, distribution of hair.

self The individual as represented in his or her own awareness and in the setting of those things with which he or she identifies. The ego and its external involvements.

self-actualization The postulated fifth and last level in Maslow's hierarchy of human motivation; the motivation to realize one's potential, whatever it may be, to the fullest, regardless of the rewards involved; doing what one is best-suited to do or intended to do. The term is controversial because it is said to lack a precise definition.

self theory An approach to the study of personality and therapy which emphasizes the role of the individual in shaping his or her own destiny. Particularly important is the individual's self-concept, which is that person's consistent, organized perception of himself or herself. In this view, the stress is on the subjective side of human existence, and an individual's self concept is regarded as more important than the conditions in the environment. A viewpoint in humanistic psychology

semicircular canals The three canals of the inner ear, which mediate sensitivity to rotation.

sensation Theoretically, an irreducible sensory experience such as might exist the first time a particular receptor is stimulated—i.e., a receptor process as such, devoid of meaning.

sense organ An organ, such as the eyes or ears, which contains receptors.

sensitivity Susceptibility to stimulation.

sensorimotor response Any overt, motor act initiated by sensory processes.

sensory adaptation Adaptation of some sensory function, as in dark adaptation, where objects not seen at first in dim light gradually become visible. See also *adaptation*.

sensory memory The first of three postulated stages in human memory; the memory which consists only of the residual stimulation in the sensory systems. After direct stimulation ceases, sensory memory is only momentary. See also *short-term memory* and *long-term memory*.

sensory-motor period Approximately, the period from birth to eighteen months of age, during which time the infant's thinking apparently is limited largely to sensory and motor responses. The basic intellectual achievement at this stage, according to Piaget, is gaining the idea of object permanence, meaning that objects which are not in one's direct sensory awareness can continue to exist and can be thought about in their absence.

sensory neuron A neuron connected to a receptor; also known as an *afferent neuron*.

septal area A region of the limbic system which plays a role in emotional reactions.

set A readiness to perceive or to respond in a certain way; an attitude which usually facilitates or predetermines an outcome.

sexual deviation Behavior involving sexual practices which are relatively infrequent in a particular culture.

shape constancy The tendency to perceive objects as maintaining their shape despite marked changes in the retinal image.

shaping Molding an organism's responses, as in experiments involving successive approximations, where each closer approximation to a desired response is reinforced. See also *successive approximations*.

shock therapy See *electroconvulsive therapy* and *insulin shock therapy*.

short-term memory (STM) Memory involving intervals less than half a minute in length.

sibling rivalry Competition among children in the same family, presumably for parental affection and attention.

similarity, principle of A principle of perceptual organization which states that objects with similar properties tend to be grouped together.

simple schizophrenia A type of schizophrenia involving decreased emotional responsiveness and indifference to the environment.

simplification The tendency for details to be forgotten.

simultaneous conditioning A method of classical conditioning in which the conditioned stimulus and unconditioned stimulus always are presented at the same time.

single-blind procedure In research, any method used to prevent the subject from knowing what treatment, such as a drug, he or she has received.

situational test A test situation in which a candidate is observed as he or she reacts to a daily task or actual sample of the job or role to be filled.

size constancy The tendency for an object to be seen as maintaining its absolute size despite changes in the size of the retinal images.

skeletal muscles Muscles on the outer body which, when stimulated, move parts of the skeleton, such as the arms and legs.

skewed distribution A frequency distribution in which scores are much more frequent toward one end or the other than in the middle. In a positive skew, there is a "tail" of extra scores toward the high end; in a negative skew, the "tail" is toward the lower end. Compare with *normal curve*.

social behavior Behavior which is influenced by or influences the behavior of others; behavior involving interaction of individuals or groups.

social class A structure of subgroups within a society, often on the basis of economic status, education, and vocation.

social comparison Evaluating oneself in relation to the observed behavior of others.

social facilitation Occurs whenever the individual in a group situation exceeds his or her characteristic performance level when working alone. It does not necessarily mean that the person is more efficient in the group situation, for he or she may have increased output but may make more mistakes.

social leader A group member who determines or plays a role in group morale and group cohesion. Contrast with *task leader*.

social learning theory A view which stresses that learning occurs through interacting with and especially by observing others. Also called observational learning. The observed person serves as a model and the learner is prompted to imitate that person, especially when the model's behavior results in favorable consequences, called reinforcement. See *modeling* and *reinforcement*.

social motives Motives originating in what one learns from others. Motives of this type are common to many members of a culture.

socialization Learning to conform to group ways; acquiring a specific culture.

sociogram A graphic representation of the results obtained with a sociometric questionnaire, showing interactions between group members in terms of acceptance and/or rejection.

sociometric questionnaire A method of determining preferences and choices in interpersonal relations. For example, each person names the person with whom he or she would most like to carry out certain activities.

sociopathic disorder A disorder in which the person fails to observe rules which govern conduct in his or her society. There are several forms, including the *antisocial reaction* and *dyssocial reaction*.

somatic (sō-mat'-ik) Pertaining to the body.

somatotherapy (sō-mat-uh-ther'-uh-pee) Altering body states by medical procedures for the purpose of alleviating mental illness. The methods include brain surgery, administration of drugs, and use of shock.

somatotonia (sō-mat-uh-tō'-nee-uh) Temperament characterized by marked vigor, directness of manner, competitiveness, need for action.

somatotypes Types of physique according to Sheldon's system, in which the somatotype 1-1-7, for example, is low in the endomorphic, low in the mesomorphic, and high in the ectomorphic dimension.

somesthetic Pertaining to body feeling or to sensitivity originating in the skin, muscles, and body cavity.

source traits Underlying traits central to the personality, as opposed to surface traits. See *depth factors*.

space perception Perceiving or otherwise reacting to the size, distance, or depth aspects of the environment.

spatial visualization An aspect of mechanical aptitude; the ability to perceive objects in two or three dimensions.

specific hunger Hunger for specific foodstuffs, such as fat, protein, or salt.

spinal cord The part of the central nervous system which runs up the spine as far as the medulla. These neurons are grouped together, somewhat like the various strands of a cord or rope.

spinal nerves Thirty-one pairs of nerves extending from spaces between the vertebrae to various parts of the body.

split-brain technique A method of research, sometimes modified for use in therapy, where the corpus callosum is severed, leaving the two hemispheres connected essentially at subcortical levels only. When the optic chiasma is also severed, visual information presented to one eye is limited to one hemisphere, as well.

split-litter method In research, assigning the offspring of a litter to different experimental and control groups, thus providing animals of comparable heredity for each group of subjects when the mammalian stock from which the animals come is inbred. Similar to the co-twin method.

split personality See *multiple personality; schizophrenia.*

spontaneous recovery Return of a conditioned response after apparent extinction.

spontaneous remission In psychiatry, disappearance of symptoms without formal treatment. Causes for their disappearance are assumed to exist but these are not yet known.

S-R approach Focusing research upon stimulus-response relationships. Concerned with behavior which is relatively independent of the conditions of individual organisms.

standard deviation (SD) A statistical index of the variability within a distribution. It is the square root of the average of the squared deviations from the mean.

standard error of the difference A statistical index of the probability that a difference between two sample means is greater than zero.

standard error of the mean A statistical index of the probability that a sample mean is representative of the mean of the population from which the sample was drawn.

standardization of a test Developing definite procedures for administering, scoring, and evaluating the results of a given test.

Stanford-Binet Intelligence Scale A widely used individual, verbal test of intelligence—an American revision of the Binet-Simon test.

startle pattern A constellation of characteristic reactions in response to unexpected stimulation: the eyes open wide, the mouth sometimes opens, shoulder and neck muscles become tense, the fingers sometimes are spread apart, and other associated reactions occur.

statistical significance The probability that an obtained value occurred by chance. When a difference between two means is said to be statistically significant at the .05 level, this statement means that the probability of obtaining a difference this large or larger would occur by chance less than 5 times in 100 trials.

status A position or rank held by an individual in a group.

stereophonic effects Artificial reproduction of sounds, and presentation of these to the two ears, so that they simulate the spatial aspects of the sound of everyday life, as in types of motion picture projection and stereophonic records.

stereoscopic effects Presentation of artificial depth cues to the two eyes so that the visual depth perception of everyday life is simulated through the fusion of two slightly different images. The eyes are separately stimulated by scenes which each eye would normally see under monocular conditions.

stereotype A general description applied to all members of a given group or race without regard to individual differences. It may be a concomitant of prejudice.

stimulus Any factor inside or outside the organism but external to the receptors of the living cell groups under consideration, which initiates activity of some kind.

stimulus generalization The eliciting of a response by stimuli similar to a particular conditioned stimulus.

stimulus variable A changeable aspect of stimulation in a psychological experiment. Often, the independent variable.

stirrup A small stirrup-shaped bone of the inner ear, attached to the oval window.

stress interview A confrontation in an interview designed to discover an individual's capacity to withstand emotional tension. For example, the interviewer may make derogatory comments about the subject's character in order to observe the subject's reaction. The interviewee is deliberately subjected to stress.

Strong–Campbell Interest Inventory An inventory in which the subject's interest patterns are compared with those of persons engaged in various fields of work.

structural psychology A system of psychology focusing on the study of conscious experience. Its emphasis is on "conscious content," such as sensation or feeling. Also called *structuralism*.

subconscious Generally speaking, what is below the level of awareness. The term *unconscious* is more widely used. See also *preconscious; unconscious motivation*.

subject An organism which participates in an experiment and whose responses are the dependent variables of the experiment.

subjective Known only to the individual concerned; not directly observable by others; private. Contrasted with *objective* or socially observable. A pain is subjective, but the person's verbal response, since others may witness it, is objective. Compare with *phenomenology*.

subjective fatigue A need for rest which is caused by psychological factors, not physical ones; usually caused by repetition of the same behavior. The fatigue is said to be subjective when a different response can be performed readily using the same muscles.

subliminal Below the level of awareness; below the threshold of stimulation, as when an auditory or visual presentation is too weak to have an effect, or at least any effect of which the individual is aware. Below the absolute threshold.

successive approximations, method of The method of reinforcing every operant response which approximates a desired behavior more closely than the one just preceding it. Thus, a pigeon may be rewarded as its pecking is closer and closer to a certain disk. See also *shaping*.

superego Generally, internal controls or standards. In the Freudian view, the superego is derived from early influences and has two parts. The conscience pertains to ethical and moral behavior; the ego ideal concerns the individual's aspirations. The superego is one of the three chief intrapsychic forces in the Freudian view; the others are the ego and id.

superordinate goal A goal of two or more groups which has a higher value than any goal held by only one group; a common cause deemed more important than individual causes.

suppression Conscious inhibition of activity, as when someone suppresses a desire to strike someone else. Compare with *repression*, which is unconscious.

surface traits Personality characteristics which are readily apparent, such as sociability or shyness. See also *depth factors*.

survey research Collection of information from representative groups of people by use of questionnaires and interviews.

suspensory ligaments Fibrous tissues holding the lens of the eye in place.

symbolic processes Mental operations which represent aspects of past experience. Images and words are symbolic. Thought processes are symbolic in that they involve the implicit manipulation of external objects, situations, and relationships.

sympathetic nervous system The division of the autonomic system which plays a predominant role in emotion and which functions in opposition to the parasympathetic system. When the sympathetic system assumes control, secretion of adrenalin is accelerated, heartbeat is accelerated, and stomach secretions are inhibited.

synapse (sin′-aps) The junction where nerve impulses pass from one neuron to another.

syndrome (sin′-drōm) A group of symptoms which characterize a particular adjustment, disease, or disorder.

system of psychology A way of ordering the facts of psychology so that they have meaning in relation to each other. A theoretical model which embraces as many relevant facts as possible and serves as a framework to be filled in as new information is obtained. The various schools of psychology, such as behaviorism, gestalt psychology, or psychoanalysis, are designed to systematize psychological knowledge and point the way for further research.

systematic desensitization A therapeutic method based upon procedures in classical conditioning. Anxiety reactions are reduced by gradually increased exposure to the conditioned stimulus and by training in relaxation.

tabes dorsalis (tay′-beez dor-sal′-us) Injury to the dorsal columns of the spinal cord, ordinarily by syphilis, resulting in a motor incoordination.

tabetic gait (tuh-bet′-ik) A jerky gait associated with advanced tabes dorsalis.

tachistoscope (tuh-kis′-tuh-skōp) A device which exposes visual stimuli—pictures, digits, letters, or words—for controlled, brief time intervals.

tact A term used by Skinner to represent verbalizations which name, symbolize, or otherwise represent aspects of the individual's world. It comes from the idea that these form a type of "contact" with the things or events symbolized. Compare with *mand*.

task leader A group member who assumes responsibility for determining and achieving the group's goals.

taste buds Receptors for taste stimulation on the inner surface of the tongue.

teaching machine A device for presenting programmed instruction. With children, the machine also may increase motivation to study programmed materials.

telegraphic utterances Word combinations which convey the essential elements of a message while omitting non-essential elements; frequent among children in the early stages of language acquisition.

temperament Such aspects of personality as joviality, moodiness, tenseness, and activity level. The term implies "emotional."

temperature senses The senses of warmth and cold, from which heat is perhaps synthesized.

temporal lobes Areas of the cerebrum below the lateral fissure, adjacent to the temples. They contain auditory areas and auditory association areas.

terminal threshold See *threshold*.

test An examination designed to reveal the relative standing of an individual in the group with respect to intelligence, personality, aptitude, or achievement.

test battery A group of tests given for a particular purpose.

test-retest reliability The consistency of measurement obtained when a test is administered on two different occasions to the same subjects.

T-group See *encounter groups*.

thalamus (thal′-uh-mus) A structure between the brain stem and cerebrum which serves as a switchboard mechanism to relay sensory impulses to the appropriate regions of the cerebral cortex and which also mediates sensitivity and modifiability at a primitive level.

Thematic Apperception Test (TAT) A projective test in which the subject makes up stories appropriate to a series of pictures; themes of his or her stories give an indication of basic personality structure.

theory A set of principles with some explanatory value.

therapy A procedure designed to cure or alleviate some disorder.

thinking Manipulating aspects of past experience implicitly, as in recalling, daydreaming, and reasoning.

third-force psychology See *humanistic psychology*.

threshold The point at which an experience just barely occurs. A stimulus of threshold strength is one which, if it were weaker, would have no typical effect. A more specific term is absolute threshold. A difference threshold is one in which a difference is just barely perceptible; the just noticeable difference or j.n.d. The terminal threshold is the upper limit of sensitivity; the point beyond which further increases in intensity have no typical effect. "Typical effect" in these definitions means no change in the type of experience being studied. If increasing the intensity of light stimulation brings pain, that is not a visual effect, hence not typical for this kind of stimulation. *Limen* is a synonym for threshold.

thyroid gland (thī'-royd) An endocrine gland situated near the windpipe. Its secretion (thyroxin) is important for metabolism. A marked deficiency of thyroxin in early life may produce a form of mental deficiency known as *cretinism*.

thyroxin (thī-rok'-sun) The secretion of the thyroid gland.

timbre Sound quality, as in the difference between the same note played on a piano and on a cello. A function of the complexity of sound waves, i.e., the overtones produced.

time-and-motion study A procedure for finding the most efficient methods for accomplishing specified tasks.

token economy A program of therapy based upon operant conditioning in which secondary reinforcement is widely used. The secondary reinforcers are tokens or chips, awarded for certain behaviors, and they can be exchanged later for some desirable event. The token economy is most widely used in mental hospitals, where the tokens are exchanged for permission to leave the ward, attend movies and dances, and make purchases on shopping trips.

token rewards Secondary reinforcers, such as coins or poker chips which can be used to "purchase" primary satisfactions.

tone Periodic vibration to which a particular pitch can be assigned, as compared with noise, which is aperiodic.

trace conditioning A method of classical conditioning in which the conditioned stimulus is removed before the appearance of the unconditioned stimulus.

traits Relatively constant aspects, characteristics, or dimensions of behavior. Usually applied to personality and exemplified by such terms as introversion, dominance, sociability, persistence, and honesty.

transfer of training A condition in which learning in one situation influences learning in another situation. A carry-over of learning. It may be *positive* in effect, as when learning one behavior facilitates the learning of something else, or it may be *negative,* as when the one habit interferes with acquisition of a later one.

transference In psychoanalysis, situations in which the patient transfers to the therapist feelings and behaviors appropriate to significant other persons in the patient's life. For example, the patient responds to the therapist as though the therapist were his or her father, fiancé, or teacher.

transmitter substance A chemical material which is responsible for making the synaptic connection. It is discharged from the presynaptic neuron into synaptic space, where it acts upon the membrane of another fiber, causing it to become activated. A different substance, when discharged into synaptic space, is presumed to cause inhibition, causing the receiving membrane to become more resistant to firing.

transposition experiment An experiment in which the subject is required to transpose or "carry over" a learned principle to a new stimulus situation. For example, a chimpanzee is exposed to a two-inch and a four-inch square and trained to select the larger one. Then, when shown a four-inch and an eight-inch square, which will the animal select? If it selects the larger, it is said to have transposed; it is responding on the basis of the relationship in the earlier situation, rather than simply to the four-inch stimulus.

trial A single response on a test, such as one trip through a maze, one reading of a poem to be memorized, or one practice period.

trial and error The apparently random, haphazard, hit-or-miss exploratory activity which often precedes the acquisition of new adjustments. It may be *overt,* as exemplified in a rat's running here and there in a maze, or covert (*vicarious*), as when one thinks of this and then that way of coping with a situation. Contrasted with *insight.*

tropism An unlearned orienting movement of the whole organism which causes it to move toward or away from the stimulus. Examples are a moth flying into the flame (positive phototropism) and a cockroach running away from light (negative phototropism). A synonym in many cases is *taxis.*

two-factor theory In learning theory, the view that feelings, attitudes, and other meanings are acquired through classical conditioning and that learning what to do about these circumstances is learned in terms of operant conditioning, known as solution learning. Learning is considered as involving both processes.

tympanic canal The descending canal of the cochlea at the lower end of which is the round window.

tympanic membrane The eardrum.

typology (tī-pol'-uh-jee) The attempt to classify persons according to types—such as physique, temperament, introversion or extraversion.

unconditioned response An original or inborn response, such as salivation stimulated by food in the mouth, withdrawal from an injurious stimulus, or contraction of the pupil to light. Ordinarily reflex in character. In classical conditioning, it is elicited by the unconditioned stimulus. See also *classical conditioning.*

unconditioned stimulus A stimulus which arouses an unconditioned response.

unconscious Below the level of awareness. Compare with subconscious, preconscious. See also *collective unconscious.*

unconscious motivation Urges, such as fears, hopes and desires, of which the individual is not aware, presumed to be repressed. See also *repression.*

utricle (yoo'-tri-kl) Part of the vestibule, just below the semicircular canals. It plays a part in the sense of equilibrium.

validation Determination of the validity of tests, usually by correlation procedures.

validity A test is said to be valid or to have validity when it actually does what it has been designed to do, such as predicting an individual's success in school or in a vocation. It is valid to the degree that test scores correlate with criteria of success.

variability The degree to which individuals, or measurements in a frequency distribution, differ from the average. The standard deviation is a measure of variability.

variable A changeable aspect of a situation which can be manipulated or measured, as in the case of independent and dependent variables in an experiment.

variable interval reinforcement See *schedule of reinforcement.*

variable ratio reinforcement See *schedule of reinforcement.*

verbal skills Linguistic abilities, as in speaking, writing, reading, or reciting.

vertebrates Animals with backbones.

vestibular system Structure at the base of the semicircular canals. Here are located receptors for the perception of rectilinear motion and acceleration.

viscera The organs of the body cavity, such as the stomach, spleen, and intestines.

visceral reactions Stomach contractions, secretion of adrenalin, and other responses of visceral organs. Visceral reactions underlie such experiences as nausea and "butterflies" in the stomach.

viscerotonia (vis-uh-ruh-tō'-nee-uh) A personality dimension or type characterized by preoccupation with the viscera, especially the stomach; for example, unusual enjoyment of eating.

visual accommodation Changes in the lens so as to focus light from sources at different distances from the eye and thus form sharp images on the retina.

visual cliff An apparent but not actual drop-off, designed to test the visual depth or distance perception of infants. They crawl on a plate of glass where there is linoleum pasted underneath for a certain distance. At the "cliff" or drop-off, the linoleum is placed some distance below the glass, and most infants refuse to go beyond this point—an indication that depth perception is present.

vitreous humor (vi'-tree-us) The transparent jelly-like substance between the lens and the retina of the eye.

vocal cords Membranes in the larynx, vibrations of which produce voiced sounds.

vocalization A sound made with the vocal mechanisms; it does not constitute speech, however, unless the sounds have communicative significance.

vocational guidance Providing opportunities, through testing, counseling, and interviews, for an individual to discover fields of work most suited to his or her intelligence, aptitudes, interests, and other personal traits.

volley theory The theory that the pitch of sounds is determined by the frequency of volleys of nerve impulses reaching the brain. These volleys are carried by groups of nerve fibers, not by a single fiber. Intensity, according to this theory, is determined by the number of impulses per volley. See also *frequency theory*.

wavelength The distance between two corresponding positions in a wave, as from crest to crest.

Weber's law (vay'-ber) A law stating that whether or not a subject can detect an increase or decrease in intensity of stimulation depends upon the ratio of the change in stimulus intensity to the original stimulus intensity.

Wechsler Adult Intelligence Scale (WAIS) (wek'-sler) An individual intelligence test designed for adults. It includes both verbal and performance items. Formerly, the Wechsler-Bellevue Scale.

Wechsler Intelligence Scale for Children (WISC) An individual intelligence test much like the adult scale in content but separately standardized for children.

X-chromosome One of the sex chromosomes. The male has only one, the female two.

Y-chromosome One of the sex chromosomes, possessed only by males.

Yerkes-Dodson law An observation which states that for performance of a given task, the optimal level of arousal varies with the complexity of the task. The more complex the task the lower the optimal arousal level.

Young-Helmholtz theory This theory of color vision assumes that there are three primary colors (red, green, and blue) and that there are cones especially receptive to the wavelengths of each. Yellow is assumed to result from simultaneous activation of the "red" and "green" cones.

Zeigarnik effect (zī-gar'-nik) The tendency, when one is ego-involved in completing a series of tasks, to recall more of the unfinished than completed ones.

References and Author Index

Listed here are the complete sources for works cited and illustrations used in the text. The boldface numbers following each reference are the pages of this text on which the work is cited. Many journal titles have been abbreviated; the most commonly cited ones are listed below.

Amer. J. Physiol.—American Journal of Physiology
Amer. J. Psychiat.—American Journal of Psychiatry
Amer. J. Psychol.—American Journal of Psychology
Amer. J. Sociol.—American Journal of Sociology
Amer. Psychol.—American Psychologist
Educ. psychol. Measmt.—Educational and Psychological Measurement
Genet. Psychol. Monogr.—Genetic Psychology Monographs
J. abnorm. Psychol.—Journal of Abnormal Psychology
J. abnorm. soc. Psychol.—Journal of Abnormal and Social Psychology
J. appl. Psychol.—Journal of Applied Psychology
J. clin. Psychol.—Journal of Clinical Psychology
J. comp. physiol. Psychol.—Journal of Comparative and Physiological Psychology
J. comp. Psychol.—Journal of Comparative Psychology
J. consult. clin. Psychol.—Journal of Consulting and Clinical Psychology

J. consult. Psychol.—Journal of Consulting Psychology
J. educ. Psychol.—Journal of Educational Psychology
J. educ. Res.—Journal of Educational Research
J. exp. Psychol.—Journal of Experimental Psychology
J. gen. Psychol.—Journal of General Psychology
J. genet. Psychol.—Journal of Genetic Psychology
J. Pers.—Journal of Personality
J. Pers. soc. Psychol.—Journal of Personality and Social Psychology
J. soc. Psychol.—Journal of Social Psychology
J. verb. Learn. verb. Behav.—Journal of Verbal Learning and Verbal Behavior
Percept. mot. Skills—Perceptual and Motor Skills
Psychol. Bull.—Psychological Bulletin
Psychol. Monogr.—Psychological Monographs
Psychol. Rec.—Psychological Record
Psychol. Rep.—Psychological Reports
Psychol. Rev.—Psychological Review

Aarons, L. (1976) Sleep-assisted instruction. *Psychol. Bull., 83,* 1–40. **284**

Abelson, R. P. (1972) Are attitudes necessary? In King, B. T., and McGinnies, E. (Eds.), *Attitudes, conflict and social change.* New York: Academic Press. **518**

Adolph, E. F. (1941) The internal environment and behavior: Water content. *Amer. J. Psychiat., 6,* 1365–1373. **300, 301**

Adorno, T. W., Frenkel-Brunswik, E., Levinson, D. J., and Sanford, R. N. (1950) *The authoritarian personality.* New York: Harper. **520, 521**

Agranoff, B. W. (1967) Memory and protein synthesis. *Scientific American, 216,* 115–122. **256**

Ahmad, F. Z. (1971) Social class and mental disorders in Pakistan. *Pakistan J. Psychol., 4,* 5–15. **538**

Akert, K., Koella, W. P., and Hess, R. (1952) Sleep produced by electrical stimulation of the thalamus. *Amer. J. Physiol., 168,* 260–267. **306**

Allen, H. (1972) Bystander intervention and helping on the subway. In Bickman, L., and Hency, T. (Eds.), *Beyond the laboratory: Field research in social psychology.* New York: McGraw-Hill. **529**

Allport, G. W. (1935) Attitudes. In Murchison, C. (Ed.), *Handbook of social psychology.* Worcester, Mass.: Clark University Press. **518**

Allport, G. W. (1937) The functional autonomy of motives. *Amer. J. Psychol., 50,* 141–145. **330**

Allport, G. W. (1965) *Letters from Jenny.* New York: Harcourt, Brace, and World. **395, 401, 408, 409, 413, 419**

Allport, G. W., and Odbert, H. S. (1936) Trait-names: A psycho-lexical study. *Psychol. Monogr., 211.* **407**

Allport, G. W., and Postman, L. (1947) *The psychology of rumor.* New York: Holt. **251**

Alluisi, E. A., and Morgan, B. B. (1976) Engineering psychology and human performance. In Rosenzweig, M. R., and Porter, L. W. (Eds.), *Annual review of psychology, 27.* Palo Alto, Calif.: Annual Reviews, Inc. **56**

Alper, T. G. (1946) Memory for completed and incompleted tasks as a function of personality: An analysis of group data. *J. Abnorm. soc. Psychol., 41,* 403–421. **262**

Altman, I. (1975) *The environment and social behavior.* Monterey, Calif.: Brooks/Cole. **149, 545**

American Dental Assistants Association (1977) Personal communication, April 11, from the Executive Director, 211 East Chicago Avenue, Chicago, Ill. 60611. **388**

American Psychological Association (1970) Psychological assessment and public policy. *Amer. Psychol., 25,* 264–266. **349, 368**

American Psychological Association, American Educational Research Association, and American Council on Measurement in Education (1974) *Standards for educational and psychological tests.* Washington, D. C.: American Psychological Association. **363, 368, 369**

Ames, L. B. (1967) *Is your child in the wrong grade?* New York: Harper and Row. **90**

Amoore, J. E., Johnston, J. W., and Rubin, M. (1964) The stereochemical theory of odor. *Scientific American, 210,* No. 2, 42–49. **146**

Anand, B. K., and Brobeck, J. R. (1951) Hypothalamic control of food intake. *Yale J. Biol. Med., 24,* 123–140. **303**

Anastasi, A. (1958) *Differential psychology* (3rd ed.). New York: Macmillan. **89**

Anastasi, A. (1964) *Fields of applied psychology.* New York: McGraw-Hill. **307**

Anastasi, A. (1976) *Psychological testing* (4th ed.). New York: Macmillan. **361, 365, 369**

Anderson, B. F. (1975) *Cognitive psychology: The study of knowing, learning and thinking.* New York: Academic Press. **242**

Anderson, C. L. (1965) Development of an objective measure of orientation toward public dependents. *Social Forces, 44.* **520**

Anisfeld, M. (1966) Psycholinguistic perspectives on language learning. In Valdman, A. (Ed.), *Trends in language teaching.* New York: McGraw-Hill. **230**

Apter, M. J., and Westby, G. (1973) *The computer in psychology.* New York: Wiley. **231, 232**

Ardrey, R. (1970) *Social contract.* New York: Atheneum. **326**

Argyros, N. S., and Reusch, R. R. (1974) Trimodal programmed instruction in reading. *J. exp. Educ., 42,* 1–5. **274**

Aronson, E. (1972) *The social animal.* San Francisco: W. H. Freeman. **545**

Asch, S. E. (1946) Forming impressions of personality. *J. abnorm. soc. Psychol., 41,* 258–290. **180**

Asch, S. E. (1955) Opinions and social pressure. *Scientific American, 193,* 31–35. **530, 531**

Asch, S. E. (1956) Studies of independence and submission in group pressure. *Psychol. Monogr., 70,* No. 416. **530, 531**

Aserinsky, E., and Kleitman, N. (1953) Regularly occurring periods of eye motility, and concomitant phenomena during sleep. *Science, 118,* 273–274. **41**

Aserinsky, E., and Kleitman, N. (1955) Two types of ocular motility during sleep. *J. appl. Physiol., 8,* 1–10. **41**

Atkinson, J. W. (1964) An introduction to motivation. Princeton, N. J.: Van Nostrand. **329**

Atkinson, J. W. (1965) The mainsprings of achievement oriented activity. In Krumboltz, J. D. (Ed.), *Learning and the educational process.* Chicago: Rand McNally. **331**

Atkinson, J. W., and Raynor, J. O. (1974) *Motivation and achievement.* New York: D. Van Nostrand. **329**

Ausubel, D. P., and Robinson, F. G. (1969) *School learning: An introduction to educational psychology.* New York: Holt, Rinehart and Winston. **275, 276**

Ax, A. F. (1953) The physiological differentiation between fear and anger in humans. *Psychosomatic Medicine, 15,* No. 5. **337**

Ayllon, T. (1963) Intensive treatment of psychotic behaviour by stimulus satiation and food reinforcement. *Behav. Res. Therapy, 1,* 53–61. New York: Pergamon Press. **207**

Ayllon, T., and Azrin, N. H. (1965) The measurement and reinforcement of behavior of psychotics. *J. exp. Anal. Behav., 8,* 357–383. **468, 469**

Azrin, N. (1967) Pain and aggression. *Psychol. Today,* May, 27–33. **325**

Bachrach, A. J., Erwin, W. J., and Mohr, J. P. (1965) The control of rating behavior in an anorexia by operant conditioning techniques. In Ullman, L. P., and Krasner, L. (Eds.), *Case studies in behavior modification.* New York: Holt. **468**

Bakal, D. A. (1975) Headache: A biopsychological perspective. *Psychol. Bull., 82,* 369–382. **338**

Bale, R. M., Rickus, G. M., and Ambler, R. K. (1973) Prediction of advanced level aviation performance criteria from early training and selection variables. *J. appl. Psychol., 58,* 347–350. **365**

Bales, R. F. (1951) *Interaction process analysis.* Chicago: University of Chicago Press. **541**

Ball, W., and Tronick, E. (1971) Infant responses to impending collision: Optical and real. *Science, 171,* 818–820. **176**

Bandura, A. (1965) Influence of models' reinforcement contingencies on the acquisition of imitative responses. *J. Pers. soc. Psychol., 1,* 589–595. **270, 325, 412**

Bandura, A. (1969) *Social-learning theory of identificatory processes.* In Goslin, D. A. (Ed.), *Handbook of socialization theory and research.* Chicago: Rand McNally. **270, 477**

Bandura, A. (1971) *Psychological modeling: Conflicting theories.* Chicago: Aldine-Atherton. **270, 276**

Bandura, A. (1973) *Aggression: A social learning analysis.* Englewood Cliffs, N.J.: Prentice-Hall. **270, 510**

Banerji, B. S. (1973) Prevention of mental retardation. *Indian J. ment. Retard., 6,* 33–42. **378**

Banuazizi, A., and Movahedi, S. (1975) Interpersonal dynamics in a simulated prison: A methodological analysis. *Amer. Psychol., 30,* 152–160. **533**

Barber, T. X. (1969) *Hypnosis: A scientific approach.* New York: Van Nostrand. **184, 185**

Barber, T. X., Walker, P. C., and Hahn, K. W. (1973) Effects of hypnotic induction and suggestions on nocturnal dreaming and thinking. *J. abnorm. Psychol., 82,* 414–427. **44**

Barker, R. G., and Wright, H. F. (1951) *One boy's day.* New York: Harper. **30**

Baron, R. A., and Byrne, D. (1977) *Social psychology: Understanding human interaction.* Boston: Allyn and Bacon. **545**

Barron, F. (1958) The psychology of imagination. *Scientific American, 199,* No. 3, 151–166. **237, Plate 6**

Barron, F. (1961) Creative vision and expression in writing and painting. In Institute of Personality Assessment and Research, *The creative person.* Berkeley: University of California, and Extension, Liberal Arts Department. **236**

Barron, F. (1975) The solitariness of self and its mitigation through creative imagination. In Taylor, I. A., and Getzels, J. W. (Eds.), *Perspectives in creativity.* Chicago: Aldine. **236**

Bartlett, F. C. (1932) *Remembering.* New York and London: Cambridge University Press. **251**

Bash, K. W. (1939) An investigation into a possible organic basis for the hunger drive. *J. comp. Psychol., 28,* 137–160. **302**

Bates, R. W., Riddle, O., and Lahr, E. L. (1937) The mechanisms of the anti-gonad action of prolactin. *Amer. J. Physiol., 119,* 610–614. **294**

Bateson, G. (1972) *Steps to an ecology of the mind.* New York: Ballantine. **452**

Bateson, P. G. (1966) The characteristics and context of imprinting. *Biol. Rev., 41,* 177–220. **514**

Baumrind, D. (1964) Some thoughts on ethics of research: After reading Milgram's "Behavioral study of obedience." *Amer. Psychol., 19,* 421–423. **532**

Bayley, N. (1940) Mental growth in young children. In Whipple, G. M. (Ed.), *Thirty-ninth yearbook, National Society for the Study of Education, II. Intelligence: Its nature and nurture.* Bloomington, Ill.: Public School Publishing Co. **94**

Bayley, N. (1970) Development of mental abilities. In Mussen, P. H. (Ed.), *Carmichael's manual of child psychology,* Vol. I. New York: Wiley. **93**

Bayley, N., and Oden, M. H. (1955) The maintenance of intellectual ability in gifted adults. *J. Gerontology, 10,* 91–107. **97**

Becker, H. (1967) History, culture and subjective experience: An exploration of the social bases of drug-induced experiences. In Hollander, C. (Ed.), *Background papers on student drug involvement.* Washington, D.C.: U.S. National Student Association. **509**

Beckwith, J., and Miller, L. (1976) The XYY male: The making of a myth. *Harvard Magazine,* October, 30–33. **325**

Beers, C. W. (1908) *A mind that found itself.* New York: Longmans. **513**

Békésy, G. von (1960) *Experiments in hearing.* New York: McGraw-Hill. **143**

Bell, C. (1811) *Idea of a new anatomy of the brain.* London: Strahan and Preston. See also *Med. Classics, 1* (1936), 105–120. **107**

Bell, C. (1821) On the nerves; giving an account of some experiments on their structure and functions, which lead to a new arrangement of the system. *Philos. Tr. Roy. Soc. London, 111,* 398–424. **109**

Belvedere, E., and Foulkes, D. (1971) Telepathy and dreams: A failure to replicate. *Percept. mot. Skills, 33,* 783–789. **31**

Benedict, R. (1949) Child rearing in certain European countries. *Amer. J. Orthopsychiat., 19,* 342–350. **323**

Bergin, A. E., and Suinn, R. M. (1975) Individual psychotherapy and behavior therapy. In Rosenzweig, M. R., and Porter, L. W. (Eds.), *Annual review of psychology, 26.* Palo Alto, Calif.: Annual Reviews, Inc. **466, 477, 478**

Bergler, E. (1974) *Principles of self-damage.* New York: Intercontinental Medical Book Corporation. **438**

Berkowitz, L. (1974) Some determinants of impulsive aggression: Role of mediated association with reinforcements for aggression. *Psychol. Rev., 81,* 165–176. **326, 434**

Berkowitz, L., and LePage, A. (1967) Weapons as aggression-eliciting stimuli. *J. Pers. soc. Psychol., 7,* 202–207. **326**

Berlyne, D. E., Craw, M. A., Salapatek, P. H., and Lewis, J. L. (1963) Novelty, complexity, incongruity, extrinsic motivation, and the GSR. *J. exp. Psychol., 66,* 560–567. **163**

Bernard, L. L. (1924) *Instinct: A study in social psychology.* New York: Holt. **296**

Berne, E. (1961) *Transactional analysis in psychotherapy: A systematic individual and social psychiatry.* New York: Grove Press. **476**

Bexton, W. H., Heron, W., and Scott, T. H. (1954) Effects of decreased variation in the sensory environment. *Canadian J. Psychol., 8,* 70–76. **308, 309**

Bindra, D. (1974) A motivational view of learning, performance, and behavior modification. *Psychol. Rev., 81,* 199–213. **207**

Bindra, D. (1976) *A theory of intelligent behavior.* New York: Wiley. **391.**

Birch, H. G. (1945) The relation of previous experience to insightful problem-solving. *J. comp. Psychol., 38,* 367–383. **229**

Birch, H. G. (1956) Sources of order in the maternal behavior of animals. *Amer. J. Orthopsychiat., 26,* 279–284. **294**

Birch, H. G., and Rabinowitz, H. S. (1951) The negative effect of previous experience on productive thinking. *J. exp. Psychol., 41,* 121–125. **240**

Birk, L. (1974) Group psychotherapy for men who are homosexual. *J. Sex marital Therapy, 1,* 29–52. **470**

Birren, J. E. (1974) Translations in gerontology—from lab to life: Psychophysiology and speed of response. *Amer. Psychol., 29,* 808–815. **96**

Bishop, J., Herz, N., and Taylor, S. (1963) *The freshman experience.* Compiled from English Composition, Class of 1966, Cornell University, 290 pp., June 1963, mimeographed. Copy in the University Archives, Cornell University, Ithaca, N.Y. **343**

Blain, G. B. (1973) *Are parents bad for children?* New York: Coward, McCann and Geoghegan. **324**

Blanchard, E. B., and Young, L. D. (1973) Self-control of cardiac functioning: A promise as yet unfulfilled. *Psychol. Bull., 79,* 145–163. **131**

Blinkov, S. M., and Glezer, I. I. (1968) *The human brain in figures and tables: A quantitative handbook.* New York: Basic Books. **114**

Block, J. (1961) *The Q-sort method in personality assessment and psychiatric research.* Springfield, Ill.: Charles C. Thomas. **419, 426**

Blommers, P. J., and Forsyth, R. A. (1977) *Elementary statistical methods.* Boston: Houghton Mifflin. **71**

Bloom, B. S. (1956) *Taxonomy of educational objectives: Handbook I. Cognitive domain.* New York: McKay. **269**

Blum, G. S. (1954) An experimental reunion of psychoanalytic theory with perceptual vigilance and defense. *J. abnorm. soc. Psychol., 49,* 94–98. **404**

Bolles, R. C. (1975) *Learning theory.* New York: Holt, Rinehart and Winston. **198, 212, 289**

Bolles, R. C. (1975) *Theory of motivation* (2nd ed.). New York: Harper and Row. **317**

Bond, E. D. (1958) *One mind common to all.* New York: Macmillan. **425**

Boring, E. G. (1950) *A history of experimental psychology* (2nd ed.). New York: Appleton-Century-Crofts. **5, 23**

Boring, E. G. (1965) On the subjectivity of important historical dates: 1879. *J. Hist. behavior. Sci., 1,* 5–9. **6**

Boring, E. G., Langfeld, H. S., and Weld, H. P. (1948) *Foundations of psychology.* New York: Wiley. **139**

Bourne, L. E., Ekstrand, B. R., and Dominowski, R. L. (1971) *The psychology of thinking.* Englewood Cliffs, N.J.: Prentice-Hall. **243**

Bousefield, W. A. (1955) Lope de Vega on early conditioning. *Amer. Psychologist, 10,* 828. **193**

Bower, G. H. (1970) Analysis of a mnemonic device. *Amer. Scientist, 58,* 496–510. **264, 265**

Bower, G. H. (1972) Stimulus-sampling theory of encoding variability. In Melton, A. W., and Martin, E. (Eds.), *Coding processes in human memory.* Washington, D. C.: Winston. **230, 263**

Bower, G. H., and Karlin, M. B. (1974) Depth of processing pictures of faces and recognition memory. *J. exp. Psychol., 103,* 751–757. **252**

Bower, T. G. R., Broughton, J. M., and Moore, M. K. (1970) Infant responses to approaching objects: An indicator of response to distal variables. *Percept. Psychophys., 9,* 193–196. **176**

Braginsky, B. M., Braginsky, D. D., and Ring, K. (1969) *Methods of madness: The mental hospital as a last resort.* New York: Holt. **437**

Brand, W. G. (1970) Extinction in goldfish: Facilitation by intracranial injection of "RNA" from brains of extinguished donors. *Science, 168,* 1234–1236. **247**

Brand, W. G., and Hoffman, R. B. (1973) Response facilitation and response inhibition produced by intracranial injections of brain extracts from trained donor goldfish. *Physiol. Psychol., 1,* 169–173. **247**

Bransford, J. D., and Franks, J. J. (1971) The abstraction of linguistic ideas. *Cog. Psychol., 2,* 331–350. **246**

Brecher, R., and Brecher, E. (1966) *An analysis of human sexual response.* New York: American Library. **345**

Breger, L. (1974) *From instinct to identity: The development of personality.* Englewood Cliffs, N.J.: Prentice-Hall. **297**

Brehm, J. W. (1956) Postdecision changes in the desirability of alternatives. *J. abnorm. soc. Psychol., 52,* 384–389. **522**

Breland, H. M. (1973) Birth order effects: A reply to Schooler. *Psychol. Bull., 80,* 210–212. **328**

Bridges, K. M. B. (1930) A genetic theory of emotions. *J. genet. Psychol., 37,* 514–527. **340**

Brigham, C. C. (1923) *A study of American intelligence.* Princeton, N.J.: Princeton University Press. See Kamin (1974). **384**

Bringmann, W. G., Balance, W. D. G., and Evans, R. B. (1975) Wilhelm Wundt 1832–1920: A brief biographical sketch. *J. Hist. behav. Sci., 11,* 287–297. **6**

Broadbent, D. E. (1977) The hidden preattentive process. *Amer. Psychol., 32,* 109–118. **164**

Brock, T. C., and Buss, A. H. (1962) Dissonance, aggression, and evaluation of pain. *J. abnorm. soc. Psychol., 65,* 197–202. **522**

Brogden, W. J. (1951) Some theoretical considerations of learning. *Psychol. Rev., 58,* 224–229. **97**

Brogden, W. J., Lipman, E. A., and Culler, E. A. (1938) The role of incentive in conditioning and extinction. *Amer. J. Psychol., 51,* 109. **211**

Bronfenbrenner, U. (1958) Socialization and social class through time and space. In Maccoby, E. E., Newcomb, T. M., and Hartley, E. L. (Eds.), *Readings in social psychology* (3rd ed.). New York: Holt. **539**

Brown, J. S. (1948) Gradients of approach and avoidance responses and their relation to level of motivation. *J. comp. physiol. Psychol., 41,* 450–465. **430, 431**

Brown, P. L., and Jenkins, H. M. (1968) Autoshaping of the pigeon's keypeck. *J. exp. Anal. Behav., 11,* 1–8. **212**

Brown, R. W. (1965) *Social psychology.* New York: The Free Press. **525**

Brown, R. W. (1973a) *A first language: The early stages.* Cambridge, Mass.: Harvard University Press. **492, 493, 494, 503, 512**

Brown, R. W. (1973b) Development of the first language in the human species. *Amer. Psychol., 28,* 97–106. **500**

Brown, R. W., and Bellugi, U. (1964) Three processes in the child's acquisition of syntax. *Harvard educ. Rev., 34,* 133–151. **495**

Brown, R. W., Galanter, E., Hess, E. H., and Mandler, G. (1962) *New directions in psychology,* Vol. I. New York: Holt, Rinehart and Winston. **137**

Brown, R. W., and McNeill, D. (1966) The "tip of the tongue" phenomenon. *J. verb. Learn. verb. Behav., 5,* 325–337. **252**

Brownfain, J. J. (1967) Hypnodiagnosis. In Gordon, J. E. (Ed.), *Handbook of clinical and experimental hypnosis.* New York: Macmillan. **479**

Browning, P. L. (1974) *Mental retardation: Rehabilitation and counseling.* Springfield, Ill.: Charles C. Thomas. **391**

Bruner, J. S. (1960) The functions of teaching. *Rhode Island Coll. J., 1,* 35–42. **275, 276**

Bruner, J. S., Goodnow, J. J., and Austin, G. A. (1956) *A study of thinking.* New York: Wiley. **225**

Bruner, J. S., Matter, J., and Papanek, M. L. (1955) Breadth of learning as a function of drive level and mechanization. *Psychol. Rev., 62,* 1–10. **336**

Bugelski, R. B. (1964) *The psychology of learning applied to teaching.* Indianapolis: Bobbs-Merrill. **272**

Bugelski, R. B. (1975) *Empirical studies in the psychology of learning.* New York: Crowell. **289**

Bugental, J. F. T. (1967) *Challenges of humanistic psychology.* New York: McGraw-Hill. **14**

Buhler, C. (1971) Basic theoretical concepts of humanistic psychology. *Amer. Psychol., 26,* 378–386. **14**

Bureau of Labor Statistics (1974) *Occupational outlook handbook: 1974-1975 edition.* Washington, D.C.: U.S. Department of Labor, Bulletin 1785. **56**

Burghardt, G. M. (1973) Instinct and innate behavior: Toward an ecological psychology. In Nevin, J. A. (Ed.), *The study of behavior: Learning, motivation, emotion and instinct.* Glenview, Ill.: Scott, Foresman. **297**

Buros, O. K. (1972) *Seventh mental measurements yearbook.* Highland Park, N.J.: Gryphon Press. **351, 369**

Burt, C. (1970) Inheritance of general intelligence. *Amer. Psychol., 27,* 175–190. **385**

Burtt, H. E. (1932) An experimental study of early childhood memory. *Pedag. Sem. J. Genet. Psychol., 40,* 287–295. **253**

Burtt, H. E. (1937) A further study of early childhood memory. *J. genet. Psychol., 50,* 187–192. **244, 254**

Burtt, H. E. (1941) An experimental study of early childhood memory: Final report. *Pedag. Sem. J. Genet. Psychol., 58,* 435–439. **255, 257**

Butler, R. A., and Harlow, H. F. (1954) Persistence of visual exploration in monkeys. *J. comp. physiol. Psychol., 47,* 258–263. **310**

Bynum, T. W., Thomas, J. A., and Weitz, L. J. (1972) Truth functional logic in formal-operational thinking: Inhelder and Piaget's evidence. *Develop. Psychol., 7,* 129–132. **222**

Byrd, R. E. (1938) *Alone.* New York: Putnam's Sons. **308**

Calder, B. J., and Ross, M. (1973) *Attitudes and behavior.* Morristown, N.J.: General Learning. **518**

Cameron, N. (1963) *Personality development and psychopathology.* Boston: Houghton Mifflin. **440**

Campbell, B. A., and Church, R. M. (Eds.) (1969) *Punishment and aversive behavior.* New York: Appleton-Century-Crofts. **286**

Campbell, D. P. (1974) *Manual for the Strong-Campbell Interest Inventory.* Stanford, Calif.: Stanford University Press. **353**

Canning, B. A., and Rose, M. F. (1974) Clinical measurements of the speed of tongue and lip movements in British children with normal speech. *Brit. J. Disord. Commun., 9,* 45–50. **499**

Cannon W. B. (1929) *Bodily changes in pain, hunger, fear and rage* (2nd ed.). New York: Appleton-Century-Crofts. **342**

Cannon, W. B. (1934) Hunger and thirst. In Murchison, C. (Ed.), *A handbook of general experimental physchology.* Worcester, Mass.: Clark University Press. **302**

Cappon, D., and Banks, R. (1960) Studies in perceptual distortion: Opportunistic observations on sleep deprivation during a talkathon. *Arch. gen. Psychiat., 2,* 346–349. **305**

Carlsen, A. J., and Johnson, N. (1948) *The machinery of the body* (rev. ed.) Chicago: University of Chicago Press. **114**

Carlson, N. (1977) *Physiology of behavior.* Boston: Allyn and Bacon. **160**

Carlson, R. (1975) Personality. In Rosenzweig, W. R., and Porter, L. W. (Eds.), *Annual review of psychology, 26.* Palo Alto, Calif.: Annual Reviews, Inc. **420**

Carmichael, L. (1927) A further study of the development of behavior in vertebrates experimentally removed from the influence of external stimulation. *Psychol. Rev., 34,* 34–47. **86**

Carmichael, L. (1975) Becoming an open school. *New Ways,* Jan.-Feb., 10. **241**

Carpenter, T. M., and Benedict, F. G. (1909) The metabolism of man during the work of typewriting. *J. biol. Chem., 6,* 271–288. **51**

Cartwright, D. S. (1974) *Introduction to personality.* Chicago: Rand McNally. **406**

Carver, R. P. (1974) Two dimensions of tests: Psychometric and edumetric. *Amer. Psychol., 29,* 512–518. **367**

Cattell, R. B. (1957) *Personality and motivational structure and measurement.* New York: Harcourt, Brace and World. **410**

Cattell, R. B. (1973) Personality pinned down. *Psychol. Today, 7,* 41–46. **407, 410**

Cattell, R. B., Eber, H. W., and Tatsuoka, M. M. (1970) *Handbook for the sixteen personality factor questionnaire.* Champaign, Ill.: Institute for Personality and Ability Testing. **407**

Ceraso, J., and Provitera, A. (1971) Sources of error in syllogistic reasoning. *Cogn. Psychol., 2,* 400–410. **235**

Chauncey, R. (1975) Deterrence: Certainty, severity, and skyjacking. *Crim. Interdis. J., 12,* 447–473. **287**

Chen, S. C.(1938) Social modification of the activity of ants in nest building. *Physiol. Zool., 10,* 420–436. **534**

Chiang, H-M., and Maslow, A. H. (1977) *The healthy personality* (2nd ed.). New York: Van Nostrand. **317**

Chomsky, N. (1957) *Syntactic structures.* The Hague: Mouton. **489, 499**

Christensen, L. (1977) *Experimental methodology.* Boston: Allyn and Bacon. **48**

Clark, R. N., Burgess, R. L., and Hendee, J. C. (1972) The development of anti-litter behavior in a forest campground. *J. appl. Behav. Anal., 5,* 1–5. **206**

Clinchy, B. (1975) Lecture on Piaget. Wellesley College, Wellesley, Mass., February. **220**

Coch, L., and French, J. R. P. (1948) Overcoming resistance to change. *Human Relations, 1,* 512–532. **506, 507**

Cofer, C. N. (1972) *Motivation and emotion.* Glenview, Ill.: Scott, Foresman. **337, 345**

Cohen, J. (1970) *Secondary motivation: I. Personal motives.* Chicago: Rand McNally. **540**

Cohen, J. (1970) *Secondary motivation: II. Social motives.* Chicago: Rand McNally. **187**

Colby, K. M., and Gilbert, J. P. (1964) Programming a computer model of neurosis. *J. math. Psychol., 1,* 405–417. **232**

Cole, M., and Scribner, S. (1974) *Culture and thought.* New York: Wiley. **187**

Collier, G. (1962) Consummatory and instrumental responding as functions of deprivation. *J. exp. Psychol., 64,* 410–414. **302**

Collins, A. M., and Quillian, M. R. (1972) How to make a language user. In Tulving, E., and Donaldson, W. (Eds.), *Organization of memory*. New York: Academic Press. **264**

Collins, R. L. (1970) The sound of one paw dropping: An inquiry into the origin of left-handedness. In Lindzey, G., and Theissen, D. D. (Eds.), *Contributions to behavior-genetic analysis*. New York: Appleton-Century-Crofts. **79**

Conte, A., Brandzel, M., and Whitehead, S. (1974) Group work with hypertensive patients. *Amer. J. Nursing, 74,* 910–912. **506**

Coombs, J. A. (1975) A nationwide study of women in United States dental schools. Doctoral dissertation. Cambridge, Mass.: Harvard University. **388**

Cooper, R. M., and Zubek, J. P. (1958) Effects of enriched and restricted early environments on the learning ability of bright and dull rats. *Canadian J. Psychol., 12,* 159–164. **90**

Corning, W. C., and Labue, R. (1971) Reflex "training" in frogs. *Psychoan. Sci., 23,* 119–120. **152**

Cox, C. M. (1926) *Genetic studies of genius.* Stanford, Calif.: Stanford University Press. **382**

Cox, R. D. (1970) *Youth into maturity.* New York: Mental Health Materials Center. **105**

Cromwell, R. L. (1975) Assessment of schizophrenia. In Rosenzweig, M. R., and Porter, L. W. (Eds.), *Annual review of psychology, 26.* Palo Alto, Calif.: Annual Reviews, Inc. **437**

Cronbach, L. J. (1970) *Essentials of psychological testing* (3rd ed.). New York: Harper. **369**

Cronbach, L. J. (1975) Five decades of public controversy over mental testing. *Amer. Psychol., 30,* 1–14. **384, 387**

Cronbach, L. J. (1977) *Educational psychology* (3rd ed.). New York: Harcourt Brace. **289**

Crovitz, H. F. (1970) *Galton's walk: Methods for the analysis of thinking, intelligence and creativity.* New York: Harper & Row. **243**

Crowe, R. R. (1974) An adoption study of antisocial personality. *Arch. gen. Psychiat., 31,* 785–791. **448**

Crystal, D. (1973) Linguistic mythology and the first year of life: An edited version of the sixth Jansson memorial lecture. *Brit. J. Disord. Commun., 8,* 29–36. **492**

Curtis, Q. F. (1937) Experimental neurosis in the pig. *Psychol. Bull., 34,* 723. **432**

Cutler, R. L. (1958) Countertransference effects in psychotherapy. *J. consult. Psychol., 22,* 349–356. **479**

Dallett, J. (1973) Theories of dream function. *Psychol. Bull., 79,* 408–416. **47**

D'Aquili, E. (1975) The influence of Jung and the work of Claude Levi-Strauss. *J. Hist. behav. Sci., 11,* 41–48. **402**

Darley, J. M., and Batson, C. D. (1973) "From Jerusalem to Jericho": A study of situational and dispositional variables in helping behavior. *J. Pers. soc. Psychol., 27,* 100–108. **529**

Darley, J. M., and Berscheid, E. (1967) Increased liking as a result of the anticipation of personal contact. *Human Relations, 20,* 29–40. **517**

Darwin, C. (1859) *The origin of species by means of natural selection* (6th ed., 1872). New York: Appleton. **3, 4**

Darwin, C. (1873) See Darwin, C., 1965. **4**

Darwin, C. (1965) *The expression of the emotions in man and animals.* Chicago: University of Chicago Press. Originally published in 1873. **4**

Das, J. P. (1973) How to teach retardates to control their behavior. *Indian J. ment. Retard., 6,* 5–20. **380**

Dashiell, J. F. (1935) Experimental studies of the influence of social situations on the behavior of individual human adults. In Murchison, C. (Ed.), *Handbook of social psychology.* Worcester, Mass.: Clark University Press. **534**

Dashiell, J. F. (1949) *Fundamentals of general psychology* (3rd ed.). Boston: Houghton Mifflin. **428**

Davenport, H. W. (1972) Why the stomach does not digest itself. *Scientific American, 220,* 87–93. **338**

Davis, B. D. (1976) XYY: The dangers of regulating research by adverse publicity. *Harvard Magazine,* October, 26–30. **325**

Davis, C. M. (1928) Self-selection of diet by newly weaned infants. *Amer. J. Diseases of Children, 36,* 651–679. **305**

Dean, E. F. (1972) A lengthened mini: The midi-mult. *J. clin. Psychol., 28,* 68–71. **410**

Deese, J. (1972) *Psychology as a science and art.* New York: Harcourt Brace Jovanovich. **48**

Delabarre, E. B. (1899) Report on the effects of cannabis indica. *Psychol. Rev., 6,* 153–154. **184**

Delgado, J. M. R. (1971) *Physical control of the mind: Toward a psychocivilized society.* New York: Harper and Row. **120**

Delk, J. L. (1973) Some personality characteristics of skydivers. *Life-Threat. Behav., 3,* 51–57. **407**

Dement, W., Henry, P., Cohen, H., and Ferguson, J. (1967) Studies on the effect of REM deprivation in humans and in animals. In Kety, S., Williams, H., and Evarts, E. (Eds.), *Sleep and altered states of consciousness.* Baltimore: Williams and Williams. **46**

Dement, W. C. (1960) The effect of dream deprivation. *Science, 131,* 1705–1707. **45**

Denker, P. G. (1947) Results of treatment of psychoneuroses by the general practitioner: A follow-up study of 500 cases. *Arch. Neurol. Psychiat., 57,* 504–505. **477**

Dennis, W. (1940) *The Hopi child.* New York: Appleton-Century. **329**

Dennis, W. (1955) Are the Hopi children noncompetitive? *J. abnorm. soc. Psychol., 50,* 99–100. **329**

Deutsch, K. W., Platt, J., and Senghaas, D. (1971) Conditions favoring major advances in social science. *Science, 171,* 450–459. **14**

Deutsch, M. (1960) The effect of motivational orientation upon trust and suspicion. *Human Relations, 13,* 122–139. **535**

Devine, D. A., and Fernald, P. S. (1973) Outcome effects of receiving a preferred, randomly assigned, or nonpreferred therapy. *J. consult. clin. Psychol., 41,* 104–107. **478**

Dicara, L. V. (1970) Learning in the autonomic nervous system. *Scientific American, 222,* 30–39. **131**

DiLoreto, A. O. (1971) *Comparative psychotherapy: An experimental analysis.* Chicago: Aldine-Atherton. **478**

Doherty, M. E., and Shemberg, K. M. (1970) *Asking questions about behavior: An introduction to what psychologists do.* Glenview, Ill.: Scott, Foresman. **49**

Dohrenwend, B. P., and Dohrenwend, B. S. (1974) Social and cultural influences on psychopathology. In Rosenzweig, M. R., and Porter, L. W. (Eds.), *Annual Review of Psychology, 25,* Palo Alto, Calif.: Annual Reviews, Inc. **538**

Dollard, J., Miller, N. E., Doob, L. W., Mowrer, O. H., and Sears, R. R. (1939) *Frustration and aggression.* New Haven, Conn.: Yale University Press. **325, 434**

Doppelt, J. E., and Kaufman, A. S. (1977) Estimation of the differences between WISC-R and WISC IQs. *Educ. psychol. Measmt., 37,* 417–424. **373**

Dornbusch, S. M., Hastorf, A. H., Richardson, S. A., Muzzy, R. E., and Ureeland, R. S. (1965) The perceiver and the perceived: Their relative influence on the categories of interpersonal cognition. *J. Pers. soc. Psychol., 1,* 434–440. **180**

Dugdale, R. L. (1877) *The Jukes: A study in crime, pauperism, disease and heredity* (4th ed.). New York: G. P. Putnam and Sons. **377**

Dunham, W. H. (1965) *Community and schizophrenia: An epidemiological analysis.* Detroit: Wayne State University Press. **481**

Dunker, K. (1945) On problem solving. *Psychol. Monogr., 58,* 2, 59. **221**

Dunn, C. C. (1932) *Heredity and variation.* Midland Park, N.J.: The University Society. **78**

Dvorak, A., Merrick, N. L., Dealey, W. L., and Ford, G. C. (1936) *Typewriting behavior.* New York: American Book Company. **65**

Earhard, M. (1967) Subjective organization and list organization as determinants of free-recall and serial-recall memorization. *J. verb. Learn. verb. Behav., 6,* 501–507. **263**

Ebbinghaus, H. (1885) *Über das Gedächtnis.* Leipzig: Duncker. Translated by Ruger, H. A., and Bussenius, C. E. (1913), *Memory.* New York: Teacher's College, Columbia University. **252**

Eccles, J. (1965) The synapse. *Scientific American, 212,* 56–66. **113**

Ehrlich, J. (1969) Attitudes, behavior, and intervening variables. *Amer. Sociol., 4,* 29–34. **518**

Eichorn, D. H. (1973) The Berkeley longitudinal studies: Continuities and correlates of behaviour. *Canadian J. behav. Sci., 5,* 297–319. **93, 94**

Ekman, P., Friesen, W. V., and Ellsworth, P. (1971) *Emotion in the human face: Guidelines for research and a review of the findings.* New York: Pergamon Press. **336**

Ellis, A. (1959) Rationalism and its therapeutic applications. *Ann. Psychother., 1,* 55–64. **459**

Ellis, A. (1962) *Reason and emotion in psychotherapy.* New York: Lyle Stuart. **456, 461**

Ellis, A., and Harper, R. (1975) *A new guide to Rational living.* Englewood Cliffs, N.J.: Prentice-Hall. **461**

Emmons, W. H., and Simon, C. W. (1956) The non-recall of material presented during sleep. *Amer. J. Psychol., 69,* 76–81. **284**

Endler, N. S. (1965) The effects of verbal reinforcement on conformity and deviant behavior. *J. soc. Psychol., 66,* 147–154. **414**

Engel, B. T. (1972) Operant conditioning of cardiac function: A status report. *Psychophysiol., 9,* 161–177. **131**

English, H. B., and English, A. C. (1958) *A comprehensive dictionary of psychological and psychoanalytical terms.* New York: Longmans, Green. **198**

Epstein, W. (1977) *Stability and constancy in visual perception.* New York: Wiley. **187**

Erickson, M. L. (1973) Group violations, socioeconomic status and official delinquency. *Social Forces, 52,* 41–52. **539**

Erikson, E. (1963) *Childhood and society* (2nd ed.). New York: W. W. Norton. **98–103**

Erlenmeyer-Kimling, L., and Jarvik, L. F. (1963) Genetics and intelligence: A review. *Science, 142,* 1477–1479. **89**

Eysenck, H. J. (1952) The effects of psychotherapy: An evaluation. *J. consult. Psychol., 16,* 319–324. **477**

Eysenck, H. J. (1965) The effects of psychotherapy. *Internat. J. Psychiat., 1,* 97–144. **477**

Eysenck, H. J. (1972) Note on "Factors influencing the outcome of psychotherapy." *Psychol. Bull., 78,* 403–405. **478**

Ezrin, C., Godden, J. O., Volpe, R., and Wilson, R. (1973) *Systematic endocrinology.* New York: Harper and Row. **129**

Fantino, E. (1973) Emotion. In Nevin, J. A. (Ed.), *The study of behavior: Learning, motivation, and instinct.* Glenview, Ill.: Scott, Foresman. **340, 341**

Fantz, R. L. (1961) The origin of form perception. *Scientific American, 204* (5), 66–72. **85**

Fechner, G. T. *Elemente der psychophysik* [*Elements of psychophysics*]. Leipzig, 1860. **5**

Ferlemann, M. (1974) Homosexuality. *Menninger Perspect., 5,* 24–27. **322**

Fernald, L. D., Jr., Fernald, P. S., and Rines, W. B. (1966) Purdue pegboard and differential diagnosis. *J. consult. Psychol., 30,* 279. **364**

Feshback, S., and Singer, R. D. (1971) *Television and aggression: An experimental field study.* San Francisco: Josey-Bass. **509**

Festinger, L., Schachter, S., and Back, K. (1950) *Social pressures in informal groups.* Palo Alto, Calif.: Stanford University Press. **517**

Festinger, L. A. (1954) Motivations leading to social behavior. In Jones, M. R. (Ed.), *Nebraska symposium on motivation.* Lincoln, Neb.: University of Nebraska Press. **310**

Fiedler, F. E. (1964) A contingency model of leadership effectiveness. In Berokwitz, L. (Ed.), *Advances in experimental social psychology.* Vol. 1. New York: Academic Press. **542**

Fisher, R. A., and Yates, F. (1963) *Statistical tables for biological, agricultural, and medical research* (6th ed.). Edinburgh: Oliver & Boyd Ltd. **33**

Fitzgerald, H. E., and Brockbill, Y. (1976) Classical conditioning in infancy: Development and constraints. *Psychol. Bull., 83,* 353–376. **212**

Flaherty, C., Hamilton, L. W., Gardelman, R., and Spear, N.E. (1977) *Learning and memory.* Skokie, Ill.: Rand McNally. **267**

Flavell, J. H., and others (1975) *The development of role-taking and communication skills in children.* Huntington, N.Y.: Krieger. **219**

Fleming, J. D. (1974) The state of the apes. *Psychol. Today, 7,* 31–46. **503, 504**

Floyd, J. R., and Lumsden, D. B. (1973) Effects of frame size in teaching vocabulary development with programmed instruction. *Improv. hum. Perf., 2,* 267–272. **274**

Fontana, A. F. (1966) Familial etiology of schizophrenia: Is a scientific methodology possible? *Psychol. Bull., 66,* 214–227. **446**

Forlano, G. (1936) School learning with various methods of practice and rewards. *Teach. Coll. Contrib. Educ.,* No. 688. New York: Columbia University. **282**

Foster, G. M. (1973) Dreams, character, and cognitive orientation in Tzintzuntzan. *Ethos, 1,* 106–121. **32**

Foster, H. H. (1975) The conflict and reconciliation of the ethical interests of therapist and patient. *J. psychiat. Law, 3,* 39–61. **533**

Foulkes, D., and Vogel, G. W. (1974) the current status of laboratory dream research. *Psychiat. Annals, 4,* 7–27. **47**

Fouts, R. S. (1972) Use of guidance in teaching sign language to a chimpanzee. *J. comp. physiol. Psychol., 80,* 515–522. **503**

Frank, J. D. (1973) *Persuasion and healing* (rev. ed.). Baltimore: Johns Hopkins University Press. **483**

Franklin, V., and Rodman, R. (1974) *An introduction to language.* New York: Holt. **512**

Freeman, G. L. (1931) The spread of neuro-muscular activity during mental work. *J. gen. Psychol., 5,* 479–493. **162**

Freeman, W., and Meyer, R. G. (1975) A behavioral alteration of sexual preferences in the human male. *Behav. Therapy, 6,* 206–212. **466**

Freud, S. (1905) A case of hysteria: Three essays on sexuality and other works. In the *Standard edition of the complete psychological works of Sigmund Freud.* Vol. VII. London: Hogarth. **35**

Freud, S. (1914) *Psychopathology of everyday life.* New York: Macmillan. **333**

Freud, S. (1933) *New introductory lectures on psycho-analysis.* New York: W. W. Norton. **398, 424**

Freud, S. (1949) *An outline of psycho-analysis.* New York: W. W. Norton. **483**

Freud, S. (1965) *The psychopathology of everyday life.* Translated by Alan Tyson, edited by James Strachey. New York: W. W. Norton. **260, 267, 333**

Frighi, L., Coppi, R., and Pinchini, F. (1972) The extensive and graphic treatment of sociopsychiatric data relative to a population of university students. *Rivista di Psichiatria, 7,* 299–339. **538**

Frisch, K. von (1955) *The dancing bees.* New York: Harcourt, Brace. **490**

Frisch, K. von (1962) Dialects in the language of the bees. *Scientific American, 207,* August, 78–87. **490**

Fritsch, G., and Hitzig, E. (1870) Über die elekrische Erregbarkeit des Grosshirns. *Arch. f. Anat. Physiol. und wissenschaftl. Mediz.,* 300–332. See "On the electrical excitability of the cerebrum" (1960) in van Bonin, G. (trans.), *Some papers on the cerebral cortex.* Springfield, Ill.: Charles C. Thomas. **114**

Fuchs, A. H., and Kawash, G. F. (1974) Prescriptive dimensions for five schools of psychology. *J. Hist. Behav. Sci., 10,* 352–366. **16**

Fuller, C. (1974) Effect of anonymity on return rate and response bias in a mail survey. *J. appl. Psychol., 59,* 292–296. **34**

Funkenstein, D. H., King, S. H., and Drolette, M. E. (1957) *Mastery of stress.* Cambridge, Mass.: Harvard University Press. **337**

Furth, H. G. (1966) *Thinking without language: Psychological implications of deafness.* New York: Free Press. **225, 226**

Furumoto, L. (1974) Mary W. Calkins (1863–1930): First woman president of the American Psychological Association. Paper presented at the Eastern Psychological Association Convention, Philadelphia. **9**

Gage, N. L. (1952) Judging interests from expressive behavior. *Psychol. Monogr., 66* (18, Whole No. 350). **524**

Gaito, J., and Bonnet, K. (1971) Quantitative versus qualitative RNA and protein changes in the brain during behavior. *Psychol. Bull., 75,* 109–127. **247**

Gallistel, C. R. (1966) Motivating effects in self-stimulation. *J. comp. physiol. Psychol., 62,* 95–101. **121**

Galton, F. (1883) *Inquiries into human faculty and its development.* New York: Macmillan. Revised edition (1907), London: Dent. **370**

Gamzu, E. R., and Williams, D. R. (1973) Associative factors underlying the pigeon's key pecking in autoshaping procedures. *J. exp. Anal. Behav., 19,* 225–232. **212**

Garcia, E. E., and DeHaven, E. D. (1974) Use of operant techniques in the establishment and generalization of language: A review and analysis. *Amer. J. ment. Defic., 79,* 169–178. **497, 501**

Garcia, J., and Koelling, R. (1966) Relation of cue to consequence in avoidance learning. *Psychoan. Sci., 4,* 123–124. **212**

Gardner, E. (1968) *Fundamentals of neurology* (5th ed.). Philadelphia: Saunders. **444**

Gardner, E. (1975) *Fundamentals of neurology* (6th ed.). Philadelphia: Saunders. **133**

Gardner, R. A., and Gardner, B. T. (1969) Teaching sign language to a chimpanzee. *Science, 165,* 664–672. **503**

Garfield, S. L., Prager, R. A., and Bergin, A. E. (1971) Evaluation of outcome in psychotherapy. *J. consult. clin. Psychol., 37,* 307–313. **477**

Garth, T. R. (1931) *Race psychology.* New York: McGraw-Hill. **384**

Gates, A. I. (1917) Recitation as a factor in memorizing. *Arch. Psychol., 6,* No. 40. **282**

Gazzaniga, M. S. (1972) One brain—two minds? *Amer. Sci., 60,* 311–317. **124, 125**

Gazzaniga, M. S., Bogen, J. E., and Sperry, R. W. (1965) Observations on visual perception after disconnexion of the cerebral hemispheres in man. *Brain, 88,* 221–236. **124**

Gerard, H. B., and Robbie, J. M. (1961) Fear and social comparison. *J. abnorm. soc. Psychol., 62,* 586–592. **321**

Gergen, K., Gergen, M., and Meter, K. (1972) Individual orientations to prosocial behavior. *J. soc. Issues, 28,* 105–130. **529**

Getzels, J. W., and Jackson, P. W. (1962) *Creativity and intelligence.* New York: Wiley. **236**

Ghiselli, E. E. (1973) The validity of aptitude tests in personnel selection. *Personnel Psychol., 26,* 461–477. **364**

Gibb, C. A. (1968) Leadership. In Lindzey, G., and Aronson, E. (Eds.), *Handbook of social psychology. IV: Group psychology and phenomena of interaction.* Reading, Mass.: Addison-Wesley. **540**

Gibb, J. R. (1971) The effects of human relations training. In Bergin, A. E., and Garfield, S. L. (Eds.), *Handbook of psychotherapy and behavior change.* New York: Wiley. **420**

Gibson, E. J. (1969) *Principles of perceptual learning and development.* New York: Appleton-Century-Crofts. **187**

Gibson, E. J., and Walk, R. D. (1960) The "visual cliff." *Scientific American, 202,* 64–71. **175**

Gibson, J. J. (1950) *The perception of the visual world.* Boston: Houghton Mifflin. **168**

Gibson, J. J. (1966) *The senses considered as perceptual systems.* Boston: Houghton Mifflin. **156**

Ginsburg, H., and Opper, S. (1969) *Piaget's theory of intellectual development: An introduction.* Englewood Cliffs, N.J.: Prentice-Hall. **216**

Ginsburg, H., and Opper, S. (1971) *Piaget's theory of intellectual development: An introduction* (2nd ed.). Englewood Cliffs, N.J.: Prentice-Hall. **243**

Giora, Z. (1971) REM deprivation: An afterthought. *Comprehen. Psychiat., 12,* 321–329. **46**

Gleason, H. A., Jr. (1961) *An introduction to descriptive linguistics* (rev. ed.). New York: Holt. **499**

Glucksberg, S., and Danks, J. H. (1975) *Experimental psycholinguistics: An introduction.* Hillsdale, N.J.: Erlbaum. **512**

Goddard, H. F. (1912) *The Kallikak family.* New York: Macmillan. **377**

Goldfried, M. R., and Kent, R. N. (1972) Traditional versus behavioral personality assessment: A comparison of methodological and theoretical assumptions. *Psychol. Bull., 77,* 409–420. **414**

Goodenough, F. L. (1932) Expression of the emotions in a blind-deaf child. *J. abnorm. soc. Psychol., 27,* 428–433. **340**

Goodwin, L. (1975) *Can social science help solve national problems? Welfare, a case in point.* New York: Free Press. **542**

Gottesman, I. I. (1963) Heritability of personality. *Psychol. Monogr., 77* (9, Whole No. 572), 1–21. **89**

Gottesman, I. I., and Shields, J. (1966) Schizophrenia in twins: 16 years' consecutive admissions to a psychiatric clinic. *British J. Psychiat., 112,* 809–818. **445**

Gough, H. H. (1957) *The California Psychological Inventory.* Palo Alto, Calif.: Consulting Psychologists Press. **407**

Goy, R. W. (1970) Early hormonal influences on the development of sexual and sex-related behavior. In Schmitt, F. O. (Ed.), *The neurosciences: Second study program.* New York: Rockefeller University Press. **298**

Graham, R. L. (1970) Robin sails home. *Natl. Geographic,* October, 504–544. **292**

Graham, R. L. (1972) *Dove.* New York: Harper and Row. **296, 300, 308, 310, 314, 315**

Gray, C. R., and Gummerman, K. (1975) The enigmatic eidetic image: A critical examination of methods, data and theories. *Psychol. Bull., 82,* 383–407. **249, 250**

Gray, H. (1959) *Anatomy of the human body* (27th ed.). (Ed. by C. M. Goss) Philadelphia: Lea and Febiger. **439**

Gray, S. W. (1974) Ethical issues in research in early childhood intervention. *Sch. psychol. Digest, 3,* 60–67. **533**

Greenfield, P. M. (1973) Who is "Da-da"? Some aspects of the semantic and phonological development of a child's first words. *Lang. Speech, 16,* 34–43. **490**

Greeno, J. G., James, C. T., and DaPolito, F. J. (1971) A cognitive interpretation of negative transfer and forgetting of paired associates. *J. verb. Learn. verb. Behav., 10,* 331–345. **259**

Greenwald, A. G. (1976) With-subject designs: To use or not to use. *Psychol. Bull., 83,* 314–320. **42**

Greenwald, H., and Greenwald, R. (1972) *The sex life letters.* New York: Bantam. **330**

Gregory, R. L. (1966) *Eye and brain.* New York: McGraw-Hill. **160**

Grossberg, J. M. (1964) Behavior therapy: A review. *Psychol. Bull., 62,* 73–88. **477**

Gruber, J. J., and Kirkendall, D. R. (1973) Relationships within and between the mental and personality domains in disadvantaged high school students. *Amer. corr. Therapy J., 27,* 136–140. **382**

Gruenberg, B. C. (1929) *The study of evolution.* Princeton, N.J.: D. Van Nostrand. **44**

Grunt, J. A., and Young, W. C. (1953) Consistency of sexual behavior patterns in individual male guinea pigs following castration and androgen therapy. *J. comp. physiol. Psychol., 46,* 138–144. **294, 295**

Guilford, J. P. (1975) Creativity: A quarter century of progress. In Taylor, I. A., and Getzels, J. W. (Eds.), *Perspectives in creativity.* Chicago: Aldine. **236**

Guilford, J. P. (1975) Factors and factors of personality. *Psychol. Bull., 82,* 802–814. **375, 407**

Guilford, J. P., and Lovewell, E. M. (1936) The touch spots and the intensity of the stimulus. *J. gen. Psychol., 15,* 149–159. **150**

Gulick, W. L. (1971) *Hearing: Physiology and psychophysics.* New York: Oxford University Press. **160**

Guskin, S. L. (1974) Research on labeling retarded persons: where do we go from here? A reaction to MacMillan, Jones and Aloia. *Amer. J. ment. Defic., 79,* 262–264. **380**

Haan, N., and Day, D. (1974) A longitudinal study of change and sameness in personality development: Adolescence to later adulthood. *Internatl. J. Aging hum. Dev., 5,* 11–39. **94**

Haber, R. N. and Haber, R. B. (1964) Eidetic imagery: I. Frequency. *Percept. mot. Skills, 19,* 131–138. **249**

Haber, R. N., and Hershenson, M. (1973) *The psychology of visual perception.* New York: Holt, Rinehart, Winston. **165, 187**

Hahn, J. F. (1974) Somesthesis. In Rosenzweig, M. R., and Porter, L. W. (Eds.), *Annual review of psychology, 25.* Palo Alto, Calif.: Annual Reviews, Inc. **149, 150**

Haire, M. (1950) Projective techniques in market research. *J. Market., 14,* 649–656. **20**

Haldane, J. B. S. (1946) The interaction of nature and nurture. *Annals of Eugenics, 13,* 197–205. **91**

Hall, C. S. (1966) *The meaning of dreams.* New York: McGraw-Hill. **47**

Hall, C. S., and Lindzey, G. (1970) *Theories of personality* (2nd ed.). New York: Wiley. **424**

Hall, C. S., and Van de Castle, R. L. (1966) *The content analysis of dreams.* New York: Appleton-Century-Crofts. **28**

Haney, C., Banks, W. C., and Zimbardo, P. G. (1973) Interpersonal dynamics in a simulated prison. *Internatl. J. Crim. Penol., 1,* 69–97. **533**

Hanna, S. M., Jenner, F. A., Pearson, J. B., Sampson, G. A., and Thompson, E. A. (1972) The therapeutic effect of lithium carbonate on a patient with a forty-eight hour periodic psychosis. *Brit. J. Psychiat., 121,* 271–280. **474**

Harden, L. M. (1930) Effect of emotional reactions upon retention. *J. gen. Psychol., 3,* 197–221. **256**

Hare, R. D. (1970) *Psychopathy: Theory and research.* New York: Wiley. **448**

Harlow, H. F. (1932) Social facilitation of feeding in the albino rat. *J. genet. Psychol., 41,* 211–221. **534**

Harlow, H. F. (1949) The formation of learning sets. *Psychol. Rev., 56,* 51–65. **280**

Harlow, H. F. (1965) Sexual behavior in the rhesus monkey. In Beach, F. (Ed.), *Sex and behavior.* New York: Wiley. **294**

Harlow, H. F., and Harlow, M.K. (1962) Social deprivation in monkeys. *Scientific American, 207,* 136–146. **86**

Harlow, H. F., and Harlow, M. K. (1966) Learning to love. *American Scientist, 54,* 244–272. **294, 299, 311**

Harlow, H. F., Harlow, M. K., and Meyer, D. R. (1950) Learning motivated by a manipulation drive. *J. exp. Psychol., 40,* 228–235. **285**

Harlow, H. F., Harlow, M. K., and Suomi, S. J. (1971) From thought to therapy: Lessons from a primate laboratory. *Amer. Sci., 59,* 538–549. **86**

Harlow, H. F., and Suomi, S. J. (1970) Nature of love—simplified. *Amer. Psychol., 25,* 161–168. **311**

Harlow, H. F., and Zimmerman, R. R. (1959) Affectional responses in the infant monkey. *Science, 130,* 421–432. **311**

Harlow, J. M. (1869) *Recovery from the passage of an iron bar through the head.* Boston: David Clapp and Son. **444**

Harrell, T. W., and Harrell, M. S. (1945) Army General Classification Test scores for civilian occupations. *Educ. psychol. Measmt., 5,* 229–239. **387, 388**

Harriman, P. L. (1942) The experimental induction of a multiple personality. *Psychiatry, 5,* 179–188. **334**

Harris, V. A., and Katkin, E. S. (1975) Primary and secondary emotional behavior: An analysis of the role of autonomic feedback on affect, arousal and attribution. *Psychol. Bull., 82,* 904–916. **343**

Harrison, A. A. (1969) Exposure and popularity. *J. Pers., 37,* 359–377. **517**

Harry, J. (1974) Social class and delinquency: One more time. *Socio. Quart., 15,* 294–301. **539**

Hart, B. L. (1974) Gonadal androgen and sociosexual behavior of male mammals: A comparative analysis. *Psychol. Bull., 81,* 383–400. **298**

Hartley, D., Roback, H. B., and Abramowitz, S. I. (1976) Deterioration effects in encounter groups. *Amer. Psychol., 31,* 247–255. **420**

Hartmann, E. (1967) *The biology of dreaming.* Springfield, Ill.: Charles C. Thomas. **41, 43, 46, 306**

Hartmann, E., Bernstein, J., and Wilson, C. (1967) Sleep and dreaming in the elephant. Report to the Association for the Psychophysiological Study of Sleep, April. **45**

Hartshorne, H., and May, M. A. (1928) *Studies in the nature of character.* Vol. 1. *Studies in deceit.* New York: Macmillan. **411**

Hauri, P., Sawyer, J., and Rechtschaffen, A. (1967) Dimensions of dreaming: A factored scale for rating dream reports. *J. abnorm. Psychol., 72,* 16–22. **37**

Hay, N. M., and Stewart, N. R. (1974) Reliability coefficients from two administrations of the Willoughby Personality Schedule. *J. counsel. Psychol., 21,* 581–582. **360**

Hayes, C. (1951) *The ape in our house.* New York: Harper and Row. **498**

Heath, R. G., Martens, S., Leach, B. E., Cohen, M., and Feigley, L. A. (1958) Behavioral changes in nonpsychotic volunteers following the administration of tarafein, the substance obtained from serum of schizophrenic patients. *Amer. J. Psychiat., 114,* 917. **445**

Hebb, D. O. (1966) *A textbook of psychology* (2nd ed.). Philadelphia: Saunders. **255**

Hecht, S. (1928) The binocular fusion of colors and its relation to theories of color vision. *Proc. Nat. Acad. Sci., 14,* 237–240. **142**

Heckhausen, H. (1967) *The anatomy of achievement motivation.* New York: Academic Press. **328**

Heider, F. (1946) Attitudes and cognitive organization. *J. Psychol., 21,* 107–112. **521**

Hein, A., Held, R., and Gower, E. C. (1970) Development and segmentation of visually controlled movement by selective exposure during rearing. *J. comp. physiol. Psychol., 73,* 181–187. **176**

Held, R., and Hein, A. (1963) Movement produced stimulation in the development of visually guided behavior. *J. comp. physiol. Psychol., 56,* 872–876. **176**

Henle, M. (1962) On the relation between logic and thinking. *Psychol. Rev., 69,* 366–378. **235**

Hepner, H. W. (1941) *Psychology applied to life and work*. Englewood Cliffs, N.J.: Prentice-Hall. **328**

Herrnstein, R. J. (1973) *I.Q. in the meritocracy*. Boston: Little, Brown. **80, 93, 384, 391**

Herskovits, M. J., Campbell, D. T., and Segall, M. H. (1969) *A cross-cultural study of perception* (rev. by Segall and Campbell). Indianapolis: Bobbs-Merrill. **178**

Herz, M. J., Peeke, H. V. S., and Wyers, E. J. (1966) Amnesic effects of ether and electroconvulsive shock in mice. *Psychonomic Science, 4,* 375–376. **256**

Hess, E. H. (1958) Imprinting in animals. *Scientific Monthly,* March, 81–90. **514**

Hess, E. H. (1965) Attitude and pupil size. *Scientific American, 212,* 46–54. **171**

Hess, W. R. (1929) The mechanism of sleep. *Amer. J. Physiol., 90,* 386–387. **306**

Hess, W. R. (1954) *Diencephalon: Autonomic and extra-pyramidal functions*. New York: Grune and Stratton. **119**

Hewes, G. W. (1973) Primate communication and the gestural origin of language. *Curr. Onthro., 14,* 5–24. **502**

Hicks, V. C., and Carr, H. A. (1912) Human reactions in a maze. *J. Animal Behav., 2,* 98–125. **272**

Hilgard, E. R. (1972) A critique of Johnson, Maher and Barber's Artifact in the "essense of hypnosis": An evaluation of trance logic, with a recomputation of their findings. *J. abnorm. Psychol., 79,* 221–233. **185**

Hilgard, E. R. (1973) A neodissociation interpretation of pain reduction in hypnosis. *Psychol. Rev., 80,* 396–411. **185**

Hilgard, E. R., and Bower, G. H. (1975) *Theories of learning* (4th ed.). Englewood Cliffs, N.J.: Prentice-Hall. **201, 215, 259**

Hill, C. G. (1973) A psychological view of corporal punishment. *Delta, 12,* 2–5. **286**

Hill, R. M. (1974) Will this drug harm the unborn infant? *Southern Med. J., 67,* 1476–1480. **81**

Hill, W. F. (1977) *Learning: A survey of psychological interpretations* (3rd ed.). New York: Crowell. **215**

Hinde, R. A. (1963) The nature of imprinting. In Foss, B. M. (Ed.), *Determinants of infant behavior: II.* London: Methuen. **514**

Hockett, C. F. (1958) *A course in modern linguistics*. New York: Macmillan. **539**

Hockett, C. F. (1960) The origin of speech. *Scientific American, 203,* 89–96. **499, 501**

Hoke, R. E. (1922) The improvement of speed and accuracy in typewriting. The Johns Hopkins University Studies in Education, No. 7. **57, 58, 59, 61, 62**

Hollingshead, A. B. (1949) *Elmtown's youth: The impact of social classes on adolescents*. New York: Wiley. **538**

Hollingshead, A. B., and Redlich, F. C. (1958) *Social class and mental illness*. New York: Wiley. **538**

Hollingworth, L. S. (1942) *Children above 180 I.Q.* New York: World Book. **381**

Holmes, D. S. (1974) Investigations of repression: Differential recall of material experimentally or naturally associated with ego threat. *Psychol. Bull., 81,* 632–653. **260**

Holt, J. (1964) *How children fail*. New York: Pitman. **275**

Holtzman, W. H. (1971) The changing world of mental measurement and its social significance. *Amer. Psychol., 26,* 546–553. **369**

Holzberg, J. D., and Knapp, R. H. (1965) The social interaction of college students and chronically ill mental patients. *Amer. J. Orthopsychiat., 35,* 47–492. **481**

Homans, G. C. (1961) *Social behavior: Its elementary forms*. New York: Harcourt, Brace, World. **517**

Honigfeld, G., and Howard, A. (1973) *Psychiatric drugs: A desk reference*. New York: Academic Press. **483**

Honzik, M. P., and Macfarlane, J. W. (1973) Personality development and intellectual functioning from 21 months to 40 years. In Jarvik, L. F., Eisdorfer, C., and Blum, J. (Eds.), *Intellectual functioning in adults: Psychological and biological influences.* New York: Springer. **96**

Honzik, M. P., Macfarlane, J.W., and Allen, L. (1948) The stability of mental test performance between two and eighteen years. *J. exp. Educ., 17,* 309–324. **94**

Hood, A. B. (1963) A study of the relationship between physique and personality variables measured by the MMPI. *J. Pers., 31,* 97–107. **406**

Horn, C. (1953) *Horn Art Aptitude Inventory.* Chicago: Stoelting. **358**

Horn, C., and Smith, L. F. (1945) The Horn Art Aptitude Inventory. *J. appl. Psychol., 29.* **359**

Horner, M. (1969) Woman's will to fail. *Psychol. Today,* November, 36–38, 62. **329**

Horner, M. (1970) Femininity and successful achievement: A basic inconsistency. In Bardwick, J., et al., *Feminine personality and conflict.* Belmont, Calif.: Brooks/Cole. **329**

Horowitz, M. J. (1969) Flashbacks: Recurrent intrusive images after the use of LSD. *Amer. J. Psychiat., 126,* 565–569. **183**

Hovland, C. I., and Weiss, W. (1951) The influence of source credibility on communication effectiveness. *Publ. Opin. Quart., 15,* 635–650. **508**

Hubel, D. H., and Wiesel, T. N. (1962) Receptive fields, binocular interaction, and functional architecture in the cat's visual cortex. *J. Physiol., 160,* 106–154. **116**

Huff, D. (1954) *How to lie with statistics.* New York: Norton. **71**

Humphrey, G. (1962) Introduction. In Itard, J-M-G., *The wild boy of Aveyron.* New York: Appleton-Century-Crofts. **74**

Hunt, J. McV. (1969) Has compensatory education failed? Has it been attempted? *Harvard educ. Rev., 39,* 278–300. **379**

Hurvich, L. M., and Jameson, D. (1957) An opponent-process theory of color vision. *Psychol. Rev., 64,* 384–404. **142**

Hutt, M. L. (1947) "Consecutive" and "adaptive" testing with the revised Stanford Binet. *J. consult. Psychol., 11,* 93–103. **378**

Hydén, H. (1967) Biochemical and molecular aspects of learning and memory. *Proceedings of the American Philosophical Society, III,* 326–342. **247**

Isaacs, W., Thomas, J., and Goldiamond, I. (1960) Application of operant conditioning to reinstate verbal behavior in psychotics. *J. Speech and Hearing Disorders, 25,* 8–12. **203**

Isaacson, L. E. (1966) *Career information in counseling and teaching.* Boston: Allyn and Bacon. **388**

Isen, A. M., and Levin, P. F. (1972) Effects of feeling good on helping: Cookies and kindness. *J. Pers. soc. Psychol., 21,* 384–388. **529**

Itard, J-M-G. (1894) Rapports et mémoires sur le savage de l'Aveyron. Paris. Trans. by Humphrey, G. (1962), *The wild boy of Aveyron.* New York: Appleton-Century-Crofts. **75**

Izard, C. E., and Nunnally, J. C. (1965) Evaluative responses to affectively positive and negative facial photographs: Factor structure and content validity. *J. educ. psychol. Measmt., 25,* 1061–1071. **336**

Izzett, R. (1971) Authoritarianism and attitudes toward the Vietnam war as reflected in behavioral and self-report measures. *J. Pers. soc. Psychol., 17,* 145–148. **520**

Jackson, C. M. (Ed.) (1923) *Human anatomy* (7th ed.). Philadelphia: Blakiston. **84**

James, W. (1890) *The principles of psychology.* Vols. I, II. New York: Holt. **30, 261, 341**

James, W. (1908) *Psychology.* New York: Holt. **264**

Jamison, D., Suppes, P., and Wells, S. (1974) The effectiveness of alternative instructional media: A survey. *Rev. educ. Res., 44,* 1–67. **269**

Jaynes, J. (1977) *The origin of consciousness in the breakdown of the bicameral mind.* Boston: Houghton Mifflin. **133**

Jelliffe, S. E., and White, W. A. (1935) *Diseases of the nervous system* (6th ed.). Philadelphia: Lea and Febiger. **444**

Jenkins, J. G., and Dallenbach, K. M. (1924) Obliviscence during sleep and waking. *Amer. J. Psychol., 35,* 605–612. **258**

Jenner, F. A., Gjessing, L. R., Cox, J. R., Davies-Jones, A., Hullin, R. P., and Hanna, S. M. (1967) A manic depressive psychotic with a persistent forty-eight hour cycle. *Brit. J. Psychiat., 113,* 895–910. **473**

Jenner, F. A., Goodwin, J. C., Sheridan, M., Tauber, J. J., and Lobban, M. C. (1968) The effect of an altered time regime on biological rhythms in a 48-hour periodic psychosis. *Brit. J. Psychiat., 114,* 215–224. **473**

Jensen, A. R. (1969) How much can we boost IQ and scholastic achievement? *Harvard educ. Rev., 39,* 1–123. **81, 384**

Johnson, M. (1973) A new technique of testing ESP in a real-life, high-motivational context. *J. Parapsychol., 37,* 210–217. **158**

Jonas, G. (1972) Profiles: Visceral learning, II. *New Yorker, 26,* August, 30–57. **131**

Jones, E. (1953) *The life and work of Sigmund Freud.* Vol. I. New York: Basic Books. **14, 15**

Jones, E. E., David, K. E., and Jergen, K. J. (1961) Role playing variations and their informational value for person perception. *J. abnorm. soc. Psychol., 63,* 302–310. **181**

Jones, E. E., Kanouse, D. E., et al. (1972) *Attribution: Perceiving the causes of behavior.* Morristown, N.J.: General Learning Press. **180**

Jones, M. C. (1924) A laboratory study of fear: The case of Peter. *Ped. Sem., 31,* 308–315. **464**

Jones, M. C. (1974) Albert, Peter, and John B. Watson. *Amer. Psychol., 29,* 581–583. **464**

Jones, R. L. (1974) Students' views of special placement and their own special classes: A clarification. *Except. Child., 41,* 22–29. **378**

Jordan, L. S. (1974) Electrodermal activity in schizophrenics: Further considerations. *Psychol. Bull., 81,* 85–91. **445**

Jourard, S. (1964) *The transparent self: Self-disclosure and well-being.* New York: Van Nostrand. (2nd edition, 1971.) **417**

Jourard, S. M. (1974) *Healthy personality: An approach from the viewpoint of humanistic psychology.* New York: Macmillan. **424**

Jung, C. G. (1928) *Contributions to analytical psychology.* New York: Harcourt. **402**

Jung, C. G. (1963) *Memories, dreams, reflections.* New York: Pantheon Books. **156**

Jurjevich, R. M. (1974) *The hoax of Freudianism.* Philadelphia: Dorrance. **16, 35**

Kagan, J., and Moss, H. (1962) *From birth to maturity.* New York: Wiley. **328**

Kamin, L. J. (1956) The effects of termination of the CS and avoidance of the US on avoidance learning. *J. comp. physiol. Psychol., 49,* 420–424. **211**

Kamin, L. J. (1974) *The science and politics of I.Q.* Potomac, Md.: Lawrence Erlbaum. **80, 384, 385, 391**

Kamiya, J. (1968) Conscious control of brain waves. *Psychol. Today, 1,* 56–60. **131**

Kamiya, J. (1969) Operant control of the EEG alpha rhythm and some of its reported effects on consciousness. In Tart, C. (Ed.), *Altered states of consciousness.* New York: Wiley. **131**

Kaplan, B. J. (1973) Malnutrition and mental deficiency. In Rebelsky, F., and Dorman, L. (Eds.), *Child development and behavior* (2nd ed.). New York: Knopf. **378**

Kardiner, A. (1939) *The individual and his society.* New York: Columbia University Press. **322**

Karlins, M., Coffman, T. L., and Walters, G. (1969) On the fading of social stereotypes: Studies in three generations of college students. *J. Pers. soc. Psychol., 13,* 1–16. **523, 526, 527**

Kashgarian, M., and Burrow, G. N. (1974) *The endocrine glands.* Baltimore: Williams and Wilkins. **127**

Kasschau, R. A., Johnson, M. M., and Russo, N. F. (1975) *Careers in psychology.* Washington, D.C.: American Psychological Association. **23**

Katchadourian, H. A., and Churchill, C. W. (1973) Components of prevalence of mental illness and social class in urban Lebanon. *Soc. Psychiat., 8,* 145–151. **538**

Katz, B. (1952) The nerve impulse. *Scientific American, 187,* November, 61. **109**

Katz, L. G. (1969) Children and teachers in two types of Headstart classrooms. *Young Child, 24,* 242–249. **386**

Keller, H. (1903) *The story of my life.* New York: Doubleday. **497**

Kelley, E. C. (1955) Education is communication. *ETC: A Rev. of gen. Semantics, 12,* 248–256. **179**

Kelley, H. H. (1950) The warm-cold variable in first impressions of persons. *J. Pers., 18,* 431–439. **181**

Kellogg, W. N. (1968) Communication and language in the home-raised chimpanzee. *Science, 162,* 423–426. **496**

Kellogg, W. N., and Kellogg, L. A. (1933) *The ape and the child.* New York: McGraw-Hill. **495, 496**

Kellogg, W. N., and Kellogg, L. A. (1967) *The ape and the child.* New York: Hafner. **496**

Kelman, H. C. (1967) Psychological research on social change: Some scientific and ethical issues. *Internatl. J. Psychol., 2,* 301–313. **533**

Kennedy, W. A., and Willcutt, H. C. (1964) Praise and blame as incentives. *Psychol. Bull., 62,* 323–353. **286**

Kerling, F. N. (1973) *Foundations of behavior research.* New York: Holt. **49**

Kessner, R. P., and Connor, H. S. (1972) Independence of short- and long-term memory: A neural analysis. *Science, 176,* 432–434. **248**

Kety, S. S. (1960) Recent biochemical theories of schizophrenia. In Jackson, D. D. (Ed.), *The etiology of schizophrenia.* New York: Basic Books. **446**

Kiesler, C. A., and Munson, P. A. (1975) Attitudes and opinions. In Rosenzweig, M. R., and Porter, L. W. (Eds.), *Annual review of psychology.* Palo Alto, Calif.: Annual Reviews, Inc. **522, 533**

Kinkade, K. (1973) *A Walden Two experiment: The first five years of Twin Oaks Community.* New York: Morrow. **206**

Kinsey, A. C., Pomeroy, W. B., and Martini, C. E. (1948) *Sexual behavior in the human male.* Philadelphia: Saunders. **322, 538**

Kinsey, A. C., and the Staff of the Institute for Sex Research, Indiana University (1953) *Sexual behavior of the human female.* Philadelphia: Saunders. **322, 538**

Kinsey, L. R., Roberts, J. L., and Logan, D. L. (1972) Death, dying, and denial in the aged. *Amer. J. Psychiat., 129,* 161–166. **103**

Kira, A. (1976) *The bathroom.* New York: Bantam Books. **69**

Kirk, S. A. (1972) *Educating exceptional children* (2nd ed.). Boston: Houghton Mifflin. **382, 391**

Kitahara, M., and Uno, R. (1967) Equilibrium and vertigo in a tilting environment. *Ann. otol. rhinol. Laryng., 76,* 166–178. **156**

Klatsky, R. L. (1975) *Human memory: Structures and processes.* San Francisco: Freeman. **248, 267**

Klausmeier, H. J., and Ripple, R. E. (1971) *Learning and human abilities: Educational psychology* (3rd ed.). New York: Harper & Row. **283**

Klein, D. B. (1970) *A history of scientific psychology: Its origins and philosophical backgrounds.* New York: Basic Books. **23**

Klineberg, O. (1938) Emotional expression in Chinese literature. *J. abnorm. soc. Psychol., 33,* 517–520. **340**

Klineberg, O. (Ed.) (1944) *Characteristics of the American Negro.* New York: Harper. **384**

Klopfer, P.H., and Hailman, J. P. (1972) *Control and development of behavior.* Reading, Mass.: Addison-Wesley. **318**

Klopfer, W. G., and Taulbee, E. S. (1976) Projective tests. In Rosenzweig, M. R., and Porter, L. W. (Eds.), *Annual review of psychology, 27.* Palo Alto, Calif.: Annual Reviews, Inc. **404**

Knupfer, G., Jackson, D. D., and Kreiger, G. (1959) Personality differences between more and less competent psychotherapists as a function of criteria of competence. *J. nerv. ment. Diseases, 129,* 375–384. **479**

Koffka, K. (1924) *The growth of the mind: An introduction to child-psychology.* New York: Harcourt, Brace. **227**

Köhler, W. (1925) *The mentality of apes.* New York: Harcourt, Brace. **228**

Kothandapani, V. (1971) Validation of thinking, belief and intention to act as three components of attitude and their contribution to prediction of contraceptive behavior. *J. Pers. soc. Psychol., 19,* 321–333. **519**

Krasner, L. (1971) Behavior therapy. In Mussen, P. H., and Rosenzweig, M. R. (Eds.), *Annual review of psychology, 22.* Palo Alto, Calif.: Annual Reviews, Inc. **271**

Krebs, D. L. (1970) Altruism — an examination of the concept and a review of the literature. *Psychol. Bull., 73,* 258–302. **529**

Krippner, S., and Ullman, M. (1970) Telepathy and dreams: A controlled experiment with electroencephalogram–electrooculogram monitoring. *J. nerv. ment. Diseases, 151,* 394–402. **31**

Krogman, W. M. (1943) The measurement of the human body. *Ciba Sym., 5,* 1467–1477. **84**

Krueger, W. C. F. (1929) The effect of overlearning on retention. *J. exp. Psychol., 12,* 71–78. **263**

Kursh, H. (1964) Don't get trapped by a psychoquack. *Today's Health,* March, 28–31. **20**

Lacey, J. I. (1967) Somatic response patterning and stress: Some revisions of activation theory. In Appley, M. H., and Trumbull, R. (Eds.), *Psychological stress.* New York: Appleton-Century-Crofts. **338**

Ladd, G. T. (1892) Contributions to the psychology of visual dreams. *Mind, 1,* 299–304. **28**

Laird, A. (1932) How the consumer estimates quality by subconscious sensory impressions. *J. appl. Psychol., 16,* 241–246. **146**

Lamb, M. E. (1975) Physiological mechanisms in the control of maternal behavior in rats: A review. *Psychol. Bull., 82,* 104–119. **298**

Lambert, M. J. (1976) Spontaneous remission in adult neurotic disorders: A revision and summary. *Psychol. Bull., 83,* 107–119. **478**

Lambert, W. W., and Lambert, W. E. (1964) *Social psychology.* Englewood Cliffs, N.J.: Prentice-Hall. **519**

Lancet (1966) The XYY syndrome. (An unsigned article) *Lancet,* No. 7427, 583–584. **325**

Landis, C. A. (1937) Statistical evaluation of psychotherapeutic methods. In Hinsie, L. E. (Ed.), *Concept and problems of psychotherapy.* New York: Columbia University Press. **477**

Lane, H. (1975) *The wild boy of Aveyron.* Cambridge, Mass.: Harvard University Press. **88, 105**

Lang, P. J., and Melamed, B. G. (1969) Avoidance conditioning therapy of an infant with chronic ruminative vomiting. *J. abnorm. Psychol., 74,* 1–8. **469**

Langs, R. J. (1971) Day residues, recall residues, and dreams: Reality and the psyche *J. Amer. Psychoanal. Assoc., 19,* 499–523. **47**

Lashley, K. S. (1951) The problem of serial order in behavior. In Jeffress, L. A. (Ed.), *Cerebral mechanisms in behavior.* New York: Wiley. **504**

Latané, B., and Darley, J. M. (1968) Group inhibition of bystander intervention in emergencies. *J. Pers. soc. Psychol., 10,* 215–221. **529, 530**

Laurendreau, M., and Pinard, A. (1962) *Causal thinking in the child.* New York: International Universities Press. **223**

Lawrence, D. H. (1971) Two studies of visual search for word targets with controlled rate of presentation. *Percept. Psychophys., 10,* 85–89. **164**

Lefkowitz, M. M., Eron, L. D., Walder, L. O., and Huesman, L. R. (1972) Television violence and child aggression. In Comstock, G. A., and Rubenstein, E. A. (Eds.), *Television and social behavior.* Vol. III: *Television and adolescent aggressiveness.* Washington, D. C.: U. S. Government Printing Office. **509**

Lehman, H. C. (1953) *Age and achievement.* Princeton, N.J.: Princeton University Press. **239**

Leighton, D., and Kluckhohn, C. (1947) *Children of the people.* Cambridge, Mass.: Harvard University Press. **322**

Lenneberg, E. H. (1964) The capacity for language acquisition. In Fodor, J. A., and Katz, J. J. (Eds.), *The structure of language.* Englewood Cliffs, N.J.: Prentice-Hall. **499**

Lesser, G. S. (1970) Designing a program for broadcast television. In Korten, F. F., Cook, S. W., and Lacey, J. J. (Eds.), *Psychology and the problems of society.* Washington, D. C.: American Psychological Association. **509**

Lesser, G. S. (1974) *Children and television: Lessons from Sesame Street.* New York: Random House. **510**

Lewin, K. (1936) *Principles of topological psychology.* New York: McGraw-Hill. **331**

Lewin, K. (1947) Group decision and social change. In Maccoly, E. E., Newcomb, T. M., and Hartley, E. L. (Eds.), *Readings in social psychology* (3rd ed.). New York: Holt. **506**

Lewis, M. M. (1971) The linguistic development of children. In Minnes, N. (Ed.), *Linguistics at large.* New York: Viking Press. **501**

Lieberman, L. R. (1973) A letter to the editor. *Science, 180,* 361. **447**

Liebert, R. M. (1974) Television and children's aggressive behavior: Another look. *Amer. J. Psychoanal., 34,* 99–107. **509, 510**

Liebert, R. M., Neale, J. M., and Davidson, E. S. (1973) *The early window: The effects of television on children and youth.* New York: Pergamon. **509**

Lilly, J. C. (1956) Mental effects of reduction of ordinary levels of physical stimuli on intact, healthy persons. *Psychiat. Res. Rep.,* No. 5, 1–28. **308**

Linton, M., and Gallo, P. S. (1975) *The practical statistician: Simplified handbook of statistics.* Monterey, Calif.: Brooks/Cole. **71**

Locke, J. (1690) *An essay concerning human understanding.* London: C. and J. Rivington. **196**

London, H., and Nisbett, R. E. (1975) *Thought and feeling: Cognitive alteration of feeling states.* Chicago: Aldine. **345**

Long, J. L. (1974) A stereo tape recorder technique for observational data. *Hum. Factors, 16,* 154–160. **29**

LoPiccolo, J., and Stegar, J. C. (1974) The Sexual Adjustment Inventory: A new instrument for assessment of sexual dysfunction. *Archives sexual Behav., 3,* 585–595. **360**

Lorenz, K. (1935) Der Kumpan in der Umwelt des Vogels: Der Artgenosse als auslösendes Moment Sozialer Verhaltungsweisen. *J. Ornithol., 83,* 137–213. **514**

Lorenz, K. (1963) *On aggression.* New York: Harcourt, Brace and World. **324**

Lovell, K. (1965) *Educational psychology and children* (8th ed.). London: University of London Press. **374**

Luckhardt, A. B., and Carlson, A. J. (1915) Contributions to the physiology of the stomach. XVII. On the chemical control of the gastric hunger mechanism. *Amer. J. Physiol., 36,* 37–46. **302**

Luft, J. (1963) *Group processes: An introduction to group dynamics.* Palo Alto, Calif.: National Press. **421**

Luria, A. R. (1973) *The working brain: An introduction to neuropsychology.* New York: Basic Books. **133, 267**

Luttage, W. G., Hall, N. R., Wallis, C. J., and Campbell, J. C. (1975) Stimulation of male and female sexual behavior in gonadectomized rats with estrogen and androgen therapy and its inhibition with concurrent anti-hormone therapy. *Physiol. Behav., 14,* 65–73. **294**

Lynn, D. B. (1974) *The father: His role in child development.* Monterey, Calif.: Brooks/Cole. **299**

MacKinnon, D. W. (1938) Violation of prohibitions. In Murray, H. A. (Ed.), *Explorations in personality.* New York: Oxford University Press. **515**

MacKinnon, D. W. (1962) The nature and nurture of creative talent. *Amer. Psychol., 17,* 484–495. **236**

MacMahon, B., Alpert, M., and Salber, E. J. (1966) Infant weight and parental smoking habits. *Amer. J. Epidem., 82,* 247–261. **81**

MacMillan, D. L., Jones, R. L., and Aloia, G. F. (1974) The mentally retarded label: A theoretical analysis and review of research. *Amer. J. ment. Defic., 79,* 241–261. **380**

MacNichol, E. F., Jr. (1964) Three-pigment color vision. *Scientific American, 211,* 48–56. **142**

Maddi, S. R., and Costa, P. T. (1972) *Humanism in personology: Allport, Maslow and Murray.* Chicago: Aldine/Atherton. **315**

Magmer, E., and Ipfling, H. J. (1973) On the problem of special social class punishments. *Scien. Poedag. Exper., 10,* 170–192. **539**

Maier, N. R. F. (1949) *Frustration: The study of behavior without a goal.* New York: McGraw-Hill. Reprinted in 1961 by the University of Michigan Press (Ann Arbor Paperbacks). **286**

Maier, N.R.F. (1973) *Psychology in industrial organizations.* Boston: Houghton Mifflin. **518**

Makous, W.L. (1966) Cutaneous color sensitivity: Explanation and demonstration. *Psychol. Rev., 73,* 280–294. **150**

Mandell, L. (1974) When to weight: Determining nonresponse bias in survey data. *Pub. Opin. Quart., 38,* 247–252. **34**

Mandler, G. (1967) Organization of memory. In Spence, K. W., and Spence, J. T. (Eds.), *The psychology of learning and motivation.* Vol. I. New York: Academic Press. **263**

Mandler, G., and Boeck, W.J. (1974) Retrieval processes in recognition. *Mem. Cog., 2,* 613–615. **263**

Manturana, H.R., Lettvin, J.Y., McCulloch, W.S., and Pitts, W.H. (1960) Anatomy and physiology of vision in the frog. *J. gen. Physiol., 43,* 129–175. **141**

Margolese, M.S. (1970) Homosexuality: A new endocrine correlate. *Hormones Behav., 1,* 151–155. **322**

Marrow, A.J. (1938) Goal tensions and recall: I. *J. gen. Psychol., 19,* 3–35. **262**

Marshall, H. R. (1908) The methods of the naturalist and psychologist. *Psychol. Rev., 15,* 1–24. **543**

Martineau, W. H. (1972) A model of the social function of humor, In Goldstein, J. H., and McGhee, P. E. (Eds.), *The psychology of humor: Theoretical perspectives and empirical issues.* New York: Academic Press. **541**

Maslow, A. H. (1943) A theory of human motivation. *Psychol. Rev., 50,* 370–396. **314**

Maslow, A. H. (1954) *Motivation and personality.* New York: Harper. **313**

Maslow, A. H. (1957) A philosophy of psychology: The need for a mature science of human nature. *Main currents in modern thought, 13,* 27–32. **417**

Maslow, A. H. (1962) *Toward a psychology of being.* Princeton, N.J.: Van Nostrand. **14**

Maslow, A. H. (1970) *Motivation and personality* (2nd ed.). New York: Harper. **313, 314**

Massengill, D. P., Gordon, M. E., and Henry, H. G. (1975) Studies in typewriter keyboard modification: I. Relationships between individual differences in performance on standard and modified typewriters. *J. appl. Psychol., 60,* 227–230. **363**

Masters, W. H., and Johnson, V. E. (1966) *Human sexual response.* Boston: Little, Brown. **298**

Masterton, R. B., and Berkley, M. A. (1974) Brain function: Changing ideas on the role of sensory, motor and association cortex in behavior. In Rosenzweig, M. R., and Porter, L. W. (Eds.), *Annual review of psychology.* Palo Alto, Calif.: Annual Reviews, Inc. **118**

Mathis, A., Smith, T., and Hansen, D. (1970) College students' attitudes toward computer-assisted instruction. *J. educ. Psychol., 61,* 46–51. **284**

Matthews, S. A., and Detwiler, S. R. (1926) The reaction of amblystoma embryos following prolonged treatment with chloretone. *J. exp. Zool., 45,* 279–292. **86**

Maury, L. F. A. (1861) *Le sommèil et les rêves* [*Sleep and dreams*] Paris: Didier. **37**

Maxwell, A. E. (1961) Trends in cognitive ability in the older age ranges. *J. abnorm. soc. Psychol., 63,* 449–452. **96**

McCall, R. B., Hogarty, P. S., and Hurlburt, N. (1972) Transitions in infant sensorimotor development and the prediction of childhood IQ. *Amer. Psychol., 27,* 728–748. **93**

McClearn, G. E., and De Freis, J. C. (1973) *Introduction to behavioral genetics.* San Francisco: Freeman. **79**

McClelland, D. C. (1961) *The achieving society.* New York: D. Van Nostrand. **329**

McClelland, D. C. (1973) Testing for "competency" rather than for "intelligence." *Amer. Psychol., 28,* 1–14. **363**

McClelland, D. C., Atkinson, J. W., Clark, R. A., and Lowell, E. L. (1953) *The achievement motive.* New York: Appleton-Century-Crofts. **329**

McConnell, J. V. (1972) The biochemistry of memory. In Teevan, R. C. (Ed.), *Readings in introductory psychology.* Minneapolis: Burgess. **246**

McConnell, J. V., Cutler, R. L., and McNeil, E. B. (1958) Subliminal stimulation: An overview. *Amer. Psychol., 13,* 229–242. **137**

McGeoch, J. A., and Melton, A. W. (1929) The comparative retention values of maze habits and of nonsense syllables. *J. exp. Psychol., 12,* 392–414. **262**

McGuire, W. J. (1964) Inducing resistance to persuasion: Some contemporary approaches. In Berkowitz, L. (Ed.), *Advances in experimental social psychology.* New York: Academic Press. **507**

McKee, M., and Robertson, I. (1975) *Social problems.* New York: Random House. **545**

McNeill, D. (1970) *The acquisition of language: The story of developmental psycholinguistics.* New York: Harper and Row. **492**

McWilliams, S. A., and Tuttle, R. J. (1973) Long-term psychological effects of LSD. *Psychol. Bull., 79,* 341–351. **184**

Mead, M. (1939) Sex and temperament. In *From the South Seas.* New York: Morrow. **326**

Medin, D. L. (1972) Role of reinforcement in discrimination learning set in monkeys. *Psychol. Bull., 77,* 305–318. **280**

Meltzer, H. (1930) Individual differences in forgetting pleasant and unpleasant experiences. *J. educ. Psychol., 21,* 399–409. **260**

Melzack, R. (1975) The promise of biofeedback: Don't hold the party yet. *Psychol. Today, 9* (July), 18–22, 80–81. **131**

Meyers, E. S., Ball, H. H., and Crutchfield, M. (1974) Specific suggestions for the kindergarten teacher and the advanced child. *Gifted Child Quart., 18,* 25–30. **382**

Middlebrook, P. N. (1974) *Social psychology and modern life.* New York: Knopf. **519, 545**

Milgram, S. (1961) Nationality and conformity. *Scientific American, 205,* 45–51. **532**

Milgram, S. (1963) Behavioral study of obedience. *J. abnorm. soc. Psychol., 67,* 371–378. **533**

Milgram, S. (1964) Issues in the study of obedience: A reply to Baumrind. *Amer. Psychol., 19,* 848–852. **532**

Miller, G. A. (1956) The magical number seven, plus or minus two: Some limits on our capacity for processing information. *Psychol. Rev., 63,* 81–97. **263**

Miller, G. A. (1974) Psychology, language and levels of communication. In Silverstein, A. (Ed.), *Human communication: Theoretical explorations.* Hillsdale. N.J.: Erlbaum. **506**

Miller, N. E. (1948a) Studies of fear as an acquirable drive: I. Fear as motivation and fear-reduction as reinforcement in the learning of new responses. *J. exp. Psychol., 38,* 89–101. **335**

Miller, N. E. (1948b) Theory and experiment relating psychoanalytic displacement to stimulus-response generalization. *J. abnorm. soc. Psychol., 43,* 155–178. **326**

Miller, N. E. (1957) Experiments on motivation. *Science, 126,* 1271–1278. **303**

Miller, N. E. (1971) *Neal E. Miller: Selected papers.* Chicago: Aldine. **318**

Miller, N. E., Bailey, C. J., and Stevenson, J. A. F. (1950) Decreased "hunger" but increased food intake resulting from hypothalamic lesions. *Science, 12,* 256–259. **303**

Miller, N. E., and Banuazizi, A. (1968) Instrumental learning by curarized rats of a specific viceral response, intestinal or cardiac. *J. comp. physiol. Psychol., 65,* 1–7. **131**

Miller, N. E., and Dworkin, B. R. (1973) Visceral learning: Recent difficulties with curarized rats and significant problems for human research. In Obrist, P. A., et al., *Contemporary trends in cardiovascular psychophysiology.* Chicago: Aldine. **131**

Miller, R. E. (1974) Development and standardization of the Air Force Officer Qualifying Test, Form M. United States Air Force Human Relations Laboratory Technical Report, No. 74–16. **353**

Millon, T. (1975) Reflections on Rosenhan's "On being sane in insane places." *J. abnorm. Psychol., 84,* 456–461. **447**

Millward, R. B., and Spoehr, K. T. (1973) The direct measurement of hypothesis sampling strategies. *Cogn. Psychol., 4,* 1–38. **225**

Milne, L., and Milne, M. (1962) *The senses of animals and men.* New York: Atheneum. **157**

Minami, H., and Dallenbach, K. M. (1946) The effect of activity upon learning and retention in the cockroach. *Amer. J. Psychol., 59,* 1–58. **259**

Minton, J. H. (1975) The impact of Sesame Street on readiness. *Sociol. Educ., 48,* 141–151. **510**

Mischel, W. (1971) *Introduction to personality.* New York: Holt. **180**

Mischel, W. (1976) *Introduction to personality* (2nd ed.). New York: Holt. **412, 424**

Moncrieff, R. W. (1967) *The chemical senses* (3rd ed.). London: Leonard Hill. **148**

Monroe, R. R., Heath, R. G., et al. (1954) *Studies in schizophrenia.* Cambridge, Mass.: Harvard University Press. **121**

Montgomery, K. C., and Segall, M. (1955) Discrimination learning based upon the exploratory drive. *J. comp. physiol. Psychol., 48,* 225–228. **309**

Moore, B. S., Underwood, B., and Rosenhan, D. L. (1973) Affect and self-gratification. *Dev. Psychol., 8,* 209–214. **529**

Morgan, C. T. (1965) *Physiological psychology* (3rd ed.). New York: McGraw-Hill. **297**

Morphett, M. V., and Washburne, C. (1931) When should children begin to read? *Elem. Sch. J., 31,* 496–503. Chicago: University of Chicago Press. **90**

Morris, D. (1967) *The naked ape.* New York: Dell. **324, 325**

Morris, G. O., and Singer, M. T. (1961) Sleep deprivation: Transactional and subjective observations. *Arch. gen. Psychiat., 5,* 453–461. **305**

Morris, L. (1950) *William James: The message of a modern mind.* New York: Scribners. **9**

Mosel, J. N., and Goheen, H. W. (1958) The validity of the employment recommendation questionnaire in personnel selection: I. Skilled traders. *Personnel Psychol., 11,* 481–490. **349**

Moskowitz, M. J. (1959) Running-wheel activity of the white rat as a function of combined food and water deprivation. *J. comp. physiol. Psychol., 52,* 621–625. **301**

Moss, H., and Kagan, J. (1961) Stability of achievement and recognition seeking behaviors from early childhood through adulthood. *J. abnorm. soc. Psychol., 62,* 504–513. **328**

Mullare, S., and Fernald, P. S. (1971) Influences of experimentally induced expectation upon elimination of a fear response. Unpublished study, University of New Hampshire. **337, 470, 478**

Munn, N. L. (1971) *The evolution of the human mind.* Boston: Houghton Mifflin. **133, 326**

Murray, E. J. (1965) *Sleep, dreams and arousal.* New York: Appleton-Century-Crofts. **306**

Murray, H. A., and Wheeler, D. R. (1937) A note on the possible clairvoyance of dreams. *J. Psychol., 3,* 309–313. **31**

Murstein, B. I. (1972) Physical attractiveness and marital choice. *J. Pers. soc. Psychol., 22,* 8–12. **516**

Musso, J. R., and Granero, M. (1973) An ESP drawing experiment with a high-scoring subject. *J. Parapsychol., 37,* 13–36. **158**

Myers, R. E. (1956) Function of the corpus callosum in interocular transfer. *Brain, 79,* 358–363. **124**

Nappe, G. W., and Wollen, K. A. (1973) Effects of instructions to form common and bizarre mental images on retention. *J. exp. Psychol., 100,* 6–8. **264**

National Research Council (1943) Committee on selection and training of air-craft pilots. An introduction to aviation psychology. Civil Aeronautics Administration, Research Bull. No. 4. **361**

Navarre, A. (1947) Un clavier français pour les machines à écrire. (A French typewriter keyboard) *Travail hum., 10,* 100–103. **64**

Neal, F. W. (1973) Questions. In Wheeler, H. (Ed.), *Beyond the punitive society: Operant conditioning, social and political aspects.* San Francisco: W. H. Freeman. **207**

Neill, A. S. (1960) *Summerhill: A radical approach to child rearing.* New York: Hart. **289**

Neilon, P. (1948) Shirley's babies after fifteen years: A personality study. *J. genet. Psychol., 73,* 175–186. **411**

Neimark, E. D., and Santa, J. L. (1975) Thinking and concept attainment. In Rosenzweig, M. R., and Porter, L. W. (Eds.), *Annual review of psychology, 26.* Palo Alto, Calif.: Annual Reviews, Inc. **223, 226**

Neisser, U. (1967) *Cognitive psychology.* New York: Appleton-Century-Crofts. **246**

Nelson, A. G. (1954a) The college teacher as a counselor. *Educ. Forum, 18,* 349–357. **477**

Nelson, A. G. (1954b) Vocational guidance. In Marcuse, F. L. (Ed.), *Areas of psychology.* New York: Harper. **389**

Nevin, J. A. (1973) *The study of behavior: Learning, motivation, emotion and instinct.* Glenview, Ill.: Scott, Foresman. **318**

Newell, A., Shaw, J. C., and Simon, H. A. (1958) Elements of a theory of human problem solving. *Psychol. Rev., 65,* 151–166. **231**

Newman, B. M., and Newman, P. R. (1976) *Development through life: A case study approach.* Homewood, Ill.: Dorsey Press. **105**

Newman, E. B. (1944) Max Wertheimer, 1880–1943. *Amer. J. Psychol., 57,* 428–435. **13**

Newman, H. H., Freeman, F. N., and Holzinger, K. J. (1937) *Twins: A study of heredity and environment.* Chicago: University of Chicago Press. **89, 386**

Newson, J., and Newson, E. (1968) *Four years old in an urban community.* London: Allen and Unwin. **233**

Nisbett, R. E. (1972) Hunger, obesity and the ventromedial hypothalamus. *Psychol. Rev., 79,* 433–453. **303**

Norman, D. A. (1976) *Memory and attention: An introduction to human information processing.* New York: Wiley. **267**

O'Dell, S. (1974) Training parents in behavior modification: A review. *Psychol. Bull., 81,* 418–433. **206**

Okuma, T., Fukuma, E., and Hata, N. (1970) "Dream detector" and automatization of REMP-awakening technique for the study of dreaming. *Psychophysical, 7,* 508–515. **44**

Olds, J. (1956) Pleasure centers in the brain. *Scientific American, 195,* 105–116. **121**

Orne, M. T. (1951) The mechanisms of hypnotic age regression: An experimental study. *J. abnorm. soc. Psychol., 46,* 213–225. **185**

Orne, M. T. (1962) On the social psychology of the psychological experiment: With particular reference to demand characteristics and their implications. *Amer. Psychol., 17,* 776–783. **533**

Osgood, C. E., Suci, G. J., and Tannenbaum, P. H. (1957) *The measurement of meaning.* Urbana, Ill.: University of Illinois Press. **7, 522**

OSS Assessment Staff (1948) *The assessment of men.* New York: Rinehart. **363, 415**

Ottoson, D. (1971) The electro-olfactogram. In Beidler, L. M. (Ed.), *Handbook of sensory physiology: IV. Olfaction.* New York: Springer-Verlag. **145**

Owen, D. R. (1972) The 4F, XYY male: A review. *Psychol. Bull., 78,* 209–233. **325**

Owens, W. A. (1966) Age and mental abilities: A second adult follow-up. *J. educ. Psychol., 57,* 311–325. **96, 97**

Paivio, A. (1971) *Imagery and verbal processes.* New York: Holt. **264**

Palermo, D. S., and Molfese, D. L. (1972) Language acquisition from age five onward. *Psychol. Bull., 78,* 409–428. **495**

Pankove, E. (1974) Identification of the gifted. *School Psychol., 28,* 8–11. **382**

Parker, D. M., and Howard, M. (1974) Effects of repeated administration of the psycho-physiological test for motion sickness susceptibility. *J. gen. Psychol., 91,* 273–276. **154**

Patel, M. D. (1936) The physiology of the formation of the pigeon's milk. *Physiol. Zool., 9,* 129–152. **294**

Patterson, C. H. (1973) *Theories of counseling and psychotherapy* (2nd ed.). New York: Harper. **461**

Pattison, E. M. (1974) Confusing concepts about the concept of homosexuality. *Psychiat., 37,* 340–349. **322**

Pavlov, I. P. (1927) *Conditional reflexes.* Trans. by G. V. Anrep. New York: Oxford University Press. **194, 195,**

Penfield, W. (1958) *The excitable cortex in conscious man.* Springfield, Ill.: Charles C. Thomas. **117, 245**

Penfield, W., and Erikson, T. C. (1941) *Epilepsy and cerebral localization.* Springfield, Ill.: Charles C. Thomas. **125**

Perls, F. S. (1969) *Gestalt therapy verbatim.* Lafayette, Calif.: Real People Press. **476**

Pernanen, K. (1974) Validity of survey data on alcohol use. In Gibbons, R. J., et al. (Eds.), *Research advances in alcohol and drug problems.* New York: Wiley. **34**

Perry, R. B. (1920) *Annotated bibliography of the writings of William James.* New York: Longmans Green. **8**

Perry, R. B. (1935) *The thought and character of William James.* Vols. I and II. Boston: Little, Brown. **9**

Peterson, J. (1926) *Early conceptions and tests of intelligence.* New York: World Book. **370**

Peterson, L. R., and Peterson, M. J. (1959) Short-term retention of individual verbal items. *J. exp. Psychol., 58,* 193–198. **248**

Pettigrew, T. F. (1964) *A profile of the Negro American.* Princeton, N.J.: D. Van Nostrand. **91, 385**

Pfaffmann, C. (1964) Taste, its sensory and motivating properties. *American Scientist, 52,* 187–206. **148**

Pfeiffer, K., and Maltzman, I. (1974) Warned reaction times of sociopaths. *J. Res. Pers., 8,* 64–75. **448**

Piaget, J. (1929) *The child's conception of the world.* New York: Harcourt, Brace. **223**

Piaget, J. (1950) *The psychology of intelligence.* New York: Harcourt, Brace. **220**

Piaget, J. (1954) *The construction of reality in the child.* Trans. by M. Cook. New York: Basic Books. **218**

Piaget, J., and Inhelder, B. (1967) *The child's conception of space.* Trans. by F. J. Langdon and J. L. Lunzer. New York: Norton. **218**

Picton, T. W., Hillyard, S. A., Galambos, R., and Schiff, M. (1971) Human auditory attention: A central or peripheral process? *Science, 173,* 351–353. **163**

Pinel, J. P. J., and Cooper, R. M. (1966) Incubation and its implications for the interpretation of the ECS gradient effect. *Psychonomic Science, 6,* 123–124. **256**

Platt, J. R. (1966) *The step to man.* New York: Wiley. **206**

Plutchik, R., and Ax, A. F. (1967) A critique of "Determinants of emotional state" by Schachter and Singer (1962). *Psychophysiol., 4,* 79–82. **343**

Polanyi, M. (1955) From Copernicus to Einstein. *Encounter,* Winter, 54–63. **382**

Poorkaj, H. (1972) Social-psychological factor and "Successful aging." *Socio. soc. Res., 56,* 289–300. **103**

Postman, L. (1975) Verbal learning and memory. In Rosenzweig, M. R., and Porter, L. W. (Eds.), *Annual review of psychology, 26.* Palo Alto, Calif.: Annual Reviews, Inc. **248, 263, 264**

Premack, D. (1970) A functional analysis of language. *J. exper. Anal. Behav., 14,* 107–125. **504**

Premack, D. (1971) Language in chimpanzee? *Science, 172,* 808–822. **504**

Prentiss, C. W. (1901) The otocyst of dicapod crustacea: Its structure, development and functions. *Bulletin of the Museum of Comparative Zoology, Harvard College, 36,* No. 7, 165–251. **153**

Pulvermacher, G. D. (1974) Report on a home-management project at Rideau Regional Centre. *Ontario Psychol., 6,* 19–23. **380**

Quigley, J. P., Johnson, V., and Solomon, E. I. (1929) Action of insulin on the motility of the gastro-intestinal tract. *Amer. J. Physiol., 90,* 89–98. **302**

Quirk, T. J., Witten, B. J., and Weinberg, S. F. (1973) Review of studies of the concurrent and predictive validity of the National Teacher Examinations. *Rev. educ. Res., 43,* 89–113. **363**

Rachman, S. (1967) Systematic desensitization. *Psychol. Bull., 67,* 93–103. **477**

Rachman, S. (1973) The effects of psychotherapy. In Eysenck, H. J. (Ed.), *Handbook of abnormal psychology* (2nd ed.). San Diego, Calif.: Knapp. **478**

Raphelson, A. C. (1973) The pre-Chicago association of the early functionalists. *J. Hist. Behav. Sci., 9,* 115–122. **9**

Reed, S. K., Ernst, G. W., and Bonerji, R. (1974) The role of analogy in transfer between similar problem states. *Cog. Psychol., 6,* 436–450. **279**

Reekers, G. A., and Lovaas, O. I. (1974) Behavioral treatment of deviant sex-role behaviors in a male child. *J. appl. Behav. Anal., 7,* 173–190. **206**

Rees, L. (1961) Constitutional factors in abnormal behaviour. In Eysenck, H. J. (Ed.), *Handbook of abnormal psychology.* New York: Basic Books. **179, 406**

Reid, J. E., and Inbau, F. E. (1964) *Lie detection.* Baltimore: Williams and Wilkins. **126**

Reik, T. (1959) *The compulsion to confess.* New York. Farrar, Straus and Cudahy. **288**

Reitman, J. (1971) Mechanisms of forgetting in short-term memory. *Cog. Psychol., 2,* 185–195. **248**

Rhine, J. B. (1974a) A new case of experimenter unreliability. *J. Parapsychol., 38,* 215–225. **158**

Rhine, J. B. (1974b) Security versus deception in parapsychology. *J. Parapsychol., 38,* 99–121. **158**

Rhine, L. E. (1970) An interview with Dr. Robert H. Thouless. *J. Parapsychol., 34,* 262–270. **158**

Riggs, L. A., Ratliff, F., Cornsweet, J. C., and Cornsweet, T. N. (1953) The disappearance of steadily fixated visual test objects. *J. Opt. Soc. Amer., 43,* 495–501. **141**

Rimm, D. C., and Somervill, J. W. (1977) *Abnormal psychology.* New York: Academic Press. **452**

Robbins, L. N. (1974) Antisocial behavior disturbances in childhood: Prevalence, prognosis, and prospects. In Anthony, E. J., and Koupernik, C. (Eds.), *The child in his family: Children at psychiatric risks.* Vol. III. New York: Wiley. **448**

Robinson, E. A. (1948) Richard Cory. In *Collected poems of Edwin Arlington Robinson.* New York: Macmillan. **427**

Rock, I. (1975) *An introduction to perception.* New York: Macmillan. **178**

Rodman, D. H., and Collins, M. J. (1974) A community residence program: An alternative to institutional living for the mentally retarded. *Trng. Sch. Bull., 71,* 52–61. **380**

Roethlisberger, F. J., and Dickson, W. J. (1939) *Management and the worker.* Cambridge, Mass.: Harvard University Press. **331**

Rogers, C. R. (1951) *Client-centered therapy.* Boston: Houghton Mifflin. **457**

Rogers, C. R. (1959) A theory of therapy, personality, and interpersonal relationships, as developed in the client-centered framework. In Koch, S. (Ed.), *Psychology: A study of a science.* Vol. 3. New York: McGraw-Hill. **417, 457**

Rogers, C. R. (1961) *On becoming a person: A therapist's view of psychotherapy.* Boston: Houghton Mifflin. **417**

Rogers, C. R. (1967) A silent young man. In Rogers, C. R. (Ed.), *The therapeutic relationship and its impact.* Madison: University of Wisconsin Press. **457, 458**

Rokeach, M. (1964) *The three Christs of Ypsilanti.* New York: Knopf. **442**

Rosen, B. C. (1962) Socialization and achievement motivation in Brazil. *Amer. socio. Rev., 27,* 612–624. **328**

Rosenblatt, D. (1975) *Opening doors: What happens in gestalt therapy.* New York: Harper and Row. **476**

Rosenhan, D. L. (1973) On being sane in insane places. *Science, 179,* 250–258. **437, 447**

Rosenthal, R. (1966) *Experimenter effects in behavioral research.* New York: Appleton-Century-Crofts. **44**

Ross, S., Denenberg, V. H., Sawin, P. R., and Meyer, P. (1956) Changes in nest building behavior in multiparous rabbits. *Brit. J. Animal Behav., 4,* 69–74. **293**

Rumbaugh, D. M., Gill, T. V., and van Glassersfeld, E. C. (1973) Reading and sentence completion by a chimpanzee. *Science, 182,* 731–733. **504**

Rutter, M. (1970) Psychological development—predictions from infancy. *J. Child Psychol. Psychiat., 11,* 49–62. **93**

Saegert, S. C., and Jellison, J. M. (1970) Effects of initial level of response competition and frequency of exposure on liking and exploratory behavior. *J. Pers. soc. Psychol., 16,* 553–558. **517**

Sahakian, W. S. (1976) *Systems, models and theories* (2nd ed.). Skokie, Ill.: Rand McNally. **215**

Sanford, E. C. (1903) Psychology and physics. *Psychol. Rev., 10,* 105–119. **543**

Schachter, S. (1959) *The psychology of affiliation.* Stanford, Calif.: Stanford University Press. **320, 321**

Schachter, S. (1969) Cognitive effects on bodily functioning: Studies of obesity and eating. In Borgatta, E. F. (Ed.), *Social psychology: Readings and perspective.* Chicago: Rand McNally. **305**

Schachter, S. (1971) *Emotion, obesity and crime.* New York: Academic Press. **343**

Schachter, S., and Singer, J. (1962) Cognitive, social and physiological determinants of emotional state. *Psychol. Rev., 69,* 379–399. **343**

Schacter, D. L. (1976) The hypnagogic state: A critical review of the literature. *Psychol. Bull., 83,* 452–481. **306**

Schaie, K. W. (1958) Rigidity-flexibility and intelligence: A cross-sectional study of adult life span from 20 to 70. *Psychol. Monogr., 72,* No. 9. **95**

Schaie, K. W. (1974) Translations in gerontology—from lab to life: Intellectual functioning. *Amer. Psychol., 29,* 802–807. **96**

Schaie, K. W., and Gribbin, K. (1975) Adult development and aging. In Rosenzweig, M. R., and Porter, L. W. (Eds.), *Annual review of psychology.* Palo Alto, Calif.: Annual Reviews, Inc. **103**

Schaie, K. W., and Strather, C. R. (1968) A cross-sequential study of age changes in cognitive behavior. *Psychol. Bull., 70,* 671–680. **96**

Schiffman, H. R. (1976) *Sensation and perception.* New York: Wiley. **160**

Schjelderup-Ebbe, T. (1935) Social behavior of birds. In Murchison, C. (Ed.), *Handbook of social psychology.* Worcester, Mass.: Clark University Press. **537**

Schlesinger, K., and Griek, B. J. (1970) The genetics and biochemistry of audiogenic seizures. In Lindzey, G., and Theissen, D. D. (Eds.), *Contributions to behavior-genetic analysis.* New York: Appleton-Century-Crofts. **79**

Schmidt, F. L., and Hunter, J. E. (1974) Racial and ethnic bias in psychological tests. *Amer. Psychol., 29,* 1–8. **349, 366**

Schooler, C. (1972) Birth order effects: Not here, not now! *Psychol. Bull., 78,* 161–175. **328**

Schultz, D. P. (1969) *A history of modern psychology.* New York: Academic Press. **23**

Schuster, C. R., and Johanson, C. E. (1974) The use of animal models for the study of drug abuse. In Gibbons, R. J., et al. (Eds.), *Research advances in alcohol and drug problems.* New York: Wiley. **45**

Schwartz, R. M. (1974) Sexual history taking. *J. Amer. Coll. Health Assoc., 22,* 405–408. **34**

Scott, J. P. (1958) *Aggression.* Chicago: University of Chicago Press. **538**

Sears, R. R. (1936) Experimental studies of projection. I. Attribution of traits. *J. soc. Psychol., 7,* 151–163. **436**

Sears, R. R. (1977) Sources of life satisfactions of the Terman gifted men. *Amer. Psychol., 32,* 119–128. **382**

Sears, R. R., Maccoby, E. E., and Levin, H. (1957) *Patterns of child rearing.* Evanston, Ill.: Row, Peterson. **270**

Segall, A. J., Vanderschmidt, H., Burglass, R., and Frostman, T. (1975) *Systematic course design for the health fields.* New York: Wiley. **271**

Seisdedos, N. (1972) Representativeness of the norming sample and verbal aspects in the adaptation of an intelligence scale (WICS). *Rev. Psicolo. gen. aplica., 27,* 365–373. **365**

Seligman, M. E. P. (1970) On the generality of the laws of learning. *Psychol. Rev., 77,* 406–418. **212**

Seligman, M. E. P. (1975) *Helplessness: On depression, development and death.* San Francisco: Freeman. **432, 452, 534**

Sellin, J. T. (1959) *The death penalty.* Philadelphia: American Law Institute. **288, 432**

Selye, H. (1976) *The stress of life* (2nd ed.). New York: McGraw-Hill. **432**

Semeonoff, B. (1976) *Projective techniques.* New York: Wiley. **424**

Sem-Jacobsen, C. W., and Torklidsen, A. (1960) Depth recording and electrical stimulation in the human brain. In Ramey, E. R., and O'Doherty, D. S. (Eds.), *Electrical studies on the unanesthetized brain.* New York: Hoeber. **121**

Senden, M. V. (1932) *Raum und Gestaltauffassung bei operierten Blindgeborenen vor und nach Operation.* Leipzig: Barth. **176**

Shaffer, L. F., and Shoben, E. J., Jr. (1956) *The psychology of adjustment* (2nd ed.). Boston: Houghton Mifflin. **428**

Shaffer, L. H., and Hardwick, J. (1970) The basis of transcription skill. *J. exp. Psychol., 84,* 424–440. **56**

Shapiro, D., and Schwartz, G. E. (1972) Biofeedback and visceral learning: Clinical applications. *Sems. Psychiat., 4,* 171–184. **131**

Sheldon, W. H., and Stevens, S. S. (1942) *The varieties of temperament.* New York: Harper. **405**

Sheldon, W. H., Stevens, S. S., and Tucker, W. B. (1940) *The varieties of human physique.* New York: Harper. **406**

Shepard, R. N. (1967) Recognition memory for words, sentences and pictures. *J. verb. Learn. verb. Behav., 6,* 156–163. **253**

Sherif, M. (1956) Experiments in group conflict. *Scientific American, 195,* 54–58. **536**

Shirley, M. M. (1933) *The first two years: Personality manifestations.* Minneapolis: University of Minnesota Press. **87, 410**

Siegel, H. I., and Rosenblatt, J. S. (1975) Estrogen-induced maternal behavior in hysterectomized-ovariectomized virgin rats. *Physiol. Behav., 14,* 465–471. **294**

Siegel, M. H., and Zeigler, H. P. (1976) *Psychological research: The inside story.* New York: Harper and Row. **49**

Sigall, H., and Page, R. (1971) Current stereotypes: A little fading, a little faking. *J. Pers. soc. Psychol., 18,* 247–255. **525**

Siipola, E. M., and Hayden, S. D. (1965) Exploring eidetic imagery among the retarded. *Percept. mot. Skills, 21,* 275–286. **249**

Silverman, I. (1974) The experimenter: A (still) neglected stimulus object. *Canadian J. Psychol., 15,* 258–270. **44**

Simon, G., and Freudel, H. (1970) *Fetishisms.* London: Softcover Library. **330**

Simpson, W. (1957) A preliminary report on cigarette smoking and the incidence of prematurity. *Amer. J. Obstet. Gynecol., 73,* 808–815. **81**

Singh, P. J., Sakellaris, P. C., and Brush, F. R. (1971) Retention of active and passive avoidance responses tested in extinction. *Learn. Motiva., 2,* 305–323. **211**

Skeels, H. M. (1966) Adult status of children with contrasting early life experiences: A follow-up study. *Monogr. Soc. Res. Child Dev., 31,* No. 3, Serial No. 105. **102, 312, 379**

Skeels, H. M. (1973) Adult status of children with contrasting early life experiences: A follow-up study. In Rebelsky, F., and Dorman, L. (Eds.), *Child development and behavior.* New York: Knopf. **82, 83, 85**

Skinner, B. F. (1948) *Walden two.* New York: Macmillan. **289**

Skinner, B. F. (1950) Are theories of learning necessary? *Psychol. Rev., 57,* 193–216. **97**

Skinner, B. F. (1953) *Science and human behavior.* New York: Macmillan. **200, 205**

Skinner, B. F. (1956) A case history in scientific method. *Amer. Psychol., 11,* 221–233. **204**

Skinner, B. F. (1960) Pigeons in a pelican. *Amer. Psychol., 15,* 28–37. **205**

Skinner. B. F. (1961) The design of cultures. *Daedalus, 90,* 534–546. **206**

Skinner, B. F. (1971) *Beyond freedom and dignity.* New York: Knopf. **206, 215**

Skinner, B. F. (1974) *About behaviorism.* New York: Knopf. **206**

Sladen, W. J. L. (1957) The Pygoscelid penguins. *Falkland Islands Dependencies Survey, Scientific Reports,* No. 17. London: Her Majesty's Stationery Office. **29**

Sloane, R. B., et al. (1974) *Short-term behavior analytically oriented psychotherapy vs. behavior therapy.* Cambridge, Mass.: Harvard University Press. **478, 479**

Slobin, D. I. (1971) *Psycholinguistics.* Glenview, Ill.: Scott, Foresman. **492**

Slotkin, J. S. (1955) Culture and psychopathology. *J. abnorm. soc. Psychol., 51,* 269–275. **450**

Smith, J. C. (1975) Meditation as psychotherapy: A review of the literature. *Psychol. Bull., 82,* 558–564. **338**

Smith, R. W. (1975) Is biology destiny? Or is it culture? (A new look at transvestism and homosexuality.) *Counsel. Psychol., 5,* 90–91. **322**

Smode, A. F. (1958) Learning and performance in a tracking task under two levels of achievement information feedback. *J. exp. Psychol., 56,* 297–304. **283**

Somjen, G. (1975) *Sensory coding in the mammalian nervous system.* New York: Plenum Press. **160**

Sontag, L. W., Baker, C. T., and Nelson, V. L. (1958) Mental growth and personality development: A longitudinal study. *Monogr. Soc. Res. Child Devel., 23,* No. 2. **95**

Snyder, F. (1971) The physiology of dreaming. *Behav. Sci., 16,* 31–44. **46**

Solomon, R. L. (1964) Punishment. *Amer. Psychol., 19,* 239–253. **286**

Solomon, R. L., Kamin, L. J., and Wynne, L. C. (1953) Traumatic avoidance learning: The outcomes of several extinction procedures with dogs. *J. abnorm. soc. Psychol., 48,* 291–302. **287**

Spanos, H. P., and Barber, T. X. (1972) Cognitive activity during hypnotic suggestibility: Goal-directed fantasy and the experience of nonvolition. *J. Pers., 40,* 510–524. **184**

Spearman, C. (1927) *Abilities of man.* New York: Macmillan. **374**

Spence, K. W. (1937) The differential response in animals to stimuli varying within a single dimension. *Psychol. Rev., 44,* 430–444. **228**

Sperry, R. W. (1961) Cerebral organization and behavior. *Science, 133,* 1749–1757. **124**

Sperry, R. W. (1964) The great cerebral commissure. *Scientific American, 210,* 42–52. **122, 124**

Sperry, R. W. (1968) Hemisphere deconnection and unity in conscious awareness. *Amer. Psychol., 23,* 723–733. **124**

Spies, G. (1965) Food versus intracranial self-stimulation reinforcement in food-deprived rats. *J. comp. physiol. Psychol., 60,* 153–157. **121**

Spiro, M. E. (1965) *Children of the kibbutz.* New York: Schocken. **324**

Squires, P. C. (1927) Wolf children of India. *Amer. J. Psychol., 38,* 313–315. **88**

Staats, A. W., and Staats, C. K. (1958) Attitudes established by classical conditioning. *J. abnorm. soc. Psychol., 57,* 37–40. **519**

Staats, A. W., Minke, K. A., Martin, C. H., and Higa, W. R. (1972) Deprivation-satiation and strength of attitude conditioning; A test of attitude-reinforcer-discriminative theory. *J. Pers. soc. Psychol., 24,* 178–185. **519**

Staff, Psychological Section, A.A.F. (1945) Psychological activities in the training command, Army Air Forces. *Psychol. Bull., 42,* 37–54. **362**

Standing, L. (1973) Learning 10,000 pictures. *Quart. J. exp. Psychol., 25,* 207–222. **253**

Star, S. A., and Hughes, H. (1950) Report on an educational campaign: The Cincinnati plan for the United Nations. *Amer. J. Sociol., 55,* 389–400. **509**

Steers, R. M., and Porter, L. W. (1975) *Motivation and work behavior.* New York: McGraw-Hill. **345**

Stein, A. H., and Bailey, M. M. (1973) The socialization of achievement orientation in females. *Psychol. Bull., 80,* 345–366. **329**

Steinberg, D. D. (1972) Truth, amphigory, and the semantic interpretation of sentences. *J. exp. Psychol., 93,* 217–219. **235**

Stellar, E., and Jordan, H. A. (1970) Perception of satiety. *Perception and its Disorders, 48,* 298–317. **304**

Stemmer, N. (1973) Language acquisition and classical conditioning. *Lang. Speech, 16,* 279–282. **501**

Stone, L. J., and Church, J. (1975) *Childhood and adolescence* (3rd ed.). New York: Random House. **105**

Strange, J. R. (1965) *Abnormal psychology: Understanding behavior disorders.* New York: McGraw-Hill. **443**

Strauss, M. E. (1973) Behavioral differences between acute and chronic schizophrenics: Course of psychosis, effects of institutionalization, or sampling biases? *Psychol. Bull., 79,* 271–279. **441**

Strobel, M. G. (1972) Social facilitation of operant behavior in satiated rats. *J. comp. physiol. Psychol., 80,* 502–508. **534**

Strodtbeck, F. L. (1958) Family interaction, values and achievement. In McClelland, D. D., et al., *Talent and society.* Princeton, N.J.: Van Nostrand. **328**

Strongman, K. T. (1973) *The psychology of emotion.* New York: Wiley. **337, 342**

Strupp, H. H. (1971) *Psychotherapy and the modification of abnormal behavior: An introduction to theory and research.* New York: McGraw-Hill. **479**

Subotnik, L. (1972) Spontaneous remission: Fact or artifact? *Psychol. Bull., 77,* 32–48. **478**

Sundstrom, E., and Altman, I. (1974) Field study of territorial behavior and dominance. *J. Pers. soc. Psychol., 30,* 115–124. **416**

Supa, M., Cotzin, M., and Dallenbach, K. M. (1944) Facial vision: The perception of obstacles by the blind. *Amer. J. Psychol., 57,* 133–183. **176**

Super, D. E. (1957) *The psychology of careers.* New York: Harper. **390**

Swain, P. B., and Crary, D. D. (1953) Genetic and physiological background of reproduction in the rabbit. II: Some racial differences in the pattern of maternal behavior. *Behavior, 6,* 128–146. **293**

Szasz, T. S. (1956) Some observations on the relationship between psychiatry and the law. *Amer. Med. Assoc. neurol. Psychiat., 75,* 297–317. **450**

Szasz, T. S. (1960) The myth of mental illness. *Amer. Psychol., 15,* 113–118. **437**

Szasz, T. S. (1970) *The manufacture of madness.* New York: Harper & Row. **450, 452**

Tanner, J. M. (1971) Sequence, tempo and individual variation in the growth and development of boys and girls aged twelve to sixteen. *Daedalus, 100,* 907–930. **100, 101**

Tanur, J. M., and ASA-NCTM Joint Committee on Statistics (Eds.) (1972) *Statistics: A guide to the unknown.* San Francisco: Holden-Day. **71**

Tarpy, R. M. (1975) Basic principles of learning. Glenview, Ill.: Scott, Foresman. **193, 196, 212, 215, 287**

Tart, C. T. (1969) *Altered states of consciousness.* New York: Wiley. **183**

Taylor, I. A., and Getzels, J. W. (1975) *Perspectives in creativity.* Chicago: Aldine. **243**

Tedeschi, J. T., and Smith, R. B. (1974) A reinterpretation of research on aggression. *Psychol. Bull., 81,* 540–562. **326**

Telfer, M. A., Baker, D., Clark, G. R., and Richardson, C. E. (1968) Incidence of gross chromosomal errors among tall criminal American males. *Science, 159,* 1249–1250. **325**

Terman, L. M. (1954) Scientists and non-scientists in a group of 800 gifted men. *Psychol. Monogr., 68,* No. 7. **382, 524**

Terrace, H. S. (1973) Classical conditioning. In Nevin, J. A. (Ed.), *The study of behavior: Learning, motivation, emotion and instinct.* Glenview, Ill.: Scott, Foresman. **212**

Thigpen, C. H., and Cleckley, H. (1957) *Three faces of Eve.* New York: McGraw-Hill. **440**

Thomas, A., Hertzig, M. E., Dryman, I., and Fernandez, P. (1971) Examiner effect in IQ testing of Puerto Rican working-class children. *Amer. J. Orthopsychiat., 41,* 809–821. **360**

Thompson, G. G., and Hunnicutt, C. W. (1944) The effects of praise or blame on the work achievement of ''introverts'' and ''extroverts.'' *J. educ. Psychol., 35,* 257–266. **286**

Thompson, R., and McConnell, J. V. (1955) Classical conditioning in the planarian, dugesia dorotocephaea. *J. comp. Psychol., 48,* 65–68. **246**

Thompson, R. F. (1975) *Introduction to physiological psychology.* New York: Harper and Row. **133**

Thompson, R. F. (1975) The search for the engram. *Amer. Psychol., 31,* 207–227. **302, 303**

Thompson, T., and Dockens, W. S. (1975) *Applications of behavior modification.* New York: Academic Press. **483**

Thorndike, E. L. (1898) Animal intelligence: An experimental study of the association process in animals. *Psychol. Monogr., 2,* No. 8. **199**

Thorndike, E. L. (1924) Mental discipline in high school studies. *J. educ. Psychol., 15,* 1–22, 83–98. **279**

Thorndike, E. L., et al. (1921) Intelligence and its measurement: A symposium. *J. educ. Psychol., 12,* 123–147. **374**

Thurstone, L. L. (1950) The factorial description of temperament. *Science, 111,* 454–455. **407**

Thurstone, L. L., and Thurstone, T. G. (1941) Factorial studies of intelligence. *Psychometric Monogr.,* No. 2. **374**

Timmons, B., Salamy, J., Kamiya, J., and Girton, D. (1972) Abdominal-thoracic respiratory movements and levels of arousal. *Psychonom. Sci., 27,* 173–175. **306**

Tinbergen, N. (1951) *The study of instinct.* Oxford: The Clarendon Press. **295**

Tinbergen, N. (1953) *Social behavior in animals.* New York: Wiley. **295**

Tinbergen, N. (1958) Curious naturalists. *Country Life* (London), 22–23. **29**

Tinbergen, N. (1965) *Animal behavior.* New York: Time, Inc. **28**

Titchener, E. B. (1898) *A primer of psychology.* New York: Macmillan. **7**

Tobias, L. L., and MacDonald, M. L. (1974) Withdrawal of maintenance drugs with long-term hospitalized mental patients: A critical review. *Psychol. Bull., 81,* 107–125. **475**

Tolman, E. C., and Honzik, C. H. (1930) Introduction and removal of reward, and maze performance in rats. *Univ. Calif. Publ. Psychol., 4,* 257–275. **285**

Touhey, C. E. (1975) Prior information, credibility, and attitude change. *J. soc. Psychol., 95,* 287–288. **508**

Tourney, G., Petrilli, A. J., and Hatfield, L. M. (1975) Hormonal relationships in homosexual men. *Amer. J. Psychiat., 132,* 288–290. **322**

Trezise, R. L. (1976) The gifted child: Back in the limelight. *Phi Delta Kappan,* November, 241–243. **381, 383**

Trowill, J. A. (1976) *Motivation and emotion.* St. Louis: Mosby. **345**

Tryon, R. C. (1940) Genetic differences in maze-learning ability in rats. *39th Yearbook, Nat. Soc. Stud. Educ., Part I,* 111–119. **79**

Tsang, Y. C. (1938) Hunger motivation in gastrectomized rats. *J. comp. Psychol., 26,* 1–17. **302**

Tulving, E. (1966) Subjective organization and effects of repetition in multi-trial free-recall learning. *J. verb. Learn. verb. Behav., 5,* 193–197. **263**

Turner, L. H., and Solomon, R. L. (1962) Human traumatic avoidance learning: Theory and experiments on the operant-respondent distinction and failures to learn. *Psychol. Monogr., 76* (40, Whole No. 559). **198**

Turner, R. H., and Vanderlippe, R. H. (1958) Self-ideal congruence as an index of adjustment. *J. abnorm. soc. Psychol., 57,* 202–206. **419**

Twardosz, S., and Sajway, T. (1972) Multiple effects of a procedure to increase sitting in a hyperactive, retarded boy. *J. appl. Behav. Anal., 5,* 73–78. **206**

Tyler, L. E. (1965) *The psychology of human differences* (3rd ed.). New York: Appleton-Century-Crofts. **388**

Tyler, L. E. (1971) *Tests and measurements* (2nd ed.). Englewood Cliffs, N.J.: Prentice-Hall. **369**

Tylor, E. B. (1863) Wild men and beast-children. *Anthro. Rev., 1,* 21–32. **88**

Ulrich, L., and Trumbo, D. (1965) The selection interview since 1949. *Psychol. Bull., 63,* 100–116. **349**

Underwood, B. J. (1957) Interference and forgetting. *Psychol. Rev., 64.* **257**

U.S. Department of Labor (1970) Bureau of Labor Statistics; *Employment and earnings.* Washington, D.C.: U.S. Government Printing Office. **388**

Valenstein, E. S., Reiss, W., and Young, W. C. (1955) Sex drive in genetically heterogeneous and highly inbred strains of male guinea pigs. *J. comp. physiol. Psychol., 47,* 162–165. **294**

Van Cott, H. P., and Kinkade, R. G. (Eds.) (1972) *Human engineering guide to equipment design.* Washington, D.C.: U.S. Government Printing Office. **71**

Vander, A. J., Sherman, J. H., and Luciano, D. S. (1975) *Human physiology* (2nd ed.). New York: McGraw-Hill. **127, 128**

Van Hemel, P. E. (1975) Rats and mice together: The aggressive nature of mouse-killing by rats. *Psychol. Bull., 82,* 456–459. **326**

Van Lawick-Goodall, J. (1967) Mother-offspring relationships in free ranging chimpanzees. In Morris, D. (Ed.), *Primate ethology.* London: Werdenfeld and Nicolson. **309**

Van Lawick-Goodall, J. (1971) *In the shadow of man.* New York: Dell. **297, 487, 488, 490, 512**

Van Tilborg, P. W. (1936) The retention of mental and finger maze habits. *J. exp. Psychol., 19,* 334–341. **262**

Verhave, T. (1966) The pigeon as a quality control inspector. *Amer. Psychol., 21,* 109–115. **206**

Vidmar, N., and Rokeach, M. (1974) Archie Bunker's bigotry: A study in selective perception and exposure. *J. Comm., 24,* 36–47. **182, 183**

Wagner, H. G., MacNichol, E. F., Jr., and Wolbarsht, M. L. (1960) The response properties of single ganglion cells in the goldfish retina. *J. gen. Physiol., 43,* 45–62. **142**

Walker, R. N. (1962) Body build and behavior in young children. *Monogr. Soc. Res. Child Dev., 27,* Serial No. 84. **179, 406**

Wallace, E. R. (1976) A critical reappraisal of certain Freudian tenets. *Psychiat. Forum, 5,* 38–45. **456**

Wallace, R. K. (1970) Physiological effects of transcendental meditation. *Science, 167,* 1751–1754. **338**

Wallace, R. K., and Benson, H. (1972) The physiology of meditation. *Scientific American, 226,* February, 85–90. **131, 338, 339**

Walster, E., and Festinger, L. (1962) The effectiveness of "overheard" persuasive communications. *J. abnorm. soc. Psychol., 65,* 395–402. **507**

Ward, J., and Fitzpatrick, T. F. (1970) The new British intelligence scale: Construction of logic items. *Res. Educ., 4,* 1–23. **374**

Warner, W. L., and Lunt, P. S. (1941) *The social life of a modern community.* New Haven: Yale University Press. **539**

Warren, J. M. (1965) Primate learning in comparative perspective. In Schrier, A. M., Harlow, H. F., and Stollnitz, F. (Eds.), *Behavior of nonhuman primates.* Vol. I. New York: Academic Press. **280**

Wason, P. C. (1960) On the failure to eliminate hypotheses in a conceptual task. *Quart. J. exp. Psychol., 12,* 129–140. **234**

Watson, J. B. (1925) *Behaviorism.* New York: Norton. **11**

Watson, J. B., and Rayner, R. (1920) Conditioned emotional reactions. *J. exp. Psychol., 3,* 1–14. **464**

Watson, R. I. (1971) *The great psychologists: From Aristotle to Freud* (3rd ed.). Philadelphia: Lippincott. **23**

Watson, S. G. (1972) Judgment of emotion from facial and contextual cue combinations. *J. Pers. soc. Psychol., 24,* 334–342. **336**

Waugh, N. (1961) Free versus serial recall. *J. exp. Psychol., 62,* 496–502. **263**

Wax, D. E. (1972) Social class, race, and juvenile delinquency: A review of the literature. *Child Psychiat. Hum. Dev., 3,* 36–49. **539**

Webster, W. G. (1972) Functional asymmetry between the cerebral hemispheres of the cat. *Neuropsychologia, 10,* 75–87. **125**

Wechsler, D. (1975) Intelligence defined and undefined: A relativistic appraisal. *Amer. Psychol., 30,* 135–139. **376**

Weintraub, D. J., and Walker, E. L. (1969) *Perception.* Belmont, Calif.: Brooks/Cole. **169**

Weisberg, P., and Waldrop, P. B. (1972) Fixed-interval work habits of Congress. *J. appl. Behav. Anal., 5,* 93–97. **204**

Weiss, W. (1970) Effects of the mass media of communication. In Lindzey, G., and Aronson, E. (Eds.), *Handbook of social psychology.* Reading, Mass.: Addison-Wesley. **509**

Welker, W. I. (1956) Some determinants of play and exploration in chimpanzees. *J. comp. physiol. Psychol., 49,* 84–89. **309**

Welty, J. C. (1934) Experiments in group behavior of fishes. *Physiol. Zool., 7,* 85–128. **534**

Wender, P. H. (1969) The role of genetics in the etiology of the schizophrenics. *Amer. J. Orthosychiat., 39*(3), April. **80, 445**

Wertheimer, M. (1945) *Productive thinking.* New York: Harper. **227**

Wexler, D. A., and Rice, L. N. (1974) *Innovations in client-centered therapy.* New York: Wiley. **483**

Wheeler, R. H. (1940) *The science of psychology* (rev. ed.). New York: Crowell. **114**

Wheelis, A. (1958) *The quest for identity.* New York: W. W. Norton. **456**

White, R. W. (1956) *The abnormal personality* (2nd ed.). New York: Ronald. **256**

White, R. W. (1965) *The abnormal personality.* New York: Ronald. **435**

Whitehead, C. S., and Hoff, C. A. (1926) *Ethical sex relations or the new eugenics: A safe guide for young men—young women.* Chicago: John A. Hertel. **322**

Whitehurst, G. J., and Vasta, R. (1977) *Child behavior.* Boston: Houghton Mifflin. **105**

Whorf, B. L. (1956) *Language, thought and reality.* Cambridge, Mass.: M.I.T. Press, and New York: Wiley. **226**

Whyte, W. F. (1955) *Street corner society: The social structure of an Italian slum* (enlarged edition). Chicago: University of Chicago Press. **538**

Whyte, W. H. (1956) *The organization man.* New York: Simon and Schuster. **517**

Wickelgren, W. A. (1973) The long and the short of memory. *Psychol. Bull., 80,* 425–438. **248**

Wiesner, B. P., and Sheard, N. M. (1933) *Maternal behavior in the rat.* London: Oliver and Boyd. **293**

Wildman, R. W., and Wildman, R. W., II (1967) The practice of clinical psychology in the United States. *J. clin. Psychol., 23,* 292–295. **480**

Williams, C. D. (1959) The elimination of tantrum behavior by extinction procedures. *J. abnorm. soc. Psychol., 59,* 269. **201**

Williams, F. (1972) *Language and speech: Introductory perspectives.* Englewood Cliffs, N.J.: Prentice-Hall. **512**

Willis, R. H. (1965) Conformity, independence, and anti-conformity. *Hum. Relations, 18,* 373–389. **532**

Wilson, G. T., Leaf, R. C., and Nathan, P. E. (1975) The aversive control of excessive alcohol consumption by chronic alcoholics in the laboratory setting. *J. appl. Behav. Anal., 8,* 13–26. **470**

Winkelmann, R. K. (1960) Similarities in cutaneous nerve end-organs. In Montagna, W. (Ed.), *Advances in biology of skin. I. Cutaneous innervation.* Proceedings of the Brown University Symposium on the Biology of Skin, 1959. New York: Pergamon Press. **149**

Wohlwill, J. F. (1960) Developmental studies of perception. *Psychol. Bull., 57,* 249–288. **169**

Wolf, S., and Wolff, H. G. (1943) Evidence of the genesis of peptic ulcer in man. In Tompkins, S. S. (Ed.), *Contemporary psychopathology.* Cambridge, Mass.: Harvard University Press. **338**

Wolf, T. H. (1973) *Alfred Binet.* Chicago: University of Chicago Press. **383**

Wollen, K. A., Weber, A., and Lowry, D. H. (1972) Bizarreness versus interaction of mental images as determinants of learning. *Cogn. Psychol., 3,* 518–523. **264**

Wolpe, J. (1961) The systematic desensitization treatment of neurosis. *J. nerv. ment. Diseases, 132,* 189–203. **465**

Wolpe, J. (1969) *Practice of behavior therapy.* New York: Pergamon Press. (2nd edition, 1973.) **465, 466**

Wood, C. G., and Hokanson, J. E. (1965) Effects of induced muscular tension on performance and the inverted U function. *J. Pers. soc. Psychol., 1,* 506–510. **341**

Woods, S. C., Decke, E., and Vasselli, J. R. (1974) Metabolic hormones and regulation of body weight. *Psychol., Rev., 81,* 26–43. **303**

Woodworth, R. S., and Schlosberg, H. (1954) *Experimental psychology* (rev. ed.). New York: Holt. **282**

Wright, D. M. (1975) Impairment in abstract conceptualization in schizophrenia. *Psychol. Bull., 82,* 120–127. **441**

Wright, S. H., and Shrader, R. R. (1965) Influence of open and closed mental hospitals on attitudes in the United States and Britain. *J. counsel. Psychol., 12,* 372–378. **481**

Young, P. T. (1936) *The motivation of behavior.* New York: Wiley. **305**

Young, P. T. (1961) *Motivation and emotion.* New York: Wiley. **305**

Youtz, R. P. (1965) A letter to the editor. *Scientific American, 212,* June, 8–10. **150**

Zajonc, R. B. (1968) Attitudinal effects of mere exposure. *J. Pers. soc. Psychol. Monogr. Suppl., 9,* 1–27. **517**

Zajonc, R. B., Crandall, R., Kail, R. V., and Swap, W. (1974) Effect of extreme exposure frequencies on different affective ratings of stimuli. *Percept. mot. Skills, 38,* 667–678. **517**

Zajonc, R. B., and Markus, G. B. (1975) Birth order and intellectual development. *Psychol. Rev., 82,* 74–88. **81**

Zarrow, M. X., Sarwin, P. B., Ross, S., and Denenberg, V. H. (1962) Maternal behavior and its endocrine basis in the rabbit. In Bliss, E. L., *The roots of behavior.* New York: Hafner. **293**

Zax, M., and Stricker, G. (1963) *Patterns of psychopathology.* New York: Macmillan. **442**

Zax, M., and Stricker, G. (1974) *The study of abnormal behavior: Selected readings.* New York: Macmillan. **452**

Zeigarnik, B. (1927) Über das Behalten von erledigten und unerledigten Handlungen. *Psychol. Forsch., 9,* 1–85. **262**

Zeiler, M. D. (1963) The ratio theory of intermediate size discrimination. *Psychol. Rev., 70,* 516–533. **228**

Zeller, A. H. (1950) An experimental analogue of repression. II. The effect of individual failure and success on memory measured by relearning. *J. exp. Psychol., 40,* 411–422. **260**

Zingg, R. M. (1940) Feral man and extreme cases of isolation. *Amer. J. Psychol., 53,* 487–517. **88**

Zipf, S. (1960) Resistance and conformity under reward and punishment. *J. abnorm. soc. Psychol., 61,* 102–109. **286**

Zuckerman, M., and Wheeler, L. (1975) To dispel fantasies about the fantasy-based measure of fear of success. *Psychol. Bull., 82,* 932–946. **329**

Index

and emotion, 339–341
and genetics, 77–80
goal directed, 300–301
hormonal influences on, 126–129
instinctive, 293–297
instrumental, 197
integration of, 394–483
modification, 463–470
multiple basis of, 40
operant, 197–198
personality, 394–424
physiological bases of, 106–133
prosocial, 528–529
respondent, 197–198
sexual, 294–298, 322, 538
social, 513–545
therapy, 453–483
TV's effect on, 509–510
verbal, 539
behavior chains, 207–209
behavior genetics, 79–80
behaviorism, 10–14
behavior modification, 463–470
aversive therapy, 466
classical conditioning, 464–466
combined methods, 469–470
contingency management, 467–468
deep muscle relaxation, 465–466
desensitization, 466
operant conditioning, 466–469
by punishment, 469–470
self-reinforcement, 470
token economies, 468–469
Bell, Charles, 106–109, 152
bell-shaped curves, 52–53
Bell's palsy, 109
Berkeley Growth Study, 94
Beyond Freedom and Dignity (B.F. Skinner), 206
Binet, Alfred, 371–373, 383
Binet-Simon test, 371–372
binocular space perception, 172, 175
biochemical basis
of memory, 246–247
of psychosis, 445–446
biofeedback, 131
biology, and early psychology, 3–4
biosocial science, 17
blame, use in learning, 185–186
blind spot in retina, 140–141
blood sugar level, 302–303
body
brain, 114–126
endocrine system, 126–129
maintenance systems, 126–131
measuring responses of, 125–126
needs, 302–307
nervous system, 106–114, 129–131
senses, 136–160
structure and behavior, 406
types and personality, 405–406
boys, slower development of, 90
brain, 113–126
areas for specialized functions,
115–117

association areas, 118
and consciousness, 122–126
convolutions of, 115
corpus callosum, 122–124
damage and psychotic behavior, 444,
472
deeper areas of, 118–122
electrical stimulation of, 118–122
fetal growth, 92–93
fissures, 115–116
hemispheres, 115–125
hypothalamus, 119–120, 303
integration in, 114
lobes, 115–116
measuring states of, 125–126
memory storage in, 245–246
motor control areas, 116
organization of, 122
outer structures of, 114–118
paresis of, 444
sensory areas of, 116–118
septal area, 120–121
size of, 114
split-brain technique, 122–125
surgery as therapy, 471–472
waves, 41
weight, 114
See also nervous system
brainstorming, 382
branching programs, 274
brightness, 139
Brook Test, 414–415
bulls, brain stimulation of, 120
Bunker, Archie, 179–183
Burtt, Benjamin, 244–245, 249, 253–257
Byrd, Richard E., 292, 308
bystander intervention, 528–529

CA (chronological age), 372
CAI (computer-assisted instruction), 39,
283–284
California Personality Inventory, 409–410
Calkins, Mary Wilton, 9
Cannon, Walter, 342
Cannon-Bard theory, 342
carpentered-world hypothesis, 178
case history, 34
caste systems, 538–540
castration, 294–295
catatonic reaction, 442–443
catharsis, 326, 456
cats
brain research on, 119
monk's conditioning of, 190–213
cell body of neurons, 107
cell division, 77
cellular dehydration, 301–302
cellular division, 77
central nervous system, 110–114
central tendency, 51, 56–57
central traits, 180–181
centration, 219
cephalocaudal development, 84
cerebellum, 122
cerebral cortex, 115, 155

cerebrotonia, 406
cerebrum, 115
chaining, 207–209
Charcot, Jean Martin, 15
chemical, *see* biochemical basis
chemotherapy, 475
childrearing, cultural differences in,
323–324. *See also* maternal behavior
children
cognitive processes of, 216–222
developmental stages, 98–101
feral, 74–77, 87–89
retarded, 377–380
Skeels-Skodak study of, 81–85,
99–102
chimpanzees, language and
communication of, 486–488, 491,
495–496, 502–504
Chomsky, Noam, 499
chromosomes, 75–77, 325
chunking, 263–264
Churchill, Winston, 349, 508, 542
clairvoyance, 31
class structure
behavioral differences, 538–539
caste system, 538–540
fluid vs. fixed, 539–540
and intelligence, 384
classical conditioning, 190–197
and attitude formation, 519
basic terms, 192
influence of, 195–197
principles of, 192–195
procedures of, 191–192
as therapy, 464–466, 469–470
client-centered therapy, 456–459
clinical approach
case histories, 34
idiographic analysis, 34–35
interviews, 35–36
nomothetic research, 34
to personality, 396
to psychology, 18
tests, 36
closure principle, 166–167
cochlea, 143–144
The Cocktail Party (T. S. Eliot), 322
coefficient of correlation, 61
cognition
in animals, 227–229
computer models of, 230–233
concepts, 222–227
concrete operations, 220–221
creative thinking, 235–241
defined, 217
development stages, 216–222
dissonance theory, 522
egocentrism, 219
and emotion, 342–343
formal operations, 221–222
information processing, 230–233
language's role in, 225–227
in learning, 269, 275
and motivation, 331–332
preoperational, 218–220

sweat glands, 126
sweating young man, therapy for, 453–483
syllogisms, 235
symbolic activity, 190–289
    conditioning and learning, 190–215
    cognitive processes, 216–243
    forgetting, 255–261
    instruction and learning, 268–289
    memory, 245–267
    reasoning, 227–235
    thinking, 222–227, 235–241
symbolism, unconscious, 400–401
sympathetic nervous system, 129
symptom substitution, 477
Synanon, 476
synapses, 111–113
syntax, 489, 493
systematic desensitization, 466
systems of psychology, 9–16
    behaviorism, 10–12
    gestalt, 12–13
    humanistic, 13–14
    psychoanalysis, 14–16

tabes dorsalis, 152
tabula rasa, 3
tact, 497–498
task analysis, 354
task specialist, as leader, 540–542
taste, 146–148
TAT (Thematic Apperception Test), 404
teacher, as model, 269–271
teaching
    machines for, 273
    for transfer, 279
    See also instruction; learning
telegraphic utterances, 492
television, influence of, 508–510
temperature sensitivity, 148–150
temporal lobes, 115–116
Terman, L.N., 382
terminal threshold, 138
"termites," 382
testes, 297
testosterone, 295
tests, 348–369
    achievement, 352
    administration of, 356–357
    alternatives to, 349
    aptitude, 350
    Army General Classification Test (AGCT), 388
    categories of, 351–353
    criterion-referenced, 366–367
    culture-free, 384
    evaluation of, 358–364
    field trials for, 356
    group, 349–350
    improving on, 366–368
    individual, 350–351
    intelligence, 349–351, 355, 371–374
    interest inventories, 352–353
    item analysis, 357
    items for, 350, 353–358

nonverbal, 351
normative study, 364–366
norm-referenced, 366–367
pencil-and-paper, 349
person who uses, 367–368
of personality, 353, 403–404
posttest, 366
potential of, 367
preparation of, 353–358
pretest, 366
projective, 403–404
psychological, 36–37
reliability of, 360, 366
revisions of, 357
situational, 413–414, 416
standards for, 367–368
task analysis for, 354
testing movement, 348–353
verbal items, 350
T-groups, 420
thalamus, 342
Thematic Apperception Test (TAT), 404
theory
    defined, 96
    role in psychology, 97
theory of evolution, 3–4
therapist, 478–479
therapy, 453–483
    behavior modification, 463–470
    classical conditioning, 464–466, 469–470
    client-centered, 456–459
    contingency management, 467–468
    defined, 453
    drug treatments, 472–475
    effectiveness of, 478–480
    evaluation problems, 476–478
    existential, 461–463
    factors in, 478–479
    group context, 475–476
    logotherapy, 462–463
    modeling, 470
    operant conditioning, 466–470
    preventive mental health care, 4, 480–481
    psychoanalysis, 454–456
    psychosurgery, 471–472
    psychotherapy, 453–463
    punishment, 469–470
    rational-emotive, 459–461
    shock, 470–471
    somatic, 470–475
    spontaneous remission, 477–478
    token economies, 468–469
thinking
    artificial, 231–233
    autistic, 235–236
    cognitive processes, 216–243
    and conditioning, 213
    convergent, 236
    creative, 235–241
    divergent, 236
    language as determining, 225–227
    reasoning, 233–235

role in rational-emotive therapy, 459–461
    See also cognition
third-force psychology, 14
thirst drive, 300–302
Thorndike, E.L., 198–199
thought, see cognition; thinking
Thouless, Robert, 158
Three Faces of Eve, 440
thresholds of stimulation, 137–139
Thurstone, Louis, 374
Thurstone, Thelma, 374
thyroid gland, 127–129
timbre, 143
time, as memory factor, 247–248
tip-of-the-tongue feeling, 252
toilet training, 398–401
token economies, 468–469
tongue, 146–148
tools, use by animals, 228
trace, memory, 245–248, 256
training, transfer of, 277–281. See also conditioning; learning
trait theory of personality
    basic traits, 407
    compared with other theories, 420–421
    defects in, 411–412
    personality inventories, 409–410
    personality typology, 405
    somatotyping, 405–406
    traits defined, 407
transactional analysis, 475–476
transcendental meditation, 338–339
transfer of training, 277–281
    bases of, 279–281
    formal discipline, 278–279
    phrenology, 277–278
    teaching for, 278
    types of, 279–280
transference, psychoanalytic, 454–455
transformations, linguistic, 500
transposition experiment, 228
transvestism, 323
trial-and-error, 229–230
tropism, 197
Twain, Mark, 156
twins
    fraternal, 89
    genetics of, 76
    heredity-environment studies, 89
    identical, 43, 89, 444–445
    intelligence studies, 385–386
    prenatal influence on, 81
two-factor theory, 210–212
typing
    chaining in, 209
    intersensory nature of, 155–157
    and typewriter design, 50–69
typology, personality, 405

unconditional positive regard, 457
unconscious
    collective, 402
    concept of the, 16